OUR "REGULAR" READERS RAVE!

"I want to sit down and be counted! Uncle John's Bathroom Readers have just bowled me over. You guys are really on a roll. And now you've got a website! It almost makes one consider getting a tanktop computer (rim shot). Thank you for providing endless hours of quality reading material for the porcelain library."

"The Bathroom Readers are my number one (and number two) source of facts to amaze my friends."

"I love you guys!! I've been an avid reader since your first book in 1988. I actually built a book shelf in my bathroom just to hold your books!!"

"I think they're GREAT! I've bought all the books, and have thoroughly enjoyed each one. I can hardly have a conversation with someone that I am not reminded of a relevant article that provides meat for discussion. Keep up the good work!"

"I am unable to relax on the 'throne' without a copy of Uncle John's good book within reach. To me, the book is more essential than toilet paper. I have finally found a way to get inner peace at last!! Thanks, Uncle John!!!!"

"Just think if all the political meeting places around the world were equipped with Bathroom Readers, BRI could use its influence and wisdom to promote peace and prosperity for all! Doable? I think so!"

Uncle John's

BIGGEST EVER

BATHROOM READER®

containing
**Uncle John's Great Big
Bathroom Reader**
and
**Uncle John's Ultimate
Bathroom Reader**

THUNDER BAY
P · R · E · S · S

San Diego, California

UNCLE JOHN'S BIGGEST EVER BATHROOM READER®
is a compilation of the following two previously published
Bathroom Reader titles:

Uncle John's Great Big Bathroom Reader®
ISBN: 1-879682-69-9
First Printing 1998
and
Uncle John's Ultimate Bathroom Reader®
ISBN: 1-879682-65-6
First Printing 1996

plus 20 articles from
Uncle John's Giant 10th Anniversary Bathroom Reader®
and 3 *articles from*
Uncle John's All-Purpose Extra Strength Bathroom Reader®

For information, write The Bathroom Readers' Hysterical Society,
5880 Oberlin Drive, San Diego, CA 92121
www.unclejohn@advmkt.com

Cover design by Michael Brunsfeld
BRI Technician on back cover: Larry Kelp

ISBN: 1-57145-814-X
Library of Congress Control Number: 2002106433

Printed and bound in Canada

12 11 10 9   05 06 07 08 09

THE TEAM

*This compilation of great Uncle John
titles was put together by...*

Allen Orso, Publisher, Portable Press
Ann Ghublikian, Publisher, Thunder Bay
Jeff McLaughlin, Associate Publisher, Thunder Bay
JoAnn Padgett, Director, Editorial & Production
Allison Bocksruker, Project Manager
Victoria Bullman, Associate Editor
Mana Monzavi, Assistant Editor
Dan Mansfield, Editorial Assistant
Cindy Tillinghast, Staff Editor
Georgine Lidell, Inventory Manager

As for the many writers, editors, and
other contributors from the Bathroom
Readers' Institute who provided
the material for this book, we'd
like to thank them too.
So we gave them the next page.

THANK YOU!

*We're grateful for the people whose advice and assistance
made this book possible.*

Bo Adan
Jeff Altemus
Erin Barrett
Harry Bartz
Tom Boerman
Jonah Bornstein
Ben Brand
Michael Brunsfeld
Karen Carnival
Jeff Cheek
Nancy Chew
Thomas Crapper
Shawn Davis
William Davis
John Dollison
Leeann Drabenstott
Andrea Freewater
Moira Gleason
Paul Hadella
Shailyn Hovind
John Javna
Gordon Javna
Jesse & Sophie, B.R.I.T.
Larry Kelp
Lonnie Kirk
Lenna Lebovich
Eric Lefcowitz
Erik Linden

Leni Litonjua
Rachael Markowitz
Max, Lucy & Alice
Richard Moeschl
Gary Morris
Antares Multimedia
Jay Newman
Andy Nilsson
Bass Pike
Gary Pool
Sherry Powell
Mustard Press
Julie Roeming
Chris Rose-Merkle
Melissa Schwarz
Adam Silver
Betty Sleep
Bennie Slomski
Dee Smith
Morgan Smith
Andy Sohn
Rich Stim
Gordon Van Gelder
Bill Varble
Jessica Vineyard
Jennifer Wahpahpa
Bob Weibel

Special thanks to Leder Norah

Hi Nancy, Pam, Joelle, Laurie, Alice & Sherrel!

CONTENTS

NOTE
Because the B.R.I. understands your reading needs, we've
divided the contents by length as well as subject.
Short—a quick read
Medium—1 to 3 pages
Long—for those extended visits, when something
a little more involved is required.
*Extended—for a leg-numbing experience.

*   *   *

PREDICTION FOR THE YEAR 2000

"When Jane cleans house she simply turns the hose on everything...Why not? Furniture (upholstery included), rugs, draperies, unscratchable floors—all are made of synthetic fabric or waterproof plastic. After the water has run down a drain in the middle of the floor (later concealed by a rug of synthetic fiber), Jane turns on a blast of hot air and dries everything."

—Popular Mechanics, 1950

AN ARTFUL HOAX

On display: Vincent Van Gogh's ear (that's how it was labeled).

Where: In New York's Museum of Modern Art in 1935, during the first exhibition of Van Gogh's art in the U.S.

Background: Hugh Troy, a New York artist, suspected that most Americans were more interested in Van Gogh the man than they were in Van Gogh the artist. To prove this, he mounted a shrivelled object in a velvet shadow box an wrote: "This is the ear which Vincent Van Gogh cut off and sent to his mistress, a French prostitute, Dec. 24, 1888." Then he visited the Van Gogh exhibit, and when no one was looking he put it out on display.

What Happened: The "ear" was mobbed, while Van Gogh's paintings were virtually ignored. It wasn't until later that Troy admitted that he had fashioned the ear out of a piece of chipped beef.

INTRODUCTION

I f you're a longtime Bathroom Reader fan, you've probably already noticed that this edition is bigger than our previous volumes. That's because we took two of our favorite but older volumes—*Uncle John's Ultimate Bathroom Reader* and *Uncle John's Great Big Bathroom Reader*—and combined them to create this foot-crushing volume called *Uncle John's BIGGEST EVER Bathroom Reader.* We've gotten plenty of requests to add as many pages as possible, so the book will keep you company through even more sit-down sessions. And we've done our best to comply.

We at the BRI often feel we have the most satisfying job in the world. We get to spend the year poring through old magazines, newspapers, and obscure books, looking for off-the-wall subjects to write about...and then we get to "field-test" the materials.

Amazingly, after fifteen years and over 5,000 pages of *Bathroom Readers,* it's still easy to find new things to write about. The material keeps on flowing.

Keep those cards and letters coming—let us know what you like and send us your own favorite bathroom reading material. We can always make use of it, one way or another.

Happy reading—and *Go with the flow!*

—Uncle John and the Bathroom Readers' Institute

YOU'RE MY INSPIRATION

It's fascinating to find out the inspiration
behind cultural milestones like these.

CLINT EASTWOOD. "Developed his distinctive manner of speech by studying the breathy whisper of Marilyn Monroe."

THE WWI GERMAN ARMY. Kaiser Wilhelm, the leader of Germany, was so impressed with the efficiency of Buffalo Bill's Wild West Show when it toured Europe in the early 1900s, that he modeled his army on it.

THE CHEVROLET INSIGNIA. Billy Durant, founder of General Motors, liked the wallpaper pattern in a Paris hotel so much that he ripped off a piece and brought it back to Detroit to copy as the symbol for his new Chevrolet car.

THE QUEENS in a deck of cards were originally depictions of Queen Elizabeth, wife of Henry VII of England.

LUCY. Perhaps the most famous human fossil ever discovered. The bones were dug up in Ethiopia in 1975—at the time, the oldest human remains in the world (3.2 million years old). They were named after the song playing on a tape recorder at the time— "Lucy in the Sky with Diamonds."

ROMEO and JULIET. Were real lovers in Verona, Italy in the early 1300s—and they really did die for each other. The story was passed from writer to writer until Shakespeare found it, apparently in a 1562 poem by Arthur Brooke, called *Romeo and Juliet, containing a rare example of loves constancie...*

FAT ALBERT. The slow-witted, good-natured cartoon character was modeled after Bill Cosby's dyslexic brother, Russell.

Ugh! If you're average, you'll swallow three spiders this year.

COURT TRANSQUIPS

We're back, with one of our regular features. Do court transcripts make good bathroom reading? Check out these quotes. They're things people actually said in court, recorded word for word.

Q: "Well, sir, judging from your answer on how you reacted to the emergency call, it sounds like you are a man of intelligence and good judgement."
A: "Thank you, and if I weren't under oath I'd return the compliment."

Q: "And you're saying because she's dead she's no longer alive; is that what you're saying?"
A: "Is there a dispute there?"

Q: "What did he say?"
A: "About that? All the way back he—I've never been called so many names."
Q: "You're not married, I take it."

Q: "You say that the stairs went down to the basement?"
A: "Yes."
Q: "And these stairs, did they go up also?"

Q: "What is the meaning of sperm being present?"
A: "It indicates intercourse."
Q: "Male sperm?"
A: "That is the only kind I know."

Q: "You said he threatened to kill you."
A: "Yes. And he threatened to sue me."
Q: "Oh, worse yet."

Q: And lastly, Gary, all your responses must be oral. O.K.?"
A: "Oral."
Q: "How old are you?"
A: "Oral."

Q: "Please state the location of your right foot immediately prior to impact."
A: "Immediately before the impact, my right foot was located at the immediate end of my right leg."
Q: "Doctor, how many autopsies have you performed on dead people?"
A: "All my autopsies have been on dead people."

Q: "Now, Mrs. Marsh, your complaint alleges that you have had problems with concentration since the accident. Does that condition continue today?"
A: "No, not really. I take a stool softener now."

The "Ye" in "Ye Olde Taverne," is pronounced "the," not "yee."

GOOD LUCK!

You're familiar with these lucky customs.
Here's where they come from.

LUCKY STAR. Centuries ago, people believed that every time a person was born, a new star appeared in the sky. The star was tied to the person's life: it would stay in the sky until the person died, and it rose or fell as the individual's fortunes rose and fell (that's where the expression "rising star" comes from). The Hebrew phrase *mazel tov*, which means "good luck," also translates as "good constellation," or "may the stars be good to you."

LUCKY CHARM. "Charm" comes from the Latin word *carmen*, which means "song" or "incantation." People once believed that certain words or phrases had magical powers when recited—something which survives today in words like "abracadabra" and "open sesame." In time, anything that brought luck, not just "magic words," became known as charms.

STARTING OUT ON THE RIGHT FOOT. A term from the ancient Romans, who believed that entering a building with the left foot was bad luck. They took the belief to extremes, even stationing guards or "footmen" at the entrances of buildings to make sure every visitor "started out on the right foot."

THIRD TIME'S A CHARM. Philip Waterman writes in *The Story of Superstition,* "Of all the numbers in the infinite scale, none has been more universally revered than three." The Greek philosopher Pythagoras thought the number three was the "perfect number," and many cultures have used triangles to ward off evil spirits. The reason it's bad luck to walk under a ladder (aside from the obvious ones) is that you're "breaking" the triangle that the ladder makes with the ground.

LUCKY SEVEN. Seven is the sum of three and four, the triangle and the square, which ancient Greeks considered the two "perfect figures." The lunar cycle, which is 28 days, is divided into four seven-day quarters: New Moon, First Quarter, Full Moon, and

In its ancient form, the carrot was purple, not orange.

Third Quarter. It may also come from the game of craps, where rolling a seven wins the roll.

LUCKY HUNCHES. Believe it or not, this is from the days when rubbing a hunchback's hump was considered good luck. The ancient Egyptians worshipped a hunchbacked god named Bes, and the ancient Romans hired hunchbacks as servants because they thought it brought the household good luck.

* * *

AMAZING LUCK

"In December 1948, Navy Lieutenant Jimmy Carter was on night duty on the bridge of his submarine, the USS Pomfret, which was riding on the surface, recharging its batteries. Suddenly, an enormous wave crashed over Carter's head and across the sub. Unable to keep his hold on the railing, Carter found himself swimming inside the wave with no sense of what was up or down. Had the current been broadside, he would have been lost. By pure chance, the wave set Carter down on the submarine's gun turret thirty feet from the bridge. He felt he was watched over by Providence, and said, 'I don't have any fear at all of death.'"

—*Oh Say Can You See,* by John and Claire Whitcomb

"In March 1997, the Sunday Oklahoman profiled Oklahoma City homemaker Mary Clamser, 44, whose deterioration with multiple sclerosis had been abruptly halted in 1994 when lightning struck her house while she was grasping metal objects with each hand and wearing her metal leg brace....

"Suddenly, she began walking easily, and though doctors told her the condition was probably only temporary, she still walks easily today. As if that weren't enough good luck, Clamser, in order to fly to California for a TV interview in April 1995, was forced to cancel a local appointment she had made at the Oklahoma City federal building for 9 a.m. on April 19."

—*News of the Weird*

Only female mosquitoes bite; they need the blood to nourish their eggs.

OOPS!

Everyone's amused by tales of outrageous blunders—probably because it's comforting to know that someone's screwing up even worse than we are. So go ahead and feel superior for a few minutes.

WANT FRIES WITH THAT?

"The building of a new staff canteen in 1977 gave the U.S. Department of Agriculture the opportunity to commemorate a famous nineteenth-century Colorado pioneer.

"Amidst a blaze of enthusiastic publicity, the Agriculture Secretary, Robert Bergland, opened The Alfred Packer Memorial Dining Facility, with the words: 'Alfred Packer exemplifies the spirit and care that this agriculture department cafeteria will provide.'

"Several months later the cafeteria was renamed when it was discovered that Packer had been convicted of murdering and eating five prospectors in 1874."

—The Book of Heroic Failures

NEXT TIME, ORDER OUT

"Astronomers using the radio telescope at Parkes Observatory in Australia thought they had important evidence of alien life when they picked up a distinctive radio signal at 2.3 to 2.4 gigahertz every evening about dinnertime. They later discovered that the signal was coming from the microwave oven downstairs."

—Strange Days #2

VICTOR VICTORIA

"An unidentified, 31-year-old man was sentenced to 20 lashes in Tehran [Iran] in October after a prank backfired.

"He had bet his father about $30 that he could dress in robe and veils and ride unnoticed in the women's section of a segregated municipal bus, but he was detected because he failed to wear women's shoes underneath the robe. A court ruled the prank obscene."

—Universal Press Syndicate

Ooh la-la! The average French person uses two bars of soap a year.

JUST SAY NO

"Police in England pounced on an elderly man when they raided a pub looking for a drug dealer. The suspect explained that his bag of white powder was actually the ashes of his late wife, Alice, which he carried everywhere."

—*Fortean Times*

THE KINDER, GENTLER IRS

"As a public service to taxpayers, the Internal Revenue Service provides a free tax information service by phone. All you have to do is call the 800 number listed in your local directory, and you can get your tax questions answered.

"But in Portland, Oregon, taxpayers got a different type of service. When the phone was answered, callers heard a sultry voice breathing, 'Hi, sexy.' The embarrassed IRS later explained that the Portland phone directory had misprinted the number. Instead of the IRS, callers were reaching Phone Phantasies."

—*The 176 Stupidest Things Ever Done*

HOLY MATRIMONY!

"A 22-year-old Los Angeles man advertised in a magazine as a lonely Romeo looking for a girl with whom to share a holiday tour of South America. The joyful Juliet who answered his plea turned out to be his widowed mother."

—*The World's Greatest Mistakes*

COOL CUSTOMER

"Robert Redford was making a movie in New Mexico...[and a] lady who encountered him in an ice cream parlor on Canyon Street between takes was determined to stay cool....She pretended to ignore the presence of the movie star....But after leaving the shop, she realized she did not have the ice cream cone she'd bought and paid for. She returned to the shop....to ask for her ice cream cone. Overhearing, Robert Redford said, 'Madame, you'll probably find it where you put it—in your purse.'"

—**Paul Harvey's *For What It's Worth***

THE STORY OF ECHO AND NARCISSUS

This ancient Greek myth tells how the echo was created...and explains why the word "narcissistic" means "self-involved." It's from a BRI favorite, Myths and Legends of the Ages.

In ancient times, the fields and forests were peopled by lovely enchanted creatures called nymphs. Their homes were the trees and flowers and streams. Their food was fairy food.

Echo was one of these charming creatures. She was lovely to look at as she flitted about the forests. She might have been a perfect delight to her companions—except for one thing. Echo talked too much! Not only that, but she insisted on having the last word in every conversation.

This annoying habit finally so angered Juno, the queen of the gods, that she decided to punish Echo.

"This shall be your punishment," Juno said. "You shall no longer be able to talk—with this exception: you have always insisted on having the last word; so, Echo, you will never be able to say anything but the last word!"

Now in the forest where the nymphs dwelt, a handsome young man named Narcissus used to go hunting. So handsome was he, even the lovely nymphs fell in love with him at first sight. But Narcissus was terribly vain. He felt that no one was good enough to deserve his love.

One day, Echo caught sight of Narcissus and straightaway fell in love with him. She yearned to tell him of her love; but because of Juno's punishment, she was powerless to speak. Echo followed Narcissus adoringly wherever he went. But now, in her affliction, Echo became very shy.

One day, while out hunting, Narcissus became separated from his companions. Hearing a sound in the woods nearby, he called out, "Who's there?"'

It was Echo. But all she could answer was the last word.

"There!"

Brasilia, founded in 1960, is one of the newest cities in the world.

Narcissus called again.

"Come!" he said.

"Come! replied Echo.

Still seeing no one, Narcissus cried, "Why do you shun me?"

"Shun me!" came back the reply.

"Let us join each other," called Narcissus.

Then Echo, full of love, stepped out from between the trees.

"Each other!" she said, giving Narcissus both of her hands.

But Narcissus drew back in his pride. "Go away," he said.

"How dare you be so forward! I would rather die than that you should have me."

"Have me," wept Echo.

But in his cold pride Narcissus left her.

Echo was heartbroken. From then on, she pined away. Echo grew thinner and thinner. Finally, nothing was left of her—but her voice.

Echo still lives among the rocks and caves of the mountains where she answers anyone who calls. But she answers with only the last word.

But cruel Narcissus did not escape punishment. He continued his vain self-love until such a day when he spurned another nymph who sought his affection. The hurt creature in her anguish entreated the goddess of Love:

"Oh, goddess," she prayed, "make this hard-hearted young man know what it is to love someone who does not return his love. Let him feel the pain I now suffer."

The nymph's prayer was heard. In the middle of the forest, there was a clear fountain. Here Narcissus wandered one day, and bending over to drink, he caught sight of his own reflection in the water. He thought he saw a beautiful water nymph. Gazing in admiration, Narcissus fell in love with himself!

He stretched out his arms to clasp the beautiful being he saw in the water. The creature stretched out its arms, too. Narcissus plunged his arms into the water to embrace his beloved. Instantly, the water shivered into a thousand ripples and the creature disappeared.

A few moments later his beloved reappeared. Now Narcissus brought his lips near to the water to take a kiss.

Women look at other women more than they look at men.

Again the image fled!

He begged his adored one to stay.

"Why do you shun me?"he begged. "If I may not touch you, at least let me look at you."

Narcissus would not leave the pool. Now he knew the pain of loving in vain. Gradually, he grew pale and faded away. As he pined in hopeless love, he lost his beauty. The nymph Echo hovered near him and sorrowed for him. And when he murmured, "Alas, alas!" she answered, "Alas!"

Finally, he died in grief. The nymphs prepared to bury him. But when they came for him, he was nowhere to be found. In his stead, bending over the pool, they found a beautiful flower.

And to this day, this lovely flower grows near the water and is called narcissus.

*   *   *

ASK THE EXPERTS

Q: Why do we use only 10 percent of our brains?

A: We don't. "The 10 percent myth dates back to the nineteenth century, when experiments showed that stimulation of small areas of the brain could have dramatic results. Touch a tiny part of brain tissue and you might be able to induce the patient to extend a limb. There was an easy, if unscientific, extrapolation: If a small percentage of the brain could do so much, then obviously most of the brain was unused.

"In reality, most of the brain mass is used for thinking. Any small-brained creature can extend limbs or see what's across the room, but it takes a big brain to handle the wiring necessary for a profound and abstract thought, such as, 'I think, therefore I am.'

"Today it is possible to watch brain activity through positron-emission tomograms, or PET scans, which show electrical firing among billions of brain cells. Not every cell is involved in every thought or nerve impulse, but there is no evidence that any gray matter is superfluous. The brain has no unused parts, no equivalent of the appendix." (From *Why Things Are, Vol II: The Big Picture*, by Joel Achenbach)

The District of Columbia has one lawyer for every 19 residents.

"ALWAYS SPIT AFTER A FISHERMAN"

*Want people from other countries to think you're polite?
Of course you do. So here are a few BRI tips about
what's considered good manners around the world.*

In Japan: Wear a surgical mask in public if you have a cold.

In Switzerland: Buy wine for your table if you drop your bread in the fondue.

In Italy: Don't allow a woman to pour wine.

In Samoa: Spill a few drops of kava, the national beverage, before drinking.

In Belgium and Luxembourg: Avoid sending a gift of chrysanthemums. They are a reminder of death.

In Sweden: Wait until you're outside your guest's house before putting your coat on.

In Jordan: Leave small portions of food on your plate. Also, refuse seconds at least twice before accepting.

In Greece: Cheerfully participate in folk dancing if invited.

In Fiji: Fold your arms behind you when conversing.

In Portugal: Signal you enjoyed a meal by kissing your index finger and then pinching your earlobe.

In China: Decline a gift a few times before accepting. Use both hands to give or receive one.

In Iran: Shake hands with children. (It shows respect for their parents.)

In Spain: Say "buen provecho" to anyone beginning a meal.

In Finland: If you pass the salt at the dinner table, don't put it in anyone's hand—put the salt shaker down and let them pick it up.

In Norway: When a fisherman walks by, spit after him. It's a way of wishing him good luck.

In Korea: Allow others to pass between you and the person you are conversing with. Don't make anyone walk behind you.

The blue whale's tongue weighs as much as an adult elephant.

MODERN MYTHOLOGY

These characters are as famous in our culture as Pegasus or Hercules were in Greek myths. Where did they come from?

SMOKEY THE BEAR. In 1942, at the peak of World War II, U.S. officials realized that forest fires could jeopardize national security. They began a poster campaign about fire prevention. In 1944, the posters featured Disney's Bambi. But in 1945, the Forest Service introduced its own character—Smokey the Bear (named after "Smokey Joe" Martin, assistant fire chief in New York City from 1919 to 1930). The campaign was successful, but really took off in 1950, when an orphaned bear cub was rescued from a fire in New Mexico and was nursed back to health by a forest ranger's family. They named him Smokey and sent him to the National Zoological Park in Washington, D.C....where he became a popular attraction as a living icon. He got so much mail that the postal service gave him his own zip code.

UNCLE BEN. From 1943 to 1945, Texan Gordon Harwell sold a special "converted" rice—made by special process, so it would last longer than usual—to the U.S. government. After World War II, Harwell and his business partner decided to sell it to the general public. But what would they call it? They were in a Chicago restaurant one night when Harwell remembered a black farmer in the Houston area who'd been famous for the high quality of his rice. He was known simply as Uncle Ben. Since Ben was long dead, Harwell asked Frank Brown, maître d' of the restaurant, to pose for the now-famous portrait on every box of Uncle Ben's Converted Rice.

CHIQUITA BANANA. During World War II, almost no bananas made it to U.S. shores—the United Fruit Company's fleet of ships had been commandeered to move war supplies. After the war, the company wondered how to reintroduce the fruit to the American public. Their solution: a radio ad campaign featuring a singing banana. ("I'm Chiquita Banana and I'm here to say / Bananas have to ripen in a certain way...") Their calypso-style jingle became so popular that it was even released as a record...and hit #1 on the pop music charts!

Onions have no flavor, only a smell.

People clamored to know what Chiquita looked like. So the company hired cartoonist Dik Browne (later, creator of "Hagar the Horrible") to create her. He gave her a familiar Latin look by "borrowing" movie star Carmen Miranda's fruit-salad hat and sexy dress. Chiquita became so famous dancing on TV commercials that in 1990, United Fruit changed its name to Chiquita Brands.

LEO, THE MGM LION. In 1915 Howard Dietz, a young adman who had just graduated from Columbia University, was ordered by his boss to create a trademark for the Goldwyn Movie Company. He was stumped...until he remembered that his alma mater's insignia was a lion. "If it's good enough for Columbia, it's good enough for Goldwyn," he said...and Leo began roaring at the beginning of each Goldwyn film. A few years later, Goldwyn merged with the Metro and Mayer film companies, forming Metro-Goldwyn-Mayer. Leo became their logo, too. Today, he is Hollywood's most durable star—featured in films for over 80 years.

JUAN VALDEZ. "This is the tale of Juan Valdez / Stubborn man, as the story says / Lives way up on a mountaintop / Growing the finest coffee crop." In the early 1960s, about 25% of all coffee sold in America came from Colombia, but consumers didn't know it. So Colombian coffee-growers hired an ad agency to make Americans aware of their product. The agency hired New York singer José Duval and sent him to Colombia with a film crew. Clothed in traditional garb—a "mulera" (shawl), a straw sombrero, white pants and shirt—José was filmed picking coffee beans and leading a bean-laden burro down mountain trails. It was a huge success—people in New York greeted Duval with "Hi, Juan" wherever he went. Today, a stylized picture of Juan Valdez is part of the Colombian coffee logo.

JACK, (the Cracker Jack boy) and BINGO (his dog). The sailor boy was added to Cracker Jack packages during World War I as a salute to "our fighting boys." But he was modeled after the company founder's young grandson, Robert, who often wore a sailor suit. The dog was named Bingo after the children's song ("B-I-N-G-O, and Bingo was his name-O"). Sad footnote: As the first "sailor boy" packages rolled off the presses, Robert got pneumonia and died. So the logo can also be seen on his tombstone in Chicago.

Good news: There are no hog lips or snouts in SPAM.

FAMOUS FOR 15 MINUTES

Here it is again—our feature based on Andy Warhol's prophetic comment that "in the future, everyone will be famous for 15 minutes." Here's how a few people have been using up their allotted quarter hour.

THE STAR: Alan Hale, a backyard astronomer in New Mexico.

THE HEADLINE: Hale, Hearty Fellow, Finds Comet but No Job.

WHAT HAPPENED: Late in the evening of July 22, 1995, Hale set up his telescope and was observing star clusters when he noticed a fuzzy blur that didn't appear in any astronomical charts. It turned out to be a comet, the brightest one to pass near the earth in more than 20 years. The same night another amateur astronomer, Thomas Bopp, made a sighting in Arizona. The comet was named Hale-Bopp in their honor.

AFTERMATH: Hale and Bopp appeared on TV talk shows, and made personal appearances all over the country. For a time they were the most famous astronomers in America. But Hale, who had a Ph.D. in astronomy when he discovered the comet, was unemployed—the only job he could find in his field was a temporary one in a space museum two hours away. Even after the discovery, he remained unemployed. He made news again when he posted a letter on the Internet in 1998, saying that because of lack of jobs, he couldn't encourage kids to be scientists when they grew up.

THE STAR: Jessie Lee Foveaux, a 98-year-old great-great grandmother living in Manhattan, Kansas.

THE HEADLINE: Great-Great-Granny Lays Golden Egg.

WHAT HAPPENED: In 1979, Foveaux signed up for a senior-citizen writing class and began compiling her memoirs as a Christmas present for her family. In 1997, the Wall St. Journal ran a front-page story on the class...and featured Jessie's work. The article ignited a bonfire of interest in her life story. The next day her phone rang off the hook as publishers fought to buy the manuscript. Foveaux chose Warner Books, which paid her $1 million for the rights.

It's lonely at the top: Only one-third of Americans say they'd want their boss's job.

AFTERMATH: *Any Given Day: The Life and Times of Jessie Lee Brown Foveaux,* hit bookstore shelves a few months later, spurring articles in *People* and other magazines and an appearance on the Rosie O'Donnell show. "I never thought anyone would read it but my own," Foveaux says. "If I had, I probably wouldn't have told as much." Book sales were disappointing, but Foveaux became rich off the book. She was able to leave more than just a manuscript to her family.

THE STAR: Kato Kaelin, moocher ordinaire—O.J.'s house guest on the night Simpson's wife and her companion were murdered.
THE HEADLINE: Trial of the Century Makes O.J.'s Sidekick House Guest of the Century.
WHAT HAPPENED: His eyewitness account was central to the O.J. murder trial—he was the last person to see Simpson before the murders, and he heard a thump outside his guest-house wall near where the bloody glove was found. His testimony helped exonerate Simpson at the criminal trial, but helped convict him in the civil trial. Kato later admitted that he, too, thought Simpson was guilty.
AFTERMATH: Kaelin's aging surfer-boy persona helped make him one of the most recognizable celebrities to come out of the trials. He appeared in photo spreads for *GQ* and *Playgirl* magazine, endorsed hair products and cigarettes, and even wrote an article for *P.O.V.* magazine on "How to Score a Free Pad."

An aspiring actor before the trials, he was now a famous aspiring actor. He got bit parts in a handful of movies, but not much more.

For a while he was also a talk show host at KLSX radio in Los Angeles. Topics included "Don't you hate waiting," and other equally stimulating fare. That fizzled too, and not just because listeners were bored. "He quit," a spokesperson for the station reports. "He found out it was hard work."

THE STAR: Divine Brown, a Hollywood, California hooker.
THE HEADLINE: Hugh's Hooker a Huge Hit.
WHAT HAPPENED: In June 1995, a police officer observed a white BMW parked off a side street on LA's seedy Sunset Strip, a boulevard notorious for streetwalkers. He checked it out…and observed a prostitute performing a sex act on actor Hugh Grant.

Doctors say: People who have pet fish fall asleep easier than people who don't.

Both suspects were arrested. Grant was fined $1,800 for the incident; Brown was fined $1,350 and spent 180 days in jail. Overnight she went from down-and-out streetwalker to celebrity.

AFTERMATH: In the months that followed she made more than $500,000 from interviews, appearances, and TV commercials in England, Brazil, and the U.S. She spent the money on designer clothes, an expensive apartment, two Rolls-Royces, a Mercedes, a stretch limo, and other goodies. "I'm blessed by God," Brown told a reporter in 1996. "I ruined his life, but he made mine."

Grant rebuilt his career and even his relationship with girlfriend Elizabeth Hurley. Brown burned through her money in about a year. She was evicted from her home, her cars were repossessed, her kids were sent back to public schools. By June 1996, she was working in a strip joint for $75 a night. In 1997, she attempted suicide. "She tasted the good life and knows she can't have it anymore," her publicist told reporters. "No wonder she's depressed."

THE STAR: William "Refrigerator" Perry, defensive lineman for the Chicago Bears.

THE HEADLINE: Rotund Refrigerator Romps in End Zone.

WHAT HAPPENED: Perry was a 1st-round draft pick for the Bears in 1985. When he reported to training camp at 330 pounds —too fat even by football standards—the Bears benched him.

He might have stayed there if the Bears hadn't lost the 1984 NFC title game to the SF 49ers. With the score 23-0, the 49ers used a 271-pound guard in the backfield. Bears coach Mike Ditka took it as a personal insult....So the next time he faced the 49ers, he had Perry, the team's fattest player, carry the ball on two plays.

People loved it. A week later, Ditka did it again...and Perry scored a touchdown. For some reason, it became national news.

AFTERMATH: By midseason, Perry was making appearances on David Letterman and the Tonight Show. By the time the Bears won the Super Bowl he was a media superstar, making a tidy sum on product endorsements. Perry's fame lasted until the next season, when Ditka realized Perry had a life-threatening weight problem, and put him on a diet. He retired from pro football in 1994, then signed on with the World League of American Football, a league that plays American football in Europe.

Smallest mammal on Earth: The bumblebee bat. It weighs less than a penny.

FAMILIAR PHRASES

Here are still more origins of everyday phrases.

GET SOMEONE'S GOAT
Meaning: Annoy someone; make them lose their temper.
Origin: "This very American phrase came from the practice of putting a goat inside a skittish racehorse's stall because it supposedly had a calming influence. A gambler might persuade a stable boy to remove the goat shortly before the race, thereby upsetting the horse and reducing its chance of winning (and improving the gambler's odds)." (From *It's Raining Cats and Dogs*, by Christine Ammer)

THE HIGH MUCKY MUCK or HIGH MUCK-A-MUCK
Meaning: A person in charge who acts like a big shot.
Origin: "The dictionaries usually give the spelling high-muck-a-muck, and that's a bit closer to the original Chinook version hiu muckamuck, which means 'plenty of food.' In the Alaska of a century or more ago, a person with plenty to eat was a pretty important fellow—and that's what the expression means. A high-muck-a-muck is usually not only a person of authority but one who likes to be sure that everyone knows how important he is." (From the *Morris Dictionary of Word and Phrase Origins*, by William and Mary Morris)

HERE'S MUD IN YOUR EYE
Meaning: A toast wishing good luck.
Origin: "The expression is not a toast to another; it is a toast to yourself—because it means, 'I hope I beat you.' The allusion is to a horse race. If the track is at all muddy, the rider of the losing horse is very likely to get mud in his eye from the horse that is winning." (From *Why Do We Say...?*, by Nigel Rees)

Second most popular place to eat breakfast in the U.S.: The car.

LEGENDARY BETS

Some of history's most famous bets may never have happened at all.
Here are a few you may have heard of. Did they really happen?

PEARL JAM
The Wager: According to Roman historian Pliny the Elder, Cleopatra once bet her lover Marc Antony that she could spend the equivalent of over $3 million in "one evening's entertainment." He didn't believe it.

The Winner: Cleopatra. Here's how she supposedly did it:

> There were dancers garbed in specially-made costumes of gold and rare feathers; there were jugglers and performing elephants; there were a thousand maid-servants attending to the couple's every need; and there was a seemingly endless banquet of indescribable splendor. At the end of the evening, Cleopatra proposed to toast her lover with a vessel of vinegar. But first she dropped her exquisite pearl earrings, each worth a small kingdom, into the cup and watched them dissolve. Then she raised the sour cocktail of untold value to her lips and drank it down.

Truth or Legend? It's possible, but not likely. Pearls are "largely carbonate, and will dissolve in a mild acidic solution such as vinegar." But it would take at least a few hours, and the vinegar would have to be so strong you could hardly drink it. However, if Cleo crushed the pearls first, they would have dissolved immediately.

THE SECRET WORD IS...

The Wager: In 1780, James Daly, manager of a theater in Dublin, Ireland, bet that he could coin a word that would become the talk of the town overnight—even though it had no meaning. Daly's boast seemed so preposterous that everyone within earshot took him up on it.

Daly immediately paid an army of children to run around town and write a single word in chalk on walls, streets, billboards, etc.

The Winner: Daly. The next morning, Dubliners were asking what this strange word meant...and why it was written everywhere they looked. People speculated that it was "indecent," but no one knew for sure. The word was quiz. According to the *Morris*

The wild turkey is the only bird with a beard.

Dictionary of Word and Phrase Origins:

> At first it became synonymous with 'practical joke'—for that was what Daly had played on the citizenry. Gradually it came to mean making fun of a person by verbal bantering. In time, it came to mean what 'quiz' means today—a question asked of a person in order to learn the extent of his knowledge.

Truth or Legend? No one knows. The tale has never been authenticated, and as far as most lexicographers are concerned, the definitive origin of the word quiz is still unknown.

THE FIRST MOVIE?

The Wager: In 1872, Leland Stanford, former governor of California, railroad tycoon, and dabbler in horses, bet newspaperman Frederick MacCrellish that for a fraction of a second, a trotter has all four feet off the ground simultaneously. The bet was for anywhere from nothing to $50,000 (depending on who tells the story). To settle the question, Stanford hired English photographer Eadward J. Muybridge to photograph one of his prime racers, Occidental, in motion. There was one problem: photographic technology in 1872 was still too primitive to capture the desired image. The bet was left unsettled and all parties moved on.

The Winner: Stanford. Five years later, Stanford was still burning to know whether he was right. This time, using the latest technology, Muybridge was able to take a picture that showed all four of Occidental's feet off the ground at once. Fascinated with the results of the new photographic technology, Stanford told Muybridge to spare no expense and buy state-of-the-art photographic equipment for another test. In 1878, with the new equipment in hand, Muybridge set up a battery of 24 cameras alongside Stanford's private track, and by precisely timing the exposures, successfully captured every position in a horse's stride. This approach to rapid-motion photography paved the way for development of the movie camera.

Truth or Legend? The story about the photo is true, but it probably didn't happen as part of a bet for two reasons. Stanford wasn't a betting man, and, in 1872, MacCrellish was using the Alta Californian to lambast Stanford for unsavory business practices—hardly conducive to a "friendly wager."

Poll results: 50% of all Oreo-eaters say they pull them apart before eating them.

STRANGE TOURIST ATTRACTIONS

Next time you're traveling across America, set aside some time to visit these unusual attractions. From the hilarious book, Roadside America.

THE CEMENT OX
Location: Three Forks, Montana
Background: The ox, nicknamed "New Faithful," is one of two 12-foot tall cement oxen statues that stand outside the Prairie Schooner Restaurant, and appears to be pulling the restaurant, which is shaped like an enormous covered wagon.
Be Sure to See...the cashier gleefully asking customers, "Have you seen old faithful?" and then adding, "Well, take a look at new faithful!" She pushes a secret button, and the cement ox starts peeing.

THE HAIR MUSEUM
Location: Independence, Missouri
Background: This museum is all that remains of an art form developed by cosmetology schools in the 19th century to keep hair clippings from going to waste.
Be Sure to See...the museum's collection of 75 items made entirely from hair, including hair wreaths, hair bookmarks, and a hair diary that belonged to a convict. You can even get a discount haircut, performed by "fully licensed" cosmetology students.

THE HOEGH PET CASKET CO.
Location: Gladstone, Michigan
Background: Hoegh makes seven different sizes of coffins for pets, including boxes tiny enough for birds and large enough for Great Danes.
Be Sure to See...the "model" pet cemetery and demonstration. Note the brass sign over the crematorium that reads, "If Christ had a dog, he would have followed Him to the cross."

NATIONAL MUSEUM OF HEALTH AND MEDICINE
Location: Bethesda, Maryland
Background: The museum is actually quite respectable and has been around for more than a century, but the definition of what is "respectable" has changed a lot over the years. Some of the older items on display are pretty disgusting.
Be Sure to See...the amputated leg of Major General Daniel E. Sickles, who lost the leg during the Civil War when it was hit by a 12-lb. cannonball—which is also on display. "For many years," the sign reads, "Sickles visited the museum on the anniversary of its amputation." Also: the computer terminal that lets you play doctor to a mortally wounded Abraham Lincoln. "Congratulations! You've scored an 84 out of a possible 100. The nation applauds your effort as a doctor and as a responsible member of society. Unfortunately, the president is dead."

THE WORLD'S SECOND-LARGEST BALL OF TWINE
Location: Cawker City, Kansas.
Background: When Frank Stoeber learned of the existence of the World's Largest Ball of Twine (12 feet in circumference, 21,140 lbs. of twine) in Darwin, Minnesota, he set out to roll an even bigger one...but died when his ball was still one foot too small in circumference. The city fathers put it on display anyway.
Be Sure to See... Stoeber's ball of twine, displayed outside in a gazebo. Note the aroma: a musty smell, kind of like damp, rotting...twine.

THE HOLE 'N' THE ROCK
Location: Moab, Utah
Background: In 1940, a man named Albert Christensen took some dynamite and started blasting holes in a rock. He kept blasting until 1952, when he had enough holes—14 in all—to build a house, a cafe, and a gift shop. The Hole 'N' the Rock attracts 40,000 visitors a year.
Be Sure to See...the bathroom, which has an entire cavern to itself. Christensen named it "a toilet in a tomb."

Fart Fact: The average human body has about 100 milliliters of bowel gas at one time.

THE MUSEUM OF QUESTIONABLE MEDICAL DEVICES
Location: In a strip mall in Minneapolis, Minnesota
Background: Operated by Bob McCoy, the museum was founded to encourage interest in science and medicine.
Be Sure to See...the Prostate Warmer, which plugs into a light socket and "stimulates the abdominal brain," and the Nemectron Machine, which "normalizes" breasts through the application of metal rings of various sizes.

THE CORAL CASTLE
Location: Homestead, Florida
Background: Edward Leedskalnin was a young man when his 16-year-old fiancée, Agnes Scuffs, ended their engagement. Leedskalnin spent the next 20 years carving a massive memorial castle to Agnes out of coral, using tools he made from junked auto parts. By the time he died in 1951, Leedskalnin (who weighed approximately 100 lbs.) had quarried, carved and positioned more than 1,100 tons of coral rock for the castle. Some of the blocks weighed more than 25 tons—but because Leedskalnin worked alone, in secret, and usually at night, nobody knows how he managed to position the blocks in place. He never explained, other than to say, "I know how the pyramids were built."
Be Sure to See...a coral sundial that tells time, a throne for Agnes that rocks, and a heart-shaped table that made it into *Ripley's Believe It or Not* as the world's biggest valentine.
Note: Leedskalnin's ex-fiancée Agnes Scuffs was still alive in 1992. She had never visited the castle.

*   *   *

BONUS DESTINATION: O'Donnell, Texas, hometown of Dan Blocker, who played Hoss on TV's *Bonanza*.
Be Sure to See... The Dan Blocker Memorial Head. When Blocker made it big, the town fathers had a likeness of his head, carved in granite, installed on a stand in the town square.

Food fact: Only 3% of Americans prefer their hot dogs plain.

IF YOU LIKE "IKE"

*Here are a few thoughts from former
president Dwight D. Eisenhower.*

"There is one thing about being a president—nobody can tell you when to sit down."

"Farming looks mighty easy when your plough is a pencil and you're a thousand miles from the cornfield."

"You do not lead by hitting people over the head—that's assault, not leadership."

"When people speak to you about a preventive war, you tell them to go and fight it."

(On Vietnam): "We are going to have peace even if we have to fight for it."

"Politics should be the part-time profession of every citizen."

"Things have never been more like the way they are today in history."

"Do not needlessly endanger your lives…until I give you the signal."

"The middle of the road is all of the usable surface. The extremes, right and left, are in the gutters."

"There are no easy matters that come to you as president. If they are easy, they are settled at a lower level."

"Every gun that is made, every warship launched, every rocket fired, signifies, in the final sense, a theft from those who hunger and are not fed, those who are cold and are not clothed."

"An intellectual is a man who takes more words than necessary to tell more than he knows."

"There is no amount of military force that can possibly give you real security. You wouldn't have that amount in the first place, unless you felt there was a similar amount that could threaten you, somewhere else in the world."

The American goldfinch's nest is so thick-walled it will hold water…some hatchlings drown.

IT'S JUST SERENDIPITY...

The word "serendipity" means "making happy and unexpected discoveries by accident." It was coined by the English writer Horace Walpole, who took it from the title of an old fairy tale, The 3 Princes of Serendip. The heroes in the story are always "making discoveries they are not in quest of." For example, it's just serendipity...

THAT BUBBLE GUM IS PINK

Background: In the 1920s, the Fleer Company of Philadelphia wanted to develop a bubble gum that didn't stick to people's faces. A 23-year-old employee, Waiter Diemer, took the challenge. He started experimenting with different mixtures, and in a year, he had the answer. In 1928, the first workable batch of bubble gum was mixed up in the company mixing machines. "The machines started groaning, the mix started popping, and then I realized I'd forgotten to put any coloring in the gum," Diemer recalled.

Serendipity: The next day, he made a second batch. This time he remembered to color it. But the only color he could find was pink. "Pink was all I had at hand," he says. "And that's the reason ever since, all over the world, that bubble gum has been predominantly pink."

...THAT WE PLAY BASKETBALL INSTEAD OF BOXBALL

Background: When James Naismith invented his game in 1891, he decided to put a horizontal "goal" high over players' heads. He figured that would be safer—there would be no violent pushing and shoving as people tried to block the goal...and shots would be lobbed, not rocketed, at it.

Serendipity: As one historian writes: "The goal was supposed to be a box. Naismith asked the janitor for a couple of suitable boxes, and the janitor said he didn't have any...but he did have a couple of round peach baskets in the storeroom. So it was baskets that were tacked to the walls of the gym." A week later one of the players suggested, "Why not call it basketball?" The inventor answered: "We have a basket and a ball...that would be a good name for it."

The Italian flag was designed by Napoleon Bonaparte.

...THAT MEL GIBSON GOT HIS BIG BREAK

Background: According to *The Good Luck Book*, "When director George Miller was looking for someone to play the male lead for his 1979 post-apocalyptic road movie *Mad Max*, he was specifically looking for someone who looked weary, beaten-up, and scarred.

Serendipity: "One of the many 'wannabes' who answered the cattle call for the part was a then-unknown Australian actor named Mel Gibson. It just so happened that the night before his scheduled screen test, Gibson was attacked and badly beaten up by three drunks. When he showed up for the audition the next morning looking like a prize fighter on a losing streak, Miller gave him the part. It launched Gibson's career as an international movie star in such films as *The Year of Living Dangerously*, *Lethal Weapon*, and the 1995 Oscar-winning *Braveheart*."

...THAT YELLOW PAGES ARE YELLOW

Background: The phone was invented in 1876, and the first Bell business directory came out in 1878. As we wrote in our Ultimate Bathroom Reader, it was printed on white paper. So were subsequent editions all over the country.

Serendipity: In 1881, the Wyoming Telephone and Telegraph Company hired a printer in Cheyenne to print its first business directory. He didn't have enough white paper to finish the job and didn't want to lose the company's business. So he used the stock he had on hand—yellow paper. Other companies around the country adopted it, too...not realizing it was an accident.

...THAT HOLLYWOOD STARS PUT THEIR PRINTS IN CEMENT AT GRAUMAN'S CHINESE THEATER

Background: In the early days of Hollywood, Sid Grauman's movie theater, fashioned after a Chinese pagoda, was the biggest and fanciest of its kind.

Serendipity: One day in 1927, movie star Norma Shearer accidentally stepped in wet cement as she walked in the courtyard of the theater. Rather than fill the prints in, Graumann got other stars to put their hand- and footprints in the cement. That turned it into one of Hollywood's biggest tourist attractions.

Yum! You swallow and recycle about a quart of mucus a day.

FOUNDING FATHERS

*Some people have achieved immortality because their
names became identified with products. You already
know the names—now here are the people.*

JAMES DRUMMOND DOLE. In 1899, his cousin, the governor of Hawaii, helped him get some land to pursue his dream of growing pineapples for export. He revolutionized the fruit industry by packing the highly perishable pineapple in cans, shoving pieces through a small slit in the top and sealing it with a bead of solder.

FRANK GERBER. In 1928, his seven-month-old granddaughter, Sally, became seriously ill. The girl's physician suggested she might benefit from a diet of strained fruits and vegetables, and he put his tomato-canning factory to work on it. When Sally recovered, mothers in the area began requesting samples of the food. He started marketing the product, and within six months, Gerber Strained Peas, Prunes, Carrots, and Spinach were available across the U.S.

CHARLES PILLSBURY. Bought his first flour mill in St. Anthony Falls, Minnesota in 1865, at a time when the state imported most of its flour. Minnesota flour was hard and brittle, and considered inferior to the imported flour. Charles installed a purifier that enabled him to produce flour which made more and better bread per barrel than the softer imported winter wheat. Ten years later, his plant was turning out 10,000 barrels of flour a day.

JOHN LANDIS MASON. In 1858, he worked with glass blowers to produce an alternative to home-canning with tin. His solution: a threaded glass container with a screw-top lid. It preserved flavor better, enabled housewives to see the contents at a glance, and was easy to clean and reuse. Over a hundred billion Mason jars have been made since then.

LEON LEONWOOD (L.L.) BEAN. Sewed leather uppers to rubber overshoe bottoms in 1912 to keep his feet dry on deer-hunting trips. He sold a few pairs to friends and neighbors and as the word spread, orders for his boots came pouring in. He turned it into an outdoor clothing business.

WORDS OF WISDOM

*Jon Winokur compiled these pearls of
wisdom in his book* Friendly Advice.

"Wise men don't need advice.
Fools don't take it."
—**Benjamin Franklin**

"Always obey your superiors. If
you have any."
—**Mark Twain**

"Life is a sh—sandwich. But if
you've got enough bread, you
can't taste the sh—."
—**Jonathan Winters**

"Rise early. Work late. Strike
oil."
—**J. Paul Getty**

"To succeed in the world it is
not enough to be stupid, you
must also be well-mannered."
—**Voltaire**

"Never take top billing. You'll
last longer that way."
—**Bing Crosby**

"It is better to be beautiful than
to be good, but it is better to be
good than to be ugly."
—**Oscar Wilde**

"It is fatal to look hungry. It
makes people want to kick
you."
—**George Orwell**

"If you see a snake, just kill it—
don't appoint a committee on
snakes."
—**H. Ross Perot**

"It's not whether you win or
lose, it's how you play the
game."
—**Grantland Rice**

"Grantland Rice can go to hell
as far as I'm concerned."
—**Gene Autry**

"I always advise people never
to give advice."
—**P.G. Wodehouse**

"Honesty is the best policy, and
spinach is the best vegetable."
—**Popeye the Sailor**

"To succeed with the opposite
sex, tell her you're impotent.
She can't wait to disprove it."
—**Cary Grant**

PAGE 42

*Here's a page we've never tried before. It was
sent to us by BRI member Tim Harrower.*

Elvis Presley died at **42**.

The angle at which light
reflects off water to create a
rainbow is **42** degrees.

The city of Jerusalem covers an
area of **42** square miles.

The Torah (the holy book of
Judaism) is broken into
columns, each of which always
has exactly **42** lines.

Fox Mulder *(The X-Files)* lives
in apartment number **42**.

There are **42** decks on the
Enterprise NCC1701-D (the
Next Generation ship).

Bill Clinton is the **42**nd U. S.
president.

A Wonderbra consists of **42**
individual parts.

There are **42** Oreo cookies in a
1-pound package.

"The beast was given a mouth
uttering proud boasts and blas-
phemies, and it was given
authority to act for **42**
months."

—***Revelations 13:5***

In Romeo and Juliet, Juliet
sleeps for **42** hours.

The right arm of the Statue of
Liberty is **42** feet long.

Jimi Hendrix and Jerry Garcia
were born in 19**42**.

The number of dots on a pair
of dice: **42**.

Dogs have a total of **42** teeth
over their lifetimes.

In *The Catcher in the Rye*,
Holden Caufield lies and says
that he is **42**.

The world-record jump by a
kangaroo is **42** feet.

The natural vibration
frequency of white mouse
DNA: **42**.

The natural vibration
frequency of human DNA: **42**.

There were **42** generations
from Abraham to Jesus Christ.

And most important:
According to Douglas Adams'
*The Hitchhiker's Guide to the
Galaxy*, "the meaning of life,
the universe, and everything" is
the number **42**.

HEADLINES

These are 100% honest-to-goodness headlines.
Can you figure out what they were trying to say?

Textron Inc. makes offer to
screw company stockholders

**SQUAD HELPS DOG BITE
VICTIM**

Man Minus Ear Waives
Hearing

IRAQI HEAD SEEKS ARMS

**MAN SHOT, STABBED;
DEATH BY NATURAL
CAUSES RULED**

*Police begin campaign to run
down jaywalkers*

**Once-sagging cloth diaper
saved by full dumps**

BILLS OVERWHELM
CHARGERS

**32 Ignorant Enough to Serve
on North Jury**

UTAH GIRL DOES WELL IN
DOG SHOWS

**Local High School Dropouts
Cut In Half**

*TYPHOON RIPS THROUGH
CEMETERY; HUNDREDS
DEAD*

Pastor Aghast At First Lady
Sex Position

Padres Hit On Penguins

*Death Causes Loneliness,
Feelings of Isolation*

SKI AREAS CLOSE DUE
TO SNOW

*Child's Stool Great For Use In
Garden*

FIRE OFFICIALS GRILLED
OVER KEROSENE HEATERS

**Woman Improving After Fatal
Crash**

STUD TIRES OUT

Death in the Ring: Most
Boxers Are Not the Same
Afterward

*FFA proposes name change to
FFA*

**REAGAN WINS ON
BUDGET, BUT MOORE
LIES AHEAD**

Man Struck By Lightning Faces
Battery Charges

**British Union Finds Dwarfs
in Short Supply**

MAN FOUND DEAD IN
CEMETERY

*Legislators Tax Brains to Cut
Deficit*

The world's most expensive spice: Spanish saffron. It can cost more than $2,000 per pound.

HITS OF THE 1970S: A QUIZ

Now it's time to find out how much you know about a few of the hits of the '70s. (Answers on page 755.)

1. "You Don't Bring Me Flowers," a duet by Barbra Streisand and Neil Diamond, was a #1 song in 1976. How did this unlikely pair get together?
a) They each recorded the song separately, and a disc jockey spliced the two recordings together.
b) They ran into each other at a recording session and—as a joke—decided to record the sappiest song they knew.
c) It was the dying request of Diamond's mother that he record a song with Streisand—her favorite singer.

2. Led Zeppelin's "Stairway to Heaven" was the most-requested FM song of the decade...but some Christian fundamentalists cite it as an example of devil-worship in rock. Robert Plant, the group's singer, composed the lyrics. He says...
a) Even he doesn't know what they mean.
b) It's strange that fundamentalists would criticize it, because he's a born-again Christian.
c) He purposely put "satanic" messages on the record to shock his critics. "If they're idiotic enough to play it backwards, they deserve it," he said.

3. Cheap Trick's "I Want You to Want Me" sold a million copies in 1979. It was an incredible turnaround for the group. Their third album had just flopped, and Epic Records had pretty much given up on them. So how did they become stars?
a) An L.A. deejay became their champion, urging listeners to write to Epic and release "I Want You to Want Me" as a single.
b) The group was asked to tour as an opening act for the Rolling Stones, which sparked new interest in their album.
c) Somehow, a quickie album that they made exclusively for the Japanese market wound up receiving air time on U.S. FM radio.

A cow has four stomachs.

4. The #1 song of 1975 was "Love Will Keep Us Together," by The Captain and Tennille who were, according to news reports, blissfully married. But few of the fans who heard the song knew it was really about...
a) Two men.
b) Two pets—a dog and a chipmunk.
c) A mother and child.

5. Melanie had a huge hit in 1971 with "I've Got a Brand New Key." She had an innocent voice, but the lyric "I've got a brand new pair of roller skates, you've got a brand new key" sounded like sex to most people. The truth would have disappointed them— the song was really inspired by...
a) A new pair of roller skates she got for her birthday.
b) A McDonald's hamburger.
c) A sporting goods store near her house.

6. The Bee Gees were the hottest group of the late '70s, and the record that started their meteoric comeback—before *Saturday Night Fever* was released—was "Jive Talkin'," a #1 hit in 1975. The song actually started out as...
a) "Jive Walkin'"—inspired by the British comedy troupe Monty Python and their "Department of Silly Walks."
b) "Drive Talkin'"—inspired by a rickety wooden bridge.
c) "Hive Stalkin'"—inspired by their hobby of keeping bees.

7. One of the biggest-selling records of the '70s was Terry Jacks's "Seasons in the Sun." He didn't plan to release it as a single, but...
a) His paper-boy heard his demo tape and really liked it...then brought his friends to Jacks's house to hear it.
b) The Beach Boys heard his demo tape and talked about recording it themselves. Jacks figured if they liked it, it must be good.
c) He'd recently broken up with his wife, Susan Jacks (of the Poppy Family), and needed a quick $10,000 to pay his divorce lawyer.

A bloody wound on your body starts to clot in less than 10 seconds.

WELCOME TO WASHINGTON!

*Politicians aren't getting much respect these days—but then,
it sounds like they don't think they deserve much, either.*

"If hypocrisy were gold, the Capitol would be Fort Knox."
—**Senator John McCain**

"It is perfectly American to be wrong."
—**Newt Gingrich**

"My choice early in life was either to be a piano player in a whorehouse or a politician. And to tell the truth, there's hardly any difference."
—**Harry S. Truman**

"My God! What is there in this place (Washington D.C.) that a man should ever want to get into it?"
—**President James Garfield**

"I think the American public wants a solemn ass as president and I think I'll go along with them."
—**President Calvin Coolidge**

"Political promises go in one year and out the other."
—**Anonymous**

"The single most exciting thing you encounter in government is competence, because it's so rare."
—**Senator Daniel Patrick Moynihan**

"You can lead a man to Congress, but you can't make him think."
—**Milton Berle**

"If...everybody in this town connected with politics had to leave town because of [chasing women] and drinking, you'd have no government."
—**Senator Barry Goldwater**

"If you don't want to work for a living, this is as good a job as any."
—**Congressman John F. Kennedy in 1946**

"There they are—See No Evil, Hear No Evil, and Evil."
—**Bob Dole, on a gathering of ex-presidents Gerald Ford, Jimmy Carter, and Richard Nixon**

The three foods Americans say they hate the most: #1 tofu; #2 liver; #3 yogurt.

LET *ME* WRITE SIGN— I SPEAK ENGLISH GOOD

When signs in a foreign country are written in English, any combination of words is possible. Here are some real-life examples.

"Guests are prohibited from talking around in the lobby in large groups in the nude."
—*Havana hotel*

"If this is your first visit to the USSR, you are welcome to it."
—*Moscow hotel*

"It is forbidden to enter a woman even if a foreigner is dressed as a man."
—*Seville cathedral*

"Visitors two to a bed and half an hour only."
—*Barcelona hospital*

"All customers promptly executed."
—*Tokyo barbershop*

"We highly recommend the hotel tart."
—*Torremolinos hotel*

"I slaughter myself twice daily."
—*Israel butcher shop*

"Because of the impropriety of entertaining persons of the opposite sex in the bedroom, it is requested that the lobby be used for this purpose."
—*Colon restaurant*

"All vegetables in this establishment have been washed in water especially passed by the management."
—*Sri Lanka restaurant*

"Gentlemen's throats cut with nice sharp razors."
—*Zanzibar barbershop*

"Very smart! Almost pansy!"
—*Budapest shop*

"Swimming is forbidden in the absence of the savior."
—*French swimming pool*

"Dresses for street walking."
—*Paris dress shop*

"Go away."
—*Barcelona travel agency*

George Washington was named after England's King George.

MADE IN FRANCE

*This started out as a "Random Origins" page...until we
noticed that everything on the page was invented
by French people. Ooh La-La!*

DRY CLEANING
In 1825, the maid of a Frenchman named Jean-Baptiste
Jolly knocked over a camphene (distilled turpentine)
lamp on a table, spilling the camphene all over the table cloth.
The harder she rubbed the tablecloth to get up the camphene, the
cleaner and brighter it became. Jolly, who made a living dyeing
fabrics, added fabric cleaning to his business. By the mid-1850s
there were thousands of dry cleaners (the process used no water)
all over France.

NON-STICK FRYING PANS
Teflon or polytetrafluorethylene (PTFE) was discovered by the
DuPont company in 1938. Teflon pans were invented in the mid-
1950s by an engineer named Mark Gregoire, who got the idea
from something his wife said to him as he was leaving to go fishing. Gregoire used PTFE to keep his fishing line from sticking, and
his wife complained that there was nothing like PTFE to keep her
pots and pans from sticking. He founded the Tefal company to
make Teflon coated pans in 1955. Today, more than 75% of U.S.
kitchens contain at least one non-stick pan.

STETHOSCOPES
In 1816, a French pathologist named René Théophile Hyacinthe
Laënnec happened to walk through the courtyard of the Louvre as
some kids hunched over two ends of some long pieces of wood.
When the kids at one end tapped the wood with a small pin, the
kids at the other end could hear it as it traveled through the
wood. Laënnec wondered if the same principle could be used to
study diseases of the heart. That afternoon he rolled up a piece of
paper into a narrow tube and placed it on the chest of a man
suffering from heart disease. He called it a "stethoscope," from
stethos, the Greek word for "chest."

When gold was discovered in California it was still officially Mexican territory.

THE WORLD'S TALLEST BUILDINGS, PART I

Last winter, Uncle John was reading a book on architecture (you know where he was). He was looking at a Picture of the Empire State Building, and it suddenly occurred to him that everyone knows the building—but hardly anyone knows its history. His Bathroom Reader antennae went up—it sounded like a perfect subject for this edition. And here it is—an expanded version that includes other skyscrapers as well.

HOW HIGH CAN YOU GO?

Question: What was the invention that made tall buildings feasible? *Answer:* The elevator.

In 1850, few buildings were taller than 4 stories tall. This was partly because construction materials and techniques weren't suitable for tall buildings yet. But even if they had been, there was no reason to bother going any higher—no one would have wanted to walk up that many flights of stairs.

The closest thing anyone had to an elevator was a hoist. This was simply a platform connected to ropes and a pulley that could be used to move heavy objects from one floor of a building to another. Guide rails running from floor to ceiling kept the hoist from swinging back and forth, but it was still very dangerous—if the rope broke, there was nothing to stop it from plummeting to the ground, killing anyone riding in it...or standing nearby. Accidents were common.

MR. OTIS REQUESTS

In 1852, the hoist at the Bedstead Manufacturing Company in Yonkers, New York, broke and the superintendent assigned a master mechanic named Elisha Graves Otis to fix it; Otis had seen many brutal mishaps with hoists....So he decided to add a safety feature to the one he was building.

He took a spring from an old wagon and connected it to the top of the platform where the rope was tied. When the rope was

---

Each year, more people are killed by bee stings than by sharks.

pulled taut, the spring was compressed. But if the rope broke, the spring released and shoved two hooks into the guide rails, holding it in place and preventing it from falling.

Otis' contraption was simple, and was intended primarily to carry freight. But it was actually the first "safety" elevator—the first one that could reliably carry human passengers.

STARTING OVER

Not long after, the Bedstead Manufacturing Company went out of business and Otis lost his job. He decided to head west to join the California Gold Rush…but before he could leave, another furniture company hired him to build two new "safety hoisters;" two men had recently been killed using an old one.

The company paid Otis with cash, a gun and a carriage which convinced him to stay. On September 20, 1853, he opened a business in Yonkers selling "Patented Life and Labor Saving Hoisting Machinery."

Seeing is Believing

Unfortunately, Otis couldn't sell even one more elevator. So he decided to demonstrate his contraption personally. He entered it in an exhibition on "progress in industry and arts" at the Crystal Palace in New York City. When a substantial crowd had gathered, Otis climbed into his hoist, went up about 30 feet, and as onlookers gasped in horror, had his assistant cut the rope with a knife. The rope snapped, the hoist lurched briefly…and then stopped in place. "All safe, gentlemen, all safe," Otis called down to the crowd.

Public demonstrations like this generated some sales, but business remained slow for the first few years: Otis sold 27 hoists in 1856, all of them designed to carry freight. In 1857, in an attempt to expand his business, he designed his first passenger elevator, a steam-powered model capable of lifting 1,000 pounds 40 feet per minute.

UNSUNG HERO

Otis died from diphtheria in 1861 at age 49. He left a business that employed fewer than a dozen people and was only worth about $5,000. The first true skyscraper was still many years off, so it's likely Otis never fully realized the impact his invention would have on mankind.

Barry Manilow wrote the "Stuck on Me" Band-Aid jingle.

UPS AND DOWNS

Otis's sons, Charles and Norton, took over the business following his death. In 1868, they patented a speedier and more elaborate steam elevator. But since there were no electric controls, the elevators required a lot of manpower: Someone had to ride inside the car to operate it (via a rope connected to the steam engine in the basement), and elevator "starters" had to be posted on every floor. Their job was to yell into the elevator shaft to the elevator operator whenever someone needed a lift.

The shouting system was crude, but it worked. The only problem was that it meant buildings could only be as high as the elevator starters could shout. Also, since the elevator was powered by a steam engine that burned coal, the elevator shaft eventually filled with steam and thick smoke, limiting the amount of time people could stand to spend riding in it. This also served to restrict the height of buildings. Elevators, which made tall buildings feasible, were starting to become an obstacle to further growth.

Picking up the Pace

That changed when the first high-speed hydraulic elevator was introduced in the early 1870s. It could travel an amazing 700 feet per minute—which created new problems: Otis's original safety mechanism stopped a falling elevator instantly by grabbing the guide rails that held the elevator in place. It worked fine when the elevator was only traveling 40 feet per minute. But at 700 feet per minute a sudden, jarring stop could be as bad for the passengers as letting the car plunge to the ground. The Otis brothers fixed this in 1878 when they patented a braking system that slowed the elevator gradually. In 1890, they perfected the first electric elevator...and the skyscraper era was underway.

OTIS FACTS

Today, the Otis Elevator Company is the largest elevator company on earth, with 66,000 employees in 1,700 different offices. It has built elevators for the White House, Eiffel Tower, Vatican, and even the space shuttle launch pad.

Part II of the World's Tallest Buildings is on page 137.

Speed demon: The ruby-throated hummingbird's heart beats 615 times per minute.

FAMOUS HOLLYWOOD PUBLICITY STUNTS

*Publicity is the mother's milk of Hollywood, and over the years,
it has been refined to an art by a handful of practitioners. Here
are three publicity stunts that built Hollywood legends.*

"I VANT TO BE ALONE."
Background: When Greta Garbo came to Hollywood from Sweden in the 1920s, she didn't realize how conservative America was. In her first newspaper interview, she mentioned casually that she was living with director Mauritz Stiller. Today that's no big deal, but in the '20s, it was a shocking revelation.
Publicity Stunt: When MGM head Louis B. Mayer heard about the interview, he was furious. He banned Garbo from ever speaking to the press again. That suited Garbo fine—she was shy anyway. But how to explain it to the press? Someone in the MGM publicity department came up with the famous quote: "I vant to be alone."

THE SEARCH FOR SCARLETT
Background: Producer David O. Selznick wanted the perfect actress to play Scarlett O'Hara in the film adaptation of *Gone with the Wind,* so he launched a nationwide talent search that lasted (coincidentally) for the two years it took to prepare for filming. Joan Crawford, Bette Davis, and Tallulah Bankhead all wanted the part. So did Katharine Hepburn, who told Selznick, "the part was practically written for me." "I can't imagine Rhett Butler chasing you for ten years," Selznick replied.

"George Cuckor, the intended director, was sent scurrying southward to scout locations, but also, supposedly, to check out high school plays for ingenues," explains a film historian. "To keep the game of who-will-play-her alive, every female willing to try out was tested." Newspapers and radio stations kept the country updated on the progress of the search.

According to legend, just when the search seemed hopeless, Selznick's brother escorted a young British actress named Vivian

---

Surveys say: If you watch at least 2 prime-time comedies a week, you probably drive a foreign car.

Leigh onto the set. They signed her on the spot.

Publicity Stunt: Selznick had Leigh in mind for the part from the very beginning. But there were two problems: Leigh was a foreigner, which might not go over well with Southern audiences, and she was in the middle of a scandalous affair with actor Laurence Olivier (both were married to other people at the time). M. Hirsch Goldberg writes in *The Book of Lies:*

> A scenario was devised in which Vivian Leigh would be discovered at the last minute after an extensive search for the right Scarlett had not been successful. In this way the foreign-born aspect would be diffused, especially since Scarlett, the character, and Vivien, the actress shared the same Irish-French background. And with Olivier and Leigh agreeing not to move for a divorce at the time, the scandal would be abated in the flurry of good news that the Scarlett part had finally been settled.

WONG KEYE, PIANO TUNER

Background: When Barbra Streisand announced that she wouldn't give any interviews to promote *On a Clear Day You Can See Forever*, publicity man Steve Yeager was stuck—if the star wouldn't cooperate, he'd have to find another publicity angle.

Publicity Stunt: Yeager called AP gossip columnist Jim Bacon and "suggested we do a story on one Wong Keye, a mythical tone-deaf Chinese piano tuner who was tuning all the pianos on the Streisand movie." Bacon agreed. According to Bacon, in his book *Made in Hollywood:* "The story was written with appropriate tongue-in-cheek. It told how Wong Keye had started out in life as a fortune-cookie stuffer in a Chinatown bakery, then sold exotic fish for awhile until he found his niche tuning pianos. Since then he had been in great demand because he was such a superb piano tuner."

What Happened: It worked—the story ran all over the country, and was picked up by the *London Daily Mirror*, which even ran a photo (an actor hired to dress up in Chinese costume). Bacon even got calls from piano owners asking how they could get in touch with Keye. "But the funniest repercussion of all," Bacon writes, "came when Streisand—who had refused to give interviews in the first place—complained to the producer because the piano tuner in the movie was getting more publicity than the star."

By any other name: Apples are part of the rose family.

THE BIRTH OF POST-ITS

Post-it Notes now seem like a logical and obvious product. In fact, you're probably so used to seeing Post-Its around your house or office that some- times it's hard to imagine there was a time when they didn't exist. Actually, they began as a mistake, and almost didn't even make it into the market. Here's Jack Mingo's story of how they were invented.

STICKIES

In 1964, a 3-M chemist named Spencer Silver was experimenting with a new adhesive. Out of curiosity, he added too much of a "reactant" chemical…and got a totally unexpected result: a milky white liquid that turned crystal-clear under pressure. He characterized it as "tacky" but not "aggressively adhesive."

He also found that it was "narcissistic"—i.e., it tended to stick to itself more than anything else. If you put it on one surface and stuck a piece of paper on it, either all or none of the adhesive would come off when you peeled off the paper.

STICKY SITUATION

Silver was intrigued with the stuff, but couldn't get his superiors at 3-M excited. So he wandered the hallways of the company giving demonstrations and presentations. He nearly had to beg 3-M to patent it.

Silver was sure there was a use for his adhesive—he just didn't know what it was. "Sometimes I was so angry because this new thing was so obviously unique," he says. "I'd tell myself, 'Why can't you think of a product? It's your job!'"

EUREKA

Finally, in 1974, someone came up with a problem to match Silver's solution.

Every Sunday, Arthur Fry, another 3-M chemist, directed the choir in his church. He always marked songs in the hymnal with little scraps of paper. But one Sunday, while signaling the choir to stand, he fumbled his hymnal and all the bookmarks fell to the floor. As he frantically tried to find his place, he thought, "If only there was a way to get them to stick to the page." That's when he

---

Geography lesson: How many Rhode Islands would you need to make one Texas? 268.

remembered seeing Silver's "now-it-sticks, now-it-doesn't" demonstration years earlier.... And while the choir sang, he started thinking of situations where semi-sticky paper might be helpful. The next morning, he rushed to work and tracked down some of Silver's adhesive. He found there were still problems to work out—like how to make sure the adhesive didn't come off on the document—and he worked with company chemists to solve them. He even created a machine in his basement that would make manufacturing easier by applying the adhesive in a continuous roll. When he was done, he found that the machine was bigger than his basement doorway...and it couldn't be disassembled without ruining it. So he knocked out a part of his basement wall.

NOT YET

Fry and his team began producing prototype Post-Its. As a form of informal marketing research, they distributed the sticky notes to offices around the building. They were a hit. "Once you start using them," one enthusiastic co-worker told him, "you can't stop."

Despite in-house success, the 3-M marketing department didn't believe Post-Its would sell. They kept asking: "Why would anybody buy this 'glorified scratch paper' for a dollar a package?" Their lack of enthusiasm showed up in test marketing. It failed miserably.

STUCK ON YOU

Fry's boss couldn't believe that they wouldn't succeed if marketed properly. After all, they were using thousands of them at 3-M. The company decided to try a one-shot test-market blitz in Boise, Idaho. Their sales reps blanketed Boise with free samples and order forms. The result: a 90% reorder response from the companies that received samples—more than twice the 40% the company considered a success.

Post-Its went into full national distribution in 1980 and caught on across America. They've since become an international hit as well.

"The Post-It was a product that met an unperceived need," says Fry. "If you had asked somebody what they needed, they might have said a better paper clip. But give them a Post-It Note, and they immediately know what to do with it."

"Seersucker" comes from a Persian word—shir-o-shakar—that means "milk and sugar."

Q&A: ASK THE EXPERTS

Everyone's got a question or two they'd like answered.
Here are a few of those questions, with answers from
some of the nation's top trivia experts.

MAKE A WISH

Q: *How do trick birthday candles (which keep relighting after being blown out) work?*
A: "The wicks are treated with magnesium crystals. The crystals retain enough heat to reilluminate the wick after the candles are blown out. Because the magnesium-treated wicks retain heat so well, experts recommend extinguishing the candles permanently by dipping them in water." (From *Why Do Dogs Have Wet Noses?*, by David Feldman)

FOILED AGAIN

Q: *Does it matter which side of the aluminum foil is used?*
A: "The dull and shiny sides of the foil have no special meaning; they are simply a result of the way that the foil is made. In the final rolling step of the manufacturing process, two layers of aluminum foil are passed through the rolling mill at the same time. The side that comes in contact with the mill's highly polished steel rolls becomes shiny. The other side, which does not come in contact with the heavy metal rolls, comes out dull.

"Shiny or dull, it does not matter." (From *Why Does Popcorn Pop?*, by Don Voorhees)

UMM...WHAT WAS THAT?

Q: *Is it true that elephants never forget?*
A: Believe it or not, yes. "We know this because of an experiment many years ago by a professor in Germany. He taught an elephant to choose between two wooden boxes, one marked with a square, the other with a circle. The box with a square had food in it, the other didn't.

"It took 330 tries before the elephant figured out that 'square' meant 'food.' Once it got the idea, though, things went a lot quicker. Soon the professor could put any two markings on the boxes. The elephant would experiment a few times, figure out which sign meant 'food,' then pick the right box from there on out.

Second Street is the most common street name in the U.S.; First Street is the 6th.

"The professor came back a year later and tested the elephant again using the old markings—circles, squares, and so on. Amazingly enough, the elephant still remembered which markings were the signs for food.

"That's why elephants are so popular in circuses. It may take them a while to learn the act, but once they've got it, they've got it for good." (From *Know It All!*, by Ed Zotti)

TEE-HEE
Q: *Why don't we laugh when we tickle ourselves?*
A: "The laughter which results from being tickled by someone else is not the same as laughter that comes from being amused. When someone tickles us, the laugh is a reflex action [that] is really a cry of distress, essentially begging the person to stop stimulating our sensitive skin. When we tickle ourselves, we're not at the mercy of someone else. If the feeling becomes too intense, we stop. Therefore, no distress signal is needed." (From *A Book of Curiosities*, by Roberta Kramer)

OIL'S WELL
Q: *What's the world's tallest man-made structure?*
A: "It is not the Sears Tower, which is 110 stories and 1,454 feet high. A Shell Oil company offshore oil rig in the Gulf of Mexico is more than twice as tall as Chicago's Sears Tower. Altogether, it rises 3,280 feet from seabed to flare top. Thirty-five 'stories' are above water level. Installed in 1994, it is the world's deepest oil platform. The $1.2 billion rig is called the Auger Tension Leg Platform, or Auger TLP for short. It's the first tension leg platform that combines both oil and gas drilling and production in U.S. waters. Designed to withstand 72-foot-high waves in 100-year hurricanes, it can sway up to 235 feet off center without damage. It was built to survive a 1,000-year storm." (From *Blue Genes and Polyester Plants*, by Sharon Bertsch McGrayne)

"Too bad 90% of the politicians give the other 10% a bad reputation." —Henry Kissinger

THE TOP 10 HITS OF THE YEAR, 1956–1959

In our last Bathroom Reader, we included lists of the annual Top 10 TV shows. That prompted requests for a similar list of the Top 10 songs of each year. So here's the first of our series of lists, compiled from a number of sources with help from New York's #1 oldies deejay, Bob Shannon of WCBS-FM.

1956
(1) Heartbreak Hotel—*Elvis Presley*
(2) Don't Be Cruel—*Elvis Presley*
(3) My Prayer—*The Platters*
(4) Lisbon Antigua—*Nelson Riddle*
(5) Hound Dog—*Elvis Presley*
(6) The Wayward Wind—*Gogi Grant*
(7) Poor People of Paris—*Lee Baxter*
(8) Que Sera, Sera—*Doris Day*
(9) Memories Are Made Of This—*Dean Martin*
(10) Rock And Roll Waltz—*Kay Starr*

1957
(1) All Shook Up—*Elvis Presley*
(2) Little Darlin'—*The Diamonds*
(3) Young Love—*Tab Hunter*
(4) Love Letters In The Sand—*Pat Boone*
(5) So Rare—*Jimmy Dorsey*
(6) Don't Forbid Me—*Pat Boone*
(7) Singin' The Blues—*Guy Mitchell*
(8) Young Love—*Sonny James*
(9) Too Much—*Elvis Presley*
(10) Round And Round—*Perry Como*

1958
(1) Volare (Nel Blu Dipinto Di Blu)—*Domenico Modugno*
(2) All I Have To Do Is Dream—*The Everly Brothers*
(3) Don't—*Elvis Presley*
(4) Witch Doctor—*David Seville*
(5) Patricia—*Perez Prado*
(6) Tequila—*The Champs*
(7) Catch A Falling Star—*Perry Como*
(8) Sail Along Silvery Moon—*Billy Vaughn*
(9) It's All In The Game —*Tommy Edwards*
(10) Return To Me—*Dean Martin*

1959
(1) Mack The Knife—*Bobby Darin*
(2) The Battle Of New Orleans —*Johnny Horton*
(3) Personality—*Lloyd Price*
(4) Venus—*Frankie Avalon*
(5) Lonely Boy—*Paul Anka*
(6) Dream Lover—*Bobby Darin*
(7) The Three Bells—*The Browns*
(8) Come Softly To Me—*The Fleetwoods*
(9) Kansas City—*Wilbert Harrison*
(10) Mr. Blue—*The Fleetwoods*

What's your favorite? One of every three Girl Scout cookies sold are Thin Mints.

THE HISTORY OF ASPIRIN

*Today we take aspirin so much for granted that it's hard to believe that
when it was first discovered, it was considered one of the
most miraculous drugs ever invented. It turns out that
the history of aspirin also makes a good story.*

PAIN KILLER

In the late 1890s, Felix Hoffman, a chemist with Germany's
Friedrich Bayer (pronounced "By-er") & Company, started
looking for a new treatment to help relieve his father's painful
rheumatism.

Drugs to treat the pain and inflammation of rheumatism had
been around for 2,000 years. In 200 B.C., Hippocrates, the father
of medicine, observed that chewing on the bark of the white
willow tree soothed aches and pains. In 1823, chemists had finally
succeeded in isolating the bark's active ingredient. It was salicylic
acid.

TOUGH STUFF

The problem was, salicylic acid wasn't safe. In its pure form, it was
so powerful that it did damage at the same time it was doing good.
Unless you mixed it with water, it would burn your mouth and
throat. And even with water, it was so hard on the stomach lining
that people who took it became violently ill, complaining that
their stomachs felt like they were "crawling with ants." Salicylic
acid had given Hoffman's father multiple ulcers. He had literally
burned holes in his stomach trying to relieve his rheumatism pain,
and was desperate for something milder. So Hoffman read through
all the scientific literature he could find. He discovered that every
scientist who had tried to neutralize the acidic properties of salicylic acid had failed...except one. In 1853, a French chemist
named Charles Frederic Gerhart had improved the acid by adding
sodium and acetyl chloride—creating a new compound called
acetylsalicylic acid. However, the substance was so unstable and
difficult to make that Gerhart had abandoned it.

Total number of concerts played by the Grateful Dead: 2,317.

No Pain, No Gain
Hoffman decided to make his own batch of Gerhart's acetylsalicylic acid. Working on it in his spare time, he managed to produce
a purer, more stable form than anyone had ever been able to
make. He tested the powder on himself successfully. Then he gave
some to his father. It eased the elder Hoffman's pain, with virtually no side effects.

The Bayer Facts
Hoffman reported his findings to his superiors at Bayer. His immediate supervisor was Heinrich Dreser, the inventor of heroin. (At
the time, it was thought to be a non-addictive substitute for
morphine. Heroin was a brand name, selected to describe the
drug's *heroic* painkilling properties.) Dreser studied Hoffman's acid,
found that it worked, and in 1899 Bayer began selling their
patented acetylsalicylic acid powder to physicians under the brand
name *aspirin*. The name was derived from the Latin term for the
"queen of the meadow" plant, *Spiraea ulmaria*, which was an
important source of salicylic acid. A year later, they introduced
aspirin pills.

IN THE BEGINNING
Within ten years of its introduction, aspirin became the most
commonly prescribed patent medicine in the world for two
reasons: (1) it actually worked, and (2) unlike heroin, morphine,
and other powerful drugs of the time, it had few side effects. There
was nothing on the market like it, and when it proved effective at
reducing fever during the influenza epidemics at the start of the
twentieth century, its reputation as a miracle drug spread around
the world.

"This was a period of time when a person only had a life
expectancy of 44 years because there were no medications available," says Bayer spokesman Dr. Steven Weisman. "Aspirin very
quickly became the most important drug available." It seemed to
be able to solve any problem, large or small—gargling aspirin
dissolved in water eased sore throats, and rubbing aspirin against a
baby's gums even helped soothe teething pain.

A cow spends eighteen hours of every day chewing.

UPS AND DOWNS

Aspirin was initially a prescription-only medication, but it became available over the counter in 1915. Sales exploded, and demand for the new drug grew at a faster rate than ever. Since Bayer owned the patent on aspirin—and there were no other drugs like it—the company didn't have to worry about competition; it had the worldwide market to itself.

But the forces of history would soon get in the way.

HEADACHE MATERIAL

In 1916, Bayer used its aspirin profits to build a massive new factory in upstate New York. They immediately started manufacturing the drug for the American market and sold $6 million worth in the first year.

Then they ran into problems. World War I made Germany America's enemy, and in 1918 the U.S. Government seized Bayer's American assets under the Trading With the Enemy Act. They auctioned the factory off to the Sterling Products Company of West Virginia. (The two Bayers would not reunite again until 1995, when the German Bayer bought Sterling's over-the-counter drug business for $1 billion.) Sterling continued marketing aspirin under the Bayer brand name, which by now had been Americanized to "Bay-er."

The original American patent for aspirin expired in 1917, and the "Aspirin" trademark was lost in 1921. Anyone who wanted to make and sell aspirin was now legally free to do so. By the 1930s there were more than a thousand brands of pure aspirin on the market; there were also hundreds of products (Anacin, for example) that combined aspirin with caffeine or other drugs. A bottle of aspirin in the medicine cabinet was as common in American households as salt and pepper were on the kitchen table.

Ready for more? "Aspirin: the Miracle Drug" is on page 246.

Ready for more? "Aspirin: the Miracle Drug" is on page 246.

Historical note: In 1763, an English clergyman named Edward Stone administered tea, water, and beer laced with powdered willow bark to more than fifty people suffering from fever. They all got better, proving that willow bark reduced fever, too.

Crazy drivers: The highest speed ever reached by a motorcycle doing a wheelie was 157.87 mph

STRAIGHT FROM MICK'S LIPS

Mick Jagger is like the Energizer Bunny—still going...and going... and going. He's had over 30 years to come up with enough comments to make at least one interesting page of quotes.

"People have this obsession: They want you to be like you were in 1969. They want you to, because otherwise their youth goes with you."

"I'd rather be dead than singing 'Satisfaction' when I'm forty-five."

"You get to the point where you have to change everything—change your looks, change your money, change your sex, change your women—because of the business."

"Of course we're doing this for the money....We've always done it for the money."

"Sometimes an orgasm is better than being onstage. Sometimes being onstage is better than an orgasm."

"People ask me, 'Why do you wear makeup? Why don't you just come off the street?' The whole idea is you don't come off the street. You put on different clothes, you do your hair and you acquire this personality that has to go out and perform. When you get off the stage, that mask is dropped."

"Fame is like ice cream. It's only bad if you eat too much."

"The best rock 'n' roll music encapsulates a certain high energy—an angriness— whether on record or onstage. That is, rock 'n' roll is only rock 'n' roll if it's not safe."

"When I'm 33, I'll quit. That's the time when a man has to do something else. I can't say what it will definitely be. It's still in the back of my head—but it won't be in show business. I don't want to be a rock star all my life. I couldn't bear to end up as an Elvis Presley and sing in Las Vegas with all those housewives and old ladies coming in with their handbags. It's really sick." (1972)

WORDS OF WISDOM

More points to ponder while poised upon the pot.

"The two biggest sellers in any bookstore are the cookbooks and the diet books. The cookbooks tell you how to prepare the food, and the diet books tell you how not to eat any of it."

—Andy Rooney

"I never believed in Santa Claus because I knew no white dude would come into my neighborhood after dark."

—Dick Gregory

"If you have a job without aggravations, you don't have a job."

—Malcolm Forbes

"The way to make money is to buy when blood is running in the streets."

—John D. Rockefeller

"Glory is fleeting, but obscurity is forever."

—Napoleon

"The length of a film should be directly related to the endurance of the human bladder."

—Alfred Hitchcock

"My grandmother is over eighty and she still doesn't need glasses. Drinks right out of the bottle."

—Henny Youngman

"Happiness is having a large, loving, caring, close-knit family in another city."

—George Burns

"Children today are tyrants. They contradict their parents, gobble their food, and tyrannize their teachers."

—Socrates (470–399 B.C.)

"Just because your voice reaches halfway around the world doesn't mean you are wiser than when it reached only to the end of the bar."

—Edward R. Murrow

"Few things are harder to put up with than a good example."

—Mark Twain

"Wise men talk because they have something to say; fools talk because they have to say something."

—Plato

Before Columbus, no Indian had type B blood.

STRANGE LAWSUITS

These days, it seems that people will sue each other over practically anything. Here are a few real-life examples of unusual legal battles.

THE PLAINTIFF: Mortimer Hetsberger, a 22-year-old bank robber.
THE DEFENDANT: Laura Gonzalez, a teller at the Fleet Bank in Atlantic City, New Jersey.
THE LAWSUIT: In July 1998, Hetsberger handed Gonzalez a note at her teller window. It said: "I want the money now." According to Gonzalez, he also told her "Now, or I'll shoot." She handed him $4,000. He was captured the same day. When he heard that Gonzalez had accused him of threatening her, he filed a $1.5 million lawsuit for slander, explaining that he'd never even spoken to her.
VERDICT: No ruling yet.

THE PLAINTIFF: A 25-year-old mortuary driver.
THE DEFENDANT: A California Highway Patrol officer.
THE LAWSUIT: The driver was stopped in Orange County and given a ticket for driving in a carpool lane with no passengers. He protested that he had four passengers—the frozen corpses he was transporting. He went to court to overturn the ticket.
VERDICT: He had to pay the fine.

THE PLAINTIFF: Kevin McGuinness.
THE DEFENDANT: The University of New Mexico.
THE LAWSUIT: When McGuinness flunked out of the University of New Mexico Medical School, he sued for reinstatement under the Americans with Disabilities Act. What's his disability? He gets very anxious when he takes exams, and doesn't do well on them.
VERDICT: Unknown.

Despite having six wives, Henry VIII only had three children and no grandchildren.

THE PLAINTIFF: David Earl Dempsey, a 27-year-old inmate at the Pima County, Arizona jail.
THE DEFENDANT: Pima County and state prison officials.
THE LAWSUIT: In February 1998, Dempsey tied a sheet around his neck and jumped out the jailhouse window, trying to commit suicide. The sheet broke, and he plummeted to the concrete below. He sued for negligence.
VERDICT: Case dismissed. While waiting for the trial, Dempsey tried suicide again. This time he succeeded.

THE PLAINTIFF: Carol Ann Bennett.
THE DEFENDANT: Warren Woodrow Bennett, her husband.
THE LAWSUIT: When Ms. Bennett moved out of their condo, she left her breast implants behind. She sued to get them back.
THE VERDICT: Implants returned.

THE PLAINTIFF: Sheila Tormino.
THE DEFENDANT: Montclaire Bowl, in Edwardsville, Illinois.
THE LAWSUIT: While she was bowling, Torino got a piece of popcorn caught in her shoe, and during her approach, she slipped and fell. She sued for $50,000, claiming the alley was negligent for not putting up warnings about popcorn on the floor.
THE VERDICT: Unknown.

THE PLAINTIFF: Eric Edmunds.
THE DEFENDANT: Humana Hospital Bayside, in Virginia Beach.
THE LAWSUIT: In 1987, Edmunds went into the hospital to get his stomach stapled, making it smaller. According to reports, "within 48 hours of the surgery, he snuck out of his room and raided the hospital refrigerator and ate so much he burst his staples." Edmunds sued the hospital for $250,000 for "failure to keep its refrigerator locked."
VERDICT: Unknown.

The Wright brothers built their first airplane for less than $1,000.

I DREAM OF JEANNIE

It wasn't a huge hit in the 1960s, when it first aired... but 30-plus years later, I Dream of Jeannie is still airing in reruns all over the world. How did the beautiful female in harem pants wind up living, unmarried, with her "master" in suburbia? Here's the story.

HOW IT STARTED

Before Sidney Sheldon was one of America's best-selling schlock authors, he applied his talents to screenplays and television scripts.

He arrived in Hollywood in 1939, when he was 22. By 1947, he'd won an Oscar for best original screenplay, for *The Bachelor and the Bobby Soxer*, starring Cary Grant and Shirley Temple. In 1962, he gave up film work to write and create *The Patty Duke Show* for Screen Gems. The one-joke sitcom about identical cousins was an immediate hit—the #18 show for the 1963–64 season. So Screen Gems asked him for another sitcom and all but guaranteed they'd air anything he created.

Sheldon worked fast. It took him two days to come up with a whole new show. As he told Richard Barnes in *Diary of a Genie*, it was a Saturday, and he was planning to fly from New York to L.A. the next day to meet with studio execs. "I decided to bring them an outline of [the] show that I wanted to do....On Saturday I started dictating the outline of *I Dream of Jeannie*." It started out as a few ideas, but "as I started dictating, it began to get fuller and fuller....[So] I decided to turn it into an entire script."

He handwrote most of the script the next day on the plane heading west and presented it at the meeting. Screen Gems bought it as the pilot for Jeannie. "The moral of the story," Sheldon says, "is that when you get an idea, write it down immediately." The show aired for five years, from 1965 to 1970.

INSIDE FACTS

The inspiration for Jeannie was the 1964 Universal motion picture, The Brass Bottle. The familiar plot: A portly ancient genie (Burl Ives) appears from a lamp to serve his master (Tony Randall). Though he's filled with good intentions, the genie keeps getting Randall into trouble. Sheldon said: "I thought that it

---

Medically speaking, the correct order of intelligence is: Moron, imbecile, idiot.

would be fun to make the genie a beautiful young girl who says, 'What can I do for you, Master?'"

Sheldon got one other thing from the film—his star. Barbara Eden played Randall's girlfriend. Sheldon thought she'd be perfect for what he described as "the all-American fantasy," and never even considered anyone else for the part.

THE GREAT NAVEL WAR
Although Sheldon and the network censors had no objection to Barbara Eden's sexy costume or the fact that the unmarried Jeannie was living with a man for whom she would do anything, they refused to let her show her navel on network TV.

The solution: She put a flesh-colored cloth plug in it during filming. The joke on the set was that genies weren't born with navels.

When George Schlatter, producer of TV's *Laugh-In* wanted to debut Eden's navel on his program, Sheldon and NBC censors stopped him. It wasn't until the reunion movies that Jeannie ever appeared on TV with a belly button.

THE NASA CONNECTION
The astronauts in Jeannie were often bumbling idiots, but NASA was happy to cooperate fully with the show. All they really cared about was eliminating anything that smacked of militarism. They wanted to guarantee that the show would "project the image of the space program as a peaceful, scientific exploration of space."

BOTTLED UP
The recognizable "Jeannie bottle" used in the series was originally made from a 1964 Jim Beam liquor decanter that had been given to producer Sidney Sheldon for Christmas. It was painted by the show's prop department. In October, 1995, a bottle used on the series was auctioned off for $10,000.

FLOP TREATMENT
Screen Gems didn't think *Jeannie* was going to be a hit, so they decided to save money and shoot the first season in black and white. It was one of NBC's last black-and-white shows ever.

BATHROOM ORIGINS

We've all heard of these products before.
Here's where they come from.

EX-LAX
In 1906 Max Kiss (that's his real name), a Hungarian-born pharmacist living in the U.S., came up with an over-the counter version of a new prescription laxative called phenolphthalein. Kiss called his new chocolate tablets Bo-Bos, but one afternoon he happened to read in the local Hungarian language newspaper about a deadlock in Hungary's parliament. The Hungarian words for "parliamentary deadlock" are sometimes shortened to "ex-lax" in print. Kiss thought it sounded like "excellent laxative."

PAY TOILETS
So few people owned indoor toilets in Terre Haute, Indiana in 1910, that when the Pennsylvania Railroad installed some at the train station, they became one of the town's major attractions. Some locals came to use the facilities, others, merely to marvel. But the restrooms were so jammed with admirers that when the trains pulled into the station, passengers literally had no place to go. So the railroad installed coin-operated locks, and gave the stationmaster a key to let ticket holders in for free.

WASH 'N DRY MOIST TOWELETTES
Ross Williams served in the Navy during World War II, and one of the things he hated most about life onboard a ship was that during water shortages he could not wash up before going to bed at night. Unfortunately for him, it wasn't until 1953 that he finally figured out a solution to the problem: paper towels soaked in liquid soap and sealed in tinfoil. According to Colgate-Palmolive, makers of Wash 'n Dry, one towelette provides as much cleaning power as a quart of water.

THE JIG IS UP

Everything has a history—even jigsaw puzzles. They started as a toy for rich kids…became a hobby for wealthy adults…and then, when mass production made it possible, became a pastime for the rest of us.

THE FIRST JIGSAW PUZZLE

Jigsaw puzzles were one of Western Europe's first educational toys. In 1762, a London mapmaker/printer named John Spilsbury glued a few of his maps onto thin wood panels. Then, using a small hand-saw, he cut them up along the borders of each country. He called them "dissected maps," and sold them to well-to-do parents "for the edification of the young." It was the beginning of an industry.

Spilsbury's timing was excellent—the first children's books had been published only a year earlier, and there was a blossoming interest in new ways to educate the young. By 1800 twenty different London publishers were cranking puzzles out. Most featured historical subjects and moral lessons—and Bible stories. Religious puzzles were an especially popular diversion on Sundays, when ordinary "secular" play was not permitted.

REAL JIGSAW PUZZLES

Until the late 19th century, jigsaw puzzles were made one at a time, gluing expensive prints to fine mahogany or cedar. Each piece was cut out with a hand saw, and each puzzle had no more than 50 pieces. Only the border pieces interlocked; anything more complicated would have cost too much money—and there was a limit to what even wealthy parents were willing to pay. Early jigsaw puzzles cost the equivalent of a week's wages for a common laborer.

Then, in 1876, the power scroll saw, also known as the jigsaw, was exhibited at the Philadelphia Centennial Exposition. It was inexpensive (some foot-powered treadle saws sold for as little as $3), and was capable of making incredibly intricate cuts. It immediately revolutionized furniture design. By the 1890s it had an impact on puzzles, too: craftsmen began making completely interlocking puzzles with smaller pieces…which could challenge adults as well as children.

So far, every U.S. president with a beard has been a Republican.

PUZZLE-MANIA

The new puzzles were a hit in high-society circles. Their popularity grew until, in 1908, a jigsaw puzzle craze swept America. No one was left out; if you couldn't afford to buy puzzles, there were puzzle lending libraries, and even puzzle rental companies. Sales were so strong that Parker Brothers gave up manufacturing games for a year to focus exclusively on puzzles. (It was during the 1908 craze that the company pioneered the idea of cutting the pieces into shapes that people could recognize—stars, ducks, dogs, flowers, snowflakes, etc.).

THE GOLDEN AGE OF PUZZLES

When the craze died down, jigsaw puzzles had become a part of American life. By the 1920s, they were so cheap that just about anyone could afford them...manufacturers were using softer woods, which were easier to saw, and fancy engraving had been replaced by black and white lithographs that kids could paint with stencils and watercolors. By 1930, wood and jigsaws had given way to cardboard and die-cutting, so it was possible to buy a beautiful puzzle for as little as 10¢.

As America got deeper into the Great Depression, these inexpensive puzzles became increasingly attractive family entertainment. The result: people went on another puzzle-buying binge. For about six months in the early 1930s, the U.S. could not get enough puzzles. At the peak of the fad, Americans were purchasing 6 million puzzles a week. Things got so frantic that newsstands began offering a service called "puzzle-a-week," with new puzzles hitting the shelves every Wednesday. In less than a year, manufacturers sold more than $100 million worth of jigsaw puzzles (in 1930s money!).

STAND-UP GUY

Puzzles remained more or less unchanged after the 1930s. The artwork improved and special "luxury" puzzle makers sprang up to handcraft custom puzzles for movie stars and captains of industry, but they were really just more of the same thing. By the 1980s, puzzles had become a stale staple of the toy industry.

Then in 1989, a Canadian broadcasting executive named Paul Gallant decided to start a toy company. But he wasn't sure what kind of toys he wanted to make. "I started thinking about puzzles, and how they hadn't changed much since the 1700s," he told the New York Times in 1997, "and wondered why no one had ever made a three- dimensional puzzle." He experimented with ordinary cardboard puzzle pieces, but they fell over when he tried to stand them up. So he made some out of the same kind of polyethylene foam that is used to insulate airliner cockpits. The pieces were sturdy enough to build miniature walls.

Gallant made a 3-D puzzle resembling a Victorian mansion and took it to the F.A.O. Schwartz toy store in Manhattan, where he showed it to the store's toy and game buyer. "I took the puzzle and I threw it in the air," Gallant says. It didn't break. "I said, 'No glue, no pins, no nothing, it just stays like this interlocking.' And I pushed the wall off and I separated the pieces and showed him this was really a puzzle. And he said, 'Wow, where did you get that?'" F.A.O. Schwartz bought 74 puzzles that afternoon in 1991; Gallant's company now sells more than $100 million worth of 3-D puzzles—shaped like skyscrapers, castles, the Eiffel Tower, the Titanic, and even Star Wars spaceships—every year, making it another of the biggest puzzle fads in history.

PUZZLING INNOVATIONS

Has it been a while since you've bought a puzzle? Here are some new products you might find on your next trip to the toy store:

• Mono-colored Puzzles. No pretty pictures, just puzzle pieces, hundreds of them, all painted the same color so that there are no clues as to where they belong in the puzzle.

• Multiple-border Puzzles. Pieces with straight edges that appear to be border pieces, but actually are inner pieces.

• Impossibles. 750-piece borderless puzzles with too many pieces. No taking the easy way out by connecting outer edges first, because edge pieces look like inner pieces. To make it even more puzzling: five extra pieces that don't fit anywhere in the puzzle.

• Triazzles. All of the pieces are triangle shaped with similar designs, but with only one correct solution.

• The World's Most Difficult Jigsaw Puzzles. Double-sided puzzles with 529 pieces. The same artwork is on both sides, rotated 90 degrees with respect to each other.

Mosquito eggs can survive in a dried-up state for 5 years.

THE GROUCHO WARS

One of Uncle John's favorite Marx Brothers scenes is from Duck Soup.
*Groucho is Rufus T. Firefly, head of a country called Freedonia...
which is close to war with its neighbor, Sylvania. At the 11th hour, a
conference is arranged with the Sylvanian ambassador to make an effort
to avert the conflict. Groucho is amenable...until he works himself up
into such a state that when the Sylvanian ambassador enters, Groucho
slugs him. And, of course, there's war. We bring this up because, as
preposterous as it seems, that kind of thing has happened more than once
in the real world. We call these occurrences the Groucho Wars.*

DIPLOMACY...GROUCHO-STYLE
Here's Groucho's Duck Soup soliloquy about war and peace.

Mrs. Teasdale (Margaret Dumont): "I've taken the liberty of
asking the ambassador to come over here, because we both felt
that a friendly conference would settle everything peacefully. He'll
be here in a moment."

Rufus T. Firefly (Groucho): "Mrs. Teasdale, you did a noble
deed. I'd be unworthy of the high trust that you've placed in me if
I didn't do everything in my power to keep our beloved Freedonia
at peace with the world. I'd be only too happy to meet Ambassador Trentino and offer him, on behalf of my country, the right
hand of good fellowship. And I feel sure that he will accept this
gesture in the spirit in which it is offered....

"But what if he doesn't? A fine thing that would be. I hold
out my hand, and he refuses to accept it. (Sarcastically) That'll
add a lot to my prestige, won't it? Me, the head of a country,
snubbed by a foreign ambassador. Who does he think he is, that
he can come here and make a sap out of me in front of all my
people? Think of it...I hold out my hand, and that hyena refuses
to accept it. WHY THE CHEAP, FOUR-FLUSHING SWINE—
HE'LL NEVER GET AWAY WITH IT, I TELL YOU—HE'LL
NEVER GET AMAY WITH IT! (The ambassador enters) So!
You refuse to shake hands with me, eh?" (Groucho slaps him in
the face)

Ambassador: "...There's no turning back now. This means
WAR!"

There are no turkeys in Turkey.

THE REAL GROUCHO WARS
These are not out of a movie script. People really died in them.

Napoleonic Wars (1865)
Between: Paraguay and its neighbors—Argentina, Brazil, Uruguay
What Started It: Francisco Solano Lopez, president of Paraguay
believed he was Napoleon. To prove it, he declared war simultaneously on all three countries.
Outcome: Paraguay was decimated. Nearly half its population was
killed in five years of battle.

War of the Oaken Bucket (1325)
Between: The independent Italian states of Modena and Bologna
What Started It: Modena soldiers invaded the state of Bologna to
steal a bucket. They succeeded, but hundreds of Bologna citizens
were killed in the process. Bologna declared war to avenge the
deaths...and to get the bucket back.
Outcome: They fought for 12 years, but Bologna never did get the
bucket. To this day it's still in Modena, stored in the bell tower of
a 14th century cathedral.

War of the Whiskers (1152)
Between: England and France
What Started It: King Louis VII of France had a beard when he was
married, but shaved it off when he got home from the Crusades.
According to The Book of Lists, his wife, Duchess Eleanor,
thought he looked ugly without it and insisted he grow it back. He
refused—so Eleanor divorced him to marry King Henry II of
England. Louis wouldn't relinquish control of Eleanor's ancestral
lands, so Henry declared war to get them back.
Outcome: This conflict lasted longer than any of the people who
started it—301 years.

War of the Stray Dog (1925)
Between: Greece and Bulgaria
What Started It: A Greek soldier's dog ran across the Bulgarian
border. When he followed it across the border, a Bulgarian border
guard shot him. Greece declared war and invaded Bulgaria.
Outcome: The League of Nations called an emergency session to
deal with the crisis, and convinced the two nations to end it
quickly.

First female boxing match in the U.S.: March 16, 1876. The winner got a silver butter dish.

The War of Jenkins' Ear (1739)
Between: Spain and Britain
What Started It: The British ship Rebecca, under the command of Robert Jenkins, was sailing off the coast of Cuba when it was boarded by the Spanish coast guard. After looting the ship, the coast guard commander cut off Jenkins' ear—which Jenkins saved and carried around with him, preserved in a jar. Seven years later the British Parliament invited Jenkins to the House of Commons to tell his story and show off the mummified ear. It became the rallying point of a war with Spain.
Outcome: The Spanish were defeated.

The Soccer War (1969)
Between: El Salvador and Honduras
What Started It: The neighboring countries were facing each other in a World Cup soccer match on June 27, 1969. Late in the game, a referee gave El Salvador a penalty kick. They scored from the penalty spot and won, 3-2. When news of the ref's call spread, riots broke out in both capital cities. Fans went on the rampage, looting and beating up opposition supporters. On July 3, war was declared.
Outcome: 2,000 people were killed and the Central American Common Market—on which both countries depended—collapsed. The result: serious food shortages and starvation. To add insult to injury, El Salvador lost the next round and was eliminated from World Cup competition.

The Cricket War (1896)
Between: Britain and Zanzibar
What Started It: According to one source, "a British ship stationed near Zanzibar entered the harbor in plain sight of Khalid Ben Bargash, the Sultan of Zanzibar. The crew wanted to watch a cricket match on shore." The Sultan, incensed that they hadn't asked his permission, declared war on Britain.
Outcome: The shortest war in history. The Brits sank the sultan's only ship, an old steamer, and destroyed his palace, in 37 minutes.

Per capita, what U.S. city has the greatest number of psychiatrists? Washington, D.C.

THEY WENT THAT-A-WAY

Malcolm Forbes wrote a fascinating book about the deaths of famous people. Here are a few of the stories he found.

JOHN JACOB ASTOR IV
Claim to Fame: Heir to an enormous fur-trading and real estate fortune. He was one of the wealthiest men in the U.S. in the early 1900s.
How He Died: On the *Titanic*.
Postmortem: One measure of Astor's social stature was the way he learned the *Titanic* was doomed—the captain warned him privately before he sounded the general alarm. According to the accounts of several *Titanic* survivors, Astor and his wife waited until the last lifeboat was loading, then Madeline climbed aboard. When it appeared there would be enough room for him, Astor climbed in and joined her. But just as the boat was about to be lowered into the water, some women appeared on deck. Astor gave up his seat, telling his wife, "the ladies have to go first." He then lit a cigarette and said to his wife, "Good-bye dearie. I'll see you later."

Astor's body was found floating in the ocean 10 days later, his pockets filled with more than $2,500 in cash.

GEORGE WASHINGTON
Claim to Fame: First President of the United States.
How He Died: Bled to death by doctors who were treating him for a cold.
Postmortem: On December 12, 1799, Washington, 67, went horseback riding for five hours in a snowstorm. When he returned home he ate dinner without changing his clothes and went to bed. Not surprisingly, he woke up feeling hoarse and complaining of a sore throat. But he refused to take any medicine. "You know I never take anything for a cold," he told an assistant. "Let it go as it came."

Washington felt even worse the next day. He allowed the estate supervisor at Mount Vernon (a skilled veterinarian, he was the best person on hand for the job) to bleed him. In those days people thought the best way to treat an illness was by removing the "dirty" blood that supposedly contained whatever was making the patient sick. In reality, it only weakened the patient, making it harder to fight off the original illness.

That didn't work, so three doctors were called. First, they dehydrated Washington by administering laxatives and emetics (chemicals that induce vomiting). Then they bled the former president three more times. In all, the veterinarian and the doctors drained 32 ounces of Washington's blood, weakening him severely. He died a few hours later while taking his own pulse.

BABE RUTH

Claim to Fame: One of the greatest baseball players who ever lived.

How He Died: Cancer of the nose and throat.

Postmortem: When Ruth fell ill in 1946, "his condition became a matter of nationwide concern, exceeding that usually accorded to the country's most important public officials, industrialists and princes of the church," wrote the *New York Times*. By the time of his last ceremonial trip to Yankee Stadium on June 13, 1948, Ruth was so weak that he had to use a baseball bat for a cane.

The Bambino knew he was sick, but no one ever told him what he was suffering from. One afternoon he paused while entering New York's Memorial Hospital and said to his nurse, "Hey, isn't this a hospital for cancer?" "Cancer and allied diseases," his quick-thinking nurse replied, apparently leaving Ruth none the wiser.

As Ruth got closer to death, Hollywood quickly threw together *The Babe Ruth Story*, a low-budget movie about his life, starring William Bendix (who was so inept an athlete that he had to be coached on how to hold a baseball bat). The Babe managed to live long enough to see it…but apparently, he didn't approve. In the last public gesture of his life, he walked out in the middle of the film. Ruth never left the hospital again, and died on Aug. 16, 1948.

"Death is Nature's expert advice to get plenty of Life."
—Johann von Goethe

A well-known jail was once located on Clink Street, in London. That's why jails are called "clinks."

LIFE IMITATES ART

When Wag the Dog *came out in 1997, Uncle John was reminded of a few other examples of films that seemed to predict a real-life event. Is it just coincidence…or are people in Hollywood psychic?*

ON THE SCREEN: *The China Syndrome*, a 1979 film about a near-meltdown at a nuclear power plant. The "China syndrome" refers to the potential of nuclear materials to melt "all the way to China" when a reactor goes bad. The film spurred debate between anti- and pro-nuke forces. One pro-nuke executive for Southern California Edison told reporters, "[The movie] has no scientific credibility, and is in fact ridiculous."

IN REAL LIFE: *The China Syndrome* opened on March 16, 1979. Twelve days later, the nuclear plant on Three Mile Island near Harrisburg, Pennsylvania, reported a partial core meltdown. The incident was so similar to the movie's plot that its executive producer feared "someone had seen the picture and sabotaged the plant." Costar Jack Lemmon said incredulously: "Every goddamned thing we had in there came true."

ON THE SCREEN: *The Godfather,* the 1972 film adaptation of Mario Puzo's novel about the Mafia. The Oscar-winner featured Marlon Brando as the crime boss known as "the Godfather."

IN REAL LIFE: People assumed "Godfather" was a word the mob really used. Actually, according to Puzo, "The term 'godfather' was one I invented…nobody ever used the term 'godfather' in reference to criminals, not even the Mafia." Nonetheless, it immediately began showing up in news stories, and is reportedly now even used in the crime world.

ON THE SCREEN: *Wag the Dog,* a political satire starring Dustin Hoffman and Robert De Niro, about political spin doctoring and an administration that "orchestrates a war with Albania to divert attention from a president caught with his pants down."

IN REAL LIFE: Released in late 1997, the film seemed eerily prophetic when the Clinton-Lewinsky scandal broke in January 1998—only a few weeks later. Soon after the scandal hit the headlines, the U.S. was threatening air strikes against Iraqi leader

Saddam Hussein for breaking a United Nations treaty. "It's surreal," said Hoffman. "It's the first time I've ever felt so clearly that the actual news is like a movie."

ON THE SCREEN: *Back to the Future Part II*. Marty McFly's (Michael J. Fox) nemesis, Biff Tannen, brings a copy of Gray's Sports Almanac back from the future to his younger self and tells him to use the book to bet on sporting events. Biff, skeptical, looks through it and comes across an unlikely entry. "Florida's going to win the world series in 1997," he reads. "Yeah, right." At the time there wasn't even a major league baseball team in Florida.

IN REAL LIFE: By 1997, Florida did have a baseball team—the Florida Marlins. And amazingly, they did win the World Series in 1997.

ON THE SCREEN: *The Chase*, an action film spoof starring Charlie Sheen as a wrongly convicted guy whose pursuit by cop cars is captured live on TV. It was released in March 1994.

IN REAL LIFE: A couple of months later, the world watched as O.J. Simpson sped along the freeway with police cars and news helicopters close behind. About 75 million people tuned in to the live chase. The film's writer/director, Adam Rifkin, told reporters: "People called and said it was just like my movie. I told them, 'No, no, my movie is just like this.' It's a perfect case of art imitating life imitating art."

ON THE SCREEN: *2001: A Space Odyssey*, a 1968 science-fiction film written by Arthur C. Clarke. In one scene, HAL, the talking computer, informs NASA of a malfunction with, "Houston, we've got a problem."

IN REAL LIFE: Just before the explosion that ended the Apollo 13 mission, as the crew played *2001*'s theme song (Thus Spake Zarathustra), Captain Jack Swigert radioed to Mission Control, "Houston, we've got a problem." Later, NASA Administrator Tom Paine sent Clarke a copy of a report, and noted under Swigert's words: "Just as you always said it would be, Arthur." Clarke writes: "I still get a very strange feeling when I contemplate this whole series of events—almost, indeed, as if I share a certain responsibility."

Dream on: The odds of the average golfer making a hole-in-one are 33,676-to-1.

LOST NAMES

*When something's named after someone, we automatically assume
it's an honor, and they're proud of it. But not always.
Here are three examples of people who felt they'd
lost their names…and wanted them back.*

OLDSMOBILE

Named After: Ransom Eli Olds

How He Got It: In 1897, Olds formed a car company
called the Olds Motor Works in Lansing, Michigan. He didn't
have enough money to go into production, so he gave Samuel L.
Smith 95% of the Olds stock in exchange for working capital. In
1899, their factory burned down; the only thing left was one little
buggy with a one-cylinder engine and a curved dashboard, called
the "Oldsmobile." They concentrated all efforts on this model. It
took off and became the first car in the world to be mass-
produced.

How He Lost It: In the early 1900s, the "Merry Oldsmobile" was
America's best-selling car. But Smith wanted to drop it to start
producing a larger, heavier family car. When Olds angrily left the
company to form the R.E. Olds Co., Smith sued for infringement,
and won—Olds was never again allowed to use his own name in
business. (He changed his company name to REO.)

SEATTLE, WASHINGTON

Named After: Chief Sealth

How He Got It: In the 1850s, Chief Sealth, a Suquamish Indian,
was friendly to white settlers (who called him Seattle)—at least at
first. The chief and his tribe traded flour and sugar to the whites
for metal, cloth, guns and tobacco. To make trading easier, Sealth
encouraged Dr. David Maynard to open a store at the little settle-
ment of Duwanmps. Maynard, in turn, suggested changing the
name of the town to Seattle in honor of the friendly Indian chief.

How He Lost It: From Sealth's point of view this wasn't a compliment—it was an attack. It violated a tribal custom that forbade
naming a place after a person who was still alive because it would
offend his guardian spirit. When the townspeople refused to
change the name, Sealth asked the residents for gifts to repay him
for problems that using his name would cause him in the next life.

Top three condiments in America today: 1. Ketchup; 2. Mustard; 3. Salsa.

They refused that, too.

Ultimately, the Suquamish tribe was exiled from their homeland and driven onto the Port Madison Indian Reservation. Tourists can visit Chief Sealth's grave today on Bainbridge Island where the inscription on his tombstone, I.H.S.—Latin for "in this spirit"—was interpreted by his Indian kinsmen to stand for "I have suffered."

FAMOUS AMOS COOKIES

Named After: Wally Amos

How He Got It: Amos was a talent agent at the William Morris Agency who used home-baked chocolate chip cookies as a calling card (he found it put producers and executives at ease and in a good mood for negotiations). After awhile, some of his famous clients began encouraging him to sell the cookies. They even invested in the Famous Amos Cookie Company, which he started in 1975—making him one of the pioneers of the gourmet cookie trend. Sales at Famous Amos hit $12 million by 1982.

How He Lost It: His cookies were a success, but he was no manager, and his company started losing money. Amos had to bring in new money; from 1985 to 1988 he went through four different co-owners. Each time a change was made, Amos gave up more of his share of the pie. By the time the Shanby Group bought it in 1988, Amos had nothing left; he even signed away his trademark rights. In 1992, when he started a new company called "Wally Amos Presents: Chip and Cookie," the Famous Amos Corp. sued him for infringement and libel.

After an acrimonious dispute, Wally Amos agreed not to use his own name or a caricature of himself on his cookies and not to bad- mouth the company that owns his name. Wally Amos then moved to Hawaii and started another cookie company called the "Uncle Noname Cookie Co."

*　　*　　*

"Names are not always what they seem. The common
Welsh name Bzjxxllwcp is pronounced Jackson."

Most unusual perspiration: Hippopotamuses exude red sweat when hot, excited, or in pain.

THE POPCORN CHRONICLES

*Whenever people at the BRI crave junk food, we pop a bunch
of popcorn. As we were munching away the other day,
Uncle John asked if anyone knew why popcorn popped,
or where it came from. That sent us scrambling for
a few answers.Here's what we found.*

BACKGROUND
There are five strains of corn on the family tree: sweet,
dent, flint, pod, and popcorn. The first four are essential to
world nutrition; 23% of all arable land in the world is used to
grow corn. Their country cousin, popcorn, is grown on less than
half of 1% of those acres. It's less productive—the kernels and ears
are smaller—but it's the only one that pops.

What makes it pop? The popcorn kernel has a hard shell.
When it dries, microscopic droplets of water are sealed inside. If a
kernel is heated above 212°F, the water inside boils and turns to
steam, creating internal pressure. When the pressure reaches about
135-165 pounds per square inch, the kernel explodes, or pops. It
literally turns inside out as the soft white interior bursts out.

EARLY HISTORY

- Popcorn is native to the Americas. Corn cobs dating back to
  5,600 B.C. have been found in excavations in a bat cave in
  New Mexico.

- Native Americans believed that a tiny demon lived in each
  kernel. When the demon's house was heated, the demon
  became so angry that it exploded. (Another version: the demon
  escaped in the explosion).

- Popcorn was introduced to European settlers at the first Thanksgiving in 1621. Chief Massasoit's brother, Quadequinea, arrived
  with a deerskin sack of popcorn. It was part of the feast, but the
  next morning some was leftover—so the Pilgrims ate it with
  milk and sugar for breakfast. They had no way of knowing they
  had just eaten the first puffed breakfast cereal.

Most popular names for U.S. high school sports teams: 1. Eagles; 2. Tigers.

- Settlers learned about popcorn from each other and from local Native American tribes. For 250 years, it remained a home-grown treat—not a national phenomenon. Farmers planted a few rows of popcorn for their children or to share with their neighbors. At first, they called it popped corn, parching corn, or rice corn. Finally, around 1820, it became popcorn.

THE POPCORN BOOM

It wasn't until the 1880s that popcorn moved from the family kitchen to the public market. In 1885, C. Cretors and Company of Chicago patented a popcorn machine. Soon street vendors were selling bags of popcorn all over the country.

In 1893, Chicago celebrated its 100th birthday with a world's fair, the Columbian Exposition. The firm of F.W. Rueckheim and Brother opened several booths at the fair, selling a new treat made of caramelized popcorn and peanuts. When the fair closed, Rueckheim decided to package and sell it on the national market. He called it Cracker Jack—contemporary slang for something first rate. "Before long," says food historian John Mariani, "Cracker Jack was a staple at baseball games throughout America."

Over the next 20 years, a number of other innovations kept popcorn interesting for vendors and consumers. For example:

- In 1914, an Iowa farmer developed a new strain of popcorn that left only about 2% of the kernels unpopped (until then, as much as 30% of the kernels were duds). The more efficient popcorn made it possible for vendors to keep selling bags at 1-5¢ each—and still turn a profit.

- In 1918, a company named Butter-Kist added a new twist—and a lot more calories. Their popcorn machines squirted melted butter on the popcorn after it was popped.

But the two innovations that really established popcorn in American culture were the movies…and the microwave.

AT THE MOVIES

Today, popcorn is synonymous with moviegoing. But for a while, theater owners resisted the idea.

In the early 1920s, during the reign of silent films, street vendors would park their popcorn machines outside theaters, and movie patrons would buy a bag or two before entering. At first,

---

Julia Ward Howe sold her "Battle Hymn of the Republic" to the *Atlantic Monthly* for **$4.**

owners objected because they had to clean up the mess. Some even refused to let customers bring popcorn into their theaters. But disgruntled movie buffs simply walked to another theater with less rigid standards.

The lesson wasn't lost on an enterprising popcorn entrepreneur in Chicago. He developed a commercial popper, and convinced several theater owners that they could make a profit by installing it in their lobbies. The profits would more than pay for the cost of cleaning up the mess.

Saving Hollywood

He was right, of course. In fact, some historians credit popcorn with saving the movie industry during the Great Depression. Money was so tight that theaters had to resort to gimmicks to attract customers—like "dish nights" (free dishes) and "ladies nights" (girlfriends or wives got in free), etc. This cut into profits so deeply that without the extra revenue from popcorn stands, many theaters would have closed.

To a lesser degree, the same conditions prevail today. About $3 of every $4 the customer pays for a movie ticket goes to the distributor (although there's a sliding scale; if the movie is popular enough to have an extended run, the percentage to the distributor is reduced). Often, the difference between a profit or loss for the theater is the sales of food. Popcorn accounts for 35% of all sales at the "refreshment" stand.

THE POPCORN HERO

Popcorn was still a long way from being an international agribusiness in 1941 when a 34-year-old, Purdue-educated agronomist named Orville Redenbacher decided to make popcorn his life's work. His axiom was: "Learn one thing, but know it better than anyone else."

The self-proclaimed "King of Popcorn" began a series of crossbreeding experiments to increase fluffiness. Up to that time, the popped grain was 15 to 20 times the size of the uncooked kernel. Redenbacher's new strains of popcorn doubled that. They had a volume of 40 times the original kernel.

For the next three decades, Redenbacher continued his pursuit of the perfect popcorn kernel. At least five new strains were developed and tested. Finally, in 1960, he announced his

Captain Jean-Luc Picard's fish was named Livingston.

ultimate discovery—a new strain he labeled Gourmet Popcorn.

Redenbacher tried to sell it to large food companies, but no one was interested. Finally, he decided to market it himself. He planned to call it Redbow, a combination of his and his partner's (Bowman) names. But a consulting firm insisted that he use his own name and photo instead.

Orville Redenbacher Gourmet Popcorn was first sold at the Marshall Fields Department Store in Chicago. Five years later, it was the leading brand in the U.S.—and popcorn had been reborn as a sophisticated snack.

Redenbacher was so closely identified with popcorn that, when his company was sold to the giant Hunt-Weston conglomerate, they kept his name on the package.

MEANWHILE...

From 1980 to 1990, two consumer products combined to double America's popcorn consumption: the microwave oven and the VCR. People were starting to watch movies at home. When Pillsbury invented microwave popcorn in 1982, it was suddenly simple to make popcorn part of the experience.

A year later, Redenbacher developed the first "shelf-stable" microwave popcorn. "Pillsbury came out with the first microwave popcorn," he explained, "but it had to be refrigerated to preserve the fat and everything that's in there to pop it with. 'Shelf-stable' meant we could put it on the shelf for a minimum of seven months [without spoiling]." This shifted popcorn consumption back to where it all started—the home. Today about 90% of retail popcorn sales are microwave popcorn.

POPCORN TRIVIA

- Americans today eat 17.3 billion quarts of popcorn a year. The average American eats about 68 quarts.

- About 70% of all popcorn is prepared and eaten in the home. Most of the remaining 30% is sold at the movies, sports events, etc.

- A popped kernel will form either a "snowflake" shape (popped big and shaped like an unruly cloud) or "mushroom" shape (popped into a ball).

- Newly harvested popcorn is better than old corn—the water

content is higher, which means more of the kernels will pop. One way to preserve moisture content: keep popcorn in the refrigerator, in an airtight container.

Nutrition

- According to The Almanac of Food, four cups of air-popped, plain popcorn have only 92 calories, with 1 gram of fat. If oil is used, the calorie and fat content more than doubles.

- Nutritional content: 71% starch and other carbohydrates, 10.5% protein, 3% fat, a sprinkling of vitamins and minerals, and up to 14% water.

Popcorn Weirdness

- Orlando, Florida created the world's largest box of popcorn on December 17, 1988. A square box, measuring 25 feet on each side, was built at Jones High School. Thousands of citizens showed up, with popcorn and poppers. When the signal was given, the poppers were turned on. Volunteers dumped the popcorn into the box. When the day ended, the box was filled to an average depth of 6.06 feet, and ended up in the *Guinness Book of World Records*.

- Marion, Ohio is the Popcorn Capital of the U. S. Every year, a quarter of a million visitors show up for their three-day Popcorn Festival. There are the usual beauty pageants, popcorn sculptures, popcorn foods, and guided tours of the popcorn museum, which features displays of antique corn poppers dating back to 1892.

And…

- The Aztecs threw ears of popcorn into the fire, then collected the popped grains. Or, if time permitted, they heated stones in the fire, then spread a layer of popcorn on the flat surface.

- Corn is the most hybridized of any major plant in the world. It can grow in more places than any other plant—from the polar regions to the hottest rain forest.

- More popcorn is eaten in the fall than any other time of year.

Sports note: A healthy pig should be able to run a mile in 7.5 minutes.

FOR YOUR READING PLEASURE...

Recently, we stumbled on Bizarre Books, a collection of weird-but-true book titles, compiled by Russell Ash and Brian Lake. Hard to believe, but these titles were chosen and published in all seriousness. How would you like to spend your time reading...

Why People Move, edited by Jorge Balan (1981)

Oh Angry Sea (a-ab-ba, hu-luh-ha): the History of a Sumerian Congregational Lament, by Raphael Kutscher (1975)

Animals as Criminals, by J. Brand (1896)

A Pictorial Book of Tongue Coating, Anonymous (1981)

The Dentist in Art, by Jens Jorgen Pindborg and L. Marvitz (1961)

How to Get Fat, by Edward Smith (1865)

A Frog's Blimp, by Shinta Cho (1981)

The Fangs of Suet Pudding, by Adams Farr (1944)

How to Cook Husbands, by Elizabeth Stong Worthington (1899)

Cold Meat and How to Disguise It, by Ms. M.E. Rattray (1904)

How to Boil Water in a Paper Bag, Anonymous (1891)

Sex Life of the Foot and Shoe, by William Rossi (1977)

How to Be Happy Though Married, by E.J. Hardy (1885)

Let's Make Some Undies, by Marion Hall (1954)

Be Bold With Bananas, by the Australian Banana Growers Council

One Hundred and Forty-one Ways of Spelling Birmingham, by William Hamper (1880)

Children Are Wet Cement, by Ann Orlund (1981)

Scouts in Bondage, by Geoffrey Prout (1930)

Do Snakes Have Legs? by Bert Cunningham (1934)

Let Me Hold It Till I Die, by H. Lovegrove (1864)

Life and Laughter 'midst the Cannibals, by Clifford White-ley Collison (1926)

Unmentionable Cuisine, by Calvin W. Schwabe (1979)

Nasal Maintenance: Nursing Your Nose Through Troubled Times, by William Alan Stuart (1983)

Old Age: Its Cause and Prevention, by Sanford Bennett (1912)

Who invented the coat hanger? Historians say Thomas Jefferson.

LUCKY FINDS

*Ever find something valuable? It's a great feeling. Here's
a look at some people who found some valuable stuff
and got to keep it! You should be so lucky...*

HOLY GRAIL
The Find: A first edition copy of a book called
Tamerlane.
Where it was Found: In a New Hampshire antique shop.
The Story: In the winter of 1988, an antique dealer named Robert
Webber paid $500 for a large collection of musty old books at
another dealer's estate auction.

One of the books was titled *Tamerlane and Other Poems,* and
was dated 1827. "It was an awful looking thing," Webber recalled.
The slim brown book had a ring stain from a drinking glass. Its
edges were faded and the printing was poor. Even if the book had
been new, it wouldn't have looked pretty. "By a Bostonian" was all
it said about the author.

Webber put a price tag of $18 on it. "My wife wanted to keep
it and read it," he said. "But I said, 'What do you want that dirty
old thing for?'" It sat there for a few days in his antique bar, with a
pile of pamphlets on fertilizer and farm machinery. A man came
into the store, saw the book and the $18 price tag, and offered $15
for it. Sold.

The customer was either really cheap or just slow to realize
what he'd bought. *Tamerlane* is nicknamed "the black tulip" by
book collectors because it is the rarest and most valuable book in
American literature. "A Bostonian" was Edgar Allen Poe and
Tamerlane was his first book of poetry, a self-published failure.
Eventually, the man who bought the book (his identity is secret)
notified Sotheby's of his find; they picked it up in an armored
truck and later auctioned it for $198,000.

WAGGA WAGGA TREASURE
The Find: An etching of a river scene.
Where It was Found: On a pig breeding trophy at Charles Stuart
University in Southeastern Australia.
The Story: In the 1950s, the Wagga Wagga Agricultural College

---

Yikes! The Pentagon spends $8,612 per second; about $271.6 billion a year.

created the Brighton Trophy to be awarded to the "five highest-producing sows of one sire." Someone in town donated the etching to serve as the centerpiece of the trophy.

When the college was taken over by Charles Stuart University in 1989, administrators put the trophy on top of a filing cabinet and forgot about it. It sat there, gathering dust, for almost a decade. Then someone decided to include it in a local exhibit of Wagga Wagga memorabilia. When the show was over, they sent it directly to Charles Stuart University. The university's art curator happened to walk past it...and recognized it as an original work of the French impressionist Auguste Renoir. Estimated value: $25,000.

MISSING LINK
The Find: A flat, jagged rock about the size of a quarter.
Where It Was Found: On a camping trip, in Rio Puerco, New Mexico.
The Story: In 1995, the Shiffler family was returning from a camping trip when they decided to stop and explore the desert. With a toy shovel in his hand, David, the three-year-old son, began digging for dinosaur eggs. He had just seen The Land Before Time, a cartoon about dinosaurs, and according to his father, "everything he picked up that day was a dinosaur egg." One rock attracted him more than any other. He insisted they take it home.

The Shifflers put the rock on a shelf in the garage. It was just a jagged fragment of some kind, but David insisted it was a dinosaur egg, and his father decided to humor him. He took it to scientists at the New Mexico Museum of Natural History and Science and asked them to look at it.

To his shock, they told him it is a dinosaur egg (a fragment of one)—and not just any dinosaur egg, either. It is believed that a meat-eating dinosaur laid it 150 million years ago—which makes it 80 million years older than any other egg like it ever found in North America. David Shiffler's egg may force scientists to revise many of their theories about dinosaurs in the Jurassic period. David's reaction: "I knew it was an egg," he announced.

According to astronautical footnotes, the moon smells a little like exploded firecrackers.

MYTH AMERICA

Here are a few more Patriotic stories we all learned when we were young...all of which are 100% baloney . The information is from Bill Bryson's book, Made in America.

THE MYTH: Representatives from the 13 colonies met in Philadelphia in 1787 and drafted the U.S. Constitution.
THE TRUTH: Rhode Island and Vermont didn't send delegates, and Maryland almost didn't, because officials there had a hard time finding anyone who wanted to go. The first five people who were asked refused, and the state was still looking for people to send when the convention opened for business. New Hampshire was willing to send two delegates, but it refused to pay their expenses, and went for weeks without any representation at the convention. "Many delegates attended only fitfully, and six never came at all," Bryson writes. "Altogether only about thirty of the sixty-one elected delegates attended from start to finish."

THE MYTH: The framers of the U.S. Constitution saw it for the great document that it was.
THE TRUTH: A lot of the delegates at the Constitutional Convention hated it. So many compromises had to be made in order to secure agreement that many participants viewed it, as Alexander Hamilton put it, "a weak and worthless fabric." Fifteen delegates refused to sign it, and even the Constitution's biggest supporters saw it as little more than a stopgap measure—after a few years passed, new delegates could meet at another convention and try to pass something better.

THE MYTH: The founding fathers believed in democracy.
THE TRUTH: "The Founding Fathers, that is, the men who framed the Constitution, disagreed about many things," writes Paul Boller in Not So!, "but on one point they were in complete agreement: that democracy meant mob rule and if unchecked, it would pose a grave threat to life, liberty and property....There was nothing unusual in the Founding Fathers' distrust of democracy; it was conventional wisdom in the 18th century. Even well into the 19th century, in the United States as well as Western Europe, the

word 'democracy' had an unsavory connotation, especially among conservatives."

THE MYTH: The United States came very close to making German the official language of the country.

THE TRUTH: For some reason, history books occasionally report that German missed being designated our language by one vote at the Continental Congress. The reason they give: Colonists wanted to put as much distance between themselves and England as possible. Actually, dumping English was never considered—in fact, it's an absurd notion. By 1790, 90% of the white population of the U.S. was of English descent. "The only known occasion on which German was ever an issue was in 1795," Bryson writes, "when the House of Representatives briefly considered a proposal to publish federal laws in German as well as in English as a convenience to recent immigrants, and the proposal was defeated."

THE MYTH: Samuel Morse invented the telegraph in 1844.

BACKGROUND: That was the version that Morse liked to tell.

THE TRUTH: Morse did invent Morse Code, but the telegraph itself was invented in 1831 by a Princeton University professor named Joseph Henry, who never bothered to patent it. Morse's telegraph was based largely on Henry's design. Morse "not only stole lavishly from Henry's original papers," Bryson writes, "but when stuck would call on the eminent scientist for guidance. For years, Henry encouraged and assisted his efforts. Yet later, when Morse had grown immensely famous and rich, he refused to acknowledge even the slightest degree of debt to his mentor."

THE MYTH: The first message sent by Morse Code was, "What hath God wrought?"

THE TRUTH: Morse's first message was, "Everything worked well." It wasn't until a later public demonstration that the message, "What hath God wrought?" was sent. Morse didn't even choose the words: the daughter of the Commissioner of Patents did that.

Spain's name comes from Span or Spania, meaning "Land of rabbits."

FAMILIAR PHRASES

Here are more origins of everyday phrases.

KIT AND CABOODLE
Meaning: All of something; the whole thing.
Origin: "The Dutch word boedel means 'effects'—what a person owns. Robbers, especially housebreakers, adopted the term—calling whatever they stole 'boodle.' They carried their burglar's tools in a 'kit.' If they were able to enter a house, gather up everything valuable, and make a clean escape, they said they had gotten away with 'kit and boodle.' In time, the phrase was shortened to 'caboodle'—the 'ca' standing for the 'kit.' The 'kit' was reintroduced into the phrase—probably for emphasis." (From *Why Do We Say It*, by Webb Garrison)

GUINEA PIG
Meaning: The subject of an experiment; the first person to try something untested.
Origin: "This small South American rodent first came to Europe in the 17th century and was either misnamed 'guinea' (Guinea being in West Africa) for Guiana (in South America) or it was named for the Guineamen, slave traders who took blacks from Guinea to the West Indies and then conveyed a variety of goods from the Indies and North America to Britain.

"In the 19th century 'guinea pig' became British slang for a person of standing who allowed his name to be put on a company's roster of directors for a fee paid in guineas, but who was not active in the company." In the 20th century, guinea pigs "came to be widely used in scientific and medical experiments— leading to the transfer of the name to the subject of any kind of experiment." (From *It's Raining Cats and Dogs*, by Christine Ammer)

(TO GIVE—OR GET) THE THIRD DEGREE
Meaning: An intense and sometimes brutal grilling to get information from someone.
Origin: "The term 'third degree' has no connection with criminality or brutal treatment....It refers to the third and final stage of

The term "karaoke" means "empty orchestra" in Japanese.

proficiency demanded of one who seeks to become a master Mason… Before the candidate is fully qualified for the third degree he must undergo a very elaborate and severe test of ability. It is from this examination that 'third degree' became applied to the treatment of prisoners by the police, and it was through the fact that the police sometimes did employ brutality in efforts to extort confession or information that our present expression obtained its common modern meaning." (From *Heavens to Betsy!*, by Charles Earle Funk)

A SPINSTER
Meaning: An older, unmarried woman.
Origin: "Until spinning was mechanized in the late eighteenth century, turning wool or flax into yarn or thread was almost always 'woman's work.' A spinster was a woman spinner—often a professional; in the seventeenth century, it came to mean an unmarried woman—presumably because, having neither husband nor children, she could devote herself full-time to her spinning." (From *The Book of Lost Metaphors*)

TO BLACKMAIL SOMEONE
Meaning: To extort money from someone.
Origin: "Blackmail has nothing whatever to do with the post office. Black is used in the figurative sense of 'evil' or 'wicked.' Mail is a Scots word meaning 'rent' or 'tribute.' The term 'blackmail' originated in Scotland, where Highland chiefs at one time extorted tribute from Lowlanders and Englishmen on the Scottish border in return for protection from being plundered." (From *Word Mysteries & Histories*, by the Editors of the American Heritage Dictionaries)

THE GRAVEYARD SHIFT
Meaning: A night shift for workers.
Origin: It wasn't coined by morticians, but by shipbuilders. "The name originated during World War I, when for the first time shipbuilders and munitions workers found it necessary to work 'round the clock in order to produce enough for the war effort. It is still used today for any shift covering the midnight and early morning hours." (From *Fighting Words*, by Christine Ammer)

Typical life span of a cow: 30 years.

COURT TRANSQUIPS

Here's more real-life courtroom dialogue.

Q: "Do you remember what shoes you were wearing?"
A: "You mean the day I fell down?"
Q: "Yes."
A: "The same shoes I'm wearing."
Q: "What do you call those shoes? Are they flats…or how would you describe them?"
A: "I'd describe them as 'these shoes.'"

Q: "Please review this document. Do you know what a fax is?"
A: "Yeah, I do, man. It's when you tell the truth, man, tell it like it is. That is what the facts is."

Q: "What is the relationship?"
A: "She's my aunt."
Q: "Who's brother or sister to whom here?"
A: My mother is his brother—is her—my mother is—what is it? By marriage, I guess you would say. My mother is her brother—is his brother by marriage, so she's just an aunt."

A: "You know, I don't know, but I mean, you know—you don't know but you know. You know what I'm saying?"
Q: "Do I? No. Do I know? No."

Q: "You assumed narcotics in reaching your opinions."
A: "Yes."
Q: "You didn't assume a Frito or a Chee-to or a banana. You assumed narcotics."
A: "It was a narcotics raid. It wasn't a Frito raid, counselor."

Q: "So you remember who the doctor was who performed that?"
A: "Yes. Very easy name to remember, Mee."
Q: "Martin?"(The witness's name.)
A: "No, Mee."
Q: "You?"
A: "That was his name."
Q: "Me?"
A: "Mee."
Q: "M-e?"
A: "M-e-e. That was his name, Dr. Mee"

Q: "Mr. Jones, do you believe in alien forces?"
A: "You mean other than my wife?"

Q: "Were you acquainted with the decedent?"
A: "Yes, sir."
Q: "Before or after he died?"
Q: "Did he ever kill you before?"
A: "Pardon me?"

BRAND NAMES

*We all know these names—many are a part of our
everyday lives. But where did they come from?*

SEALY MATTRESS. In 1881, an inventor from Sealy, Texas developed a cotton-filled mattress. Word spread around the Southwest, and people began asking for the "mattress from Sealy." Eventually it became known simply as the "Sealy mattress."

SAMSONITE LUGGAGE. Named after Samson, the biblical strong man, to symbolize "strength and durability."

DORITOS. Rough translation from Spanish: "little bit of gold."

SANYO. Means "three oceans" in Japanese. Toshio Iue, who founded the company in 1947, planned to sell worldwide—across the Atlantic, Pacific, and Indian Oceans.

HUSH PUPPIES. At a dinner in 1957, Jim Muir, sales manager for Wolverine World Wide, Inc., was served tiny fried balls of corn dough known in the South as "hush puppies." When he wondered about the name, his host explained that local farmers used the food to quiet barking dogs. Muir decided it was a perfect name for a new pigskin shoe his company was developing. The reason: the shoe "could soothe a customer's aching feet, a.k.a. their 'barking dogs.'"

AMANA. In 1854, a German religious sect moved to Iowa and founded the Amana Colonies. Nearly a century later (1932) George Foerstner, a member of the group, started a business making freezers. It was run by the Amana community under their own brand name until 1943, when they sold it back to Foerstner. He kept the name.

MINOLTA. A loose acronym for **M**achinery and **IN**struments Optica**L** by Kazuo **TA**shima (founder of the Japanese-German Camera Company). The first Minolta-brand camera was introduced in 1932.

The mouse is the most common mammal in the U.S.

CHEESE GEOGRAPHY

This started out as a "How did the cheeses get their names?"
page. Then we found out that most of the cheeses we're interested
in are named for the places they were first made. So here's
what we wound up with, for you cheeseheads.

BRIE. In 1815, following the Napoleonic Wars, diplomats at the Congress of Vienna were served Brie; they enjoyed it so much they pronounced it the King of Cheeses. Birthplace: a northeastern region of France known as (surprise) Brie.

PARMESAN. A hard, well-aged cheese named after the Italian city of Parma (where it is called parmigiano).

COLBY. A granular cheese first made in Colby, Wisconsin at the end of the 19th century.

CAMEMBERT. Originated in the village of Camembert in France's Normandy region. To test the ripeness of Camembert, touch your eye with one finger and the cheese with another. If they feel the same, the cheese is ripe.

LIMBURGER. Created by Trappist monks in the Belgian town of Limburg.

CHEDDAR. The world's most popular cheese. Gets its name from the village of Cheddar in Somerset, England, where it was first produced in the 16th century.

GOUDA. A compressed sphere of cheese named for the Dutch town of Gouda.

SWISS. In Switzerland, where it originated, they call it Emmenthaler. "Swiss" is the generic term for imitations. The holes, by the way, come from pockets of natural carbon dioxide gases expanding in the cheese as it ages.

MONTEREY JACK. Created in Monterey, California by David Jacks, in the 1890s.

TILLAMOOK. American Cheddar made in Tillamook County, Oregon.

Time magazine's "Man of the Year" in 1938 was Adolf Hitler.

THE ORIGIN OF
THE WHITE HOUSE

*The White House is more than just a building—it's an important
national symbol—as well one of the most recognizable buildings
on Earth. How much do you know about its history?
Here's an introduction.*

BOOM TOWN
When the founding fathers began making plans for the
nation's capital city in 1789, they couldn't agree on a location. The northerners wanted a northern city to serve as the capital; the southerners wanted a southern city. Finally, they
compromised: Instead of establishing the capital in an existing
city, they'd create a new one from scratch. And they'd build it
somewhere in the middle of the country, not too far north and not
too far south.

On July 12, 1790, President Washington signed an Act of
Congress declaring that on "the first Monday in December 1800,"
the federal government would move to a new Federal District "not
exceeding ten miles square…on the river Potomac." Philadelphia
would serve as a temporary capital until then.

LOCATION, LOCATION, LOCATION
But the act didn't say exactly where on the Potomac the new city
should be. A lot more arguing took place before Secretary of State
Thomas Jefferson and Secretary of the Treasury Alexander Hamilton finally agreed on a ten-mile by ten-mile area of farmland and
swamps, a mile east of Georgetown, Maryland, and just over the
Potomac from Arlington, Virginia.

Maryland and Virginia donated the land, and George Washington hired engineer Pierre L'Enfant, a friend of Jefferson, to lay
out the new city. Washington also appointed three federal district
commissioners to oversee the work that was done in the new capital. One of their first decisions: they named the new city "Washington." (Although, for the rest of his life, George Washington
insisted on calling the city the "Federal District.")

AD HOC

Since the idea of a president was so new—most European countries were still ruled by royalty—nobody really knew what a president's house should look like. So in 1792, Thomas Jefferson took out a newspaper ad offering $500 to the architect who came up with the best design for a president's house, with George Washington making the final decision. Newspaper contests were an unusual way to solicit architectural designs even in the 1790s, but Jefferson figured it was the only way to guarantee that the architect would be chosen based on the merits of his design and not on favoritism or connections. Jefferson probably came to regret the newspaper contest idea, because he entered his own plans in the contest under the pseudonym "Mr. AZ" and lost.

TEMPORARY HOUSING

George Washington admired the work of architect James Hoban, an Irish immigrant who had designed the State Capitol of South Carolina. Washington encouraged Hoban to enter the contest…and then decided in his favor.

Hoban's design called for a three-story mansion and, as asked, included plans for wings that could be added on later when the time came. (They were never built.) He set the dimensions of the presidential palace at 170 feet long, 85 feet deep, and three stories high. Washington thought Hoban's building was beautiful, but he also complained that it was too small. He suggested increasing its size by about 20%. Since that would have cost a fortune, the suggestion was politely ignored.

HOUSE PAYMENTS

Hoban estimated that the president's house would cost about $400,000 to build. But no one knew how to pay for it. George Washington thought he could raise the funds through the sale of building lots in the Federal District. But building an entire city from the ground up, in the middle of farmlands and swamps, for a republic barely ten years old, seemed such an impossible undertaking that many people doubted whether the city would ever really be built. In fact, the new city was the laughing stock of New York and Philadelphia; the state of Pennsylvania had even begun building its own permanent federal buildings in the expectation that Washington, D.C. would eventually be abandoned.

C3PO is the first character to speak in Star Wars.

In the face of such skepticism, the few District of Columbia lots that sold at all, sold at much lower prices than anticipated.

So the planners had to cut corners. The third floor of the president's house was eliminated, as were the North and South Porticoes (the large, columned overhangs that were planned for the front and rear of the building). The marble fireplaces that had been ordered were canceled and replaced with simpler ones made of wood. The "presidential palace" was becoming less palatial.

Part II of the "Origin of the White House" is on page 158.

* * *

FRUSTRATIONS OF THE RICH & FAMOUS

"When his car broke down on a busy New York road, William Shatner (of "Star Trek" fame) stuck out his thumb and tried to hitch a ride. But no one stopped.

"'Eventually, I tried to play the celebrity card,' the actor said. 'I made this pickup truck slow down by jumping out and shouting, "Hi, it's me, Captain Kirk!"'

"The woman driving said, 'Yeah?' then stuck up her middle finger and went 'Well, beam THIS up!'

"As she sped off down the road, Shatner decided to walk."

—The Edge, Portland Oregonian

"Treasury Secretary Michael Blumenthal found himself in an embarrassing situation in Beethoven's, an expensive San Francisco restaurant in 1979. Blumenthal was confronted with a sizable dinner bill, an expired Visa card, and a waiter who wanted proof of signature to back up an out-of-town check. Blumenthal thought for a minute, and solved his predicament the only way he could: He produced a dollar bill and pointed to his own signature, W. M. Blumenthal, in the bottom right-hand corner. The signatures matched, and Blumenthal's personal check was accepted."

—Strange Facts and Useless Information, by Scot Morris

NOT FOR EXPORT

It's not easy selling things in the global economy—a lot of product names lose something in translation. These products are real...but you probably aren't going to find them at your Wal-Mart any time soon:

Strange Taste—a popular Chinese candy.

Zid!—a German "gourmet chocolate and fruit confection."

Pschit—a French soft drink, and Mucos, a soda sold in the Philippines.

Ass Glue—a Chinese patent medicine that is marketed as a "blood nourishing paste."

Koff—a Finnish beer sold briefly in the United States.

Shitto—a spicy pepper sauce from Ghana.

Super Piss—a Finnish solvent that unfreezes car locks.

Little Hussy—a writing tablet

AND FROM JAPAN...

Japanese cars displayed at a 1997 Tokyo auto show:

- Subaru Gravel Express
- Mazda Bongo Friendee
- Nissan Big Thumb Harmonized Truck
- Suzuki Every Joy Pop Turbo
- Mazda Scrum
- Mitsubishi Delica Space Gear Cruising Active
- Mazda Proceed Marvie
- Daihatsu Town Cube
- Isuzu Giga 20 Light Dump

Kowpis—a "popular fermented milk drink."

Homo Sausage—beef jerky.

Ease Your Bosoms—coffee marketed as an antidote to stress.

Pokari Sweat—a sports drink.

Green Piles—lawn fertilizer.

Hand Maid Queen Aids—Band-Aid shaped chocolates.

"One-fifth of the people are against everything all the time." —Robert F. Kennedy

IRONIC, ISN'T IT?

There's nothing like a good dose of irony to put the problems of day-to-day life in proper perspective.

IRONIC DEATHS

• "Evan Wheeler, a veteran actress, was playing a death scene in a Baltimore production of *The Drunkard* in November, 1986, when she dropped to the stage and, to tremendous applause, died." (*Hodgepodge II*)

• "The wife of Claudius I tried to poison her husband with poisonous mushrooms in 54 A.D. Claudius' doctor tried to make him throw up by tickling his throat with a feather. Claudius choked on the feather and died." (*Oops*)

• In 1955, actor James Dean made an ad warning teens about driving too fast. ("The life you save may be mine," he said.) Shortly after, he died when his Porsche Spider, going 86 mph, hit another car.

• In 1871, attorney Clement Vallandigham was demonstrating to a jury that the man his client was accused of shooting could have accidentally done it himself. Vallandigham took out a gun, held it as it was held at the scene of the crime, and pulled the trigger. The gun was loaded; he proved his point.

MUSICAL IRONY

• The man who wrote "Home Sweet Home," John Howard Payne, "never had a permanent residence." (*The Book of Lists*)

• "The man who wrote 'Dixie,' Dan D. Emmett, was a Northerner. He was born in Ohio and wrote the song in a New York boarding house." (*The Book of Lists*)

• Joni Mitchell, who wrote "Woodstock," wasn't at the Woodstock music festival. She watched it on TV.

• The couple who wrote "Take Me Home Country Roads" had never been to West Virginia. They had only seen pictures of it on postcards a friend sent.

• The men who wrote "Take Me Out to the Ballgame," Albert von Tilzer and Jack Norworth, had never been to a baseball game.

In 1659, it was illegal to celebrate Christmas in Massachusetts.

• "The music that played as President Bush stepped to the podium at the 1992 Republican convention in Houston—following his wife's speech on family values—was taken from the gay musical *La Cage Aux Folles.*" (*Forbes*)

BITTER IRONY

• The inmates at the prison in Concord, New Hampshire, spend their days making the state's license plates, which bear the motto LIVE FREE OR DIE.

• "The memorial statue erected in Vienna to the memory of composer Franz Schubert cost more than the luckless genius earned from his work during his lifetime." (*Oops*)

• "In 1853 John Coffee built the jail in Dundalk, Ireland. He went bankrupt on the project and became the first inmate of his own jail." (*Not a Good Word About Anybody*)

• "I. N. Terrill, a member of the legislature, wrote the criminal law statutes for Oklahoma…and was the first person convicted under the law for murder." (*Ripley's Believe It or Not*)

• "Fernande Olivier lived with Picasso for seven years when she was young and poor. She was not impressed with his paintings, which included many portraits of her that she thought unflattering. In 1912 she moved out and took with her a little heart-shaped mirror as her only memento of the years with her Spanish painter. She never saw Picasso again, and died in poverty in 1966. A few years after her death, a cubist painting of her by Picasso sold for $790,000." (*Not a Good Word About Anybody*)

PRESIDENTIAL IRONY

• "Ronald Reagan was rejected for the leading role in the 1964 movie The Best Man because "he doesn't look presidential." (*Not a Good Word About Anybody*)

• The man known as the Father of Our Country, George Washington, may well have been sterile.…He fathered no children, and according to experts, suffered from a variety of debilitating diseases, including smallpox, rotten teeth, consumption, amoebic dysentery, pleurisy, malaria, and a genetic impairment called Kleinfelter's syndrome, "which could well have rendered him sterile."

The first TV commercial: a Bulova watch ticking onscreen for exactly 60 seconds.

"MAKE MY DAY..."

Feelin' lucky, punk? Are ya? Then, go ahead...
read this stuff from Clint Eastwood.

"In the complications of society as we know it today, sometimes a person who can cut through the bureaucracy and red tape is a hero."

"I don't like the idea of anybody getting killed, but especially me. I'm against war, all war."

"They say marriages are made in Heaven. So are thunder and lightning."

"I see my films as first aid to the modern male psyche. Most jobs today can be held by women. Many men have become defensive and enjoy being taken to another time, another period, where masculinity was important to survival."

"Women are superior to men. You see a lot of smart men with dumb women, but you don't see a lot of smart women with dumb guys. A lot of guys will go out with a bimbo, but women who are smart don't do that."

"The self-sufficient human being has become a mythological character in our day and age."

"I'm interested in the fact that the less secure a man is, the more likely he is 'to have extreme prejudice.'"

"There's nothing wrong with glamorizing the gun. I don't think that hurts anybody. I'm for gun legislation myself."

"It's not the bloodletting that people come to see in the movies. It's vengeance. Getting even is important to the public. They go to work every day for some guy who's rude and they can't stand, and they just have to take it. Then they go see me on the screen and I kick the s—t out of him."

"If I just wanted to go out and make some dough I could gun 'em down as good as I ever did. But I'd rather not do movies where there are 800 guys in the theater and one chick who was coerced into going by her brother."

Guinness world record: Minnie the cat killed 12,480 rats between 1927 and 1933.

THE BIRTH OF BASEBALL CARDS, PART I

People in the U.S. have been collecting baseball cards for over 100 years. Bubblegum hadn't even been invented yet when Old Judge cigarettes gave birth to this American institution.

BACKGROUND

Baseball cards have grown from a kid's hobby to a $2 billion-a-year industry. Their history goes back to the early days of baseball.

The Duke of Tobacco. Until the 1880s, when "Buck" Duke took over the Duke Tobacco Company (later The American Tobacco Co.) from his father, most tobacco was sold loose, in tins; people would roll their own cigarettes. In 1885, Buck bought the rights to a machine that put out 200 ready-made cigarettes at a time. Now he was able to concentrate on selling cigarettes instead of tobacco. What he needed was more customers. So he began a huge ad campaign. Soon Duke had 40% of the cigarette market.

To cut costs, Duke replaced tobacco tins with paper cigarette packs. As Pete Williams recounts in *Card Sharks:*

> When he discovered that many of the packs were crushed in shipping, Duke came up with the idea of placing a cardboard insert to stiffen the pack. Not only would they prevent damage, but the "cards" would serve as advertising pieces and premiums to boost sales...He included cards of actors and actresses...[and] his idea inspired competitors to place baseball cards in their products.

The first cards were sold with Old Judge Cigarettes in 1886. They were 1-1/2" X 2-1/2"—much smaller than today—and pictured stoic-looking players wearing neckties with their uniforms. Eventually they started using "action" shots, which were actually staged photographs of players reaching for, or swinging at, balls on a string. Instead of the statistics and trivia found on the back of today's cards, these early cards had advertising.

"Fleas can be taught nearly anything that a congressman can." —Mark Twain

WHY BASEBALL?

Baseball cards had three advantages for tobacco companies:

1) They capitalized on the growing popularity of the sport, which was just coming into its own; 2) The connection with sports heroes helped combat the notion that store-bought cigarettes were effeminate; and 3) They were collectible. Pete Williams notes:

> With the cards came card collecting, which presented a challenge since the cards came one to a pack. Collecting became something of a family affair, as young boys would obtain the cards from their fathers and urge them to buy more tobacco products. Non-tobacco users who wished to collect had to pick up the tobacco habit—as the companies hoped—or find a user willing to part with the cards.

THE PRECIOUS SET

Duke Tobacco got out of the baseball card business in 1890, when it combined with other tobacco companies to form American Tobacco. With a virtual monopoly on cigarettes, there was no need for promotions.

But from 1909 to 1911, anti-trust laws were used to break American Tobacco up, so the company went back to using baseball cards as a promotion. They came out with a 524-card set called the "T206"— which has turned into the most valuable baseball card series in history. According to Card Sharks, here's why:

> Shortly after production began, shortstop Honus Wagner of the Pittsburgh Pirates (now a Hall of Famer) objected to the use of his photo and threatened legal action if his card was not removed from the set. American Tobacco complied, but not before a quantity of Wagners had been printed and shipped with tobacco.

For a long time, baseball historians believed Wagner objected because he disapproved of cigarette smoking. Then they found out he'd once endorsed a brand of cigars...and realized he just didn't want them using his likeness without paying for it.

Today, the few Wagner cards that slipped out have become the Holy Grail of baseball card collecting. In 1997, one was sold at auction for $641,000!

There's more. For Part II of the baseball card story, turn to page 357.

The most men ever to ride on one motorcycle: 47 (Army Corps of Brasilia team, 1995).

TALL IN THE SADDLE: WESTERN FILM QUOTES

Peggy Thompson and Saeko Usukawa have put together a collection of great lines from Westerns called Tall in the Saddle. *Some samples:*

Young Eddie: "He don't look so tough to me."
Cowboy: "If he ain't so tough, there's been an awful lot of sudden natural deaths in his vicinity."
—*The Gunfighter* (1950)

"I always say the law was meant to be interpreted in a lenient manner. And that's what I try to do. Sometimes I lean to one side of it, sometimes I lean to the other."
—**Paul Newman,** *Hud* (1963)

"Sonny, I can see we ain't going to have you 'round long enough to get tired of your company."
—**Richard Widmark,** *The Law and Jake Wade* (1958)

Cowboy: "For a long time I was ashamed of the way I lived."
Dance hall girl: "You mean to say you reformed?"
Cowboy: "No, I got over being ashamed."
—*Goin' to Town* (1935)

J. W. Grant: "You bastard!"
Hired gun Henry "Rico" Fardan: "Yes, sir. In my case an accident of birth. But you, you're a self-made man."
—*The Professionals* (1966)

Fletch McCloud (Roy Rogers): "Ever hear what William Shakespeare said? 'All's well that ends well.'"
Cowboy Bob Seton (John Wayne): "Shakespeare, huh? He must have come from Texas. We've been saying that for years."
—*The Dark Command* (1940)

Trampas: "When I want to know anything from you, I'll tell you, you long-legged son of a—"
"The Virginian": "If you want to call me that, smile."
—*The Virginian* (1929)

Sheriff Bullock: "How is he, Doc?"
Doc: "Well, he suffered lacerations, contusions, and a concussion. His jugular vein was severed in three places. I counted four broken ribs and a compound fracture of the skull. To put it briefly, he's real dead."
—*Rancho Notorious* (1952)

"I like my coffee strong enough to float a pistol."
—**Ernest Borgnine,** *Jubal* (1955)

"I don't want trouble with anybody—unless I start it."
— **"Wild Bill" Elliott,** *The Showdown* (1950)

Coincidence? 40% of people who move to a new address change their brand of toothpaste at the same time.

WHEN YOU GOTTA GO...

Here's the BRI's quick, all-purpose language lesson. Now, no matter where you're traveling, you'll be able to ask the essential question: "Where is the bathroom?" Are you ready? Okay, now repeat after us...

Spanish: Donde ésta el baño?

Danish: Hvor er toilettet?

Japanese: Torie wa doko desu ka?

Russian: Gde zdes tualet?

Hawai'I (Hawaiian): Ai hea lua?

Tâi-oân Hö-ló-oë (Taiwanese): Piän-só. tï tó-üi?

Italian: Dove e il bagno?

Cymraeg (Welsh): Ble mae'r toiled?

Magyar (Hungarian): Hol a mosdó?

Kiswahili (Swahili): Choo kiko wapi?

Dutch: Waar is het toilet?

Bahasa (Indonesian): Kamar kecil di mana?

Afrikaans: Waar is diebadkamer? Waar is die toilet?

Romāna (Romanian): Unde este toaleta?

Bosanski (Bosnian): Gdje je toalet?

French: Ou sont les toilettes?

Czestina: Kde je záchod?

Esperanto: Kie estas la necesejo?

German: Wo ist die Toilette?

Eesti (Estonia): Kus on väljakäik?

Íslenska (Icelandic): Hvar er snyrtingin?

Interlingua: Ubi es le lavatorio?

Polski (Polish): Gdzie jest toaleta?

Tagalog: Nasaan ang kasilyas?

Yiddish: vu iz der bodtsimer?

Latviski (Latvian): Kur atrodas vannas istaba?

Lietuvis (Lithuanian): Kur yra tualetas?

Srpski (Serbian): Gde je toalet?

Ivrit (Hebrew): eifo ha'sherutim?

Surveys say: Only about 1/4 of all American adults eat 3 meals a day.

NUDES & PRUDES

It's hard to shock anyone with nudity today. But stupidity is always a shock. These characters demonstrate that whether you're dressed or naked, you can still be dumber than sin.

NUDE... "In 1831, when Edgar Allen Poe was at West Point, parade dress instructions called for 'white belts and gloves, under arms.' According to legend, Poe took them literally. He appeared on parade ground, rifle balanced on his bare shoulder, wearing nothing but white belt and gloves. He was expelled."

PRUDE... "Madama de la Bresse directed that her life savings of 125,000 francs be used to buy clothing for naked Paris snowmen. In 1876 the courts upheld the validity of her bequest, making French snowmen the best dressed in the world." (*More Best, Worst, and Most Unusual*)

NUDE... "When state police in Ogdensburg, New York, caught William J. Hess, 39, burglarizing a greenhouse, he was wearing nothing. He replied that he was naked so that anyone who saw him in the greenhouse couldn't identify him by describing his clothing." (*Dumb, Dumber, Dumbest*)

PRUDE... "The Dallas grocery chain Minyard's pulled the November 1993 issue of *Discover* magazine from its shelves because of the cover photo of a sculpture of two apes, the 3.2-million-year-old *Australopithecus afarensis*, with their genitals exposed. The apes are believed to be our earliest ancestors. 'When it shows the genitals or the breasts,' Minyard's president Jay L. Williams said, 'we're going to pull it.'" (*Dumb, Dumber, Dumbest*)

NUDE... "In Greenfield, Wisconsin, owners of the Classic Lanes bowling alley decided to jazz up their sport with a little humor. Outside their building, they posted signs reading BOWL NAKED, BOWL FREE. Obviously, no one took them up on their offer...until April 16, 1996. That's the day 21-year-old Scott Hughes strolled into the bowling alley, rented a pair of shoes, and proceeded to take off his clothes. As a local church group watched

Pontius Pilate was born in Scotland.

in horror, Hughes went on to bowl a 225 game—wearing nothing but a cowboy hat and bowling shoes." *(Knuckleheads in the News)*

PRUDE... Francesca Nortyega, a well-known European reformer, willed her estate to a niece on the condition that she keep the family goldfish outfitted in pants.

NUDE... In 1995, San Francisco mayor Frank Jordan, running for re-election, tried to show he was a "regular guy' by accepting a challenge from two disc jockeys to take a nude shower with them. Photos of the shower circulated all over the city. He lost in a land-slide.

PRUDE... "East German swimmer Sylvia Ester set a world 100-meters record of 57.89 seconds in 1967—but officials refused to recognize it because she swam in the nude." *(World's Biggest Mistakes)*

NUDE... "Peter Archer, 47, was arrested for running naked down a street in Melbourne, Australia, but was released when police learned he was fleeing a mortuary where a doctor had officially pronounced him dead." *(Portland Oregonian)*

PRUDE... "Three small figurines in an exhibit at Dallas City Hall happened to be nude. So the thoughtful city officials, worried that the nudity might offend some viewers, had the figurines covered with tiny, handmade fig leaves." *(The 176 Stupidest Things Ever Done)*

NUDE... Irene Wachenfeldt, a Swedish high school teacher, illustrated a lesson on loving your body by taking her clothes off in class. "My body is good enough," she said. "I want you to feel the same about your bodies." When she was forced to quit, students objected. One wrote: "It was one of our best lessons."

PRUDE... Noah Webster, well known for his dictionaries, once published a censored version of the Bible as well. "Many words are so offensive, especially for females," he explained. He changed words like *teat* to *breast*, and *stones* (testicles) to *peculiar members*. It flopped.

BEGINNINGS

Of course you've heard of all the things listed below.
But you may not have heard how they got started.

SCOTCHGARD

In 1944, a laboratory assistant at the 3M company spilled an experimental chemical on her tennis shoes. She tried to wash the stuff off, but couldn't. As the weeks passed, she noticed that the chemical-stained part of her shoe remained clean while the rest of it collected dirt and grime. 3M researchers, who had been trying to find practical uses for the chemical, realized it was ideal as a fabric protector.

THE SODA STRAW

The first straws, made of parafinned paper, were introduced in 1888 by an inventor named Marvin Stone. They didn't catch on—the hand-rolled tubes cracked easily and were unsanitary. Then in the early 1900s—not long after concessionaire Harry Stevens introduced hot dogs to New York Giant baseball games—he noticed that when fans drank from their soda bottles, they had to take their eyes off the game for a moment. So he hired a paper maker to roll some straws out of paper, and began including one with every soda he sold. It increased his sales, and made straws a permanent part of American culture. In 1905, Stone's company came up with a machine to mass-produce them.

HIGHWAY DIVIDERS

Invented by Dr. June A. Carroll of Indio, California. Carroll lived near a particularly dangerous stretch of highway, so in 1912, she painted a stripe down the middle of the road for about a mile to help drivers stay on the right side of the road. The California Highway Commission liked the idea so much that it painted stripes down the middle of every paved road in the state.

KEEP HONKING ...I'M RELOADING

BRI member Debbie Thornton sent in this list of real-life bumper stickers. Have you seen the one that says...

Horn broken.
Watch for finger.

*He who laughs last
thinks slowest.*

What has four legs and an arm?
A happy pitbull

**I love cats...they taste
just like chicken.**

Rehab is for quitters.

No radio–already stolen.

**I don't suffer from insanity,
I enjoy every minute of it,**

*Smile. It's the second best thing
you can do with your lips.*

**Give me ambiguity...
or give me something else.**

We are born naked,
wet, and hungry.
Then things get worse.

*Always remember you're
unique, just like everyone else.*

**Very funny Scotty.
Now beam down my clothes.**

There are three kinds of
people: those who can count...
and those who can't.

*Keep honking...
I'm reloading.*

**i suuport
publik edekashun.**

Make it idiot-proof and someone will make a better idiot.

*Puritanism: The haunting fear
that someone, somewhere
may be happy.*

**It IS as bad as you think, and
they ARE out to get you.**

Cover me. I'm changing lanes.

*I want to die peacefully in my
sleep like my grandfather, not
screaming and yelling, like the
passengers in his car*

**Where there's a will, I
want to be in it.**

So many lawyers,
so few bullets.

The Earth is .02 degrees hotter during a full moon.

THE ANIMALS
AT THE ZOO, Part 1

*If you've ever gone to a zoo, you probably know what it's like to
stare at animals for a few hours with no idea of what you're
looking at. Why do they keep growling that way? Why are they
digging like that? And so forth. We can't give you a complete
rundown on every animal behavior, but here are a few tips that
we hope will make your next visit to the zoo more interesting.*

WATCHING LIONS

Lions are very social animals. They live in groups called
prides, which normally consist of about 3 to 12 females
and 2 to 4 males. There is one dominant male. They depend on
each other for hunting, grooming, raising young, etc. Here are
some things you might see them do:

Behavior: Peeing backward, onto a tree or wall (male).
What It Means: Marking a territory. Normally, males pee in a
crouch. But when they want to mark an area, they spray backward
onto a vertical object—sometimes even onto people watching
them. If a zoo lion backs up to you with his tail raised, watch out.

Behavior: Excessive self-grooming (male).
What It Means: Stress. Male lions normally spend a lot of time
grooming their manes and paws. But when they're under a lot of
stress—which happens when they don't feel comfortable with
other lions or with their surroundings—they do it more frequently.

Behavior: Lying on back with legs spread out.
What It Means: It's cooling off. A lion's fur is thinnest on its
stomach, so it's letting the air circulate there.

Behavior: Yawning.
What It Means: Boredom? You might think so. But actually a
lion's yawn, a familiar sight at zoos, is not a commentary on its life
in captivity. Even wild lions are habitual yawners. Yawning is
simply a biological reflex that increases the flow of oxygen to the

blood. You'll see lions yawn after waking from rest or just before feeding—a sign that they are gearing up to do something. And, yes, yawning is just as contagious among lions as it is among people.

Behavior: Roaring.
What It Means: In the jungle, it would be a territorial statement. In the zoo, it's more likely to be a response to some sort of loud noise.

Interesting sight: Watch how one lion's roar will set off the rest of them. Soon, there will be a bunch roaring at the same time. It's as contagious as yawning.

OTHER ANIMALS

BEAR—Behavior: Pacing.
What It Means: Mental stress. Zoos have come a long way from the days when animals were displayed in caged cells. Today's zookeepers rely on the latest research, and their own creativity, to keep animals in good physical and mental shape. But the sad truth is that even the best efforts do not guarantee results. Bears in captivity are particularly likely to show signs of under-stimulation, such as pacing. One way that zookeepers try to keep animals spirited is by reducing "handouts" at mealtime. The animal is encouraged to work for its food. In the case of bears, honey placed inside a log often does the trick of challenging them, keeping them in touch with wild food-gathering instincts.

CROCODILE—Behavior: Biting each other's tails.
What It Means: Are they fighting or playing? Animals play rough, so sometimes it's hard to tell whether two animals engaged in aggressive physical contact are angry or having a good time. But with crocodiles, it's no mystery: they're not getting along. Playful or friendly behavior is virtually nonexistent among crocs. Most of the day, they tolerate each other at best (though, they will practice cooperative hunting and feeding). The rules of their biting battles are pretty basic: lock your opponent's tail in your jaw, and you win.

For more of "The Animals At The Zoo," see page 249.

THE TOP 10 HITS OF THE YEAR, 1960–1963

Here's another installment of BRI's Top Ten of the Year list.

1960
(1) Theme From "A Summer Place"—*Percy Faith*
(2) He'll Have To Go—*Jim Reeves*
(3) Cathy's Clown—*The Everly Brothers*
(4) Running Bear—*Johnny Preston*
(5) Teen Angel—*Mark Dinning*
(6) It's Now Or Never—*Elvis Presley*
(7) Handy Man—*Jimmy Jones*
(8) I'm Sorry—*Brenda Lee*
(9) El Paso—*Marty Robbins*
(10) The Twist—*Chubby Checker*

1961
(1) Tossin' And Turnin'—*Bobby Lewis*
(2) I Fall To Pieces—*Patsy Cline*
(3) Michael—*Highwaymen*
(4) Crying—*Roy Orbison*
(5) Runaway—*Del Shannon*
(6) My True Story—*Jive Five*
(7) Pony Time—*Chubby Checker*
(8) Will You Love Me Tomorrow?—*The Shirelles*
(9) Take Good Care of My Baby—*Bobby Vee*
(10) Runaround Sue—*Dion*

1962
(1) The Twist—*Chubby Checker*
(2) I Can't Stop Loving You—*Ray Charles*
(3) Mashed Potato Time—*Dee Dee Sharp*
(4) Roses Are Red (My Love)—*Bobby Vinton*
(5) Big Girls Don't Cry—*Four Seasons*
(6) Johnny Angel—*Shelley Fabares*
(7) The Loco-Motion—*Little Eva*
(8) Let Me In—*Sensations*
(9) Stranger On The Shore—*Mr. Acker Bilk*
(10) Soldier Boy—*Shirelles*

1963
(1) Sugar Shack—*Jimmy Glimer & the Fireballs*
(2) Surfin' U. S. A.—*Beach Boys*
(3) The End of the World—*Skeeter Davis*
(4) Rhythm of the Rain—*Cascades*
(5) He's So Fine—*Chiffons*
(6) Blue Velvet—*Bobby Vinton*
(7) Hey Paula—*Paul And Paula*
(8) Fingertips (Part 2)—*Little Stevie Wonder*
(9) My Boyfriend's Back—*The Angels*
(10) It's All Right—*Impressions*

The triangular part of the underside of a horse's hoof is called a frog.

THE LAST LAUGH:
EPITAPHS

Some unusual epitaphs and tombstone rhymes, sent in by our wandering BRI tombstone-ologists.

In England:
Anna Lovett
Beneath this stone
   & not above it
Lie the remains of
   Anna Lovett;
Be pleased good reader
   not to shove it,
Least she should come
   again above it.
For 'twixt you & I,
   no one does covet
To see again this
   Anna Lovett.

In Topeka, Kansas:
Tim McGrew
Here lies Sheriff Tim
McGrew who said
he would arrest Bill
Hennessy or die—
He was right.

In London, England:
Anonymous
Beneath this silent
   stone is laid
A noisy antiquated
   maid
Who from her cradle
   talked to death,
And ne'er before was
   out of breath.

In England:
Edgar Oscar Earl
Beneath this grassy
   mound now rests
One Edgar Oscar Earl,
Who to another
   hunter looked
Exactly like a squirrel.

In Cleveland, Ohio:
Anonymous
I thought it was a
   mushroom when
I found it in the woods
   forsaken;
But since I sleep
   beneath this mound,
I must have been
   mistaken.

*In Northumberland,
England:*
**Matthew
Hollingshead**
Here lieth Matthew
   Hollingshead,
Who died from cold
   caught in his head.
It brought on fever and
   rheumatiz,
Which ended me—
   for here I is.

In Boston, Mass.
Owen Moore
Owen Moore:
Gone away
Owin' more
Than he could pay.

In Tombstone, Ariz.
John Timothy Snow
Here lies John
Timothy Snow, who
died fighting for a
lady's honor. (She
wanted to keep it)

*In Wolverhampton,
England:*
Joseph Jones
Here lies the bones
Of Joseph Jones
Who ate whilst he was
   able
But, once o'er fed
He dropt down dead
And fell beneath the
   table.
When from the tomb
To meet his doom,
He rises amidst
   sinners;
Since he must dwell
In Heav'n or Hell
Take him—which
   gives best dinners.

The original Godzilla costume weighed 220 lbs. It was made of urethane and bamboo.

A COMIC STRIP IS BORN

Ever wonder how the creators of your favorite comic strips came up with the idea? Uncle John got curious and did some research. Here are a few of the stories he found.

THE FAR SIDE

Background: In 1976, jazz guitarist Gary Larson was on the verge of getting a dream gig with a big band in Seattle…but they hired somebody else. Crushed with disappointment, Larson spent the weekend drawing animal cartoons (something the "frustrated biologist," as he called himself, had done since he was a kid). On Monday, he took his drawings to a small California wilderness magazine to sell, and to his surprise, the magazine bought them all.

A Strip Is Born: Meanwhile, he kept drawing. To pay the rent, he took a job as an animal cruelty investigator with the Seattle Humane Society. (In true "Far Side" fashion, he ran over a dog on the way to the interview.) One day, while Larson was on assignment, a reporter for the *Seattle Times* noticed the drawings in his notebook. She asked if she could show them to her editor…who hired Larson to do a cartoon called "Nature's Way." Unfortunately, it ran right next to the children's crossword puzzle. Parents complained about its warped humor, and it was canceled.

Luckily, Larson had just shown his cartoons to an editor at the *San Francisco Chronicle.* The editor immediately bought the strip. The only thing he changed was the name. "Nature's Way" became "The Far Side."

DILBERT

Background: Scott Adams' career as an artist didn't look promising. He got the lowest grade in a drawing class at college, and had cartoons rejected by *Playboy, The New Yorker* and a long list of comic strip syndicators. He was stuck in cubicle-land, working first at the Crocker National Bank for eight years, then at Pacific Bell for nine.

A Strip Is Born: In the late 1980s, while he was still at Pac Bell, he decided he wanted to earn a living as a cartoonist. He invented "Dilbert" and sent samples to six comic strip syndicates. Four rejected him, one suggested he take drawing lessons, and one—United Features—offered him a contract. But since "Dilbert" wasn't a hit yet, Adams kept his day-job.

The turning point came in 1993. "I asked the syndicate for ideas on what they would like me to write more about," Adams recalls. "They said, 'Do more on downsizing, more on things getting harder in the workplace.'" To find out what people were thinking in cubicles around America, Adams began posting his e-mail address in every strip. The feedback he got helped him make "Dilbert" the first comic strip to capture the frustrations of modern office workers. In 1995, he was finally able to leave Pac Bell and become a fulltime cartoonist. Today, "Dilbert" is in over 1,000 newspapers; about 20% of his story ideas still come from readers.

CALVIN & HOBBES

Background: Bill Watterson graduated from college in 1979, and immediately got a job as a political cartoonist for the *Cincinnati, Ohio Post.* He was fired after six months. So in 1980, he tried a new career—as a comic strip artist. His first effort was called "Spaceman Spiff," about a character who "wore flying goggles, smoked a cigar, and explored space in a dirigible." It was rejected by every syndicate.

A Strip Is Born: Five years and several flops later, he finally got someone interested in his work. The United Features Syndicate picked out two minor characters in a strip he'd submitted—the lead character's little brother and a stuffed tiger who came to life—and paid Watterson to develop a strip about them. He called them Calvin (after theologian John Calvin) and Hobbes (after the pessimistic philosopher Thomas Hobbes). United Features actually rejected the finished product, so Watterson took it to Universal Press Syndicate. They liked it. "Calvin and Hobbes" debuted on November 18, 1985, and didn't bow out until ten years later, at the end of 1995. At that time it was America's most popular strip, appearing in 2,400 newspapers.

"There is no deodorant like success."
—Elizabeth Taylor

CELEBRITY GOSSIP

*Here's this edition's installment of the BRI's cheesy tabloid
section—a bunch of gossip about famous people.*

SEAN CONNERY
Believes in reincarnation. According to one report, he's convinced that in a past life, he was "an alcoholic railroad builder in Africa who lived with two native women, both of whom bore him sons, and who died of alcohol poisoning."

CHARLES LINDBERGH
• When Lindbergh took his first flying lesson, he learned two things: (1) how to fly, and (2) that he was afraid of heights.
• To cure himself of vertigo, he first tried "wing walking" (climbing on the wings of a biplane while it was in flight), which didn't work, and then parachute jumping, which did.
• "When Lindbergh crossed the Atlantic," Jack Mingo writes in The Juicy Parts, "he didn't carry a radio because it added too much weight. His navigation was an iffy thing. At one point near the end of his journey he spotted a fishing fleet, dove his plane down to within shouting distance, cut the engines, and screamed, 'Which way to Ireland?'"

PABLO PICASSO
Picasso wasn't breathing when he was born, and his face was so blue that the midwife left him for dead. An uncle revived him by blowing cigar smoke up his nose.

DONALD TRUMP
• In his book Trump: *The Art of the Comeback,* Trump confesses to being a "clean-hands freak" who washes his hands whenever he can and who hates shaking hands with strangers, especially when the stranger has just come from the restroom, "perhaps not even having washed his hands."
• One year Trump visited the Bronx's Public School 70 (located in a poor neighborhood) for the school's annual Principal for a Day event. On his way out, Trump dropped a $1 million bill in

the bake sale cash box. (It was fake, of course—Trump's idea of a joke.)

WILLIAM SHATNER
Swears he's seen a UFO. "You'd almost think he was joking," writes Tim Harrower in the *Portland Oregonian*, "but, no, Shatner was serious when he reported that a silver spacecraft flew over him in the Mojave Desert as he pushed his inoperative motorcycle. He also claims to have received a telepathic message from the beings in the craft advising him which direction to walk."

PRESIDENT LYNDON BAINES JOHNSON
• "It was well known," biographer Robert Dallek writes in *Flawed Giant: Lyndon Johnson and His Times*, "that he had ongoing affairs with a secretary, a beautiful Hispanic woman people called the 'chili queen,' and a woman at his ranch dubbed the 'dairy queen'....When the wife of television newscaster David Brinkley accepted an invitation to visit Lyndon and Lady Bird at the ranch on a weekend her husband couldn't be there, Johnson tried unsuccessfully to get her into bed."
• Johnson could be extremely abusive to his aides, even the Secret Service officers sworn to defend him with their lives. Once, while driving across a field at the LBJ Ranch in Texas, Johnson stopped to relieve himself. "One of the Secret Service men standing near him 'felt warm water on his leg,'" Dallek writes. "He looked down and said, 'Mr. President, you are urinating on me.' And Johnson's response was, 'I know I am...it's my prerogative.'"

HENRY FORD
• One of his closest friends was Thomas Edison, and he was with the inventor when Edison died. At the moment of death, Ford captured Edison's last breath in a bottle. It was one of his most prized possessions.
• Once while fiddling with a microscope, Ford had a close-up look at some granulated sugar crystals...and was horrified by their sharp points. He swore off of sugar for the rest of his life, fearing it would slice up his internal organs.

Until President Kennedy was killed, it wasn't a federal crime to assassinate the President.

WEIRD MEDICAL CONDITIONS

You never know what's going to happen, right? Like, you might get stuck on that seat, have to call 911, and wind up in the next edition of the Bathroom Reader....Or you might find you've got one of these conditions. Don't laugh—it could happen to YOU!

THE STENDHAL SYNDROME
Diagnosed In: Florence, Italy, 1982

Medical Report: "Some visitors to Florence panic before a Raphael masterpiece. Others collapse at the feet of Michelangelo's statue of David," reports the Reuters News Service. "At least once a month on average, a foreign tourist is rushed to the psychiatric ward of Florence's Santa Maria Nuova Hospital suffering from acute mental imbalance, seemingly brought on by an encounter with the city's art treasures. "Psychiatrists call it the Stendhal Syndrome, after the French writer who recorded a similar emotional experience on his first visit to the city in 1817. After viewing some of the city's famous art, he wrote: 'I felt a pulsating in my heart. Life was draining out of me, while I walked fearing a fall.'

"More than half the patients are tourists from European countries. Italians, on the other hand, seem to be immune to the condition, along with the Japanese, who are apparently so organized in their sight-seeing that they rarely have time for emotional attacks."

MUSCLE DYSMORPHIA SYNDROME
Diagnosed In: The United States, 1997

Medical Report: According to the *New York Times:* "Some body-builders appear to be suffering from an emotional disorder that is, in effect, the opposite of anorexia. Despite their muscular bodies and being in tiptop shape, they are convinced that they look puny. "Their preoccupation with their bodies can become so intense that they give up desirable jobs, careers and social engagements so they can spend many hours a day at the gym bulking up. Some often refuse to be seen in a bathing suit out of

---

Average growing time for Christmas trees to reach proper height: 7 to 10 years.

fear that others will regard their bodies as too small and out of shape.

"The first description of the disorder, called muscle dysmorphia, appeared in an issue of the journal *Psychosomatics*."

KORO

Diagnosed In: Indonesia

Medical Report: According to Fenton & Fowler's *Best, Worst and Most Unusual*: "Indonesian men occasionally fall prey to an obsessive fear that their penis is withdrawing into the body and that, if they do not take the matter into their own hands, so to speak, the process will ultimately kill them. The prescribed treatment is to grasp the disappearing organ and hold on for dear life until it stops receding.

"Since a typical bout of the malady, called koro, can last for hours or even days, the embarrassed victim must often ask friends, wife, witch doctor, and others to spell him in holding onto the vanishing member while he rests. He may also use a small, specially designed, notched box. The disease is purely psychological, of course, but the 'treatment' frequently leaves victims exhausted, temporarily impotent, and black and blue about the privates."

THE JERUSALEM SYNDROME

Diagnosed In: Jerusalem, Israel, 1994

Medical Report: According to the Associated Press: "A new condition is affecting visitors to the holy city of Jerusalem. Upon arriving there, people become convinced they are biblical figures reborn—including Moses, Jesus and Abraham.

"Yari Bar-El, the psychiatrist who has treated 470 of the tourists for the syndrome, chalks it up to the approach of the year 2000. 'We know that every millennium there's an increase of religious feelings,' he explains, adding that 'most patients recover in a week.'"

SEINFELD SYNCOPE

Diagnosed In: United States, 1998

Medical Report: According to *TV Guide*: "This newly identified medical condition caused a 62-year-old man to laugh so hard while watching Seinfeld that he became unconscious and fell face first into his dinner."

Fart fact: The average person passes 1 to 3 pints of gas a day, in 14 different episodes.

BRITS VS. AMERICANS: A WORD QUIZ

We both speak English, but we don't necessarily use the same words. For instance, the British call trucks "lorries." See if you can match the British words to their American counterparts. Words are from I Hear America Talking, *by Stuart Berg Flexner.*

BRITISH

1) Tower Block
2) Booter
3) Note
4) Fringe
5) Graughts
6) Caravan
7) Track
8) Cash Desk
9) Polka Dots
10) Candy Floss
11) Boarding
12) Motion
13) Accumulator
14) Fascia (panel)
15) Cubbyhole
16) Pantechnicon
17) Lie-by
18) Verge
19) Chucker Out
20) Push Chair
21) Wing
22) Patience
23) Sponge Bag
24) Braces
25) Spanner

AMERICAN

a) Cotton Candy
b) Checkout Counter
c) Moving Van
d) Dash (board)
e) Battery
f) Tread
g) Shaving kit
h) Stroller
i) Fender
J) Bangs (of hair)
k) Bill (paper money)
l) Billboard
m) Bouncer
n) Shoulder (of a road)
o) High-rise Apartment
p) Chocolate Chips
q) Horn, Siren
r) Trailer
s) Rest Area
t) Bowel Movement
u) Glove Compartment
v) Suspenders
w) Checkers
x) Wrench (tightening tool)
z) Solitaire (a card game)

Answers

1-o, 2-q, 3-k, 4-j, 5-w, 6-r, 7-f, 8-b, 9-p, 10-a, 11-l, 12-t, 13-e, 14-d, 15-u, 16-c, 17-s, 18-n, 19-m, 20-h, 21-i, 22-z, 23-g, 24-v, 25-x

Poll results: Nachos is the food most craved by moms-to-be.

THE CONCRETE CAMEL AND THE NEW SOUTH WHALE

Colorful language and sardonic humor carried Australians through convict days, settler hardship, war...and the building of the Sydney Opera House.

CRAWLED FROM UNDER A LOG

On January 30, 1957, the *Sydney Morning Herald* screamed the headline, "Dane's Controversial Design wins Opera House Contest." The judges called Joern Utzon's work, "original." One architect described it as "a piece of poetry." Another, in the same article, called it "an insect with a shell on its back, which has crawled out from under a log."

IT'LL NEVER FLY

Joern Utzon said he liked to be "modern and work at the edge of the possible." Like viewing a "Gothic church" the eye would "never get tired... of it." "It'll never fly," said onlookers as three giant cranes from France were erected like big birds. They had a point. The highest shell was 70 meters high, with a very steep pitch. It took the architect and engineers three years to solve the problem of constructing the "fifth façade" or sails. Over 2000 precast concrete segments were tensioned by 350 kilometers of steel cables and covered by one million specially glazed Swedish tiles in tile-lid segments, each containing two colours.

CONCRETE CAMEL

Sydneysiders watched through 16 years of construction. Nay-sayers sharpened their knives. The Opera House was a "concrete camel," "copulating turtles," "the hunchback of Bennelong Point," "a pack of French nuns playing football," "a petrified Moby Dick and all his children risen from the sea," "the first building to be built upside down," and "the biggest New South Whale." "It might have been cheaper if they'd built it overseas and sailed it across," they said. Today this work of genius is internationally recognized as one of the great buildings of the 20th century.

The world's largest rhinestone (115,000 carats) is stored at the Liberace Museum in Las Vegas.

THE SYDNEY OPERA HOUSE'S ARCHITECT
Did you know…?

- He was Danish.

- He was only 38 years old when he designed the Sydney Opera House.

- He had never visited Australia, but studied sea charts of Sydney Harbor to show him elevations. He watched the only available film on Sydney at the Australian Embassy in Copenhagen.

- He realised people would look down onto the structure and said, "One could not have a flat roof filled with ventilation pipes—in fact one must have a fifth façade which is just as important as the other façades…Therefore instead of a square form I have made a sculpture."

- He signed his winning entry drawings with an elongated cartoon of himself—with a pen dipped in his cranium like an ink bottle.

- An Australian women's magazine dubbed him, "the Danish Gary Cooper, only better looking."

- On the wall of his Sydney office he had a poster showing a disassembled telephone with the slogan, "Put them together and dial anywhere." He often said, "when some clever people have been able to produce a number of elements, put them together and talk through the result, then we must be able to solve this much more simple problem even if it seems impossible." (Utzon, Glass Walls Zodiac, No. 14)

- One of his favourite books was a centuries old manual on Chinese architecture called Ying zao fa shi which influenced his architecture. The plinth for the Opera House was inspired by Mexican Mayan temples and the tiles by Japanese ceramics.

- It took nearly a week to reach Sydney by plane from Copenhagen.

- The surface of each curved roof section would fit a large spherical surface. They are like bits of peel cut out of an orange, thus prefabricated sections could be made to speed up construction.

- Joern Utzon became an Australian hero.

Surveys say: Nearly 1/10 of American households dress their pets in Halloween costumes.

OH, MARLENE!

Here are a few thoughts from Marlene Dietrich,
the great actress from the 1930s and 1940s.

"If there is a supreme being, he's crazy."

"My legs aren't so beautiful, I just know what to do with them."

"Tenderness is greater proof of love than the most passionate of vows."

"In America sex is an obsession. In other parts of the world, it's a fact."

"The average man is more interested in a woman who is interested in him than he is in a woman with beautiful legs."

"A man would prefer to come home to an unmade bed and a happy woman than to a neatly made bed and an angry woman."

"Once a woman has forgiven a man, she must not reheat his sins for breakfast."

"It's the friends you can call up at 4:00 a.m. who matter."

"They thought of us glamour girls as they used to think of color photography. When the story was weak, they shot it in color as a cover-up. If the feminine lead was a weak role, they cast a glamour girl in it. But if you tried to find the girl's part on paper, it wasn't there."

"Most women set out to change a man, and when they have changed him, they do not like him."

"It is a joy to find thoughts one might have, beautifully expressed by someone wiser than oneself."

"How do you know when love is gone? If you said that you would be there at seven and you get there by nine, and he or she has not called the police yet—it's gone."

"Superstitions are habits rather than beliefs."

Victory is joyful only back home. Up at the front it is joyless."

A coffee tree yields about one pound of coffee in a year.

INSIDE THE X-FILES

Is the truth really out there? Our investigation into the TV phenomenon The X-Files *has turned up some fascinating pieces of information.*

HOW IT STARTED
Inspiration: The highest-rated TV movie of the 1972–73 season was a low-budget thriller called *The Night Stalker*. In it, a wisecracking Las Vegas reporter named Carl Kolchak discovers that the serial killer terrorizing his city is really a vampire. Of course, no one believes him...and when he finally defeats the killer, all evidence vanishes. Only he realizes the dark truth—everyone else thinks he's a kook.

A year later, Kolchak returned in a film called *The Night Strangler*—this time chasing a killer zombie in Seattle. Once again, Neilsen ratings were high, and ABC commissioned a series for the 1974–75 season: *Kolchak: The Night Stalker*. It wasn't a huge success, but it did attract a cult following. One avid fan was a California teenager named Chris Carter. "It really shook me up to think there might be a twilight world of blood-sucking creatures," he recalls. "It made a big impression on me."

The TV Experience Ten years later, Carter was in the TV biz himself. After kicking around for awhile, he finally signed a deal to develop new programs for the fledgling Fox Network. "When I got to Fox in 1992," he explains, "I had the luxury of being asked what I would like to do. So I said I wanted to create a scary show, something as dark and mysterious as I remember Kolchak was when I was a kid."

Two other influences played into his work:

• *The Avengers*, an English spy program of the mid-1960s that featured a bantering man/woman team. They had an extraordinary chemistry that never turned into romance. Carter loved them.

• America's growing obsession with UFOs and the supernatural. Carter wasn't a "believer," but in 1991 he'd had a conversation with a Yale professor who claimed that as many as 3% of the American population actually thought they'd been abducted by aliens. Carter was shocked. "I realized there was a topicality to this

---

Average number of Santas hired by a U.S. shopping mall: 3.73.

theme of the unknown," he says, "and *The X-Files* grew out of that fascination."

THE STARS

David Duchovny (Agent Fox Mulder) planned to be an English Lit. professor, but while working on his doctorate in English Literature at Yale in 1985, he got a part in a Löwenbraü beer commercial. He made $9000—twice the annual salary of his teaching assistantship—and was hooked.

• After that, he had a variety of small roles in TV and films. He figured he was a break or two away from movie stardom when the *X-Files* pilot script showed up. He wasn't interested in more TV, but thought he'd get a free trip and a few weeks of work from it. He was so uninterested in the part that when producer Chris Carter told him to wear a tie to the audition, he wore one covered with pink pigs. Carter jokes, "I think that got him the job."

Gillian Anderson (Agent Dana Scully) landed a role in the off-Broadway play *Absent Friends* six months after graduating from college in 1990…and won the Theatre World Award as the "outstanding new talent of 1990-91" for it.

• Before reading the *X-Files* pilot script, she vowed never to do TV. But she was broke, and "couldn't put it down." Her audition was only the second time she'd ever been in front of a camera…and Duchovny toyed with her. "I already knew I had the part, so I played the scene in a kind of sarcastic way," he says, "—much more sarcastic than it was written—and Gillian was just completely thrown by it….She was shocked that anybody would talk to her that way."

• It turns out that was exactly the reaction Chris Carter was looking for. He wanted to hire her, but Anderson recalls that Fox protested. "They wanted somebody leggier, somebody with more breasts, somebody drop-dead gorgeous." Carter hired her anyway.

INSIDE FACTS

The Truth Is Out There?
The pilot episode ("The X Files") was supposedly based on a real incident. That claim hasn't been made for any other episodes… but stories are often based on real events. For example:

• In "Young at Heart," Barnett grows a "salamander-like" hand. Carter's inspiration: a news story about a London researcher "who grew an extra limb on a salamander's back."

• The toxic fumes given off by characters in "The Erlenmeyer Flask" and "Host" episodes were inspired by the unexplained fumes that came from a woman patient in a Riverside, California, hospital in 1994, making doctors and nurses seriously ill.

• According to the *Fortean Times*, the episode called "Humbug" was inspired by "the real-life killing of a sideshow character called 'Lobsterboy.'"

Close Encounters
Gillian Anderson barely held onto her job in the initial season. First she had trouble learning her lines and mastering the show's scientific jargon. Then she had a hard time with the grueling schedule. About six months into the first season she got married...and came back from her honeymoon pregnant. She was sure she'd be fired. She told Duchovny first. "It looked like his knees buckled," she says. "I think he said, 'Oh, my God.'"

A few weeks later, she told Carter. His reaction? Depends on who you ask. According to on-the-set sources, "He went ballistic. He wanted to get rid of her." But Carter says: "I never, ever considered replacing her." In any case, she stayed. During pregnancy, her condition was covered up with loose-fitting lab coats. When her due date hit, she had an emergency C-section. Ten days later, she was back to work.

What's In A Name?
Fox Mulder: Fox was the name of a boyhood friend of Carter's. Mulder is his mother's maiden name.
Dana Scully: Fans assumed she was named after UFOlogist Frank Scully. But Carter says the inspiration was L.A. Dodgers announcer Vin Scully.
Episode titles: Carter intentionally keeps them mysterious. "If titles come in that I don't think are up to our standard of vagueness or seriousness," says Carter, "I ask the writer to change them." One episode title— "Piper Maru"—sounds obscure...but it's really just the name of Anderson's daughter.

NEVER SAY NEVER

A *few pearls of wisdom from* 599 Things You
Should Never Do, *edited by Ed Morrow.*

"Never accept a drink from a urologist."

—**Erma Bombeck**

"Never hit a man with glasses. Hit him with something much bigger and heavier."

—**Anonymous**

"Never insult seven men if you're only carrying a six-shooter."

—**Harry Morgan**

"Never judge a man by the opinion his wife has of him."

—**Bob Edwards**

"Never eat Chinese food in Oklahoma."

—**Bryan Miller**

"Never get caught in bed with a live man or a dead woman."

—**Larry Hagman**

"Never hunt rabbit with dead dog."

—**Charlie Chan**

"Never miss a chance to have sex or appear on television."

—**Gore Vidal**

"Never put off till tomorrow what you can get someone else to do today."

—**Douglas Ottati**

"Never put off until tomorrow what you can do the day after tomorrow."

—**Mark Twain**

"Never put off until tomorrow what can be avoided altogether."

—**Ann Landers**

"Never keep up with the Joneses. Drag them down to your level. It's cheaper."

—**Quentin Crisp**

"Never take a job where the boss calls you 'Babe.'"

—**Brett Butler**

"Never trust a man who has only one way to spell a word."

—**Dan Quayle, quoting Mark Twain**

"Never expect to steal third base while keeping one foot on second."

—**American Proverb**

Why do puppies lick your face? They're instinctively searching for scraps of food.

THE TOP 10 HITS OF THE YEAR, 1964–1967

Here's another installment of BRI's Top Ten of the Year list.
Is it a squib or is it an eyebrow???

1964
(1) I Want To Hold Your Hand
—*The Beatles*
(2) She Loves You—*The Beatles*
(3) Hello, Dolly
—*Louis Armstrong*
(4) Pretty Woman—*Roy Orbison*
(5) I Get Around—*Beach Boys*
(6) Louie, Louie—*The Kingsmen*
(7) My Guy—*Mary Wells*
(8 We'll Sing in the Sunshine
—*Gale Garnett*
(9) Last Kiss—*J. Frank Wilson*
& The Cavaliers
(10) Where Did Our Love Go
—*Diana Ross & the Supremes*

1965
(1) (I Can't Get No) Satisfaction
—*The Rolling Stones*
(2) I Can't Help Myself (Sugar
Pie, Honey Bunch)
—*Four Tops*
(3) Wooly Bully—*Sam The Sham*
& The Pharoahs
(4) You Were On My Mind
—*We Five*
(5) You've Lost That Lovin'
Feelin'—*The Righteous*
Brothers
(6) Downtown—*Petula Clark*
(7) Help!—*The Beatles*
(8) Can't You Hear My Heartbeat?—*Herman's Hermits*
(9) Turn, Turn, Turn—*The Byrds*
(10) My Girl—*The Temptations*

1966
(1) The Ballad Of The Green
Berets—*Sgt. Barry Sadler*
(2) Cherish—*The Association*
(3) (You're My) Soul And Inspiration—*The Righteous Brothers*
(4) Reach Out I'll Be There
—*The Four Tops*
(5) Monday, Monday
—*The Mamas & The Papas*
(6) Last Train To Clarksville
—*The Monkees*
(7) California Dreamin'
—*The Mamas & The Papas*
(8) You Can't Hurry Love
—*The Supremes*
(9) Good Vibrations
—*The Beach Boys*
(10) These Boots Are Made For
Walkin'—*Nancy Sinatra*

1967
(1) To Sir With Love—*Lulu*
(2) The Letter—*The Box Tops*
(3) I'm A Believer—*The Monkees*
(4) Windy—*The Association*
(5) Ode To Bille Joe
—*Bobbie Gentry*
(6) Light My Fire—*The Doors*
(7) Somethin' Stupid—*Nancy*
Sinatra and Frank Sinatra
(8) Happy Together—*The Turtles*
(9) Groovin'—*The Rascals*
(10) Incense & Peppermints
—*The Strawberry Alarm Clock*

Supermarket survey: 90% of the U.S. population rode in a grocery cart when they were kids.

BEGINNINGS

You've heard of all the products listed below.
Here's a look at how they were invented.

THE CLUB

In 1985, Jim Winner, Jr. bought a brand-new Cadillac with all the whistles and bells, including GM's sophisticated new antitheft system. He added a car alarm to go with it, but it didn't do any good—the car was stolen a short time later. Winner thought back to his Army days, when he used to secure his jeep by running a thick chain through the steering wheel and around the brake pedal to keep his friends from driving off with it. He decided to make a simpler, similar device—one that fastened only to the steering wheel—for civilian use. He tested 50 prototypes in bad neighborhoods before settling on a design for The Club.

WIRE COAT HANGERS

Albert Parkhouse worked for the Timberlake Wire and Novelty Co. at the turn of the century. The company had a lot of employees, but not enough hooks for everyone to hang their coats and hats on. One morning in 1903, Parkhouse became so frustrated looking for a hook that he grabbed a piece of wire, bent it in half and twisted the two ends together to make a hook, then shaped the rest of the wire so that he could hang his coat on it. Timberlake patented the idea and made a fortune; according to his relatives, Parkhouse did not.

THE ZAMBONI

Frank Zamboni owned an ice skating rink in Paramount, California in the early 1940s. He hated paying five men for the 1-1/2 hours it took to smooth out the ice every night, and after seven years of experimenting, he finally invented a machine that could do it in 15 minutes. Olympic skating star Sonja Henie practiced at Zamboni's rink; she made the machines famous when she paid Zamboni $10,000 for two of them and brought them with her on her nationwide tour. By 1960, Zambonis were in use at the Winter Olympics.

Simon Robinson of Australia once screamed at 128 decibels—almost as loud as a jet engine.

SAY UNCLE

Uncle John would like to take a few minutes to talk about some of the other famous "uncles" in American history.

UNCLE SAM, a symbol of the United States
Birth: Sam Wilson owned a meat-packing plant in Troy, New York. When the War of 1812 broke out, the government contracted him to supply meat to troops stationed nearby. He started stamping crates for the army with a big "U.S." But when a government inspector visited the plant and asked a worker what the initials meant, the worker shrugged and guessed it stood for his employer, "Uncle Sam."
Everyone's Uncle: The nickname spread among the soldiers. Soon, all army supplies were said to come from "Uncle Sam." Then a character called Uncle Sam began showing up in newspaper illustrations. The more popular he got, the more patriotic his outfit became. In 1868, Thomas Nast dressed Uncle Sam in a white beard and Stars-and-Stripes suit for a political cartoon. Nast borrowed the look from a famous circus clown named Dan Rice.

UNCLE TOM, title character of *Uncle Tom's Cabin*
Birth: Harriet Beecher Stowe wanted the title character of her novel, *Uncle Tom's Cabin*, to be "simple, easygoing and servile"…but also "noble, high-minded, and a devout Christian." She found inspiration in conversations with her cook, a free woman who was married to a slave in Kentucky. As Stowe explained in an 1882 letter to the Indianapolis Times, the cook said her husband was so faithful, his master trusted him to come alone and unwatched to Cincinnati to market his farm product. Now this, according to the laws of Ohio, gave the man his freedom, de facto. But she said her husband had given his word as a Christian, his master promising him his freedom. Whether he ever got it, I know not.
Everyone's Uncle: The book was published in 1852 and quickly became one of the best-selling novels of the 19th century. It played an important role in arousing anti-slavery passions that resulted in the Civil War. When Lincoln met Stowe, he greeted her by asking, "Is this the little woman whose book made such a great war?" Over time, "Uncle Tom" became a derogatory term to

African-Americans, referring to someone too servile, or who cooperated too closely with whites—not entirely fair, since Uncle Tom was ultimately flogged to death by slave owner Simon Legree after he refused to reveal the hiding place of two female slaves.

UNCLE REMUS, narrator of a popular series of folk tales
Birth: Joel Chandler Harris grew up in the South after the Civil War listening to folk tales told by former slaves. As an adult, he began collecting them and publishing them. One of the most helpful people he talked to was an elderly gardener in Forsyth, Georgia, called Uncle Remus. Harris made him the narrator of his books.
Everyone's Uncle: In the enormously popular *Uncle Remus: His Songs and His Sayings* (published in the late 1800s), Uncle Remus, a former slave, entertains his employer's young son by telling him traditional "Negro tales" (believed to have come from Africa) involving Brer Rabbit, Brer Fox, and Brer Wolf. Harris' books preserved the tales in print form and introduced them to a world-wide audience. Disney's animated *Song of the South* made Uncle Remus a part of modern American pop culture (Zip-a-dee-doo-dah!).

UNCLE FESTER, crazed character from the *Addams Family* TV series
Birth: The ghoulish family in Charles Addams' *New Yorker* cartoons was never identified by (first) name—so it was never clear exactly who the bald fiend in the family portraits was. But in 1963, Addams agreed to let ABC make a TV sitcom out of his characters. All he had to do was give the characters names and family relationships. The bald guy officially became Morticia's Uncle Fester.
Everyone's Uncle: The TV show was a Top 20 hit in 1964-65. Fester was brought to life by Jackie Coogan, who had been the first child star of the silent film age. In 1923, he was the biggest box office star in the country, but his appeal faded as he got older. By 23 he was broke and out of work. After a tragic life that included arrests for drugs and booze, Coogan made a comeback. He showed up for the Addams audition with a huge walrus mustache and hair on the sides of his head. Told that Fester was hairless, he returned the next day shaved completely bald and got the part.

Polar bears can eat 50 lbs. of meat in one sitting.

STRANGE BREWS

Are Bud and Miller too bland? You can always try one of these…

CALLING HOMER SIMPSON…

"A brewery in Bulgaria recently announced that brewmaster Yordan Platikanov has developed a beer that neutralizes any residual uranium 134 or strontium in the body after exposure to nuclear radiation. Platikanov said the new beer should be urged on nuclear power plant workers relaxing at the end of a shift."—*Universal Press*

BEER FOR THE BATH

"The Kloser brewery in Nuezelle, Germany, announced it would soon begin selling dark beer concentrate for foam baths and eczema treatment. The new product differs from beer only in that the yeast is left in, creating its skin-soothing quality. Said owner Helmut Fritsche, 'You can bathe in it or drink it. Whoever wants to, can do both.'"—*The Edge, Portland Oregonian*

ANCIENT BEER

"An Egyptologist, two scientists and Britain's largest brewer announced plans to brew an ale from a recipe dating back 3,500 years to the time of Tutankhamun. 'Tutankhamun Ale' will be based on sediment from old jars found in a brewery housed inside the Sun Temple of Nefertiti….The team gathered enough materials to produce just 1,000 bottles of the ale. 'We are about to unveil a great Tutankhamun secret,' said a spokesman at Newcastle Breweries. '—the liquid gold of the Pharaohs. It's a really amazing inheritance they have left us—the origins of the beer itself.'"
—*San Francisco Examiner*

HEAVY METAL BEER

"Mötley Crüe promoted a new album with a bright, blue-colored beverage called Motley Brüe, a drink 'for people who are done with the whole drugs and alcohol thing but still want to have fun.'"—*TV Guide*

The average American credit card holder owes almost $3,900.

THE FORGOTTEN MEN

*U.S. vice presidents are the forgotten men of politics...and some-
times that's just as well; some pretty strange characters have
been elected vice president over the years. Ever heard
of any of these ex-veeps? We'll bet you haven't.*

RICHARD MENTOR JOHNSON (served with Martin
Van Buren, 1837–41)
Background: Democratic congressman from Kentucky.
Described by one witness as "the most vulgar man of all vulgar
men in this world." His personal affairs scandalized Washington
society. He married three times, each time to a slave woman.
When his second wife ran off with the man she truly loved, Johnson had her captured, then sold her at a slave auction.
VP Achievements: The only VP ever elected by Congress rather
than by popular vote (he was so disliked that he couldn't get
enough electoral votes). He was ahead of his time in one way—he
cashed in on his newfound celebrity by opening a tavern and spa
on his Kentucky farm. During his term, he chose to stay there and
manage it most of the time, rather than live in Washington.

WILLIAM RUFUS DE VANE KING (served with Franklin
Pierce, 1853)
Background: Democrat from Alabama. Known more for his
effeminate clothing and demeanor than his politics. In 1834, he
struck up a lasting friendship with future president James
Buchanan, with whom historians speculate he had a homosexual
relationship.
VP Achievements: On Inauguration Day, he was in Cuba trying
to recover from tuberculosis, and was too sick to make it to Washington. He did make it to his home state for a victory celebration—and then died. The length of his term as VP: six weeks.
This made him the only bachelor VP, the only VP to be sworn in
outside the country, and the only one never to enter Washington,
D.C., during his term. No one lost any sleep finding a replace-
ment. The VP position remained vacant until the next election,
which Buchanan won.

Among older men, vanilla is the most erotic smell.

HANNIBAL HAMLIN (served with Abraham Lincoln, 1861–64)

Background: Republican senator from Maine. Described by one historian as "a keen opportunist with a short attention span." Once Lincoln was nominated, the Republicans needed someone from the east to balance the ticket. Hamlin's qualifications: He had political experience but wasn't controversial. In fact, he had almost no legislative record. He looked forward to the vice presidency, because it would "be neither hard nor unpleasant."

VP Achievements: Perhaps the most invisible VP ever. Being Lincoln's VP during the Civil War should have earned him a prominent spot in history books. But Lincoln quickly lost faith in his colleague's political skills and completely ignored him. Hamlin went home to his farm in Maine, sulking, "I am the most unimportant man in Washington." He only went back there once each year to open each new session of Congress, then returned to Maine. Lincoln dumped him in 1864 in favor of Andrew Johnson.

GARRET AUGUSTUS HOBART (served with William McKinley, 1897–99)

Background: Republican from New Jersey. Lost in his only bid for office (U.S. Senate) before becoming VP. Got the nomination because, as one of the richest men in the country, he had been willing to spend a lot of money on Republican causes.

VP Achievements: According to some historians, Hobart was one of the most influential VPs ever. No one has ever heard of him because he preferred wielding power behind the scenes. Most of his deals went down during intimate parties at his rented D.C. mansion, where senators were treated to cigars, liquor, and poker in exchange for their votes.

WILLIAM ALMON WHEELER (served with Rutherford B. Hayes, 1877–81)

Background: Republican congressman from New York. According to one historian, "The most boring of all the Republican vice presidents, and friends, that is saying something." Had a reputation for complete honesty—which made him a rarity in 1876.

VP Achievements: The only VP nominated as a joke. According to Steven Tally in *Bland Ambition:*

> Because presidential nominee Rutherford B. Hayes was from
> Ohio, the delegates to the Republican convention of 1876

First and last time the Roadrunner spoke: a 1951 Bugs Bunny cartoon called Operation: Rabbit.

needed to pick someone from the important state of New York. They really didn't care who it was; it was just the vice presidency, after all, and most of the delegates had to be getting home. The delegates from New York began joking about which of them would take the nomination. Somebody yelled to future vice president Chester Arthur, "You take it, Chet!" and somebody else said, "You take it, Cornell!" The delegates were nearly beside themselves with merriment when one of the delegates said, "Let's give it to Wheeler!"

They thought this was such a good one that they presented the nomination to the floor. Wheeler's nomination was approved by acclamation, and according to a newspaper account of the event, "the delegates did not wait to continue the applause, but rushed off in every direction for the hasty dinner...and the out-speeding trains." This prompted the presidential nominee Hayes to write to his wife, "I am ashamed to say, who is Wheeler?"

THOMAS MARSHALL (served with Woodrow Wilson, 1912–1920)

Background: Democratic governor from Indiana. Diminutive man described as "120 pounds of 'glad to see ya, how ya doin'?' ...a shorter version of George Bailey from *It's a Wonderful Life*." He claimed he wasn't surprised to be nominated vice president, because "Indiana is the mother of vice presidents, the home of more second-class men than any other state."

VP Achievements: First vice president to publicly treat the office as a joke. Asked how he got elected, he credited an "ignorant electorate." After the election, he sent President Wilson a book inscribed, "From your only vice." (Wilson was not amused.) When groups visiting the Capitol peered into his office, he would tell them to "be kind enough to throw peanuts at me."

According to *Bland Ambition*, however, Marshall's major achievement "came after a particularly tedious catalog of the nation's needs by a particularly bellicose senator—What this country needs is more of this! What this country needs is more of that! Marshall leaned toward an associate and said, 'What this country needs is a really good five-cent cigar!' The coining of this phrase may stand as the greatest accomplishment of a vice president in the nation's history."

THE WORLD'S TALLEST BUILDINGS, PART II

On page 49, we told you the story of Elisha Craves Otis, inventor of the world's first safety elevator—which makes him one of the fathers of the modern skyscraper. Here's the story of another key figure in the quest to touch the sky...without ever leaving the ground.

BOOMTOWN
If ever a city needed tall buildings in a hurry, it was Chicago in the 1880s. Located in the center of America's farmland, with rail links to every coast, it was a natural hub of commerce for the entire continent, and one of the fastest growing cities in the country. The population more than doubled between 1880 and 1890, and commercial land prices shot up even faster: An acre of prime commercial real estate that cost $130,000 in 1880 was worth $900,000 by 1890. Building across the landscape became so expensive that people were forced to begin thinking of ways to build straight up into the air.

Out of the Ashes...
The Great Chicago Fire of 1871 made the need for tall buildings urgent even before the 1880s. The fire raged for only two days, but it wiped out one-third of all the buildings in the city—including most of the financial district. The fire was so devastating that when architect William LeBaron Jenney began work on the Home Insurance Building twelve years later, rebuilding was still underway.

MAN OF STEEL
Jenney was an uninspired architect— "a rather heavy-handed designer," one critic says, "who never turned out anything of great beauty." And if he hadn't had a noisy parrot, he might be forgotten today. Instead, he is the man historians consider the father of the modern skyscraper.

According to legend, Jenney was working on his design for the Home Insurance Building one afternoon in 1883 when the bird began making so much noise that he couldn't concentrate.

He got so angry that he grabbed the heaviest book he could find and pounded furiously on the bird's steel-wire cage to shut it up.

The cage should have broken after such abuse, Jenney thought afterwards, but it didn't. It didn't even dent. If steel cages were so strong, he realized, why not make buildings out of steel! Why not build the Home Insurance Building with steel?

BRICK BY BRICK

By the early 1880s, buildings were still rarely taller than six or seven stories, and it wasn't just because people hated slow elevators or climbing stairs. Bricks, the standard construction materials of the time, were too heavy to build much higher than that. To support a tall structure, the lower walls would have to be so thick that there would be little floor space left. Besides, why use so many bricks to add just one floor when the same number of bricks could be used to construct an entire building someplace else?

Steel, on the other hand, is so much lighter and can carry so much more weight than brick that you can build more than 100 floors before you run into the same type of problem.

REACH FOR THE SKY!

Jenney was one of the first people to realize that steel made it possible to construct buildings with a strong inner "skeleton" to support the building's weight from the inside—so the outer walls didn't have to be built heavy and thick. As George Douglas writes in *Skyscrapers: A Social History in America,*

> In this great decisive step in architectural history, Jenney had perceived the advantages of a building whose exterior wall becomes a mere curtain or covering that encloses the building but does not support it. All the support is provided by the interior framing…in a way, one might say this was a new kind of building that had no wall, only a skin.

And thanks to the invention of the safety elevator, for the first time it was possible to transport people to the upper floors quickly and safely.

Ugly Duckling

The Home Insurance building stood ten stories tall when finished, but that was the only thing interesting about it. Otherwise, it was plain and undistinguished. It didn't even inspire other architects, let alone the public. However, even if it had been beautiful, it wouldn't have attracted much attention: Ten-story buildings didn't tower over their neighbors the way modern skyscrapers do. Douglas writes:

> By a strange irony of history, the importance of the Home Insurance Building did not dawn on either the general public…or the Chicago architects working with Jenney on other building projects….It was only years later that critics and historians came to view the Home Insurance Building as the first real skyscraper.

CHICAGO STYLE

Nevertheless, the Home Insurance Building was the right building in the right city at the right time.

Chicago needed to replace as much office space as quickly, as economically and as efficiently as possible, and skyscrapers were made to order for the task: buildings like the Home Insurance Building provided more usable floor space for the money, materials, and land spent than was possible with any other construction method.

There was another bonus: Since the steel skeleton reduced the number of interior walls to a minimum, the precious office space inside could be partitioned however the tenants wanted it; when they moved away, the office space could be re-partitioned to suit the new tenants. That kind of versatility was ideal for a city that was reinventing itself day by day.

Numerous skyscrapers were built in Chicago over the next several years, including the Tacoma Building, the Rand McNally Building, and the tallest of them all, the Masonic Temple—a 21-story edifice that stood an amazing 302 feet high. It was the tallest building in the world.

Into the Dustbin…

It turned out that these large buildings created new problems: they didn't allow in as much light and air as smaller buildings, and they could be unsafe in fires. Landlords of smaller buildings were afraid skyscrapers would suck tenants away and cause rent prices to collapse.

By 1892, even the city government had turned against skyscrapers. Not long after the Masonic Temple was finished, the city passed a new height limitation of 130 feet on all future build-ings—less than half the height of the temple. The limit was raised to 260 feet in 1900, but the die was cast: Chicago, birthplace of the skyscraper, would soon take a back seat to New York as home to the tallest buildings on earth.

As for the Home Insurance Building, it was demolished in 1934 to make way for the Field Building, the last skyscraper built in Chicago before the Great Depression halted new construction for more than a decade.

Part III of the World's Tallest Buildings is on page 182.

* * *

DID YOU HEAR THE ONE ABOUT...

Muriel B. Mihrum sent us this article from the Wilmington, N.C. *Star News*. It's by Dave Peterson, their outdoor columnist.

Did you hear the one about the black bear caper in Louisiana?

It seems that someone reported a bear clinging to small branches in the top of a tall pine. County officers responded and confirmed that there was, indeed, a bear in that tree.

Meanwhile, game wardens and wildlife biologists had been alerted, because the black bear is not common in that part of the state and has even been considered for the endangered list....To save the bear, wildlife people said they needed a veterinarian, a tranquilizer gun, and a substantial net beneath the tree.

The vet arrived and delivered the tranquilizer darts, but there was no visible reaction from the bear. We were now into about the eighth hour of rescue efforts and the area was ringed with 50 or more avid spectators.

After the tranquilizer darts failed, they decided that the only reasonable option was to cut the tree in a manner that would cause it to fall slowly to soften the blow to the bear.

When the tree came down, everyone rushed to secure the bear and it was at that point when faces turned red. It wasn't a bear! They had spent over eight hours rescuing a large black garbage bag that had blown into the tree.

Highest annual per capita consumption of Spaghetti-Os in the U.S.: Grand Rapids, Michigan.

STRANGE LAWSUITS

Here are a few more real-life examples of unusual legal battles.

THE PLAINTIFF: Gloria Sykes, 25-year-old resident of the San Francisco Bay area.
THE DEFENDANT: The City of San Francisco.
THE LAWSUIT: Sykes was hit by a San Francisco cable car while crossing the street. The only visible injuries were a few cuts and bruises. But later, she claimed, she realized that the accident had turned her into a nymphomaniac. She sued, seeking compensation for neurological and psychological damages.
VERDICT: She was awarded $50,000.

THE PLAINTIFF: Anoki P. Sultan.
THE DEFENDANT: Roman Catholic Archbishop James Hickey.
THE LAWSUIT: Sultan blamed the church for allowing the devil to take over his body. He knew the devil was present, because he hadn't been able to hold a job, had dropped out of school, smoked cigarettes, and had committed other unspeakable acts. He sued, asking for either $100 million or an exorcism.
VERDICT: Case dismissed.

THE PLAINTIFF: Mukesh K. Rai, a devout Hindu living in California.
THE DEFENDANT: Taco Bell.
THE LAWSUIT: In January 1998, Rai ordered a bean burrito at a Ventura, California Taco Bell. They gave him a beef burrito instead. He took a bite, then realized the mistake. When he complained, he was told: "So you ate meat. What's the big deal?" He sued for severe psychological damage and emotional distress because cows are sacred in the Hindu religion, and may not be eaten. "This is the equivalent of eating his ancestors," his lawyer told reporters.
VERDICT: Not settled out of court yet (but it will be).

Good taste: Catfish have 100,000 taste buds.

ON THE CABLE

Cable television was introduced in the 1950s as a way to bring distant TV signals to rural areas. It wasn't until the 1970s that people thought of using it to expand programming—and even then, experts said it would never have a large audience; after all, who would pay for TV when they could get it for free? Today, most of us who watch cable TV don't realize how new it is…or where the stations we watch came from. Maybe in a future Bathroom Reader *we'll do a long piece on how cable made its big breakthrough. In the meantime, here are thumbnail histories of some of the better-known cable channels. (There's more on page 309.)*

HOME BOX OFFICE (HBO)
Background: In 1965, a small company called Sterling Communications won the exclusive rights to provide cable service to lower Manhattan. Their selling point: Better reception. But people weren't buying. After spending $2 million in two years—and still picking up only a few hundred customers—the company was in trouble. Time, Inc., a minor partner in the operation, loaned Sterling enough money to keep it afloat. But in 1970, Time decided the company was losing too much. Desperate to keep his business going, Sterling's founder came up with a new concept: "The Green Channel."
On the Air: The idea was simple: rent first-run movies from Hollywood studios, the way theaters do—but show them on television. Add in some sports events, and consumers would finally have a reason to pay for cable service. The cost of the movies would be high but could be covered by selling the service to other cable companies. Intrigued, Time gave Sterling enough money to test the idea, and the channel (now called HBO) went on the air in 1972. It started with a market-test of 325 homes in Wilkes-Barre, Pennsylvania. By the 1980s, it had become Time's largest source of profit.

TURNER BROADCASTING SYSTEM (TBS)
Background: Ted Turner was twenty-four in 1963 when his father committed suicide. He took over the family's billboard/advertising company and saved it from bankruptcy. In 1970, he bought a small Atlanta UHF television station that ran network reruns and old movies. A few years later, he purchased the rights to Atlanta

---

Look up: At least two people have actually been hit by meteors.

Braves baseball games and built his network around them. Meanwhile, in 1975 the FCC issued a ruling that independent TV stations could send their signals outside local areas to distant markets. This opened the door for the growth of cable, and Turner walked through.

On the Air: He immediately bought space on the first orbiting telecommunications satellite (owned by RCA) and began broadcasting his newly-christened TBS "SuperStation" to cable systems from coast to coast. Almost overnight, his little UHF station doubled its audience to two million households. Baseball was TBS's main attraction, and Turner realized that he couldn't afford to lose the rights to the Braves. So he bought the team. With them, he flourished.

USA NETWORK

Background: In 1975, United Artists and Columbia Cablevision joined forces to create an all-sports station, the Madison Square Garden Sports Network.

On the Air: They hired a 34-year-old consultant, Kay Kaplovitz, to set the network up. Two years later, the station made history by naming Koplovitz its president—the first woman to head a national TV network. She changed its name to USA and moved to diversify programming. Her strategy was a success. In 1981, she proudly announced that USA had become the first advertiser-based cable network to turn a profit, having earned "a few pennies" that year. Today, sports aren't a part of their programming at all.

THE ENTERTAINMENT AND SPORTS PROGRAMMING NETWORK (ESPN)

Background: Before cable, sports fans had to wait until the weekend to find sports on TV. William Rasmussen, the announcer on local Connecticut broadcasts of the World Hockey Association's Hartford Whalers, guessed that die-hard fans would pay to have sports brought into their living rooms every day. So he signed up for space on the RCA telecommunications satellite (which beamed signals to cable stations). Then he tried to raise money to pay for it. By the time ESPN debuted on September 7, 1979, the Getty Oil Company had bought 85% of the network for $10 million.

On the Air: ESPN's first broadcasts were of University of Connecticut games, but plans were in the works for bigger things:

The network contracted with the National Collegiate Athletic Association (NCAA) to telecast hundreds of NCAA events nationally. College athletics remain the station's bread and butter, though it now provides some coverage of professional sports and off-the-wall events like the Strong Man competition. It's now owned by Disney.

LIFETIME

Background: Billed as "the first woman's cable network," Lifetime arose in 1984 out of the ashes of two failing cable stations: Daytime (a diet and talk-show channel) and the Cable Health Network.

On the Air: Lifetime premiered as a mixed bag of talk and call-in shows featuring, among others, Regis Philbin, Richard Simmons, and sex therapist Ruth Westheimer. Dr. Ruth was a hit, but little else was. Losses of $36 million in the first two years proved that women weren't interested. In fact, a poll of viewers revealed that some believed Lifetime was a religious channel. In 1988, Lifetime hired a new head of programming, who switched the focus to drama and reruns of shows like *Moonlighting* and *L.A. Law*. The formula worked. Today, about 70% of Lifetime's viewers are female.

TURNER NETWORK TELEVISION (TNT)

Background: TBS and CNN were well-established in the mid-1980s when Ted Turner made two financial decisions that sent him deep into debt. First, he failed in a hostile takeover attempt of CBS. Then he paid $1.6 billion to acquire 3,650 films from the MGM library, including *The Wizard of Oz* and *2001: A Space Odyssey*. Some analysts estimated he'd overpaid for the films by a half-billion dollars.

On the Air: Beleaguered by unpaid bills, on the verge of losing control of his empire, Turner made a surprising decision: He started yet another cable channel—TNT—and offered many of the MGM movies on it. One problem: Many of the films were in black and white, and contemporary audiences prefer color. So Turner colorized the films, over the objections of directors like Woody Allen and Steven Spielberg. (Congress even held hearings on the subject.) The controversy turned into the fledgling network's biggest publicity break. It debuted in 1988 with *Gone with the Wind*, carried by more cable systems than any new network in history.

The 1st presidential news conference shown on TV was in 1955. Eisenhower was president.

VIDEO TREASURES

How many times have you found yourself at a video store staring at the thousands of films you've never heard of, wondering which ones are worth watching? It happens to us all the time—so we decided to offer a few recom- mendations for relatively obscure, quirky videos you might like.

SOLDIER OF ORANGE (1978) Drama / Foreign
Review: "Rutger Hauer became an international star as a result of his remarkable performance in this Dutch release, in which he plays one of four college buddies galvanized into action when the Nazis invade the Netherlands. This is an exceptional work; an exciting, suspenseful, and intelligent war adventure." *(Video Movie Guide) Stars:* Rutger Hauer, Jeroen Krabbe, Edward Fox, Susan Penhaligon. *Director:* Paul Verhoeven.

MONA LISA (1986) Drama
A sort of noir mystery in the tradition of *Chinatown*.
Review: "A wonderful, sad, sensitive story of a romantic, small-time hood who gets personally involved with the welfare and bad company of the high-priced whore he's been hired to chauffeur." *(Video Hound's Golden Movie Retriever) Stars:* Bob Hoskins, Cathy Tyson, Michael Caine. *Director:* Neil Jordan.

COMFORT AND JOY (1984) Comedy
One of Uncle John's favorite Christmas movies.
Review: "Quirky, fun little comedy. When a mild-mannered Scottish disk jockey's girl moves out on him, his world begins to fall apart. He decides to find more meaning in his life by throwing himself into a noble struggle to reconcile two groups battling over territorial rights for their ice cream trucks. Full of dry wit and subtle humor. Sophisticated viewers are more likely to find this good fun." Music by Mark Knopfler of Dire Straits. *(Illustrated Guide To Video's Best) Stars:* Bill Paterson, Eleanor David, C.P. Grogan, Alex Norton. *Director:* Bill Forsyth.

BABETTE'S FEAST (1987) Foreign / Drama
Review: "Exquisite, delicately told tale of two beautiful young minister's daughters who pass up love and fame to remain in their small Dutch village. They grow old, using religion as a substitute

---

Cats can make over 100 different vocal sounds; dogs can make about ten.

for living life…and then take in Parisian refugee Audran, a woman with a very special secret. Subtle, funny and deeply felt, with several wonderful surprises, an instant masterpiece that deservedly earned a Best Foreign Film Academy Award. [Director] Axel wrote the screenplay, from an Isak Dinesen short story." *(Leonard Maltin's Movie & Video Guide) Stars:* Stephane Audran, Jean-Phillippe Lafont, Gudmar Wivesson, Jarl Kulle, Bibi Andersson, Birgitte Federspiel, Bodil Kjer. *Director:* Gabriel Axel.

HOW TO GET AHEAD IN ADVERTISING (1989) Certifiably weird comedy.
Review: "A cynical, energetic satire about a manic advertising idea man who becomes so disgusted with trying to sell pimple cream that he quits the business. Ultimately he grows a pimple of his own that talks and begins to take over his life. Acerbic and hilarious." *(Video Hound's Golden Movie Retriever) Stars:* Richard E. Grant, Rachel Ward, Richard Wilson. *Director:* Bruce Robinson.

BAGDAD CAFE (1988) Comedy /Drama
Review: "This delightfully off-beat comedy-drama concerns a German businesswoman who appears in the minuscule desert town in California called Bagdad. She and the highly strung owner of the town's only diner-hotel have a major culture and personality clash. Jack Palance as a bandanna-wearing artist is so perfectly weird he practically walks off with the film." *(Video Movie Guide) Stars:* Marianne Sägebrecht, C.C.H. Pounder, Jack Palance. *Director:* Percy Adlon.

HOUSE OF GAMES (1987) Mystery
Review: "A very unusual and fascinating thriller. An uptight pop psychiatrist and best-selling female author decides to rescue one of her clients from a charismatic con artist. Instead, she is nearly conned out of $6,000 of her own money and she has also become fascinated with this man. She is both drawn to him and challenged by him. And, she quickly gets in over her head….Quickly the twists and cons get so thick that she doesn't know who is conning who. A slick thriller well worth watching, but pay attention." *(Illustrated Guide To Video's Best) Stars:* Lindsay Crouse, Joe Mantegna, Lilia Skala, Mike Nussbaum, J.T. Walsh. *Director:* David Mamet.

The Pacific island of Nauru's economy is based almost entirely on bird droppings.

PUSS IN BOATS

*In sailing ship days cats went to sea to keep rats and mice down,
but Trim became a personal pet and companion to
British explorer Captain Matthew Flinders.*

BIRTH

The timbers creak and the sails flap as the vessel pitches and tosses. We're aboard the British ship *Reliance* sailing eastward across the Indian Ocean from Cape Town to Botany Bay. The winds are howling and the waves are huge. The year is 1799.

Below deck (that's downstairs to anyone not up on sea speak) a birth is taking place. A birth in a berth, as it were.

A litter of mewing, blind, flat-eared kittens is arriving. But I don't suppose either mother or new arrivals are taking much notice of the noisy, heaving weather. Doubtless Mother Cat just purposefully gets on with purring, licking and suckling her kittens.

CATS GALORE

It was nothing unusual, of course. Cats and ships went together like burgers and ketchup. They were a form of rodenticide. Almost all vessels were badly infested with nibbling rats and mice. No doubt this particular mother cat had been born at sea herself and knew no other life.

No, what is unusual about this feline happy event is that it was chronicled. That's why we know about it. It's also why, nearly two hundred years later, it was solemnly commemorated in Sydney.

TRIM AND FLINDERS

One of the kittens was a nice little Tom named Trim. He became a personal pet and companion to Captain Matthew Flinders, British explorer. And they shared some pretty hair-raising adventures. For five years Captain and cat were inseparable friends and, together, they travelled tens of thousands of pretty eventful miles.

Flinders, ably assisted by Trim, was the first chap to chart much of the Australian coast. Eventually he recorded his doings and deeds in a book *Voyage to Terra Australis*, which was published in Britain after his death in 1814. The enterprising Captain also invented the Flinders Bar to offset the effects of iron on the compass needle. He was the first person to use a barometer to predict wind changes, too.

They saw service together on the *Investigator*. Then, in 1800, Trim and Flinders returned to England—a journey which would have taken many tedious and uncomfortable weeks. There Trim made the acquaintance of Mrs. Flinders, the Captain's wife. She seems to have seen a great deal less of her husband than his cat did, although there are no records of her having minded particularly.

WAR

Britain was—yet again—at war with France between 1802 and 1815. But a little thing like that didn't stop Captain Flinders and his intrepid feline sailing back to the Antipodes in 1802, where they enjoyed (or at least survived) a "friendly" meeting with French ships at Encounter Bay on Australia's south coast.

How did the conversation go? "Bonjour. Permettez-moi de vous presenter mon chat, Trim." Perhaps. The presence of a cat has always been a useful icebreaker in sticky situations. Perhaps Trim, had he but known it, was doing a bit of international diplomatic work.

By 1803 Trim and Flinders were on the *Porpoise*. It was shipwrecked and together they waited two months for rescuers before setting sail again on the *Cumberland*. The destination was Britain where Flinders hoped to find a better ship. Alas, the poor *Cumberland* was no more seaworthy than its predecessor and Flinders was forced to put in to the (French, and therefore enemy) island of Mauritius for help.

Oh dear. Luck had run out. There was no one to vouch for this Englishman on enemy territory in war time. Moreover, the 'passport' given to Flinders by the French offering him French hospitality, should he ever need it, was in the name of the *Investigator*, not the *Cumberland*. One can just imagine the heated exchange and level of misunderstanding between the British sea captain and de Caen, the French governor.

The results were grim for both man and cat. Flinders was held as a spy in captivity for seven years before his release to retirement in Britain, but Mauritius put an end to poor old Trim.

Heavy thought: Iron weighs more after it rusts.

He disappeared in mysterious circumstances: "An untimely death, being devoured by the Catopophagi of that island," surmised his master, sadly.

FLINDERS KEEPS RECORD
We know all this because Flinders kept boredom at bay during his period of detention by writing in his journal. The original manuscript is now held at the Maritime Museum at Greenwich in England. And a long extract has been published in Australia. In the journal he is very affectionate about Trim.

Flinders hoped that there would one day be a memorial to Trim which would call attention to the cat's "little merriment with delight and his superior intelligence with surprise" and to remind us all that "Never will his like be seen again!"

TRIM'S MEMORIAL
It took nearly two centuries, but the State Library of New South Wales, Sydney finally got around to carrying out Flinders's wishes in 1996.

There's been a statue of Captain Flinders outside the library in Macquarie Street in Sydney since 1925. In 1996 the explorer was joined by a beautiful life-sized statue of his cat Trim, cast in bronze by the sculptor John Cornwell.

It was the late Vaughan Evans's idea. Evans was a keen amateur maritime historian who worked as a volunteer at the library for many years. Trim now stands, nose up and best paw forward, inside the building on a sunny windowsill. So that loyal and much loved puss has found a warm, peaceful and permanent resting place.

Money for the 'Trim Project' was raised by public subscription. Many of the donors sent gifts in the names of their own cats: Sir Basil, Stripey, Smokey and Jellicle to name but a few. The feline monument was unveiled on March 28, 1996 by Rear-Admiral David Campbell AM, RAN Naval Command, Sydney in the presence of 400 admirers and The Naval Reserve Band.

Identity crisis? Approximately 10% of Jewish households have Christmas trees.

ED WOOD'S MASTERPIECE

As a follow-up to Greg Walcott's piece about Ed Wood (immediately preceding this), we thought we'd include a few comments from critics about Plan 9 from Outer Space.

ONLY HUBCAPS

"Some say [*Plan 9 from Outer Space*] is the worst movie anyone ever made. Certainly it's the worst movie Ed Wood ever made. And nobody but Wood could have made it. The lunacy begins with a portentous introduction from our old friend Criswell, the clairvoyant. 'Greetings my friends,' Criswell reads from his cue card. 'We are all interested in the future because that's where you and I are going to spend the rest of our lives.' While we're still mulling over the meaning of that statement, Wood hits us with the heavy-duty special effects—UFOs flying over Hollywood Boulevard. Actually, they're only hubcaps, superimposed on a pseudo-sky."

—*The Worst Movies of All Time*, by Michael Sauter

ATTACK OF THE UNDEAD

"God knows what the first eight "Plans" were, but *Plan 9* is a doozy....Aliens Dudley Manlove and Joanna Lee (today a successful scriptwriter) were sent by The Ruler to raise the dead so that they'd attack the living. That's just about what Wood tried to do with his dead friend Bela Lugosi, billed as the star of the film although he died prior to production. Wood had a couple of minutes of footage of Lugosi from an aborted project, so he simply inserted the snippets into this film and repeated them over and over so that Lugosi had adequate screen time. Lugosi's character— The Ghoul Man—was played in the rest of the movie by a chiropractor, an extremely tall fellow who spends his screen time with a cape covering his face so we won't know he's an impostor. The ruse doesn't work, but I don't think Wood really cared."

—*Guide for the Film Fanatic*, by Danny Peary

If you shake a can of mixed nuts, the larger nuts go to the top.

BEYOND RIDICULE

"Words such as amateurish, crude, tedious and aaarrrggghhhh can't begin to describe this Edward D. Wood film with Bela Lugosi in graveyard scenes made shortly before his death....

The unplotted plot by Wood has San Fernando Valley residents troubled by UFOs of the worst encounter. Humanoid aliens Dudley Manlove and Joanna Lee land their cardboard ship with a ninth plan to conquer the world (the first eight failed, you see). They resurrect corpses, including Vampira, Tor Johnson and Lugosi's double. The results are unviewable except for masochists who enjoy a good laugh derived from watching folks making fools of themselves."

—*Creature Features Movie Guide Strikes Again*, by John Stanley

MASTERFUL SPECIAL EFFECTS

"The graveyard set provides the film with many of its eerie moments, thanks to a number of dead tree branches and cardboard tombstones; in one scene a policeman accidentally kicks over one of the featherweight grave markers.

"Despite the resourcefulness of the director, there are slight technical shortcomings in the final version of *Plan 9*. Even Wood's staunchest defenders will admit that the Old Master seemed to have a tough time with lighting. In one scene, as Mona McKinnon runs in horror from Bela Lugosi's double, she goes directly from a graveyard at midnight to a nearby highway at high noon. This same confusion between night and day occurs several times in the course of the film."

—*The Golden Turkey Awards*, by Harry and Michael Medved

CHEAP, CHEAP, CHEAP

"Money was always a problem for Wood. Budgets were routinely non-existent, forcing him to film on the cheap, scrimping...as best he could....How cheap was *Plan 9*? The flying saucers are hubcaps suspended by wires. In several scenes the movie jumps from daylight to nighttime and back. And outdoor lawn furniture doubles as bedroom furniture....In all of the literature about Plan 9 (and there's reams of the stuff) one question about the movie has never been answered. If *Plan 9* was to revive the dead, what were the other eight plans?

—*Why The People of Earth Are "Stupid,"* by Tom Mason

FOUNDING FATHERS

You already know their names. Here's who they belonged to.

Jerome Smuckers. Started out selling apple butter in Orrville, Ohio in 1897; in 1923 he branched out to jams and jellies.

Abraham and Mahala Stouffer. Cleveland, Ohio restaurateurs. Their Stouffer's restaurants were so popular that they began freezing entrees for customers to eat at home. By 1957, they were selling frozen foods in supermarkets; and by the late 1960s they were supplying frozen dinners for the Apollo space program.

John Deere. In 1837, Deere invented the first practical steel plow, which unlike iron plows, cut through black, sticky prairie soil without bogging down in the thick muck. Today John Deere is the largest agricultural machinery manufacturer in the world.

Jack Mack. Mack and his brother Augustus were wagon builders in Brooklyn at the turn of the century. In 1900, they built the first bus in the U.S. It was used to carry tourists around Brooklyn's Prospect Park. The bus was so reliable—it logged more than 1 million miles over 25 years—that Jack and Augustus were swamped with orders. They and three other brothers formed the Mack Brothers Company a short time later. Jack designed the company's first truck in 1905.

The Smith Brothers. The first commercial typewriters were available in 1873, but it wasn't until 1895 that someone invented a typewriter that allowed you to see the words as you were typing. When Union Typewriter Co. balked at making the new machine in 1903, Lyman, Wilbert, Monroe, and Hurlbut Smith left the company and founded the L.C. Smith Brothers Typewriting Co. In 1925 they merged with the Corona Typewriting to become Smith-Corona.

Herman Fisher and Irving Price. Together with Helen Schelle, they founded the Fisher-Price toy company in 1930 to make toys out of Ponderosa Pine. Their first big hit: Snoopy Sniffer, a "loose-jointed, floppy-eared pull toy who woofed when you pulled his wagging spring tail," in 1938. The company made its first plastic toys in 1949.

A chameleon's tongue is twice the length of its body.

INTERNATIONAL LAW

Believe it or not, these laws are real.

In England, it's illegal to name your pet "Queen" or "Princess" without the Queen's permission.

If you aren't a member of the royal family in Japan, it's illegal for you to own a maroon car.

In Equatorial Guinea, you can name your daughter anything you want—except Monica.

In India, women—but not men—are allowed to marry goats.

Old English law: if an object is smaller than a husband's little finger, he can beat his wife with it.

In Canada, if a debt is higher than 25¢, it's against the law for you to pay with pennies.

In Vancouver, British Columbia, the speed limit for tricycles is 10 miles per hour.

In Baluchistan, Pakistan, the law allows a man to "acquire" a wife by trading in his sister.

In Athens, Greece, driving on public roads while "unbathed" or poorly dressed can cost you your driver's license.

If a man is wearing a hat in Cheshire, England, the law requires him to raise it when a funeral passes.

You can keep cows in sheds in the Northern Territories of Canada, and you can keep chickens in sheds. But you can't keep cows and chickens in the same shed.

Makes sense: in London, England, it's illegal to operate a motor vehicle while sitting in the back seat.

In Australia, the pictures of convicted drunk drivers are published in newspapers with the caption, "He's drunk and in jail."

Cigarettes are legal in Nicaragua; cigarette lighters aren't.

Boxing is illegal in China (too brutal); capital punishment isn't.

Largest dinosaur: the Seismosaurus. They grew to 119 feet in length and weighed 90 tons.

ELEMENTARY, MY DEAR SHERLOCK

Here are a few of the more interesting comments author Arthur Conan Doyle had Sherlock Holmes make in his books.

"Eliminate all other factors, and the one which remains must be the truth."

"I never guess. It is a shocking habit—destructive to the logical faculty."

"You can never foretell what any one man will do, but you can say with precision what an average number will be up to."

"As a rule, the more bizarre a thing is, the less mysterious it proves to be."

"Life is infinitely stranger than anything which the mind of man could invent."

"There is nothing more deceptive than an obvious fact."

"You know my method. It is founded on the observance of trifles."

"It is always dangerous to reason from insufficient data."

"Crime is common. Logic is rare."

"Any truth is better than indefinite doubt."

"I cannot agree with those who rank modesty among the virtues."

"It is stupidity rather than courage to refuse to recognize danger when it is close upon you."

"Mediocrity knows nothing higher than itself; but talent instantly recognizes genius."

"I can discover facts, Watson, but I cannot change them."

"A man always finds it hard to realize that he may have finally lost a woman's love, however badly he may have treated her."

"The most difficult crime to track is the one which is purposeless."

MENTAL AEROBICS

Here's something else to do while you're sitting there—exercise your mind. We've adapted some standard mental exercises for bathroom readers, so when you're feeling sluggish, or just haven't woken up yet, you can use this time to make yourself more alert.

STRETCH YOUR MIND
Use this exercise to warm-up or refresh your mental muscles, anytime during the day.

Complete some or all of the following seven steps. If you can, try saying them out loud.

1. Count backwards from 100 to zero, quickly.

2. Recite the alphabet, assigning a word for each letter (like, "A, apple; B, ball; etc."). Do this quickly.

3. List 20 names of men you know, assigning a number to each ("1, Brian; 2, Pete, etc."). Quickly.

4. Do the same thing as #3, but list 20 women you know assigning a number to each ("1, Jennifer; 2, Andrea; etc."). Quickly.

5. Name and number 20 foods as quickly as you can ("1, burger; 2, cookies, etc.").

6. (Feeling much more alert by now!) Choose one letter of the alphabet and name 20 words that begin with that letter as quickly as you can AND number them ("1, news; 2, nice, etc.").

7. Close your eyes and count to 20 slowly, then open them. Your mind is now geared-up to meet whatever mental challenges you might face today.

TAKE CREATIVE LEAPS
One way to become more creative is to change your normal routine. Experts say that most big shifts in our lives come from a lot of little shifts. Don't underestimate their potential!

Try some of the following:

1. Wipe with your opposite hand!

2. Walk out of the bathroom backwards.

Black whales are born white.

3. If you normally flush while you're sitting, wait until you stand up; if you normally flush standing up, do it while sitting.

4. Put your pants on the way you normally do, paying attention to which leg you put in first. Take them off again. Put them back on using the "wrong" leg first.

5. Turn on the faucet. Now turn it off; turn it on again, using the other hand.

6. Wear your watch on the opposite wrist.

7. Brush your teeth with the opposite hand.

...Or come up with some more of your own.

MENTAL SPRINT
Helps increase creativity and sharpness.

1. Flip to any other page in this book (make sure you dog-ear or leave your finger on this one so that you can find it again).

2. Select the first noun that you see on that page (e.g., "ball").

3. Look at your watch.

4. For the next minute or two (or longer), list as many words or phrases that you can relate to that noun ("ball: bounce, play, games, red, etc."). Don't stop to think or analyze, just go as quickly as you can.

To enhance results, do this exercise aloud...if you dare.

AND IF NONE OF THESE WORK...
Here are some good excuses for sleeping on the job:

1. "They told me at the blood bank this might happen."

2. "Whew! I musta left the top off the liquid paper."

3. "This is one of the seven habits of highly effective people!"

4. "Oh, I wasn't sleeping! I was meditating on our mission statement and envisioning a new paradigm!"

RANDOM AMERICANA

A few bits of info we've put aside to entertain you.

PURVIS' FOLLY

"The first person ever to belch on national radio was Melvin Purvis, head of the Chicago office of the FBI. Purvis was the guest on a show sponsored by Fleischmann's Yeast, in 1935, and in the middle of reading a commercial, the famed G-man emitted a loud burp. For many years thereafter, Fleischmann's Yeast was nicknamed 'Purvis' Folly.'"

—*The Book of Strange Facts and Useless Information,* by Scot Morris

LUCKY DOG

"The Crystal Beach Cyclone in Crystal Beach, Ontario, (sic) was once considered the most terrifying of all roller coaster rides. A nurse was kept on duty at all times. The first drop in the ride featured an 85% turn to the right that caused patrons to lose hats, coats, teeth, and wigs, and to careen into each other, sometimes cracking ribs. However, in its 20 years of existence, there was only one fatality—in 1943. A man stood up to remove his suit jacket as the coaster started. His arms locked, and he couldn't sit back down. He was thrown from the car and run over. His heirs sued, claiming that the lap bar didn't hold him. The judge put a dog in the coaster to test it, the dog emerged healthy and happy, and the suit was denied. Turns out, the dog, a British bulldog, belonged to the park's maintenance supervisor and rode the coaster daily."

—*The Worst of Everything,* contributed by Paul Ruben

AMERICAN KNOW-HOW

"A baby conceived with the help of a $2.95 turkey baster was born on Mother's Day. Julie Johnson, 34, of Cary, N.C., volunteered to be a surrogate mother for her sister, Janet, after Janet's $15,000 in vitro failed. So Julie stood on her head and received the sperm via the sterilized kitchen baster. "I figured gravity couldn't hurt," she said. Her sister added, "We're going to be completely honest with the kid. We'll tell him Aunt Julie had to have him because we couldn't."

—*San Francisco Examiner*

Wettest city in the U.S.: Quillayute, Washington. Driest: Yuma, Arizona.

ORIGIN OF THE WHITE HOUSE, PART II

Here's the second part of our story of how the White House was built. Part I is on page 96.

BUILDING THE HOUSE
The cornerstone for the president's house was laid on October 13, 1792 (nobody knows for sure where—the exact location was not recorded), and work on the four-foot-thick outer walls began. They were built by masons and slave laborers, all of whom lived in shanties on the property because there was no place else in the as-yet unbuilt city for them to live. (At one point, a brothel was set up on the White House grounds, for their "convenience.")

The exterior would be faced with freestone, a form of sandstone that was chosen because it can be cut like marble. But freestone is also very porous and is highly susceptible to water damage, so the masons sealed the stone with a wash of salt, rice and glue. It was the building's first coat of white paint; soon it would be nicknamed the "White House."

STOP AND GO
Work on Washington, D.C. was moving slowly due to shortages of skilled labor, raw materials, and—especially—dollars, thanks to the disappointing land sales in the district and a Congress that was reluctant to commit any extra money.

The White House had more than its share of its own problems: Despite all the cuts that had been made, it was still way over budget, and when the Congress learned in 1798 how much money had been spent, it refused to pay any more. When the roof was finished the building was sealed up and abandoned, sitting empty for more than a year until new funds could be raised to pay for the interior.

The Wet House
When work resumed, an architect named Benjamin Henry Latrobe examined the structure to determine its structural

---

On average, it takes 660 days from conception for an elephant to give birth.

soundness. He found that the structural timbers, which weren't the highest quality of wood to begin with, had been exposed to so much cold, dampness, and rain during the seven years of construction that they were now dangerously decayed. But there was no money to replace them, so Latrobe repaired them as best he could and work on the house continued.

By now the White House was hopelessly behind schedule. "We do not believe it will be possible to prepare the building for the reception of the President until October or November next," the commissioners wrote in February 1800.

FIRST NIGHT
George Washington didn't live to even see the finished White House, let alone live in it. He left office in 1797 and died two years later, at about the same time the exterior walls were completed.

The White House was still unfinished when Washington's successor, John Adams, arrived in Washington, D.C., but he moved in anyway on November 1, 1800. The rest of the federal government—which consisted of 130 federal employees—moved to the new capital a month later.

A WORK IN PROGRESS
"Unfinished" is the polite way to describe the condition of the White House. The roof leaked, the ceilings were crumbling, and the windows were so loose that rain and wind blew into just about every room. "Not one room or chamber is finished," First Lady Abigail Adams wrote. "It is habitable only by fires in every part....This is such an inconvenience that I know not what to do!" The White House didn't even have an enclosed yard, so she took to hanging her wet laundry in the unfinished East Room.

The exterior looked even worse. As Ethel Lewis writes in The White House, the grounds were strewn with "dump heaps, old brick kilns, and water holes giving off evil odors…it looked more like a ruin than a Presidential Palace." The workers and slave laborers were still living in shanties on the lawn, and it would be nearly a month before the White House had an outhouse.

IN AND OUT
But the Adamses would suffer for only four months—in 1800,

Adams lost the presidential election to his political rival, Thomas Jefferson. Adams avenged the defeat in three different ways:

(1) He stayed up late on Inauguration eve appointing judges that he thought would be embarrassing to Jefferson.

(2) He boycotted the Inauguration the following morning.

(3) He moved out of the White House as required, which meant that Jefferson would have to move in.

Jefferson preferred to stay at Monticello whenever possible, but he also did a lot to improve the White House. He removed the shanties, landscaped the grounds, installed a fence, and filled the mansion with fashionable furniture. And for safety's sake, "mixed in with the fine furniture," Ethel Lewis writes, "were eight fire buckets."

By the time Jefferson left office in 1809, the White House was finally a comfortable home, though not by today's standards— there was no electricity, no telephones, no central heating, no air conditioning, and there was only the most primitive system of running water, designed by Jefferson himself. There weren't even any closets (in those days few people owned more than a cedar chest full of clothes, and built-in closets were unheard of).

By 19th-century standards, the White House would do just fine...but not for long—in 1814 British soldiers burned it to the ground, leaving the mansion's white stone walls an empty shell.

For more on the history of the White House, turn to page 251.

For more on the history of the White House, turn to page 251.

*　*　*

CAN'T HOLD A CANDLE TO IT

Q: Why do some flames burn blue while others burn yellow?

A: "It's a matter of how much oxygen is available to the burning fuel. Lots of oxygen makes blue flames, while a limited amount of oxygen makes yellow ones." (From *What Einstein Didn't Know*, by Robert L. Wolke)

All the gold ever mined could be molded into a cube 60 feet high and 60 feet wide.

KNOCK YOURSELF OUT!

"Knock yourself out" usually means something like, "Have a good time." But these people took the phrase literally.

STANLEY PINTO
Usually a skilled professional wrestler, he got tangled in the ropes in a Providence, Rhode Island, match. Trying to get free, he pinned his own shoulders to the mat for three seconds. The referee counted him out.

HARVEY GARTLEY
"In 1977, Gartley fought Dennis Oulette in a Golden Glove boxing competition. Gartley was counted out in a knock-out 47 seconds after the opening bell. Oulette never made contact with Gartley. The young Gartley was so excited during the match that he 'danced himself into exhaustion and fell to the canvas'—knocking himself out and losing the fight." (*Oops*)

THE USS SCORPION
The last U.S. nuclear submarine lost at sea sank with two nuclear weapons on board. Apparently, one of Scorpion's conventional torpedoes became activated and threatened to explode. To save the ship, the crew ejected it. But the torpedo "became fully armed, and sought its nearest target—the Scorpion."

HMS TRINIDAD
Sailing in the Arctic in 1941, the British ship fired a torpedo at a German destroyer—forgetting the effect that the icy water would have on the oil in the torpedo's steering mechanism. The torpedo curved, and in less than a minute it was headed straight at the Trinidad. It blasted right into the ship's engine room and put HMS Trinidad out of action for the duration of the war.

SPANISH AIR FORCE JET
"In 1979, a Spanish Air Force jet was participating in a target practice run near a hillside in Spain. The jet's gunfire ricocheted off the mountain and blew up the plane." (*Oops*)

Four most common arrests in the U.S.: drunk driving, theft, drugs, and drunkenness.

BOBBY CRUICKSHANK.

"It was the final round of the 1934 U.S. Open," write Ross and Kathryn Petras in *The 176 Stupidest Things Ever Done*, "and the pressure was on. Cruickshank was two strokes ahead of his competitors. He had to make the next hole in four strokes to keep his lead.

"Cruickshank's drive off the tee was fine. But his following approach shot was too weak. With horror, he watched the ball sink with a splash into the stream in front of the green.

"A split second later, the ball bounced back out of the water—apparently ricocheting off of a submerged rock—and rolled onto the green only ten feet from the hole.

"It was a miracle. With a whoop, Cruickshank tossed his club in the air, tipped his hat, and yelled to the heavens, 'Thank you, God!' Unfortunately, the club landed on his head. It knocked him down and upset his balance for the rest of the day. He lost the lead and came in third."

HENRY WALLITSCH

In 1959, Wallitsch fought a heavyweight match against Bartolo Soni in Long Island, New York. In the third round, he took a wild swing at Soni and missed. The force of his swing made him lose his balance, and he fell through the ropes head-first. His chin hit the floor so hard, it knocked him out.

JACK DOYLE

In the mid-1930s, Doyle was considered a promising heavyweight boxer. When a reporter declared him "the next heavyweight champion," he stopped training—and didn't even fight for a year and a half. In October, 1938, after the long lay-off, he announced he was going to fight Eddie Phillips—and he was taking this bout very seriously.

He arrived a half hour late for the match. Then, in the second round, "he swung such a mighty punch that, when Phillips stepped sideways, Doyle knocked himself out, plunged through the ropes and landed next to the time keeper who solemnly counted to ten." (*The Return of the Book of Heroic Failures*)

DUMB CROOKS

Here's proof that crime doesn't pay.

HI, THIS IS A ROBBERY. HERE'S MY I.D.

DALLAS, Texas— "Ronnie Darnell Bell, 30, was arrested in Dallas for attempting to rob the Federal Reserve Bank. According to police, Bell handed a security guard a note that read: This is a bank robbery of the Dallas Federal Reserve Bank of Dallas, give me all the money. Thank you, Ronnie Darnell Bell. The guard pushed a silent alarm while an oblivious Bell chatted amiably, revealing to the guard that only minutes earlier he had tried to rob a nearby post office but that 'they threw me out.'"

—*The Edge, The Portland Oregonian, 6/18/98*

TAKE THE MONEY AND...?

BALTIMORE, Maryland— "Bank robbers usually take the money and run. Not Jeffrie Thomas, police said. Thomas, 35, walked into a Signet Bank on Monday and handed the teller a note demanding money. When police arrived and asked which way he went, employees pointed to a man counting cash near a teller's station. It was Thomas, adding up the take, police said. Thomas, who was unarmed, was taken into custody."

—*The Baltimore Sun, 4/13/97*

HOT TIPS

DADE COUNTY, Florida— "On several break-ins, Ronald Bradley, 21, carefully wore gloves. But...he wore golf gloves—the kind that left his fingertips naked. He was sent to prison for three years."

—*Sports Illustrated, 6/20/78*

A HELPFUL ATTITUDE

MINNEAPOLIS, Minnesota— "Suspected purse-snatcher Dereese Delon Waddell in suburban Minneapolis last winter stood on a police lineup so the 76-year-old female victim could have a look at him. When police told him to put his baseball cap on with the bill facing out, so as to be presentable, he protested, 'No, I'm

---

Tallest U.S. President: Abraham Lincoln (6'4"). Shortest: James Madison (5'4").

gonna put it on backwards. That's the way I had it on when I took the purse.'"

—*Jay Leno's Police Blotter*

CAREFUL DRIVER

SYRACUSE, New York— "In 1992, Philip S. Whaley, Sr., was captured and charged with grand larceny and other crimes after a twenty-eight-minute chase involving numerous route changes. For all twenty-eight minutes, Whaley signaled every single turn that he made. Said an officer, 'We knew exactly where he was going.'"

—*America's Least Competent Criminals*

MISSING PIECES

GRAPEVINE, Texas— "In 1993, 24-year-old David Bridges stole a television set so he could watch the Dallas Cowboys. He was arrested when he went back a second time, to get the remote control."

I'LL BE RIGHT OVER, OFFICER

PANAMA CITY, Florida— "Brandon Lamont Dawson, 20, was captured after police found a pager he'd left in his car following a homicide, traced it to Dawson, called him on the phone, and asked him to come to retrieve the device. He was arrested when he walked into the Panama City police station."

—*TV Guide, 12/13/97*

DUMB DRIVE-IN

VIRGINIA BEACH, Virginia— "A man charged with auto theft came to court in, of all things, a stolen car.

"Tony Brite appeared in court Friday like he was supposed to, then left with two companions after his preliminary hearing. A detective followed Brite outside, then watched as the three got into a new Volvo with New York license plates.

"Suspicious, Detective Gary Nelson ran a check on the plates and was told they belonged to a Mercedes. The Volvo had been stolen the day before from a Virginia dealership. Nelson followed the Volvo into a convenience store parking lot across the street from Virginia Beach's First Precinct. All three were arrested peacefully."

—**From a 1997 wire service report**

FAMILIAR PHRASES

Here are more origins of some everyday phrases.

THE WHOLE NINE YARDS
Meaning: Everything; the whole shebang.
Origin: "Curiously enough, the nine yards does not refer to distance gained or lost in any kind of athletic contest....The reference is to the amount of cement contained in one of the rotating cement-mixer trucks used by construction companies. When emptied, it would discharge the whole nine yards, thereby completing its mission." (From the *Morris Dictionary of Word and Phrase Origins*, by William and Mary Morris)

IT'S ALL GREEK TO ME
Meaning: Something doesn't make sense.
Origin: "During the Middle Ages, as for centuries thereafter, any educated Englishman or woman knew Latin, but only a minority also knew Greek. A major reason was that Greek uses its own alphabet, so before even starting to learn the language you have to learn the letters. The phrase itself comes from Shakespeare's Julius Caesar." (From *Loose Cannons & Red Herrings*, by Robert Claiborne)

MIND YOUR P's AND Q's
Meaning: To be on your best behavior.
Origin: According to Edwin Radford and Alan Smith in *To Coin a Phrase:* "The most likely origin of this traditional warning is the practice of tavern owners 'chalking up' the pints and quarts consumed by a thirsty customer in the course of an evening." Customers had to keep track of how much they'd drunk...and how much they owed.

BULL IN A CHINA SHOP
Meaning: To be clumsy, especially in a delicate situation.
Origin: A common expression in English since the 1830s—and probably a political one. In 1834, China terminated trade with John Bull (England). This, says Robert Hendrickson in *Animal Crackers*, "had something to do with the coining of the phrase—

The five animals most often mentioned in the Bible are sheep, lambs, lions, oxen, and rams.

perhaps through a political cartoon showing an angry John Bull threatening to destroy a 'China' shop if trade wasn't resumed." He adds: "The 'china' in the phrase refers to the fine porcelain from China brought to Europe from the Far East as early as the 16th century."

TO REST ON YOUR LAURELS
Meaning: To be content with success already achieved; stop going after more glory.
Origin: "For centuries, wreaths of laurel were used to crown victors, great poets, and people who had achieved distinction. This 'evergreen' was chosen to signify that they will be remembered for all time (hence the term 'poet laureate'). Once someone had been crowned, they didn't have to prove themselves anymore—and could 'rest on their laurels.'" Another meaning: Traditionally, "anyone who aspired to greatness placed laurel leaves under their pillow—literally resting on their laurels—to acquire strength for victory, or inspiration for their poetry." (From *Everyday Phrases*, by Neil Ewart)

LEFT IN THE LURCH
Meaning: Left far behind, often in difficult circumstances.
Origin: "The key word apparently comes from the French *lourche*, a 16th century game said to have resembled backgammon. To be 'in the lurch' started off as a way of saying a player was far behind in a game" and evolved into a term that could apply to any situation. (From *The Dictionary of Clichés*, by James Rogers)

THE DIE IS CAST
Meaning: A final decision has been made.
Origin: "The term comes from Suetonius's account of Julius Caesar's invasion of Italy in 49 B.C. When Caesar crossed the River Rubicon into Italy, thereby advancing against [Pompey] and the Roman Senate, he supposedly said, 'Jacta alea est' (The dice have been thrown), Meaning that now there was no turning back." (From *Fighting Words*, by Christine Ammer)

First woman to win a Nobel Prize: Marie Curie, for Physics, in 1903.

CRUM'S LEGACY

Ever wonder how potato chips were invented? Here's BRI food historian Jeff Cheeks' account. It's not clear whether Vanderbilt was really Crum's first customer, but that's the legend. We'll leave that for you to decide.

BACKGROUND
Cornelius "Commodore" Vanderbilt was born on May 27, 1794 and grew up on Staten Island. When Cornelius was 14, he quit school to help his father with the family skiff...and by the time he was 16, he'd saved enough to buy a small ferry of his own.

During the War of 1812, he made his first fortune, carrying troops and supplies to forts in the New York area. In 1829, at age 35, he started a steamship line; 25 years later, thanks to passengers lured by the 1849 Gold Rush, he was one of the richest men in the world.

I SAY POTATO...
Vanderbilt's wealth allowed him to live lavishly. He built a number of stately homes, one of which was near Saratoga Springs in upstate New York. In 1853, while summering there, his tactless, imperious manner may have led to the creation of a favorite American snack.

In those days, potatoes were usually served baked, boiled, or mashed; oil was too expensive to waste on frying them. But one night a customer having dinner at Moon's Lake House—legend says it was Vanderbilt—told the waiter to bring him fried potatoes like the ones he'd tasted in France. He gave detailed instructions on how to prepare them.

The chef, George Crum, had the ego of a master chef—reinforced by the fact that he was a proud Native American, a chief in the Algonquin tribe. He made the fries as directed. The customer sent them back. They were too large and not crisp enough. The chef prepared another batch, but they, too, were sent back. They were still too big and not crisp enough. Furious, Crum sliced the next potatoes paper thin, dipped them in hot fat, and dusted them with salt. The customer loved them—they were better than French fries!

Was the customer really Vanderbilt? No one knows for sure...but it's a fact that Vanderbilt loved Crum's creation so much that he offered to put up the money if Crum wanted to start his own restaurant...and that Crum turned him down.

A koala bear sleeps 22 hours of every day.

BRAIN TEASERS

BRI member Tim Harrower sent us these puzzles and dared us to solve them. They were a favorite in the BRI "research lab," so we're "passing" them on to you. See page 759 for the answers.

1. A married couple goes to a movie. During the film, the husband strangles the wife. No one notices—and he's able to get her body back home without attracting attention. How did he do this?

2. A man goes to a party, drinks some punch, and then leaves early. Everyone else at the party who drinks the punch dies of poison. Why didn't the man die?

3. One day Kerry celebrates her birthday. Two days later, her older twin brother Terry celebrates his birthday. How could this be, when they were born a half-hour apart?

4. How quickly can you find out what is unusual about this paragraph? It looks so ordinary that you would think that nothing is wrong with it at all —and, in fact, nothing is. But it is a bit odd. Why? If you study it and think about it, you may find out, but I am not going to assist you in any way. You must do it without coaching. No doubt, if you work at it for long, it will dawn on you. Who knows?

5. It's the ninth inning. The pitcher delivers; the batter hits a deep fly ball. The outfielder starts to catch it—then deliberately lets it fall from his glove. Why?

6. John's mother has three children. The oldest is a boy named Herbert, who has brown eyes—everyone calls him Herb. Next youngest is a girl named Penelope. Everyone calls her Penny. The youngest child has green eyes and can wiggle his ears. What is his first name?

7. Three men decide to share a hotel room for the night. The desk clerk charges them $30. They each pay $10. After they go to their room, the desk clerk realizes the room is only $25, so he gives a bellhop $5 to take up to the men. On his way up, the bellhop decides to tip himself $2 for his trouble. In the room, he gives each man $1—which means that each guy actually paid $9 for the room.

J. Edgar Hoover liked to fire FBI agents whose palms were sweaty when shaking hands.

So: 3 x $9 = $27; the bell-hop kept $2; that adds up to $29. Where did the other dollar go?

What's going on here? Why doesn't the math add up right?

8. An hour later, two women check into another room. The room is $30; they each pay $15. Again, the desk clerk realizes the room is only $25, so he gives the bellhop $5 to take up to the women. This time, the bellhop keeps $3 for himself and gives $1 to each of the two women. So each woman actually paid $14 for the room.

So: 2 x $14 = $28; the bellhop kept $3; that adds up to $31.

And that's where the missing dollar shows up again.

9. A man lies dead in a room with 53 bicycles in front of him. What happened?

10. Bob and Carol and Ted and Alice all live in the same house. One night, Bob and Carol go to a movie; when they return, Alice is lying dead on the floor in a puddle of water and glass. It's obvious that Ted killed her—but Ted is never arrested or punished. How could this be?

11. A deaf-mute goes into a hardware store. He wants to buy a pencil sharpener, so he walks up to the clerk, sticks a finger in his ear and rotates his other hand around his other ear. The next customer is a blind man. How does he let the clerk know he wants a pair of scissors?

BAD PUNS

From *Best Book of Puns*, by Art Moger

• They say all sheep are alike—actually, they have mutton in common.

• Many folks believe that legalized gambling has made Atlantic City a bettor place.

• Adam and Eve lived appley ever after.

• A soldier hid inside a cannon to avoid guard duty, but he was finally discharged.

Can you think of an English word that rhymes with "month"? Our sources say there is none.

THE TOP 10 HITS OF THE YEAR, 1968–1971

Here's another installment of BRI's Top Ten of the Year list.

1968

(1) Hey Jude —*The Beatles*
(2) Love Is Blue —*Paul Mauriat*
(3) Honey —*Bobby Goldsboro*
(4) People Got To Be Free —*Rascals*
(5) (Sittin' On) The Dock Of The Bay —*Otis Redding*
(6) Sunshine Of Your Love —*Cream*
(7) This Guy's In Love With You —*Herb Alpert*
(8) The Good, the Bad, and the Ugly —*Hugo Montenegro*
(9) Mrs. Robinson —*Simon & Garfunkel*
(10) Woman, Woman —*Gary Puckett & the Union Gap*

1969

(1) Sugar, Sugar —*The Archies*
(2) Aquarius/Let The Sunshine In —*The Fifth Dimension*
(3) I Can't Get Next To You —*The Temptations*
(4) Honky Tonk Women —*The Rolling Stones*
(5) Everyday People —*Sly & The Family Stone*
(6) Dizzy —*Tommy Roe*
(7) Hot Fun In The Summertime —*Sly & The Family Stone*
(8) Get Back —*The Beatles*
(9) Build Me Up Buttercup —*The Foundations*
(10) Crimson & Clover —*Tommy James & The Shondells*

1970

(1) Bridge Over Troubled Water —*Simon And Garfunkel*
(2) (They Long To Be) Close To You —*The Carpenters*
(3) American Woman—*Guess Who*
(4) War —*Edwin Starr*
(5) Raindrops Keep Fallin' On My Head —*B.J. Thomas*
(6) Ain't No Mountain High Enough —*Diana Ross*
(7) Let It Be —*The Beatles*
(8) Get Ready —*Rare Earth*
(9) I'll Be There —*The Jackson Five*
(10) Band Of Gold —*Freda Payne*

1971

(1) Joy To The World —*Three Dog Night*
(2) Maggie May —*Rod Stewart*
(3) It's Too Late/I Feel The Earth Move —*Carole King*
(4) How Can You Mend A Broken Heart —*Bee Gees*
(5) One Bad Apple —*The Osmonds*
(6) (The Lament of the Cherokee Reservation Indian) Indian Reservation —*The Raiders*
(7) Take Me Home, Country Road —*John Denver*
(8) Go Away Little Girl —*Donny Osmond*
(9) Just My Imagination (Running Away With Me) —*The Temptations*
(10) Knock Three Times —*Dawn*

World's heaviest primates: "morbidly" obese humans. After that: gorillas, at 485 lbs.

ABOMINABLE FACTS

Here's an interesting scenario: You're climbing Mt. Everest, and nature calls. You find a cave, take out your Bathroom Reader, and are lost in "thought" when suddenly, a big hairy creature appears in front of you. It's the Abominable Snowman! What do you do? Well, that's up to you— but our advice is, go ahead and give him the book. You can always get another one back in the States, and he's got nothing to read while he's...uh...you know. No wonder he's abominable.

HOW HE GOT HIS NAME

Abominable Snowman is a great name, but it actually means nothing; it was a mis-translation.

In 1921, Lt. Col. Charles Kenneth Howard-Bury was climbing in the Himalayas when he spotted a number of "dark forms" moving about on a snowfield above his party. But they were too far away to tell for sure what they were, and by the time the climbers reached the snowfield, the animals were gone. All that was left was a trail of some very large footprints.

Barking up the wrong tree
Howard-Bury thought the forms were large grey wolves; the sherpas with him described the animals as Meto-Kangmi or "snow creatures," a generic term used to describe a number of familiar animals that might have made the tracks.

Howard-Bury reported his findings to Katmandu, Nepal, and from there they were transmitted to London. In the process, something changed: meto-kangmi became metch-hangmi, which means "abominable snowman"—a meaningless, but intriguing phrase.

As Ivan Sandersen writes in *Abominable Snowmen,* "The result was like the explosion of an atom bomb. Nobody, and notably the press, could possibly pass up any such delicious term."

Articles on the "snowman" appeared in newspapers around the globe, turning the abominable snowman from a sleepy regional mystery into something that people were talking about all over the world. Ironically, because the creature was popularly referred

---

Mexico has more American residents than any other country except the United States.

to as a "snowman," it was assumed that it's white. Actually, people who claim to have seen it say its long, shaggy hair is reddish.

THE FIRST REPORT OF FOOTPRINTS

In 1889, Major L.A. Waddell, an English explorer, stumbled onto a trail of giant footprints in the snow while trekking through the Himalayas. The footprints were discovered on a mountain more than 17,000 feet above sea level. His native guides told him that they belonged to the Yeti, a vicious ape-like creature known to eat humans. The guides advised him to run downhill if attacked, because the creature's long hair blocked its vision when it ran downhill.

THE FIRST EVIDENCE

Eric Shipton, a mountain climber, was flying home from an expedition to Mount Everest in 1951. The flight out of Karachi, Pakistan, was uneventful—until the stewardess notified him that a throng of reporters would be waiting for him when the plane landed in London. He couldn't figure out what they wanted. Then he realized they were interested in some photos he'd taken on the Menlung Glacier and sent back home.

The photos in question had, in fact, captured the attention of the entire world. They depicted huge footprints in the snow—more than 13 inches wide and 18 inches long—that apparently belonged to a two-legged animal much larger than a human being. The only problem: no such animal is known to exist in the Himalayas. People speculated that Shipton had finally found proof that the Yeti, or abominable snowman exists.

OTHER SIGHTINGS

• In 1958, Dr. Alexander Pronin of Leningrad University reported seeing a humanoid creature in the Pamir mountains located mainly in Tajikistan. He watched the creature for more than three minutes before it ran away, and then saw it again the next day.

• In 1988, the Soviet news agency TASS reported that some researchers had come within 35 yards of an abominable snowman in the Pamir mountains. After the sighting the researchers planned a second trip into the region, but no further sign of the creature was ever found.

THE HILLARY EXPEDITION

In the late 1960s, Sir Edmund Hillary, the first man to conquer Mt. Everest, returned to the Himalayas to study human physiology at high altitudes. Before he left, he announced that he would investigate the question of the abominable snowman.

Sure enough, Hillary found some "Yeti tracks" in the snow. But as it turns out, they weren't made by a Yeti. In the shade, the tracks were small and had clearly been made by a fox...but wherever the tracks emerged from the shade and into the sunlight, they melted into enlarged, distorted footprints, creating the illusion that they had been made by an animal much larger than a fox. Hillary also noticed that when he let his own footprints melt, some of them grew to nearly a foot wide and two feet in length.

Later in the trip Hillary borrowed a "Yeti scalp" from a Buddhist monastery and had it examined. It turned out to be from a goatlike animal called a serow. Then he examined fur purportedly taken from a Yeti. It was from a Tibetan blue bear.

By the time he returned from the Himalayas, Hillary was convinced that Yetis were purely legendary animals.

THE SLICK EXPEDITION

In 1958, explorer Tom Slick visited the Pangboche monastery in Nepal and photographed a large, shrivelled hand that was kept there.

In 1959, the thumb and other parts of the hand were smuggled out of the country. Dr. Osman Hill of the London Zoological Society performed blood tests that showed the skin was "not human or from any known primate." Dr. Hill became convinced they were Neanderthal.

In 1991, the *Unsolved Mysteries* TV show had the fragments analyzed at the University of California biology laboratories in Los Angeles; these tests showed that the skin was not human, but that it was "close to human." In May 1991, someone broke into the Pangboche monastery and stole a Yeti skullcap and what was left of the Yeti hand. The monastery burned down a few months later.

Coincidence? Conspiracy? To this day, there is not a single shred of tangible, incontrovertible evidence that the Yeti exist. But many people believe it's just a matter of time.

About 10% of U.S. households pay their bills in cash.

RUMORS

Why do people believe wild, unsubstantiated stories? According to some psychologists, "rumors make things easier than they are." And besides, they're fun. Here are a few you might have heard.

RUMOR: If you mail your old sneakers to Nike, they'll send you a new pair free.
HOW IT SPREAD: Over the Internet, in 1998. An announcement sent via e-mail claimed Nike had started the promotion "to help make playgrounds for the underprivileged from old tennis shoes." It said: "Pass this e-mail to everyone you know so that everybody can help out." It also listed a mailing address for what it called the "Nike Recycling Center."
THE TRUTH: It was a fake. The address belonged to a Nike warehouse. Nike now receives an average of 100–150 pairs of old shoes a day at the warehouse, and public-minded corporations like Time-Warner began collecting old shoes for Nike until they learned it was a hoax.

RUMOR: Don't throw rice at weddings. Birds eat it, it expands in the stomachs, and they explode.
HOW IT SPREAD: Via the Ann Landers advice column. In 1996 Landers fell for the rumor and published a warning in her column. "Please throw rose petals instead," she implored her readers. "Rice is not good for the birds."
THE TRUTH: The USA Rice Federation, which admittedly has a vested interest in keeping the rice flying, sent an angry letter to Landers. "This silly myth pops up periodically, and it is absolutely unfounded," spokeswoman Mary Jo Cheesman insists.

RUMOR: The pre-printed label on your federal tax forms contains a secret code that tells the IRS auditors whether or not to audit you. If you throw the label away, you won't be audited.
HOW IT SPREAD: From one worried (and hopeful) taxpayer to another, especially in the weeks leading up to April 15.
THE TRUTH: The label is actually there to reduce processing costs, lower the risk for error, and speed the delivery of tax refunds. "It does contain coding information," says Mary Turville,

an accountant with the National Society of Accountants, "but it has to do with mail routes and the form package you used in the past. There is no way to trace your tax return from the label."

RUMOR: When the TV show *Green Acres* went off the air in 1971, the cast and crew killed Arnold the Pig and ate him at the farewell barbecue.

HOW IT SPREAD: In 1995 *Starweek* magazine published a letter from a Green Acres fan who wrote to complain about the alleged incident. "Arnold was a valuable member of the cast," the letter writer said. "Just because he was a pig was no reason to eat him. I had fond memories of *Green Acres*, but not now. I hope the cannibals burn in hell! Forever!" From there, the story took on a life of its own.

THE TRUTH: At least twelve different pigs played Arnold, and according to trainer Frank Inn, they all lived to old age and died of natural causes. Similar rumors circulated about the pigs that starred in the 1995 film *Babe*.

RUMOR: There's a seeing-eye dog in Germany named Lucky. He has led four of his owners to their deaths so far, but the agency that places him is making plans to give him to a fifth owner…without revealing Lucky's checkered past. "It would make Lucky nervous," trainer Ernst Gerber supposedly explained.

HOW IT SPREAD: The story is attributed to a newspaper called the *Europa Times*. It appeared in 1993. Since then it has spread via the Internet and word of mouth. "I admit it's not an impressive record," Gerber supposedly told the newspaper, explaining:

Lucky led his first owner in front of a bus, and the second off the end of a pier. He actually pushed his third owner off a railway platform…and he walked his fourth owner into heavy traffic, before abandoning him and running away to safety. But, apart from epileptic fits, he has a lovely temperament. And guide dogs are difficult to train these days….

THE TRUTH: It's a complete fabrication.

SCOOBY-DOO, WHERE ARE YOU?

Who's the most famous made-for-TV
cartoon character ever? It could be Scooby.

HOUSE OF MYSTERY

In 1969, Fred Silverman, daytime programming director at CBS, asked Bill Hanna and Joe Barbera, TV's most prolific animators, to develop an animated series called House of Mystery. It was supposed to be a supernatural/whodunit series based loosely on a combination of a 1940s radio show called *I Love a Mystery* (considered by critics to be the best radio serial ever) and the 1959–1963 sitcom *Dobie Gillis*, which centered around a group of teenagers.

Hanna-Barbera quickly created the characters. The show, was called *Mysteries Five*, then renamed *Who's S-s-s-cared?* It was to revolve around four teenagers and their dog (who at that time only had a small part). Silverman took the idea to New York and presented it to the top CBS brass. To his surprise, they rejected it. The reason: it was too frightening for little children. That posed a big problem to Silverman: he had already reserved his best Saturday morning slot for the show. He was determined to change their minds.

THE CHAIRMAN COMES THROUGH

Silverman spent most of his flight back to L.A. trying to figure out how on earth he would be able to sell the show. Finally, to relax, he put on his headphones. The first thing he heard was Frank Sinatra singing "Strangers in the Night"…which ends with the nonsense lyrics, "Scooby-Dooby-Doo." Silverman suddenly had an inspiration—that could be the dog's name. And if he made the dog the star of the show with the other characters supporting him, it would be funny rather than scary.

The CBS executives bought it, and Scooby Doo was born.

Henry Ford, father of the Model T, is also father of the charcoal briquet.

WHO'S WHO?

The final cast of characters for the show included:

• **Scooby-Doo, a Great Dane.** Don Messick, who voiced everyone from Bamm-Bamm to Papa Smurf in Hanna-Barbera cartoons, had to invent a new type of speech for Scooby. "I had to come up with what I call 'growl talk,'" he said. "The words were there. Joe [Barbera] liked things starting with R's, for the dogs especially. He got that from watching Soupy Sales in the early days." (Go ahead, say "Rooby-Rooby Roo"—you know you want to.)

• **Norville "Shaggy" Rogers,** Scoob's best friend, was based on Bob Denver's characterization of Maynard G. Krebs in Dobie Gillis. He was voiced by Top 40 deejay Casey Kasem. (Famous quote: "Zoiks!")

• **Velma Dinkley** (voice: Nicole Jaffe), the brains of the outfit, was blind as a bat without her glasses. Seemed to know every language on earth. (Famous quote, whenever she figured out a clue: "Jinkees!")

• **Daphne Blake** (voice: Heather North), the wealthy redheaded beauty who seemed to have no purpose on the show at all. Occasionally, she'd accidentally stumble on a clue. (Famous quote: "Oops!")

• **Freddie Jones** (voice: Frank Welker), the good-looking leader of the gang, who always made Shaggy do the dangerous stuff. (Famous quote: "We'll split up. Velma, you go with Scooby and Shaggy, and I'll go with Daphne.") Hm-m-m—maybe Daphne did have a purpose.

THE NUMBERS

The show was an instant success. It took over Saturday morning in the 1970s and eventually set a still-unbroken record as the longest running continuously-produced children's animated show. Eighteen years passed before television was without some new incarnation of Scooby-Doo. In all, there were eleven different series with the name "Scooby Doo" in them. The most recent series (1990) was A Pup Named Scooby-Doo. Ten other dogs appeared in the series, all related to Scooby. The most famous, but least liked, was Scooby's nephew, Scrappy-Doo. According to a recent poll on the Internet, Scrappy was the most annoying cartoon character of all time.

Time-killer: Check out the Internet to find numerous recipes for Scooby snacks.

HOW THE BALLPOINT PEN GOT ROLLING

Look carefully at the point of a ballpoint pen. There's a tiny little ball there, of course, which transports the ink from the ink reservoir onto the paper. It looks simple. But actually developing a workable ballpoint pen wasn't easy. Here's the story of how it became a "Bic" part of our lives, from Jack Mingo.

BACKGROUND

On October 30, 1888, John J. Loud of Massachusetts patented a "rolling-pointed fountain marker." It used a tiny, rotating ball bearing that was constantly bathed on one side in ink. That was the original ballpoint pen. Over the next thirty years, 350 similar ballpoint patents were issued by the U.S. Patent Office—but none of the products ever appeared on the market.

The main problem was getting the ink right. If it was too thin, the pens blotched on paper and leaked in pockets. If it was too thick, the pens clogged. Under controlled circumstances, it was sometimes possible to mix up a batch of ink that did what it was supposed to do... until the temperature changed. For decades, the state-of-the-art ballpoint would (usually) work fine at 70° F, but would clog at temperatures below 64° and leak and smear at temperatures above 77°.

OUR HEROES

That's how it was until the Biro brothers came along. In 1935, Ladislas Biro was editing a small newspaper in Hungary. He constantly found himself cursing his fountain pen; the ink soaked into newsprint like a sponge and the pen's tip shredded it. Eventually, he recruited his brother Georg, a chemist, to help him design a new pen. After trying dozens of new designs and ink formulations, the brothers—unaware that it had already been done at least 351 times before— "invented" the ballpoint pen.

A few months later, while they were vacationing at a Mediterranean resort, the brothers began chatting with an older gentleman about their new invention. They showed him a working model, and he was impressed. It turned out that the gentleman was Augustine Justo, the president of Argentina. He suggested that the Biros open a pen factory in his country. They declined…but when World War II began a few years later, they left Hungary and headed to South America. The Biros arrived in Buenos Aires with $10 between them.

Surprisingly, Justo remembered them and helped them find investors. In 1943, they set up a manufacturing plant. The results were spectacular—a spectacular failure, that is. They'd made the mistake everyone else had made—depending on gravity to move the ink onto the ball. That meant the pens had to be held straight up and down at all times. Even then, the ink flow was irregular and globby.

A PEN SAVED IS A PEN EARNED

Ladislas and Georg returned to the lab and came up with a new design. The ink was now siphoned toward the point no matter what position the pen was in. The Biros proudly introduced their new improved model in Argentina—but the pens still didn't sell. They ran out of money and stopped production.

That's when the U.S. Air Force came to the rescue. American flyers, sent to Argentina during the war, discovered that Biro ball-points worked upside down and at high altitudes. So the wartime U.S. State Department asked American manufacturers to make a similar pen. The Eberhard Faber Company paid $500,000 for the American rights in 1944, yielding the Biro brothers their first profitable year ever.

RIPOFF CITY

About this time, a Chicagoan named Milton Reynolds saw a Biro pen in Argentina. When he returned to the U.S., he discovered that similar pens had been patented years earlier. Since the patents had expired, he figured he could get away with copying the Biro design. He began stamping out pens and selling them for $12.50 each through Gimbels department store in New York City. They were such a novelty that Gimbel's entire stock—a total of 10,000 pens—sold out the first day. Other manufacturers jumped on the bandwagon.

The Reynolds Pen Company hired swimming star Esther Williams to show that the pen would write underwater. Other manufacturers showed their pens writing upside down or through stacks of a dozen pieces of carbon paper. But despite the hoopla,

Cool customers: The U.S. eastern seaboard consumes almost 50% of all ice cream sandwiches.

ballpoint pens still weren't dependable. They plugged up or leaked, ruining many documents and good shirts. People bought one, tried it, and—frustrated—vowed never to buy another ballpoint as long as they lived. Sales plummeted.

LA PLUME DE MARCEL

Meanwhile, Marcel Bich, a French manufacturer of penholders and cases, watched with professional interest as the ballpoint industry took off and then crashed. He was impressed by the ballpoint pen's innovative design, but appalled by the high cost and low quality. He realized that if he could come up with a dependable, reasonably priced pen, he could take over the market. So he licensed the Biro brothers' patents, and began experimenting.

For two years, he bought every ballpoint pen on the market and systematically tested them, looking for their strengths and weaknesses. Then in 1949, Bich unveiled his triumph: an inexpensive ballpoint with a six-sided, clear plastic case. It wrote smoothly and didn't leak or jam. They were a huge hit in Europe.

Looking ahead, he knew that his name would eventually be a problem in America. Rather than risk having his product referred to as a "Bitch Pen," he simplified his name so it would be pronounced correctly no matter where it was sold— "Bic."

CONQUERING AMERICA

In 1958, Bic set up shop in the U.S. As it turned out, it wasn't his name that proved a problem—it was those shoddy pens people had bought a decade earlier. The American public had come to trust expensive pens, but refused to believe a 29¢ pen would really work.

So Bic launched an ad campaign to demonstrate that his pens would work the "first time, every time." He flooded the airwaves with TV commercials—many live—showing that Bic pens still worked after "being shot from guns, drilled through wallboard, fire-blasted, and strapped to the feet of ice-skaters and flamenco dancers." He also began selling them in grocery stores, and little shops near schools, where he knew students would see them.

The result: By 1967, Bic was selling 500 million pens—60% of the U.S. market. His competitors also began selling cheap, high-quality pens...and ballpoints were changed forever.

As *Time* magazine said in 1972: "Baron Bich has done for ballpoints what Henry Ford did for cars."

Good taste: Mosquitoes prefer children to adults, blondes to brunettes.

HE SAID, SHE SAID

Ronald B. Schwartz collected these gems in his book,
Men are Lunatics, Women are Nuts!

"There's no such thing as a man...Just a little boy in a man's body."
—**Elvis Presley**

"If you want anything said, ask a man. If you want anything done, ask a woman."
—**Margaret Thatcher**

"If you want to resist the feminist movement, the simple way to do it is to give them what they want and they'll defeat themselves. Today, there are women who don't know if they want to be a mother, have lunch, or be secretary of state."
—**Jack Nicholson**

"A man's home may seem to be a castle on the outside; inside, it's often his nursery."
—**Clare Booth Luce**

"I require three things in a man. He must be handsome, ruthless, and stupid."
—**Dorothy Parker**

"As long as you know that most men are children, you know everything."
—**Coco Chanel**

"The best way to get most husbands to do something is to suggest that perhaps they're too old to do it."
—**Shirley MacLaine**

"If men can run the world, why can't they stop wearing neckties? How intelligent is it to start the day by tying a little noose around your neck?"
—**Linda Ellerbee**

"Talking with a man is like trying to saddle a cow. You work like hell, but what's the point."
—**Gladys Upham**

"Men are gluttons for punishment. They fight over women for the chance to fight with them."
—**Vincent Price**

* * *

"Marriage is a three ring circus: engagement ring, wedding ring, and suffering."—**Anonymous**

Get out the stomach pump: Sales of Rolaids, Alka-Seltzer, and Tums jump 20% in December.

THE WORLD'S TALLEST BUILDINGS, PART III

*Here's the story of how New York became the skyscraper
capital of the world. (Part II is on Page 137.)*

NEW YORK'S FIRST SKYSCRAPER
In 1888, a young silk manufacturer named John Noble
Stearns bought a skinny strip of land in lower Manhattan. He wanted to build something on it, but wasn't sure what. He
just knew he wanted to make a lot of money.

It happened that Stearns' architect was familiar with the
skeleton-construction method becoming popular in Chicago. He
suggested constructing an 11-story building 159 feet long, 158 feet
tall...but only 21-1/2 feet wide. Stearns liked the idea, and work
on the Tower Building, New York's first true skyscraper, began.

White Elephant
The Tower Building was so flat and thin that many people were
afraid it would blow over in the first high wind. Stearns' friends
laughed at him when the building went up, and they refused to go
inside when it was finished. Nobody wanted to be in it when it
finally fell over.

But when several months passed and the Tower Building
didn't collapse, people began venturing in and climbing to the
eleventh floor, one of the highest points in the entire city. New
York's love affair with tall buildings had begun.

UP, UP AND AWAY
The subsequent growth of the New York City skyline mirrored the
improvements in elevator technology. From 1841 to 1894, the
tallest building in the city was Trinity Church on lower Broadway,
which had a steeple 284 feet high. For a few cents you could climb
the rickety wooden staircase inside the steeple and take in the
highest view the city had to offer.

But in the 1890s, after the Otis brothers had perfected the
first electric elevator, a burst of new construction completely
transformed the business district of Manhattan. In 1894, the

17-story Manhattan Life Insurance Building became the first to top Trinity Church, making it the tallest building east of Chicago. It was quickly followed by scores of other skyscrapers, including the 21-story American Surety Building, the 23-story American Tract Society Building, and the 32-story Park Row Building—which, at 391 feet, finally beat out Chicago to make New York City the home of the tallest building on Earth.

THE SKYSCRAPER RACE

The Park Row Building was only the beginning. As George Douglas writes in *Skyscrapers: A Social History in America:*

> New York hadn't seen anything yet. In the years between 1900 and the First World War…skyscrapers rose like tall grasses on the summer prairie….New York business leaders came to see in the skyscraper not only convenient and economical office space, but a possible means of corporate glory and aggrandizement. A great tower, obviously, could not only house management but glorify it.

The Singer Building

In the 1890s, the Singer Sewing Machine Company built a 10-story office building at Broadway and Liberty St. in Manhattan. They added to the building repeatedly over the years, and in 1906 announced the addition of a 612-foot-tall, 47-story tower that would be "higher than all existing skyscrapers by 200 to 300 feet."

The building also boasted every state-of-the-art convenience the early 1900s had to offer: centralized steam heat complete with individual thermostats, a central vacuum cleaning system, hot and cold running water in every office, and 16 elevators—more than in any other building in the world.

The tower opened on May 1, 1908, and held the title of the world's tallest building for a mere 18 months. Sixty years later this precious architectural gem set another record: it became the tallest building ever demolished, when it was razed to make way for the "banal and colorless" United States Steel Building.

The Metropolitan Life Building

Next on the list of "tallest buildings in the world" was the Metropolitan Life Building, which in 1909, became the first office building to pass the 700-foot mark. It was 88 feet higher than the Singer Building.

giant crayon 35' wide and 100' taller than the Statue of Liberty.

The land and the building cost an astronomical $6 million, a shocking sum that was difficult for Metropolitan's conservative shareholders to stomach. But the head of Metropolitan justified the expense by explaining that since the building was fully occupied, it cost almost nothing in the long run...and generated invaluable free advertising for the company.

Metropolitan capitalized on its headquarters in ways the Singer company never dreamed of: It made the massive lantern at the very top of the pointed roof into its corporate symbol, as well as the inspiration for the company's slogan, "The light that never fails." And on election night in 1908, it even used the beacon to beam the results of the presidential election out to the rest of the city.

The Metropolitan Building still stands, and is still the home office of the Metropolitan Life Insurance Company.

JUST THE BEGINNING

Both the Singer Tower and the Metropolitan Life Tower were impressive sights to behold, but the first building to really capture the public's imagination—and cement its love affair with the skyscraper—was the Woolworth Building, a magnificent 60-story edifice that to this day is considered one of the most beautiful skyscrapers ever built.

For that story, turn to page 200.

* * *

RANDOM "THOUGHTS"

"It is wonderful to be here in the great state of Chicago."

—*Former U. S. Vice-President Dan Quayle*

"The streets are safe in Philadelphia. It's only the people that make them unsafe."

—*Former Philadelphia Mayor Frank Rizzo*

The BBC reported in 1964 that Ringo Starr had his toenails removed. It was really his tonsils.

THE TOP 10 HITS OF THE YEAR, 1972–1975

Here's another installment of BRI's Top Ten of the Year list.

1972

(1) The First Time Ever I Saw Your Face —*Roberta Flack*
(2) Alone Again (Naturally) —*Gilbert O'Sullivan*
(3) American Pie —*Don McLean*
(4) I Gotcha —*Joe Tex*
(5) Candy Man —*Sammy Davis, Jr.*
(6) Without You —*Nilsson*
(7) Lean On Me —*Bill Withers*
(8) Brand New Key —*Melanie*
(9) Baby Don't Get Hooked On Me —*Mac Davis*
(10) Daddy, Don't You Walk So Fast —*Wayne Newton*

1973

(1) Tie A Yellow Ribbon Round The Old Oak Tree —*Tony Orlando and Dawn*
(2) Bad, Bad Leroy Brown —*Jim Croce*
(3) Let's Get It On —*Marvin Gaye*
(4) Killing Me Softly With His Song —*Roberta Flack*
(5) My Love —*Paul McCartney / Wings*
(6) Why Me —*Kris Kristofferson*
(7) Will It Go Round In Circles —*Billy Preston*
(8) Crocodile Rock —*Elton John*
(9) You're So Vain —*Carly Simon*
(10) Touch Me In The Morning —*Diana Ross*

1974

(1) The Way We Were —*Barbra Steisand*
(2) Seasons In The Sun —*Terry Jacks*
(3) Come And Get Your Love —*Redbone*
(4) Love's Theme —*Love Unlimited Orchestra*
(5) Dancing Machine —*Jackson Five*
(6) The Loco-Motion —*Grand Funk Railroad*
(7) The Streak —*Ray Stevens*
(8) TSOP —*MFSB*
(9) Bennie And The Jets —*Elton John*
(10) One Hell Of A Woman —*Mac Davis*

1975

(1) Love Will Keep Us Together — *The Captain & Tennille*
(2) Rhinestone Cowboy —*Glen Campbell*
(3) Philadelphia Freedom —*Elton John*
(4) Shining Star —*Earth, Wind & Fire*
(5) My Eyes Adored You —*Frankie Valli*
(6) Before The Next Teardrop Falls —*Freddy Fender*
(7) Fame —*David Bowie*
(8) One Of These Nights —*Eagles*
(9) Laughter In The Rain —*Neil Sedaka*
(10) Thank God I'm A Country Boy —*John Denver*

Supermarket News: The top 3 products for coupon redemption are cold cereal, soap, and deodorant.

YOUR GOVERNMENT AT WORK

Concerned about the government's priorities? Now you can breathe a sigh of relief, knowing your tax dollars are being well-spent on things like...

• Real estate. "In 1986 the National Park Service bought a half acre of land in southwest Washington, D.C., for $230,000. In 1988 someone discovered that the Park Service already owned the land—they bought it in 1914." *(Great Government Goofs)*

• Streamlining the Pentagon. "During the 1980s Department of Defense efficiency experts saved between $27 million and $136 million each year! However, the efficiency experts cost between $150 million and $300 million each year." *(Stupid Government Tricks)*

• Physical fitness. "When $122 million was allocated for an addition to the Dirksen Office Building in Washington, D.C., it went to give the senators a third gymnasium." *(Goofy Government Grants & Wacky Waste)*

• Reimbursement. "According to a 1989 report by the State Department Watch, a private watchdog organization, the Department of State issued eighteen thousand travel expense checks without getting corroborating evidence for the expenses. One check for $9,000 was issued to 'Ludwig van Beethoven,' whose Social Security number was listed as '123–45–6789.'" *(Stupid Government Tricks)*

• Sociology. "$84,000 [was] approved by Congress for a project to discover why people fall in love." *(Great Government Goofs)*

• Fighting Poverty. $5 million was approved by Congress as an interest-free loan to Sears, Roebuck under the federal "antipoverty" funds program. *(Great Government Goofs)*

• Space travel. "The National Aeronautics and Space Administration spent $23 million to build a prototype toilet for the space

Peter Dowdeswell holds 25 records for speed-eating, including eating 1 lb. of eels in 13.7 seconds.

shuttle—a 900% increase over the original estimate. Why the overrun? The astronauts wanted a manual flush rather than an automatic one." *(From Goofy Government Grants & Wacky Waste)*

• Natural history. "$107,000 was appropriated by Congress for a project to study the sex life of the Japanese quail." *(Great Government Goofs)*

• "The Illinois Department of Conservation spent $180,000 to study the contents of owl vomit." *(Great Government Goofs)*

• Medical research. "In 1993 the Physicians Committee for Responsible Medicine termed 'outlandish' a $3 million federally funded research project to determine whether marijuana will make rabbits more susceptible to syphilis and mice more prone to contract Legionnaires' disease." *(Stupid Government Tricks)*

• On-the-spot research. "More than $7 million is spent each year by politicians on junkets to popular vacation spots around the world. It's called 'business travel.' As a matter of fact, when the government's fiscal year is about to run out, there's an estimated 48% increase in government business travel." *(Goofy Government Grants & Wacky Waste)*

*   *   *

AND SPEAKING OF DUMB...

News of the Weird reports that "Annette Montoya, 11, of Belen, New Mexico, and her parents were arrested for forgery after Annette, in the company of her father, attempted to open a bank account with a $900,000 check. The girl told sheriff's deputies that she earned the money doing 'some yard work.' During the interrogation, she crossed her heart and said, 'Hope to die if I'm lying.'"

From the BRI files: Lagos, Nigeria—Two small buses collided when their drivers tried to slap each others' hands in greeting, the News Agency of Nigeria reported. Seven people died; the two drivers were among them.

DAEDALUS AND ICARUS

This Greek tale about man's first attempt to fly is still used today to illustrate both the dangers of hubris and the impetuous nature of youth. This version is from Myths and Legends of the Ages.

On the island of Crete, during the reign of King Minos, there lived a most skillful artisan named Daedalus. Daedalus was the greatest inventor and craftsman of his time, and his fame spread to the far corners of the world.

It was Daedalus who built the famous labyrinth in which King Minos kept that terrible beast, the Minotaur. This labyrinth was a building with hundreds of winding halls and passages so complicated that no one who went into it could ever find his way out again.

But although Daedalus performed great services for King Minos, the king feared him. Minos was afraid that Daedalus, with his great wisdom and skill, might some-day gain the throne of Crete. So King Minos imprisoned Daedalus and his young son, Icarus, in a dark stone tower.

But no locks could hold Daedalus! For he could open them all. And one dark night,

Daedalus and Icarus escaped from the tower.

After they had fled, Daedalus and Icarus did not find it so easy to escape from Crete. You see, Crete is an island, and King Minos had his soldiers search every ship that left its shores.

Daedalus and Icarus lay in hiding in a cave along the seashore. One bright day, Daedalus was idly watching the seagulls soaring and swooping over the water in their search for food. Suddenly, an idea struck him.

"King Minos may control the land and the sea," he cried, "but he does not control the air. That is how Icarus and I shall escape."

Then Daedalus set to work to study the birds and learn the secret of their flight. For endless hours he watched the birds flying. He caught a bird and studied the clever structure of its wings. Then he put to use his knowledge and skill to copy the wings of a bird. The boy,

Last 2 European countries to let women vote: Switzerland (1971) and Leichtenstein (1984).

Icarus, spent his days trapping the seagulls and plucking their feathers. Daedalus took the feathers which his son had obtained, and sewed them together with marvelous skill. Soon, wings began to take shape, so wonderfully made that, except for their great size, they looked exactly like the real wings of a bird. And then Daedalus took these wings, and with melted wax attached them to a wooden framework.

When he had made a pair of wings for himself and a pair of wings for his son, Daedalus fastened them in place. A wing was strapped to each arm. Then Daedalus proceeded to teach his son to fly, just as a mother bird teaches her young. How happy and excited young Icarus was when he found that he could fly through the air, that he could circle and float on the wind! He was impatient to be off.

Finally the time came when Daedalus felt they were ready to make the escape from Crete. He turned to his young son and said, "Icarus, listen carefully to my words. Follow close behind me in your flight. Do not fly too low or the dampness from the sea will cling to your wings and make them too heavy for you to lift. Do not fly too high or the sun will melt the wax of your wings."

Then Daedalus kissed his son fondly and began to rise into the air. Icarus followed his father. As the two of them flew across the sky, people looked up in amazement. The ploughmen in the fields gazed upward, the shepherds marveled! They thought they were watching the flight of gods.

At first, Icarus stayed close behind his father. But then, exalting in his new-found power, he flew off on little side trips. Soon he forgot everything his father told him and flew high into the heavens.

Then the blazing sun did its work and the wax of his wings melted. Icarus fluttered his arms, but there were not enough feathers left to beat the air. He called his father, but in vain. Down he fell into the sea!

Daedalus sped to the aid of his son, but when he saw the feathers floating on the ocean, he knew to his grief that Icarus had been drowned. So ended man's first attempt to fly; for Daedalus, heartbroken at the loss of his son, flew on to Sicily, took off his wings and never flew again.

Cats' urine glows under a blacklight.

NAME YOUR POISON

*You may not like the products…but it's always interesting
to find out where familiar brand names come from.*

Pall Mall cigarettes: Named for one of the most fashionable streets in London. The British pronunciation is "Pell Mell."

Cutty Sark scotch: Named after the clipper ship that won a trans-Atlantic sailing race in the 1870s.

Lucky Strike cigarettes: Dr. R. A. Patterson, a Virginia doctor, gave the name to plug tobacco that he sold to miners during the California Gold Rush of 1856. It was first introduced as a cigarette in 1917.

Bourbon whiskey: When Louis XVI of the Bourbon dynasty of France assisted the struggling colonists during the Revolutionary War, they named a region of Virginia and Kentucky Bourbon County in his honor. The county later became the birthplace of bourbon whiskey.

Chesterfield cigarettes: Named after the 4th Earl of Chesterfield, 18th-century trend-setting socialite. The Chesterfield couch and jacket are also named after him.

Old Crow scotch: Named in 1835 after Dr. James Crow, the Scottish surgeon and chemist who introduced sanitation and modern distillation methods to the domestic whiskey industry.

Kent cigarettes: Herbert A. Kent, a Lorillard Tobacco Company executive, was so popular at the office that the company named Kent cigarettes after him in 1952.

White Horse scotch: Originally served in the White Horse Inn in Edinburgh, Scotland.

I. W. Harper whiskey: When Isaac W. Bernheim and his brother started a whiskey business in 1872, they named their product I. W. Harper—I. W. for Bernheim's initials…and Harper after their star salesman. The firm's customers already called it Mr. Harper's whiskey. Bernheim figured there was no point in tampering with a well established name.

CAUGHT IN THE SPOTLIGHT

Everyone wants to be famous these days—but sometimes people forget that it's not always a good idea. Take these guys—they hopped into the limelight…and ended up making headlines they wished they hadn't.

HEADLINE: *Man Wins Largest Prize in Game Show's History…and Free Trip to Jail*
The Story: In December 1987, a man identifying himself as "Patrick Quinn" went on the TV game show Super Password and won $58,600, the largest one-day jackpot in the show's history.
Caught: The show aired on January 8, 1988…and within minutes phones at the Password offices began to ring. "We started getting calls from people…saying, 'That's not Patrick Quinn, there is no Patrick Quinn,'" executive producer Bob Sherman told reporters.

The man was actually Kerry Ketcham, who was wanted by the Secret Service for faking a $100,000 life insurance claim on his wife (who had not died). When Ketcham showed up at the Super Password offices to pick up his check, he was arrested. He pled guilty to two counts of mail fraud…and forfeited his winnings from the show. Reason: he gave a false name when applying to be a contestant.

HEADLINE: *Man Loses Nearly $10 million in Lottery; Wins Prison Sentence.*
The Story: On October 19, 1990, a real estate executive named Joseph A. Sutera won the "Mass Millions" prize in the Massachusetts lottery, collecting a jackpot of $9,916,540 to be paid out in annual installments over 20 years.
Caught: Years earlier, Sutera had swindled hundreds of seniors in Connecticut, Rhode Island, New Hampshire, and other states out of their retirement savings in bogus real estate deals. When Sutera won the lottery, more than a thousand swindled retirees spotted his name in news stories. So many claims were filed against the

---

First four countries to have television: England, the U.S., the U.S.S.R., and Brazil.

winnings that Sutera was forced into bankruptcy. A federal judge awarded Sutera's winnings to his victims in 1994. By then, Sutera was already serving a five-year prison sentence on federal fraud charges.

HEADLINE: *Large Donor at Political Fundraiser Earns a Seat at President Bush's Table...and a Ticket to Jail.*

The Story: On April 28, 1992, Los Angeles businessman Michael Kojima contributed $500,000 to a Republican Party Fundraiser called "The President's Dinner" for then-President George Bush, who was pushing "Family Values" as a major theme in his campaign. That made Kojima the largest contributor at the event (which raised a record $9 million in one night, the largest political fundraiser ever) and earned him a spot at President Bush's table. He appeared in photographs and news footage broadcast around the world.

Caught: Los Angeles prosecutors immediately recognized Kojima as the man dubbed "America's Most-Wanted Deadbeat Dad," wanted on a fugitive warrant for failing to pay more than $200,000 in child support to two of his five ex-wives. According to the *Los Angeles Times*, Kojima "had eluded investigators for four months, moving frequently and living under assumed names."

Authorities arrested him a few days later as he was preparing to leave on vacation with his sixth wife. But rather than turn the money over to Mrs. Kojima and her children, Republican fundraisers put the $500,000 in an escrow account and asked a judge to decide who should get the money, while maintaining that the party "has a valid interest in and is entitled to the political contributions." In the end, the GOP got to hang on to about half of the money.

HEADLINE: *Hijacked Honeymooners Receive Key to City; Trip to Prison.*

The Story: In 1977, Jerry and Darlene Jenkins of Burlington, Vermont, were honeymooning in New York City when a mentally ill man hijacked their car and took them on a terrifying ride that ended when the car jumped a curb and plowed into a crowd of people, killing one pedestrian and injuring 12 others.

Most sought after Cracker Jack prizes: toy rings. Reason: they're often used as engagement rings.

New Yorkers were so shocked by the senselessness of the crime that they showered the couple with dinner invitations, tickets to Broadway plays, and free hotel rooms paid for by the *New York Daily News,* the New York Telephone Company, and other big corporations. Mayor Abraham Beame even had the couple over to City Hall, where he presented them with a public apology and an engraved silver plate.

Caught: The incident made headlines all over the country, including Burlington, Vermont—where law enforcement officials recognized Jerry Jenkins as the man who was wanted for passing more than $2,500 worth of bad checks in area stores. And, as *The Washington Post* reported a week later, "there was some question as to whether the couple was even married. His woman companion, who previously identified herself as his 21-year-old bride, Darlene, apparently left New York for parts unknown." Jenkins was arrested.

ON THE OTHER HAND...

HEADLINE: *Viewers of "America's Most Wanted" TV Show Nab Another Desperado.*

The Story: David Adams, a Tennessee man wanted in connection with a number of fraud and arson cases, was nabbed at a Nashville country fair after two women recognized him from an "America's Most Wanted" episode that had aired two days earlier. The women alerted park rangers, who took Adams into custody.

Caught: "David Adams" turned out to be actor Christopher Cotton, the man hired by "America's Most Wanted" to portray the crook in the show's crime reenactment sequences.

Cotton showed proof of identification to the rangers, but it didn't win his release—at least not right away. According to news reports, "Adams had often used fake identification and disguises to elude authorities, so the authorities had to take Cotton into custody until a photo and fingerprints could be compared."

"I guess it's an occupational hazard," Cotton told reporters, "but I never expected it. You never know how people are going to react to television."

The first language of African-American heroine Sojourner Truth was Dutch.

BEGINNINGS

At the BRI, we enjoy finding out where things come from.
Here are some items we picked at random:

THE SQUARE HANDKERCHIEF

Among her many eccentricities, Marie Antoinette hated the fact that handkerchiefs came in so many sizes and shapes. She decided that she liked the square ones the best, and, in 1785, she had her husband, Louis XVI, issue a law that henceforth, "the length of handkerchiefs shall equal their width, throughout my entire kingdom." Non-square handkerchiefs have been hard to find ever since.

ERASERS

In 1770, an American friend gave renowned English scientist Joseph Priestly a ball made out of a material Priestly had never seen before. He observed that the material, which was sap from a South American tree, could rub away pencil marks from paper, so he called it "rubber." It wasn't until the discovery of vulcanized rubber in 1839 that rubber erasers became practical, and even then it took another 20 years before a Philadelphia inventor named Hyman Lipman patented the first pencil with an eraser.

AIRLINE STEWARDESSES

Before 1930, only men served on airplane crews. Then, Ellen Church, a nurse and student pilot, convinced United Airlines that having females on board would help ticket sales...but not for the reason you'd think: "Don't you think it would be good psychology to have women up in the air?" she asked the directors. "How is a man going to say he is afraid to fly when a woman is working on the plane?" United agreed and told her to hire seven women. The women had to be under 5'4" and 115 pounds, age 25 or less, single, and—registered nurses. Their wage: $125 a month for each 100 hours in the air. On top of serving passengers, the first stewardesses also had to help the crew clean the plane, load the baggage, gas the plane, and push it from the hangar.

More people have seen David Copperfield perform live than any other performer in the world.

RED BARNS

BRI-member Douglas Ottati sends us this information: "Why are barns painted red? In the early nineteenth century, farmers learned that the color red absorbed sunlight extremely well and was useful in keeping barns warm during winter. The farmers made their red paint from skim milk mixed with the rust shavings of metal fences and nails."

GUIDE DOGS

It probably seems as though seeing-eye dogs have been around forever. Actually, they are a 20th-century development.

Near the end of World War I, a doctor and his dog were walking the grounds of a German military hospital with a soldier who'd lost his sight in the war. The doctor stepped inside the hospital for a minute. When he returned, he found that the dog had led the soldier around the grounds on its own. That inspired him to do some experiments. When the doctor showed that he had successfully trained dogs to lead the blind, the German government lent its support. Later, an American named Dorothy Eustis visited Germany to see the trained dogs, and wrote an article about it in *The Saturday Evening Post*. In 1929, the first school for seeing-eye dogs was set up in the U.S.

BASEBALL'S "MOST VALUABLE PLAYER" AWARD

According to *Wheels of a Nation*, by Frank Donovan, the award started out as an effort to publicize a now-forgotten car called the Chalmers: "Hugh Chalmers announced in 1910 that he would give a car to the champion batters of each league. He was delighted when Ty Cobb, a Detroiter, won the American League championship. But his elation turned to fury when Cobb promptly sold his prize."

THE RUBBER BAND

In 1820, Thomas Hancock, an Englishman, was given a bottle made of rubber by some Central American Indians. He cut it into strips and created the first rubber bands (although he sold them as garters and waistbands).

MYTH AMERICA

*Here are a few "facts" about the Wild West that you may
have heard...which are 100% baloney. Most of the information
is from Bill Bryson's excellent book,* Made in America.

THE MYTH: Cowboys talked like cowboys—they said things like "get along little dogie," and "I've got an itchy trigger finger."
THE TRUTH: A lot of the words associated with cowboys were invented by novelists and movie scriptwriters, and not until long after the age of the cowboy had passed. Motherless calves were not called dogies until 1903, jails didn't become hoosegows until 1920, and the expressions bounty hunter, gunslinger, and I've got an itchy trigger finger were all invented in Hollywood.

MYTH: Settlers traveled west in huge Conestoga wagons pulled by horses.
THE TRUTH: Conestoga wagons were too heavy, and horses were too weak, for the long trip west. Settlers used smaller, nimbler wagons called prairie schooners, and they pulled them with mules or oxen, which were stronger and hardier than horses.

MYTH: Wagon trains traveled in straight, single-file lines across the prairies.
THE TRUTH: The trip across much of America was so dusty, Bryson writes, that whenever possible, wagons "fanned out into an advancing line up to ten miles wide to avoid each other's dust and the ruts of earlier travelers."

MYTH: If your wagon train was attacked by Indians, the way you defended yourself was by circling the wagons.
THE TRUTH: Another invention of Hollywood filmmakers, who liked the way circled wagons looked on film. The wagons didn't circle, Bryson writes, "for the simple reason that the process would have been so laborious and time consuming to organize that the participants would very probably have been slaughtered long before the job was accomplished." Some wagon trains did circle

---

The 5 smartest primates, after humans: chimpanzees, gorillas, orangutans, baboons, and gibbons.

when they stopped at night, but not specifically for protection. They needed a way to corral the animals.

MYTH: If you wanted to make it as a gunfighter in the Old West, you had to be man enough to take a bullet in the shoulder or thigh, and keep on shooting.
THE TRUTH: Taking a bullet "like a man" is such a standard plot device in cowboy novels that, as one film critic put it, "One would think that the human shoulder was made of some self-healing material, rather like a puncture-proof tire." Actually, most people who were shot never got up again. Bullets were slower and softer in the 19th century—which sounds nice, but can actually make them more lethal. Instead of shooting straight through the body and exiting quickly out the other end, they tend to bounce around like a pinball, then exit "with a hole like a fist punched through paper," Bryson writes. "Even if they miraculously missed the victim's vital organs, he would almost invariably suffer deep and incapacitating shock and bleed to death within minutes."

MYTH: As marshall of Dodge City, Wyatt Earp helped tame the Wild West.
THE TRUTH: Earp was never the marshall of Dodge City. He did serve two terms as deputy marshall, but according to historian Peter Lyon in American Heritage, the only reason he took the job was because it was good for his gambling career. "Every professional gambler needed a star," Lyon writes. "The badge of office permitted its wearer to carry a gun....Only peace officers were permitted to carry guns in Dodge City; all others were obliged to check their weapons in racks provided for that purpose." Wyatt wasn't even an honest card player, let alone a standup lawman, which may be why he wanted a gun. According to historian Floyd Streeter, Earp had a reputation for being "up to some dishonest trick every time he played."

"There's two ways for a fellow to look for adventure:
By tearing everything down, or building everything up."
—The Lone Ranger

THE TOP 10 HITS OF THE YEAR, 1976–1979

Here's another Top Ten of the Year list.

1976
(1) Silly Love Songs
    —*Paul McCartney / Wings*
(2) Don't Go Breaking My Heart
    —*Elton John / Kiki Dee*
(3) Disco Lady —*Johnnie Taylor*
(4) December, 1963 (Oh, What
    A Night) —*The Four Seasons*
(5) Kiss And Say Goodbye
    —*The Manhattans*
(6) Play That Funky Music
    —*Wild Cherry*
(7) 50 Ways To Leave Your Lover
    —*Paul Simon*
(8) Love Machine, Pt. 1
    —*Miracles*
(9) Love Is Alive —*Gary Wright*
(10) A Fifth Of Beethoven
    —*Walter Murphy & The Big
    Apple Band*

1977
(1) Tonight's The Night
    —*Rod Stewart*
(2) I Just Want To Be Your Every-
    thing —*Andy Gibb*
(3) Best Of My Love —*Emotions*
(4) Love Theme From "A Star Is
    Born" —*Barbra Streisand*
(5) I Like Dreamin'
    —*Kenny Nolan*
(6) Angel In Your Arms —*Hot*
(7) Don't Leave Me This Way
    —*Thelma Houston*
(8) Higher and Higher
    —*Rita Coolidge*

(9) Torn Between Two Lovers
    —*Mary MacGregor*
(10) Undercover Angel
    —*Alan O'Day*

1978
(1) Shadow Dancing
    —*Andy Gibb*
(2) Stayin' Alive —*The Bee Gees*
(3) You Light Up My Life
    —*Debby Boone*
(4) Night Fever —*The Bee Gees*
(5) Kiss You All Over —*Exile*
(6) How Deep Is Your Love
    —*The Bee Gees*
(7) Baby Come Back —*Player*
(8) (Love Is) Thicker Than
    Water —*Andy Gibb*
(9) Three Times A Lady
    —*The Commodores*
(10) Boogie Oogie Oogie
    —*A Taste Of Honey*

1979
(1) My Sharona —*The Knack*
(2) Bad Girls —*Donna Summer*
(3) Reunited —*Peaches And Herb*
(4) Do Ya Think I'm Sexy?
    —*Rod Stewart*
(5) Le Freak —*Chic*
(6) Y.M.C.A. —*The Village People*
(7) Hot Stuff —*Donna Summer*
(8) I Will Survive
    —*Gloria Gaynor*
(9) Ring My Bell —*Anita Ward*
(10) Sad Eyes —*Robert John*

Uh-oh. The population of Earth has more than doubled since 1950.

THE CLASSIFIEDS

Have you ever been in a place where all you can find to read in the bathroom is an old newspaper? Try this: just flip to the classifieds and look for funny goofs like these. Most were collected by Richard Lederer for his book Fractured English.

FOR SALE

An antique desk suitable for lady with thick legs and large drawers.

GREAT DAMES FOR SALE

Four-poster bed, 101 years old. Perfect for antique lover.

Pit Bull For Sale: Owner deceased.

Eight puppies from a German Shepherd and an Alaskan Hussy.

WANTED

Looking for hanging cage for my daughter. Must have exercise wheel.

Unmarried girls to pick fresh fruit and produce at night.

Girl wanted to assist magician in cutting-off-head illusion. Salary and Blue Cross.

Preparer of food. Must be dependable, like the food business and be willing to get hands dirty.

Man wanted to work in dynamite factory. Must be willing to travel.

Hard working, experienced farm woman. Household and field work; know how to cook; must own tractor—send photo of tractor.

Hair-cutter. Excellent growth potential.

MISCELLANEOUS

Lost: Beagle, partly blind, hard of hearing, castrated; answers to the name of Lucky.

For rent: 6-room hated apartment

Illiterate? Write today for free help.

The license fee for altered dogs with a certificate will be $3 and for pets owned by senior citizens who have not been altered the fee will be $1.50.

Free—Three Kittens: Siamese coloring. Will do yard work. To a loving home only.

THE WORLD'S TALLEST BUILDINGS, PART IV

Here's the story of how F.W. Woolworth used nickels and dimes
to pay for one of the most popular skyscrapers ever constructed.
(Part III on page 182.)

KING OF COMMERCE

At the turn of the century, Frank Winfield Woolworth was one of the richest merchants in the world. And every penny of his fortune was earned in nickels and dimes.

Woolworth had opened the world's first "5 & 10 Cent Store" in 1879. As the name implied, he priced everything at either a nickel or a dime—and started a revolution in retailing. With that kind of pricing, he didn't need skilled (or high-salaried) salespeople; customers just picked out what they wanted and brought it to the register. Shoppers flooded his store with business. Woolworth had five stores by 1886, 28 by 1895, and 59 by 1900. In 1910, he merged with several rivals to create a retailing empire with more than 600 stores.

MONUMENT TO EXCESS

In 1909, Woolworth decided to build a magnificent world headquarters to commemorate his rags-to-riches story. He bought a plot of land on Broadway in lower Manhattan and commissioned architect Cass Gilbert to build what would later be dubbed a "cathedral of commerce"—the tallest building in the world.

Woolworth had an enormous ego, which is one reason he wanted his building to be taller than the Metropolitan Tower. But he may have had a more personal reason for knocking Metropolitan out of the #1 slot: revenge. Earlier in his career, Metropolitan had turned Woolworth down for a loan. Dwarfing the Metropolitan Tower with his own Woolworth building would be his way of evening the score.

Opposition

The Woolworth building would eventually become one of the most beloved buildings in the world; but during construction it

Switzerland has the highest per-capita consumption of soft drinks in the world.

made a lot of enemies. The industry journal *Engineering Record* was a particularly adamant critic, and in its pages it argued that construction of the building should be halted. It warned of what would happen to New York if buildings as tall as the one Woolworth proposed continued to be built.

> There is no such excuse…for the rearing of this great pile, shutting off the light of its neighbors, darkening the streets, and containing a population of several thousand people whose concentration on a little piece of ground will add another heavy burden to the transportation facilities in the vicinity.

The Record's complaints were ignored and the construction went forward. But this and similar warnings would soon prove accurate, and would change the quality of life in cities forever.

TAKING CHARGE

Woolworth obsessed over every detail of construction, As George Douglas writes in *Skyscrapers: A Social History in America*:

> [Woolworth] argued with Gilbert about the width of corridors, the layout of offices, the style of radiators, the light fixtures, the elevators, and everything else that came to his attention. When it was time to pick out the plumbing fixtures, Woolworth himself visited the offices of the Sanitas Manufacturing Company to look at the line of toilets and other bathroom fixtures available. He personally picked out the levers that he wanted for the urinals in the men's rooms.

Woolworth spared no expense to make his building one of the most opulent skyscrapers ever built.

> The main entrance on Broadway was a magnificent arch treated to rich Gothic detail and filigree. The lobby might well have served as the entrance to a Turkish sultan's palace or harem. The walls were of golden marble from the Isle of Skyros….For his own private offices Woolworth had ransacked the galleries and auction houses of Europe, and, impressed by Napoleon's tastes and zest for power, he emulated the decor of Napoleon's palace at Compiegne.

Another item gracing the lobby was a sculpture of Woolworth himself, holding a nickel.

The building was also a technological marvel. There were air cushions at the bottom of every elevator shaft, a restaurant and a swimming pool in the basement. The exterior of the building was illuminated with 80,000 light bulbs. "Highest, Safest, Most Perfectly Appointed Office Structure in the World," one advertisement read, "Fireproof Beyond Question, Elevators Accident Proof."

BRAVE NEW WORLD

The building was finished in 1913 and opened its doors for business on April 24. It was 60 stories high and more than 800 feet tall; it cost $13.5 million to build—every penny of which Woolworth paid in cash. From the White House, President Woodrow Wilson himself pushed the button that illuminated the exterior. The Woolworth Building was now officially the tallest building on Earth, and it would remain so until 1930.

It was also one of the most important skyscrapers ever built. "Before that day in 1913," George Douglas writes, "the skyscraper had been a thing of architectural and engineering curiosity. Now at last it was clearly revealed as one of the great wonders of the modern world."

Feeling high? Part V of "The World's Tallest Buildings" is on page 240.

* * *

RANDOM "THOUGHTS"

"It isn't pollution that's harming the environment. It's the impurities in our air and water that are doing it."

—Former U.S. Vice-President Dan Quayle

"China is a big country, inhabited by many Chinese."

—Former French President Charles de Gaulle

Walter Matthau's real name: Walter Matuschanskaysasky.

ART IMITATES LIFE

Ever wonder where screenwriters get their ideas?
Sometimes it's from news stories like these.

In Real Life: "Ed Gein was a soft-spoken, hard-working handy-man in a small town in Wisconsin. His entire life was dominated by his stern, repressive mother, Augusta, and after her death, he turned her room into a shrine.

"In the fall of 1957, a policeman investigating the disappear-ance of a local shopkeeper checked up on the last purchase listed in her receipt book—the sale of a can of antifreeze to Ed Gein." The officer went to Gein's house to ask about it and found the woman's body—along with female "masks" made from other bodies he'd apparently unearthed from a local cemetery. (*It's a Weird World*, by Paul Hagerman).

On Screen: Gein was the inspiration for the character of Norman Bates, played by Anthony Perkins in Alfred Hitchcock's classic thriller, *Psycho*.

In Real Life: Geoffrey Francis Bowers was an attorney with the world's largest law firm, Baker & McKenzie. In 1986, he was dismissed because he had AIDS and filed a lawsuit against them charging discrimination. He died while the case was still being tried but was posthumously awarded $500,000 by a jury.

On Screen: His life-and-death story became *Philadelphia*, the Oscar-winning 1993 drama starring Tom Hanks. But when Bowers' parents complained that their son's life story had been appropriated for the movie without permission, Tri-Star denied it was him. The family sued for $10 million. They settled out of court, with Tri-Star admitting publicly that Hanks's character was, indeed, Bowers.

In Real Life: "In 1961," according to the *Fortean Times*, "the small California seaside resort of Rio del Mar, near Santa Cruz, was bombarded by hordes of crazed birds. They pecked people, smashed into houses or cars, knocked out car headlights, broke windows, chased people around the streets and staggered around vomiting pieces of anchovy over local lawns. Eight people were nipped.

On Screen: Two years later, in 1963, director Alfred Hitchcock—who had been living in a nearby town at the time (and had called local newspapers for information)—released *The Birds*, starring Rod Taylor and Tippi Hedren. The film was based partly on a Daphne du Maurier story…and partly the strange occurrence at Rio del Mar.

In Real Life: In 1936, the small town of Hollister, California, began an annual motorcycle race called the Gypsy Tour. They stopped it in 1947, when 4,000 bikers from a group called the Angelenos showed up for the event, took over the town, and reportedly turned it into a bottle-throwing riot. Photos of the bikers that ran in *Life* magazine shocked the nation. They also shocked some of the witnesses, who said the photos had been faked and the story grossly embellished by reporters.

On Screen: Whether or not it really happened, the story inspired John Paxton to write the screenplay for the immensely popular 1953 film, *The Wild One*, starring Marlon Brando as "Johnny," the motorcycle gang leader. It made him a teen/screen idol. In 1997, Hollister tried to resurrect the Gypsy Tour as a nostalgia event.

In Real Life: Kim Peek's brain was damaged during fetal development, and it left him with "diminished motor capacities." His parents had no idea he had any special talents until 1984, when he was thirty-three years old. That's when a screenwriter named Barry Morrow interviewed him. After the interview, Morrow asked Peek's father: "Do you know that he knows all the ZIP codes in the United States?" It turned out that Kim could also remember incredibly detailed information about history, sports, geography, and many other subjects.

On Screen: Morrow used the interviews to write *The Rain Man*, starring Tom Cruise and Dustin Hoffman. The success of the film influenced Peek. For the first time, he felt confident enough to interact with people. He even gave speeches in which he urged tolerance for people who are different.

Fear of cancer is known as "cancerophobia"; fear of heart attacks is known as "cardiophobia."

GONE, BUT NOT FORGOTTEN

You can see them in museums or in books—but you won't see
them on the road, because no one makes them anymore.
Here's some info about four automobile legends.

THE RICKENBACKER (1922–1927): One of the first cars named for a celebrity. Before World War I, Eddie Rickenbacker was one of the most famous race car drivers in the United States. After the war he was even more famous as "America's first hero in the air," a title he earned by shooting down 26 German airplanes in dogfights. When he returned home, a group of Detroit businessmen backed him in his own car company. Rickenbacker's cars boasted six-cylinder engines with two flywheels instead of one, which made them among the smoothest-running automobiles on the road.
FATE: In 1927, huge losses forced the company to close its doors. Ironically, the last Rickenbacker designs were sold to the German automaker Audi; Rickenbacker himself became president of the Indianapolis Speedway.

THE OAKLAND (1908–1931): An early luxury car manufacturer. It was nearly bankrupt by the second year of its existence, but General Motors saw its potential. They bought it in 1909, and every year from 1910 to 1926, the Oakland was one of the 15 best-selling cars in the country. Its biggest claim to fame was its 1924 "True Blue" model—the first car ever mass-produced that wasn't painted black.
FATE: Oakland was headquartered in Pontiac, Michigan. In 1926, the division introduced a new, lower-priced car called the Pontiac that quickly overshadowed the Oakland, selling 140,000 cars in 1927 to Oakland's 50,000. GM discontinued the Oakland in 1931 and renamed the division Pontiac in 1933.

THE HUPMOBILE (1908–1930s): Founded by Robert C. Hupp, who was quickly recognized as one of the most gifted auto-makers of his day. "I recall looking at Bobby Hupp's roadster at the first show where it was exhibited," Henry Ford remarked years later, "and wondering whether we could ever build as good a small car for as little money." The company's most famous design was its 1934 model—one of the first ever designed with aerodynamics in mind. But its biggest claim to fame today is the fact that it's the only car ever commemorated on U.S. money. That's a Hupmobile in the illustration on the back of the $10 bill.

FATE: Hupmobile had reliable sales until it moved upmarket, building larger, more luxurious cars to earn higher profits. The strategy backfired during the Great Depression, when auto industry sales plunged more than 75%. Hupmobile never fully recovered, and in 1940 it abandoned automaking altogether, diversifying into electronics, auto parts, kitchen appliances, and other businesses.

THE MAXWELL (1904-1925): In 1903, John Maxwell designed his own automobile and joined with Benjamin Briscoe, owner of a sheet metal plant in Detroit, to form the Maxwell-Briscoe Motor Company. Briscoe hoped to become a major player in the auto industry. He copied General Motors, forming a holding company and buying other car companies, but for him, the strategy didn't work. His United States Motor Company bought up 150 different automakers…and then, in 1912, went belly-up. The Maxwell Motor Company managed to stay afloat until 1920, but by then it was 85 million in debt and there were more than 26,000 unsold Maxwells gathering dust in warehouses all over the country.

FATE: In 1921, the bankers who controlled Maxwell hired Walter P. Chrysler, a former president of Buick who'd developed a reputation as a "doctor" for sick companies, to turn Maxwell around. Chrysler wasted no time—he sold off the 26,000 Maxwells by slashing prices to $5 over cost; then he used the money to engineer a new car he named the "Good Maxwell," to counter consumer fears that Maxwells weren't well-built. Somehow, it worked—Maxwell sold nearly 49,000 cars in 1922 and earned more than $2 million in profits.

In 1924, Chrysler introduced the Chrysler Six, Maxwell's first six-cylinder car. It sold so well that Chrysler discontinued the Maxwell models the following year, and on June 6, 1925 reorganized Maxwell as the Chrysler Corporation.

Bluebirds cannot see the color blue.

THE CREAM OF
THE CRUD

It may be hard to believe, but these recordings are real.
We guarantee it. Who made them…and why? We'll never know.
Some mysteries are beyond human understanding.

THE WORLD'S WORST RECORDINGS

"Music to Make Automobiles By"
Volkswagen made this recording "to inspire their workers." It
features the exciting sounds of an auto assembly line, backed with
an orchestra. (We mentioned this in the *Giant BR*, but it really
does belong here too.)

"Granny's Mini-skirt"
A bluegrass "rap" song from Irene Ryan, who played Granny on
The Beverly Hillbillies. According to the lyrics, she decided to learn
to Twist and Jerk, and started wearing a mini-skirt. Only trouble
is, the sight of her knobby knees is makin' ol' Grandpa sick.

"Buddy Ebsen Says Howdy in Song and Story"
Another atrocity from a *Beverly Hillbillies* alumnus. Critic's
comment: "Jed Clampett goes a-shootin' at some tunes, and up
from his throat comes a-bubblin' crud."

"Elvis' Greatest S--t"
A bootleg album on the Dog Vomit label, with the National
Equirer shot of Elvis in his coffin on the front cover. It contains
the absolute worst of Elvis Presley. Tracks include: "Old McDonald Had a Farm," "Song of the Shrimp," "Fort Lauderdale Chamber of Commerce," and "Dominic the Impotent Bull."

"Sound Effect of Godzilla One" (Japanese import)
Critic's comment: "You can drop the needle anywhere and basically you'll hear Godzilla going 'Rarr…Rarr.' That's it."

Pumpkin rule of thumb: the darker the shell, the longer the pumpkin lasts.

"Sound Effects: U.S. Air Force Firepower"
Stuart Swezey, who actually owns a copy of this one, says, "[It has] tracks like 'Mass napalm attack by F-100s' and 'Psychological warfare, public address from C-47,' where they announce [with helicopter sounds in the background] 'Clear the village! We are about to strafe and bomb it!'"

"Laverne & Shirley Sing!"
According to the authors of Hollywood Hi-Fi, "An entire album of early '60s girl group tunes, as interpreted by Cindy Williams (who can almost carry a tune) and Penny Marshall (who sounds like a lovelorn goose honking for a mate). Since they are shown on the cover eating Popsicles, a more accurate title might've been Laverne and Shirley Suck."

"Bobby Breaux and the Pot-Bellied Pig"
Drummer Bobby Breaux collaborated with a 450-lb boar named Rebel after noticing he grunted in tunes. Features "Amazing Grease" and "Hava Nasquela." Breaux backed the pig up on drums and synthesizer.

"The Sound of Combat Training"
Recorded live at the United States Army Training Center, Fort Knox, Kentucky. Tracks include: "Innoculation," "Mess Hall," and "Gas Chamber Exercise."

"The Crepitation Contest" (The Power of Positive Stinking)
A whole album of nothing but farting. From the liner notes: "If you put your fingers in your ears, you can't hold your nose. If you hold your nose, you'll have to listen...."

NORAD Tracks Santa
A Cold War classic recorded in 1962. NORAD's (North American Air Defense) job was to protect us from enemy air attack. According to Ken Sitz, who owns a copy: "Interspersed with standard Christmas music are NORAD reports on Santa Claus—basically, whether or not he's going to be shot down!"

And don't miss... "Muhammed Ali Fights Mr. Tooth Decay: A Beautiful Children's Story."

Even Antarctica has an area code. It's 672.

IRONIC, ISN'T IT?

*More irony to put the problems of your
day-to-day life in proper perspective.*

BUREAUCRATIC IRONY
• In 1974, the Consumer Product Safety Commission
ordered 80,000 buttons promoting toy safety. They said:
"For Kids' Sake, Think Toy Safety." The buttons were recalled
when the agency found out they had "sharp edges, parts a child
could swallow, and were coated with toxic lead paint."
• "The town council of Winchester, Indiana, passed an anti-
pornography law, but the editors of the town's only newspaper
refused to publish it on the grounds that the statute itself was
pornographic. Unfortunately, a law does not take effect in
Winchester until it has been published in the newspaper." *(Fenton
and Fowler)*
• When the public clamored for campaign finance reform, a
columnist in *USA Today* reported that Republicans favored "a let-
the-good-times-roll proposal that would eliminate all contribution
limits....This bill is called the (I'm not making this up) Doolittle
Bill, named for its sponsor, California GOP Rep. John Doolittle."
(*USA Today*, October 1, 1997)
• Shortly after passing a bill that prohibited pornography on the
Internet, the House of Representatives released the Starr
Report...on the Internet.

IRONIC APPEARANCES
• "On the night of September 20, 1996, author Bertil Torekul
gave a lecture to an audience of 300 in the Stifts-och Landsbib-
liotek Library in Linkoping, Sweden. He spoke about...book-burn-
ing. The fire alarm sounded about a minute after he finished his
speech. The Linkoping library burned to the ground." *(Fortean
Times)*
• "After the world premiere at England's Leeds Playhouse of *The
Winter Guest*, a play featuring a community cut off by a blizzard,
the audience found themselves snowbound and were put up for
the night in the theater." *(Fortean Times)*

The ancient Egyptians bought jewelry for their pet crocodiles.

IRONIC FIRES

• In 1613, the town of Quimper, France, was burned down by its fire equipment. The fire started in a canvas fire bucket. *(Ripley's Believe It Or Not)*

• "To warn the public about Fourth of July brush fires, sheriff's deputies and firefighters gathered at a remote bomb-disposal range outside San Diego to blow up thousands of illegal fireworks for the news media. Sparks from the demonstration fell onto a nearby hill, causing a ten-acre brush fire that required 50 firefighters, two water-dropping helicopters and a bulldozer to extinguish." *(Dumb, Dumber and Dumbest)*

• On December 31, 1903, the Iroquois Theater in Chicago burned down. Thirty days earlier, it had opened with much fanfare as the "World's First Fireproof Theater."

IRONIC DEATHS

• Dr. Alice Chase, who wrote *Nutrition for Health* and other books on the science of proper eating, died recently...of malnutrition. *(Fenton and Fowler)*

• "Dr. Stuart M. Berger, an author of best-selling diet and health books who contended that his weight-loss programs would result in increased longevity, died on February 23, 1994. At the time, he was 40 years old and weighed 365 pounds." *(Dumb, Dumber, and Dumbest)*

• "The famous physician, Semmelweis, who fought against operating room contamination by unclean doctors, died of an infection caused by cutting his hand with dirty dissection instruments." *(Oops)*

• J.I. Rodale, publisher of books on health and nutrition, appeared on The Dick Cavett Show in 1971, when he was 72 years old, and predicted he would live to be 100. Later in the show, Cavett noticed Rodale appeared to have fallen asleep. Actually, he was dead.

DELICIOUS IRONY

• "In 1996, a landslide near Los Angeles broke a sewer line and sent tons of human waste into the Pacific Ocean, closing the stretch of beach where the TV show 'Baywatch' was filmed." (From news services.)

UNCLE JOHN'S PAGE OF LISTS

For years, the BRI has had a file full of lists. We've never been sure what to do with them...until now.

5 FILMS THAT FEATURE FARTS

1. Airplane! The pilot is affected by mild food poisoning.
2. Blazing Saddles. Bean-eating cowboys toot up a storm by the old campfire.
3. Amadeus. Mozart rips one mockingly after caricaturing Salieri at the piano.
4. Le Grande Bouffe. A character farts himself to death.
5. Fanny and Alexander. Uncle Karlchen astonishes children by blowing out candles.

—From *The Research Book of Bodily Functions*

THE 7 DEADLIEST DOGS

1. Pit bull
2. German shepherd
3. Chow
4. Malamute
5. Husky
6. Wolf hybrid
7. Akita

6 WORDS YOUR DIGITAL CLOCK CAN SPELL

1. ZOO (2:00)
2. S.O.S. (5:05)
3. SOB (5:08)
4. SIS (5:15)
5. BOO (8:00)
6. BOB (8:08)

7 LAWS OF TV

1. The hero will always find a parking space.
2. Police never wait for backup.
3. If a woman is running away from someone, she will trip and fall.
4. Cars will explode in all accidents, no matter how slight.
5. Haunted houses are never locked.
6. If a hero jumps hundreds of feet into water, it will always be deep enough.
7. Nobody on TV has time to watch TV.

—From *Reader's Digest*

6 THINGS THE AVERAGE RAT CAN DO

1. Wriggle through a hole no larger than the diameter of a quarter.
2. Scale a brick wall as though it had rungs.
3. Swim a half mile and tread water for 3 days.
4. Gnaw through lead pipes and cinder blocks.
5. Multiply so fast, a pair could have 15,000 descendants in a year.
6. Plummet five stories to the ground and scurry off unharmed.

—From *Hodge Podge*

4 GRAFFITI FROM GRACELAND

1. Elvis, no matter where you go, there you are.
2. Elvis, I'm having your baby 29 Sept.'91.
3. Elvis, can I use your bathroom?
4. Elvis, you came, you saw, you conquered, you croaked.

The word "Mrs." cannot be written in full.

WRONG ABOUT WRIGHT

Judging from what we've been told in history books, when the Wright brothers invented powered flight, they were rewarded with parades, medals and headlines. But that's a lie. The truth is, the U.S. government insisted that one of the greatest technological achievements of all time simply hadn't happened. Here's the true story.

CHANCE—THE UNINVITED GUEST

On December 8, 1903, Samuel Langley, head of the Smithsonian Institution and America's foremost expert on flight, was ready to make his most important attempt at manned flight. Since 1891 he'd been flying unmanned models powered by internal combustion engines; the U.S. government considered his experiments so promising that they'd given him $50,000 to continue. Now he planned to fly his gasoline-powered, manned plane off of a houseboat in the Potomac River. The press was on hand, waiting expectantly.

But it didn't happen. Unfortunately, the launching device, which was supposed to hurl the plane into the air, snagged the plane at the last second instead…and it went into the water "like a handful of mortar."

The *New York Times*, scornful of attempts at powered flight anyway, heaped abuse on Langley. They editorialized: "The ridiculous fiasco…was not unexpected. The flying machine might be evolved by the combined and continuous efforts of mathematicians and mechanicians in from one to ten million years."

THE REAL THING

It didn't take that long. Only nine days later, on December 17, two bicycle makers from Dayton, Ohio—Wilbur and Orville Wright—achieved the goal of all the world's would-be aviators: powered flight. It was a revolutionary development in the history of humankind…but few people even noticed. Only a few papers carried the Associated Press story of the flight. Most editors considered the whole thing a scam. When the Wrights set up the world's first airstrip outside Dayton in 1904 and flew daily all summer, only a few reporters came to see.

In fact, the first published eyewitness account of flight appears, amazingly enough, in a bee-keeping journal called

---

Dolphins nap with one eye open.

Gleanings in Bee Culture. And this almost a year after they started flying. The editor, A.I. Root, saw the Wrights make aviation's first turn on Sept. 20, 1904 and wrote:

> I have a wonderful story to tell you, a story that in some respects outrivals the Arabian Nights fables...It was my privilege to see the first successful trip of an airship without a balloon to sustain it, that the world has ever made...These two brothers have probably not even a faint glimpse of what their discovery is going to bring to the children of men.

The scientific press was also slow to acknowledge the Wrights' accomplishment. As Sherwood Harris writes in *The First to Fly*:

> As late as January 1906, *Scientific American* had been skeptical of reports about the Wrights long flights, its editorial board feeling that if the reports were true, then certainly the enterprising American press would have given them great attention. When the reports persisted, the magazine finally obtained confirmation by letter from many reputable people who had witnessed actual flights. In its December 15 [1906] issue, the magazine stated its complete acceptance of the Wright flights.

MILITARY INTELLIGENCE

You'd think the U.S. government would leap to purchase one of the most revolutionary weapons ever. Not so. In 1904, after making flights of five minutes, the Wrights wrote their Congressman, Robert Nevin, offering to license their device to the government for military purposes. Their letter said they'd made 105 flights up to 3 miles long at 35 mph. The flying machine, they said, "lands without being wrecked" and "can be made of great practical use in scouting and carrying messages in times of war." (Interestingly enough, for many years the only use the Wrights could imagine for their creation was war.)

The War Department, under future president William Howard Taft, responded that they weren't interested. They'd gotten many requests for "financial assistance in the development of designs for flying machines" and would only consider a device that had been "brought to the stage of practical operation without expense to the U.S. government." But, they added, do get in touch "as soon as it shall have been perfected."

In Oct. 1905, the Wrights wrote that they'd built a better

plane and made flights of up to 39 minutes and over 20 miles. The War Department again declined in a letter with almost the same wording—a form letter! Obviously, either no one was reading their letters, or no one understood what they were saying.

Showing incredible patience, the frustrated Wrights politely wrote back again. This time they said they'd build a flying machine to any specifications the government would name. The War Department, still clinging to the obvious impossibility of powered flight, wrote back saying it "does not care to formulate any requirements for the performance of a flying machine…until a machine is produced which by actual operation is shown to be able to produce horizontal flight and to carry an operator"—even though they had already produced it. They were so dejected that they didn't fly again for two and a half years.

ACCEPTED AT LAST

In 1907 a young balloon racer named Frank Lahm got a job with the Army Signal Corps office in Washington, D.C. He knew all the early flight pioneers and had heard from them about the miracle achieved by the Wrights. That, finally, was the Wrights' big break. Fred Howard writes in *Wilbur and Orville*:

> Lahm wrote a letter to the Board of Ordnance and Fortification (of the Army Signal Corps), urging that the brothers' latest proposal for the sale of a Flyer receive favorable action. It would be unfortunate, he said, if the U.S. should not be the first to take advantage of [the] unquestioned military value of the Wright Flyer. Lahm's letter had the desired effect….
>
> Wilbur decided a fair price for the Flyer would be $25,000. The Board had only $10,000….When Wilbur went to Washington to attend a formal meeting of the Board, his frankness of manner and self-confidence worked their usual magic and the Board assured him the entire $25,000 would be forthcoming by drawing on an emergency fund left over from the Spanish-American War.

MORE BUREAUCRATIC INSANITY

Apparently nothing much has changed: Even though the Wrights were the only ones in the world making practical airplanes, the U.S. government still had to put the matter out for bids. So in Dec. 23, 1907, it issued an "Advertisement and specification for a

49er faithful: The town of Ismay, Montana has changed its name to Joe, Montana.

Heavier-Than-Air Flying Machine," capable of carrying two men at 40 mph and staying up for at least an hour, then landing without serious damage. Critics howled. The *American Magazine of Aeronautics* wrote, "There is not a known flying machine in the world which could fulfill these specifications." Amazingly, the Signal Corps got 41 bids, with price tags ranging from $850 to $1 million. One was from a federal prisoner who would build a plane for his freedom. Another had plans written on wrapping paper and a third bidder offered to build planes by the pound.

The Wrights, of course, got the contract.

I SEE LONDON, I SEE FRANCE

Still, it was the French and British who first acknowledged the Wright Brothers' feats publicly. Shortly after winning the government contract (but before they'd proved themselves by building the U.S. a plane), Wilbur went to France to demonstrate their machine. The French were avid aviators, and welcomed him enthusiastically...at first. Then, as he rebuilt his plane (it had been damaged in shipping), working long hours and living simply in a nearby room, they became suspicious. Why wasn't he more flamboyant? Why didn't he attend the rounds of parties, like other celebrated French air pioneers?

Eventually, the French and British press decided he was a charlatan. But on August 8, 1907, they changed their minds. "To make a long story short," recalled an American named Ross Browne, who was there to see Wilbur's first European flight, "he got into the machine that afternoon, got into the air and made a beautiful circular flight. You should have seen the crowd there. They threw hats and everything."

STILL DUMB

Finally, four years after the first flight, the Wright Brothers were heroes. But there was one final insult: The Smithsonian Institution insisted that the first manned flight had been Langley's slam-dunk into the Potomac. They didn't want the Wright Flyer, so it sat in a shed in Dayton until 1928...when Orville finally gave it to the London Museum of Science. Only in 1942 did the Smithsonian bow to common knowledge, reverse its position, and humbly ask for the plane. The Smithsonian restored it and dedicated it in 1948, on the 45th anniversary of flight.

FAMILIAR PHRASES

Here are more origins of everyday phrases.

CLOSE, BUT NO CIGAR

Meaning: Nice try, but not quite!

Origin: "In the old-time fair or carnival, local lads were invited to exhibit their strength or skill by throwing baseballs at targets, pounding with a mallet to raise a weight, and so on—and the prize was a cigar. Since these devices were almost always rigged, the ambitious youths seldom won. The concessionaire would encourage them to further efforts (at a nickel a time) with, 'Close, but no cigar!'" (From *Loose Cannons and Red Herrings*, by Robert Claiborne)

THE BIG CHEESE

Meaning: An important or self-important person.

Origin: Sounds like it comes from a big wheel of cheese, but actually is derived from chiz, the Persian and Urdu word meaning "thing." It also might have been a play on the word "chief."

SPICK AND SPAN

Meaning: Neat and well turned out.

Origin: "This expression was first used to describe ships fresh from the shipwrights and carpenters. A spick was a 'spike' or 'nail,' and span was a 'wood chip.'" (From *To Coin a Phrase*, by Edwin Radford and Alan Smith)

THE WHOLE SHEBANG

Meaning: Everything.

Origin: "Shebang"—from the Irish word shebeen—was coined in America by Irish immigrants. According to the *Morris Dictionary of Word and Phrases*, "A shebeen in Ireland was a very lowly public house, one where drinks were sold without a license…[It] was regarded as a relatively valueless piece of real estate, and the expression 'I'll give you so much for the whole shebeen' became current. Gradually the original reference was lost and shebeen—now shebang after the trip across the Atlantic—came to mean any kind of…business affair."

Who looked after the knight's estate while he was away on the crusades? Usually his lawyer.

OOPS!

More examples of Murphy's Law—anythng that can goe wroong will!

COME AND LISTEN TO A STORY...

"[Using] the very latest equipment, Texaco workmen set about drilling for oil at Lake Peigneur in Louisiana during November, 1980.

"After only a few hours of drilling they sat back expecting oil to shoot up. Instead, however, they watched a whirlpool form, sucking down not only the entire 1,300-acre lake, but also five houses, nine barges, eight tugboats, two oilrigs, a mobile home, most of a botanical garden and ten percent of nearby Jefferson Island, leaving a half-mile-wide crater. No one told them there was an abandoned salt mine underneath.

"A local fisherman said he thought the world was coming to an end."

—*The Return of Heroic Failures*

DETAILS, DETAILS

"A group of Russian counterfeiters produced a near-perfect run of bogus 50,000-ruble bank notes (worth about $22). Once they went into general circulation, officials agreed that it was an excellent job and [the bills] appeared to be genuine currency. Their only error was misspelling 'Russia.'"

—*Dumb, Dumber, Dumbest*

AND WAS THAT IN 1492...OR 1865?

"Ads that ran in national newspapers last week for the forthcoming movie Jefferson in Paris used images of the Constitution of the United States.

"Then it was learned at Walt Disney Co., where the film and ad were created, that neither Thomas Jefferson nor Nick Nolte, who plays him in the movie, had written the Constitution.

"We all walked in Monday morning and said, 'Oh, s--t, it should have been the Declaration of Independence!' an unnamed

Disney executive told *Newsweek*.

"The magazine notes that Disney is the company that planned to build a Virginia theme park to celebrate American history."

—*San Francisco Chronicle*

SO MUCH FOR THE "MEDIA ELITE"
"On June 9, 1978, Mr. Bob Specas was ready to beat a domino record by knocking down 100,000 dominoes in a row. The media was there to broadcast the historic event. A TV camera recorded his progress as Specas set up the last dominoes for his performance.

"97,497...97,498...97,499. Then a TV cameraman dropped his press badge...and the dominoes went off."

—*The 176 Stupidest Things Ever Done*

HAPPINESS IS A STRANGE GUN
"When police in Saginaw, Michigan, pulled over a motorist on a traffic violation, they made a discovery: the guy was carrying a pistol in his car. Despite his protestations that he had never seen the weapon before, the cops knew their duty and they arrested him. Imagine the officers' embarrassment when they had to let the suspect go the following day with an apology! Seems the gun had dropped out of a cop's holster into the car when they were questioning the motorist about the traffic charge."

—*Oops*

ALL IN THE FAMILY
"Ian Lewis, 43, of Standish, Lancashire (England), spent 20 years tracing his family tree back to the 17th century. He traveled all over Britain, talked to 2,000 relatives and planned to write a book about how his great-grandfather left to seek his fortune in Russia and his grandfather was expelled after the Revolution. Then he found out he had been adopted when he was a month old and his real name was David Thornton. He resolved to start his family research all over again."

—*Strange Days*, by the editors of *Fortean Times*

Pink plastic lawn flamingoes were inspired by a 1957 photo in a *National Geographic* magazine.

THE DUKE WEARS RUBBERS

The Duke of Wellington wasn't a Victorian rubber fetishist.
He just found it easier to be brave if his feet weren't wet.

Arthur Wellesley was born in 1769 in the notoriously wet Emerald Isle of Ireland. Unluckily for him, he couldn't think straight unless his feet were dry. And they often weren't, given the climate and the leaky footwear, which was all you got in the late 18th and early 19th centuries. It was fine for the ladies who hardly ventured outdoors or for blokes who only sat on horses or inside carriages. But it was moistly miserable for anyone who wanted to, or had to, connect feet with ground.

WATERLOO
In his prime, Wellesley was hot stuff as a professional soldier, and there was plenty of the enemy to practice on—after the French Revolution in 1789, Britain was almost continuously at war with neighboring France.

Wellesley was created Viscount, then Earl, and finally, in 1814, the first Duke of Wellington. It was Wellington who finally led the British troops to victory in 1815 against Napoleon Bonaparte at Waterloo, that tiny dot on the map a few miles south of Brussels, capital of Belgium.

WELLINGTON BOOTS
Whether leading an army, or just hanging out, Wellesley was the outdoor type. His feet were out in the mud and long grass in all weathers. He knew that rubber, as long as it's properly sealed, doesn't leak. Which led him to his brilliant idea. "Make me some rubber boots," he said . And that's why rubber boots—at least in some English-speaking countries—have been known as Wellingtons or 'wellies' ever since.

A BATTLE WON
Poor old Napoleon didn't stand a chance. Historians tell us he was distinctly under the weather on June 18, the day of the battle. The poor man is supposed to have suffered badly from

hemorrhoids. So sitting astride a horse would have made it hard to concentrate on the job in hand. But Wellington, his feet securely dry and cosy in the famous boots, even after hours of overnight rain, was in a victorious mood.

THE REST OF HIS LIFE

After Waterloo, Wellington went on to have a long and distinguished political career. He represented Britain at summit conferences all over Europe. He advised Queen Victoria, and was even prime minister twice.

In old age "The Iron Duke" spent much of his time at Walmer Castle in Kent, a residence complete with sea view. He had the use of it as Lord Warden of the Cinque Ports—one of the many honors showered upon him. He died at Walmer in 1852.

Today the castle is open to the public. The room in which old Arthur breathed his last is maintained in ghoulish authenticity. See the bed he slept in and the chair he died in. And, of course, a pair of those boots is on display.

LIFE AFTER DEATH

He got a massive state funeral with lots of pomp and circumstance, an honor Britain rarely accords to anyone who isn't royal. The carriage that bore his coffin is on display at St. Paul's cathedral in London. A statue of Wellington dominates Waterloo Place—a relatively quiet area between Trafalgar Square and Buckingham Palace.

WELLINGTON THIS, WELLINGTON THAT

The boots weren't the only thing named for Wellington. They named the capital of New Zealand after him in 1840, for example. British pubs are often named for the great and the good, so Wellington has his fair share. There are plenty of Wellington Streets in the United Kingdom, too.

Not many of us get a tree named after us, either, but Wellington did. *Wellingtonia* is a member of the sequoia family, redwoods that are quite common in parks and large gardens in Wellington's United Kingdom stamping ground.

And if you're thinking about Beef Wellington—that delectable filet of beef on a bed of liver pate inside a pastry crust—be advised that it wasn't named after the duke. Because of the way it looks when it's done, it was named after the boot.

When pitched, the average major league baseball rotates 15 times before it's hit by the batter.

THERE ONCE WAS A LADY FROM FRANCE...

Limericks have been around since the 1700s. Here are a few of the more "respectable" ones that readers have sent us.

A certain young chap named Bill Beebee
Was in love with a lady named Phoebe;
"But," he said, "I must see
What the clerical fee
Be before Phoebe be Phoebe Beebee."

There was a young artist called Saint,
Who swallowed some samples of paint;
All shades of the spectrum
Flowed out of his rectum
With a colorful lack of restraint.

A flea and a fly in a flue
Were imprisoned, so what could they do!
Said the fly: "Let us flee,"
Said the flea: "Let us fly!"
So they flew through a flaw in the flue.

When a jolly young fisher named Fisher
Went fishing for fish in a fissure,
A fish, with a grin,
Pulled the fisherman in;
Now they're fishing the fissure for Fisher.

There was young fellow called Cager,
Who, as the result of a wager,
Offered to fart
The whole oboe part
Of Mozart's Quartet in F Major.

The fabulous Wizard of Oz
Retired from business becoz
What with up-to-date science,
To most of his clients,
He wasn't the Wizard he woz.

There was an old spinster from Fife,
Who had never been kissed in her life:
Along came a cat,
And she said "I'll kiss that!"
But the cat meowed: "Not on your life!"

I sat next to the Duchess at tea,
Distressed as a person could be.
Her rumblings abdominal,
Were simply phenomenal,
And everyone thought it was me!

Said an eminent, erudite ermine:
"There's one thing I cannot determine:
When a dame wears my coat,
She's a person of note—
When I wear it, I'm called only vermin."

---

2 people most admired by teenagers in 1983: Eddie Murphy and Ronald Reagan, in that order.

HELLO, DOLLY

Besides music, singer Dolly Parton is known for three things.
The third is her straight talk. Here's a bit of what she has to say.

"I'm not offended by all the dumb blonde jokes, because I know I'm not dumb...and I also know that I'm not blonde."

"One of the surest signs that a woman is in love is when she divorces her husband."

"It's important that, though I rely on my husband for love, I rely on myself for strength."

"I was the first woman to burn my bra—it took the fire department four days to put it out."

"I buy all those (fitness) videos—Richard Simmons, Jane Fonda. I love to sit and eat cookies and watch 'em."

(On her acting) "I'm never going to be a Meryl Streep. But then, she'll never be a Dolly Parton either."

"I've never left the Smoky Mountains, I've taken them with me wherever I go, and (pointing to her chest) I'm not referring to these either."

"You'd be surprised how much it costs to look this cheap."

"Radio doesn't seem interested in old folks like me, [even though] I feel like I'm doing the best work of my career right now. They say wisdom comes with age. Well, so does talent."

"The way I see it, if you want the rainbow, you gotta put up with the rain."

"I've got more confidence than I do talent, I guess. I think confidence is the main achiever of success."

"If people think I'm a dumb blonde because of the way I look, then they're dumber than they think I am. If people think I'm not very deep because of my wigs and outfits, then they're not very deep."

"I look just like the girl next door...if you happen to live next door to an amusement park."

It takes about a week to make a jellybean.

STEINEM SPEAKS

Some of Gloria Steinem's comments about women are controversial…but whether you agree with them or not, you'll find them thought-provoking.

"I have yet to hear a man ask for advice on how to combine marriage and a career."

"Men should think twice before making widowhood women's only path to power."

"Some of us are becoming the men we wanted to marry."

"A woman without a man is like a fish without a bicycle."

"Jacqueline Onassis has a very clear understanding of marriage. I have a lot of respect for women who win the game with rules given you by the enemy."

"Law and justice are not always the same. When they aren't, destroying the law may be the first step toward changing it."

"Women may be the one group that grows more radical with age."

"Every country has peasants— ours have money."

"We can tell our values by looking at our checkbook stubs."

"Women age, but men mature."

"On why she never married: "I can't mate in captivity.

"One day, an army of gray-haired women may quietly take over the earth."

"Someone once asked me why women don't gamble as much as men do, and I gave the common sense reply that we don't have as much money. That was a true but incomplete answer. In fact, women's total instinct for gambling is satisfied by marriage."

"It may eventually turn out that men and women have similar degrees of aggressiveness, but for the next fifty years or so, until the sex roles are… reformed, women will be a good and peaceful influence in politics."

Take your height and divide by eight. That's how "tall" your head is.

MODERN MYTHOLOGY

*These mythological characters may be as famous in our culture
as Hercules or Pegasus were in ancient Greece.
Here's where they came from.*

SNAP!, CRACKLE!, & POP! In 1933, commercial artist
Vernon Grant was working at his drawing board when he
heard this Rice Krispies ad on the radio:

> Listen to the fairy song of health, the merry chorus sung by
> Kellogg's Rice Krispies as they merrily snap, crackle and pop in
> a bowl of milk. If you've never heard food talking, now is your
> chance.

Inspired, he immediately drew three little elves—which he named
after the noises the cereal supposedly made. Then he took the
sketches to N.W. Ayer, the Philadelphia ad agency that handled
Kellogg's advertising; they bought the cartoons on the spot. They
also hired Grant to keep illustrating the little trio for cereal boxes,
posters, and ads. He made a good living working for Kellogg's over
the next decade, but wasn't happy with the arrangement. So he
decided to sue Kellogg's for sole ownership of the characters. Bad
move: he lost, Kellogg's fired him, and Grant never made another
cent off the characters he'd created.

THE SUN-MAID RAISIN GIRL. "The sun-bonneted
woman...who smiles on every box of Sun-Maid raisins was a real
person," writes Victoria Woeste in *Audacity* magazine. "Her name
was Lorraine Collett and in 1915 she was sitting in her front yard
letting her hair dry before participating in Fresno's first Raisin Day
parade. A Sun-Maid executive was passing by and was struck by
the sight. He had a photographer come take her picture, then had
artist Fanny Scafford paint the picture from it." All Collett made
from it was a $15 modeling fee and a bit part in a 1936 film called
Trail of the Lonesome Pine. The original bonnet is now in the
Smithsonian.

MR. PEANUT. Amadeo Obici founded the Planters Nut &
Chocolate Company in 1906, in Wilkes-Barre, Pennsylvania.
Roasted and salted peanuts were still new to most Americans, and
the company was an immediate success. As it got bigger, Obici

decided he needed a logo. In 1916, he sponsored a contest to find one. The winner: 13-year-old Antonio Gentile, from Suffolk, Virginia, who submitted a drawing of "a little peanut person" and got $5 for it. A commercial artist took Gentile's sketch, added a hat, cane, and monocle (to lend a touch of class to the lowly legume), and Mr. Peanut was born. The elegant gentle-nut made his debut in 1918, in *The Saturday Evening Post*.

MCGRUFF THE CRIME DOG. In the late 1970s, the Ad Council made a deal with the U.S. Justice Department to create an anti-crime ad campaign. Their first task: invent a spokes-character (like Smokey the Bear) to deliver the message in commercials. Adman Jack Keil began riding with the New York police to get ideas. He remembers:

> We weren't getting anywhere. Then came a day I was flying home from the West Coast. I was trying to think of a slogan— crunch crime, stomp on crime. And I was thinking of animal symbols— growling at crime, roaring at crime. But which animal? The designated critter had to be trustworthy, honor-able, and brave. Then I thought, you can't crunch crime or defeat it altogether, but you can snap at it, nibble at it—take a bite out of crime. And the animal that takes a bite is a dog.

A bloodhound was the natural choice for a crimefighter, but they still needed a name...so they sponsored a nationwide name-the-dog contest. The most frequent entry was Shure-lock Bones. Others included: Sarg-dog, J. Edgar Dog, and Keystone Kop Dog. The winner was submitted by a New Orleans police officer. In the ads, Keil supplies McGruff's voice.

TONY THE TIGER. In 1952, Kellogg's planned to feature a menagerie of animals—one for each letter of the alphabet—on packages of its Sugar Frosted Flakes. They started with K and T: Katy the Kangaroo and Tony the Tiger. But they never got any further. Tony—who walked on all fours and had a much flatter face than today—was so popular that he became the cereal's official spokes-character. In the first Frosted Flakes commercials, only kids who ate Tony's cereal could see him. His personality has changed a number of times since then, but his voice hasn't. It's Thurl Ravenscroft, an ex-radio star who jokingly claims to have made a career out of just one word: "Grr-reat!"

BIRTHDAY TRADITIONS

In her book Happy Birthdays Around the World, *Lois Johnson explains how people in other countries celebrate their birthdays. A few examples:*

CHINA. "A baby's birthday is celebrated when he is thirty days old, and when he is a year old. Then there are no more celebrations until the tenth birthday. After that, every tenth year is celebrated for as long as the person lives. The most important date is the thirtieth anniversary, when a child becomes an adult."

NIGERIA. "Many children follow the old tribal custom of celebrating their birthdays as an age group, instead of having an individual birthday. The custom began in very early times, when there was no calendar. The only way the people had of marking their birthdays was by the reign of a certain king, or by some important event. People then, who were born during one of these periods, became an age group, and celebrated their birthdays together."

THAILAND. "According to tradition, if the parents of the child can afford it, the father and mother buy as many birds or fish, sometimes both, as their child is years old, plus one extra animal for the child to 'grow on.' After sprinkling each animal with blessed water, the boy or girl lets the birds fly free, and returns the fish to the waters of the river or canal. This ceremony is believed to insure the favor of the gods for the coming year."

INDIA. "On this day, the Hindu child does not have to go to school. Hindus believe that a special day such as a birthday is meant for prayer and celebration."

KOREA. "A baby's first birthday is celebrated with great ceremony. The same sort of custom that is followed in other Asian countries is observed in Korea. The mother and father lay all kinds of articles on a table—pencils, pieces of money, books, and strips of cloth. The baby is then set down in the middle, and whatever the baby reaches for is supposed to show what his future skills will be."

GREAT BRITAIN. "Sometimes well-meaning classmates may follow the British custom of 'bumping.' To wish the birthday child well, some of his friends will pick him up by the ankles while others will lift him under the armpits, and then they 'bump' him on the ground as many times as he is years old—with, of course, an extra 'bump' to grow on."

SRI LANKA. "The first birthday celebration comes when a Sri Lankan baby is thirty-one days old. Then, customarily, a close relative brings the baby a special gift. For a boy baby, it may be a gold chain; for a girl, gold arm bangles. The parents also present the new baby with a charm, made of copper in a scroll design, which is rolled into a gold-enclosed cylinder or tube. This charm is worn all through the person's life and is supposed to protect them from harm."

* * *

GOOD OL' AMERICAN INGENUITY

"Paragon Cable in New York recently began a new approach to customers with delinquent accounts. Instead of cutting off service altogether, which would create additional expense to restart when the customer paid up, Paragon merely fills the customer's entire 77-channel lineup with C-SPAN. Paragon said the project had been successful."

—*U.S. News & World Report,* July 31, 1995

Levi Strauss didn't call 'em jeans. He called 'em "waist overalls."

BANDS THAT NEVER EXISTED

*You've heard the expression, Don't believe everything you hear?
Well, it turns out the rule also applies to rock bands.*

THE MASKED MARAUDERS

In 1969, Greil Marcus wrote a story for *Rolling Stone* magazine claiming that the biggest rock stars of the day had gotten together and recorded an album. "This is indeed what it appears to be," he wrote, "John Lennon, Mick Jagger, Paul McCartney, and Bob Dylan, backed by George Harrison and a drummer as yet unnamed—the 'Masked Marauders.' The album was recorded with impeccable secrecy in a small town near the site of the original Hudson Bay Colony in Canada." The magazine even printed a Masked Marauders album cover with the article.
The Truth: Marcus made the whole thing up. When the article generated attention, he cashed in on it, hiring some "musicians" to record an album—complete with songs like "Mammy" and "I Can't Get No Nookie." It was an outrageous rip-off, but nothing on the album cover indicated that it was a joke. So people who believed what they read in *Rolling Stone* and rushed out to buy the album had no idea they were really getting a tone-deaf fake.

MILLI VANILLI

In 1990, Arista Records released Girl, You Know It's True, the debut album for a pop duo Milli Vanilli, made up of Fabrice Morvan, a Frenchman, and Robert Pilatus, a German.

It was a spectacular hit, selling more than 10 million copies world-wide—including 7 million in the United States. The album won several American Music Awards, as well as the 1990 Grammy for best new artists. "Musically," Pilatus told reporters, "we are more talented than any Bob Dylan. Musically, we are more talented than Paul McCartney. Mick Jagger, his lines are not clear. He don't know how he should produce a sound. I'm the new modern rock 'n' roll. I'm the new Elvis."

The battle hymn of the Ethiopian army used to be "The St. Louis Blues."

The Truth: In December, 1989, a rap singer named Charles Shaw informed a *New York Newsday* reporter that Morvan and Pilatus hadn't even sung on their album. He retracted the claim a few weeks later (it turned out that he was paid $150,000 for the retraction), but Milli Vanilli's horrible live performances fueled suspicions that they weren't the genuine article. Finally in November, 1990, Milli Vanilli's producer, Frank Farian, confirmed it. The pair, it turned out, had been hired because they would add sex appeal to the music videos.

Morvan and Pilatus were stripped of their Grammy and were even named in a class action suit filed by angry fans. They eventually regrouped as "Rob and Fab: The German and the French," but the new act bombed.

THE ARCHIES
When the Archie comic strip became a half-hour CBS cartoon show in 1968, sales of everything connected to Archie characters, from lunch boxes to comic books, skyrocketed. The executives who created the show wanted to sell records, too. So, they hired Don Kirshner, the man behind the Monkees' hits, to put together a group that would make records as the Archies. The band released an album in 1968. Their first single, "Bang Shang-A-Lang," was a modest success, but their second single, "Sugar, Sugar"—a song the Monkees had turned down in 1967—was the biggest selling record of 1969, with total sales of over $4 million.
The Truth: There was no band. Kirshner had endured so many problems with the Monkees that the last thing he wanted was another group. He simply hired two studio singers—Ron Dante (who provided the voices for Archie, Jughead, and Moose) and Toni Wine (who sang the Veronica and Betty parts)—and recorded everything with them.

A number of "Archies" bands toured the country claiming to be the genuine article, but the "real" Archies never toured. It wasn't from lack of trying: "At one point they wanted me to dye my hair and put freckles on and go out as Archie," Dante remembers. "I said, 'Oh boy, is this a career move or what?'"

* * *

"On behalf of all white people, I'd like to say we're sorry about Vanilla Ice." —**Dennis Miller**

If your feet just smell bad, it's foot odor. If they smell really bad, it's "bromidrosis."

GREASY, GRIMY GOPHER GUTS

We were looking for some new ways to entertain you, when someone came up with the idea of a singalong/poetry reading. You know, while you're sitting in there, you can make some…uh…other kinds of noise. But we wondered—what should we include? That's when Aunt Jenny came up with a book called Greasy, Grimy Gopher Guts, *compiled by Joseph Sherman and T.K.F. Weisskopf. Its full of those ditties you used to know when you were in 1st grade. Sing it out, now!*
(Explain it to your family later.)

(Sung to the tune of
"The Old Grey Mare")
Great green gobs of greasy, grimy
gopher guts,
Mutilated monkey meat,
Little birdies' dirty feet.
Great green gobs of greasy, grimy
gopher guts,
And I forgot my spoon.

Jingle Bells, Santa smells,
A million miles away.
Stuffed his nose With Cheerios
And ate them all the way—hey!

I'm gonna go eat worms.
Big ones and little ones,
Ishy guishy squishy ones,
I'm gonna go eat worms.
I'm gonna die,
Everybody cry,
I'm gonna eat some worms.

Eeny meeny miney moe,
Catch your teacher by the toe.
If he squirms, squeeze it tight
Then you take a great big bite.

'Twas the night before Christmas
And all through the garage,
Not a creature was stirring,
Not even the Dodge.
The tires were hung by the chim-
ney with care.
In hopes that St. Nicholas would
fill them with air.

Little Miss Muffet
Sat on a tuffet
Eating her curds and whey.
Along came a spider
And sat down beside her
And she ate that, too.

Mary had a little lamb.
She fed it castor oil.
And everywhere that Mary went,
It fertilized the soil.

(To be sung to the tune of
"The Star-Spangled Banner")
Oo-oh say can you see
Any bedbugs on me?
If you do, pick a few—
'Cause I got them from you.

20% of tuxedo rentals take place in May.

NEVER SUCK ON A CHOPSTICK

Planning on traveling abroad? Many cultures frown on behavior we consider "normal"—fingerpointing, yawning without covering your mouth, even eating while walking on the street. Here is a list of rude or vulgar behavior from around the world...which just might help you avoid touching off an international incident.

China: Never suck on your chopsticks.

Russia: Never squeeze through a theater aisle with your backside turned to the people sitting there.

Turkey: Don't talk to elderly people in a louder-than-normal voice.

Thailand: Avoid stepping on doorsills. (It's believed that a domestic deity lives in them.)

Taiwan: Never move an object with your foot.

Chile and Bolivia: Don't pour wine with your left hand.

Bali: Never take pictures of topless or nude bathers.

Arab countries: Don't sit so that the sole of your shoe ("the lowest and dirtiest place on your body") is pointing at someone.

Germany: Never shake hands while your other hand is in your pocket.

Poland: Don't drink everything in your glass if you hadn't intended getting a refill.

Indonesia: Never touch anyone's head.

Japan: Don't scribble on someone's business card.

Brazil: Don't give the "O.K." sign—it's considered obscene.

Chile: Don't slap your fist into the palm of your hand.

Portugal: Never use your bread to soak up the juices from your meal.

Kenya: Never accept a gift with your left hand.

India: Don't whistle in public.

Iran: Never blow your nose in public.

England: Don't start a conversation with "What do you do?"

Ireland: Avoid discussion of religion or politics.

Iceland: Never use a person's last name when greeting them.

How does a shark find fish? It can hear their hearts beating.

YOU'RE MY INSPIRATION

It's always fascinating to find out who, or what, inspired familiar characters. Here are some we've come across.

DON CORLEONE, the Mafia leader in *The Godfather,* Mario Puzo's bestselling novel.
Inspired by: Puzo's mother. "Like the don," he explains, "she could be extremely warm and extremely ruthless....[For example], my father was committed to an insane asylum. When he could have returned home, my mother made the decision not to let him out—he would have been a burden on the family. That's a Mafia decision."

MOBY DICK, the Great White Whale, title character of Herman Melville's classic novel.
Inspired by: Mocha Dick, a real white sperm whale that was the terror of the seas in the first half of the 19th century. (He was named for Mocha Island, near Chile.) Mocha Dick was said to have wrecked or destroyed nearly thirty whaling boats and killed thirty men, beginning in 1819. Historians say Melville first read of him in an 1839 issue of *Knickerbocker* magazine.

WINNIE THE POOH, Christopher Robin's stuffed bear.
Inspired by: A Canadian black bear. In 1914, Harry Colebourne, a Canadian soldier, was traveling east on a troop train headed for England and World War I. When the train stopped in White River, Ontario, Harry bought a black bear cub from a hunter. He called it Winnie, after his hometown of Winnipeg, and took it to England as a mascot.

Colebourne was eventually stationed in France, and while he was gone, he loaned Winnie to the London Zoo. By the time he returned, the bear had become so popular that he decided to leave it there.

A few years later, a four-year-old named Christopher Milne brought his favorite stuffed bear, Edward, to the zoo. Christopher saw Winnie and became so excited that he decided to rename Edward. "Pooh" was his nickname for a swan he loved—he appropriated it for the bear, and Edward became Winnie the Pooh.

MARY, the classic nursery rhyme character ("Mary had a little lamb, its fleece was white as snow…").
Inspired by: An eleven-year-old girl in Boston, Massachusetts. In 1817, a young man named John Roulstone saw young Mary Sawyer on her way to school…followed by a pet lamb. He thought it was so amusing, he jotted down a little poem about it.

Thirteen years later, Mrs. Sarah Josepha Hale added 12 more lines to the poem and published the whole thing under her own byline. Today there's some controversy about the authorship of the poem…but not the inspiration.

OLIVER BARRETT IV, the romantic hero in *Love Story,* a #1 bestselling book by Erich Segal and a hit movie in the 1970s.
Inspired by: Two students Segal knew at Harvard in the 1960s. The side of Barrett that was "the tough, macho guy who's a poet at heart" was fashioned after Tommy Lee Jones (now an actor). The side that "had a controlling father and was pressured to follow in the father's footsteps" was inspired by Jones's roommate—Al Gore.

MICKEY MOUSE, the most famous cartoon character in history.
Inspired by: A real mouse…and maybe actor Mickey Rooney. The mouse, whom Disney called Mortimer, was a pet that the cartoonist kept trapped in a wastebasket in his first art studio in Kansas City. Rooney, a child movie star, says in his autobiography that he inspired the mouse's new name, in the early 1920s:

> One day I passed a half-open door in a dirty old studio and peeked in. A slightly built man with a thin mustache…looked up and smiled. "What's your name, son?"
>
> "Mickey…What are you drawing?"
>
> "I'm drawing a mouse, son." Suddenly he stopped drawing, took me by the shoulders, and looked me in the eye. "Did you say your name was Mickey?"
>
> "Yes sir."
>
> "You know what I'm going to do?…I'm going to call this mouse Mickey—after you."

Florida has more tornadoes per square mile than any other state.

THE CURSE OF THE WEREWOLF, PART I

We've all heard the werewolf legend, seen it in films and on TV. In real life, it's called Lycanthropy. Here's a little of its history.

ANIMAL TALES

Nearly every society has legends about people who change into animals. In Russia there are stories of were-bears. In Africa, they have were-leopards, were-hyenas, and were-hippos. In Asia there are tales about were-tigers, elephants, crocodiles, snakes, and even sharks.

Why are these animals singled out? "In almost all cases," Nancy Garden writes in her book, *Werewolves*, "the animal has these characteristics: 1) It is commonly found in the area; 2) It is feared by the inhabitants; and 3) It has been known to attack people and/or farm animals."

In Europe, wolves fit that profile: As the population grew over the centuries, Europeans settled in parts of the continent where wolves had roamed freely. As the wildlife that wolves depended on for food began to disappear, they often preyed on livestock. And when food was really scarce, they might even go after humans. As late as 1875, an estimated 160 people were attacked by starving packs of wolves in Russia. So it's not surprising that when Europeans told scary stories by the fireside, wolves were a common subject. Their spooky habit of howling at the moon made them that much more fearsome.

THE WEREWOLF TRIALS

No one (or at least hardly anyone) believes in werewolves today, but in the Middle Ages, they were taken quite seriously. "Of all the world's monsters," says Daniel Cohen in his book, *Werewolves*, "the werewolf is the one that has been most widely believed in, and the most widely feared."

Here are some of the things people commonly believed:
• A person could become a werewolf in a number of ways: if he was cursed, drank water from a wolf's pawprint, ate the meat of an

---

In the time it takes to hatch one egg, the male emperor penguin loses 1/3 of its body weight.

animal killed by a wolf, wore a girdle made of wolfskin, or used a magic salve. "The business about becoming a werewolf after being bitten by another werewolf is basically a creation of the movies," says Cohen. "'Real' werewolves didn't just bite people, they tore their victims to pieces and ate them."

• In some versions of the legend, the werewolf remained human, but took on wolf characteristics, such as fur, fangs, and paws. In other variations, the person literally turned into a wolf.

• Werewolves could be killed any way that a normal wolf could be killed.

DEMON WOLVES

It was commonly accepted that werewolves were in league with the devil. Even educated churchmen who didn't believe human beings could really transform into other animals assumed that the devil was involved. "They often said that the devil created the 'illusion' of transformation," Cohn writes. "He made people 'think' they had turned into wolves, and made the victim 'think' they were being attacked by the creature."

Some "authorities" believed a real wolf could be turned into a werewolf when the spirit of an evil person entered it. "It was possible therefore," Cohen explains, "for an evil person to be asleep in his bed at night, or even locked in a cell under the eyes of his jailers, and yet his spirit could roam free as a werewolf. As a result, a lot of people were convicted of being werewolves even after it was proven that they were nowhere near the place where the werewolf had allegedly committed its crimes."

This was serious business. In Europe, as late as the 18th century, if you were suspected of being a werewolf you could be put on trial and then put to death. Untold thousands were put to death—between 1520 and 1630, an estimated 30,000 cases of "werewolfery" trials were recorded in central France alone, and thousands more trials took place in other parts of Europe.

"The Curse of the Werewolf, Part II" is on page 342.

BOWDLERIZING THE SEXY BITS OUT OF SHAKESPEARE

Thomas Bowdler gave his name to a new word for censorship.

Thomas Bowdler had an insatiable appetite for what he regarded as the dirty bits in literature—Shakespeare's plays, Gibbon's *History of the Decline and Fall of the Roman Empire*, and even the Bible—which he chopped out, or "bowdlerized," so that no one else could read them.

A KILLJOY IS BORN
Bowdler was born in Bath in 1754 just a few years before King George II's 22-year-old grandson George III came to the throne—the one who eventually "lost the American colonies" as the British put it. Mr. Bowdler Sr. used to read the Bible and Shakespeare to the family, but censored the passages he thought a little too naughty for the wife and kids. This is probably where young Thomas first picked up his prissy ideas.

The Bowdlers were an old family (if you know what we mean), sufficiently well off so that young Thomas didn't need to worry much about earning a living. He trained as a doctor in Scotland but never seemed to like practicing much. Maybe it was because he had to deal with actual bodies. Ick.

So, while the Brits fought the French, and Napoleon's fortunes rose and declined, Bowdler wrote some pretty dull medical treatises and did a bit of charity work, living first on the Isle of Wight off the south coast and then near Swansea in Wales.

THE FAMILY SHAKESPEARE
In 1818, when Bowdler was in his 60s, his famous ten-volume expurgated—and completely boring—version of Shakespeare appeared. "Words and expressions are omitted which cannot with propriety be read aloud in a family," he said in his intro. "Many words and expressions occur which are of so indecent a nature (oh, dear!) as to render it highly desirable that they should be

erased." And that's what he did.

He believed, in his high-handed way, that nothing—not even the genius of the finest writer who ever put quill to paper in the English language—was "an excuse for profaneness or obscenity; and if these could be obliterated the translucent genius of the poet would undoubtedly shine with more unclouded lustre." Everybody's a critic.

THE SEXY BITS

So Shakespeare's lusty Juliet, whose hormone-mad hots for Romeo make her long for "love-performing night" that "Romeo may leap to these arms" in order to perform "amorous rites," is reduced by Bowdler to a simpering, sexless—and pretty tedious—teenybopper with a crush.

And remember King Lear: old, deranged, and driven out into the stormy wilderness by two of his daughters? Shakespeare has him bellowing like a bull: "Let copulation thrive; for Gloucester's bastard son was kinder to his father than my daughter got 'tween lawful sheets." Well, Bowdler, the literary castrator, would have none of that: he hacked the 22-line speech down to seven.

He got rid of most of the drunken porter's speech in *Macbeth* too. Lewd cracks about brewer's droop and booze-induced leaky bladders were definitely off-limits for Bowdler's family audience.

Doll Tearsheet is Falstaff's floozy in *Henry IV: Part II*. In Shakespeare's play she keeps the fat, charismatic, but not-very-well-behaved Falstaff—and by implication anyone else with money for a few drinks—happy. Bowdler simply expunged her. Alas, poor Doll.

GOD GOES TOO

He had no truck with blasphemy either. Bowdler replaced every casual reference in Shakespeare to God with the word "heaven." It hardly enhanced old Will's carefully contrived rhythms.

NO S-E-X, PLEASE, WE'RE BRITISH

It was an unlikely preoccupation in 1818. Compared with what came later in the century—the Victorian Age—most people were relatively relaxed about sex and sexuality, although four editions of the cleaned-up Shakespeare were published in the first six years, so Bowdler must have done pretty well on royalties.

State sport of Maryland: Jousting.

Bowdler's big moment really came when Victoria took the throne in 1837—even though he was already dead. In 1825 he'd departed temporal life, presumably for the spiritual joys of a sex-free heaven. As high Victorian "morality" gripped the country, several more editions were published—some of which were still around in British girls' schools staffed by shy lady teachers a century later in the 1950s.

RULE, BRITANNIA!

Morality? The Victorians were actually obsessed with sex, of course. Perhaps in mixed polite society sex wasn't talked about but it was certainly thought about—constantly. Why else would they have spent so much energy pretending to suppress it? It was a time when prospective brides from "nice" families were traditionally told to have no truck with the unpleasant obligations which marriage would impose on them, but "to lie back and think of the British Empire."

Their men, meanwhile having done a bit of child-engendering duty at home, could go and get their real pleasures with some of the million or two prostitutes on the streets of the big cities: Sir John Simon's Privy Council Report of 1868 reckoned that there were 18,000 working in London alone. And when all that was over, presumably the happy Victorian family could settle down by the fireside to a joyful home-reading of Bowdler's "clean" Shakespeare. Strange times.

And that, dear children, is how the word "bowdlerize" came to be. Sweet dreams.

* * *

Strange Scholarships

Want some help with college tuition? You might qualify for one of these. In 1994, it was announced that:
- The Frederick & Mary F. Beckley Fund for Needy Left-handed Freshmen offers up to $1,000 for left-handers who want to go to Juanita College in Pennsylvania.
- The John Gatling Scholarship Program offers $6,000 to anyone with the last name Gatlin or Gatling who wants to go to the University of North Carolina.
- Tall Clubs International offers two scholarships of $1,000 each for females 5'10" or taller, and males 6'2" or taller.

A killer whale's heart beats 30 times a minute under water, 60 times a minute on the surface.

THE TOP 10 HITS OF THE YEAR, 1980–1983

Yet another installment of BRI's Top Ten of the Year list.

1980

(1) Call Me —*Blondie*
(2) Another Brick In The Wall —*Pink Floyd*
(3) Rock With You —*Michael Jackson*
(4) Magic —*Olvia Newton-John*
(5) Crazy Little Thing Called Love —*Queen*
(6) Do That One More Time —*Captain & Tennile*
(7) Coming Up —*Paul McCartney*
(8) Funkytown —*Lipps, Inc.*
(9) It's Still Rock And Roll To Me —*Billy Joel*
(10) The Rose —*Bette Midler*

1981

(1) Bette Davis Eyes —*Kim Carnes*
(2) (Just Like) Starting Over —*John Lennon*
(3) Lady —*Kenny Rogers*
(4) Endless Love —*Diana Ross & Lionel Richie*
(5) Jessie's Girl —*Rick Springfield*
(6) Celebration —*Kool & The Gang*
(7) Kiss On My List —*Daryl Hall & John Oates*
(8) Keep On Loving You —*REO Speedwagon*
(9) I Love A Rainy Night —*Eddie Rabbitt*
(10) 9 To 5 —*Dolly Parton*

1982

(1) Physical —*Olivia Newton-John*
(2) Eye Of The Tiger —*Survivor*
(3) I Love Rock N' Roll —*Joan Jett & The Blackhearts*
(4) Centerfold —*J. Geils Band*
(5) Ebony And Ivory —*Paul McCartney & Stevie Wonder*
(6) Don't You Want Me —*Human League*
(7) Hurts So Good —*John Cougar*
(8) Jack And Diane —*John Cougar*
(9) Abracadabra —*Steve Miller Band*
(10) Hard To Say I'm Sorry —*Chicago*

1983

(1) Every Breath You Take —*Police*
(2) Billie Jean —*Michael Jackson*
(3) Down Under —*Men At Work*
(4) Flashdance…What A Feeling —*Irene Cara*
(5) Beat It —*Michael Jackson*
(6) Total Eclipse Of The Heart —*Bonnie Tyler*
(7) Maneater —*Daryl Hall & John Oates*
(8) Maniac —*Michael Sembello*
(9) Baby Come To Me —*Patti Austin with James Ingram*
(10) Sweet Dreams (Are Made Of This) —*Eurythmics*

Half of all Americans over the age of 55 have no teeth.

PART V: THE CHRYSLER BUILDING

*Part V of the World's Tallest Buildings is the story of a
skyscraper that's still regarded by many as the most beautiful
building ever built. (For Part IV, see page 200.)*

TOP THIS

By the late 1920s, the Woolworth Building had held the
title of "world's tallest building" for more than a decade.
But its reign clearly wouldn't last much longer—skyscrapers were
going up all over Manhattan, and many of their owners publicly
aspired to be the new record-holder.

However, no one knew who would actually pull it off—it was
a "rule" in this building competition that the heights of prospective skyscrapers be kept secret to prevent rival architects from
planning even taller structures.

One man who was determined to own the world's tallest
building was Walter P. Chrysler, a former machinist's apprentice
who had worked his way up to vice president at General Motors—
and then left to head his own successful auto company.

For years Chrysler had wanted to build a skyscraper. But it
wasn't until he took a trip to France that he finally decided how
tall it should be. "Something that I had seen in Paris kept coming
back to me," he later explained. "I said to the architects, 'make
this building higher than the Eiffel Tower.'"

GETTING OFF THE GROUND

Chrysler's architect, William Van Alen, knew that two former
partners of his, H. Craig Severance and Yasuo Matsui, were
designing a building for the Bank of Manhattan at 40 Wall St. He
didn't know how high it was going to be, and they weren't about
to tell him. So Van Alen announced that the Chrysler Building
would be 925 feet tall, expecting them to make their design just
tall enough to beat it. He was right—as it neared completion it
became clear that 40 Wall Street was going to be 927 feet tall, a
scant two feet higher than the Chrysler Building's announced
height.

Slow food: The average French citizen eats 500 snails a year.

MAKING A POINT

Now Van Alen knew what number to beat, and he had an idea about how to do it.

In its original plans, the 71-story Chrysler Building was topped by a hollow 142-foot art-deco dome. Van Alen used it as a sort of Trojan Horse. While construction went on as planned outside, a new construction crew was operating in secret inside the dome, building a 123-foot high spire.

Just as 40 Wall St. was nearing completion, Van Alen had the workers lift the spire up through the hole in the top of the dome and bolt it into place. The spire pushed the Chrysler Building's height to 1,048 feet, making it the first building to pass the 1,000 foot mark—as well as the tallest building in the world. It was also the first building to be built taller than the Eiffel Tower, just as Walter Chrysler had asked.

HIGH WATER MARK

The Chrysler building is considered by many to be the most beautiful skyscraper ever built, the pinnacle of art deco architectural design. Van Alen incorporated numerous automotive themes into the building's exterior. At each corner of the base of the tower at the 31st floor, he placed a gargoyle in the form of a winged helmet of Mercury—the symbol on Chrysler's radiator caps at the time. And on the 61st story he added eagle's-head gargoyles that were modeled after the hood ornament on the 1929 Chrysler Plymouth.

One architectural historian describes the building as "the skyscraper of skyscrapers. It is perhaps the sort of building one might dream in a primitive dream....Its silvery tower kindles the imagination of those who believe there is some life and glory in urban existence. The Chrysler Building remains one of the most appealing and awe-inspiring of the skyscrapers. It has few equals anywhere."

The Chrysler Building's beauty has endured for decades, but its status as the world's tallest building only lasted a year. Even as it was opening for business, the construction of the Empire State Building was already underway.

Part VI of the World's Tallest Buildings is on page 293.

No laughing matter: William Shakespeare invented the expression, "Laugh it off."

TITANIC COINCIDENCES

There's something almost mystical about the Titanic. There are so many bizarre coincidences associated with it, you'd think it was an episode of The Twilight Zone.

THE TITAN/TITANIC

In 1898, a short novel called *The Wreck of the Titan or Futility*, by Morgan Robertson, was published in the U.S. It told the story of the maiden voyage of an "unsinkable" luxury liner called the *Titan*. Robertson described the boat in great detail.

The *Titan*, he wrote, was 800 feet long, weighed 75,000 tons, had three propellers and 24 lifeboats, and was packed with rich passengers. Cruising at 25 knots, the *Titan's* hull was ripped apart when it hit an iceberg in April. Most of the passengers were lost because there weren't enough life boats. Robertson apparently claimed he'd written his book with the help of an "astral writing partner."

Eerie Coincidence: Fourteen years later, the real-life *Titanic* took off on its maiden voyage. Like the fictional *Titan*, it was considered the largest and safest ship afloat. It was 882.5 feet long, weighed 66,000 tons, had three propellers and 22 life boats, and carried a full load of rich passengers. Late at night on April 14, 1912, sailing at 23 knots, the *Titanic* ran into an iceberg which tore a hole in its hull and upended the ship. At least 1,513 people drowned because there weren't enough lifeboats.

THE TITANIAN/TITANIC

In 1935, a "tramp steamer" was heading from England to Canada. On watch was a 23-year-old seaman named William Reeves. It was April, the month when the Titanic hit an iceberg and went down. As the *Reader's Digest Book of Amazing Facts* tells it:

> Young Reeves brooded deeply on this. His watch was due to end at midnight. This, he knew, was the time the Titanic had hit the iceberg. Then, as now, the sea had been calm. These thoughts swelled and took shape as omens…as he stood his

---

When you walk down a steep hill, the pressure on your knees is equal to three times your body weight.

lonely watch....He was scared to shout an alarm, fearing his shipmates' ridicule. But he was also scared not to.

Eerie Coincidence: All of a sudden, Reeves recalled the exact date of the *Titanic* accident—April 14, 1912—the day he had been born. That was enough to get him to act.

He shouted out a danger warning, and the helmsman rang the signal: engines full astern. The ship churned to a halt—just yards from a huge iceberg that towered menacingly out of the night.

More deadly icebergs crowded in around the tramp steamer, and it took nine days for icebreakers from Newfoundland to smash a way clear.

The name of the ship Reeves saved from a similar fate to the *Titanic's*? The *Titanian*.

THE LUCKLESS TOWERS

Talk about coincidences! BRI member Andrew M. Borrok (hope we got that right—the fax is hard to read) submitted the following excerpt just as Uncle John was writing this piece. Obviously we had to include it. Thanks!

The stoker on the *Titanic* was named Frank Lucks Towers. Charles Pelegrino writes in his book, *Her Name, Titanic:*

Though he would survive this night (Titanic) without injury, his troubles were just beginning. In two years he'd be aboard the Empress of Ireland when it collided with another ship, opening up a hole in the Empress' side. (Note: it was the worst peace-time maritime disaster—over 2000 lost.) It would be an usually hot night, and all the portholes would be open as she rolled onto her side in the St. Lawrence River. In minutes she would be gone—yet miraculously, Frank Towers was going to survive— virtually alone. He'd take his next job aboard the Lusitania, (sunk by German U-boats in 1915) and would be heard to shout "Now what!" when the torpedo struck. He'd swim to a lifeboat, vowing every stroke of the way to take up farming.

His story was destined to inspire a young writer to script a teleplay entitled Lone Survivor. The teleplay was so well received that it paved the way for a series. The writer's name was Rod Serling and the series became *The Twilight Zone.*

Smallest post office in the United States: Ochopee, a town in the western Everglades.

URBAN LEGENDS

In our last Bathroom Reader *(the* Giant 10th Anniversary *edition),
we ran a piece on urban legends. Since then, we've come across so
many more good ones that we just had to include them. Remember
the rule of thumb: if a story sounds true, but also seems too
"perfect" to be true, it's probably an urban legend.*

THE STORY: Two speeding semi trucks crash head on in a
heavy fog. The drivers survive, but the two trucks are too
smashed together to separate, so the towing company tows
them to the junkyard in one piece. A few weeks later, junkyard
workers notice a terrible smell coming from the wreck. They pry
the cars apart…and discover a Volkswagen beetle with four
passengers crushed flat in between the two trucks.
THE TRUTH: Urban legends featuring small cars smashed by
big vehicles are so numerous that they're practically a category by
themselves. What keeps them alive is the general fear of meeting
a similar fate.

THE STORY: Rock Hudson and Jim Nabors (TV's Gomer Pyle)
were married in a secret Hollywood ceremony.
THE TRUTH: According to Rock Hudson biographer Sam
Davidson, Hudson and Nabors barely knew one another. Davidson
says she believes the rumors were started "by some gay guys who as
a joke sent out invitations to the wedding of Nabors and Hudson."
The invitations were mistakenly taken seriously, and the rumors
became so pervasive that Nabors and Hudson "made a point of
not being seen together at Hollywood events."

THE STORY: In a South African hospital, a number of patients
have died mysteriously while convalescing in a particular bed. The
hospital investigated…and discovered that the cleaning lady had
been inadvertently killing a patient every time she polished the
floor.
HOW IT SPREAD: On the Internet, in 1996. The e-mail was
supposedly taken from a June 1996 *Cape Times* article headlined
"Cleaner Polishes Off Patients." The story follows:

> "It seems that every Friday morning a cleaner would enter the
> ward, remove the plug that powered the patient's life support

system, plug her floor polisher into the vacant socket, then go about her business. When she had finished her chores, she would plug the life support machine back in and leave, unaware that the patient was now dead. She could not, after all, hear the screams and eventual death rattle over the whirring of her polisher.

"We are sorry, and have sent a strong letter to the cleaner in question. Further, the Free State Health and Welfare Department is arranging for an electrician to fit an extra socket, so there should be no repetition of this incident. The enquiry is now closed."

THE TRUTH: Rumors of death-by-cleaning-lady incidents floated around South Africa for years before reporters at a South African newspaper named *Die Volksblad* decided, in 1996, to see if there was any truth to them. They ran an article asking relatives of any of the victims to come forward. No one did…but another South African paper picked up the story—and finally the *Cape Times* mistakenly ran the story as an actual occurrence, rather than a regional newspaper's attempt to track down an urban legend.

THE STORY: A medical school student prepares to work on a cadaver during her gross anatomy laboratory. She lifts the cover off of the body…and discovers that the cadaver is an ex-boyfriend.
THE TRUTH: Finding out that the cadaver assigned to you is a friend, relative or loved one is a fear as old as medical school anatomy classes themselves. Tales of such a thing happening have been traced back hundreds of years. One version, involving the English novelist Laurence Sterne, dates back to 1768.
Note: It actually did happen at least once. In 1982, a student at the University of Alabama School of Medicine learned that the body of her great aunt was one of the nine cadavers assigned to her anatomy class. The state anatomy board replaced it with another body.

*   *   *

"Nothing in education is so astonishing as the amount of ignorance it accumulates in the form of inert facts." **—Henry Adams**

ASPIRIN: THE MIRACLE DRUG

Here's more on the history of aspirin.
The first part of the story is on page 59.

The first part of the story is on page 59.

MID-LIFE CRISIS
In 1950, aspirin earned a place in the *Guinness Book of World Records* as the world's best-selling painkiller. But if the medical community had paid attention to Dr. Lawrence Craven, an ear-nose-throat specialist, in 1948, aspirin would have been recognized as much more than that.

Dr. Craven had noticed that when he performed tonsillectomies, patients who took aspirin bled more than the ones who didn't. He suspected the aspirin was inhibiting the ability of blood to clot, something that might be useful in preventing strokes and heart attacks—both of which can be caused by excessive clotting of the blood.

Craven decided to test his theory. He put 400 of his male patients on aspirin, then watched them over several years to see how many had heart attacks. Not one did, so Craven expanded his research. He began following the histories of 8,000 regular aspirin-takers, to see if any of them had a heart attack. None of them did, either.

Dr. Craven published his findings in a medical journal. But nobody listened. "The medical community shunned his findings," says Dr. Steven Weisman. "He wasn't a cardiologist, he wasn't in the academic community and he was publishing in a lesser-known journal."

ASPIRIN SCIENCE
The biggest problem was that as late as 1970 nobody had any idea how aspirin worked. That year John Vane, a researcher with London's Royal College of Surgeons, discovered what Dr. Craven had known intuitively—that aspirin blocks an enzyme that causes blood platelets to stick together, which is what happens when blood clots. By inhibiting clotting, aspirin helps to prevent

strokes, heart attacks, and other cardiovascular ailments.

Not long afterwards, researchers in Sweden discovered that aspirin also blocks the production of prostaglandins, hormone-like chemicals that affect digestion, reproduction, circulation, and the immune system. Excess levels of prostaglandins can cause headaches, fevers, blood clots, and a host of other problems. Scientists quickly began to discover that aspirin's ability to block the prostaglandin production makes it an effective treatment for many of these problems.

WONDER DRUG

For the first time in 70 years, researchers were beginning to understand aspirin's potential beyond reducing pain, fever and inflammation. Thousands of studies have since been conducted to test aspirin's effectiveness against a number of diseases, and many more are planned.

The results have been astounding. In 1980, the U.S. Food and Drug Administration (FDA) recommended aspirin to reduce the risk of stroke in men experiencing stroke symptoms. In 1985, it recommended aspirin to heart attack patients as a means of reducing the risk of second heart attacks. One 1988 heart attack study was so successful that researchers shut it down five years early so that the test subjects who weren't taking aspirin could begin to take it. In 1996, the FDA recommended administering aspirin during heart attacks as a means of lowering the risk of death.

And that's only the beginning. Aspirin is believed to lower the risk of colon cancer by as much as 32%, and scientists are also exploring aspirin's ability to slow the progression of Alzheimer's disease, cataracts, diabetes, numerous other forms of cancer, and even HIV, the virus that causes AIDS.

"No little white pill does everything, that's for sure," says the University of Pennsylvania's Dr. Garret Fitzgerald, one of the world's top aspirin experts. "But the strength of the evidence for aspirin working where it has been shown to work is probably greater than the strength of the evidence for any drug for human disease."

Iron man competition: The most pushups ever performed in one day was 46,001.

Bathroom Reader Warning: Aspirin isn't for everyone. Consult a doctor before taking aspirin regularly. Aspirin is still an acid, and it can irritate the lining of the stomach and cause pain, internal bleeding and ulcers. "'An aspirin a day' does not apply to everyone," says Dr. Paul Pedersen, a doctor of internal medicine. "It's not like apples."

• Also: In 1986, scientists established a link between aspirin and Reye's syndrome, a rare but sometimes fatal disease that strikes children suffering from acute viral infections like influenza and chicken pox.

ASPIRIN FACTS

• Americans take an estimated 80 million aspirin a day—about the same amount as the rest of the world combined. 30-50% of them are taken as preventative medicine for cardiac disease.

• How you take aspirin depends on where you live: Americans prefer pills; the English like powders that dissolve in water; Italians like fizzy aspirin drinks, and the French like aspirin suppositories.

• Roughly 6% of Americans cannot take straight aspirin because it irritates their stomachs. That's where coated or "buffered" aspirin comes in—each pill is treated with a special, slow-to-dissolve coating that prevents the aspirin from being absorbed by the body until it has left the stomach and gone into the intestines.

• One of the remaining unsolved aspirin mysteries is why it only works on you when you're sick. "If your body temperature is normal, it won't lower it," says Roger P. Maickel, a professor of pharmacology at Purdue University. "If you don't have inflammation, it doesn't have any antiarthritic effects on your joints. It's beautifully simple to work with, yet the damn thing does everything."

MIGRAINE MATERIAL

What did Felix Hoffman, inventor of aspirin, have to show for his work? Not much—aspirin made the Bayer family fabulously wealthy, and it earned Felix Hoffman's supervisor, Heinrich Dreser, enough money to retire early. Hoffman was not so lucky—he was entitled to royalties on anything he invented that was patented, but since aspirin was never successfully patented in Germany, the really big bucks eluded him.

If you're typical, you can guess someone's sex with 95% accuracy just by smelling their breath.

THE ANIMALS AT THE ZOO, Part 2

Here's more info on animal-watching at the zoo, from
Beastly Behaviors, by Janine M. Benyus

WATCHING ELEPHANTS

The typical elephant herd is made up of adult females and the young of both sexes. It is a very tight-knit group. In the wild, adult males wander by themselves or congregate in small bachelor groups. Bulls are extremely irritable, unpredictable, and dangerous when in "must" (heat). For this reason, many zoos refuse to keep them.

Behavior: Elephants do most of their "talking" with their trunks. Here's what the different trunk positions mean.

Position: Hanging straight down.
What It Means: The elephant has nothing in particular on its mind. This is how it holds its trunk while going about its normal, everyday business.

Position: Held up in "tea spout" position (U-curve in the middle, pointed outward at the tip).
What It Means: It's the elephant's sniffing position. Usually, an elephant's first reaction to something new is to try to pick up its scent.

Position: Hanging down with tip curled in.
What It Means: Fear or submission.

Position: Thrust straight outward.
What It Means: Aggression. Threat. Elephants hold their trunks this way when they're charging.

Behavior: Touching each other's trunk.
What It Means: Greeting. Take note of the ears as one elephant approaches another. If they're high and folded, it's going to be a friendly encounter.

First meal eaten on the moon: 4 bacon squares, 3 sugar cookies, peaches, pineapple-grapefruit drink, coffee.

Behavior: Flapping their ears.
What It Means: The elephant is cooling itself. Its favorite way to beat the heat, though, is to roll in mud.

Behavior: Trumpeting.
What It Means: Excitement. Elephants get vocal only when they're excited. Generally, the more excited they are—either with joy or anger—the longer and louder they'll trumpet. At zoos, they'll give a short, sharp toot when they're impatient to be fed.

Behavior: Bold trumpeting; lots of rubbing and bumping against each other. Could be accompanied by urinating and defecating.
What It Means: The scene may sound and look scary, but it's probably a celebration. Elephants reunited after a long separation can become very raucous. It's just their way of telling each other, "It's great to see you. I missed you."

OTHER ANIMALS

DOLPHINS
Behavior: Rubbing.
What It Means: Affection. When you see dolphins nuzzling, you probably think they're expressing care for one another. And you're right. Dolphins use touch as a way to bond. They also use rubbing to remove social tensions, and parasites, such as barnacles, from each others' skin. A dolphin may rub its body, fluke, or flippers against a neighboring dolphin. Or two dolphins may engage in a full-body rub or pat each other repeatedly in a "pat-a-cake" maneuver.

OSTRICHES
Behavior: Pretending to feed.
What It Means: Think of it as a way for a male and female to test their compatibility during a complicated courtship ritual. Together, the couple will peck at the ground. Though it might look like they're feeding, they're not. It's more like a dance—with their goal being to move in unison.

Poll results: 12% of Americans say they think Joan of Arc was Noah's wife.

TEARING DOWN
THE WHITE HOUSE

*The White House wasn't always a national treasure. A number of
presidents once seriously considered tearing it down or turning it into a
museum and building a new residence somewhere else.
But today, that's unthinkable. Here's why.*

NOT ENOUGH SPACE

At first, most Americans didn't think there was anything
particularly special about the White House. Few had ever
seen it or had any idea what it looked like, and even the families
who lived there found it completely inadequate.

When it was built, the White House was the largest house in
the country (and it remained so until after the Civil War). But it
served so many different purposes that little of it was available for
First Families to actually live in. The first floor, or "State Floor,"
was made up entirely of public rooms; and half of the second floor
was taken up by the president's offices, which where staffed by as
many as 30 employees. The First Family had to get by with the
eight—or fewer—second-floor rooms that were left.

By Lincoln's time, the situation was intolerable. Kenneth
Leish writes in *The White House*, "The lack of privacy was
appalling. The White House was open to visitors daily, and office
seekers, cranks, and the merely curious had no difficulty making
their way upstairs from the official rooms on the first floor."

THE LINCOLN WHITE HOUSE

Lincoln was so uncomfortable with the situation that he had a
private corridor (since removed) constructed. This at least allowed
him to get from the family quarters to his office without having to
pass through the reception room, where throngs of strangers were
usually waiting to see him.

He also received a $20,000 appropriation to improve the
furnishings of the White House, which had become, as one visitor
put it, "bare, worn and spoiled," like "a deserted farmstead," with
holes in the carpets and paint peeling off of the walls in the state
rooms.

Lincoln was busy with the Civil War, so he turned the matter over to his wife, who spent every penny and went $6,700 over budget. Lincoln was furious, and refused to ask Congress to cover the balance. "It would stink in the nostrils of the American people," he fumed, "to have it said that the President of the United States had approved a bill overrunning an appropriate [amount] for flub dubs for this damned old house, when the soldiers cannot have blankets."

The new furnishings did not last for more than a few years. When Lincoln was assassinated in 1865, the White House fell into disarray. "Apparently," writes The White House Historical Society, "no one really supervised the White House during the five weeks Mrs. Lincoln lay mourning in her room, and vandals helped themselves."

SAVING THE HOUSE

Ironically, at the same time the White House was being ransacked, it was gaining a new respect with Americans... attaining an almost shrine-like status.

National tragedy turned the White House into a national monument. It wasn't just the White House anymore—it was the place where the great fallen hero, Lincoln, had lived. Photography had only been invented about 30 years earlier. Now for the first time, photos of the White House circulated around the country. It became a symbol of the presidency...and America.

The Founding Fathers had assumed that future presidents would add to, or even demolish and rebuild the official residence as they saw fit. But after 1865, no president would have dared to suggest tearing it down.

Feeling patriotic? There's more on the White House
on page 682.

* * *

"I'll be glad to be going—this is the loneliest place in the world."
—President William Howard Taft, on leaving the White House

Only male fireflies can fly.

WHY ASK WHY?

Sometimes, answers are irrelevant—it's the question that counts.
These cosmic queries are from a variety of readers.

Why do psychics have to ask your name?

Why don't sheep shrink when it rains?

How much deeper would the ocean be without sponges?

What happens if you get scared half to death twice?

Despite the cost of living, have you noticed how it remains so popular?

How do you tell when you run out of invisible ink?

Did ancient doctors refer to IVs as "fours"?

Why are they called "apartments" when they're all stuck together?

If bankers can count, how come they have eight windows and only four tellers?

Is Dan Quayle's name spelled with an e at the end?

Why do we play in recitals and recite in plays?

If the #2 pencil is so popular, why is it still #2?

If most car accidents occur within five miles of home, why doesn't everyone just move 10 miles away?

Why can't I set my laser printer on "stun"?

If all the world is a stage, where is the audience sitting?

Why do they call them "hemorrhoids" instead of "asteroids"?

Why is the alphabet in that order? Is it because of that song?

If you write a book about failure and it doesn't sell, is it a success?

Would a fly without wings be called a walk?

If white wine goes with fish, do white grapes go with sushi?

If the funeral procession is at night, do folks drive with their lights off?

Poll result: 30% of people asked to participate in an opinion poll refuse.

TWO FORGOTTEN INVENTORS

*Here's a look at two people who made great inventions,
only to see the credit go to someone else.*

FORGOTTEN INVENTOR: John Fitch
CLAIM TO FAME: He had been George Washington's
gunsmith at Valley Forge, and had skills as a silversmith,
brass founder, surveyor and clockmaker. But he should have been
known as the man who invented the steamboat—not Robert
Fulton. He built his first model of a "boat propelled by steam" in
1785, and successfully tried out a full-size version the following
year. He obtained exclusive rights in five states for mechanically-
propelled boats and, by 1790, was operating regularly scheduled
services between Philadelphia, Pennsylvania and Trenton, New
Jersey.
HIS LEGACY: Over the years Fitch's debts piled up and squat-
ters took over his lands. He died sad and broke in 1798 at the age
of 55, five years before Fulton "invented" the steamboat. Congress
later honored Fitch with a mural in the U.S. Capitol, but Fulton is
still the one who gets all the credit.

FORGOTTEN INVENTOR: Nathan B. Stubblefield
CLAIM TO FAME: Stubblefield was the real inventor of the
radio—not Marconi. He first demonstrated a "wireless telephone"
for a few friends on his farm in 1890, when Marconi was still a
teenager. He filed no patent at the time, he "just went on tinkering." On January 1, 1902 (less than a month after Marconi had
transmitted the letter "S" across the Atlantic in Morse code), he
finally got around to doing a demonstration for the public. About
1,000 friends and neighbors watched as, "speaking softly into a
two-foot-square box, he was heard at half a dozen listening
[stations] around town." Later that year, he gave a better-publi-
cized and better-attended demonstration in Washington, D.C.,
from a steam launch on the Potomac River.
  Marconi, known today as the father of radio, actually
pioneered wireless telegraphy, the transmission of Morse code.

Why is the celtuce plant called a celtuce? It tastes a little like celery, a little like lettuce.

Stubblefield sent voices and music (played by his son) over the air, and he did it years before Marconi sent his first dots and dashes. In a 1908 patent he described how to put radios in horseless carriages, making him the father of the car radio—another invention he did not capitalize on.

INTO THE DUSTBIN: None of Stubblefield's inventions, "including a battery devised for radios," made him much money. His marriage broke up, his house burned down. Still he continued to work on new inventions. But we don't know much about them—Shortly before his death Stubblefield destroyed all his inventions and burned their plans. He was a lonely, impoverished hermit when he was found starved to death in a shack near his hometown of Murray, Kentucky in 1928. His body went into an unmarked grave.

*   *   *

AND SPEAKING OF
THE DUSTBIN OF HISTORY...

Here's another historic figure who's been swept out of the history books:

FORGOTTEN FIGURE: Captain James Iredell Waddell, Confederate war hero and commander of the warship Shenandoah.

CLAIM TO FAME: Under Waddell's command, the Shenandoah disrupted Yankee whaling operations in the Pacific, captured numerous Union vessels, destroyed over $1 million worth of shipping, and took more than 1,000 prisoners.

Much of this success came after General Lee's surrender at Appomattox on April 9, 1865. Even when Waddell learned of the surrender, he chose to ignore it, believing the South would keep fighting a guerrilla war.

INTO THE DUSTBIN: Waddell made plans to attack San Francisco by sea. But on his way there, the Shenandoah met up with a friendly British merchant ship, whose captain informed Waddell that the war was definitely over. Realizing he would be tried and probably hanged for piracy if he made port in America, Waddell and crew sailed for England. The Shenandoah surrendered to the British in Liverpool on November 6, 1865.

Most popular soap opera in the world: Mexico's *The Rich Also Cry.*

FAMOUS FOR BEING NAKED

Here are a few celebrities who are remembered for not wearing any clothes. (Or for looking like they weren't.)

CHERI BRAND, child model.
Famous For: Posing for the original portrait of Little Miss Coppertone, the girl whose bottom is exposed because a dog is pulling down her bathing suit.
The Bare Facts: In 1953, a Miami advertising agency hired graphic artist Joyce Ballentyne to design the logo for Coppertone suntan lotion. For models, she used her 3-year-old daughter Cheri and a cocker spaniel she borrowed from a neighbor. The image appeared in ads on billboards all over the U.S., accompanied by slogans like "Don't be a paleface," and "Tan, don't burn." The image became a pop icon, as well as one of the most recognized logos in the country. Today, it's a reminder of innocent 1950s and of summer vacations past.

Brand, now a health club manager, is proud to be a part of pop culture. "If I get teased, I suppose I would blush," she says, "but what child doesn't have a photo like that in their album. Mine just happens to be more public."

Little Miss Coppertone faded as a corporate symbol in the late 1970s as deep tanning became synonymous with skin cancer, but the company brought her back in 1987 when it launched Water Babies, a sunscreen for children. The character's new role: "teaching the importance of sun protection to kids."

ANNETTE KELLERMAN, a Hollywood actress in 1916.
Famous For: Being the first person to appear completely naked in a feature film, in 1916.
The Bare Facts: The film was called *A Daughter of the Gods*, and was filmed on location in Jamaica. In one memorable scene Kellerman, formerly a professional swimmer, jumps from a 100-foot-high tower into a pool supposedly filled with alligators, then crashes against some rocks and falls down a waterfall. She is nude

the entire time.

Amazingly, the film was so bad that not even the novelty of film nudity could save it. William Fox, head of the Fox Film Corporation, hated it so much that he re-edited it himself, then removed the director's name from it and barred him from the premiere.

ADAH ISAACS MENKEN, stage actress of the 1860s.
Famous for: Performing as the "Naked Lady" of the theater. She toured the world with a play called *Mazeppa,* in which she wore in a loose-fitting tunic that showed off her "uncovered" calves (actually flesh-colored tights).
The Bare Facts: Ironically, the woman known internationally as the "Naked Lady" always appeared fully clothed. She wore a skimpy, loose-fitting tunic over flesh-colored tights, which, as Edward Marks writes in *They All Had Glamour,* "were completely unknown in 1861. The audiences thought they were gazing on bare skin."

In 1860, a theater owner in Albany, NY decided to spice up the well-known play *Mazeppa.* Until then, the play's highlight had always been when a live horse performed a stunt onstage. To make it more exciting, the theater owner tied the provocatively dressed Adah to the horse. A star was born. As one historian writes:

> Adah, whose acting career had gotten off to a slow start due to lack of talent, found herself completely at home in the role of celebrity. She took *Mazeppa* to New York, where she opened to rave reviews, then went to wow'em out west. Adah's curvaceous calves did the trick. Neophyte journalist Mark Twain was smitten. Mormon leader Brigham Young, though expressing shock, managed to sit through the whole show.

Menken traveled to Europe, where she was equally popular. *The London Review* observed that Adah looked like "Lady Godiva in a slip," noting that "of course, respectable people go to see the spectacle and not her figure." At one performance Napoleon III, the King of Greece, the Duke of Edinburgh were all in attendance; Charles Dickens considered her a close friend.

Then in 1868, at the height of her fame, she collapsed onstage. A month later she was dead of tuberculosis.

The average coach airline meal costs the airline $4.00. The average first class meal: $50.

THE BIRTH
OF THE BURGER

*BRI member and food editor, Jeff Cheek, contributed
this fascinating history of the hamburger*

WILD HORSEMEN

In the 13th Century, wild, nomadic horsemen known as Tartars overran most of Asia and Eastern Europe. They had a distinct way of preparing meat: slice off a large chunk of horsemeat or beef and slip it under a saddle. A day of hard riding would tenderize it. Then it was chopped up and eaten raw.

This custom was introduced into the area we now call Germany by traders traveling down the Elbe River to Hamburg.

The German people did not eat horsemeat—but they did start serving ground, raw beef flavored with garlic, spices and a raw egg. (Today, it's called steak tartare, and is still popular in Europe.) And for those who preferred cooked beef, the raw beef patties became the first hamburger steaks. But they weren't the hand-held sandwiches we call hamburgers. Those came hundreds of years later.

BIRTH OF THE BURGER

It began around 1879, in a restaurant near the docks of the Hamburg-Amerika Line in Germany. Owner Otto Kuase began serving a sandwich American sailors loved: two slices of buttered bread, pickle strips, and a fried beef patty with a butter-fried egg on top. Add a mug of good German beer, and this sandwich made an excellent, inexpensive dinner.

So many Yankee seamen came to his restaurant for the sandwich that Kuase listed it on his menu as "American Steak." When the sailors returned home, they taught restaurants along the Eastern Seaboard how to make it. Soon, all a customer had to say was "bring me a hamburger." The name stuck, even when the recipe changed.

THE BURGER STARTS SIZZLING

In 1904, to celebrate the centennial of the Louisiana Purchase, St. Louis staged a huge World's Fair. There were hundreds of vendors

15 million gallons of wine were destroyed in the 1906 San Francisco earthquake.

selling foods—including German immigrants peddling their native fare. This included a new version of the old hamburger. The slices of bread were replaced with dinner rolls, which fit the round meat patty. Butter was expensive, so the rolls were smeared with the cheaper Heinz ketchup. The butter-fried egg was replaced by slices of onion, tomato, and pickles.

The new hamburger was inexpensive because cheaper cuts of beef could be used...and it was an instant success. People from all over the country attended the fair, and returned home ready to eat more.

THE BUN

There was one flaw—the dinner rolls made burgers harder to eat. So for another dozen years or so, people kept using the traditional slices of bread. Then an enterprising cook in Wichita, Kansas invented the last component of the modern hamburger: he created a round, soft bun that absorbed the juices of the meat patty.

His name was J. Walter Anderson. He was working as a short order cook when he made his discovery. Soon after, he bought an old trolley and converted it into a five stool diner, specializing in burgers at 5¢ each. This was in 1916, but it was a real bargain even then. In 1920, Anderson added two more diners, stressing their cleanliness with the name White Castle Hamburgers. Others followed and White Castle became the first national hamburger chain.

* * *

THE NAME'S THE SAME?

At the beginning of World War I, Kaiser Wilhelm had a treaty with Belgium guaranteeing its neutrality. When he sent his armies through Belgium to attack France, the U.S. protested—and the Kaiser replied that the treaty was just "a scrap of paper." It was a public relations disaster—anti-German hysteria swept the world. In Britain, the Royal Family changed its name from the House of Saxe-Coburg to the English-sounding House of Windsor. On American menus, sauerkraut became "victory cabbage" and hamburger steak became Salisbury Steak. But against pressure to call burgers "ground meat patty sandwiches," burger-lovers held their ground. Today, a hamburger is still a hamburger.

The U.S. Army accidentally ordered an 82-year supply of freeze-dried tuna salad mix for troops in Europe.

FIREWORKS FACTS

Next July 4th, you'll have something new to talk about.

A **FLASH IN THE PAN**
The first fireworks were hollowed out bamboo stalks stuffed with black powder. The Chinese called them "arrows of flying fire," and shot them into the air during religious occasions and holidays to ward off imaginary dragons.

According to legend, the essential ingredient—black powder—was first discovered in a Chinese kitchen in the 10th century A.D. A cook was preparing potassium nitrate (a pickling agent and preservative) over a charcoal fire laced with sulfur. Somehow the three chemicals—potassium nitrate, charcoal, and sulfur—combined, causing an explosion. The meal was destroyed, but the powder, later known as gunpowder, was born.

SAFETY FIRST
According to the fireworks industry's own estimates, as many people have been killed by 4th of July fireworks as were killed in the Revolutionary War. Nearly all of the victims were killed setting off their own fireworks, not watching public displays. And most fatalities occurred before World War II, when fireworks were almost completely unregulated. The carnage became so widespread that the 4th of July actually came to be known as the "Bloody Fourth" and even the "Carnival of Lockjaw," due to the large number of people who died from infected burns.

Then in the 1930s, several organizations began a campaign to outlaw fireworks. Pressured by the Ladies' Home Journal (which printed photographs of dozens of maimed victims), the federal government and individual states outlawed just about every kind of firework imaginable...to the point where many states now ban them entirely. Since then, the number of firework-related injuries plummeted. Today, the Consumer Safety Commission ranks them as only the 132nd most-dangerous consumer item, behind such things as beds, grocery carts, key rings, and plumbing fixtures.

COLORS
• Because black powder burns at a relatively low temperature, for

Stop complaining: Senegalese women spend an average of 17.5 hours a week just collecting water.

more than 800 years fireworks burned only with dull yellow and orange flames. It wasn't until the 19th century that pyrotechnicians discovered that mixing potassium chlorate into the powder made it burn much hotter, enabling it to burn red when strontium was added, green when barium was added, and bright yellow when sodium was added.

• White was impossible to produce until the mid-1800s, when scientists developed ways to add aluminum, magnesium, and titanium to black powder.

• Blues and violets (caused when copper and chlorine are added) are the hardest colors to create; even today, fireworks manufacturers judge their skills according to how well their blues and violets turn out.

FIREWORKS LINGO
Here are some names the fireworks industry gives to its creations:

• Willows: Fireworks with long colorful "branches" that stream down towards the ground.

• Palm Trees: Willows that leave a brightly-colored trail from the ground as they're shot into the air.

• Chrysanthemums: Fireworks that explode into perfect circles.

• Split comets: Fireworks that explode into starlets, which explode again into even more starlets.

• Salutes: A bright, white flash, followed by a boom.

• Triple-break Salutes: Salutes that explode three times in rapid succession.

• Cookie-Cutters: Created by filling the inside of a cardboard container with black powder and gluing individual starlets to the outside. When the black powder charge explodes, the starlets explode in the same shape as the cookie-cutter. Shapes include stars, hearts, ovals, etc.

Fattest paper ever printed: *The New York Times,* 10/17/65, at 946 pages it weighed 7 1/2 lbs.

EDWARDS: THE UNLUCKIEST KINGS OF ENGLAND

*Being a royal Edward in England wasn't such a great deal.
Every king (and a few princes) of that name came to grief of
some kind, and often shared it with their friends and relatives.*

EDWARD THE ELDER (869-924) Before the Norman
Conquest in 1066, English kings weren't numbered
(although sometimes their days were). So, instead, the three
Saxon Edwards have nicknames. The first of them was called
Edward the Elder (for reasons that should be obvious). During this
Edward's 25 years on the throne, he ran a lot of Danes out of
England and ran through three wives. On his death, his son by
wifey #2, Aelfweard (the Unpronounceable) mounted the throne,
and was kicked off it less than a month later, by Athelstan, son of
wifey numero uno. (Boys, boys! Stop that squabbling!)

EDWARD THE MARTYR (963-978) This Edward came to the
throne at the age of 12, and hardly had time to warm it. Eddie was
murdered, possibly at the instigation of his wicked stepmother
Elfriday, whose ten-year-old son took over. After miracles at his
tomb, Edward was declared a saint and martyr. Such a shame he
wasn't around to enjoy the attention.

EDWARD THE CONFESSOR (1003-1066) The fact that his
father's name was Ethelred the Unready should have told us something, even though the term "unready" is not supposed to mean
unprepared, but instead...stubborn and unwilling to accept outside
advice.

His own name as "Confessor" meant that he had lived his
life in the faith (the Roman Catholic faith, that is), including
initiating the construction of Westminster Abbey, and didn't die
as a martyr. History is divided as to whether his reign consisted of
24 years of peace, or simply being too lazy to do anything. A
declared celibate, he married, but left no children. On his
deathbed he named his brother-in-law Harold as his successor.

When Sir Henry Royce died in 1933, the "RR" Rolls-Royce monogram was changed from red to black.

He was canonized 100 years after his death. Also much too late to enjoy it.

KING EDWARD I (1239-1307) Now we're getting into the numbers. Edward I seized the moment at age 32. He stomped Wales into submission, kicked all the Jews out of England, and kept up a running battle with Scotland because the Scots just wouldn't lie down and say "I give." When he finally defeated them in 1298, he took their Stone of Scone—which isn't a week-old pastry, but a 336-pound lump of yellow sandstone—the traditional rock upon which all kings of Scotland were crowned. (It was returned to Scotland in 1996.) That, and his capture and execution in 1305 of William Wallace (as played by Mel Gibson), made Edward *Plantagenet non grata* in the land of kilts and bagpipes. He expired on his way to yet another Scottish campaign, this time to crush a revolt by Robert Bruce. Serves him right, the bully.

KING EDWARD II (1284-1327) The first Prince of Wales should have cut his ship of state loose from the Piers. Piers Gaveston, that is, who became notorious as Edward's lover. When Edward married Princess Isabella of France in 1308, the coquettish Piers decked himself out in the bride's jewels. The 16-year-old queen was not amused; her ire earned her the name "She-Wolf of France."

Edward's reign was typified by upheaval, terminating with his abdication and murder by Isabella's supporters. Next to join him in death were Piers and Hugh Despenser, the king's next favorite. Edward and Isabella's son (who's coming up next) eventually wrested the throne from his mother, the She-Wolf, and had her lover, Roger Mortimer, executed.

KING EDWARD III (1312-1377) We already know this Edward is trouble (see above). And because his mother was a French princess, he laid claim to the throne of France in 1337, which lit the wick of the Hundred Years War (technically a string of battles and skirmishes, but who's counting?) His reign was plagued, literally, by three waves of the Black Death and its fallout: labor and food shortages, inflation, and unrest. Two of his sons, John of Gaunt and Edmund, would sow the seeds for the War of the Roses. A fertile family...but feisty!

Legend has it that Edward picked up the garter of the Countess of Salisbury when it fell from her leg to the floor during

---

Surveys say: About 2/3 of American men prefer boxers to briefs.

a dance. He founded the Order of the Garter (a kind of collective of knights) on his pronouncement "Honi soit qui mal y pense" (Shame on him who thinks evil of it)—a reference to those who wondered just how close the two were. She later married his son Edward, better known as the Black Prince.

EDWARD, THE BLACK PRINCE (1330-1376) This Edward died a year before his father, Edward III, so he never got to be king. If he'd lived, his son Richard II wouldn't have inherited the throne in 1377, and wouldn't have been deposed by Parliament, setting the stage for the ascension of the house of Lancaster (the red side of the War of the Roses). The Black Prince's lasting contribution to the family is the Prince of Wales motto: "Ich Dien" (I serve). But it seems like his serve was a little off.

KING EDWARD IV (1442-1483) After a decades-long gap in important Edwards, this one put a white York rose on the throne in 1461, after defeating and executing his cousin Henry VI. He also disposed of another Edward, Henry's son. Finding murder a handy way to avert trouble, he had his second brother, George Duke of Clarendon, executed for treason in 1478. His reign was otherwise unremarkable except for the fact that his heir, little Edward V, was left in the hands of the king's brother Richard, whose reign—if the stories are true—would be even more murderous than his own. (Well, he started it!)

KING EDWARD V (1470-1483) What can you say about the shortest reign in English history? Popular opinion has it that King Edward V and his younger brother, Richard Duke of York, were either murdered by Richard III or Henry VII. Take your pick.

Imprisoned in the Tower of London on their father's death in 1483, Uncle Richard brought a claim of pre-contract of marriage against their mother, making the boys illegitimate, and naming himself King Richard III. Edward remained uncrowned and unfound for 200 years. In 1674, bones were located under a wall of the tower and "identified" as his and his brother's by Thomas More's account in *The History of Richard III*. The bones were placed in a white urn and moved to St. George's Chapel, Windsor, where they remain today. And await DNA tests that would put the story, if not the king and his brother, to rest.

Mammal rule of thumb: in just about every species, the female lives longer than the male.

KING EDWARD VI (1447-1563) Left to follow in father Henry VIII's really big footsteps at age nine, Edward became engaged to his cousin, Mary Queen of Scots. If he'd lived, she surely would have been ahead of the game. Weak of heart and body, Edward declared his half-sisters ("Bloody") Mary and (Virgin Queen) Elizabeth to be bastards, and passed the throne to Henry VIII's great-niece, Jane Grey. Jane was promptly married off to a court intriguer, made queen, and reigned (but not officially) for nine whole days. Poor Jane was dethroned and executed by the previously mentioned Mary, the daughter of Henry VIII and his first wife, Katherine of Aragon. She was just 17. (You know what we mean.)

Edward VI would be the last royal Edward for 400 years.

KING EDWARD VII (1841-1910) They're back! Eddie became an expert at the game of patience, waiting till age 60 to ascend the throne. (Hang in there, Charles. There's hope for you yet!) Denied any meaningful role as a royal prince, he threw off Queen Victoria's apron strings with a vengeance, and plunged into the excesses of food, drink, gambling, and women. Despite marrying the unbelievably tolerant Princess Alexandra in 1863, he continued his profligate ways, while also building a fair image as politician and statesman. Never one to take a warning, he died in 1910 after a string of heart attacks.

KING EDWARD VIII (1894-1972) Love. More important than the "Land of Hope and Glory"? Apparently so. The second shortest reign in English history ended in 1936, less than a year after it started. Edward abdicated to marry "the woman I love," a twice-divorced American. As the Duke of Windsor (although the lady in question, Wallis Simpson, would never be granted the right to be called Duchess), he had a cushy life: a little royal visiting here, serving as a non-combatant general in WWII there. He even passed some time as the Governor of the Bahamas. Not bad. On Edward's death in 1972, Wallis was finally admitted to the palace, and in 1986 she was buried beside him at Frogmore, Windsor, where she'd never been invited in life.

EDWARD ? (1964-) Don't think you need to worry, Ed old son. You're only seventh in line to the throne. And court intrigues certainly aren't what they used to be. (Sigh.)

Whoopi Goldberg's real name is Caryn Elaine Johnson.

WORD ORIGINS

Ever wonder where words come from?
Here are some interesting stories.

CURFEW

Meaning: A prescribed time to leave certain places.
Origin: "In medieval times the danger from fire was especially great because most buildings were made of wood. With a wind blowing, a single burning house could start a conflagration. Hence the practice developed of covering fires before retiring for the night. During the reigns of Williams I and II, a bell was sounded at sunset to give notice that the time had come to extinguish all fires and candles. This came to be called 'curfew,' a word borrowed almost directly from the French couvre feu, which, in translation, is 'cover the fire.'" (From *The Story Behind the Word*, by Morton S. Freeman)

SHAMPOO

Meaning: Soap for washing hair.
Origin: "Early travelers in India were intrigued by a native custom. Sultans and nabobs had special servants who massaged their bodies after hot baths. From a native term for 'to press,' such a going-over of the body with knuckles was called a 'champo' or 'shampoo.'" (From *Why You Say It*, by Webb Garrison)

ALIMONY

Meaning: An allowance made to one spouse by the other for support pending or after legal separation or divorce.
Origin: "The word aliment means food. This traces to the Latin alo, 'nourish.' So the way the many divorce laws are written now, if a wife sues for release from her bonds, she expects alimony, which, etymologically, is really 'eating money.'" (From *Word Origins*, by Wilfred Funk)

CANNIBAL

Meaning: A person who eats humans.
Origin: "When Christopher Columbus landed in Cuba, he asked the natives what they called themselves. In their dialect they said

that they were Canibales, or people of Caniba. (This was a dialectal form of Caribe, and the Cuban natives were Caribes.) Later explorers used either name, Canibales or Caribes, in referring to any of the people of the West Indies. All of these people were very fierce; some were known to eat human flesh. Less than a century after Columbus's voyages, all Europeans associated the name Canibales with human-eaters." (From *Thereby Hangs a Tail*, by Charles Earle Funk)

ONION
Meaning: A pungent, edible vegetable.
Origin: "In Latin there is a word union which is translated as 'oneness' or 'union.' The word onion is derived from this...because it consists of a number of united layers. There is also another interesting analogy between 'union' and 'onion.' The rustics about Rome not only used the word unio to mean onion, but they also thought it a suitable designation for a pearl. And even today a cook will speak of 'pearl onions' when she means the small, silvery-white variety." (From *Word Origins*, by Wilfred Funk)

HORS D'OEUVRE
Meaning: A small treat served before a meal.
Origin: "These tasty treats before a fancy meal get their name from a French expression meaning 'outside of work.' Preparing the meal was part of the ordinary labor of the kitchen staff, and any extras for special occasions or feasts were not part of the regular chores." (From *Where in the Word?*, by David Muschell)

POSTMAN
Meaning: Deliverer of mail.
Origin: "The term 'post' to describe mail or message delivery originated in the 13th century with Marco Polo. He described Kublai Khan's network of more than 10,000 yambs, or relay stations, calling them in Italian poste, or 'posts.' They were located every 25 to 45 miles on the principal roads throughout the empire. In addition, at three-mile intervals between the poste there were relay stations for runners, who...wore wide belts with bells to signal the importance of their business." (From *Remarkable Words with Astonishing Origins*, by John Train)

Nearly 50% of the world's scientists are assigned to military projects.

WRETCHED REVIEWS

Doesn't it bother you when a movie you love gets a thumbs-down from those two bozos on TV? Us, too. The Critics Were Wrong, by Ardis Sillick and Michael McCormick, compiles hundreds of misguided movie reviews like these.

FRANKENSTEIN (1931)

"I regret to report that it is just another movie, so thoroughly mixed with water as to have a horror content of about .0001 percent....The film...soon turns into sort of comic opera with a range of cardboard mountains over which extras in French Revolution costumes dash about with flaming torches."

—Outlook & Independent

THE GRADUATE (1967) *Nomination for best actor*

"The Graduate is a genuinely funny comedy which succeeds despite an uninteresting and untalented actor (Dustin Hoffman) in the title role."

—Films In Review

LETHAL WEAPON (1987)

"As a thriller, it lacks logic. As a cop film, it throws standard police procedures, and with them any hope of authenticity, to the wind. As a showcase for the martial arts, it's a disappointment....And as action-adventure, it's pointlessly puerile."

—Johanna Steinmetz, Chicago Tribune

M*A*S*H* (1970)

"At the end, the film simply runs out of steam, says goodbye to its major characters, and calls final attention to itself as a movie—surely the saddest and most overworked of cop-out devices in the comic film repertory."

—Roger Greenspun, The New York Times

ROCKY (1976) *Top box-office hit / Oscar winner for best picture and director / Nomination for best actor and screenplay*

To win at bingo in the old days you had to ring a small bell. That's where the bing comes from.

"An overly grandiose script, performed with relentless grandiloquence....Up to a point I'm willing to overlook the egg on a guy's face, but, really, there's such a thing as too much—especially when they're promoting this bloated, pseudo-epic as a low-budget Oscarbound winner.

—*Washington Star*

2001: A SPACE ODYSSEY (1968)

"Not a cinematic landmark. It compares with, but does not best, previous efforts at filmed science-fiction....It actually belongs to the technically-slick group previously dominated by...the Japanese."

—*Variety*

ANNIE HALI, (1977) *Oscar winner for best picture and director*

"Woody Allen has truly underreached himself....His new film is painful in three separate ways: an unfunny comedy, poor moviemaking and embarrassing self-revelation.... It is a film so shapeless, sprawling, repetitious and aimless as to seem to beg for oblivion."

—**John Simon,** *New York*

PSYCHO (1960) *Oscar nomination for best director*

"Hitchcock seems to have been more interested in shocking his audience with the bloodiest bathtub murder in screen history, and in photographing Janet Leigh in various stages of undress, than in observing the ordinary rules for good film construction. This is a dangerous corner for a gifted moviemaker to place himself in."

—**Moira Walsh,** *America*

SATURDAY NIGHT FEVER (1977)

"Nothing more than an updated '70s version of the...rock music cheapies of the '50s. That is to say...more shrill, more vulgar, more trifling, more superficial and more pretentious than an exploitation film....A major disappointment."

—*Variety*

Avocados have more protein than any other fruit.

THE WORLD'S SECOND DUMBEST OUTLAW

Here's another example of someone who's gone down
in history as the worst there ever was.

"**B**LACK JACK" TOM KETCHUM (1862?–1901)
Background: Ketchum was an ordinary cowboy before turning to crime. He returned from a cattle drive one day and learned that his girlfriend had eloped with another man. The rejection pushed him over the edge.

Claim to Fame: Ketchum has been dubbed the "second stupidest outlaw who ever lived." He ran with members of Wyoming's notorious Hole-in-the-Wall gang, but bungled so many stick-ups that getting away with a few dollars was the best he usually managed.

He had a strange reaction to failure, as Jay Robert Nash explains in *American Eccentrics:*

> Whenever a caper of his went wrong, he would methodically beat himself on the head with the butt of his six-shooter snarling, "You will, will you? (slam!)...Now take that (pop)...and that (bang)!"
>
> Many of Black Jack's planned crimes turned into disasters, and if each member of his gang got $10 for his share, it could be considered a superior outing. Needless to say, Black Jack's gun and skull both took regular beatings.

But even stupid outlaws have their day. In 1898, Ketchum and his boys robbed a train in New Mexico of about $500. Not exactly a king's ransom, but it was enough to keep Ketchum coming back for more. He didn't bother to vary his routine even a little. Ketchum went after the same train, at exactly the same remote spot, a total of four times. On the fourth, lawmen were waiting for him. There was a shoot-out, and Ketchum was wounded and captured.

So why was Ketchum only the second-stupidest outlaw? Because his brother, Sam, was even dumber. While Black Jack was in prison, Sam masterminded yet another identical robbery of the same train. He got himself killed in the attempt.

THE "ART" OF ROCK

What do rock stars really think of their "art?"
Maybe not what you'd expect.

Q: "If you had to put into 25 words or less what it is you're trying to say when you get up on stage, what would it be?"
A: "LOOK AT ME!"
　　—Joe Strummer (the Clash)

"Rock 'n' roll is a bit like Las Vegas; guys dressed up in their sisters' clothes pretending to be rebellious and angry, but not really angry about anything."
　　　　　　　　—Sting

"I may be a living legend, but that sure don't help when I've got to change a flat tire."
　　　　—Roy Orbison

"Somebody said to me, 'But The Beatles were antimaterialistic.' That's a huge myth. John and I literally used to sit down and say, 'Now, let's write a swimming pool.'"
　　　　—Paul McCartney

"People got my face up on their walls. You turn on TV, that's my head. That's sick, man. I used to have a…McDonald's costume on. I used to make hamburgers."
—Mark White (Spin Doctors)

"If you want to torture me, you'd tie me down and force me to watch our first five videos."
　　　　　—Jon Bon Jovi

"Mick Jagger would be astounded if he realized to many people he's not a sex symbol, but a mother image."
　　　　—David Bowie

"In rock 'n' roll, you're built up to be torn down. Like architecture in America, you build it up and let it stand for ten years, then call it shabby and rip it down and put something else up."
　　　　　—Joni Mitchell

"Art is the last thing I'm worried about when I write a song. If you want to call it art, yeah, okay, you can call it what you like. As far as I'm concerned, 'Art' is just short for 'Arthur.'"
　　　　—Keith Richards

"To have a huge hit record with only three chords is one of the best tricks a writer can do."
　　　　—Burton Cummings
　　　　(the Guess Who)

Troubled waters: "Caribbean" is derived from the same root as "cannibal."

LUCKY FINDS

*Here's a look at a few more lucky people
who found some real valuable stuff.*

GRANDMA'S GARBAGE

The Find: An old painting
Where It Was Found: At grandma's house.
The Story: In 1964, a Connecticut woman happened to be visiting her grandparents' house on a day when they were throwing out some old junk. She saw an old painting she liked, and her grandparents let her have it. She hung it over her bed, where it stayed for the next 25 years.

In 1989, the woman took the painting into an art appraiser to see if it was worth anything. The appraiser offered her $1,000 for it. She refused. A little while later, he called and offered her $100,000. Now she was suspicious, and contacted an auction house. It turned out to be a rare work by the 19th-century artist Martin Johnson Heade. The painting sold at auction a few months later for $1.1 million.

STEPPING OUT

The Find: An animated cartoon film made in 1922.
Where It Was Found: In a film rental library in London, England.
The Story: In the mid-1970s, film collector David Wyatt paid two pounds (about $3) for a 7-minute-long, black-and-white silent cartoon titled "Grandma Steps Out."

Twenty years later, Wyatt showed the film to Russell Merritt, a film scholar working on a book called Walt in Wonderland: The Silent Films of Walt Disney. Merritt recognized "Grandma Steps Out" as the only known copy of "Little Red Riding Hood," Disney's first film—and one of the American Film Institute's ten "most-wanted" lost films. Disney drew the film when he was a 21-year-old commercial artist in Kansas City. Six years later he finished "Steamboat Willie," his first Mickey Mouse cartoon. Wyatt's copy may have been a bootleg—which explains the new title—but it's still the only copy of a film that, for decades, was

---

Franklin D. Roosevelt's 3 favorite foods: frog legs, pig knuckles, and scrambled eggs.

assumed to be lost forever. Estimated value: priceless. "Its value historically is inestimable," says Scott MacQueen, at Walt Disney studios. "Not only is this the very first Disney cartoon, but there are also very few examples of work in Disney's own hand. It represents the beginning of the dynasty."

PICTURE PERFECT

The Find: A daguerreotype photograph of a young man, taken in 1847.

Where It Was Found: At an antique photograph auction in Pittsburgh, Pennsylvania.

The Story: In 1996, Paul and Maria Pasquariello saw an original daguerreotype at the auction. It was identified as a picture of George Lippard, an obscure 19th century novelist and historian, but they knew they'd seen the picture somewhere before. They were almost positive the picture was actually of the famous abolitionist John Brown.

But the Pasquariellos couldn't be sure—because this picture was of a young, cleanshaven man, and most pictures of Brown were taken when he was older and had grown an enormous beard.

That night they pored through history books until they finally found the same picture—a portrait of Brown described as coming from "a long lost daguerreotype."

The next day the Pasquariellos bought the daguerreotype for $12,075. Sotheby's later auctioned it to the Smithsonian Institute's National Portrait Gallery for $129,000, the highest price ever paid by the gallery for a photograph.

WHAT A DOLL

The Find: An old doll.

Where It Was Found: On a garbage heap in Bochum, Germany.

The Story: Five-year-old Nicole Ohlsen found the doll in some trash. Her mother was about to throw it away when she discovered a cache of diamonds inside. Estimated value: $72,000. The mother took the diamonds to the police, who told her no one had reported them missing—and let her keep them.

Stilts were invented by French shepherds who needed a way to get around in wet marshes.

NATURE'S REVENGE

What happens when we start messing around with nature, trying to make living conditions better? Sometimes it works...and sometimes nature gets even. Here are a few instances when people intentionally introduced animal or plants into a new environment...and regretted it.

Import: Kudzu, a fast-growing Japanese vine.
Background: Originally brought into the Southern U.S. in 1876 for use as shade. People noticed livestock ate the vine and that kudzu helped restore nitrogen to the soil. It seemed like a perfect plant to cultivate. So in the 1930s, the U.S. government helped farmers plant kudzu all over the South.
Nature's Revenge: By the 1950s, it was out of control, blanketing farmers' fields, buildings, utility poles and—often fatally—trees. Today, utility companies spend millions of dollars annually spraying herbicides on poles and towers to keep them kudzu-free. And instead of helping plant kudzu, the government now gives advice on how to get rid of it.

Import: The mongoose.
Background: The small Asian mammals famous for killing cobras were brought to Hawaii by sugar planters in 1893. Their reason: They thought the mongooses would help control the rat population.
Nature's Revenge: The planters overlooked one little detail: the mongoose is active in the daytime while the rat is nocturnal. "In Hawaii today," says one source, "mongooses are considered pests nearly as bad as rats."

Import: The starling, an English bird.
Background: In 1890, a philanthropist named Eugene Schieffelin decided to bring every type of bird mentioned in Shakespeare's plays to New York City's Central Park. He brought in hundreds of pairs of birds from England. Unfortunately, most (like skylarks and thrushes) didn't make it. Determined to succeed with at least one species, Schieffelin shipped 40 pairs of starlings to Central Park and let them loose just before the mating season on March 6, 1890.

Morphine addiction became known as the "soldier's disease" following the Civil War.

Nature's Revenge: There are now more than 50 million starlings in the U.S. alone—all descendants from Schieffelin's flock—and they have become a major health hazard. They fly in swarms, littering roads and highways with their droppings, which carry disease-bearing bacteria that are often transmitted to animals and people. They've also become pests to farmers, screeching unbearably and destroying wheat and cornfields.

Import: The gypsy moth.
Background: In 1869, Leopold Trouvelot, a French entomologist, imported some gypsy moth caterpillars to Massachusetts. It was part of a get-rich-quick scheme: he figured that since the caterpillars thrive on oak tree leaves, which are plentiful there, he could crossbreed them with silkworm moths, and create a self-sustaining, silk-producing caterpillar. He'd make a fortune!

Unfortunately, the crossbreeding didn't work. Then one day, a strong wind knocked over a cage filled with the gypsy moth caterpillars. They escaped through an open window and survived.
Nature's Revenge: At first, the moths spread slowly. But by 1950, gypsy moths could be found in every New England state and in eastern New York. They've since spread to Virginia and Maryland—and beyond. Populations have become established as far away as Minnesota and California, probably due to eggs unknowingly transported by cars driven from the Northeast to those regions. They're not a major threat, but can cause severe problems: In 1981, for example, they were reported to have stripped leaves from 13 million trees.

Import: Dog fennel.
Background: At the turn of the 19th century, Johnny Appleseed wandered around the Ohio territory, planting apples wherever he went. It's not widely known that he also sowed a plant called dog fennel, which was believed to be a fever-reducing medicine.
Nature's Revenge: It's not only not medicine, it's bad medicine; farmers are sick of it. "The foul-smelling weed," says the People's Almanac, "spread from barnyard to pasture, sometimes growing as high as fifteen feet. Today, exasperated midwestern farmers still cannot rid their fields of the plant they half-humorously call 'Johnnyweed.'"

The average city dog lives three years longer than the average country dog.

ODDBALL FOOD NAMES

Can you imagine being offered a nice, big helping
of Burgoo? Sounds appetizing, doesn't it?

ANADAMA BREAD

A Gloucester, Massachusetts, fisherman was married to a woman named Anna and every night, she fed him corn-meal and molasses for dinner. He got so sick of it that one evening he stormed into the kitchen, threw some yeast into the mix, and baked a sodden, lumpy loaf…muttering "Anna, damn 'er" the whole time. His Yankee-accented phrase came out as Anadama, giving the bread its name.

This story first appeared in print in 1915—and though it sounds like a tall tale, it's cited so often that most food historians believe it.

BURGOO

Politics and Burgoo go hand in hand in Kentucky. This Southern beef and fowl stew was cooked for people at political rallies. There are several versions about how it was created, but this one is the most colorful: During the Civil War, a Yankee soldier managed to kill a number of wild birds which he promptly made into a stew, using a copper kettle normally used for mixing gunpowder. He invited his buddies to join him, and-having eaten nothing but hardtack and bacon for days—they jumped at the offer. The soldier suffered from a speech impediment. When he was asked what the dish was, he tried to say "bird stew," but it came out as "Burgoo."

JANSSON'S TEMPTATION

In 1846, Eric Jansson fled Sweden to escape religious persecution for his radical theology. He and his followers settled in Illinois. Jansson told his followers that eating was a sin that turned their thoughts away from God, and he allowed them only a starvation diet. His downfall came when they found him consuming a rich dish of potatoes, onions, and cream, now known as Jansson's Temptation.

Hollywood fashion tip: wearing yellow makes you look bigger on camera; green, smaller.

BAPTIST CAKE
Many churches settle for a symbolic sprinkling of holy water during baptism, but Baptists insist on full immersion. When deep-fried doughnut-like confections were introduced in New England in the 1920s, they were named Baptist Cakes because they were "baptized" in hot oil.

HOPPIN' JOHN
A New Orleans dish of cowpeas and rice, traditionally served on New Year's Day to ensure good luck in the coming year. The name dates back to 1819 and is derived from a New Year's ritual of having the children hop around the table before being served.

LIMPING SUSAN
A variation on Hoppin' John, with red beans substituted for cowpeas.

JOHNNY CAKE
Blame the Yankee accent for Johnny Cakes, too. In Colonial America, travelers would bake a supply of cakes to take on trips, called Journey Cakes. "Journey" comes out as "johnny" when pronounced with a broad, New England accent. In 1940, the Rhode Island Legislature ruled that only cakes made from flint corn could carry the proud title of Johnny Cakes. There is a Johnny Cake Festival in Newport every October...as well as a Society for the Propagation of the Johnny Cake Tradition.

MONKEY GLAND
A cocktail made with "orange juice, grenadine, gin and an anise cordial." According to food historian John Mariani:

> It became popular in the 1920s, when Dr. Serge Voronoff, a Russian emigre to Paris and director of experimental surgery at the Laboratory of Physiology of the College de France, was promoting the benefits of transplanting the sex glands of monkeys into human beings to restore vitality and prolong life....

The cocktail, which facetiously promised similar restorative powers, may have been invented at Harry's New York Bar in Paris, by owner Harry MacElhone.

It takes a drop of ocean water more than 1,000 years to circulate around the world.

STAR TREK: THE NEXT GENERATION

Uncle John's very first Bathroom Reader came out in 1988—a year after Star Trek: The Next Generation *debuted. In that book, we profiled the original* Star Trek. *Now, because readers have asked for it, we're finally getting around to writing about TNG.*

HOW IT STARTED
As soon as the original *Star Trek* became a syndicated hit in the early 1970s, Paramount and *Trek* creator Gene Roddenberry started planning a sequel (working title: "Star Trek II").

But in 1975, Paramount switched directions and decided to make a feature film instead. *Trek's* writers worked for three years on the concept…but they couldn't come up with a script that the studio felt had a "big enough" plot to justify a full-length movie. So Roddenberry and his crew went back to work on the new TV series.

In 1978, three weeks before production of the show was supposed to begin, Paramount stepped in again—and canceled it. The reason: *Star Wars* was making a killing at the box office, and studio execs decided a big-budget feature film would make more money than a TV series. By March 1978, all of the original cast of *Star Trek* had been signed to make *Star Trek: The Motion Picture.*

Resurrection. Eight years later, in 1986, two events inspired Roddenberry to resurrect "Star Trek II": A *Star Trek* 20th reunion party got Roddenberry's team excited about doing TV again; and *Star Trek IV: The Voyage Home*, the best of the Trek movies to that point, was a critical and box office success. It convinced Roddenberry that the time was right for a new small-screen *Star Trek*—but not a sequel. The new show, he decided, would have…

• A new cast. Creating all-new characters had two major advantages for Paramount: (1) It left the original *Star Trek* cast free to make feature films; and (2) a cast of unknowns would be cheaper.

• A new setting. Roddenberry figured about "a century after

Mammal rule of thumb: if you eat meat, you have at least four toes on each foot.

Kirk" (later refined to 78 years), which put it in the 24th century.
- No "retread" Vulcans, Klingons, or other beings.
- A longer mission (ten years or more instead of the original five) and a different philosophy for the Enterprise. The vessel was to feel less like a battleship and more like a family-friendly exploration/peacekeeping craft with services to support its population.

Given the original *Trek*'s popularity, it seems logical to assume that one of the big networks grabbed the show, right? Wrong. No one wanted to foot $1 million per episode for sci-fi, which still didn't have a prime-time track record. Instead, Paramount ended up selling it directly to local stations. But once again, *Star Trek* proved that the network experts didn't understand the lure of good science fiction. It quickly became the most successful syndicated drama in television history.

INSIDE FACTS

High-priced Gamble
The Next Generation was TV's most expensive program in 1987, and the highest-priced syndicated show ever. In fact, by the second season, it already had pushed its budget to $1.5 million per episode. This led panicky execs to institute some unexpected cost-cutting measures. For example, in the third season, new crew uniforms were unveiled, at a cost of $3,000 each. To save money, no one on the set below the rank of ensign was allowed to have one.

Still on the Cheap
On the other hand, the special-effects budget was only about $85,000 per episode. When adjusted for inflation, that's less than the special effects of the original show. The result: some surprisingly low-budget effects were used. In one episode, for example, when they needed to show the surface of a sun, they used "vibrating dry oatmeal on a light box." In another, the corona of a sun was achieved by "bouncing a laser beam off of a beer can onto a piece of white cardboard." And to get the texture of a planet, visual-effects producer Dan Curry says, "I did a macro shot of a rock in my garden, with my camcorder."

A Bald Englishman?
Gene Roddenberry was looking for a Frenchman to play Captain

Picard, but couldn't find the right actor. Then *Trek* producer Bob Justman saw Patrick Stewart address a drama conference and decided he'd be perfect. But Roddenberry took one look at Stewart's photo and said, "I'm not going to have a bald Englishman for a captain." In the end, Stewart was the best they could find. They auditioned him wearing a toupee, but hated it. "That wasn't the Patrick we wanted," recalled Roddenberry. "He looked like a drapery clerk."

Name Game
• Geordi LaForge, the blind navigator played by Levar Burton, was named in tribute to George LaForge—a young, wheelchair-bound Trekkie who died in 1975 from complications related to muscular dystrophy.
• Wesley Crusher, the doctor's son, was named after Gene Roddenberry, whose middle name was Wesley. "He is me at 17," Roddenberry said. "He is the things I dreamed of being and doing."

Making Whoopi
No one believed it when Oscar winner Whoopi Goldberg sent word (through a friend) that she'd love to be on the show. Finally, she took a more direct route, phoning the *Star Trek* offices herself.

"Since I was a little girl on the streets, *Star Trek* was always my guide to morality," she explained. She appeared as Guinan, hostess of the ship's lounge, in the first episode of the second season, and appeared in 26 more shows over the next six years.

Brief Notes
• It wasn't until the third season, when ratings were strong and the show was fully accepted by Trekkies, that Roddenberry began bringing in characters from the first series. Mark Lenerd, who played Sarek, Spock's father, was the first to cross over.
• Jonathan Frakes auditioned for the part of Riker seven times—and was actually the second choice for the role. The first choice blew his final audition so badly that Frakes got the job.
• Roddenberry eventually agreed to have a Klingon on the bridge because it showed that Starfleet had made "progress" in its relations with other worlds in the years since the first show.

LOONEY LAWS

Believe it or not, these laws are real.

In Kentucky, it's against the law to throw eggs at a public speaker.

In Shawnee, Oklahoma, it's illegal for three or more dogs to "meet" on private property without the consent of the owner.

In Hartford, Connecticut, transporting a cadaver by taxi is punishable by a $5 fine.

In Michigan, it's illegal for a woman to cut her own hair without her husband's permission.

You can ride your bike on main streets in Forgan, Oklahoma, but it's against the law to ride it backwards.

If you tie an elephant to a parking meter in Orlando, Florida, you have to feed the meter just as if the elephant were a car.

California law forbids sleeping in the kitchen...but allows cooking in the bedroom.

It's a felony in Montana for a wife to open a telegram addressed to her husband. (It's not a crime for the husband to open telegrams addressed to his wife.)

You can gargle in Louisiana if you want to, but it's against the law to do it in public.

In Maryland it's against the law for grandchildren to marry their grandparents.

It's against the law to anchor your boat to the train tracks in Jefferson City, Missouri.

In Columbus, Montana, it's a misdemeanor to pass the Mayor on the street without tipping your hat.

It's illegal to throw an onion in Princeton, Texas.

Kentucky law requires that every person in the state take a bath at least once a year.

It's against the law to pawn your wooden leg in Delaware.

To take an oath, ancient Romans put a hand on their testicles...that's where *testimony* comes from.

THE TOP 10 HITS OF THE YEAR, 1984–1987

Another installment of BRl's Top Ten of the Year list.

1984

(1) When Doves Cry —*Prince*
(2) What's Love Go To Do With It —*Tina Turner*
(3) Against All Odds (Take A Look At Me Now) —*Phil Collins*
(4) Footloose —*Kenny Loggins*
(5) Say Say Say —*Paul McCartney & Michael Jackson*
(6) Jump —*Van Halen*
(7) Owner Of A Lonely Heart —*Yes*
(8) Hello —*Lionel Richie*
(9) Ghostbusters —*Ray Parker, Jr.*
(10) Karma Chameleon —*Culture Club*

1985

(1) Careless Whisper —*Wham! featuring George Michael*
(2) Like A Virgin —*Madonna*
(3) Wake Me Up Before You Go-go —*Wham!*
(4) Everybody Wants To Rule The World —*Tears For Fears*
(5) I Feel For You —*Chaka Khan*
(6) Money For Nothing —*Dire Straits*
(7) I Want To Know What Love Is —*Foreigner*
(8) Out Of Touch —*Daryl Hall & John Oates*
(9) Crazy For You —*Madonna*
(10) Take On Me —*A-ha*

1986

(1) That's What Friends Are For —*Dionne & Friends*
(2) Say You, Say Me —*Lionel Richie*
(3) On My Own —*Patti Labelle & Michael Mcdonald*
(4) I Miss You —*Klymaxx*
(5) Broken Wings —*Mr. Mister*
(6) How Will I Know —*Whitney Houston*
(7) Party All The Time —*Eddie Murphy*
(8) Kyrie —*Mr. Mister*
(9) Burning Heart —*Survivor*
(10) Addicted To Love —*Robert Palmer*

1987

(1) Walk Like An Egyptian —*Bangles*
(2) Alone —*Heart*
(3) Shake You Down —*Gregory Abbott*
(4) I Wanna Dance With Somebody —*Whitney Houston*
(5) Nothing's Gonna Stop Us Now —*Starship*
(6) C'est La Vie —*Robbie Nevil*
(7) The Way It Is —*Bruce Hornsby & The Range*
(8) Here I Go Again —*Whitesnake*
(9) Livin' On A Prayer —*Bon Jovi*
(10) Shakedown (from Beverly Hills Cop II) —*Bob Seger*

The famous lover Giovanni Casanova ended his life working as a librarian.

HURRY UP AND PAY!

"In China," the New York Times *reports, "it's common for sales clerks to abandon their posts without notice, and to ignore—or even insult—customers." In 1995, as part of a national politeness campaign, the Chinese government banned 50 commonly-used phrases from retail stores. Here's a sample list.*

The busier I am, the more you bother me. How annoying!

Who told you not to look where you're going?

Didn't you hear me? What do you have ears for?

Get out of the way, or you'll get killed.

Are you finished talking?

If you're not buying, what are you looking at?

Are you buying or not?

Have you made up your mind?

Go ask the person who sold it to you.

What are you yelling about?

Don't you see I'm busy? What's the hurry?

I can't solve this. Go complain to whoever you want.

I just told you. Why are you asking again?

Buy if you can afford it, otherwise get out of here.

Why didn't you choose well when you bought it?

Hurry up and pay.

Ask someone else.

Time is up, be quick.

The price is posted. Can't you see it yourself?

If you're not buying, don't ask.

Stop shouting. Can't you see I'm eating?

It's not my fault.

We haven't opened yet. Wait awhile.

I'm not in charge. Don't ask me so many questions.

Didn't I tell you? How come you don't get it?

Don't push me.

If you want it, speak up; if you don't, get out of the way.

Don't talk so much. Say it quickly.

You're asking me? Whom should I ask?

Don't stand in the way.

Why don't you have the money ready?

Attics were invented in Attica.

JAWS, JR.

They're just little fishes, but piranhas can turn you
into a skeleton in a few seconds flat. Nice thought, huh?

THE NAME. The word "piranha" comes from the Tupi language of South America and means "toothed fish." In some local dialects of the Amazon region, the name for common household scissors is also "piranha."

NOT A SHARK. A piranha only has one row of upper and lower teeth, not several, as many sharks do. But its teeth are sharper than almost any shark teeth. When the piranha snaps them together, says one expert, "the points in the upper row fit into the notches of the lower row, and the power of the jaw muscles is such that there is scarcely any living substance save the hardest ironwood that will not be clipped off." Natives often use the teeth as cutting blades.

FISHING TIP. Piranhas are capable of biting through a fishing net. If caught on a hook, they usually die from the injury. So a good way to "bring them in alive" is to throw a chunk of meat in the water. The fish will bite into it so hard that you can lift bunches of them out of the water before they let go.

BEHAVIOR. Some things that attract piranhas are blood and splashing. Experts disagree over whether the fish will attack a calm, uninjured person, but piranhas are definitely territorial. That's why Amazon fishermen know that if they catch a piranha, they'd better try another spot if they expect to catch anything else.

DEADLY DIET. Surprisingly, only a few species of piranha are meat-eaters; many eat fruits and other plants that fall into the river. But those meat-eaters can do exactly what you think they can. In the 19th century, for example, Teddy Roosevelt wrote about his adventures along the Amazon. He claimed to have seen piranhas quickly make a skeleton of a man who had fallen off his horse and into the river.

MORE DUMB CROOKS

More proof that crime doesn't pay.

GIVING HIM THE SLIP

SAN FRANCISO, Ca.— "Talk about dumb, here's a beaut....A would-be San Francisco bank robber recently cased two different banks. He even picked up a deposit slip at one of them. But his carefully planned robbery began to fall apart when he presented a holdup note—written on the Bank of America deposit slip he'd picked up—to a teller at Wells Fargo.

"Sorry, this is a Bank of America slip; we can't honor this. Why don't you try them? They're just down the street,' a quick-thinking teller said.

"Off went the robber to try his luck at the other bank.

"The teller called the cops, who happily greeted the would-be robber a few minutes later with open arms (and handcuffs) as he walked in the door."

—San Francisco Chronicle, **Jan. 7, 1996**

HOW DID YOU KNOW?

PITTSBURGH, Pa.— "MacArthur Wheeler, 46, was sentenced to 24 years in prison in Pittsburgh last month, a conviction made possible by clear photography from the bank's surveillance camera. Wheeler and his partner did not wear masks and, in fact, were not concerned about the camera at all, because they had rubbed lemon juice all over their faces beforehand, believing the substance would blur their on-camera images."

—Medford, Oregon Mail Tribune, **February 22, 1996**

BOOK 'EM!

BUFFALO, Okla.— "The only explanation police have is that the two teenagers must have gotten the bank mixed up with the library.

"It's the first attempted library robbery I ever heard of," policeman Ray Dawson said Thursday. Dawson said the teenagers held out an empty pillow case and told the library attendant, 'Put it in.'

Harry S. Truman was the last president with no college degree.

"'Put what in?' the attendant asked.

"'The money. Put it in and nobody'll get hurt,' the youth demanded.

"The attendant, who said there was less than $1 in collected library fines in his petty cash box, ran out the door and escaped. The teenagers were arrested hours later in Garden City, Kansas."

—*United Press International, 1975*

OH, THAT

WANDSWORTH, England— "On July 20, 1979, an armed robber dashed into a little grocery store and told the proprietor 'Give me the money from your till or I will shoot.' The owner was perplexed.

'Where's your gun?' he asked. There was an awkward silence....Then the robber replied that he didn't actually have a gun, but if the owner gave him any trouble, he'd go out and get one and come back. After a moment, the crook quietly left."

—*The Return of Heroic Failures*

RIGHT ON SCHEDULE

VERNON, British Columbia— "Raymond Cuthbert entered a drugstore in Vernon, and announced that he and his partner would be back in half an hour to rob the place. Employees called the Royal Canadian Mounted Police, who arrested Cuthbert and Robert Phimister when they returned as promised."

—*Dumb, Dumber, Dumbest*

COPS AND ROBBERS

CHICAGO, Ill.— "Terry Johnson had no trouble identifying the two men who burglarized her Chicago apartment at 2:30 A.M. on August 17, 1981. All she had to do was write down the number of the police badge that one of them was wearing and the identity number on the fender of their squad car. The two officers— Stephen Webster, 33, and Tyrone Pickens, 32—had actually committed the crime in full uniform, while on duty, using police department tools."

—*Crime/16 Stupid Thieves*

In ancient Greece, if a woman watched even one Olympic event, she was executed.

THE POLITICALLY CORRECT QUIZ

As we pointed out in the last Bathroom Reader, *"political correctness"
isn't as bad as it's made out to be—after all, there's nothing wrong with
becoming more sensitive to people's feelings. On the other hand, people
can get pretty outrageous with their ideas of what's "appropriate."
Here are seven real-life examples of politically correct—or
"incorrect"—behavior. How sensitive are you? Can you
spot the "correct" one? (Answers on page 760.)*

1. In 1997, the "Beetle Bailey" comic strip moved toward political
correctness when cartoonist Mort Walker wrote a story in
which...

a) Cookie began offering vegetarian meals.
b) Sarge apologized for calling Beetle "dehumanizing" names.
c) After taking sensitivity training, General Halftrack admitted to
being "sexist."

2. In 1993, Hempstead, Texas school officials banned pregnant
girls from their high school's sixteen-member cheerleading squad.
Then they rescinded the rule because...

a) They would have been illegally discriminating against the four
pregnant cheerleaders on the squad.
b) An angry cheerleader threatened to sue them for not providing
birth control.
c) Church groups picketed the school, protesting the implication
that cheerleading causes pregnancy.

3. In February 1998, it was announced that the latest group to
take offense at "insensitive" language was...

a) British sanitation workers, who objected to being called
"garbage men."
b) Barroom bouncers in New York City, who began a letter-writing campaign to local newspapers to get them to use the term
"crowd control engineers."

In 1948 four men took a cow to the top of the Matterhorn. They all froze to death.

c) Meat shop owners in France, who objected to newspapers describing murderers as "butchers."

4. Political correctness goes both ways. In 1962, for example, a woman wrote to the Sears, Roebuck and Co. Catalog (then the world's largest) and complained that the women modeling maternity lingerie...

a) Should not be on display unless they are really pregnant.
b) Weren't wearing wedding rings.
c) Should be holding baby bottles, to take the focus off their breasts.

5. More reverse political correctness. In 1996, a Laurens, South Carolina man told reporters that he was shocked local African-Americans were so prejudiced. What was he referring to?

a) Their objection to a local school's "slave auction" fundraising event.
b) Their objections to a Ku Klux Klan "museum and apparel store."
c) Their objections to "flesh-colored" crayons being used in classrooms, and their insistence that "black" crayons be referred to as "flesh-colored" also.

6. At the University of Pennsylvania, a woman was asked to leave a meeting of a group called "White Women Against Racism" because...

a) She protested that the initials in the group's name spell out WAR (WWAR).
b) She was black.
c) She was a transsexual.

7. When Connecticut's Canine Control Office issued dog tags in the shape of a fire hydrant...

a) Firefighters objected that it ridiculed their profession.
b) Women called the office to object that it discriminated against female dogs.
c) Church groups called the office and complained that the tag's shape resembled a male sex organ.

The U.S. has more bagpipe bands than Scotland does.

THE ANIMALS AT THE ZOO, Part 3

Here's even more info for zoo-lovers and animal watchers.

WATCHING GORILLAS

Gorillas are highly intelligent, social animals. Groups are led by a dominant "silverback" male. Gorillas were once thought to be ferocious people-eating beasts. In reality, they're peaceful vegetarians.

Behavior: Chest beating.
What It Means: Usually excitement, but it depends on the context. A gorilla could thump his chest in the middle of play, for example, or as part of a threat display. The sound can travel as far as a mile.

Behavior: "Smiling." Teeth not bared.
What It Means: Invitation to play. Gorillas, especially young ones, like to have fun. As a sort of "come and get me" gesture, one gorilla will direct a happy face at another. Within seconds, the two may be chasing each other and wrestling.

Behavior: Inspecting and picking each other's skin and hair.
What It Means: Grooming. This practice is common among primates. It's important for group hygiene. But it's just as important for social bonding. You can learn a lot about the social structure of a gorilla group by observing who grooms whom.

Behavior: Various sounds.
What They Mean: All gorillas enjoy a good belch to express satisfaction with a meal. The silverback does most of the specialized vocalizing. He grunts when he wants to call the group together. He gives a call that sounds something like a dog's bark when he wants to hurry the group along to a different spot.

Behavior: Back riding.
What It Means: Foreplay. Mother gorillas will carry their babies

If you could drive your car straight up in the air, you'd reach outer space in an hour.

on their backs. Among grown gorillas, though, playing "horsey" means that the two are definitely an item.

Despite the male gorilla's reputation as the "Don Juan" of the animal kingdom, it's typically the female who is more sexually assertive. She's the one who climbs up onto her mate's back and rides him like a horse. If you're lucky enough to see this rare courtship display at a zoo, you won't need an interpreter to explain what's going on.

WATCHING GIRAFFES

Giraffes are the tallest land mammals, measuring 15–17 feet (male) or 13–15 feet (female) from horn tip to toe. Our fascination with these animals is nothing new. In ancient times, a giraffe was transported 2,000 miles along the Nile from southern Africa to a royal zoo, in Egypt.

Behavior: Neck held erect while walking.
What It Means: Dominance. You can pick out the dominant bull from the rest of the herd by its proud walk. The other giraffes, in comparison, hold their necks lower, at an angle.

Behavior: Necking.
What It Means: Conflict. Giraffes are generally peaceful. When they do spar, they rub and wrap their necks together. You know the situation is getting serious when they begin to slam heads and jab with their horns.

Behavior: Mother nuzzling her young.
What It Means: Giraffe I.D. The mama giraffe is filing some very important information as she lovingly noses and licks a newborn. She's learning the youngster's distinctive smell and skin pattern. The information will come in handy some day when she needs to pick her kid out of the crowd.

Behavior: Nosing, rubbing, and/or licking each other.
What It Means: Bonding. Group harmony is important to giraffes. But giraffes don't necessarily spread their affection around equally. Researchers have found that certain herd members are touched more than others.

Five oldest words still in use in the English language: Town, priest, earl, this, and ward.

THE TOM AND JERRY STORY

The cartoon world's most famous cat and mouse are almost sixty years old. But with cable TV airing their cartoons daily, a whole new generation knows (and apparently loves) them.

BACKGROUND

In the late thirties, MGM had a full-time animation studio. But while Disney and Warner Brothers cartoons became more popular each year, MGM's list of cartoon flops kept growing. One reason was their disorganized and indecisive management. Another was weak characters; MGM had nothing to compare with Bugs Bunny or Mickey Mouse.

William Hanna and Joe Barbera, two young MGM animators, were convinced that the studio would soon fold, so they decided they might as well develop a cartoon of their own. After all, what did they—or MGM—have to lose? They picked a cat and mouse as their subjects because, as Joe Barbera put it, "half the story was written before you even put pencil to paper."

DON'T CALL US...

In 1940, they finished "Puss Gets the Boot" about a cat named Jasper trying to catch an unnamed mouse. The brass at MGM didn't care for it, but since they didn't have anything else in the works, they released it to theatres. To their surprise, the public loved it. It was even nominated for an Academy Award.

It was just what MGM needed. So Hanna and Barbera were shocked when MGM executives called them in and told them to "stop making the cat and mouse cartoons." Why? Because they "didn't want to put all our eggs in one basket."

"Of course," Barbera says wryly, "before 'Puss Gets the Boot,' MGM didn't have a single good egg to put in any basket." But orders were orders. Shortly after, however, MGM got a letter from a leading Texas exhibitor asking, "When are we going to see more of those adorable cat and mouse cartoons?" He was too important

Wettest inhabited place on earth: Buenaventura, Colombia, with 265 inches of rain per year.

to ignore, so Hanna and Barbera were given the green light to develop the series.

WHAT'S IN A NAME?

Now that the team was going to make more cat and mouse cartoons for MGM, they needed names for their characters. Instead of painstakingly researching and developing a title for the pair, Hanna and Barbera asked fellow workers to put pairs of names into a hat. The pair they picked: "Tom and Jerry." An animator named John Carr won fifty dollars for the idea. MGM, on the other hand, made millions.

For seventeen years, Hanna and Barbera, still unknown to the public, made over 120 Tom and Jerry cartoons in the basement at MGM. Because their lead characters didn't talk, the cartoon's success was dependent on top-notch animation, plus writing that relied heavily on facial expressions and timing. This was all held together by composer Scott Bradley's complex music scores for each cartoon. Tom and Jerry cartoons won seven Academy Awards. Due to financial constraints at the studio, however, the series was dropped in 1958. Hanna and Barbera went on to create their own animation studio and churn out more made-for-TV cartoons than anyone in history, including The Flintstones, The Jetsons, Yogi Bear, and Scooby Doo.

MEANWHILE...

In 1963, five years after the last Tom and Jerry cartoon was made, legendary Warner Brothers animator Chuck Jones moved to MGM to resurrect the series. Not only did he have the unenviable task of toning down the violence in a cartoon that revolved around it, but by Jones' own admission, he didn't understand the characters. What came out was a wimpy copy of the Roadrunner and Coyote cartoons that didn't have the budget of the previous Tom and Jerry series. Not only were the plots and animation static, but Scott Bradley's carefully constructed scores were replaced by stock '60s music. After three unsuccessful years, MGM dropped the cat and mouse for good.

Since then, the series has been resurrected for TV in a number of different varieties (like *Tom and Jerry Kids*)...by Hanna-Barbera Studios.

The Netherlands has more burglaries per capita than any other country on earth.

PART VI: THE EMPIRE STATE BUILDING

It isn't the world's tallest skyscraper anymore, but the Empire State Building is still one of the most popular skyscrapers in the world, and as enduring a symbol of New York City as the Statue of Liberty. Here's the story of how it was built. (Part V is on Page 240.)

FAMILY PLOT

In 1827, William Backhouse Astor, son of New York land baron John Jacob Astor, bought a large plot of farmland in what is now mid-Manhattan. He didn't do much with it; he just held on to it because he figured that one day it might be worth more than the $20,500 he paid for it.

By the mid-1850s, several of the Astors had built mansions on the property, including William's daughter-in-law, Caroline. Much of the surrounding area was still farmland and pasture, but that was okay—Mrs. Astor liked the peace and quiet.

PAIN IN THE ASTOR

As the years passed, the property surrounding the Astor mansions was also developed, first into mansions for other millionaires, and later into upscale shops and other commercial buildings. In 1893, Mrs. Astor's nephew, William Waldorf Astor, built a 13-story hotel right next door to her mansion. He named it the Waldorf, after himself.

The Waldorf soon became the finest hotel in New York, playing host to royalty, captains of industry, and visiting heads of state—but Mrs. Astor, the queen of New York society, was furious that her own flesh and blood had forced her to live next door to transients. So she struck back—she tore down her mansion and in its place, built a 16-story hotel whose only purpose was to steal business from the Waldorf. Like her nephew, Mrs. Astor named her hotel—the Astoria—after herself.

Eventually, Mrs. Astor and her nephew patched up their differences and began operating the hotels jointly as the Waldorf-Astoria. It was more than a hotel—it was the gathering-place for the city's high society. The millionaires who lived nearby would

---

Heaviest U.S. president: William Howard Taft (332 lbs.). Lightest: James Madison (100 lbs.).

frequently drop in for dinner, drinks or tea while out on their daily strolls. But as time went on and the relentless commercialization of the neighborhood continued, many wealthy neighbors abandoned the area. With fewer and fewer of the city's elite living in walking distance, the hotel faded in importance. By the 1920s, the Waldorf-Astoria was passé; its fading velvet-tassle Victorian decor completely out of step with contemporary fashion. In 1929, the Astors sold the hotel(s) and some surrounding property to the Bethlehem Engineering Corporation for $16 million.

STARTING OVER
Bethlehem planned to demolish the building and replace it with a 55-story structure that would be the largest (though not the tallest) office building in the city.

But they couldn't arrange the financing. In September 1929, they sold the property to the Empire State Building Corporation.

Dynamic Duo
This new group of developers had financial and political clout that Bethlehem could only have dreamed of. Two of the most important members were John J. Raskob a former vice president of General Motors, and Al Smith, the scrappy former governor of New York and Democratic presidential nominee.

Raskob was in charge of coming up with the money to build what was going to be called the Empire State Building. Smith was in charge of public relations. His job was to sell the building, not just to the public, but also to prospective tenants. He was the right man for the job—nicknamed "the Happy Warrior," he'd worked his way up from the sidewalks of New York City into the governor's mansion, and was one of the most popular politicians New York had ever seen. Besides, a lot of people owed him favors.

BACK TO THE DRAWING BOARD
Bethlehem had planned to make its 55-story building low and wide. Raskob and his partners figured that a taller, skinnier building would make more money. So they told their architectural firm, Shreve, Lamb & Harmon, to come up with a design for one.

"Bill, how high can you make it so that it won't fall down?" Raskob supposedly said to architect William Lamb. Lamb replied that it was possible to construct a building 80 stories tall or higher.

The sailfish is the fastest fish in the world. It has a top speed of 68 miles per hour.

When the architects asked what the building should look like, either Smith or Raskob (both men later claimed credit) pulled out a big pencil and pointed it skyward. "It should look like this," they supposedly said.

Competing with Chrysler
Raskob decided to build the biggest building on Earth, and not just for the bragging rights. He had a personal motive—revenge. Apparently, Raskob had once made a deal with Walter P. Chrysler to join the Chrysler company...and Chrysler had reneged. Now Mr. Chrysler was building his own world's-tallest-skyscraper several blocks away. As John Tauranac writes in The Empire State Building, "Raskob wanted a building that would literally and figuratively put Walter Chrysler's building in the shade."

The only problem was that nobody except Walter Chrysler himself knew how tall the Chrysler building was going to be, and he wasn't talking.

One-Upsmanship
When the Chrysler Building was finally completed at 1,048 feet, Raskob was free to make new plans. He had announced the height of the Empire State Building as 1,000 feet. But it was still on the drawing board. So he ordered Shreve, Lamb & Harmon to add 5 stories to the building, making it 85 stories and 1,050 feet tall— two feet higher than the finished Chrysler Building. At this stage, the Empire State Building called for a flat-topped building with no tower or spire on the roof. That would come a little later...and it, too, would outdo the Chrysler building.

TRIAL BALLOON
In December 1929, Al Smith announced a change in the design of the building that would increase the height from 1,050 feet to 1,250 feet. Smith wasn't talking about adding a flagpole. He was talking about constructing a mooring mast for dirigibles, which would enable the building to serve as a sort of downtown airport for lighter-than-air balloons. The airships would tie up to the building in much the same way that a ship ties up to a pier. Passengers would then disembark via a gangplank that extended from the airship to the mooring mast. The topmost floors of the Empire State Building would be arrival and departure lounges,

ticket counters, and passenger services.

This may sound absurd today, but at the time, dirigibles seemed like the future of long-distance air travel. "No kidding," Smith told reporters. "We're working on the thing now." In September 1931, a small zeppelin actually did tie up to the mooring mast, and two weeks later a Goodyear blimp picked up a stack of newspapers from the top of the New York Evening Journal magazine and delivered them to the top of the Empire State Building. The stunt was an attempt to demonstrate that roof-to-roof deliveries might be a way to reduce congestion in the traffic-clogged streets below.

HOT AIR

Nobody knew whether the plan was really feasible, but that didn't stop Raskob and Smith. John Tauranac explains:

> No estimate of the additional cost of the project had been made at the time of the announcement, nor had feasibility studies been made or any market research done to determine whether people were actually willing to walk a gangplank from a dirigible to a mooring mast suspended almost 1,250 feet in the air. Nevertheless, Raskob had told Smith to proceed....The whole job was estimated at about $750,000, a paltry addition to the final costs.

The dirigible mast remained a part of the building's design and actually did get built. The idea of actually using it, however, was quietly dropped, and the landing gear that would have enabled dirigibles to use it was never installed. As for the space that was set aside for the ticket counter and passenger lounge, it was converted to "the world's highest soda fountain and tea garden."

As long as you're already visiting the Empire State Building,
why not turn to the next installment, Part VII?
It's on page 313.

IRONIC, ISN'T IT?

*More irony to put the problems of your
day-to-day life in proper perspective.*

DELICIOUS IRONY
"A 1978 newsletter edited at a branch of Mensa, an organization for high-IQ people, had numerous misspellings—including the word, 'intelligense.'"—*The Literary Life and Other Curiosities*

• "The U.S. Postal Service suffered a courtroom setback in 1992. USPS needed to get an expert-witness list to a Dayton, Ohio, judge by the next day in an unemployment discrimination case in order to be able to use the witnesses at trial. The list was sent from Washington, D.C., by the Postal Service's overnight Express Mail but did not arrive for ten days."—*The Concrete Enema*

• "In 1993 near Alvin, Texas, Andrea Guerrero, 18, and her brother came across a man who was slumped over his truck and not breathing. Andrea saved his life by administering CPR until an ambulance arrived. At the time, Guerrero was on her way home from a CPR certification exam, which she had flunked."
—*The Concrete Enema*

• "[In 1986,] our *For What It's Worth Department* concludes that Orlando, Florida has one prejudiced jury! In the Orange County Courthouse, a jury of twelve…was stuck for twenty minutes in a courthouse elevator…On their way to the courtroom to hear a case against the Otis Elevator Company!" —*Paul Harvey's For What It's Worth*

• "In 1978 Ray Wright of Philadelphia, Pennsylvania was promoting his burglar alarm business, leaving flyers on autos. They read, 'If you didn't see me put this on your windshield, I could just as easily have stolen your car.' While he busy advertising, someone stole his truck."—*Encyclopedia Brown's Book of Facts*

EMBARRASSING IRONY

• "[In 1994,] author James Herriot, whose gentle accounts of the life of a British country veterinarian (such as *All Creatures Great*

Foot fetish: 15 percent of Americans secretly bite their toenails.

and Small) are sold throughout the world and have inspired a television series, was in the hospital yesterday after being attacked by a flock of sheep."—*News Report*

• "The always-so-correct British Broadcasting Corporation was severely embarrassed when news leaked out that they had paid white film extras up to five times as much as black extras during African location shooting of a documentary film series. Its title: The Fight Against Slavery."—*The World's Greatest Mistakes*

• "Human Kindness Day took place in Washington, D.C. on May 10, 1975. At a press conference afterwards, police said there had been 600 arrests, 150 smashed windows, and 42 looted refreshment stands."—*The Book of Heroic Failures*

IRONY FROM ABOVE

• "In 1979 the Allied Roofing and Siding Company of Grand Rapids, Michigan was engaged in cleaning snow from roofs in the area to prevent damage or collapse from the weight of heavy snow. But guess what roof did collapse from the weight of snow? The roof over the Allied Roofing and Siding Company."—*The Book of Blunders*

• "In Jacksonville, the Riverside Chevrolet Company launched a sales campaign featuring the slogan, 'Look for it! Something BIG is going to happen!' A few hours later, the showroom ceiling collapsed on six new cars."—*Not a Good Word About Anybody*

• "The American Institute of Architects held their 1979 annual conference in Kansas City, to be near the Kemper Arena, to which they had awarded their prize as 'One of the finest buildings in the nation.' On the first day of the conference, hordes of architects toured the inspired structure, with its wide spanning roof trusses, which The Architectural Record described as having 'an almost awesome muscularity.' On the second day, the roof of the $12 million building fell down. Twenty-six architects were hospitalized."—*The Book of Heroic Failures*

THE TOP 10 HITS OF THE YEAR, 1988–1991

Here's another installment of BRI's Top Ten of the Year list.

1988
(1) Faith —*George Michael*
(2) Need You Tonight —*INXS*
(3) Got My Mind Set On You
    —*George Harrison*
(4) Never Gonna Give Up
    —*Rick Astley*
(5) Sweet Child O' Mine
    —*Guns N' Roses*
(6) Heaven Is A Place On Earth
    —*Belinda Carlisle*
(7) So Emotional
    —*Whitney Houston*
(8) Hands To Heaven —*Breathe*
(9) Could've Been —*Tiffany*
(10) Roll With It
    —*Steve Winwood*

1989
(1) Look Away —*Chicago*
(2) My Prerogative —*Bobby Brown*
(3) Every Rose Has Its Thorn
    — *Poison*
(4) Miss You Much
    —*Janet Jackson*
(5) Straight Up —*Paula Abdul*
(6) Wind Beneath My Wings
    (from *Beaches*) —*Bette Midler*
(7) Cold Hearted —*Paula Abdul*
(8) Girl You Know It's True
    —*Milli Vanilli*
(9) Baby, I Love You Way/Free-
    bird Medley —*Will To Power*
(10) Giving You The Best That I
    Got —*Anita Baker*

1990
(1) Hold On —*Wilson Phillips*
(2) Nothing Compares 2 U
    —*Sinead O'Connor*
(3) It Must Have Been Love
    (from *Pretty Woman*)
    —*Roxette*
(4) Poison —*Bell Biv Devoe*
(5) Vogue —*Madonna*
(6) Another Day In Paradise
    —*Phil Collins*
(7) Vision Of Love
    —*Mariah Carey*
(8) Hold On —*En Vogue*
(9) Cradle Of Love (from *Ford
    Fairlane*) —*Billy Idol*
(10) Blaze Of Glory (from *Young
    Guns II*) —*Jon Bon Jovi*

1991
(1) (Everything I Do) I Do It For
    You (from *Robin Hood*)
    —*Bryan Adams*
(2) I Wanna Sex You Up (from
    New Jack City)
    —*Color Me Badd*
(3) Gonna Make You Sweat
    —*C&C Music Factory*
(4) One More Try —*Timmy T.*
(5) Rush Rush —*Paula Abdul*
(6) Unbelievable —*EMF*
(7) I Like The Way (The Kissing
    Game) —*Hi-Five*
(8) More Than Words —*Extreme*
(9) The First Time —*Surface*
(10) Baby Baby —*Amy Grant*

pumpkin pie, lavender, cucumbers, baby powder, and Good 'n' Plenty candy.

WHAT'S FOR BREAKFAST?

We take it for granted that bacon, eggs, orange juice, and coffee are breakfast foods. But it's really just a matter of tradition.

COFFEE AND TEA. People started drinking coffee and tea in the morning not because they were pleasant, but because they were hot, dark, and mysterious. Until the 17th century, it was common for Europeans to start their day with alcohol. Queen Elizabeth, for example, had a pot of beer and a pound of beefsteak for breakfast every day. Scottish breakfasts routinely included a dram of whiskey. Coffee, tea, and sugar had the same illicit appeal as alcohol when they reached Europe in the 1600s—so they became suitable substitutes for booze.

EGGS & BACON, SAUSAGE, OR HAM. Colonists brought chickens and pigs with them to America because they were easy to transport by ship, and could provide food on the long voyage. Besides that, it was traditional to eat meat in the morning—and pork was the colonists' first choice. (It was so popular that one writer suggested they rename the U.S. "the Republic of Porkdom.") Eggs probably became a staple at breakfast because "they're freshest when just gathered from the previous night's roosting."

CITRUS FRUIT / ORANGE JUICE. Believe it or not, people started eating oranges in the morning because they thought it would warm them. The ancient Greeks taught that some foods heat your body, and other foods cool it—regardless of the temperature at which they're served. Peas were cold, for example, onions were hot...and oranges were very hot. People still believed this in the Middle Ages, which is why the Spanish began eating candied orange peels the first thing in the morning. The habit was picked up by the British, who brought it to the Colonies. (In Scotland, the orange peel became orange marmalade, which they put on toast with butter—starting another breakfast tradition.)

Orange juice became a staple of the American breakfast table in the 1920s. In 1946, concentrated orange juice was introduced.

More than 10% of the world's annual production of salt is used to de-ice American roads.

IS IT KOSHER?

*Everyone has heard the term "kosher." In American slang, that means
"on the up-and-up." Most people also know it's actually a religious
term—a part of Judaism. But what does it really mean? Even many
less-observant Jews aren't 100% sure.*

KOSHER BASICS

Kosher means "fit" or "acceptable" in Hebrew. According
to the Torah, or Old Testament (Leviticus, chapter 11),
only certain types of animals are considered kosher and can be
eaten. In addition, three verses (Exodus 23:19, 24:26, and
Deuteronomy 14:21) forbid the cooking of a baby goat in its own
mother's milk.

From these origins, the rabbis in the Talmud (the book of
ancient writings that are the basis of religious authority for Orthodox Jews) developed a detailed set of requirements for raising,
slaughtering, preparing, storing, cooking, and eating animals.

For Jews who "keep kosher" (many do not), everything from
the animal's birth to its consumption at mealtime must be done in
accordance with these rules. And for a processed food to be
labeled kosher, it must be certified by a rabbi who has overseen all
of the ingredients…as well as the manufacturing process and
equipment.

WHAT FOOD IS KOSHER?

It's detailed, but here are some general rules:

Meat: Animals must be raised without hormones and growth stim-
ulants, and must be slaughtered quickly to minimize pain. Within
three days of slaughter, kosher butchers are required to de-vein
meat, salt it, and rinse it three times in fresh, flowing water to
remove blood—which people are forbidden to eat.

Kosher: Any animal that chews its cud and has split hooves
(e.g., cows); fish with both fins and scales; all birds except scav-
engers and birds of prey.

Non-kosher: Pigs, rabbits, shellfish, reptiles, invertebrates,
amphibians and underwater mammals.

Country with the highest crime rate: Dominican Republic. Lowest crime rate: Togo.

Milk: Meat and dairy products must be kept completely separate from one another. They not only have to be stored apart, but cooked and eaten with separate dishes, utensils, pots and pans. (Glass dishes, which are non-porous, can be used for anything.) Especially devout Jews wait six hours after eating meat before eating a milk product, so that the foods don't mix even in their stomachs.

Pareve Foods: Pareve is Yiddish for "neutral." Eggs, fish, tofu, and fruits and vegetables are neither dairy nor meat and can be eaten with either milk or meat (if prepared with neutral utensils).

KOSHER COMPLICATIONS

Some rules governing how kosher foods must be manufactured and prepared make it hard to tell if a food really is kosher. For example: kosher foods can't be produced on the same assembly lines as non-kosher foods. So if a "kosher" spaghetti sauce is manufactured on the same assembly line as spaghetti sauce containing non-kosher meat, it's not kosher. And nondairy creamers that contain sodium caseinate, a milk derivative, are considered a dairy product; they can't be used in drinks served at meals where meat is served.

It's almost impossible for consumers to tell on their own whether a food is truly kosher. That's why more than 400 Rabbinical Supervision agencies have sprung up to evaluate foods, by overseeing the manufacturing process and certifying it to be kosher. The oldest and largest of these is the Union of Orthodox Jewish Congregations of America. Foods they certify have a letter U in a circle on the package. Another organization, The Committee for the Furtherance of Torah Observations, uses a K in a circle.

KOSHER FACTS

• As of 1997, there were 20,000 kosher products on U.S. store shelves, representing 30% of all packaged foods in supermarkets and 40% of packaged foods in health food stores.
• Roughly 7,000,000 consumers spend $3 billion a year on kosher foods, and the market is growing at a rate of 11% a year.
• Ironically, a majority of certified kosher foods (about 76% of them) are sold to non-Jews who are concerned about food safety, or whose religions have similar food restrictions.

The Great Smoky Mountains National Park gets the most visitors of any national park.

ANIMAL SUPERSTITIONS

Superstitions are intriguing, even if you don't believe in them. Here are some very old ones relating to animals, collected by Edwin and Mona Radford in their book, Encyclopedia of Superstitions.

"A strange dog following you is good luck. A dog howling is a sure sign of death."

"If a rooster crows near the door with his face towards it, it is a sure prediction of the arrival of a stranger."

"Good luck will attend anyone upon whose face a spider falls from the ceiling."

"If a cat sneezes, it is a sign of rain. If a cat sneezes three times, a cold will run through the family."

"Living pigeons cut in half and applied to the feet of a man in fever will cure him."

"To cure illness in a family, wash the patient and throw the water on a cat. Then drive the cat out of doors, and it will take the illness with it."

"If blind people are kind to ravens they will learn how to regain their sight."

"If you find a hairy caterpillar, you should throw it over your shoulder for good luck."

"If a dog passes between a couple who are going to be married, much ill-luck will result to them."

"Mice, minced, given to a sufferer, will cure the measles."

"Dried rat's tails will cure a cold."

"If a white weasel crosses your path, it presages death or misfortune; but if one runs in front of you, you will be able to beat all your enemies."

"If a cat sneezes near a bride, it means she will have good luck in her wedded life."

"When mice swarm into a house hitherto free from them, a member of the household will die"

"If the rooster crows at midnight, the Angel of Death is passing over the house."

"If a man should kill a glow-worm, it will endanger his love affair, and may cause the death of his beloved."

Crocodile babies don't have sex chromosomes; the temperature at which the egg develops determines gender.

MORE LEGENDARY BETS

Some bets achieve the status of legends because of the unexpected results they produce. Here are two classic examples of bets that got out of hand...and became folklore.

THE BOTTLE HOAX OF 1749

The Wager: In the first week of 1749, the Duke of Portland bet the Earl of Chesterfield that if he were to advertise the public performance of something obviously impossible, "there'd be enough fools in London to fill the theater and pay handsomely for it." Chesterfield took him up on it.

The Duke then placed this ad in the London papers:

> At the New Theater in the Haymarket, on Monday next, is to be seen a Person who performs most surprising things....He presents you with a common Wine Bottle, which any of the spectators may first examine; this Bottle is placed on a Table in the midst of the Stage, and he (without any equivocation) goes into it, in the sight of all the Spectators, and sings in it. During his stay in the bottle, any person may handle it, and see plainly that it does not exceed a common Tavern Bottle.

The Result: The Duke won. Soon all London was talking about the upcoming event. The theater was sold out well in advance of the day—with people paying as much as 7 shillings, 6 pence a seat to see it. But, obviously, there wasn't anything to see and things got ugly quickly. After about 20 minutes, when it became apparent that they'd been had, the audience rioted...they destroyed the theater, stealing everything in it...and then they burned the building down. The Duke had covered his tracks, and the true story of the bet didn't leak out until several years later.

THE BERNERS STREET HOAX OF 1809

The Wager: A well-known practical joker of his day, Thomas Hook, was walking in a quiet residential neighborhood near London with a friend. He pointed to a particularly quiet-looking house on Berners Street, No. 54, and bet that "within a month, that house will be the talk of London." His friend took him up on it.

According to one account: "Hook went into action. No. 54,

he discovered, was occupied by an elderly widow, a Mrs. Tottingham—and he rented a room in the house opposite. Then he wrote and posted more than a thousand letters—it took him two weeks—and when 'zero hour' dawned, he and his friend were sitting in their window to watch the fun."

The Result: Hook won. Here's how Curtiss MacDougall describes it in his book, *Hoaxes:*

> It began early in the morning, with the arrival of about a dozen chimney sweeps from all parts of London, summoned by a letter to sweep the chimneys of No. 54. While the agitated housemaid was still arguing heatedly with these disappointed men, there converged upon No. 54 several coal-carts, each with a ton of coal, "as per your esteemed order." Then came a van-load of furniture, a consignment of beer, in barrels, a huge chamber organ (carried by six men), a cartload of potatoes, and even a hearse, with a train of mourning-coaches. Shopkeepers of all kinds—confectioners, wig-makers, opticians, clockmakers, fancy-goods dealers, dressmakers and many more—arrived in large numbers, all bringing samples of their wares. Two fashionable doctors and a dentist did their best to struggle through the ever-growing crowd and pay professional visits to the unfortunate Mrs. Tottingham—who could really have done with medical attention, for she was on the verge of hysterics.
>
> By this time, Berners street was choked up with carts, furniture, barrels of beer, and a large crowd. The police had been called out—and to make matters worse, all sorts of notables began to arrive, all headed to No. 54. The Duke of York, Commander-in-Chief of the Army, came in reply to a pathetic note telling him that a brother-officer was lying dangerously ill at No. 54, and begged a parting interview. The Lord Chief Justice came—so did the Archbishop of Canterbury, the Governor of the Bank of England, and the Lord Mayor of London. Apparently, he'd been victimized by a very similar letter to the one that bagged the Duke of York.
>
> One gets the impression that if it had been possible, 'the architect of this most outrageous deception' would probably have been hanged, drawn, and quartered. As it was, nothing happened to them—because, while everybody suspected a lot, nothing could be proved. Still, Hook left his Berners Street lodging very quietly as soon as the mob had been dispersed, and he wasn't seen in London for a long time afterwards.

WHY WE HAVE SPRING AND WINTER

Here's another Greek/Roman tale from Myths and Legends of the Ages. *This one tells us how springtime and winter were created.*

Far down under the surface of the earth lay the lands of Pluto, god of the underworld. Pluto, who despised light and avoided cheer, rarely left his dark and gloomy kingdom. But one day, he paid a short visit to the surface of the earth.

As he sped along the earth in his black chariot drawn by four black horses, he was seen by Cupid.

"What great good luck!" thought the mischievous god of love, as he fitted an arrow to his bow. "Here's a target I may never get a chance at again!"

Cupid took careful aim and shot his arrow straight into Pluto's heart.

Now, anyone who is hit by Cupid's arrow doesn't die but instead falls in love with the first person he sees. The first person Pluto saw was Proserpine, the lovely daughter of Ceres, goddess of the harvest. Proserpine was gathering lilies beside a gay, bubbling stream. When Pluto saw her, he was overwhelmed with love. He swept Proserpine up in his arms and carried her off in his chariot. The terrified girl screamed for help, but there was no one to hear her cries.

Pluto struck the earth with his great three-pronged spear, and the ground opened up. Into the opening, Pluto drove his plunging black horses. The earth closed again, while down, down, deep into the earth the chariot sped with Pluto and his beautiful prisoner.

Soon they arrived at Pluto's palace. The underworld king spoke words of love to Proserpine. He begged her not to be afraid. "You shall be my beloved," he said. "You shall reign as queen over all the realms of the dead."

But Proserpine only shook her head and wept. She would not look at Pluto; she would neither eat nor drink.

Middle-class malaise: The higher the income, the more likely an American man will cheat on his wife.

Far away, on the surface of the earth, Proserpine's mother, Ceres, was enveloped in despair. She searched the world over for her missing daughter, but she could not find her.

One day, weary and sad, Ceres sat down beside a river. The place she chose to rest was a fateful one. It was the very spot where Pluto had caused the earth to open so that he could pass in with Proserpine.

The nymph who lived in the nearby river had seen everything that happened. She was terribly afraid of Pluto, and dared not tell Ceres. Instead, she lifted up the sash which Proserpine had dropped and wafted it to the feet of her mother.

Ceres cried out with grief at the sight of her daughter's sash. Now she knew that Proserpine was in the earth, but she did not know what had happened. In her grief and anger, she blamed the earth itself.

"Ungrateful soil!" cried Ceres. "I have given you richness and clothed you with greenery and nourishing grain. Is this how you repay me? Now no more shall you enjoy my favors."

In her anger, Ceres sent too much rain, which killed the crops, then too much sun, which dried the fields. The leaves fell from the trees, cattle died, and ploughs broke in the furrows. The poor earth suffered terribly.

Finally, Arethusa, the nymph, interceded for the land. "Goddess," she said, "do not blame the land. Unwillingly did it open to let your daugher in. Pluto carried her off to be queen of the underworld. As my waters seeped through the earth, they saw her there. She is sad, but she is not afraid."

When Ceres heard this, she determined to get help. She quickly turned her chariot toward heaven and threw herself before the throne of Jupiter, the king of the gods. She begged him to bring Proserpine back to the earth—to force Pluto to give up her daughter.

Jupiter consented, but he was forced to make one condition. If Proserpine had not eaten anything while in the underworld she could return; otherwise, she must stay in Pluto's kingdom.

Mercury, the messenger of the gods, was then sent to Pluto with Jupiter's orders to return Proserpine to her mother.

World's largest carnivore: The Southern elephant seal. It weighs 7,700 lbs. and is 21 feet long.

Pluto could not refuse an order from Jupiter. But first, the clever Pluto offered Proserpine a pomegranate. No longer afraid of Pluto, Proserpine started to bite into the fruit. In alarm, Mercury stopped her—but not before she had swallowed six pomegranate seeds. Now, Pluto was able to demand that Proserpine spend six months of the year with him—one month for each seed she had swallowed.

So it was arranged. For six months each year, Proserpine must leave her mother, Ceres, and be Pluto's queen. During that time, Ceres is sad and unconcerned with the earth. Everything dies. It is winter.

At the end of six months, Proserpine comes back to her mother. She brings joy to Ceres and bright springtime to the earth.

* * *

ASK THE EXPERTS

Q: *Why can't we ever buy cashews in their shells?*
A: "Cashews aren't sold in their shells because they don't have a shell. Don't all nuts have shells? Yes. Then what gives?

"A cashew is a *seed*, not a nut. The cashew is the seed of a pear-shaped fruit, the cashew apple, which is itself edible. The cashew seed hangs at the lower end of the fruit, vulnerable and exposed. Cashews grow not on trees, but on tropical shrubs, similar to sumac plants.

"A hard leathery shell is what differentiates a nut from a seed. Kernels with thin, soft shells, such as pumpkins and sunflowers, are properly called seeds." (From *Imponderables*, by David Feldman)

Q: *Does a millipede have a million legs or a thousand legs?*
A: Neither. "Although the animal's name might suggest that it has a million legs, in fact the number of limbs on a millipede won't even total a thousand. Despite the fact that the word millipede means "thousand-legged," these many-limbed creatures actually have less than two hundred legs in all....Of course, two hundred is still a lot of legs." (From *How Do Ants Know When You're Having a Picnic?*, by Joanne Settel and Nancy Baggett)

Geography quiz: Which country has the longest coastline of any on earth? Canada.

BACK ON THE CABLE

Aren't you glad you don't have a TV in your bathroom? We are, because you'd probably be sitting there for hours, watching "Dukes of Hazzard" reruns instead of reading Uncle John's Bathroom Reader. Here's more info on cable stations.

NICKELODEON

Background: In the 1970s, cable was still trying to find a niche as an alternative to network television. Kids' shows like Sesame Street and The Electric Company on PBS, were regarded as quality "alternative" shows—so when Nick was being launched in 1977 as "the first all-day, every day, something-for-every-kid programming package ever offered for cable TV," that's what they chose to emulate.

On the Air: Nick was the first television channel, cable or otherwise, that was devoted entirely to children's programming. It's hard to believe today, but there were no commercials—the company's budget was limited to the subscription fees paid to it by cable companies. "We don't take advertising because cable, to succeed, needs to be different from commercial broadcasting," Nickelodeon Vice President Cy Schneider explained in 1983. "It makes for a better product." It also made for enormous losses—by 1983, Nickelodeon was an estimated $20 million in debt. In 1984, it reversed course and began accepting commercials; a year later it was acquired by Viacom. By 1995, it was the most-watched basic-cable channel in the country, earning more than $100 million a year from advertising, cable subscription fees, and more than 400 licensed products.

CABLE NEWS NETWORK (CNN)

Background: By the mid-'70s, many AM radio stations had successfully moved to an all-news format. Ted Turner, owner of TBS, figured that if radio could make a 24-hour news profitable, so could TV. And he relished the idea of showing the Big 3 networks that news—which they thought of as their "crown jewel"—could be done well on cable, too. The only problem was that Turner didn't know anything about news broadcasting...and didn't even like it. But he was convinced that if he didn't follow through with the idea, some other cable entrepreneur would beat him to it. Analysts told Turner that there wasn't enough audience

---

President Calvin Coolidge liked to eat breakfast while having his head rubbed with Vaseline.

for an all-day news network. After a few years of waiting, he decided to do it anyway.

On the Air: Turner called Reese Schonfeld, founder of the nonprofit Independent Television News Association, and asked him: (1) if a 24-hour cable news channel was feasible; and (2) if he'd be interested in running it. Schonfeld said yes to both.

Together, Turner and Schonfeld successfully pitched CNN to cable operators at their annual convention in 1979. Turner then had to sell a TV station he owned in Charlotte, North Carolina, to raise the startup capital. CNN premiered on June 1, 1980. For years it was derided as the "Chicken Noodle Network" by the Big 3 networks and the public alike...but its respectability and clout grew steadily over time. Its crowning moment came in October 1987, when President Reagan invited "all four networks'—CBS, ABC, NBC and CNN—in for an Oval Office chat. As CNN anchor Bernard Shaw put it at the time, Reagan's invitation gave CNN "parity" with the Big-3 network news organizations for the first time.

THE FAMILY CHANNEL

Background: Pat Robertson founded the Christian Broadcasting Network (CBN) in 1960 when WYAH-TV—his little station in Portsmouth, Virginia—became the first in the country authorized by the FCC to devote more than 50% of its air time to religious programming. The network was built up with the help of donations from viewers. It started broadcasting via satellite in 1977, but continued to suffer from low ratings until 1981, when Robertson launched The Family Channel.

On the Air: The Family Channel de-emphasized religious programming in favor of reruns of wholesome shows like *Wagon Train, Burns and Allen,* and *I Married Joan.* "Only a masochist would want to watch religious shows all day," Robertson explained. The Family Channel also began to accept commercials. Over the years Robertson continued to shift the station's emphasis away from religious broadcasting toward more lucrative secular shows like Newhart. By 1991, the station was making so much money that CBN's tax exempt status was threatened. So Robertson spun it off as an independent company, naming himself as chairman. By 1995, the only preaching show left on the Family Channel was Robertson's own "700 Club." Today it is owned by media mogul Rupert Murdoch.

Only 54.3% of Louisiana high school students will ever graduate, the lowest of any state.

DUMB PREDICTIONS

An enthusiastic BRI member e-mailed us this list. We print it here as a reminder that the "experts" are as clueless as the rest of us.

C omputers in the future may weigh no more than 1.5 tons."
—*Popular Mechanics*, **1949**

"I think there is a world market for maybe five computers."
—**Thomas Watson, chairman of IBM, 1943**

"This 'telephone' has too many shortcomings to be seriously considered as a means of communication. The device is inherently of no value to us."
—**Western Union internal memo, 1876**
(after Alexander Graham Bell offered to sell them the rights to the telephone)

"The wireless music box has no imaginable commercial value. Who would pay for a message sent to nobody in particular?"
—**Associates of NBC president David Sarnoff**
(responding to his recommendation, in the 1920s, that they invest in radio)

"We don't like their sound, and guitar music is on the way out."
—**Decca Recording Company 1962**
(rejecting the Beatles)

"I'm just glad it'll be Clark Gable who's falling on his face and not Gary Cooper."
—**Gary Cooper**
(happy he didn't take the lead role in Gone With The Wind)

"A cookie store is a bad idea. Besides, the market research reports say America likes crispy cookies, not soft and chewy cookies like you make."
—**Bankers' comment to Debbi Fields**
(about her idea to start Mrs. Fields' Cookies)

Country with the most elephants: Zaire, with 195,000. Country with the fewest: Vatican City.

"Heavier-than-air flying machines are impossible."
—**Lord Kelvin, president, Royal Society, 1895**

"If I had thought about it, I wouldn't have done the experiment. The literature was full of examples that said you can't do this."
—**Spencer Silver**
(on the adhesive that led to 3-M Post-Its)

"Professor Goddard does not know the relation between action and reaction and the need to have something better than a vacuum against which to react. He seems to lack the basic knowledge ladled out daily in high schools."
—**New York Times editorial, 1921**
(about Robert Goddard's revolutionary rocket work)

"You want to have consistent and uniform muscle development across all of your muscles? It can't be done. It's just a fact of life. You just have to accept inconsistent muscle development as an unalterable condition of weight training."
—**Comment to Arthur Jones**
(inventor of Nautilus)

"Stocks have reached what looks like a permanently high plateau."
—**Irving Fisher, Professor of Economics, Yale University, 1929**

"Everything that can be invented has been invented."
—**Charles H. Duell, Commissioner, U.S. Office of Patents, 1899**

"Louis Pasteur's theory of germs is ridiculous fiction."
—**Pierre Pachet, Professor of Physiology at Toulouse, 1872**

"640K ought to be enough for anybody."
—**Bill Gates, 1981**

PART VII: BUILDING THE EMPIRE STATE BUILDING

Here's the next-to-last section of our story on the world's tallest buildings. Part VI is on page 293.

BORROWED TIME

The Empire State Building was slated to be the world's tallest building—and it was paid for with some of the world's largest construction loans. Since the loans were going to be repaid with rent money, it was essential to finish the structure quickly and get tenants moved in. So speed was factored into every phase of design and construction. Anything that could be mass-produced was, and everything that was installed in the building was specifically designed for ease of assembly.

The architects worked at a breakneck pace, completing much of the design while construction was underway. They had to hustle to stay one step ahead of the steelworkers, who were adding 4-1/2 stories to the building every week, a record setting pace.

One architect observed: "The builders were throwing steel into the sky not just higher but faster than anybody had ever dreamed possible." And as soon as the framework for a new floor was completed, the carpenters, glazers, masons, plumbers, and electricians would move in and finish the rest. In all, more than 4,000 workers were employed at the site when construction was at its peak.

OPEN FOR BUSINESS

Amazingly, eighteen months after the demolition of the Waldorf Astoria began, the Empire State Building opened its doors for business. The structure's statistics were awesome: It was 1,250 feet and 86 floors high. It boasted 1.8 million square feet of office space with 6,500 windows, 7,000 radiators, and 17 million feet of telephone and telegraph wire. It was built with enough steel to build railroad tracks from New York to Baltimore and back. And the exterior walls were faced with 10 million bricks, 200,000 cubic feet of stone, and 730 tons of aluminum and steel. It was billed as the Eighth Wonder of the World, and to admirers of the 1930s, it more than lived up to the title.

Hard Times
But the world around the building had changed almost as fast as the skyline. Only weeks after construction began in October 1929, the stock market crashed and ushered in the Great Depression. Nobody knew how long it would last—and besides, it was too late to stop construction. So work on the Empire State Building continued uninterrupted.

By the time the building was finished, the New York real estate market had collapsed. Practically speaking, filling it with paying customers was an impossible task.

WHITE ELEPHANT
When the Empire State Building opened in 1931, only 23% of the offices were occupied; and for the rest of the Depression, the "Empty State Building" would never be more than two-thirds full.

By 1936, there were still no tenants between the 41st and the 80th floors (although NBC had television laboratories on the 85th floor), and even the floors below the 41st floor were not fully occupied. Real estate experts predicted that if the top 45 floors were not torn down, the building would lose $3 million a year "for life." Things were so bad that the management even took to turning the lights in the empty floors on at night so that no one would know how empty the building was.

With so few rent-paying tenants, other sources of money came to count for a lot. "One of the greatest sources of income," Tauranac writes, "was the observatories. All those millions of dollar admissions contributed to the coffers of the Empire State Building, especially after *King Kong* (1933) had been depicted climbing to the pinnacle of the Empire State with a disheveled Fay Wray in his grasp. But even *King Kong* was not enough."

Hanging On
In 1936, the Empire State Building Corporation defaulted on the mortgage and became technically insolvent. The only reason it wasn't forced into bankruptcy was that Metropolitan Life, holder of the mortgage, didn't figure it could do a better job attracting

tenants than the current management was. Selling the building wasn't a realistic option in the glutted real estate market, so they just left it alone, lowered the interest rate on the loan, and collected whatever money they could.

The strategy turned out to be a wise one. "By 1940," Tauranac writes, "Met Life had received $3.8 million that it would not have received had they foreclosed, and although everybody might not have been particularly happy, they were satisfied."

BOUNCING BACK

The Empire State Building began to recover in the early 1940s, thanks to the slowly improving economic situation and the buildup that accompanied America's entry into World War II. In 1942, the Office of Price Administration signed a lease for five entire floors, and 19 other federal agencies would eventually move in, too. By 1944, the building was 85% full; in 1950, *Time* magazine reported that it was "jammed to the rafters," with tenants paying $10 million worth of rent in a building that cost a little over $5 million a year to operate. In 15 years, the Empire State Building had gone from bankruptcy to one of the most profitable buildings in the world. And it would remain the tallest building in the world for more than 40 years.

Newer, taller buildings would eventually be built, but for many skyscraper buffs, there would never be anything like the Empire State Building. "It has been surpassed in height," George Douglas writes, "but it has not been displaced in the hearts of New Yorkers and of millions of visitors for whom it is the great skyscraper, the building that comes first to mind as the tallest of the tall. For style, grace, and dramatic thrust it is hard to find its equal anywhere in the world."

*When you're ready for the exciting conclusion,
flip on ahead to Part VIII on page 320.*

Three largest Native American tribes in the U.S.: Cherokee, Navajo, Chippewa.

THE WORLD'S WORST ACTOR

Some people's fame endures not because they were good at what they did—but because they were mind-bogglingly bad. The BRI's eccentric collection of history books is full of tales about people like Robert Coates. But then, he's in a category all by himself.

ROBERT "ROMEO" COATES (1772-1842)
Background: Born in Antigua, Coates had dark, exotic looks that stood out in a British crowd. But he didn't rely on nature to attract attention—he dressed in costumes covered with diamonds and feathers. In 1807, a few days before his stage debut in Bath, England, he arrived in town—in a diamond-studded carriage shaped like a seashell.

Claim to Fame: Coates became wildly popular in England for butchering Shakespeare. As Margaret Nicholas writes in *The World's Greatest Cranks and Crackpots:*

> He constantly forgot his lines, invented scenes as he went along, and turned to address the audience whenever he thought it was getting out of hand. If he enjoyed playing a scene, he would quite happily repeat it three or four times. He loved dramatic death scenes and had no qualms about "breathing his last" several times over. Exasperated playgoers would yell, "Why don't you die?"

One night during *Romeo and Juliet*, Coates dashed off stage and returned with a crowbar...which he used to try to pry open Juliet's tomb. He considered it an improvement on Shakespeare.

At another performance, someone hurled a fighting cock on stage (in "tribute" to Coates' motto, "while I live, I'll crow"). The bird pecked at Coates' feet, but the actor delivered his romantic speech without missing a beat.

Coates proved that bad acting can be very profitable.

Nicholas writes:

> His fame spread and soon he was playing to packed houses. People would travel great distances to see if he really was as bad

as everyone reported. He became such an attraction that even the Prince Regent went to see him.

When he played the part of Lothario in Rowe's *The Fair Penitent* at London's Haymarket Theater, at least a thousand people had to be turned away....

At another performance...his acting was so poor that several people laughed themselves ill and had to be helped outside into the fresh air and treated by a doctor.

Eventually, the rowdy crowds became a problem. No actress, for fear of injury, would play Juliet opposite Coates' Romeo (his favorite role). And theater owners became less willing to risk damage to their property. He often had to bribe them just to get a part in their plays.

Without the income from acting to support his lavish style Coates went bankrupt. He was killed in 1848, at age 75, when he was run down by a hansom taxi.

* * *

SPEAKING OF DUMB...

"In Altoona, Pennsylvania...TV anchorman Brandon Brooks demonstrated for his viewers how to protect their homes from burglars. He used his own home to demonstrate double locks on doors, windows that will not open from the outside, burglar alarms...

"Now it appears that thieves were watching the program. They not only learned where the double locks were, but where the TV set was and the VCR and the furniture and other things.

"So nights later—while Brandon Brooks was on the air back at the studio—the thieves broke into his house and cleaned him out.

"The window that won't open from the outside: They smashed it."

—**Paul Harvey's** *For What It's Worth*

The average tastebud lives only 10 days before it dies and is replaced with a new one.

THEY WENT THAT-A-WAY

Here are a few more stories about the deaths of famous people from Malcolm Forbes' fascinating book.

MATA HARI

Claim to Fame: Nude dancer, seductress, and supposed master spy for the Germans during World War I.

Cause of Death: Firing squad.

Postmortem: Mata Hari (her real name was Margaretha Zelle) was famous before the war for dancing what she claimed was an "authentic Hindu temple ritual." It was really just an excuse for her to take her clothes off, and it gave her admirers an excuse to come and see her. "I could never dance well," she admitted. "People came to see me because I was the first who dared show myself naked to the public."

She may not have been a spy at all—just a scapegoat. But when the French lost two hundred thousand men in the Battle of the Somme, they needed someone to blame. Mata Hari, who had antagonized authorities for years, fit the bill perfectly. She was arrested, tried for espionage, and sentenced to death. She refused to be tied to the execution pole, and reportedly also turned down a blindfold. Mata Hari was seductive to the end, smiling and winking at the firing squad as they raised their rifles in her direction.

JIMI HENDRIX

Claim to Fame: Rock musician and one of the most talented guitarists who ever lived. His hits included "Purple Haze," "Foxy Lady," and an electric guitar version of "The Star Spangled Banner."

Cause of Death: Overdosed on sleeping pills and drowned in his own vomit.

Postmortem: Was Hendrix's death purely an accident? Was it a suicide? Was it a drug-induced combination of the two? We'll never know for sure. Hendrix, who'd been sliding deeper into drug addiction in the months preceding his death, was reeling from a number of poor concert performances earlier in the year. He was booed by an audience in West Germany, and he had walked offstage in mid-song during a concert at Madison Square Garden, telling the audience, "I just can't get it together." Hendrix was also battling with his record company and having financial problems. On September 13, he had to cancel a concert performance in Rotterdam, The Netherlands, because his bass player Billy Cox had a nervous breakdown.

On September 17, 1970, Hendrix and Mick Jagger's ex-girlfriend Monika Danneman were in London. They went to a party and then to a bar, and returned home some time after 3:00 a.m. When Monika went into the bedroom, she saw Jimi with a large handful of sleeping pills. He reassured her that he was only counting them, then had a glass of wine and went to bed. Monika watched him until 7:00 a.m., when she took a sleeping pill and went to bed, too. When she awoke at 10:20 a.m., she saw that Jimi was lying still and had vomit around his nose and mouth. The sleeping pills were gone. Monika panicked and called a friend for advice, who told her to call an ambulance. It was too late—when Hendrix got to the hospital he was pronounced dead on arrival. The last recording of Hendrix's voice is a message he left on his ex-manager's answering machine at 1:30 a.m. of the morning he died. On it Hendrix says, "I need help bad, man!"

LYNYRD SKYNYRD
Claim to Fame: One of the most popular rock bands of the 1970s.
Cause of Death: Plane crash.
Postmortem: In October 1977, the band released its fourth album, *Street Survivors*. The cover showed a picture of the band, surrounded by flames, and one of the featured songs was "That Smell," which included the lyrics, "Ooh, ooh that smell. The smell of death's around you."

A week later the band's plane crashed near Gillsburg, Mississippi, while en route to a concert date at Baton Rouge, Louisiana. Two people were killed, including Ronnie Van Zant, the band's lead singer and songwriter; and twenty other people on board were injured. Immediately after the crash, the band's record producer recalled every unsold copy of *Street Survivors* and replaced the fiery album cover with one portraying the band members against a black background.

The least likely time is Wednesday, between 3 and 6 P.M.

THE WORLD'S TALLEST BUILDINGS, PART VIII

With all the technological marvels taking place around us, the competition for world's tallest building may not seem as interesting or as colorful as it once did...but it continues. Here's a quick summary of the record-holders of the last 30 years.

THE WORLD TRADE CENTER

Until it was destroyed by terrorists on September 11, 2001, the World Trade Center was one of the greatest architectural landmarks of New York City. Here's how it began:

In the late 1950s, lower Manhattan was a low rent district teeming with pet shops, electronics stores, auto parts stores, and other small businesses. In 1960, David Rockefeller, chairman of the Chase Manhattan Bank, proposed building a skyscraper to help revitalize the neighborhood. In 1962, the Port Authority of New York signed on to the project, and made plans to build a single office complex that would serve the needs of the "world trade community"—importers, exporters, shippers, international bankers, and government trade agencies.

Numerous designs were considered, including building one massive 150-story building, or three or four buildings 50 or 60 stories tall. The single building idea was rejected as being too tall; the multiple buildings were nixed out of fear that they would look like a "housing project." Finally, the architects decided on two massive towers that at 1,368 and 1,362 feet tall would be scarcely more than 100 feet taller than the Empire State Building, at the time, still the tallest building in the world.

The two towers, nicknamed "David" and "Nelson" after the Rockefeller brothers, opened in 1972 and 1973...and were met with almost universal scorn. As George Douglas puts it,

> The massive towers seem entirely out of scale with the tapering tip of lower Manhattan, rising abruptly into the sky like two upended florist's boxes....They remind one of a pair of giant's legs threatening to tip the whole island on its end, perhaps

sinking everything into the sea. The effect on New York's graceful skyline has mostly been annoying and mocking.

The buildings weren't just ugly, they were also money losers for years, and they failed to revitalize lower Manhattan. They dumped so much office space onto the market at once that there wasn't any incentive to build any more...and the 9-to-5 workers who overcrowded the area during the day evacuated at night, leaving the neighborhood a ghost town.

THE SEARS TOWER

In 1974, Sears & Roebuck moved into Chicago's Sears Tower, which at 1,454 feet, eclipsed the World Trade Center in New York. For the first time in nearly 75 years, the city that was the birthplace of the skyscraper was again home to the world's tallest building. Sears planned to occupy the bottom 50 floors and rent out the rest. In *The Big Store*, Donald Katz gives us the Sears' point of view:

> "Being the largest retailer in the world," former chairman Gordon Metcalf had told Time magazine, "we thought we should have the largest headquarters in the world." The plan was to rent out the upper floors of the Tower until Sears employees occupied all 110 floors at the end of the century.... Inside the company, the Tower was named for the vainglorious executive who ordered its construction. It was called "Gordon Metcalf's erection."

Unlike the World Trade Center towers and other skyscrapers that were typical of "modernist" designs of the 1960s and early 1970s, the Sears Tower tapered gracefully as it rose skyward, with "setbacks" at the 49th, 65th, and 90th floors. It was better received than the World Trade Center, but it still had its problems—namely wind and the building's 16,000 bronze-tinted windows. As Judith Dupré writes in *Skyscrapers*:

> Tenants are subject to terrifying high winds both inside and out. An employee on the seventy-seventh floor has said, "On very windy days, the building sways noticeably...the corner columns creak and groan...and my windowpane flaps and vibrates so alarmingly that I abandon my office." The windows—shattering so frequently that the *Wall Street Journal* devoted a November 2, 1988 article to the subject—are fast becoming the stuff of myth:

More than half the population of Kenya is under the age of 15.

the article quotes a secretary who "heard that one man was blown out and then blown back in."

Sears had its own financial problems in the 1980s—it moved out of the Sears Tower in 1988 and sold the building a few years later.

END OF AN ERA?

Before the computer age, housing most or all of your employees and corporate files in one building was a necessity—people could communicate easily with one another and files were within easy reach. Computers and modern telecommunications have changed this. William Mitchell writes in *Scientific American:*

> The burgeoning Digital Revolution has been reducing the need to bring office workers together, face-to-face, in expensive downtown locations. Efficient telecommunications have diminished the importance of centrality and correspondingly increased the attractiveness of less expensive suburban sites that are more convenient to the labor force....Microsoft and Netscape battle it out from Redmond, Washington, and Mountain View, California, respectively...few of their millions of customers know or care what the headquarters buildings look like.

HEADING EAST

The Sears Tower held the record for the world's tallest building for 25 years, and there have been no buildings planned in the United States that will top it. Instead, an Asian nation has constructed a building that pushed the Sears Tower to second place. The Petronas Twin Towers in Kuala Lampur, Malaysia, rose to a height of 1,483 feet when finished in 1998, beating out the Sears Tower by 22 feet. The Kuningan Persada Tower in Jakarta, Indonesia, would have knocked the Sears Tower to third. It was planned to be 1,480 feet tall when finished—but it was never completed, due to economic fluctuations in Asia during the late 1990s.

Why so many tall buildings being built in Asia, and so few in the United States? Because for a time, the Asia of the 1990s resembled the America of the 1900s. "Buildings that grab statistics like "world's tallest" or "world's second tallest," writes *The New York Times'* Paul Goldberger, "are the product...of cultures in the first flush of excitement at moving onto the world stage. Such buildings are assertions of power, demands to be noticed, and

What city has the most taxicabs in the world? Mexico City—60,000 taxis.

there is a particular moment in the life cycle of a rising culture when those impulses are irresistible."

Of course, the collapse of the Asian economy in 1998 will affect the status of many "tallest" buildings. Just how remains to be seen.

YOU AIN'T SEEN NOTHIN' YET
Will the digital revolution put a stop to the seemingly endless contest to see who can build the world's tallest building? Not likely…at least not any time soon. "In the 21st century, as in the time of Cheops, there will be undoubtedly taller and taller buildings, built at great effort and often without real economic justification," William Mitchell writes, "because the rich and powerful will still sometimes find satisfaction in traditional ways that they're on top of the heap."

* * *

AND NOW FOR A CHANGE OF PACE

Whew! That was a long piece—eight sections on tall buildings. Kinda makes us want to write something silly—like these kids' musical bloopers collected in the Missouri School Music Newsletter.

(They insist they're real, and, of course, we believe them.)

- "Beethoven wrote music even though he was deaf. He was so deaf he wrote loud music. Beethoven expired in 1827 and later died from this."
- "A virtuoso is a musician with real high morals."
- "Refrain means don't do it. A refrain in music is the part you better not try to sing."
- "When electric currents go through them, guitars start making sounds. So would anybody."
- "My very best liked piece of music is the Bronze Lullaby."
- "Probably the most marvelous fugue was the one between the Hatfields and the McCoys."
- "Most authorities agree that music of antiquity was written long ago."
- "I know what a sextet is, but I had rather not say."

THE TOP 10 HITS OF THE YEAR, 1992–1995

The hits keep coming. Here's another BRI Top Ten of the Year list.

1992

(1) End Of The Road (from Boomerang) —Boyz II Men
(2) Baby Got Back —Sir Mix A-lot
(3) Tears In Heaven —Eric Clapton
(4) Save The Best For Last —Vanessa Williams
(5) Baby-Baby-Baby —TLC
(6) Jump —Kriss Kross
(7) My Lovin' (You're Never Gonna Get It) —En Vogue
(8) Under The Bridge —Red Hot Chili Peppers
(9) All 4 Love —Color Me Badd
(10) Just Another Day —Jon Secada

1993

(1) I Will Always Love You (from The Bodyguard) —Whitney Houston
(2) Can't Help Falling In Love (from Sliver) —UB40
(3) Whoomp! (There It Is) —Tag Team
(4) That's The Way Love Goes —Janet Jackson
(5) Weak —SWV
(6) Freak Me —Silk
(7) If I Ever Fall In Love —Shai
(8) Dreamlover —Mariah Carey
(9) Rump Shaker —Wreckx-n-Effect
(10) Informer —Snow

1994

(1) The Sign —Ace Of Base
(2) I Swear —All-4-One
(3) I'll Make Love To You —Boyz II Men
(4) The Power Of Love —Celine Dion
(5) Breathe Again —Toni Braxton
(6) Stay (I Missed You) (from Reality Bites) —Lisa Loeb & Nine Stories
(7) Hero —Mariah Carey
(8) All She Wants —Ace Of Base
(9) All For Love —Bryan Adams / Rod Stewart/ Sting
(10) Don't Turn Around —Ace Of Base

1995

(1) Gangsta's Paradise (from Dangerous Minds) —Coolio, featuring L.V.
(2) Waterfalls —TLC
(3) Kiss From A Rose (from Batman Forever) —Seal
(4) Creep —TLC
(5) On Bended Knee —Boyz II Men
(6) Another Night —Real McCoy
(7) Don't Take It Personal (Just One Of Dem Days) —Monica
(8) Take A Bow —Madonna
(9) Fantasy —Mariah Carey
(10) This Is How We Do It —Montell Jordan

The term "kangaroo court" was unknown in Australia until it was brought over from the U.S.

AUNT LENNA'S PUZZLERS

She's back by popular demand! Here are two of Aunt Lenna's favorite brain twisters. See next year's Bathroom Reader *for the answers. Just kidding. See page 758 for the answers.*

Circle Words
The letters in the circles are in the correct order. Simply find where the words begin and in which direction the word is read.

```
     T  O            S  N            S  U
1. U       P    2. H       Y    3. E       A
     A  I            P  M            A  N
```

Nine Dots
Using four straight lines, connect all nine dots without lifting the pen off the paper (i.e., a continuous line).

```
    •     •     •

    •     •     •

    •     •     •
```

Now, do it with only three straight lines!

Originally, Jack-O-Lanterns were made from turnips.

LIFE SAVERS

*Longtime BRI writer Jack Mingo contributed this story of how
one of the most popular candies in history was created.*

MELTS IN YOUR HAND
In 1913, when air conditioning was still just a dream,
candy-maker Clarence Crane was having trouble with his
business. He specialized in manufacturing chocolate—but it didn't
travel well during hot summer months. As a result, candy stores
ordered almost nothing from him between June and September.

To stay in business, the Cleveland native decided to develop a
new line of hard mints—they tasted cool in the Midwestern
summer, and they wouldn't melt. There was only one problem: His
factory was only set up for chocolates. Luckily, he found a druggist
with a pillmaking machine. Crane figured it would work for candy
as well, so he commissioned the man to stamp out a batch.

HOLE LOT OF TROUBLE
As it turned out, the pill maker's machine was malfunctioning—it
kept punching a hole in each mint's center. When he presented
the first batch to Crane, the druggist promised he'd fix the problem for the next batch. But Crane said, "Keep it the way it is.
They look like little life preservers."

That title was a little long to put on a pack, so he tried "Life
Savers" and decided that he had an irresistible hook for the mints.
He advertised his "Crane's Peppermint Life Savers" as a way of
saving yourself from "that stormy breath" and designed a round
paperboard tube with a label showing an old seaman tossing a life
preserver to a woman swimmer. Still, he considered the product to
be a sideline to his real business and didn't push it with any
enthusiasm.

MEANWHILE, BACK IN NEW YORK...
Edward John Noble made a living selling ad space on streetcars in
New York City. One day, he saw Crane' Life Savers in a candy
store and bought a roll. He was so impressed that he jumped on a
train to Ohio to convince Crane to buy streetcar ads. "If you
spend a little money promoting these mints," Noble told Crane,
"you'd make a fortune!"

Crane wasn't interested, but Noble persisted. To get rid of
him, Crane sarcastically suggested that Noble buy the Life Saver
brand. He'd even throw in the defective pill machine for free.

One in three American adults say their partner snores.

Noble asked, "How much?" Caught unprepared, Crane blurted out, "$5,000."

Noble thought the price was a steal—but he didn't have that kind of money. He returned to New York and was able to raise $3,800. He went back to Cleveland and talked Crane's price down to $2,900.

PAPER-FRESH

Noble immediately ran into problems. He found that after a week on the shelves, the candy started tasting like the paperboard it came in. So he developed a tinfoil wrapper that kept the flavor fresh. But there were thousands of stale, old rolls on candy store shelves. Store owners refused to order any more unless Noble exchanged the old rolls for new ones. He made the exchanges, but the candy still didn't sell very well. Noble started giving away samples on street corners—to no avail.

COUNTER PROPOSAL

He then came up with what was, at the time, a brilliant new marketing idea: To sell his candy in other places besides candy stores.

Noble talked to owners of drug stores, barber shops, and restaurants, convincing many to carry Life Savers. He told them, "Put the mints near the cash register with a big 5¢ card. Be sure that every customer gets a nickel with his change, and see what happens."

It worked. With change in hand, some customers flipped a nickel back to the clerk and took a pack. Noble finally began making money.

SWEET SPOT

However, his success created a new problem. Other candy manufacturers quickly discovered the magic of counter displays for impulse sales. The space around cash registers started getting overcrowded.

Noble had another brilliant idea. He designed a segmented candy bin—leaving space for other candy products—but putting Life Savers in the best position...across the top. They were so successful that Life Saver counter displays are still found next to many checkout lines.

Meanwhile, the company began expanding its line from its original Pep-O-Mint flavor. Life Savers have since become the world's best-selling candy ever—with nearly 50 billion of the familiar rolls sold.

A woman's sense of smell is most acute during ovulation.

Q&A: ASK THE EXPERTS

More random questions, with answers from America's trivia experts.

PEEPING VINCENT

Q: *Why do the eyes in a painting or photograph follow you?*
A: "This is the result of the original sitting. If the subject was looking directly at the artist or the camera when the work was executed, they will seem to be looking directly at you, no matter where you stand. If, however, the subject was looking to one side of the artist, the eyes will never focus on the observer." (From *A Book of Curiosities*, by Roberta Kramer)

I'LL EAT JUST ONE

Q: *Why are some potato chips green?*
A: "Green potato chips are the result of something called sunscald. Potatoes are supposed to grow under the ground. Once in a while, however, part of the tuber might poke above the soil and be exposed to the sun. Being a chlorophyll-containing plant, the potato begins to turn green below the spots that were in the sun. While chlorophyll isn't bad for you, the solanine (a toxic chemical) produced may not be that great for you. There are no studies of how many green chips it would take to make you ill, but you may as well play it safe and toss them back in the bag anyway." (From *Why Does Popcorn Pop?*, by Don Voorhees)

BLINDED BY THE LIGHT

Q: *Why do moths fly into the light?*
A: "Moths aren't really attracted to light. Somehow, the brightness confuses the creature's sense of direction and it can't fly straight anymore. Scientists still don't completely understand why. They do know that, unlike human beings, the moth uses light rays from the moon or sun as a guide when it flies. The moth keeps itself moving in a straight line by constantly checking its position against the angle of the light rays striking its eyes.

"Although this complicated guidance system works fine when the light source is far away, it goes haywire when the light is close by. Stimulated by a bulb or candle, the moth's nervous system

3 most landed-on Monopoly® squares: Illinois Ave., Go, and the B&O Railroad.

directs its body to fly so that both eyes receive the same amount of light. This locks the helpless creature onto a course toward the light and eventually causes it to blunder right into the bulb or flame." (From *How Do Ants Know When You're Having a Picnic?*, by Joanne Settel and Nancy Baggett)

LIKE A FISH UNDERWATER

Q: *Can a fish drown?*
A: Believe it or not, yes. "Fish, like people, need oxygen to live. There is oxygen both in the air and in the water. People breathe in the oxygen of the air through their lungs. When a man drowns, it's because he has used up his supply of oxygen and cannot get any from the water. So he dies. Fish breathe through gills rather than lungs. Gills can extract oxygen from water, but not from air. When a fish is pulled out of water, it soon exhausts its supply of oxygen, and 'drowns' because its gills can no longer function." (From *A Book of Curiosities*, by Roberta Kramer)

AFTER-DINNER DIP?

Q: *Should you really wait an hour after eating before swimming?*
A: "Water safety experts used to think…that stomach cramps caused by swimming on a full stomach were a leading cause of drowning. The cramps would cause you to double up in pain, you'd sink like a stone, and that would be the end of you. Later research, however, showed that stomach cramps were rare. It's still not wise to swim long distances on a full stomach because you might become dangerously tired. But splashing around in the pool is harmless." (From *Know It All*, by Ed Zotti)

MERRY XRISTOS

Q: *Why is the word Christmas abbreviated as Xmas?*
A: "Because the Greek letter x is the first letter of the Greek word for Christ, Xristos. The word Xmas, meaning 'Christ's Mass,' was commonly used in Europe by the 16th century. It was not an attempt to take Christ out of Christmas." (From *The Book of Answers*, by Barbara Berliner)

It's pear-adise: China grows more pears than any other country in the world.

SERENDIPITOUS HITS

*We've already done a few things with serendipity in this
Bathroom Reader, so we'll keep it going. Here are three
songs that became hits...with a little help from serendipity.*

LET THE SUNSHINE IN / AGE OF AQUARIUS
—*The Fifth Dimension*

Background: The hit musical, Hair, had been on Broadway
for about a year when the vocal group The Fifth Dimension
arrived in New York City to perform at the Americana Hotel in
1969.

Serendipity: "Billy [Davis, of the group] lost his wallet in a cab,"
recalls Florence LaRue (also a group-member). "He didn't know
where he'd lost it, but a gentleman called and said he'd found it
and wanted to return it. Billy was grateful, but the man didn't
want a reward. He just said, 'I would like you to come and see a
play that I've produced.'

"Well, as it happens, he was the producer of the play *Hair*.
And as we were sitting there listening to 'Aquarius,' we all looked
at each other and said, 'This is a song we've got to record. It's just
great.'"

They took the song to their producer, who suggested that they
combine it with "Let the Sunshine In." They recorded it in Las
Vegas, where they were performing. "It was the quickest thing we
ever recorded," says Florence. "And it was our biggest hit."

YOU AIN'T SEEN NOTHIN' YET
—*Bachman-Turner Overdrive*

Background: B.T.O. was basically a family organization. Randy,
who played lead guitar and sang, had been a charter member of
The Guess Who. His brother Robby played drums, and his brother
Tim played rhythm guitar. The bass player's name was Fred Turner
(hence Bachman-Turner), but still another brother, Gary, was
their first manager.

Gary had a speech impediment; whenever he got excited, he
stuttered. And his brothers sometimes poked mild fun at him over
it. One time, Randy brought a new song into the studio for the
group's 1974 *Not Fragile* album. He started fooling around with the

---

song, saying things like, "I'll now sing it like Frank Sinatra," and then croon away, just like Sinatra. Then he did a version in James Cagney's voice. Finally, he decided to sing it like stuttering Gary: "B-b-b-b-baby, you ain't seen nothin' yet." The brothers thought it was so funny that they decided to record it that way, intending only to send a copy of it to Gary as a gag. They planned to go back later and do a straight rendition.

Serendipity: But when they played the first takes of their album for Mercury Records, the stuttering tune was still on the tape—they'd forgotten to delete it—and Mercury wanted to include it on the record. Randy said no and tried to recut it in his regular voice, but it just didn't work. So the original rendition of "You Ain't Seen Nothin' Yet" went on the album. The next thing B.T.O. knew, Mercury wanted to release it as a single. Now Randy really objected. As the producer of the record, he could refuse to let the record company release it. And he did…for three weeks. Finally, figuring it wouldn't be a hit anyway, he relented. Within two months, it was the top record in the U.S. "It's a gold single now," he said in 1975. "I'm not so embarrassed anymore."

INCENSE AND PEPPERMINTS—*The Strawberry Alarm Clock*

Background: In 1967, a band manager brought producer Frank Slay a tape of a song that his group had recorded. "I thought it was an absolute stone smash," Slay says, "but there were no lyrics."

Slay sent the tune to a lyricist named John Carter and asked him to write "hip psychedelic" words to it. Carter wrote a song full of "meaningless nouns," which he titled "Incense and Peppermints." The group didn't like it, but they agreed to learn it.

Serendipity: Slay invited Carter to the studio for the recording session, and Carter made a major contribution. He didn't think the lead singer was right for his song, so he asked another member of the group to sing it instead. No one complained, and the group recorded "Incense and Peppermints" that day. However… the next day, the singer was gone. "Where is he?" Carter asked. "Oh, he's not even in the group," came the reply. "He's just a friend who'd dropped by for the day, to help with the harmony."

"Incense" hit at just the right time, when the "psychedelic sound" was starting to force its way into mainstream rock. It became the first psychedelic-pop hit. That anonymous singer wound up hearing himself wherever he went in 1967, on a #1 song.

Miguel de Cervantes wrote *Don Quixote* while in prison.

VIDEO TREASURES

*Here's another list of lesser-known movies available
on video that the BRI recommends.*

ROBIN AND MARIAN (1976) *Romance / Adventure*
Review: "Take the best director of swashbucklers, Richard
Lester; add the foremost adventure film actor, Sean
Connery; mix well with a fine actress with haunting presence,
Audrey Hepburn; and finish off with some of the choicest charac-
ter actors. You get Robin and Marian, a triumph for everyone
involved." *(Video Movie Guide)* Stars: Sean Connery, Audrey
Hepburn, Richard Harris, Ian Holm, Robert Shaw, Nicol
Williamson. *Director:* Richard Lester.

ATLANTIC CITY (1981) *Drama*
Review: "An absolutely stunning film by Louis Malle, this
English-language production is riveting from its first few shots and
never lets up. It has the kind of rhythmically precise direction that
bespeaks absolute artistic command, eliciting the maximum
impact from the smallest of expressed emotions... Everyone
involved is superlative, from Burt Lancaster and Susan Sarandon
to the newcomer Robert Joy (who plays a new breed of punk kid
to make your skin creep)." *(Movies On TV)* Stars: Burt Lancaster,
Susan Sarandon, Robert Joy, Kate Reid, Hollis McLaren. *Director:*
Louis Malle.

GREGORY'S GIRL (1981) Romance / Comedy
Review: "While American directors were churning out vile sex
comedies about teenagers, Scotland's inimitable Bill Forsyth was
making this charming, offbeat comedy about teenage puppy love.
Gordon John Sinclair is a tall, gangly teenager who falls for the
mysterious new girl in school (Dee Hepburn)—the star of the
school's otherwise all-male soccer team...This sweet, extremely
amusing film (which is brimming with clever sight gags) is like
nothing made in the U.S." *(Guide for the Film Fanatic)* Stars:
Gordon John Sinclair, Dee Hepburn, Chic Murray, Jake D'Arcy.
Director: Bill Forsyth.

Most common reason for hiring a private detective in the U.S.: "Tracking down a debtor."

ATOMIC CAFE (1982) *Documentary*
Review: "A chilling, humorous compilation of newsreels and government films of the 1940s and 1950s that show America's preoccupation with the A-Bomb. Some sequences are in black and white. Includes the infamous training film 'Duck and Cover,' which tells us what to do in the event of an actual bombing." *(Video Hound's Golden Movie Retriever) Director:* Kevin Rafferty.

DARK EYES (1987) *Foreign / Drama (In Italian with subtitles)*
Review: "Mastroianni gives a tour-de-force performance as a once-young, idealistic, aspiring architect, who settled for a life of wealth and ease after marrying a banker's daughter...and proved incapable of holding on to what's important to him. A rich, beautifully detailed, multileveled film that's at once sad, funny, and haunting. Based on short stories by Anton Chekov (One of which was previously filmed as *Lady with a Dog*)." *(Leonard Maltin's 1998 Movie & Video Guide) Stars:* Marcello Mastroianni, Silvana Mangano, Marthe Keller, Elena Safonova, Pina Gei. *Director:* Nikita Mikhalkov.

BIG HEAT (1953) *Noir / Suspense*
Review: "This sizzling film noir directed by Fritz Lang features [Glenn] Ford (in his best performance) as an anguished cop out to smash a maddeningly effete mobster (Scourby) and break his hold on a corrupt city administration. With sensational support from [Lee] Marvin as a sadistic hood and [Gloria] Grahame as Marvin's bad / good girlfriend... .Brutal, atmospheric, and exciting—highly recommended." *(Movies On TV) Stars:* Glenn Ford, Alexander Scourby, Lee Marvin, Gloria Grahame. *Director:* Fritz Lang.

BELIZAIRE THE CAJUN (1986) *Romance*
Review: "Belizaire the Cajun is a film that is atmospheric in the best sense of the word. The Louisiana bayou of the 1850s is richly recreated in a cadence of texture and deep, dark swamp-land colors, along with the rhythms of Cajun accents and full-bodied folk music (score by Michael Doucet). Armand Assante is Belizaire, an herbal doctor who finds himself in a mess of trouble because of his affection for his childhood sweetheart and his efforts to save a friend from persecution." *(Video Movie Guide) Stars:* Armand Assante, Gail Young, Michael Schoeffling, Stephen McHattie, Will Patton. *Director:* Glen Pitre.

The U.S. has 12,383 miles of coastline; 6,640 miles of it are in Alaska.

MEET MR. WHIPPLE

Finish this sentence: "Please don't squeeze..." See? It's obnoxious, but it's unforgettable. That's why it's considered one of the most successful commercials of all time. Here's the story of how the great American hero of toilet paper, Charmin's Mr. Whipple, was born.

PAPER TRAIL

In 1957, Proctor & Gamble bought the Charmin toilet paper factory in Madison, Wisconsin. It was the consumer product giant's first move into the toilet paper business—and not a particularly auspicious one. At the time, Charmin was a regional brand sold in the northern, rural part of the state. It had a reputation, recalls one critic, for being a "rough-hewn, backwoods toilet tissue...a heavy-duty institutional, even outdoorsy-type toilet tissue." In other words, you might put it in your bomb shelter, but you wouldn't want it in your bathroom.

Proctor & Gamble improved Charmin's quality and launched an advertising campaign featuring a cartoon character called "Gentle the Dog." The new Charmin was "fluffed, buffed, and brushed," just like Gentle's fur, the ads said.

LESS IS MORE

In 1964, Proctor & Gamble researchers made a toilet paper breakthrough: they figured out how to make the paper feel softer. Instead of pressing water out of the wood pulp as it was being made into toilet paper, they dried the pulp with streams of hot air. The hot air "would actually 'fluff it up,'" one internal memo reported. "This allows for a deeper, more cushiony texture. An added benefit...is that less wood fiber per roll is required to make the same amount of this improved tissue." Less wood fiber meant the paper was cheaper to make than competing brands; the softer feel meant it could be sold for a higher price.

Throwing Ideas Around

But how would Proctor & Gamble get the word out about Charmin's new-found fluffiness? The company's ad agency, Benton & Bowles, experimented with ads showing Gentle the Dog going to court to change his name from Gentle to "Gentler." But test

---

"Nothing can be said about our politics that hasn't already been said about hemorrhoids." —Anon.

audiences hated the ad, so Gentle the Dog was put to sleep. What could they replace it with? A three-person creative team was assigned to come up with something. They had a roll of Charmin with them to serve as inspiration, but it didn't seem to work—no one had any viable ideas. "It was one of those Grade B movie situations," creative director Jim Haines recalls. He continues:

We were having a think session, you know, a frustration session and we were not only kicking ideas around, we were tossing the roll around, and we started to get the giggles. John Chervokas [the junior copy writer] caught the roll and started to squeeze it and somebody said, "Don't squeeze it," and John said, "Please don't squeeze it," or "Please don't squeeze the Charmin," and it just happened. The thing just rolled off his tongue.

The team immediately sketched out a commercial that would have supermarket shoppers trying to squeeze Charmin the same way they would squeeze produce for freshness before buying it…and an angry store manager who tries to get them to stop, only to get caught squeezing it himself when he thinks no one is looking. "In an hour and a half," Chervokas recalls, "America's most universally despised advertising campaign became a reality."

FINDING MR. WHIPPLE

Proctor & Gamble, a conservative company, was reluctant to be associated with an ad that had people waving and squeezing rolls of toilet paper on TV. But they agreed to pay for three test commercials. B & B's creative team realized that the entire campaign depended on finding the right actor to play the grocer, whose name was Edgar Bartholomew.

"I was originally thinking of an Edmund Gwennish kind of character—you know, Miracle on 34th St. A lovable little fraud, maybe a little dumpy," Chervokas says.

What he ended up with was one of TV's biggest drunks. Until he got the Charmin part, Dick Wilson had enjoyed a long career in Vaudeville, movies and TV, playing mostly drunks. "I must have done over 350 TV shows as a drunk," Wilson recalls. "I'm the drunk on *Bewitched*. I was the drunk on *The Paul Lynde Show*. I did a lot of Disney's drunks."

Wilson still remembers the call he got from his agent about the part:

> My agent asked me, "What do you think of toilet paper?" And I told him I think everybody should use it. "No, no, no," he said, "I'm asking you how would you like to do a commercial for toilet paper, there's an audition tomorrow." I said, "How do you audition toilet paper?" and my agent said, "Please go and take a screen test." And I said a screen test would be a permanent record. But I went.

The Name Game

Wilson got the part right away, and five days later the first Charmin commercial went into production in—believe it or not—Flushing, New York. But they ran into trouble even before they started filming.

When agencies use a fictional name in an ad, it's standard procedure to find a real person with the same name and license it from them for a nominal fee—usually $1. That way, the agency can fend off anyone else who might claim their name is being used without permission. But this time, to their astonishment, the agency's lawyers couldn't find a single person named Edgar Bartholomew.

"So we looked through the Benton & Bowles employee list to see if any name there tickled our fancy," Chervokas says. "And, it just so happened that the late George Whipple, then head of Benton & Bowles' public relations department, was picked. He sold his name for a dollar." A few days later they taped the first ad, "Digby to the Rescue," in which Mr. Whipple calls on a police-man named Officer Digby to help him restore order to the toilet paper section, which is overrun with Charmin-squeezing women.

TRIAL RUN

The agency tested the first ad using what is known as a "Burke recall test"—they ran it during a television show on one TV station in the midwest, and then called viewers the next day to see if they remembered any of the commercials. Earlier advertising concepts scored as high as 27 points or as low as two points. "Officer Digby to the Rescue" scored 55 points, the highest recall score of any commercial ever tested.

The ads were just as successful when they hit the airwaves in

1964. Over the next six years Charmin shot up from zero percent of the toilet paper market into first place, beating out Scott Tissue for the number-one spot.

PROS AND CONS

The Mr. Whipple ads aired for 21 years, making it one of the longest-running and most successful advertising campaigns in history. And it made Dick Wilson a wealthy man. He was paid a six-figure salary, and only worked about 16 days a year.

Playing Mr. Whipple had its downside, though. As Dick Wilson the man became synonymous with Mr. Whipple, his life changed forever. "The face is so identifiable, I can't really do other work," he says. "And I've given up shopping in supermarkets. When I go through the toilet paper section I get some very strange looks.

He added, "I've guarded Whipple. I never go into blue movies or into sex shops. That wouldn't look nice, would it?"

SO LONG, MR. WHIPPLE

In 1985, Proctor & Gamble discontinued the Mr. Whipple ads in favor of something fresher. Can you remember what they replaced Mr. Whipple with? Neither can anyone else—Proctor & Gamble experimented with forgettable new campaigns for years after, and although they remained dominant in the toilet paper wars, they never found a campaign as memorable.

Likewise, Dick Wilson never had another success to match his long run as Mr. Whipple. He once did a spoof of the Mr. Whipple character in an A&W ad—he can't pick up a can of root beer without squeezing it and spilling it all over the place—but that was about it. A few years after the Whipple gig ended, Wilson retired from acting.

Not much more was heard from Wilson until 1996, when for no apparent reason, his lifetime supply of free Charmin stopped coming in the mail. The story made *USA Today* about a month later; the day after the article appeared Proctor & Gamble resumed the shipments. "He IS Mr. Whipple, and always will be Mr. Whipple," a company spokesperson told reporters, "and certainly we want to make sure nothing but Charmin goes in his bathroom."

FAMOUS FOR 15 MINUTES

*Here's more proof that Andy Warhol was right when he said that
"in the future, everyone will be famous for 15 minutes."*

THE STAR: Jessica McClure, an 18-month-old infant in Midland Texas.

THE HEADLINE: All's Well that Ends Well in Texas Well.

WHAT HAPPENED: In 1987, McClure fell 22 feet down a well while playing in the backyard of her aunt's home. It was only eight inches in diameter and rescuers feared the well would collapse if they widened it. So they decided to dig another hole nearby and tunnel through solid rock to where Jessica was trapped.

After 58 hours, rescuers reached "Baby Jessica" and brought her to the surface. She had a severe cut on her forehead and gangrene on one foot that cost her her right little toe, but she was in remarkably good condition. The entire country watched the rescue unfold live on television. (At the time, it was the fourth-most-watched news story in television history.)

AFTERMATH: The McClure family was flooded with donations during and after the crisis. They used some of the money to buy a new house, then put the rest—an estimated $700,000 to $1 million—in a trust fund for Jessica to collect when she turned 25.

Baby Jessica, 12 years old in 1998, emerged from the experience unscathed (except for a few scars and the missing toe). She doesn't even remember the incident, and knows about it only from looking through her family's scrapbooks. The McClures divorced in 1990.

THE STAR: Fred Tuttle, a 79-year-old Vermont dairy farmer.

THE HEADLINE: Man With a Plan No Flash in the Pan.

WHAT HAPPENED: In 1996, Vermont filmmaker John O'Brien decided to make a film called "Man With a Plan," about a dairy farmer who runs for Congress because he needs the money. The farmer's campaign catches fire and he defeats the Democratic incumbent. O'Brien cast his neighbor Fred Tuttle, a retired dairy farmer, in the lead. The movie was a low-budget art house film, but it caught on in Vermont. Tuttle became one of the most

---

Beavers can swim half a mile underwater on one gulp of air.

recognized celebrities in the state.

AFTERMATH: When PBS made plans to air the movie nation-wide in the fall of 1998, O'Brien suggested that Tuttle run against millionaire Jack McMullen for the Republican nomination for U.S. Senate as a publicity stunt to promote the film. Tuttle agreed to do it. "We thought McMullen was tremendously unqualified," O'Brien said, "but Fred's tremendously unqualified, too. So we won't hold that against McMullen."

Tuttle pledged to spend a total of $16 on his campaign. And since he was recovering from knee replacement surgery, he spent most of the campaign on his front porch, sedated with Demerol. He won the primary anyway, beating out a "carpetbagger" million-aire who'd just recently moved to Vermont. He went on to face incumbent Sen. Patrick Leahy in the general election. (He lost in a landslide.)

THE STAR: Kenneth Lakeberg, 25, father of Amy and Angela Lakeberg, conjoined or "Siamese" twins.

THE HEADLINE: Family Faces Fears with Faith.

WHAT HAPPENED: In 1993, Lakeberg's wife gave birth to twins who shared one heart and one liver. Their prognosis was bleak—both children were certain to die if they were not sepa-rated and one would surely die if they were. The Lakebergs decided to have the surgery. Angela was the healthiest of the twins, so she was the one doctors fought to save. The twins' plight, and the ethical issues surrounding the sacrifice of one's life to save the other, generated national attention. Thousands of dollars of donations poured in to help the financially strapped family pay for the surgery.

AFTERMATH: Within days, the story turned sour: Kenneth Lakeberg was revealed to have spent $8,000 of the contributions on a car, expensive meals, and $1,300 on a three-day cocaine binge before the surgery. "We ate at nice places," he explained. "We traveled good. I think we deserved at least that much." Later, Lakeberg spent time in and out of jail on a variety of charges, including stealing a friend's car. When Angela died in June 1994, he was in a drug rehab program, and his wife had to bail him out of jail so he could attend the funeral.

Female wrestlers are also known as "siffleuses."

THE STARS: Big Edie and Little Edie Beale, the aunt and cousin of Jaqueline Kennedy.

THE HEADLINE: Filmmakers Find Two Nuts in Bouvier Family Tree

WHAT HAPPENED: In 1961, Big Edie and Little Edie Beale, members of Jackie Bouvier Kennedy's family, traveled to Washington D.C. to attend John Kennedy's inauguration. Afterwards, they returned home to Grey Gardens, their 28-room mansion in East Hampton, New York…and never left the house again.

They were still there in 1973, living in two small rooms in an upstairs porch, along with raccoons, fleas, and dozens of cats in a "squalid" estate filled with overgrown weeds, when Jackie's sister, Lee Radziwill, approached filmmakers Albert and David Maysles about making a film portrait of her childhood with Jackie Kennedy.

The Maysles agreed and filmed various Bouvier kin…until they got to Big Edie and Little Edie. They found the pair so interesting that they abandoned Radziwill's project and made a film entirely about the Edies. In the film mother and daughter— surrounded by their cats—sing, dance, bicker, dress in bathing suits and bath towels secured with expensive broaches, and eat ice cream and boiled corn in bed. "I saw many signs of health in the Beales," Albert Maysles told the *Los Angeles Times* in 1996. "They don't have television, they don't drink, and they have a strong bond between them. I've always believed their lifestyle was their way of thumbing their noses at the aristocracy and all its snobbery."

AFTERMATH: *Grey Gardens* was released in 1976 and was an enormous critical success. It catapulted Big Edie and Little Edie into cult superstardom. "Perry Ellis was a huge fan," says Susan Fromke, who also worked on the film. "They used to have 'Grey Garden' parties with the film projected on the wall of a loft and people would wear their favorite Edie outfit."

Big Edie died about a year after the film was released. In 1979, Little Edie sold *Grey Gardens* to Ben Bradlee of *The Washington Post*. "Mother told me to sell it to keep it out of Jackie's hands," she explained. She moved to Miami Beach and was still living there in 1998.

It takes twelve ears of corn to make a tablespoon of corn oil.

UNCLE JOHN'S PAGE OF LISTS

Here are a few random lists from the fabled BRI files.

5 PALINDROME SENTENCES

(the same forward and backward)

1. You can cage a swallow, can't you. But you can't swallow a cage, can you?
2. Blessed are they that believe that they are blessed.
3. Parents love to have children; children have to love parents.
4. First ladies rule the state and state the rule: "Ladies first!"

THE 7 COMMANDMENTS OF ROAD RUNNER CARTOONS

1. Road Runner cannot harm coyote.
2. No outside force can harm coyote.
3. Only dialogue is "Beep-Beep!"
4. Road runner must stay on roads.
5. All locations are in the American Southwest.
6. All products must come from Acme

Corp.
7. Gravity, when applicable, is Coyote's worst enemy.
    —From *Chuck Amuck* (by Chuck Jones)

4 REAL-LIFE JOB INTERVIEW DISASTERS

1. A job applicant challenged the interviewer to arm wrestle.
2. A job candidate said he'd never finished high school because he was kidnapped and kept in a closet in Mexico.
3. A balding candidate excused himself and then returned wearing a full hairpiece.
4. An applicant interrupted the questioning to phone her therapist for advice.
    —From *Parade*

4 WORST WARS FOR LOSS OF AMERICAN LIFE

1. Civil War: 529,332.
2. World War II: 405,399.
3. World War I:

116,516.
4. Vietnam: 54,246.

4 TERMS COINED ON "STAR TREK"

1. Warp drive
2. Mind meld
3. Phaser
4. Dilithium crystal

4 THINGS FIRST CREATED FOR THE 1960s SPACE PROGRAM

1. Freeze-dried foods
2. Cordless electric tools
3. Pocket calculators
4. Aerial photos used on TV weather reports

4 THREE STOOGES GAGS & THE SOUNDS THAT WENT WITH THEM

1. Poke in the eyes—accompanied by a violin or ukulele pluck.
2. Punch in the gut—kettle drum sound.
3. Ear twist—ratchet.
4. Curly's knees bending—a musical saw.

---

10 of the tributaries flowing into the Amazon River are as big as the Mississippi River.

THE CURSE OF THE WEREWOLF, PART II

Fangs a lot for checking out Part II of our section on the werewolf legend.

ON TRIAL

Two of the best-known "werewolves" in European history are Peter Stube and Jean Grenier—famous as much for what they symbolize as for what they did. One was tortured to death; the other was confined to a mental institution. Stube lived in the 1500s; Grenier lived in the 1800s.

Peter Stube

It was big news when Stube was arrested in Cologne in 1590 and "confessed" under torture that he was a werewolf.

According to his confession, a female demon had given him a magic belt that he could use to turn into a giant wolf. For nearly 30 years, he had supposedly used this power to attack and kill villagers, livestock and even wild animals in the surrounding countryside. The townspeople accepted his confession, and he was sentenced

> to have his body laid on a wheel, and with red hot burning pincers in ten places to have the flesh pulled off from the bones, after that, his legs and arms to be broken with a wooden axe or hatchet, afterward to have his head struck from his body, then to have his carcass burned to ashes.

A pamphlet describing Stube's crimes and trial, illustrated with "gruesome" details, became a bestseller all over Europe.

Jean Grenier

By the 19th century, authorities were more enlightened about werewolves. They were skeptical when Grenier, a 13-year-old boy, "admitted" in 1849 to killing and eating "several dogs and several little girls"—all of them on Mondays, Fridays, and Sundays just before dusk, the times when he claimed to became a werewolf.

Philip Riley writes in *The Wolfman:* "The town's lawyer asked the court to set aside all thoughts of witchcraft and lycanthropy (werewolfism) and...stated that lycanthropy was a state of halluci-

---

Rudyard Kipling refused to write with anything other than black ink.

nation and the change of shape existed only in the disorganized brain of the insane, therefore, not a crime for which he should be held accountable."

Instead of sentencing Grenier to death, the judge ordered that he be confined to the monastery at Bordeaux, "where he would be instructed in his Christian and moral obligations, under penalty of death if he attempted an escape." Grenier slid even deeper into madness and died at the monastery seven years later. He was 20.

WEREWOLF DISEASES

Centuries after werewolves "roamed" Europe, scientists have found some real "curses"—diseases and physical conditions—that may have inspired the legends.

• Porphyria makes a person extremely sensitive to light...which would cause them to go out only at night. It creates huge wounds on the skin—which people used to think were caused when the afflicted person ran through the woods in the form of a wolf.

• Hypertrichosis causes excessive growth of thick hair all over the body, including the entire face. The disease is extremely rare. Scientists estimate that as few as 50 people have suffered from the disease since the Middle Ages—but it may have contributed to werewolf legends. When the sufferer shaves off the excess hair, they appear perfectly normal—which may have contributed to the idea that people were changing into wolves. Scientists believe the disease is caused by an "atavistic genetic defect," or a mutation that allows a long-suppressed gene to become active after thousands of years of dormancy. Human skin cells, the theory speculates, still have the ability to grow thick coats of fur that were normal thousands of years ago, but that evolutionary processes have "switched off."

• The belladonna plant was once eaten as medicine or rubbed on the skin as a salve. It also has hallucinogenic qualities when eaten in large quantities; eating too much can make people think they are flying or have turned into animals.

The real reason most of us know about werewolves today is because of the Wolfman horror films. That story is on page 713.

FAMILIAR PHRASES

*Here are the origins of some phrases we use all the time...
even when we don't know what we're saying.*

COOK YOUR GOOSE

Meaning: Destroy one's chances or hopes.

Origin: "From a 16th century legend: King Eric of Sweden had come to an enemy town to attack it. The town's burghers, in a show of contempt for the king and his small band of men, hung a goose from a town tower and then sent a message to King Eric that asked, in effect, 'What do you want?' 'To cook your goose,' came the king's reply...whereupon the Swedes set fire to the town, cooking the goose in the process." (From *Eatioms*, by John D. Jacobson)

BONE UP

Meaning: Study (e.g., for an examination).

Origin: It has nothing to do with real bones. "It refers to a publishing firm named Bohn, which put out a guide (sort of like Cliff's Notes) in the early 20th century that helped the students pass Greek and Latin courses. Though the students called it 'Bohn up' at first, the term was soon changed to 'bone up' because of the obvious pun on '*bone*head.'" (From *Why Do We Say...?*, by Nigel Rees)

TO PACK A WALLOP

Meaning: Have a powerful punch or impact.

Origin: "In modern English 'to wallop' means to thrash, and in noun form, a heavy blow, but originally it...was slang for ale. The verb *pack* in this expression means 'to deliver.'" So, it was, literally, "deliver the beer." (From *Have a Nice Day—No Problem!*, by Christine Ammer)

LEAVE NO STONE UNTURNED

Meaning: Look for something in every possible place.

Origin: "Goes back to the battle between forces led by the Persian general Mardonius and the Theban general Polycrates in 477 B.C. The Persian was supposed to have hidden a great treasure under

Your skeleton keeps growing until you're about 35...and then it starts to shrink.

his tent, but after he was defeated the victorious Polycrates couldn't find the valuables. He put his problem to the oracle at Delphi and was told to return and leave no stone unturned. He did—and found the treasure." (From *Dictionary of Word and Phrase Origins Vol. II*, by William and Mary Morris)

TO LOWER THE BOOM ON SOMEONE

Meaning: Attack someone unexpectedly.

Origin: "Comes from the days when pirates—or even disgruntled sailors—would rid themselves of an annoying crew member by taking advantage of the fact that he happened to be standing near the boom—a long pole which is used to extend the bottom of the sail. The sailor would quietly loosen the lines that held the boom up and quickly let it drop. The sudden drop, along with the force of wind, would cause the boom to swing violently, crashing into the unsuspecting victim, and knocking him overboard." (From *Scuttlebutt...*, by Teri Degler)

HOW NOW, BROWN COW

Meaning: What's up? What's next?

Origin: "Brown Cow' is an old (18th century) way of referring to a barrel of beer, and it is likely that the saying was originally meant as a suggestion that everybody have another beer to prolong a pleasant interlude at the tavern. The idea of 'what's next' apparently derives from the question of whether or not to have another beer." (From *The Dictionary of Clichés*, by James Rogers)

BRING HOME THE BACON

Meaning: Win; Deliver a victory.

Origin: "In Old England any married couple who swore they hadn't quarreled for over a year, or had never wished themselves 'single again'—and could prove this to the satisfaction of a mock jury—was entitled to the famed Dunmow Flitch, a prize consisting of a side of bacon that was awarded at the Church of Dunmow in Essex County. This custom—which was initiated in 1111 and lasted until late in the eighteenth century—is how 'bacon' came to mean 'prize.'" (From *Animal Crackers*, by Robert Hendrickson)

Three most common U.S. town names: 1) Midway, 2) Fairview, 3) Oak Grove.

LOST IN TRANSLATION

Have you ever thought you were communicating brilliantly, only to find out that other people thought you were speaking nonsense? That's a particularly easy mistake to make when you're speaking a foreign language. A few examples:

LAYING PIPE
When the Sumitomo Corporation in Japan developed an extremely strong steel pipe, they hired a Japanese advertising agency to market it in the United States. Big mistake: The agency named the pipe Sumitomo High Toughness, and launched a major magazine advertising campaign using the product's initials—SHT—in catchy slogans like "SHT—from Sumitomo," and "Now, Sumitomo brings SHT to the United States." Each ad ended with the assurance that SHT "was made to match its name."

PRODUCT CONFUSION

The Big Mac: Originally sold in France under the name *Gros Mec*. The expression means "big pimp" in French.

GM cars: Originally sold in Belgium using the slogan "Body by Fisher," which translated as "Corpse by Fisher."

The Jotter: A pen made by Parker. In some Latin countries, jotter is slang for "jockstrap."

Puffs tissues: In Germany, puff is slang for "whorehouse."

Cue toothpaste: Marketed in France by Colgate-Palmolive until they learned that *Cue* is also the name of a popular pornographic magazine.

Schweppes Tonic Water: The company changed the name from *Schweppes Tonic Water* to *Schweppes Tonica* when they learned that in Italian, "il water" means "the bathroom."

The Ford Caliente: Marketed in Mexico, until Ford found out "caliente" is slang for "streetwalker." Ford changed the name to S-22.

The Rolls-Royce Silver Myst: In German, mist means "human waste." (Clairol's Mist Stick curling iron had the same problem.)

Book with the longest English word in the title: *The Baron Kinkvervankotsdorsprakingatchdern.*

SERENDIPITY
SELECTS A PRESIDENT

Serendipity isn't only a factor in little things, like bubble gum
(see "It's Just Serendipity" on page 38). On at least one occasion,
it helped pick a president of the United States. Here's the story.

TIGHT SITUATION

The presidential election of 1824 was a four-way race. Andrew Jackson got the most votes—with John Quincy Adams close behind—but didn't receive a majority. That meant the election would be decided in the House of Representatives. According to law, the candidate with the most votes in each delegation would get the state's electoral vote.

The House met to pick a president on February 9, 1825. It was close, but Adams was the favorite. Although he'd come in second in the popular vote, he had put together almost enough support to win the presidency on the first ballot.

However, if he didn't make it the first time around, his opponents felt sure that his support would begin slipping away. So the anti- Adams forces concentrated on keeping the election unresolved.

A CRUCIAL DECISION

As the vote approached, Adams was one state shy of victory...and there was only one state still undecided: New York. Their delegation was evenly split—half for Adams, half against. If it remained tied, New York's ballot wouldn't count...and the election would be forced into a second round. But there was a weak link in the anti-Adams camp. As Paul Boller writes in *Presidential Campaigns:*

> One of the New York votes [that anti-Adams forces] were counting on was that of General Stephen Van Rensselaer, the rich and pious Congressman from the Albany district....The old General went to the Capitol on election day firmly resolved to vote against Adams, but on his arrival he was waylaid by Daniel Webster and Henry Clay. They took him into the Speaker's Room and painted a dismal picture of what would happen to the country if Adams wasn't chosen on the first ballot. Van Rensselaer was deeply upset by the encounter... "The election turns on my vote," he told a cohort. "*One* vote will give Adams

---

Shortest Oscar-winning performance: Anthony Quinn's 8 minutes as Gauguin in *Lust For Life* (1956).

the majority—this is a responsibility I cannot bear. What shall I do?"

His friend urged him to vote against Adams, as planned, and Van Rensselaer agreed. Boller continues:

> But Van Rensselaer wasn't really resolved. He was still perplexed when he took his seat in the House Chamber. Profoundly religious, however, he decided to seek divine guidance while waiting to cast his [anti-Adams] ballot and bowed his head in prayer.

When he opened his eyes, the first thing he saw, lying on the floor, was a ballot with Adams' name on it. Van Rensselaer took this as a sign from God. He threw his other ballot away, picked the Adams ticket off the floor, and stuck it in the ballot box. As a result of this serendipitous moment, New York went for Adams, "and Adams was elected president on the first ballot."

* * *

SERENDIPITY SAVES COLUMBUS

If it hadn't been for a serendipitous drink of water, Christopher Columbus might never have taken his trips across the Atlantic.

"In the 1480s," write Stefan Bechtel and Laurence Roy Stains in *The Good Luck Book,* Columbus "had been but one of many adventurers who believed it would be possible to reach the spice-rich Indies by sailing west." But he couldn't find a financial backer. For seven years he tried convincing the crowned heads of Europe to finance a voyage, and he always got "no" for an answer. "Eventually," say Bechtel & Stains, "he made his way back to the Spanish court for yet another audience with Ferdinand and Isabella. After listening to his plea, once again they turned him down."

> It was an insufferably hot day, so after leaving the court Columbus stopped at a nearby monastery to get a drink of water. He fell into conversation with one of the monks, and before long Columbus was pouring out his heart again, telling the holy man all about the voyage he hoped to make. The monk, it so happened, was also the Queen's confessor. And he was so taken with Columbus's speech that he spoke to Isabella, who granted Columbus yet another audience. And that time, at long last, Ferdinand and Isabella said yes.

WHAT'S FOR BREAKFAST?

We probably take it for granted that the foods we eat for breakfast have always been around. Of course, they haven't. Here's the history of five foods we've come to expect on the table in the morning.

WAFFLES. Introduced to the United States by Thomas Jefferson, who brought the first waffle iron over from France. The name comes from the Dutch "wafel." Waffles owe much of their early popularity to street vendors, who sold them hot, covered in molasses or maple syrup. It wasn't until the twentieth century that the electric waffle iron made them an American staple.

ENGLISH MUFFINS. In 1875, Samuel Bath Thomas moved to America from England, bringing with him his mother's recipe for "tea muffins." He started out baking them in New York in 1880. In 1926, he officially named them Thomas' English Muffins.

FRENCH TOAST. Really does have its origins in France, where it's known as ameritte or pain perdu ("lost bread"), a term that has persisted in Creole and Cajun cooking. Throughout its history in America, it has been referred to as "Spanish," "German," or "nun's toast." Its first appearance in print as "French toast" was in 1871.

GRAPE JUICE. In 1869, Dr. Thomas Welch, Christian, dentist, and prohibitionist, invented "unfermented wine"—grape juice—so that fellow teetotalers would not be forced into the contradiction (as he saw it) of drinking alcohol in church. Local pastors weren't interested, so he gave up and went back to pulling teeth. His son Charles began selling it as grape juice in 1875.

PANCAKES. When the first European settlers landed in the New World, they brought pancakes with them. They met Native Americans who made their own pancakes, called nokehic. Even the ancient Egyptians had pancakes; in fact it's difficult to think of a culture that didn't have pancakes of one kind or another.

The first ready-made pancake mix came in 1889, when two men in St. Joseph, Missouri, introduced "Self-Rising Pancake Flour." They named it "Aunt Jemima" after a song from a minstrel show.

THE TOP 10 HITS OF THE YEAR, 1996–1997

Here's the last installment of
BRI's Top Ten of the Year list.

1996

(1) Macarena (Bayside Boys Mix)
—*Los Del Rio*
(2) One Sweet Day
—*Mariah Carey & Boys II*
Men
(3) Because You Loved Me (from
Up Close & Personal)
—*Celine Dion*
(4) Always Be My Baby
—*Mariah Carey*
(5) Nobody Knows
—*The Tony Rich Project*
(6) Give Me One Reason
—*Tracy Chapman*
(7) Tha Crossroads
—*Bone Thugs-n-Harmony*
(8) You're Makin' Me High / Let
It Flow —*Toni Braxton*
(9) I Love You Always Forever
—*Donna Lewis*
(10) Twisted—*Keith Sweat*

1997

(1) Candle In The Wind 1997 /
Something About The Way
You Look Tonight
—*Elton John*
(2) You Were Meant For Me /
Foolish Games —*Jewel*
(3) I'll Be Missing You
—*Puff Daddy & Faith Evans*
(4) Un-break My Heart
—*Toni Braxton*
(5) I Believe I Can Fly (from
Space Jam) —*R. Kelly*
(6) Can't Nobody Hold Me Down
—*Puff Daddy, featuring Mase*
(7) Don't Let Go (Love) (from *Set*
It Off) —*En Vogue*
(8) Return Of The Mack
—*Mark Morrison*
(9) Wannabe—*Spice Girls*
(10) How Do I Live
—*Leann Rimes*

*   *   *

2000 Trivia

TIME FLIES. Dick Clark, America's perennial teenager, turned 70 years old in the year 2000.

HUH? According to a 1994 *Cosmopolitan* article, the "Cosmo Girl" in the year 2000 would be "an egg-freezing, libido-boosting dynamo with no glass ceiling, preparing for missions to Mars or donning the virtual-reality goggles for a shopping spree."

THE DUSTBIN
OF HISTORY

Think your heroes will "go down in history" for something they've done?
Don't count on it. These folks were VIP's in their time…but they're
forgotten now. They've been swept into the Dustbin of History.

FORGOTTEN FIGURE: Nicholas P. Trist, Presidential envoy to Mexico, 1847-48.
   CLAIM TO FAME: Trist negotiated the treaty that ended the Mexican-American war, and played a major role in opening the West. It should have been the crowning achievement of his diplomatic career. Instead, it cost him his job.

President Polk wasn't pleased with the way negotiations were going, so he ordered Trist to call them off and come home. Trist ignored Polk, stayed in Mexico and completed the negotiations. With the signing of the treaty in February 1848, he added the territories of California, Nevada, Arizona, Utah, and New Mexico to the United States, as well as parts of Colorado and Wyoming.
INTO THE DUSTBIN: Trist was fired for insubordination, and spent many years afterward working in obscurity as a railroad clerk. Finally in 1870, 20 years after Polk left office, Trist was officially recognized for achieving a major diplomatic coup.

FORGOTTEN FIGURE: Emile Coue, a pharmacist who dabbled in hypnotism.
CLAIM TO FAME: In 1920, Coue introduced a system of "healing through positive thinking" at his clinic in Nancy, France. As his reputation grew, he made appearances in London and, in 1923, the United States—where he was mobbed by throngs of admirers in packed lecture halls all over the country. He is best remembered for his famous phrase, "Every day, and in every way, I am becoming better and better." Frequent repetitions, Coue insisted, would spur the brain to cure just about anything.

Had Coue kept his claims modest, he would probably be remembered as one of the fathers of positive thinking. But he didn't; he claimed his chant could cure baldness, major illnesses, fight vice, reduce crime, and even determine the gender—not to

---

The U.S.S. *Phoenix* survived Pearl Harbor, was sold to Brazil, and sank in the Falklands War.

mention career—of a baby before it was born. "If a mother wants her unborn son to be a great architect," he explained, "she should visit great buildings and surround herself with pictures of architectural masterpieces and above all she should think beautiful thoughts."

INTO THE DUSTBIN: Coue returned to the U.S. for a second tour in 1924, but the crowds that greeted him this time were smaller. Reason: bald people who chanted his phrase all year were still bald, fat people were still fat, mothers gave birth to children in the wrong gender, etc. Patients began to abandon his clinic in France and Coue might have gone out of business entirely...if he hadn't dropped dead of a heart attack in 1926.

FORGOTTEN FIGURE: Cromwell Dixon, "boy" aviator
CLAIM TO FAME: The first aviator to fly over the Continental Divide. In 1911 a group of investors, which included circus owner John Ringling and the president of the Great Northern Railway, offered $10,000 to the first person who could fly over the Divide. At age 19, Dixon decided to try for the money. He left the Montana state fairgrounds in Helena on Sept 30, 1911, then headed for Blossburg, just over the Divide. His friends lit a bonfire on a high peak near the town to help him find his way. Little was known about mountain flying at the time, and a number of pilots had been killed when downdrafts slammed them into the mountains. But Dixon made it, and collected both the money and considerable attention.
INTO THE DUSTBIN: Dixon was killed a few days later at Spokane, Washington when a sudden air current slammed his plane into the ground, "crushing him under the engine."

FORGOTTEN FIGURE: "Mr. Greeler," who is apparently so forgotten that nobody knows what his first name was. He was a nineteenth-century musical composer and patriot.
CLAIM TO FAME: Greeler set the entire United States Constitution to music in the 1870s. The entire composition, a six-hour opus, was performed for enthusiastic audiences in Boston in the 1870s. His recitative of the Preamble, and his fugues of the Amendments brought the house down.
INTO THE DUSTBIN: No known copies of Greeler's score survive today.

Three most common fears: spiders, people and social situations, flying.

TARZAN AT
THE MOVIES

*There have been more movies about Tarzan than practically any other character. So it surprised us to find out that the first Tarzan movie was actually a flop. It took a smart press agent named Harry Reichenbach to make the "King of the Jungle" a box office success. He did it with the first film in 1917...and then he came back and did it again with the third one. By then, Tarzan was a movie franchise.
Here's Reichenbach's account of what happened.*

TARZAN OF THE APES

Background: In 1917, press agent Harry Reichenbach ran into a friend named Billy Parsons who'd just borrowed $250,000 to make the world's first Tarzan movie. The movie bombed at the preview and every distributor in the country turned it down. Parsons was desperate. Reichenbach watched the movie, and liked it. He agreed to publicize it if Parsons would give him a percentage of the profits.

Publicity Stunt: Reichenbach booked a theater on Broadway and filled the lobby with jungle plants, a big stuffed lion, and live monkeys in cages. And it "just happened" that on the day before the premiere, the newspapers were filled with accounts of the exploits of "Prince Charlie," an orangutan dressed in a tuxedo and top hat, who'd gotten loose inside the lobby of a fancy hotel that was filled with New York's elite. According to Reichenbach:

> Prince Charlie, timid and embarrassed, was about to introduce himself to this brilliant assemblage when he noticed a revolving door on the 42nd Street side and began to spin wildly around in it. Excited by this turn in social life, the big ape leaped into the lobby with greater confidence and cordially screeched at them to try his new sport, but they had all made a clearance in record time. The only way they could be persuaded to return was under cover of police.

When "someone" let the media know that Prince Charlie was a publicity stunt to promote *Tarzan of the Apes,* the newspapers covered the story a second time, letting the public know that the

---

Five most commonly grown fruits on earth: Grapes, bananas, apples, coconuts, and plantains.

ape would be in the lobby of the theater for the opening.

What Happened: *Tarzan of the Apes* brought in more than $1.5 million at the box office, earning Reichenbach $50,000 and establishing both the Tarzan franchise on film, and Harry Reichenbach as a master press agent.

THE RETURN OF TARZAN

Background: Reichenbach was not hired to promote the second Tarzan film, *Romance of Tarzan*…and it flopped. So when Samuel Goldwyn produced the third Tarzan film, *The Return of Tarzan*, in 1920, he insisted that Reichenbach be hired again.

Publicity Stunt: A week before the film was scheduled to open, a "music professor" named Dr. T. R. Zan checked into the Belleclaire, one of New York's fanciest hotels, and had a large piano box lifted by block and tackle into his hotel room. Dr. Zan explained that he wanted to be able to play his piano in his room.

The next morning, Dr. Zan sent for room service. "I have a very delicate stomach," he told the bellhop, and he ordered two soft-boiled eggs, a piece of toast, and a glass of warm milk. "By the way", he told the bellhop, "I also want 15 lbs. of raw meat."

"With your—your delicate stomach?" The bellhop asked.

"No, it's not for me, foolish boy! That's for my pet." And with that, Dr. Zan opened the door to the adjoining room to reveal a lion sitting on the carpet. The bellhop told the management what he'd seen. They investigated and then called the police. Meanwhile, "someone" let a newspaper reporter know what was happening.

What Happened: According to Reichenbach,

> Every morning newspaper carried the story of T. R. Zan the next day. The newsreel weeklies didn't overlook it either. It was a story that caught the imagination and spread over the wires to all the papers in the country.

A few days later, advertisements appeared announcing that *The Return of Tarzan* would open at the Broadway Theatre and only then did the stunt become apparent and the newspapers gave new publicity to the hoax, linking T. R. Zan of the Belleclaire Hotel with Tarzan of the pictures….The lion, Jim, appeared in person at the opening of the picture. We polled over 25,000 columns in news stories and established the film as a national hit.

Caution: In 1992, 55,142 people were injured by jewelry.

CROISSANT, COFFEE, AND BLOOD

*This article was contributed by BRI member Jeff Cheek.
It's a great example of the role serendipity plays in history
(and our diet). At the very least, it should make ordering
a cup of coffee and a croissant more interesting.*

ON THE ROPES

From July 17 until September 12, 1683, the Austrian capital of Vienna was besieged by a Moslem army commanded by the Turkish Grand Vizier, Kara Mustafa. Historians note this as the high-water mark of Islamic influence in Europe. If the Moslems had succeeded here, it's likely they would have taken all of Europe.

After Vienna was encircled, a Polish mercenary named Kulczyski volunteered to go for help. Disguised as a Turk, he made his way through enemy lines. He was discovered, but his linguistic ability made his cover story believable. He escaped, made his way to Bavaria, and led an 80,000-man army back to Vienna.

The Viennese people had no way of knowing this—they were completely isolated as they beat back repeated Turkish assaults on their walled city. Their outer defenses were lost, but the besieged city held out.

ROLL TO VICTORY

In the early morning hours of September 12, a Viennese baker was preparing his dough for the next day's bread. He noticed that a tray of delicate breakfast rolls was vibrating. Why? They were acting as a seismograph, transmitting vibrations made by Turkish pickaxes. The Turks, it turned out, had decided to tunnel up to Vienna's walls, then launch a final assault. The baker sent his son to warn the city fathers, and the Austrians rushed to the ramparts just in time to repel the Grand Vizier's forces.

Kulczyski and the Bavarian army arrived a few hours later, sealing the Moslem defeat. After a bloody, 15-hour battle, the Turkish army fled, abandoning their tents and stores of food. The latter included thousands of sacks of hard, black beans, which the Austrians began to burn, because they believed the beans had no value.

A NEW TWIST

When the heroic baker was told to name his own reward, he asked to become chief baker in the royal palace. The request was granted. To impress his new masters, and to commemorate their narrow escape from the Moslems, he created a new breakfast roll. The star and crescent had long been a symbol of the Islamic faith, so instead of making ordinary round or oblong rolls, he rolled the dough out, then cut it into six inch triangles. He rolled these from the top corner, creating a humpbacked center with tapering horns. Just before baking, he twisted these horns down, forming a crescent.

Eighty-five years later, in 1770, a tactless Austrian princess named Marie Antoinette married Louis XVI of France. To ensure her supply of crescent rolls, she brought her own bakers from Vienna. The Royal French bakers were furious at this insult, but didn't dare protest. Instead, they fought back by creating a new and better breakfast roll. They retained the crescent shape to appease Her Majesty, but used pastry dough. Thus, the noble croissant was born.

BACK TO 1683

Meanwhile, back in 1683, Kulczyski was asked what reward he wanted for saving Vienna. His request was surprisingly modest: all he asked for was the sacks of black beans that the Austrians were destroying...and permission to open a business in Vienna.

Both were immediately granted.

It turns out that while making his way through the surrounding Moslem army, Kulczyski had been served a sweet, black beverage, which seemed to restore his energy. It was coffee—virtually unknown in Europe at that time, but a staple for the Turks.

Kulczyski collected all the Turks' unburned sacks of coffee beans and opened the first coffee house in Eastern Europe. Soon, all of Europe was drinking Viennese coffee, and Kulczyski became a wealthy and respected citizen of his adopted homeland.

The United Kingdom eats more cans of baked beans than the rest of the world combined.

THE BIRTH OF BASEBALL CARDS II

The origin of baseball cards, on page 103, is tied in with the history of cigarettes in America. The rest of the story is about kids...and money.

KIDS' STUFF

In the years following tobacco's exit from the baseball card business, cards were marketed directly to kids. They were used as promotions for candy, chewing gum, and cookies—but none were especially successful until 1928, when the Fleer Corporation invented bubblegum. As one sports historian writes, "Baseball cards had found a marketing partner to replace tobacco."

The Goudey Company was the first to combine bubblegum and cards, and they became the most popular distributor of cards in the 1930s. Other companies joined in, adding gimmicks to make cards appealing to kids. They issued sets with players' heads superimposed on cartoon bodies, included coupons for fan clubs, offered chances to win baseball gear, and so on. By the end of the 1930s, card collecting was beginning to take off as a hobby. Then World War II broke out, and resources were diverted to the war effort. Baseball cards all but disappeared.

CUTTHROAT COMPETITION

The business of baseball cards began in earnest after the war. The Bowman Company came out with the first annual sets of cards in 1948, and secured their investment by signing baseball players to contracts that gave Bowman exclusive rights to sell cards with bubblegum.

But with the introduction of color cards in 1950, baseball card collecting became the fastest growing hobby among boys in America—and competitors began lining up. The most important one was Sy Berger, an executive at Topps (the company that made Bazooka bubblegum), who genuinely liked baseball.

Berger convinced his bosses that they should start manufacturing and selling cards. He started hanging around the clubhouses of the three New York teams, signing players to Topps contracts.

China grows the most sweet potatoes in the world; The U.S. grows the most corn.

To avoid infringing on Bowman's right to package cards with gum, Topps offered its cards with a piece of taffy. Bowman filed suit—but the court ruled that Bowman couldn't stop Topps from signing players to card contracts.

By 1955, Topps had outhustled its rival for player contracts. In 1956, Bowman conceded defeat and sold out to Topps. From the '50s through the '70s, Topps had a virtual stranglehold on the business. When the Fleer Corporation tried issuing cards with a cookie, Topps took them to court and won.

MONEY, MONEY, MONEY

Topps was selling 250 million cards a year, raking in millions of dollars in profits. But what did the players get? A whopping $125 for a five-year contract—plus a $5 "steak money" bonus. The amazing thing is, they were glad to get it; the average player salary in the 1960s was only $19,000.

Two things changed that: 1) a baseball players' union was formed and got involved in contract negotiations with Topps, and 2) in 1980, Fleer won an anti-trust suit against Topps. The judge ruled that any company was free to negotiate a card deal.

A year later, there were three companies willing to sign players to card contracts. And by 1988, there were at least a half-dozen more. Cards got fancier and more expensive…and baseball cards turned into big business.

• By 1985, baseball cards had passed stamps and coins as the most popular collecting hobby in the country.

• By 1988, card companies were selling five billion cards a year.

• By 1992, sports cards were nearly a $1 billion a year business. The industry leader, Upper Deck, was selling $250 million worth of cards and sports memorabilia annually. They paid former superstar Mickey Mantle—who made $100,000 a year at the peak of his career—$2.5 million to make 26 promotional appearances at memorabilia conventions.

PARADISE LOST

A baseball card glut, combined with the bad press that the 1995 baseball strike generated, slowed down the card business—and it may never hit its peak again. But there's no going back to the innocence of earlier decades. An adult attitude has settled over

Most popular jukebox song of all time: "Crazy," by Patsy Cline (1962).

the hobby. As one critic puts it, "Once kids stuck the cards of their favorite players to the spokes of their bicycles. Now adults store their collections in safe-deposit boxes and fret over how much to insure their 1952 Mickey Mantles for."

MISCELLANY

• The first cards to list player stats on the back were put out by Mecca Cigarettes in 1918.

• In 1969, Topps goofed on Angel's 3rd-baseman Aurelio Rodriguez's card. They photographed the Angels' batboy, thinking he was Rodriguez, and put the batboy's picture on the card.

• In 1989, a card of Baltimore Oriole Billy Ripken (brother of Cal) made headlines when it slipped past Fleer proofreaders. The card shows Ripken holding a bat over his right shoulder in a posed stance. At the bottom of the bat knob, written in black felt pen, is a "profanity." "Sometimes players play practical jokes on the photographers," said a Fleer spokesman. "We try to catch them before they go to press, but this one must have made it through."

How Baseball Cards Got Their Modern Look

Bill Hemrich owned the Upper Deck sports card and memorabilia shop, located just a short walk from the stadium where the California Angels played their home games. Around 1987, he shelled out $4000 for a stack of Don Mattingly rookie cards—which turned out to be fakes. Paul Sumner, a printing company executive, heard the story and contacted Hemrich. He sketched out an idea for a baseball card using hologram technology. The hologram design would be impossible to counterfeit, Sumner explained. Plus, it would set the cards apart from all the rest with a hip, high-tech look.

Together they formed Upper Deck Cards, got rich, and changed sports cards forever.

"I believe everyone should carry some type of religious artifact on his or her person at all times." —Bob Costas, explaining why he carried a Mickey Mantle card in his wallet.

There are $171 million worth of pennies and $2.6 billion worth of dimes in circulation.

THE SECRET CENSORS

We're guaranteed free speech by the Constitution. But, historically, there are lots of subtle ways the "free press" has kept that under control. Here are some amusing(?) examples from one of Uncle John's favorite books, If No News Send Rumors, *by Stephen Bates. (We highly recommend it for bathroom reading.)*

Dirty secret: "The *Los Angeles Times* bars the word 'smog' from its real-estate section. Ads may say 'cleaner skies,' but such phrases as 'no smog here' are forbidden."

Get them somewhere else: "The *Christian Science Monitor* refuses advertisements for, among other things, medicines and tombstones."

Speak no evil: "A 1985 regulatory ruling got almost no press coverage. The Occupational Safety and Health Administration (OSHA) had concluded that the oils in newspaper inks cause cancer and that ink barrels should include printed warnings."

What sweat?: "In the 50s and 60s, business considerations sometimes influenced newspapers' weather reports. Weather predictions in the *Sacramento Bee* never included the word 'hot,' which newspaper officials feared might dissuade businesses from relocating to Sacramento. Instead, even blistering weather was described as 'unseasonably warm.'"

No boycotts: "Some newspapers, at the urging of florists' trade associations, refuse to include the sentiment "Please omit flowers" in obituaries. A spokesman for one such paper, the *Pittsburgh Press*, explained that the phrase 'urges a boycott just like "Don't buy grapes," and we don't permit that.'"

Keeping people informed: "In 1966, CBS chose not to cover the Senate Foreign Relations Committee's hearings on Vietnam. Instead, it aired its regular reruns of *I Love Lucy* and *The Real McCoys*, among others....A few months later, CBS did interrupt its daytime programming for live coverage of the Pillsbury Bakeoff prize ceremony. The bake-off, unlike the Vietnam hearings, had a sponsor—Pillsbury."

Five largest internal organs of the body: liver, brain, lungs, heart, and kidneys.

BRANDO ON ACTING

Marlon Brando has long been regarded as one of America's great actors. Here are some surprising thoughts he had about his craft.

"Acting is fundamentally a childish thing to pursue. Quitting acting—that is the mark of maturity."

"I was down the tubes not long ago…you could see it when you rented a car; you could see it when you walked into a restaurant."

"If you've made a hit movie, then you get the full 32-teeth display in some places; and if you've sort of faded, they say 'Are you still making movies? I remember that picture, blah, blah, blah.' The point is, people are interested in people who are successful."

"An actor is at most a poet and at least an entertainer."

"Acting is like sustaining a twenty-five-year love affair. There are no new tricks. You just have to keep finding new ways to do it, to keep it fresh."

"If you play a pig, they think you're a pig."

"If you're successful, acting is about as soft a job as anybody could ever wish for. But if you're unsuccessful, it's worse than having a skin disease."

"If you want something from an audience, you give blood to their fantasies. It's the ultimate hustle."

"Acting is as old as mankind… Politicians are actors of the first order."

"An actor's a guy who, if you ain't talking about him, ain't listening."

"I'm convinced that the larger the gross, the worse the picture."

"Why should anybody care about what any movie star has to say? A movie star is nothing important. Freud, Gandhi, Marx—these people are important. But movie acting is just dull, boring, childish work. Movie stars are nothing as actors. I guess Garbo was the last one who had it."

Richest country in the world: Switzerland. Poorest: Mozambique.

DINER LINGO

Diner waitresses and short-order cooks have a language all their own—a sort of restaurant jazz, with clever variations on standard menu themes. In the second Bathroom Reader, we listed some favorites. Here are more.

Axle Grease: Butter

Baby: A glass of milk

Belch water: Plain soda water

A breath: A slice of onion

Burn the pup: A hot dog

Dough well done with cow to cover: Buttered toast

Mug of murk: Cup of coffee

On wheels: Take-out orders

A splash with dog biscuits: Soup and crackers

Black bottom: A chocolate sundae with chocolate ice cream

Mystery in the alley: A side order of hash

A bowl of bird seed: Cereal

Shake one in the hay: Strawberry milkshake

Pig between the sheets: Ham sandwich

All the way: Everything on it (mayonnaise, lettuce, onions)

High and dry: Plain

A crowd: Three of the same order

A team: Two of the same item

An order of down with mama: Toast with marmalade

Cream cheese with warts: Cream cheese and chopped olive sandwich

First lady: Spareribs

GAC: Grilled American cheese sandwich

Steak on the hoof: Rare steak

One on: Hamburger (on the grill)

21: Two burgers (two orders of one)

31: (three orders of one)

Keep off the grass: No lettuce

Cowboy: Western omelette

Warm a pig: Hot ham or pork sandwich

Put out the lights and cry: An order of liver and onions

A bowl of red: Chili

A cold spot: A glass of iced tea

Boiled leaves: A cup of hot tea

A brunette with a sand: Coffee with sugar only

Fish eyes: Tapioca pudding

Canned cow: Condensed milk

One on the country: Buttermilk

60% of American men say they normally eat a hot dog in 5 bites or less.

HANGOVER SCIENCE

If you've ever had a hangover, you've probably wondered what was going on in your body. It's surprisingly complex.

U NDER THE INFLUENCE
Here are some basic facts about drinking:

1. When you drink an alcoholic beverage, your body absorbs about 90% of the alcohol in the drink. The rest is exhaled, sweated out, or passed out in urine.

2. On average, a normal liver can process 10 grams of alcohol per hour. That's the equivalent of one glass of wine, half a pint of beer, or one shot of 80 proof spirits. (Exactly how much depends on a number of things, including your bodyweight and gender.)

3. Alcohol is a depressant, which means that it slows down the activity of your central nervous system by replacing the water around the nerve cells in your body.

4. Alcohol also changes the density of the fluid and tissue in the part of your ears that controls your sense of balance. That's why it can be difficult to walk, or even stand up, when you've had too much to drink.

WHAT CAUSES A HANGOVER?

Now we have to get a little technical:

• Your liver processes alcohol into a toxic chemical called acetaldehyde. Just as the alcohol made you feel good (or at least drunk), the acetaldehyde makes you feel bad. It's the accumulation of this chemical in your body, more than the alcohol itself, that causes hangover symptoms. (That's why the hangover comes after you've been drinking—the alcohol has been changed into acetaldehyde.) Specifically, acetaldehyde causes your blood vessels to dilate—which makes you feel warm, and can give you a headache.

• Meanwhile, the alcohol that's still in your system is raising both your pulse and blood pressure—which makes the headache even worse.

• And then there's the effect on your kidneys. When you're sober, your kidneys use a chemical called vasopressin to recycle the water in your body. But alcohol reduces the level of vasopressin in your body—which, in turn reduces your kidneys' ability to function. So instead of recycling water, you urinate it out. That makes you dehydrated…which can make your hangover worse.

• It's also possible that what you're experiencing in a hangover is a minor case of alcohol withdrawal syndrome—the same thing that chronic alcoholics experience when they stop drinking. "Your brain becomes somewhat tolerant over the course of an evening of heavy drinking," says Dr. Anne Geller, who runs the Smithers Alcoholism Treatment Center in New York City. "The next morning, as the alcohol is coming out of your system, you experience a 'rebound.' You might feel nauseous, maybe you'll have some diarrhea, maybe you'll feel a little flushed. Your tongue is dry, your head is aching and you're feeling a little bit anxious or jittery. Those are all signs of rebound, and that can be experienced as a hangover."

PREVENTATIVE MAINTENANCE

There are a few things you can do *before* you start drinking that may prevent the worst excesses of a hangover:

• Eat a substantial meal or at least have a glass of milk before you start drinking. It will help protect your stomach lining.

• Avoid champagne and dark-colored drinks, especially red wines. They contain byproducts of fermentation that may make the hangover worse.

• Drink a pint of water before you go to bed. The water will help minimize dehydration.

• The next morning, eat something sweet for breakfast, such as honey or jam. They contain fructose, which generates a chemical called nicotinamide adenine dinucleotide (NAD) that is involved in the processing of alcohol.

HANGOVER CURES

You can't cure a hangover once you've got one—it's that simple. Many "cures" only make things worse:

• Aspirin and ibuprofen (Advil, Nuprin) can irritate your

stomach lining, which is probably already upset from the alcohol. There's even some evidence that aspirin can make you feel even more drunk.

• Acetaminophen (Tylenol) can strain your liver, which already has enough on its hands processing the alcohol.

• Coffee just keeps you awake. Wouldn't you rather be asleep?

• Drinking more alcohol—the "hair of the dog that bit you"— doesn't work either; it only postpones the inevitable. The only people it helps are alcoholics, whose hangovers are compounded by symptoms of alcohol withdrawal.

Traditional Remedies
Here are some traditional hangover remedies. They don't work, either, but some are so disgusting that at least they'll take your mind off of being hungover:

• Swallow six raw owl eggs in quick succession.

• "Hangover Breakfast"—black coffee, two raw eggs, tomato juice, and an aspirin.

• Jackrabbit tea: Take some jackrabbit droppings, add hot water to make strong tea. Strain the tea; then drink. Repeat every 30 minutes until the headache goes away or you run out of droppings.

• Whip yourself until you bleed profusely. The loss of blood won't cure the hangover, but it will (1) make you groggy, and (2) serve as a distraction.

• Drink the sugary juice from a can of peaches.

• Add a teaspoon of soot to a glass of warm milk (hardwood soot is best). Drink.

• Spike some Pepto-Bismol with Coca-Cola syrup from the drugstore, or with a can of day-old Coke.

*   *   *

"A woman drove me to drink...and I never had the courtesy to thank her."
—W. C. Fields

WHO'D LOVE A PLATYPUS?

He looks suspiciously like a beaver in a duck costume (or vice versa).
He's got a name that sounds like he's friends with Socrates or Aesop.
No wonder he's such a shy little critter.

INTERESTING THINGS ABOUT THE PLATYPUS

- His real name is *Ornithorhynchus anatinus* (poor guy).
- He has one of the most waterproof coats in the world.
- He spends up to 12 hours a day in water as cold as 0°C.
- The girl platypus poos and reproduces out of the same orifice (yuck!).
- He has a spur on his foot that is venomous enough to kill a dog.
- When first sightings of the platypus were reported back to Europe, they thought it was a hoax.
- He is found only in eastern Australia, especially in Tasmania.
- He growls like a puppy when in danger.

WHAT IS IT, AND WHERE DID IT COME FROM?

Apparently, there are two theories of where the platypus came from. The scientific theory is that the platypus (and his Aussie mate, the echidna) evolved from either marsupials or a bunch of early mammals. The other theory comes from Aboriginal folklore about a naughty little duck...

> Once upon a time, there was a duck whose name was... Duck. Duck lived with his friends in a sheltered river pond. All of them were in constant fear of Mulloka the Water Devil, and never strayed far from their pond. But one day, against the advice of her elders, Duck ventured downstream and eventually found herself on a patch of grass on the riverbank. Unaware that this was the territory of the lonely Water-rat, she climbed out. Hearing Duck, Water-rat emerged, threatened her with his spear and, dragging her underground, forced her to mate with him. By the time of egg-hatching, Duck was ashamed to have to lead out two extraordinary offspring. They had bills and webbed feet, but instead of two feet they had four and instead of feathers they had fur, while on each hind leg they had a sharp spike like Water-rat's spear. The first members of the platypus race were born.

I believe the second story...

URBAN LEGENDS

*Here's another batch of too-good-to-be-true stories that
are floating around. Have you heard any of them?*

THE STORY: Firefighters cleaning up the scene of a California forest fire are shocked to find the charred remains of a scuba diver hanging from the limbs of a burnt tree. An autopsy reveals that the cause of death was massive internal injuries sustained from a fall. An investigation reveals that he was diving off a nearby coast on the day of the fire...and was scooped up into a bucket of seawater being carried by a firefighting helicopter.

THE FACTS: The story, which sometimes involves a fisherman still clutching his fishing pole, has been around since at least 1987. It falls into one of the most popular urban legend categories of all: "What a stupid/unusual way to die!" (It's even popular in France, which has also been cited as the location of the incident.)

THE STORY: After playing a round of golf, a man with a habit of chewing his golf tee between holes complains he isn't feeling well. He checks into a hospital, and a few days later he dies. An autopsy reveals that insecticide from the golf course tainted the tee he was chewing, and poisoned him.

THE FACTS: This one is actually true. In 1982, Navy Lieutenant George M. Prior played two rounds of golf at the Army-Navy Country Club in Arlington, Virginia. By the time he finished, he was complaining of a headache; that night he checked into the hospital with nausea, fever, and a severe rash. He died ten days later. An autopsy determined that he died from an extreme allergic reaction to the pesticide used on the golf course.

THE STORY: The Red Cross conducts a volunteer blood drive at a local high school...and discovers that 20% of the student body tested positive for HIV.

THE FACTS: The rumor has been traced back to 1987, when it worked its way around the country, "attaching itself to whichever high school had just hosted a blood drive." Teenage fear of the

---

Most visited country in the world: France. Most popular tourist destination there: Euro Disney.

adverse consequences of sexual activity, coupled with parents' fear that their children are having sex, keeps this one alive.

Actually, between 1985 and 1996, the Red Cross tested 1.6 million samples of donated blood for HIV. Only 28 of these donors tested positive for HIV; of the 28, only one was a high school student.

THE STORY: A truck driver loses the brakes on his 18-wheeler while driving down a steep hill. He somehow manages to avoid hitting any cars and finally turns off onto an emergency exit ramp… where he runs over a picnicking family that has mistaken the emergency ramp for a rest stop.
THE FACTS: It never happened—but it's a good example of a classic urban legend theme: the tragedy is narrowly averted, only to result in a much bigger tragedy.

THE STORY: A woman buys a pair of shrink-to-fit jeans. Rather than shrink them in the washing machine, she puts them on and soaks with them in the tub, hoping they'll contour perfectly to her body. But they shrink so much that they crush her to death.
THE FACTS: It started with a TV commercial. In the mid-1980s, Levi's ran an ad for shrink-to-fit 501 jeans in which a man climbs into a tub with jeans on and soaks until they fit perfectly. The rumors started flying soon afterward.

This legend is an example of one of the most popular themes of all: the ridiculous fashion trend that kills. In the sixties, the "fatal fashion" was beehive hairdos filled with black widow spider nests; in the eighties, it was men stuffing cucumbers down the fronts of their tight pants, only to drop dead on the disco dance floor from lack of circulation.

* * *

"Man does not live by words alone, despite the fact that sometimes he has to eat them."
—Adlai Stevenson

Cubans eat more sugar than anyone else; Irish people eat the most corn flakes.

WORDPLAY

Another page of tidbits dug up by the erstwhile
Tim Harrower while surfing the Internet.

SPECIAL WORDS

The longest word you can spell without repeating a letter: Uncopyrightable.

The longest word with just one vowel: Strengths.

The only English word with a triple letter: Goddessship.

Longest commonly-used word with no letter appearing more than once: Ambidextrously.

The word with the longest definition, in most dictionaries: Set.

The longest common word without an a, e, i, o, or u: Rhythms.

The shortest -ology (study of) word: oology (the study of eggs).

The only two common words with six consonants in a row: Catchphrase and latchstring.

The longest English word with letters appearing in alphabetical order: Aegilops (an ulcer in the eye—we've never heard of it, either).

UGLY WORDS

According to a poll by the National Association of Teachers of Speech, the ten worst sounding words in the English language are: Cacophony, Crunch, Flatulent, Gripe, Jazz, Phlegmatic, Plump, Plutocrat, Sap, Treachery.

MULTI-PURPOSE SYLLABLE

You can pronounce-ough eight different ways in the following sentence: A rough-coated, dough-faced, thoughtful ploughman strode the streets of Scarborough; after falling into a slough, he coughed and hiccoughed!

LEARN A FOREIGN LANGUAGE

Taxi is spelled the same way in nine languages: English, French, Danish, Dutch, German, Swedish, Spanish, Norwegian, and Portuguese.

EXCEPTIONAL WORD

Of is the only word in which an "f" is pronounced like a "v".

---

5 most dangerous jobs in the U.S.: logger, pilot, asbestos worker, metal worker, and electrician.

DOWN-HOME TYCOON

*Some observations from one of America's
richest men—Warren Buffet.*

"That which is not worth doing is not worth doing well."

"If at first you succeed, quit trying."

"In the end, I always believe my eyes rather than anything else."

"It takes 20 years to build a reputation and five minutes to ruin it. If you think about that, you'll do things differently."

"Chains of habit are too light to be felt until they are too heavy to be broken."

"The only way to slow down is to stop."

"Someone's sitting in the shade today because someone planted a tree a long time ago."

"If principles can become dated, they're not principles."

"I keep an internal scoreboard. If I do something that others don't like but I feel good about, I'm happy. If others praise something I've done, but I'm not satisfied, I feel unhappy."

"I remember asking that question [How does he define friendship?] of a woman who had survived Auschwitz. She said her test was, 'Would they hide me?'"

"With enough insider information and a million dollars, you can go broke in a year."

"What I am is a realist. I always knew I'd like what I'm doing. Oh, perhaps it would have been nice to be a major league baseball player, but that's where the realism comes in."

"Wall Street is the only place that people ride to work in a Rolls Royce to get advice from those who take the subway."

"I want to explain my mistakes. This means I do only the things I completely understand."

A COMIC STRIP IS BORN

*Here are more stories behind the
creation of some of the world's
most popular comic strips.*

BLONDIE
Background: Blondie is the most popular "family" comic strip in the world, appearing in 55 countries and 2,200 newspapers. But it started out in 1930 with a very different story line. The stars were Blondie Boopadoop, a gold digger looking for a rich husband, and Dagwood Bumstead—who was, believe it or not, "a playboy, party animal, and polo player," and heir to the Bumstead railroad fortune. Dagwood spent most of his time partying and chasing Blondie.

A Strip Is Born: As the Depression got more severe, the company that distributed "Blondie" to newspapers worried that rich airheads wouldn't amuse people anymore. They told the strip's creator, Chic Young, to "go back to the drawing board and start over" with something readers could relate to. He did. In 1933, Dagwood and Blondie surprised everyone by falling in love. Dagwood's parents objected to their marriage…and disinherited him. Result: He had to get a job, which made the Bumsteads "common folk." From then on, the jokes could be about the problems of ordinary life—getting up for work, missing the bus, pleasing the boss, making ends meet, etc.

CATHY
Background: In 1976, at age 26, Cathy Guisewite was already a VP at an ad agency…but she was 50 pounds overweight and not terribly happy. One night, as she waited for a boyfriend to call, she realized "how pathetic" she'd become. She drew a few humorous pictures of herself eating junk food, waiting at the phone, and sent them to her mother.

Soon, she was sending these "illustrated versions of my anxieties" to her parents regularly. "Instead of writing in my diary," she

---

Professions most likely to work nights: police, security guard. Least likely: construction worker.

says, "I sort of started summing up my life—my pathetic moments in pictures—and sending them home."

A Strip Is Born: Her parents saved the drawings and eventually suggested she try to sell them as a comic strip. "My mother had always taught me to write about things instead of talking to anyone," Guisewite says. "'If you're angry,' she'd say, 'don't scream at the person. Write about it. If you're hurt or jealous, don't go gossiping to girlfriends. Write about it. If you're lonely or sad or depressed, write about it.' Try to imagine my horror when—after a lifetime of teaching me to keep my feelings private—she insisted my drawings were the makings of a comic strip for millions of people to read."

Her timing couldn't have been better. Universal Press Syndicate had been looking for a strip dealing with women's issues, and this one, they said, was the first that had "some feeling, some soul." They bought the strip and named the main character after its author. Today, Guisewite says, "If I had ever had any idea how many people would one day be reading it, I would never have agreed to name her Cathy."

GARFIELD

Background: Jim Davis was too sickly to work on the family farm in Indiana, so his mother kept him supplied with pencils and paper and encouraged him to draw. When he graduated from college, he got a job as assistant to Tom Ryan, creator of the syndicated comic strip "Tumbleweeds."

A Strip Is Born: A few years later, Davis went to New York to sell his own strip— "Gnorm Gnat," about an insect. It was turned down. "They told me nobody could identify with a bug," Davis says. He looked for a subject people could identify with and noticed there were lots of dogs in successful comic strips—Snoopy, Marmaduke, Belvedere—but almost no cats.

So he decided to fashion a cat character after his "big, opinionated, stubborn" grandfather, James Garfield Davis, and sold it to United Features. The strip debuted on June 19, 1978, in 41 newspapers. During the 1980s, Garfield merchandising became a billion-dollar-a-year industry. For example, between 1987 and 1989, 225 million of those suction-cupped Garfield dolls sold.

Largest bell on earth: the Tsar Kolokol in Moscow. It weighs 222 tons and has never been rung.

STARWATCH 101

BRI member Jessica Vineyard contributed this illuminating piece on some astronomical basics. Perfect for reading by flashlight when you're out at night stargazing.

WHY DO STARS TWINKLE?

Have you ever tried to figure out whether something is a star or a planet by looking at the light shining from them? The easiest way to tell the difference is that stars twinkle, planets do not.

Why is this true? It's fairly simple, actually. Stars are so far away that the light from a single star—even the nearest ones (besides the Sun)—takes years to get to your eye. By that time, the beam of starlight that enters your eye is actually a delicate filament of light, easily affected by the ripples in the atmosphere. The rippling effect of the air around us is what makes the star appear to twinkle.

Planets, on the other hand, are much closer to us. In binoculars, or even with the unaided eye, you can actually see the round discs of planets. This light is from such a large, nearby source that it's not as easily affected by the turbulence in our atmosphere. Planets appear to have a strong, steady beam of light.

If you're not sure whether you're looking at a planet or a star, compare your target object with another source of light nearby. See if either of them twinkle.

WHY ARE STARS MEASURED IN LIGHT-YEARS?

A *light year* is the distance light travels in a year. How far is that? Well, light moves at 186,000 miles a second (it's the fastest thing in the universe), and there are 31,536,000 seconds in a year. So the equation is:

$$186,000 \ (miles) \ x \ 31,560,000 \ (seconds)$$

That comes out to about 6 trillion miles. Stars are incredibly far away. Our galaxy, for example, is more than 100,000 *light years* across. It's a heck of a lot easier to refer to their distances in terms of light years than any smaller measurement.

Most common German surname: Myers. Most common Italian surname: Russo.

WHY ARE STARS DIFFERENT COLORS?

A star's color usually indicates its temperature. Generally speaking, blue stars are the hottest. The coolest are often red...and very large (called "red giants" because at the end of their lives, stars simultaneously cool off and swell up to 100 times their normal size). In between blue and red, in decreasing order, are white, yellow, and orange.

WHAT ARE "SHOOTING STARS?"

Meteors.

Okay, then—what are meteors?

Meteors are often the byproduct of comets, especially when they're in "meteor showers."

Explanation: When a comet passes near the sun, it leaves particles of rock and dust in its wake, called meteoroids. If the Earth passes near or through this trail of comet debris, some meteoroids are pulled toward us by gravity. They may get so close that they pass into our atmosphere—which quickly slows them down. (A lot like throwing a small rock into a pond of water.) We see a streak of light in the night sky, caused by vaporization of the meteoroid's particles. And that's when the meteoroid becomes a meteor, or shooting star.

How big are they? Most meteors are no larger than the toenail on your little toe. Many are just the size of a grain of sand. (Really!) But some can be the size of your fist and, in rare cases, the size of a large dog or even a car. Most burn out before reaching the ground, but when a large meteor enters the Earth's atmosphere, it can survive its fall and land somewhere on the planet.

Many meteors disappear into the water, never to be seen again. But some are found on land—especially on the Antarctic icefields. (If a rock is found on an icefield, it can only be from a meteor, since there are no other rocks around.)

When a meteor lands on the solid surface of the Earth, it becomes a meteorite. They're hard to find because, to the untrained eye, they look just like any other rocks. Good luck.

---

3 most popular dogs in the U.S.: Labrador Retrievers, Rottweilers, and Cocker Spaniels.

THE ANIMALS AT THE ZOO, Part 4

Here's more research from Uncle John's trip to the zoo. For more, we recommend Beastly Behaviors *by Janine Benyus.*

WATCHING ZEBRAS

Behavior: Rubbing.
What It Means: They have an itch to scratch. Zebras rub up against trees, termite mounds or rubbing posts to scratch places they can't reach by themselves. They also rub to remove insects, loose hair…or dandruff.

Behavior: Sniffing / Rubbing noses.
What It Means: Hello. Stallions from different groups will sniff each other's noses as part of a greeting ceremony. This defuses any potential tension or aggression.

Behavior: Circling.
What It Means: They're fighting. Zebras circling one another will try to bite each other while trying to avoid being bitten. They'll continue around and around, crouching to protect their hind legs until they're practically pivoting on their haunches.

Behavior: Neck wrestling.
What It Means: Fighting. After circling for some time, zebras often begin neck wrestling (similar to humans thumb wrestling). While one places his neck on top of the other's and pushes down, the zebra underneath is pushing up. Often, the zebra on the bottom will suddenly drop down and pull his head out, trying to get his neck across his opponent's.

Behavior: Lip curling.
What It Means: Courtship. After sniffing a female's rear and urine, a zebra stallion will raise his head with a lip curl gesture— nose in the sky and lips curled back. This seals his nostrils, help- ing the odor to travel quickly to his scent receptors.

The Arabic word for "forbidden" is "harem."

Behavior: Nibbling.
What It Means: Grooming. Zebras nibble by scratching their upper incisors against the other's coat, getting rid of loose hair and cleaning the skin. They begin by nibbling one side of each other's necks and backs. They continue on to their tails, then turn around and start working on the other side.

WATCHING PENGUINS

Behavior: "Slender walking"—walking with the beak pointed up, feathers sleeked back, and flippers held to the sides.
What It Means: "I mean no harm." Since penguins live in crowded colonies, they often have to walk by many other penguins just to get a drink of water. By putting its bill in the air, the bird is "symbolically taking its weapon out of commission." The slender walk is a penguin's way of saying "Don't mind me. I'm not going to bother you."

Behavior: Panting.
What It Means: Penguins pant to cool themselves down. Their bodies are designed to keep heat in; when temperatures reach 32°F, they need to cool off. They pant with their beaks open to take advantage of the cooling effects of evaporation.

Behavior: Pecking at another penguin.
What It Means: They're fighting. Penguins spar bill to bill. They'll peck and pull at each other trying to grab hold of the other's body. When they do get a grip, they often strike each other with their flippers.

Behavior: Mutual bowing.
What It Means: Courtship. Though a pair of penguins may be attracted to each other, both need to overcome their aggressive tendencies. Bowing helps them become more comfortable with one another.

Behavior: "Ecstatic displaying."
What It Means: This is a way for male penguins to announce ownership of nest sites and to attract females. An ecstatic displaying penguin will rear his head back, point his bill at the sky, fluff his crest feathers, roll his eyes back, wave his flippers, and give a loud *gaa aah aah aah* call.

UNCLE ALBERT SAYS

Cosmic question: What would Albert Einstein think if he knew we consider his comments great bathroom reading?

"Only two things are infinite, the universe and stupidity—and I'm not sure about the former."

"God is subtle, but He is not malicious."

"'Common sense' is the set of prejudices acquired by age eighteen."

"Nationalism is an infantile disease. It is the measles of mankind."

"I never think of the future. It comes soon enough."

"Try not to become a man of success, but rather, a man of value."

"I experience the greatest degree of pleasure in having contact with works of art. They furnish me with happy feelings of an intensity such as I cannot drive from other realms."

"To punish me for my contempt for authority, Fate made me an authority myself."

"Why is it that nobody understands me, and everybody likes me?"

"A life directed chiefly toward fulfillment of personal desires sooner or later always leads to bitter disappointment."

"My political ideal is that of democracy. Let every man be respected as an individual, and no man idolized."

"Whatever there is of God and goodness in the Universe, it must work itself out and express itself through us. We cannot stand aside and let God do it."

"Science without religion is lame, religion without science is blind."

"I am a deeply religious nonbe-liever…This is a somewhat new kind of religion."

"With fame I become more and more stupid, which of course is a very common phenomenon."

Average number of bathing suits sold in America every second: 4.

CLARKE'S COMMENTS

Here are a few thoughts from the eminent science fiction writer Arthur C. Clarke, author of 2001: A Space Odyssey.

"Politicians should read science fiction, not westerns and detective stories."

"Any sufficiently advanced technology is indistinguishable from magic."

"A faith that cannot survive collision with the truth is not worth many regrets."

"It may be that our role on this planet is not to worship God but to create him."

"This is the first age that's paid much attention to the future, which is a little ironic since we may not have one."

"How can extreme forms of nationalism survive when men have seen the Earth in its true perspective—as a single, small globe against the stars?"

"Sometimes I think we're alone in the universe, and sometimes I think we're not. In either case the idea is quite staggering."

"If an elderly but distinguished scientist says that something is possible, he is almost certainly right. But if he says that it is impossible, he is probably wrong."

"The realization that our small planet is only one of many worlds gives mankind the perspective it needs to realize that our own world belongs to all of its creatures."

"I don't believe in God but I'm very interested in her."

"The production of natural meat is so inefficient a process that it may even be prohibited by the twenty-first century. (But) the biochemists are making great progress; our grandchildren will love grass, and won't even know that they're eating it."

"The only way to discover the limits of the possible is to go beyond them into the impossible."

BRAND NAMES

You already know these names.
Here's where they came from.

CLOROX. In 1913, the Electro-Alkaline Company of Oakland, California, started selling bleach in jugs carried by horse-drawn carts. A supplier pointed out that their name sounded industrial—even dangerous. He suggested combining "chlorine" and "sodium hydroxide" (two of the product's ingredients), to create Clorox.

BRILLO. From the Latin word *beryllus,* which means "shine."

LEE JEANS. At the turn of the century, Henry D. Lee was one of the Midwest's biggest wholesalers of groceries, work clothes, and other items. In 1911, because he wasn't getting shipments of work clothes on time, he decided to build his own factory. In 1924, he started making jeans for cowboys. In 1926, Lee's made the first jeans with zippers.

FORMULA 409. The two scientists who invented the "all purpose cleaner" in the late 1950s didn't get the formula right until their 409th attempt.

CONVERSE ALL-STARS. Named for Marquis M. Converse, who founded the Converse Rubber Company in 1908. He introduced the canvas-topped All-Star—one of the world's first basketball shoes—in 1917.

BAUSCH & LOMB. In the 1850s, Henry Lomb invested his life savings ($60) in an eyeglass business run by John Bausch. By 1908, they were selling over 20 million lenses a year.

TURTLE WAX. In the early 1940s, Ben Hirsch mixed up a batch of car wax in a bathtub. He called it Plastone Liquid Car Wax, and started selling it around the country. Several years later, he was walking along Turtle Creek in Beloit, Wisconsin, when "he made a mental connection between the hard shell of a turtle and his product." Plastone became Turtle Wax.

THANKSGIVING MYTHS

Historian Samuel Eliot Morison says that "more bunk has been written about Pilgrims than any other subjects except Columbus and John Paul Jones." After reading this, maybe you'll agree.

It's one of American history's most familiar scenes: A small group of Pilgrims prepare a huge November feast to give thanks for a bountiful harvest and show their appreciation to the Indians who helped them survive their first winter. Together, the Pilgrims and Indians solemnly sit down to a meal of turkey, pumpkin pie, and cranberries.

Just how accurate is this image of America's first Thanksgiving? Not very, it turns out. Here are some common misconceptions about the origin of one of our favorite holidays.

MYTH: The settlers at the first Thanksgiving were called Pilgrims.
THE TRUTH: They didn't even refer to themselves as Pilgrims—they called themselves "Saints." Early Americans applied the term "pilgrim" to all of the early colonists; it wasn't until the 20th century that it was used exclusively to describe the folks who landed on Plymouth Rock.

MYTH: It was a solemn, religious occasion.
THE TRUTH: Hardly, It was a three-day harvest festival that included drinking, gambling, athletic games, and even target shooting with English muskets (which, by the way, was intended as friendly warning to the Indians that the Pilgrims were prepared to defend themselves).

MYTH: It took place in November.
THE TRUTH: It was some time between late September and the middle of October—after the harvest had been brought in. By November, says historian Richard Ehrlich, "the villagers were working to prepare for winter, salting and drying meat and making their houses as wind resistant as possible."

Every Thanksgiving, Americans consume 45 million turkeys—one for every 5-1/2 U.S. citizens.

MYTH: The Pilgrims wore large hats with buckles on them.
THE TRUTH: None of the participants were dressed anything like the way they've been portrayed in art: the Pilgrims didn't dress in black, didn't wear buckles on their hats or shoes, and didn't wear tall hats. The 19th-century artists who painted them that way did so because they associated black clothing and buckles with being old-fashioned.

MYTH: They ate turkey.
THE TRUTH: The Pilgrims ate deer, not turkey. As Pilgrim Edward Winslow later wrote, "For three days we entertained and feasted, and [the Indians] went out and killed five deer, which they brought to the plantation." Winslow does mention that four Pilgrims went "fowling" or bird hunting, but neither he nor anyone else recorded which kinds of birds they actually hunted— so even if they did eat turkey, it was just a side dish. "The flashy part of the meal for the colonists was the venison, because it was new to them," says Carolyn Travers, director of research at Plymoth Plantation, a Pilgrim museum in Massachusetts. "Back in England, deer were on estates and people would be arrested for poaching if they killed these deer…The colonists mentioned venison over and over again in their letters back home." Other foods that may have been on the menu: cod, bass, clams, oysters, Indian corn, native berries and plums, all washed down with water, beer made from corn, and another drink the Pilgrims affectionately called "strong water."

A few things definitely weren't on the menu, including pumpkin pie—in those days, the Pilgrims boiled their pumpkin and ate it plain. And since the Pilgrims didn't yet have flour mills or cattle, there was no bread other than corn bread, and no beef, milk, or cheese. And the Pilgrims didn't eat any New England lobsters, either. Reason: They mistook them for large insects.

MYTH: The Pilgrims held a similar feast every year.
THE TRUTH: There's no evidence the Pilgrims celebrated again in 1622. They probably weren't in the mood—the harvest had been disappointing, and they were burdened with a new boatload of Pilgrims who had to be fed and housed through the winter.

SPECIAL AFFECTS

*Here are a few unexpected ways that movies have
made their mark on the American public.*

COMA (1978)

"In 1978," writes historian Scot Morris, "there was a reported 60% drop in human organs donated to U.S. hospitals, as compared to the previous year. Why?...The decline in donors occurred just after the release of *Coma*, a film in which hospital patients are murdered so their organs can be harvested and sold."

FORREST GUMP (1994)

The title character carries his favorite book, *Curious George*, around in a suitcase. Later, he gives a copy to his son. In the first three weeks after the film's release, sales of *Curious George* books jumped 25%—and have stayed high since.

IT HAPPENED ONE NIGHT (1934)

Clark Gable took off his shirt in the Oscar-winning comedy, and America saw he was bare-chested underneath. Overnight, undershirt sales plummeted.

E.T. (1982)

"In one of the film's more dramatic moments," writes Carolyn Wyman in *I'm a Spam Fan*, "the alien opens up his clenched fist and out drops—not the expected weapon—but brown, yellow, and orange pieces of both boy and extraterrestrial's favorite candy"— Reese's Pieces. "Those few minutes of screen time sent sales of Reese's Pieces into outer space. Sales increased 65%, causing the company to keep two factories open round the clock."

LOVE HAPPY (1949)

The Marx Brothers' final film was so badly underfinanced that the producer had to invent what is now known as "product placement." He devised a rooftop chase scene where the characters jumped from one neon sign to another. It was one long commercial and corporations paid to be a part of it.

"Republican" and "Democrat" are both towns in North Carolina.

PLITZ-PLATZ I WAS TAKING A BATH

As kids, we were all told that trains go "choo-choo" and cars go "beep beep." Check out the sounds they make in other languages.

AAH-CHOO!
Portuguese: Ah-chim!
German: Hat-chee!
Greek: Ap tsou!
Japanese: Hakshon!
Italian: Ekchee!

SPLASH!
Hindi: Dham!
Russian: Plukh!
Danish: Plump!
Spanish: Chof!
Greek: Plitz-platz!

EENY-MEENY-MINY-MO
Arabic: Hadi-badi
Italian: Ambaraba chichicoco
Japanese: Hee-foo-mee-yo
Swedish: Ol-uh dol-uh doff
Polish: Ele mele dudki

CHOO-CHOO!
Chinese: Hong-lung, hong-lung
Danish: Fut fut!
Japanese: Shuppo-shuppo!
Swahili: Chuku-chuku
Greek: Tsaf-tsouf!

ZZZZZZZ...
Arabic: Kh-kh-kh...
Chinese: Hulu...
Italian: Ronf-ronf...
Japanese: Gah-gah...

UPSY-DAISY!
Arabic: Hop-pa!
Italian: Opp-la!
Japanese: Yoisho!
Russian: Nu davai!
Danish: Opse-dasse!

KITCHY-KITCHY-KOO!
Chinese: Gujee!
French: Gheely-gheely!
Greek: Ticki-ticki-ticki!
Swedish: Kille kille kille!

UH-OH!
Chinese: Zao le!
Italian: Ay-may!
Japanese: Ah-ah!
Swahili: Wee!
Swedish: Oy-oy!

BEEP BEEP!
Chinese: Dooo dooo!
Hindi: Pon-pon!
Spanish: Mock mock!
French: Puet puet!
Japanese: Boo boo!

CHUGALUG!
Arabic: Gur-gur-gur!
Hindi: Gat-gat!
Hebrew: Gloog gloog!
Russian: Bool-bool!
Chinese: Goo-doo, goo-doo!

Native Americans spoke more than 133 different languages.

FAMILIAR PHRASES

Here are some origins of everyday phrases.

KNUCKLE UNDER
Meaning: Give in to someone of superior strength.
Origin: Today only the joints in your fingers are known as knuckles, but before the 14th century all joints in the body were called knuckles. In those days, "knuckling under" meant getting down on your knees before your master or conqueror.

BRAND-NEW
Meaning: Obtained very recently.
Origin: The German word for "fire" is *Brand*. Horseshoes, as well as other items that were fresh from the fire of a blacksmith's forge, were said to be *brandneu*, or "brand-new" in English.

DOUBLE-CROSS
Meaning: Betray.
Origin: Comes from boxing and describes a fixed fight. If a fighter deliberately loses, he "crosses up" the people who have bet on him to win; if he wins, he "crosses up" the people paying him to lose. Someone is betrayed no matter how the fight turns out; hence the name double-cross.

FINISH IN A DEAD HEAT
Meanings: Tie for first place.
Origin: Racing term from the days when horses ran several races, or "heats," to determine a winner. (A horse had to win two out of three, three out of five, etc.) When two horses tied in a heat, it was considered "dead," because it didn't count.

HAVING KITTENS
Meaning: Acting hysterically.
Origin: In the Middle Ages, when a pregnant woman experienced severe pains that didn't appear to be labor pains, people thought she was bewitched and "had kittens clawing at her inside her womb. " A common excuse given in court for obtaining an abortion was "to remove cats in the belly."

HERE'S THE STORY...

Inside facts on The Brady Bunch, *the syrupy TV sitcom that aired from September 26, 1969 to August 30, 1974. Like* Star Trek, *it was never very popular in prime time, but has become a monster cult show.*

HOW IT STARTED

In 1964, while TV producer Sherwood Schwartz was working on his hit show *Gilligan's Island,* he began fleshing out ideas for a new family sitcom.

In the mid-'60s, the standard *Leave It to Beaver* sitcom family was already out of date; you had to have a gimmick to have a hit. So Schwartz came up with the idea of making the wife a widow, and the husband a widower. It was a TV first—a blended family, with three kids from the dad and three from the mom. He called it *Yours and Mine.*

Schwartz wrote the script for a 1/2-hour pilot episode in which Carol and Mike Brady get so lonely on their honeymoon that they return home to get Alice and the kids. He showed it to the networks and got a mixed response. NBC liked the idea, but thought the pilot was unrealistic (who'd leave their honeymoon to be with kids?); ABC wanted Schwartz to expand it to a 1-1/2 hour TV movie (he refused because it would be too boring); CBS rejected it outright—they had their own widow-marries-widower show in the works (it never aired). So *Yours and Mine* was dead in the water.

Then four years later in 1968, Lucille Ball and Henry Fonda starred in a fairly successful movie with a plot similar to Schwartz's show, called *Yours, Mine, and Ours.* It reminded someone at ABC of the pilot they'd seen in 1964; they called Schwartz and bought the program. Once ABC was committed, Schwartz had no trouble getting Paramount TV to finance it. The show was on its way.

INSIDE FACTS

Name That Show

Paramount immediately ran into a problem with the name. A lawyer for the owners of *Yours, Mine, and Ours* threatened to sue them if they kept the title Yours and Mine. Schwartz wanted to fight—he'd registered his title first. But no one else thought it was

America's four favorite leftovers: pasta (including lasagna), pizza, chicken, and meatloaf.

worth. the effort. The choice came down to *The Brady Bunch,* or *The Brady Brood.* "Bunch" sounded like juvenile delinquents; "brood" sounded like a horror flick. Finally, they just picked one and started production.

The Bradys vs. the Censors

• It was officially established in the early episodes that Mike Brady was a widower—but the fate of Carol's first husband was never discussed. Why? Schwartz wanted to leave open the possibility that Carol was a divorcée, even though the network wouldn't allow it explicitly.
• 1969 was the peak of the "sexual revolution," and Carol and Mike joined in. They became the first contemporary TV sitcom couple to actually sleep together. Until then, censors had always required twin beds—even for married couples. But the Bradys had…a double bed!
• One thing the Bradys weren't allowed to have: a toilet. ABC removed the toilet from the Brady bathroom, leaving only a sink and tub. The running joke on the set was that the Bradys used the restroom at the corner gas station.

The Blended Family

• Schwartz interviewed 464 boys and girls to find the Brady kids.
• He wanted the sons and daughters to have the same hair color as their parents. The reason: he didn't want viewers confused about which kids belonged to whom. But when the Brady kid auditions started, Schwartz didn't know who was going to play the parents. So he hired two sets of Brady kids—blonde and brunette. When Robert Reed and Florence Henderson were hired as the parents, he fired the blonde boys and brunette girls.

In the Cast

• Barry Williams was the most popular Brady kid. He was an instant pop star, getting 6,500 letters a week in 1971.
• Robert Reed didn't want to play Mike Brady. A classically trained actor, he had the lead role in the Broadway play *Barefoot in the Park.* He wanted to star in the TV version planned for the 1970 season, and only took the *Brandy Bunch* part after ABC decided that all the actors in the *Barefoot* sitcom would be African Americans.

WHEN YOUR HUSBAND GETS HOME...

Here's a bit of advice taken directly from a 1950s Home Economics textbook. It was sent in by a reader, along with the comment: "Times have changed!" No kidding. Believe it or not, this was part of a course intended to prepare high school girls for married life.

Have dinner ready: "Plan ahead, even the night before, to have a delicious meal—on time. This is a way of letting him know that you have been thinking about him and are concerned about his needs. Most men are hungry when they come home and the prospects of a good meal are part of the warm welcome needed."

Prepare yourself: "Take 15 minutes to rest so you will be refreshed when he arrives. Touch up your makeup, put a ribbon in your hair and be fresh-looking. He has just been with a lot of work-weary people. Be a little gay and a little more interesting. His boring day may need a lift."

Clear away the clutter: "Make one last trip through the main part of the house just before your husband arrives, gathering up school books, toys, paper, etc. Then run a dust cloth over the tables. Your husband will feel he has reached a haven of rest and order, and it will give you a lift, too."

Prepare the children: "Take a few minutes to wash the children's hands and faces (if they are small), comb their hair, and if necessary, change their clothes. They are little treasures and he would like to see them playing the part."

Minimize all noise: "At the time of his arrival, eliminate all noise of washer, dryer, dishwasher or vacuum. Try to encourage the children to be quiet. Greet him with a warm smile and be glad to see him."

Some don'ts: Don't greet him with problems or complaints. Don't complain if he's late for dinner. Count this as minor compared

A record: 60.2% of the U.S. TV audience watched the last episode of M*A*S*H in 1983.

with what he might have gone through that day."

Make him comfortable: "Have him lean back in a comfortable chair or suggest he lie down in the bedroom. Have a cool or warm drink ready for him. Arrange his pillow and offer to take off his shoes. Speak in a low, soft, soothing and pleasant voice. Allow him to relax—unwind."

Listen to him: "You may have a dozen things to tell him, but the moment of his arrival is not the time. Let him talk first."

Making the evening his: "Never complain if he does not take you out to dinner or to other places of entertainment. Instead, try to understand his world of strain and pressure, his need to be home and relax."

*   *   *

THE BEST & WORST TIPPERS

According to a poll in *Bartender* magazine:

• Lawyers and doctors are the worst tippers. Normally, doctors are the #1 tightwads. In rougher times, it's lawyers. The reason: "There are more lawyers and less work."

• The biggest tippers are bartenders and "service personnel."

• As smoking gets more restricted, cigar and cigarette smokers—who are now forced to smoke at the bar instead of at restaurant tables—are becoming notably good tippers.

• Other leading tightwads: teachers, computer people, musicians, professional athletes, and pipe smokers.

• Other top tippers: hairstylists, mobsters, tavern owners, regular customers.

• Vodka drinkers are good tippers. People who order drinks topped with umbrellas are bad tippers.

• Democrats tip better than Republicans.

One in 500 humans have one blue eye and one brown eye.

FAMOUS TIGHTWADS

For some bizarre reason, really rich people are often the most uptight about spending money. Here are a few examples of people who've gone over the deep and about loose change.

MARGE SCHOTT, owner of the Cincinnati Reds. Told her staff in 1995 she couldn't afford Christmas bonuses and gave candies instead. They turned out to be free samples from a baseball-card company…and they came with coupons inviting consumers to "win a trip to the 1991 Grammys."

CARY GRANT. Nicknamed "El Squeako" by Hollywood friends, he counted the number of firewood logs in his mansion's garage and used a red pen to mark the level of milk in the milk bottles in his refrigerator, both to keep his servants from taking them.

FRANKLIN D. ROOSEVELT, U.S. president. Mooched dollar bills off of his valet to drop in the collection plate at church.

GROUCHO MARX. Wore a beret, which became one of his trademarks, "so he wouldn't have to check his hat."

CORNELIUS VANDERBILT, American financier. When his doctor told him on his deathbed that a glass of champagne a day would moderate his suffering, Vanderbilt—then the wealthiest man in America—replied, "Dammit, I tell you Doc, I can't afford it. Won't sodywater do?"

J. PAUL GETTY, oil baron. Installed a pay phone in his mansion to keep visitors from running up his long-distance bill; put locks on all the other phones. "When you get some fellow talking for ten or fifteen minutes," the billionaire explained, "well, it all adds up."

LEE IACOCCA, former head of Chrysler Corp. Threw himself lavish holiday parties and charged the gifts to underlings. Popular saying at Chrysler: "If you have lunch with someone who looks like Iacocca and sounds like Iacocca, rest assured—if he offers to pick up the check, it's not Iacocca."

The G in g-string stands for "groin."

CELEBRITY SWEEPSTAKES

There's an old saying in advertising: "If you haven't got anything to say about your product, have a celebrity say it for you." Sometimes celebrity endorsements work, sometimes they don't. Here are a few examples.

ROSEANNE AND TOM ARNOLD
In 1993, CelebSales, a clothing manufacturer, hired the outspoken couple to endorse a line of large-sized clothing.
What they wanted: A positive image. Roseanne had TV's #1 show and she was unapologetic about her size. "I think the sexiest thing a woman can do," she said, "is be as fat as me—or fatter." Roseanne also attracted publicity. *People* magazine, for example, shot an entire fashion layout for the line, with Roseanne modeling the clothes herself.
What they got: A lawsuit. A week before the clothes were to premiere in a fashion show, Roseanne pulled out of the deal, obtained a court order canceling the show, and sued CelebSales, claiming they owed her $750,000 in licensing fees. CelebSales countersued for $24 million, arguing that the Arnolds "not only reneged on agreements to market the clothes on television, but generated publicity so vile that nobody would want to buy their product."
What happened: The clothing line was canceled. In 1996, a court awarded the Arnolds the $750,000 they said they were owed. By that time, they weren't even a couple anymore.

CYBILL SHEPHERD & JAMES GARNER
In 1986, the Beef Industry Council announced that it had hired Shepherd, an ex-model and star of TV's "Moonlighting," and Garner to represent them in a $30 million "Beef: Real Food for Real People" campaign.
What they wanted: To change beef's image as an unhealthy food. "We're thrilled that two stars of such magnitude have agreed to join the beef team," one council spokesperson told reporters. "I don't think we could have two celebrities and an industry more suited for one another."

The can opener was invented 48 years after the can was.

What they got: Egg on their face. A few months later, Shepherd was interviewed in *Family Circle* magazine. "Asked to name her latest beauty tip," said a news report, "the star was quoted as saying, 'I've cut down on fatty foods and am trying to stay away from red meat.'" Shepherd claimed her publicist had made the quote up. "The comments attributed to me were released by my publicity office, but they were not entirely correct," she explained. "I do avoid 'fatty foods,' but I have retained red meat in my diet."

Then, in April 1988, Garner underwent a quintuple bypass surgery to correct clogged arteries. Was beef the cause? "It could very well be due to something else," a beef board spokesman protested. Newspapers reported that Garner was recovering. "According to his spokesman," said one, "he is 'beginning to eat a normal diet.' No word on whether beef is included."

What happened: The Beef Industry Council pledged that it would stand by Shepherd and Garner...then quietly dumped each of them when their contracts expired.

JACK KLUGMAN

The star of TV's "Odd Couple" and "Quincy" was hired as spokesperson for Canon USA copiers in 1982.

What they wanted: A recognizable TV pitchman

What they got: Unexpected competition. In 1984, Minolta hired Klugman's "Odd Couple" co-star, Tony Randall, to endorse its own line of copiers. Randall played a compulsive cleaner on the show; Klugman played a slob—which was why Minolta wanted Randall, as *Fortune* magazine reported in 1985:

> The Minolta ads, which according to his agent riled Klugman, played up the Odd Couple stereotypes and even made a thinly veiled reference to Klugman when Randall ad-libbed, "Of course, I'm not slob like, uh..." and gave his you-know-who-I-mean look. Minolta's marketing coup was to associate Canon machines in consumers' minds with Klugman's mess: jammed paper, perhaps, or ink blackened hands.

What happened: The Randall ads boosted sales of Minolta copiers, but they didn't hurt Canon's sales, so the company retained Klugman as their spokesman.

Diet Pepsi was originally called "Patio Diet Cola."

TOASTER FOODS

We wrote about how the toaster was invented back in BR #2—now here's the origin of America's two biggest-selling toaster foods.

EGGO WAFFLES

The Eggo name has probably been around longer than you think. It was coined in 1935, when three brothers—Frank, Tony, and Sam Dorsa—borrowed $35 to buy a waffle iron and started experimenting with waffle batter. When they got a batter they liked, they sold it to restaurants in Northern California. A fourth brother, George, suggested they call their product "Eggo" because "the batter has lots of eggs." In 1937, the company went public, and the brothers built a big waffle-batter factory in San Jose.

After World War II, when Americans began buying home freezers in record numbers, the Dorsas guessed there was a bigger market for frozen waffles than for waffle batter. So in 1950, they gambled and switched their entire production to ready-made waffles. Within a year, they were cranking out 10,000 an hour...and still couldn't keep up with demand. Kellogg's bought the company in 1968. Today, the brand controls an estimated 60% share of the $500 million frozen waffle industry.

POP-TARTS

The Pop-Tart story starts with dog food, not cereal...and not with Kellogg's but with its rival, Post. According to Steve Hymon, in the *Chicago Tribune:*

> In 1957, Post's pet-feed division came out with Gaines Burgers [which] were a novel concept because the dog food was semi-moist but didn't have to be refrigerated—a convenience many humans coincidentally sought in their breakfast food.
>
> In 1963, the Post research and development department, using some of the same technology that made Gaines Burgers possible, figured out a way to keep fruit filling moist while inhibiting the growth of spoilage-causing bacteria. The obvious application: a fruit-filled pastry that could be shipped and stored without having to be refrigerated.
>
> On Feb. 16, 1964, Post unveiled its new product,

Country Squares. The food industry oohed and aahed; the business press buzzed; grocers waited expectantly.

And waited.

Post blundered. It took so long to get its product to grocery stores that Kellogg's had had a chance to catch up. In just six months, Kellogg's created and test-marketed Pop-Tarts. People at Post knew they were sunk. Hymon goes on:

> The names given to the two products were one more indication of Kellogg's superior marketing savvy. Kellogg appreciated that kids were the primary target audience for Pop-Tarts because they had yet to establish breakfast habits of their own. Post seems to have been more confused. As awful a name as Country Squares seems in 1994, it was arguably worse in 1964, when the word "square" was widely used to mean "nerdy." When paired with "country," it seemed to describe a food for middle-aged rubes from the sticks.

POPPING OFF

The original Pop-Tarts came in four flavors: Strawberry, Blueberry, Brown Sugar, and Apple-Currant (which Kellogg's quickly changed to Apple-Berry when it realized most consumers didn't know what currants were). Kellogg's put its marketing muscle behind the new product, blitzing kid's TV shows with commercials featuring Milton the Toaster. By 1967, they had both created and locked up the $45 million toaster pastry market. The brand maintained a 75% market share into the 1990s, with $285 million in sales in 1990...and nearly $500 million by 1993.

What happened to Country Squares? Post changed the name to Post Toast-Em Pop-Ups, but it was too late. Post finally gave up in the early 1970s and sold the marketing rights to someone else.

TOASTER FLOPS. *Not every toaster food works. Here are some other ideas that bit the big one...and the reasons why.*
- Downyflake Toaster Eggs. Too weird.
- ReddiWip's Reddi Bacon. Bacon fat dripped to the bottom of the toaster, creating a fire hazard.
- Toaster Chicken Patties. Same problem, with chicken fat.
- Electric French Fries. Stamped out in slab form, they "looked like a picket fence, tasted like a picket fence."

BUILDING A BETTER SQUIRT GUN

When Uncle John was a kid, he had squirt guns that shot 5 to 10 feet at most, and that was only if you pulled the trigger so hard it hurt. Today, there are water toys that shoot 50 feet or more. Here's the story.

BOY WONDER

Lonnie Johnson loved to tinker. As a kid, he used to take his brothers' and sisters' toys apart to see how they worked. By high school, he'd graduated to mixing rocket fuel in the family kitchen. One year he used scrap motors, jukebox parts, and an old butane tank to create a remote-controlled, programmable robot …which won first prize in the University of Alabama science fair. Not bad for a kid from the poor side of Mobile, Alabama.

UNDER PRESSURE

Johnson got an engineering degree from Tuskeegee Institute and wound up working at the Jet Propulsion Lab in Pasadena, California. But he still spent his spare time tinkering. He recalls that one evening in 1982, "I was experimenting with inventions that used water instead of freon as a refrigeration fluid. As I was shooting water through a high-pressure nozzle in the bathtub, I thought "Wow, this would make a neat water pistol."

He built a prototype squirt gun out of PVC pipe, plexiglass, and a plastic soda bottle. Then he approached several toy companies…but none of them thought a squirt gun with a 50-foot range would sell. Johnson even looked into manufacturing the toys himself, but couldn't afford the $200,000 molding cost.

BREAKTHROUGH

In March 1989, he went to the International Toy Fair in New York and tried to sell his invention again. This time, the Larami Corporation was interested. They arranged a meeting with Johnson at their headquarters in Philadelphia. When everyone was seated, Johnson opened his suitcase, whipped out his prototype, and shot a burst of water across the entire room. Larami bought the gun on the spot. Within a year, the "Super Soaker" was the bestselling squirt gun in history.

We're outnumbered: 7,000 new insect species are discovered every year.

FAMOUS
FOR 15 MINUTES

Here it is again—our feature based on Andy Warhol's prophetic comment that "in the future, everyone will be famous for 15 minutes." Here's how a few people are using up their allotted quarter-hour.

THE STAR: Mr. Twister the Clown
THE HEADLINE: *Clown's Coins Create Controversy*
WHAT HAPPENED: Cory McDonald made his living as the balloon-sculpting Mr. Twister, performing at fairs and birthday parties. For six years, he also enjoyed wandering the streets of Santa Cruz, California, putting quarters in expired parking meters. One day in 1995, a frustrated meter maid handed him a citation; she'd found out that a local law prohibited "good Samaritans" from feeding other people's meters. McDonald was outraged. A lawyer agreed to take his case "pro-Bozo," and together they waged a publicity campaign to embarrass the city and change the law.
THE AFTERMATH: It worked. Newspapers all over the U.S. picked up the story, and Mr. Twister became the symbolic victim of all bad laws and frivolous prosecutions in America. Anti-government editorials referred scathingly to the Santa Cruz city government. Finally, Santa Cruz city council members—eager to put the matter to rest—donned big red clown noses at a council meeting and repealed the ordinance. Mr. Twister expressed his appreciation by twisting balloon animals for them.

THE STAR: Lya Graf, a 20-year-old circus midget
THE HEADLINE: *Millionaire Mogul Meets Midget & Mellows*
WHAT HAPPENED: J. P. Morgan—one of the world's most feared robber barons—was in the Senate Caucus Room on June 1, 1933, waiting to testify before the Senate Banking and Currency Committee. Suddenly a publicity man for the Ringling Brothers Barnum & Bailey Circus popped a midget onto his lap. At that instant, a newspaper photographer who was in on the stunt snapped a picture. The whole room froze; Morgan was not known for his sense of humor…and didn't like physical contact. But to

---

No matter how cold it gets, gasoline won't freeze. Below-180 degrees F, it just turns gummy.

everyone's surprise, he smiled and chatted with her. The next day, the photo and Lya Graf were famous all over the world.

THE AFTERMATH: The photograph changed public perception of the robber barons. As John Brooks writes in *American Heritage* magazine:

> Morgan, and even Wall Street as a whole, profited adventitiously from the encounter. From that day forward until his death a decade later, he was in the public mind no longer a grasping devil whose greed and ruthlessness had helped bring the nation to near ruin, but rather a benign old dodderer. The change in attitude was instantaneous and Morgan took advantage of it.

Lya Graf wasn't so lucky. "She was shy and sensitive," writes Brooks, and though she could tolerate employment as an "ordinary circus freak," she couldn't stand being a "celebrity freak."

> Two years later, hounded by fame, she left the United States and returned to her native Germany. She was half Jewish. In 1937 she was arrested as a "useless person" and in 1941 was shipped to Auschwitz, never to be heard from again.

THE STAR: Alvin Straight, a 73-year-old farmer
THE HEADLINE: *A Lawn Day's Journey: Laurens Man Mows Path to Fame*
WHAT HAPPENED: In the spring of 1994, Alvin Straight found out that his 80-year-old brother, Henry, had had a stroke. He hadn't seen Henry in seven years, and decided he'd better go see him "while I had the chance." The only problem: Alvin lived in Laurens, Iowa…and Henry lived 240 miles away in Mt. Zion, Wisconsin. Alvin didn't have a driver's license, didn't want anyone else to drive him, and wouldn't take public transportation. So he hitched a 10-foot trailer to his lawn tractor and started driving the back roads at 5 mph. It took him six weeks, and by the time he got to Mt. Zion, he was so sore "I could barely make it with two canes." CNN broadcast the story, and Alvin was an instant celebrity.

THE AFTERMATH: He was bombarded with offers to appear on talk shows—Letterman, Leno, etc.—but he wouldn't go, because he refused to fly or take the train to either coast. He did sign a contract to make a TV movie of his life, but nothing ever came of it.

THE STAR: George Holliday, general manager of an L.A. plumbing company.

THE HEADLINE: *Camcorder Creates King Controversy*

WHAT HAPPENED: George Holliday gave his first wife a camcorder for Valentine's Day. He was playing with it on the evening of March 2, trying to figure out how it worked…so when sirens awoke him early the next morning, he instinctively grabbed for it. He pulled on some pants and stood shivering on his balcony, filming while some L.A. cops beat the hell out of a man named Rodney King. The next day, he took the tape to a local TV station and for $500, let them broadcast it. The broadcast was fed to CNN and in hours, the whole world knew about it. In a few days, Holliday was famous. Camera crews were at his door, and major news publications were interviewing him.

THE AFTERMATH: Holliday had lots of offers to cash in on his celebrity: a film company wanted to make The George Holliday Life Story, a producer talked about The George Holliday TV Show, a company wanted him to endorse a George Holliday "crimebuster" toy. All but a $39.95 video called Shoot News and Make Money with Your Camcorder fell through. He filed a $100 million lawsuit against the TV stations that had aired his film clip without his permission, but lost. By the time he met his second wife a few years later, says one report, "his notoriety had waned to the point where he had to tell her who he was."

THE STAR. Fred and Selena Payton, owners of a carpet and upholstery cleaning service in Rockville, Maryland

THE HEADLINE: *Selena and Fred are Giving It Up for Arsenio*

WHAT HAPPENED: In July 1993, Arsenio Hall—looking for a ratings boost for his TV show—announced that he would host one show at a viewer's house. He picked the Paytons. For some reason, this was national news—and the Paytons, now famous for 15 minutes…for being famous for 15 minutes…were interviewed by all the major news organizations.

THE AFTERMATH: The night went off without a hitch, as 1,200 people from the neighborhood hung out with the Paytons and watched Patti LaBelle and Bobcat Goldthwait entertain. Then the Paytons' 15 minutes were up. Hall's show went off the air soon afterward.

The term "rookie" comes from the Civil War slang "reckie," which was short for "recruit."

A MUSICAL IS BORN

Some musicals are so famous that they are familiar even to people who never go to plays. Here are the origins of some favorites.

SHOWBOAT (1927)

Oscar Hammerstein, Jerome Kern, and producer Florenz Ziegfield were sick of the light, upbeat musicals that had made them famous. They wanted to do something with adult themes like alcoholism, interracial relationships, and marital troubles—even if no one came to see it. But they needn't have worried. Their adaptation of Edna Ferber's novel about life on a riverboat opened in 1927 to rave reviews and sold out so often that Ziegfield considered staging a second production in a nearby theater to handle the overflow. So far the show has had five Broadway revivals, more than any other play in history.

OKLAHOMA! (1943)

Based on a play called *Green Grow the Lilacs*, which had a limited run in the 1930-1931 Broadway season. A woman who'd helped produce it thought it would make a good musical and approached composer Richard Rodgers with the idea. He was interested, but his partner Lorenzo Hart—who'd become an unreliable alcoholic—wasn't. Rodgers's solution: he teamed up with lyricist Oscar Hammerstein...who hadn't had a hit in years and was considered a has-been. Together they wrote a musical called *Away We Go!* When it got to Broadway, it was renamed *Oklahoma!* and played to sellout crowds. It established Rodgers and Hammerstein as a team.

MAN OF LA MANCHA (1965)

In the late 1950s, a TV/film writer named Dale Wasserman went to Madrid to do research for a movie. The local press mistakenly reported that he was there to write a play about Don Quixote—which sparked his curiosity. Wasserman became so interested in Quixote and author Miguel Cervantes that he traveled all over Spain, retracing their steps. This in turn, inspired him to write a TV drama called *I, Don Quixote*, which aired on CBS in 1959. He expanded it into *Man of La Mancha* in the early 1960s.

GREASE (1972)

Originally a five-hour rock 'n' roll musical written by two amateur actor-writers for a Chicago community theater. A producer bought the rights and had it trimmed by more than half before taking it to New York. Interesting sidelight: George Lucas's film, *American Graffiti,* is usually credited with starting the 1950s nostalgia boom, but this play opened off-Broadway on Feb. 14, 1972—a year before *American Graffiti* premiered. It ran for 3,388 performances, and the 1978 film version was the #1 box-office film of the year.

ANNIE (1977)

Lyricist Martin Charnin was browsing in a bookstore, doing some last-minute Christmas shopping, when he saw a book called *Arf: The Life and Hard Times of Little Orphan Annie.* He bought it for a friend and intended to wrap it and give it away. Instead, he stayed up that night reading it...and decided to turn it into a musical. Ironically, although the musical was a smash, the movie it inspired in 1982 was such a huge disaster that it even caused the play's ticket sales to plummet...and ultimately forced it to close in 1983.

CATS (1982)

When T.S. Eliot first wrote *Old Possum's Book of Practical Cats,* a children's book of verses, he only circulated it to his friends; it wasn't published until years later. The same thing happened when Andrew Lloyd Webber, a fan of the book, put some of the poems to music. At first, he only entertained friends with them. Eventually he decided to turn them into a short, one-act musical...then changed his mind and began working on a full-length performance. *Cats* is now the longest-running musical in Broadway history, earning more than $100 million since it opened.

LES MISERABLES (1987)

French playwright Alain Boubil got the idea after seeing *Jesus Christ Superstar* on Broadway: he figured that if pop-rock music could be used to tell the story of Jesus, why not tell the story of the French Revolution? Boubil wasn't sure how to do it...until he saw *Oliver!,* adapted from the Charles Dickens novel *Oliver Twist.* He decided to adapt a classic novel from the period...and settled on Victor Hugo's novel *Les Miserables.*

Every US president with a beard has been a Republican.

PUBLIC PROPOSALS

Asking someone to marry you used to be a solemn, private matter. No longer. Now it's a public event, complete with trumpeters, billboards, and an audience—ranging from a few passersby to hundreds of thousands of TV viewers. (Incidentally, the answers to these proposals were all "yes"!)

D**AN CAPLIS**
Proposed: On television
Story: Caplis and Aimee Sporer worked for Channel 4 news in Denver—he was the legal expert, she was the anchorwoman. One night they were sitting next to each other during a broadcast. After explaining how judges decide on criminal sentences, Caplis looked at the camera and told the audience that since they were like family, he wanted to share an important moment with them. He took a ring out of his pocket and put it in front of Sporer. Choked up, she said, "I would love to marry you," then turned away from the camera. The quick-thinking cameraman cut for a commercial break.

LOU DROESCH
Proposed: At a city council meeting
Story: Pam Ferris, the city clerk of Louisville, Colorado, was taking notes at the council meeting when Droesch, a local mortgage banker, went up to the microphone to voice his opinion about an issue. It wasn't the issue anyone expected. He said: "I'm crazy about your city clerk. And I ask that the city fathers approve my asking for her hand in marriage." Then he got down on one knee and popped the question.

NEIL NATHANSON
Proposed: In a crossword puzzle
Story: Neil and his girlfriend, Leslie Hamilton, liked doing the San Francisco Examiner crossword puzzles together. "One Sunday," writes Michael Kernan in *Smithsonian* magazine, "Leslie noticed that many of the puzzle answers struck close to home."

"State or quarterback" turned out to be MONTANA, which is where she came from. "Instrument" was CELLO, which she

---

Jimmy Hoffa's middle name is, appropriately, Riddle.

plays. "I was about halfway through the puzzle," she remembers, "when I figured out that a string of letters running across the middle of the puzzle said 'DEAR—WILL YOU MARRY ME NEIL.'...Sure enough, it was Leslie."

Neil, it turns out, had been working with Merl Reagle, the *Examiner's* puzzlemaker, for four months. They invited him to the wedding. "I never did finish the puzzle," Leslie added.

JIM BEDERKA
Proposed: During a college graduation ceremony
Story: Paige Griffin was sitting with her class, ready to graduate from Ramapo College in Mahwah, New Jersey, when her boyfriend Jim showed up and asked her to leave the group for a minute. She said no—she didn't want to cause a disturbance. He kept insisting, getting more and more aggravated. Finally she gave in. As she stepped into the aisle, she saw two trumpeters decked in medieval garb standing at the stage. Between them: a sign reading "Paige, will you marry me?" When she accepted, the trumpeters held up a "She said yes" sign; 1,500 people applauded.

MARK STEINS
Proposed: At an AIDS benefit
Story: Leanza Cornett, 1933's Miss America, paused during her performance at the 1994 AIDS Mastery Benefit in Los Angeles to select a raffle winner. She stuck her hand in a bag, pulled out a piece of paper, and read: "Let's get married. Wanna? Check the appropriate response: Yes or Yes." She thought it was a joke...until she realized there was a ring attached.

BOB BORNACK
Proposed: On a billboard
Story: In the Chicago suburb of Wood Dale, Bornack put up a billboard that read: "Teri, Please Marry Me! Love, Bob." The sign company immediately got 10 calls from women named Teri who wanted to know if it was "their" Bob. "One Teri called in a total panic because she's dating two Bobs," said an employee. "She didn't know which one to answer." (It wasn't either of them.)

Cleopatra wasn't Egyptian; she was Greek. And she was the seventh queen by that name.

THE "ODD ELVIS" QUIZ

Elvis is one of the greatest rock singers of all time...as well as one of the most unusual people ever to walk the earth. Here's a little quiz based on some of the stranger recollections of his friends and associates. See if you are on the same wavelength as the King. Answers on page 761.

1. Elvis' friends learned not to show pain around him Why not?
a) He hated weaklings.
b) He'd burst out crying if a friend was hurt, and wouldn't stop blubbering for hours.
c) He thought he had the power to "cure the sick." They'd have to sit there while he "laid hands" on them...then pretend he'd cured them.

2. The King was a big eater. Take breakfast, for example: Elvis usually ate a pound of bacon, six scrambled eggs, "a platter of buttersoaked biscuits with sausage," and pots of black coffee to wash it all down. Occasionally, though, Elvis experimented with new diets—like the time he developed an interest in vegetarianism. "Because the spiritual teachings say that you have to eat right," Elvis told friends over dinner one evening in 1973, "I'll be eating a lot of vegetables now, a lot of salads, and raw fruits. I'm telling the maids, and that's what they're going to make for me." How long did Elvis's vegetarian phase last?
a) Two hours.
b) Two days.
c) Two months.

3. Elvis liked TV, but he hated the show *The Streets of San Francisco*. "We made damn sure that *The Streets of San Francisco* was never on when Elvis was around," his bodyguard once said. "I promise you, Elvis was very likely to blow a television set out with his gun if it had come on the screen." It wasn't because the plots were dull, or because the acting was bad. What was the reason?
a) He didn't like the size of Karl Malden's nose.
b) He didn't like the sponsor.
c) He didn't like the character's name.

4. Elvis hated dieting and exercise and often asked his doctor, George Nickopoulos, about other methods of losing weight. One night, "Dr. Nick" mentioned the possibility of an intestinal bypass or "shunt" that would cause food to pass through the King's body before it was completely digested. What was Elvis' reaction?
a) He said he wanted the operation that night.
b) He was so grossed out that he threw up.
c) He said he didn't want the operation himself, but wanted to watch Dr. Nick perform it on someone else "for scientific reasons."

5. In 1961, a friend of Elvis' on the Memphis police force died. What odd request did Elvis have?
a) He wanted to sing "Hound Dog" as they lowered the coffin into the grave.
b) He wanted to watch the mortician embalm his friend.
c) He wanted to prop his friend's body up in a police car and drive around Memphis with the sirens and lights on.

6. Elvis once met country singer Jimmy Dean. How did he greet him?
a) He pulled out a gun and stuck it up against his head.
b) He complained that he didn't look "anything like your cousin, James Dean."
c) He started running around, snorting and mooing.

7. Being asked to perform for the president in the White House is one of the biggest honors a musician can receive. Elvis was once asked to play at a party thrown by President Richard Nixon. It didn't work out because...
a) They insisted Elvis wear a business suit while he performed.
b) His manager snorted, "Elvis doesn't play for free."
c) Conservatives threatened to boycott the event if Elvis showed up.

8. Elvis is the only person we've ever heard of who actually died while reading in the bathroom. What was he reading?
a) A book about Nostradamus.
b) A book about the Shroud of Turin.
c) *Uncle John's Bathroom Reader.*

First President to wear long pants instead of breeches: James Madison (1809-1817).

FAMOUS LAST WORDS

It's never too early to get yours ready.

"Don't let it end like this. Tell them I said something."
—**Pancho Villa**

"I'd rather be fishing."
—**Jimmy Gass,** *murderer*

"O.K. I won't."
—**Elvis Presley,** *responding to his girlfriend's request that he not fall asleep in the bathroom*

"It's very beautiful over there."
—**Thomas A. Edison**

"Why not? Why not?"
—**Timothy Leary**

"Make my skin into drumheads for the Bohemian cause."
—**John Ziska, Czech rebel**

"I've never forgiven that smart-alecky reporter who named me 'Butterfingers'."
—**Thomas Moran,** *pickpocket*

"I'm tired of fighting. I guess this is going to get me."
—**Harry Houdini**

"Remember me to my friends, tell them I'm a hell of a mess."
—**H. L. Mencken,** *essayist*

"Monsieur, I beg your pardon."
—**Marie Antoinette,** *to her executioner, after stepping on his foot accidentally*

"Dying is a very dull affair. My advice to you is to have nothing whatever to do with it."
—*Author* **Somerset Maugham**

"But, but, Mister Colonel—"
—**Benito Mussolini,** *executed 1945*

"This isn't the worst. The worst is that they stole twenty-five years of my life."
—*Director* **Erich von Stroheim's** *last words to Hollywood*

"I'm not afraid to die, Honey…I know the Lord has his arms wrapped around this big fat sparrow."
—*Blues singer* **Ethel Waters**

"I am about to, or, I am going to die. Either expression is used."
—**Dominique Bouhours,** *grammarian*

"Never felt better."
—**Douglas Fairbanks, Sr.**

If you're an average American, you spend 4-6 hours a day watching TV.

GROUCHO GETS ELECTED, ACT I

Here's a script from a recently rediscovered radio show featuring Groucho and Chico Marx. Close your ears and listen with your eyes as you enjoy an episode of Five Star Theater, *performed on March 13, 1933.*

SCENE: *The office of Beagle, Shyster & Beagle, Attorneys at Law. Miss Dimple, the receptionist, is typing. Judge Maxwell, a local politician, is waiting for Waldo T. Flywheel, attorney, to arrive. Ravelli (Chico Marx), Flywheel's assistant, is sleeping in the corner.*

The door opens.

MISS DIMPLE: Good morning, Mr. Flywheel.

GROUCHO: Can't you think of anything else to say? You say that to me every morning.

JUDGE: (Stepping forward) Oh, Mr. Flywheel, you remember me, Judge Maxwell. I've been planning for a long time to drop in and talk to you about the coming election.

GROUCHO (impatiently): I know. I know.

JUDGE: (Surprised): Really? How did you know?

GROUCHO: Why, you just told me.

JUDGE: Mr. Flywheel, my re-election is being bitterly fought by a group of crooked politicians. Their leader is Big Boss Plunkett, who is

going to be tried for bribery shortly after the election. He doesn't want me on the bench because he knows I can't be tampered with.

GROUCHO (indignantly): See here, Judge Maxwell. Did you come here to buy my vote?

JUDGE: Why, no, of course not.

GROUCHO: Then you're wasting my time...and my time is valuable. Do you realize that while you're here talking nonsense, I could be at my desk, sleeping?

JUDGE: You don't understand, Mr. Flywheel. I am here to enlist your support in my campaign.

RAVELLI (waking up): Attsa fine. I take two bottles.

JUDGE: Two bottles of what?

RAVELLI: Two bottles of campaign. (Laugh) Attsa some joke!

JUDGE (Indignant): Gentlemen! From your attitude I can only conclude that you are in sympathy with Boss Plunkett and his crooked politics. I'm going. Good day.

Door slams.

When asked what they feel most guilty about, 34% of Americans say "nothing in particular."

GROUCHO: Ravelli, I'm ashamed of you. I saw you taking your hand out of Judge Maxwell's pocket.

RAVELLI: Well, I had to take it out sometime.

Knock, door opens.

MISS DIMPLE: Why, it's Boss Plunkett, the politician!

GROUCHO: Ravelli, take Plunkett's hat.

CHICO: You take it, boss. It won't fit me.

PLUNKETT: Flywheel, my pal. Joe Crookley tells me that if it hadn't been for the way you defended him in court, he would have gone to prison for 20 years. He says you're a pretty smart lawyer.

GROUCHO (Coyly): Oh! I don't take his flattery seriously. That Joe Crookley is just a silly old cutthroat.

PLUNKETT: Listen, Flywheel, I want to talk turkey to you.

GROUCHO (Whispering): I think you'd better talk English. I don't want Ravelli to understand.

PLUNKETT: Look here, I'm against Judge Maxwell. If you join our party, I'll see to it that you get the nomination for judge.

GROUCHO: Plunkett, I'm willing to accept the nomination, but I can't join your party.

PLUNKETT: Why not?

GROUCHO: Frankly, I haven't a thing to wear.

Does Groucho get the nomination? Find out in Act II, page 627.

*   *   *

BIG NUMBERS: A TRILLION

Trillions are the numbers we use to express the national debt. But few of us have a sense of how big they are. Tim Gutmann, a New Hampshire mathematician, came up with a way of getting proper perspective. He asks: "Where were you one trillion seconds ago?"

His answer: "One trillion seconds is over thirty one thousand six hundred and eighty-eight years. That's 31,688 years. Lots and lots longer than recorded history; indeed, writing was developed in Sumeria only 252 billion (not trillion) seconds ago. Humans were around, but they hadn't been for long. Lucy (*Australopithecus afarensis*—the oldest known human descendent) walked the earth around 110 trillion seconds ago."

First President to greet people with a handshake: Thomas Jefferson. Earlier presidents bowed.

OOPS!

Everyone's amused by tales of outrageous blunders—probably because it's comforting to know that someone's screwing up even worse than we are. So here's an ego-building page from the BRI. Go ahead and feel superior for a few minutes.

LEFT OUT

In 1994, Susan Leury was commissioned to create a 9-foot, 800-lb. bronze statue of native son Babe Ruth for the new baseball stadium in Baltimore. "During the many months of modeling and molding…Leury met countless experts and aficionados. Details were researched and debated. Did the Babe wear his belt buckle on the left or right? Was his hat cocked to the side or worn straight? No fact was too small to escape scrutiny. Except one.

"The bronze Babe, unveiled at the northern Eutaw Street entrance of Oriole Park, is leaning on a bat and clutching on his hip a right-handed fielder's glove. The real Babe was a lefty."

—from *Parade* magazine, 1/1/96

BOMBS AWAY!

"In 1994, the Northwest Herald of Crystal Lake, Illinois, ran a story about the controversy surrounding the Smithsonian Institution's exhibit of the Enola Gay, the B-29 Superfortress that dropped the atomic bomb on Hiroshima in 1945.

"Apparently, the crack journalist who wrote the headline either failed to read the story, or had forgotten how World War II ended.

"The headline read: 'Atomic Bombers Criticize Enola Homosexual Exhibit.' 'It was a stupid thing on deadline,' the editor said. 'I'm not discussing it anymore.'"

—from the *San Francisco Chronicle*, 10/23/94

ASHES TO ASHES

"In 1990 the Wilkinsons, a family in Sussex, England received what they thought was a gift package of herbs from Australian relatives. They stirred the contents into a traditional Christmas pudding, ate half of it and put the remainder in the refrigerator.

Napoleon Bonaparte, a Frenchman, designed the flag of Italy.

"Soon thereafter, a member of the family relates, 'We heard from Auntie Sheila that Uncle Eric had died, and had we received his ashes for burial in Britain.'

"Shocked, the Wilkinsons quickly summoned a vicar to bless, and bury, Uncle Eric's leftovers."

—from the *Wall Street Journal,* 12/18/90

A STIFF DRINK

"Coca-Cola is fixing an embarrassing typo in the word 'disk' in copyright information on about 2 million 12-packs of the drink.

"In the misprint, the 's' is replaced by a 'c.' The error appeared on boxes of Olympic promotional packages of Coca-Cola Classic distributed in the Atlanta area.

"Normally, the small type under the copyright information states that the 'red disk icon and contour bottle are trademarks of the Coca-Cola Co.' 'Everybody recognizes that it was an innocent mistake,' said a company spokesman, who wouldn't say how the error occurred. 'It's obviously a misprint.' "

—from wire service stories, 7/96

OOPS—WRONG AIRPORT

"Edward Valiz and Jose Gonzales were headed for the tiny Turlock, California airport, but when they emerged from their rented plane, they discovered instead that they'd landed at Castle Air Force Base…in the middle of a training exercise.

"Base officials said they had tried to warn off the plane, but never got any radio response.

"The pair were arrested when drug-sniffing police dogs found two pounds of methamphetamine, along with $1,300 in cash."

—from the *San Francisco Examiner,* 1994

WHICH PARTS?

"People calling an 800-number for Sears, Roebuck and Co. listed in the local phone directory were offered, instead, the chance to listen to 'the kinkiest group orgy line in America.'

"Apparently, a phone company clerk mistyped the number. 'I was amazed and shocked at first,' said one caller. 'After a few seconds, it seemed pretty funny. I mean, what a message to get when you're trying to reach a parts department.'"

—from wire service stories, 8/96

FABULOUS FLOPS

*Some consumer products are popular the moment they hit
the market, while others never get off the ground.
Their only legacy is a few bathroom laughs.*

Cheese-Filtered Cigarettes. In 1963, a Wisconsin businessman looking for new ways to use local cheese had a brainstorm: If smoke can be used to flavor cheese, why can't
cheese be used to flavor smokes? According to the Wall Street
Journal, Univ. of Wisconsin chemists found that Parmesan and
Romano were the best filter cheeses, using "a combination of one-
third charcoal and two-thirds cheese." The cigarette industry
didn't bite.

Grubbies Sneakers. You've heard of pre-washed jeans. In 1966,
B.F. Goodrich came up with a similar idea: "pre-tattered" sneakers.
You didn't have to wait months for your sneakers to look beat-up.
With Grubbies, all you added was the foot odor.

Indoor Archery. In the early '60s, bowling was one of America's
hottest sports. Hoping to "do for archery what automatic pinset-
ters have done for bowling," a number of entrepreneurs opened
"archery lanes," with automatic arrow-returns. They expected to
have thousands around the United States by 1970.

Look of Buttermilk/Touch of Buttermilk Shampoo. A 1970s
"health product." Were you supposed to eat it or wash with it? Did
you want to wash with it? Rubbing dairy products into their hair
didn't exactly conjure up images of cleanliness in the minds of
most consumers. "Touch of Yogurt Shampoo" also flopped.

Plastic Snow. Before snowmaking machines, how did ski resorts
keep people skiing during dry spells? In the mid-'60s, plastics
seemed like the answer. One resort spread tons of Styrofoam
pellets on their ski runs; they quickly blew away. Another
company offered mats with nylon bristles, like Astroturf, and New
Jersey's Great Gorge ski area laid them out on its slopes. They
worked well...unless you fell down. "The bristles were needle-
sharp and everybody tore his pants," founder Jack Kurlander told
reporters, "There was blood, blood, blood. Boy were we embarrassed!"

Medical studies show that intelligent people have more copper and zinc in their hair.

FLUBBED HEADLINES

These are 100% honest-to goodness headlines. Can you figure out what they were trying to say?

Man Robs, Then Kills Himself

KHRUSHCHEV IS BURIED IN ENCYCLOPEDIA

Carter Plans Swell Deficit

LIVING TOGETHER LINKED TO DIVORCE

MAYOR SAYS D.C. IS SAFE EXCEPT FOR MURDERS

Town Okays Animal Rule

Deer Kill 130,000

BOYS CAUSE AS MANY PREGNANCIES AS GIRLS

Prostitutes Appeal to Pope

DEADLINE PASSES FOR STRIKING POLICE

Stiff Opposition Expected to Casketless Funeral Plan

DRUNK GETS NINE MONTHS IN VIOLIN CASE

Bar Trying to Help Alcoholic Lawyers

Criminal Groups Infiltrating Pot Farms

Teenage Prostitution Problem Is Mounting

Delegate sex switch dvocated

DEAD EXPECTED TO RISE

LEGALIZED OUTHOUSES AIRED BY LEGISLLATURE

Lot of Women Distressing

"Dead" Woman Doesn't Recall What Happened

Blind workers eye better wages

SUN SUED IN PUERTO RICO BY CONSERVATION TRUST

Milk Drinkers Turn to Powder

U.S., China Near Pact on Wider Ties

TWO CONVICTS EVADE NOOSE; JURY HUNG

MRS. COLLINS BURNED AT DUMP

Hospitals Are Sued by 7 Foot Doctors

Farmer Bill Dies In House

JUMPING BEAN PRICES AFFECT POOR

LAWMEN FROM MEXICO BARBEQUE GUESTS

Columnist gets urologist in trouble with his peers

Antique Stripper to Demonstrate Wares at Store

When you correct for the weight difference, men are proportionately stronger than horses.

THE BIRTH OF RAMBO

*Who created Rambo? If you said Sylvester Stallone, you're
wrong—it was a mild-mannered Canadian college
professor teaching at the University of Iowa.*

Young David Morrell could not tolerate conflict of any kind.
Whenever violence appeared on TV, he had to leave the
room. Until his early teens, even news reports panicked
him; he was convinced someone would suddenly announce that a
new war had begun. As he got older, Morrell found that writing
was a way to get over some of his fears.

AN IDEA IS BORN

In 1969, while studying American literature at Penn State
University, Morrell saw a TV news program that sparked his imagination and changed his life. The first report of the evening
showed soldiers sweating out a battle in Vietnam. The second was
about National Guardsmen dodging rocks, bottles, and bullets
trying to put down urban riots.

If a viewer turned the sound off, he mused, it would seem that
both film clips were a part of the same story. That gave him an
idea for a tale in which the Vietnam war literally came home to
America. He imagined a disaffected Vietnam veteran returning,
disturbed and embittered by his Vietnam experiences, wandering
aimlessly around the backroads of the country.

THE PLOT THICKENS

Another news story provided further inspiration. "In a Southwest-
ern American town," Morrell recalled, "a group of hitchhiking
hippies had been picked up by the local police, stripped, hosed,
and shaved. I wondered what my character's reaction would be if
he were subjected to the insults those hippies had received."

Morrell decided his character would probably go nuts. He
began writing a novel about a longhaired Vietnam vet who's
driven over the edge when he's arrested and abused by a small-
town Kentucky sheriff.

The character still didn't have a name. But that changed one
afternoon when—an hour after Morrell had read a poem by

Strange stat: More boys than girls are born during the day; more girls are born at night.

Arthur Rimbaud (pronounced "Rambo") for his French class—his wife returned from the supermarket with a type of apple she'd never heard of before…the Rambo.

Morrell rushed to his typewriter and typed: "His name was Rambo, and he was just some nothing kid, for all anybody knew, standing by the pump of a gas station on the outskirts of Madison, Kentucky."

FIRST BLOOD

It took years to complete *First Blood*. Morrell finally finished it in 1971, while he was a professor at the University of Iowa. Although the book was intended to be an antiwar novel, it was extremely violent. By the end of the book, the Kentucky town is destroyed, the sherriff is killed along with 200 National Guardsmen, and Rambo is executed by his former instructor, who blows the top of his head off with a shotgun.

That summer Morrell sent the manuscript to a literary agent. He was so unsure of how people would react to it—Was it too bloody? Too violent?—that he included his Ph.D. dissertation in the package, too. That way, he figured, the agent would still have something respectable to sell if publishers hated the novel.

He needn't have worried. *First Blood* was sold in three weeks…and it was a huge success. *Time* magazine put it at the top of its book review page, observing that it was the first in a new genre of fiction— "carnography," the violence equivalent of pornography.

Columbia Pictures snapped up the movie rights for $90,000 and then sat on it for a year. They then sold it to another studio…which passed it on to someone else, and so on. Over the next ten years, 18 different screenplays based on *First Blood* were developed. Nearly every Hollywood tough guy—Clint Eastwood, Paul Newman, Robert De Niro, Nick Nolte, and even George C. Scott—was considered for the lead role and rejected.

"The novel became a Hollywood legend," Morrell says. "How could so much money and so much talent be expended on an enterprise that somehow could not get off the page?"

For part II of the Rambo story, turn to page 615.

The naked truth: People in nudist colonies play volleyball more often than any other sport.

NOT WHAT THEY SEEM TO BE

We take a lot of things for granted, based on image. But things (and people) often aren't what we think they are. Here are some examples.

AMERICAN GOTHIC

Image: Grant Wood's famous painting of an old Indiana couple posing in front of their farmhouse is considered the definitive portrait of the straitlaced Midwestern farmer.

Actually: They aren't farmers...or a couple. Wood's sister, Nan, was the model for the woman; a dentist friend named Byron McKeeby posed as the man. And the "farmhouse" in the picture was once used as a bordello.

WILLIAM ENO

Image: Considered the "Father of Traffic Safety." According to David Wallechinsky in *Significa*, he "originated stop signs, one-way streets, taxi stands, pedestrian safety islands, and traffic rotaries."

Actually: He never learned to drive. He thought cars were a passing fad. And he preferred horses anyway.

THE CHRISTMAS SONG.

Image: A classic of the Christmas season. With lyrics like "Chestnuts roasting on an open fire...Jack Frost nipping at your nose," it evokes the feeling of a cold December perfectly.

Actually: It was written during a summer heat wave in Los Angeles. According to one account: "Mel Torme and his lyricist...wrote it in less than an hour, while consuming cold drinks at the piano and putting ice to their foreheads."

THE BEACH BOYS

Image: The Kings of California Surfing. Led by Brian Wilson, who wrote and sang hits like "Surfin' Safari" and "Surfin' USA," they started a national surfing craze in the early 1960s.

Actually: Brian Wilson (and three other Beach Boys) never surfed. "I didn't really know anything about surfing at all," he

---

Vultures fly without flapping their wings.

admitted in 1995. In fact, says Stephen Gaines in his Beach Boy biography:

> Although the Beach Boys had sold an estimated 80 million records—20 million of them with surfing as a major theme—and Brian had splashed around in the water with his brothers for publicity photos, he had never mounted a surfboard... Indeed, photographing Brian in the surf was almost a cruel joke, because Brian had a deep, abiding fear of the water, and in his childlike manner he would warble in a thin voice, "The ocean scares me!"

Actually, the only Beach Boy who ever surfed was Brian's brother Dennis, the group's drummer, who drowned in 1983.

AIR JORDANS
Image: The first "air-cushioned" sneakers.
Actually: Nike tried air, and it didn't work—it leaked through the "airbag" material. They had to replace it with a gas that has larger molecules than air.

THE WEEKLY READER
Image: A benign weekly newspaper for elementary school kids.
Actually: Not so benign. In October 1994, the magazine ran an article "that discussed smokers' rights and the harm done to the tobacco industry by smoking restrictions. The article said nothing about smoking as a cause of lung cancer and heart disease." It turned out that the *Weekly Reader's* owners were also the largest shareholders in RJR Nabisco, makers of Camel cigarettes.

THE "BLACK BOX"
Image: Whenever an airplane goes down, the first thing investigators say there're looking for is the "black box" that contains a recording of all conversations in the cockpit.
Actually: It's a yellow box.

KARL MARX
Image: Enemy of American capitalism
Actually: Years after he had become famous as the author of the *Communist Manifesto*, he gratefully accepted a job as the London correspondent of the *New York Tribune*. His reason: His anticapitalist political writing hadn't earned him enough to live on.

THE GREENING OF AMERICA

Here's a fad you've probably never heard of—chlorophyll. Does it sound silly? Well, think of all the things popular today that are going to be just as laughable in 40 years.

THE GREEN STUFF

In the 1930s, Dr. Benjamin Gruskin found a way to make chlorophyll—the green stuff in plants that turns sunlight into chemical energy—soluble in water. This discovery interested scientists but didn't appear to have much practical use.

That didn't bother O'Neill Ryan, Jr., and Henry T. Stanton, two ad executives. They decided to get into the chlorophyll business and patented Gruskin's process. Then, they tried to get manufacturers to use chlorophyll in products as a breath freshener and odor killer—even though they had no proof (or reason to believe) it worked as either.

A GREENER AMERICA?

Somehow, in 1950, Ryan and Stanton managed to talk Pepsodent into coming out with a chlorophyll-based toothpaste called Chlorodent. Backed by Pepsodent's advertising muscle, it sold so well that other toothpaste companies rushed their own versions to market. By mid-1951, 30% of all toothpastes sold in the United States contained chlorophyll.

Other companies began adding chlorophyll to their products. By the end of 1952, stores were filled with chlorophyll soaps, cigarettes, dog foods, mothballs, toilet paper, diapers, shoe insoles, even popcorn. Chlorophyll beer, men's shorts, and Hebrew National chlorophyll-treated salami were in the works.

The End: In 1953, the American Dental Association and the FDA announced that chlorophyll did not cure bad breath—or any other odor. As the New York State Medical Society put it, "chlorophyll has certainly...swept the nation clean, not of odors, but of money." The public got the message. In less than a year, sales of chlorophyll-based products plunged from $120 million to $10 million—and most of them were pulled from the market.

Q: How fast does the average American adult read? A: About 150-200 words a minute.

STRANGE LAWSUITS

These days, it seems that people sue each other over practically anything.
Here are a few real-life examples of unusual legal battles.

THE PLAINTIFF: Robert Lee Brock, an inmate at the
Indian Creek Correctional Center in Chesapeake, Virginia
THE DEFENDANT: Robert Lee Brock, an inmate at the
Indian Creek Correctional Center in Chesapeake, Virginia
THE LAWSUIT: Brock (serving 23 years for grand larceny) sued
himself "for getting drunk and violating his civil rights." In a
handwritten brief, he said: "I partook of alcoholic beverages in
1993. As a result I caused myself to violate my religious beliefs.
This was done by my going out and getting arrested." Since Brock
is imprisoned and can't work, he asked the state of Virginia to pay
him and his family $5 million.
THE VERDICT: The judge acknowledged Brock's "innovative
approach to civil rights litigation," then dismissed it as "ludi-
crous."

THE PLAINTIFF: Gloria Quinan, owner of Banner Travel in
Santa Rosa, California
THE DEFENDANT: Pacific Bell
THE LAWSUIT: Pac Bell made a slight error when they listed
Quinan's travel agency in their 1988 "Smart" Yellow Pages. Her ad
was supposed to say she specialized in "exotic" travel; they
changed it to "erotic" travel. Quinan's business dropped off by
more than 50 percent, and most of the calls she did get were "from
people genuinely interested in erotic services." Pac Bell said they
wouldn't charge Quinan for the ad. She preferred to sue for $10
million.
THE VERDICT: Settled quietly out of court.

THE PLAINTIFF: Thomas Zarcone, food truck operator
THE DEFENDANT: William M. Perry, A Suffolk County, New
York, judge
THE LAWSUIT: On April 30, 1975, Judge Perry was presiding
over night court in Hauppage, New York. He sent a deputy sheriff
out to buy coffee from Zarcone, who ran a food truck outside the

---

At their closest point, the Russian and U.S. borders are less than two miles apart.

courthouse. Fifteen minutes later, the deputy sheriff returned with three police officers. "He told me that Judge Perry wanted to see me about the coffee, because it was terrible," Zarcone recounted. "I said, 'You must be joking.' " They weren't. At the judge's orders, they handcuffed him and hauled him into the courthouse while bystanders gawked. "People were saying, 'Look, they're locking up the frankfurter man,' " Zarcone told a reporter. He was taken to Perry's chambers, where the judge screamed that his coffee was "garbage" and insisted it had been watered down. Zarcone sued the state.

THE VERDICT: Zarcone was awarded an unspecified amount for damages. Perry was removed from the bench for lying to the appellate court about the incident.

THE PLAINTIFF: Bob Glaser, a San Diego attorney
THE DEFENDANT: City of San Diego
THE LAWSUIT: In 1995, Glaser attended a Billy Joel / Elton John concert. He had to pee, and while he was in the men's room, women started using it because the lines for the women's room were so long. Glaser, "angered when a woman used a urinal in front of him," sued for $5.4 million for "embarrassment and emotional trauma."
THE VERDICT: Still pending.

THE PLAINTIFF: Rhonda Cook
THE DEFENDANTS: Des Moines Chrysler-Plymouth and Fred Owens, an ex-employee
THE LAWSUIT: In 1995, Cook stopped at the Iowa care dealership to look at a new Chrysler Concorde. Salesman Fred Owens convinced her to climb into the trunk "to check out its spaciousness." Then he slammed the trunk shut and bounced the car a few times. Cook claimed emotional distress and false imprisonment, and sued for unspecified damages. She pointed out that the sales manager had previously offered $100 to anyone who could get a customer to climb in the trunk.
THE VERDICT: Still pending.

MISS AMERICA, PART I: The Origin

There she is…on TV, in the newspapers on cereal boxes. It's Miss America. You may think of it as an institution, but for all its pomp and pretension today, the Miss America Pageant started off as just a crass little money-making gimmick. See for yourself. This story may surprise you.

SUMMER'S TALE

H. Conrad Eckholm was the owner of Atlantic City's Monticello Hotel in the 1920s. The hotel made a lot of money during the summer, but business always dropped off drastically after the Labor Day weekend.

Eckholm figured that a festival of some sort, held at the end of September, might keep families at the beach a week or two longer. He pitched the idea to the Atlantic City Business Men's League, and they agreed to sponsor the "Fall Frolic" of 1920, which featured a masquerade ball and a "Rolling Chair Parade."

PUBLICITY STUNT

The Frolic was a success; the Business Men's League decided to sponsor a second one in 1921. This time, however, an Atlantic City newspaperman named Harry Finley suggested adding a new event to the schedule: a "popularity contest" for young women.

His idea was to have several Northeastern newspapers select young women to represent their cities. They'd be picked from photographs sent in by readers, and would compete against each other in Atlantic City to see who was the most popular of all.

Everyone would benefit from the contest: the newspapers would sell more papers, and Atlantic City hoteliers would get free publicity…which would draw paying customers to the boardwalk. So the Atlantic City Chamber of Commerce and the Hotelmen's Association got behind it. They agreed to add the event to the 1921 Fall Frolic.

CHOOSING A NAME

What would the popularity contest be called? At the first organizing committee meeting in 1921, someone suggested "Miss

Mel Brooks fought in the Battle of the Bulge in World War II.

America." But the rest of the committee thought that sounded weak. They insisted on "The most Beautiful Bathing Beauty in America" instead. (Winning contestants did assume the title "Miss America" as early as 1925, but the pageant itself didn't officially take the name until 1941.)

JUST IN CASE

Perhaps to guarantee that at least some genuine beauties would show up, organizers divided the Beauty category into two groups. The "professional" division was open to "actresses, motion picture players, or professional swimmers"; the "amateur" division was composed of the newspaper nominees and any other nonprofessionals who wanted to enter.

The winners from each category would face off against one another for the grand prize, a mermaid statue "valued at $5,000"…but actually only worth about $50.

THE FIRST PAGEANT

No one remembers how many "professionals" competed that first year, but Miss America Pageant records show that newspapers from only eight cities—Atlantic City, Camden (NJ), Newark, Ocean City (NJ), Harrisburg (PA), Pittsburgh, Philadelphia, and Washington, D.C.—nominated contestants.

Of these, only seven actually competed for the title: Miss Atlantic City, citing a potentially unfair hometown advantage, dropped out of the competition and assumed the role of hostess. For the next 40 years—the "Miss Atlantic City" contest was abolished in 1960—Miss Atlantic City hosted the Miss America Pageant, but did not actually compete.

LITTLE MISS WASHINGTON

One of the unintended consequences of letting anyone nominate a candidate for the newspaper competition was that some of the young ladies chosen didn't even know about the contest.

Margaret Gorman, a 15-year-old schoolgirl from Washington D.C., was playing marbles in the dirt with some friends when some reporters from the Washington Herald tracked her down and told her she'd just won the Miss Washington D.C. pageant.

Her parents had never heard of it and were a little apprehensive—but they weren't about to pass up a free trip to Atlantic

---

Future shock: 72% of Americans believe in heaven; 12% say they don't.

City. They agreed to play along. The decision was a good one: Gorman won the amateur division and went on to beat Virginia Lee, winner of the professional division, for the bathing-beauty crown. She became the very first Miss America.

A GOLDMINE

With its eight contestants and $27,000 budget, the 1921 pageant was extremely modest by today's standards. Even so, an estimated 90,000 to 100,000 people turned out to see it, making it a huge success. It was just a swimsuit contest, not a polished TV ceremony draped in patriotism like today's pageants, but that didn't matter. What counted most was that it made money for Atlantic City merchants. As A. R. Riverol writes in *Live from Atlantic City: The History of the Miss America Pageant Before, After and in Spite of Television*,

> The pageant's original aim was not to promote pageantry, beauty, scholarship, or any other such lofty ideal. Its creation was to make money, a point that many aficionados still feel uncomfortable admitting. That the pageant provided a variety of events, diversions, and entertainment was a peripheral amenity to the organizer's aims—business and self-promotion.

"We brought people here by the thousands," Mayor Edward Bader observed dryly, "and if they wished to purchase anything, the merchants profited."

Not what you expected? That's just the beginning.
For part II of the Miss America story, turn to page 479.

* * *

RANDOM THOUGHT

"When I go to the beauty parlor, I always use the emergency entrance. Sometimes I just go for an estimate."

—*Phyllis Diller*

Austrians are the world's #1 cat-lovers; 30% of Austrian households have at least one cat.

SEEDLESS FRUIT

In most cases, if there are no seeds, there is no fruit. Over time, however, several types of fruit that are good for eating have been found or created without pesky seeds inside. This piece is by Prof. David Sugar (no kidding!).

SEEDLESS WATERMELONS

The Seedless watermelon is not truly seedless—the seeds are so underdeveloped that they can be eaten while barely being noticed. It was developed by selecting watermelon strains in which the seeds matured much later than the flesh. So when the flesh is ripe for eating, the seeds still have a long way to go.

Where do seeds for planting seedless watermelon come from? When grown in parts of the world with very long, hot growing seasons, the seeds will finally mature. By that time, the flesh has deteriorated and is no longer good to eat.

SEEDLESS GRAPES

This is probably the best-known seedless fruit, especially the Thompson Seedless. In seedless grape varieties, the seed begins to form (which stimulates the grape berry's growth), but it stops developing while still very small, and becomes insignificant to the eater.

When grape seeds do develop, they produce hormones that stimulate the fruit and make it larger. So some seedless grape growers spray on a synthetic version of that hormone when the grapes are growing ... to get those really big seedless grapes.

Making new seedless grape plants doesn't require seeds— pieces of grapevine cut in the winter will make new vines after rooting in moist soil.

SEEDLESS PEARS AND APPLES

Normally, apples and pears must have seeds. Each apple or pear has the capacity to develop 10 seeds, at least one for the fruit to grow. However a good load of seeds helps the fruit to become large and have a normal shape. An apple or pear with only one or two seeds may be misshapen—since the fruit grows more in the area near the seed than in other parts of the fruit.

But warm temperatures during flowering can sometimes overcome the need for seeds. For example, the Bartlett pear grown in Oregon and Washington generally needs seeds for fruit to form. In the warmer spring weather of California, on the other hand, Bartlett pears often grow without seeds. This is called "parthenocarpy" or "virgin fruit" (the Parthenon in Greece is the temple of virgins).

SEEDLESS "STONE" FRUITS

The "stone" fruits—peaches, nectarines, plums, apricots, cherries, and almonds—all have a single seed. While an occasional fruit may be found in which the seed did not fully develop, this type of fruit will usually fall off the tree if it doesn't have a seed inside.

By the way: you may be surprised to see almonds on this list of fruits. Actually, an almond tree is very much like a peach tree… except that in the almond, the seed grows large; the fleshy "fruit" part dries up and usually splits open before harvest.

* * *

NAME THAT YEAR

How do you pronounce "2001"? Thanks to Stanley Kubrick's film *2001: A Space Odyssey,* most people think of it as "Two Thousand and One."

That's no accident. Fred Ordway, who advised Kubrick on the film, recalls: "Stanley asked me if we should say 'two thousand and one' or 'twenty-oh-one.' And we decided that 'two thousand and one' sounded better." He adds: "We often wondered… whether [the film's title] would have an influence on the English language when we got into 21st century."

It did. But William Safire, who writes a weekly column called "On Language" for the *New York Times,* opts for "twenty-oh-one." Safire explains: " 'Two thousand and one' may sound mysterious and futuristic today but by the time we get there, it will be a laborious mouth filler."

Apparently, Safire is in the minority. A poll conducted by the *Futurist* in 1993 showed that 62% of people surveyed favored "two thousand one," 18% preferred "two thousand and one," and only 10% approved of Safire's choice of "twenty-oh-one."

It takes six months to build a Rolls Royce…and 13 hours to build a Toyota.

OLYMPIC CHEATERS

Some people become famous at the Olympic games because they win a medal. Others become infamous because they don't play by the rules. Here's a look at the BRI's Olympic Hall of Shame.

ROMAN EMPEROR NERO
Year: 67 A.D.
Place: Olympia
What happened: Nero decided to compete in the chariot race. In the middle of the event, however, he fell off his chariot and was left behind in the dirt. He never completed the course.
Reaction: The Olympic judges, "under extreme pressure," declared him the winner anyway.

SPRIDON BELOKAS, Greek marathon runner
Year: 1896
Place: Athens, Greece (the first modern-day Olympics)
What happened: These Olympics were a matter of national pride for Greeks. So Belokas became a national hero when he won the bronze medal. But shortly after the games ended, he admitted "hitching a ride in a horse-drawn carriage" during the race.
Reaction: He was stripped of his medal and running shirt, and became a national disgrace overnight.

MEMBERS OF THE EAST GERMAN LUGE TEAM
Year: 1968
Place: Grenoble, France (Winter Games)
What happened: The East Germans placed first, second, and fourth in the luge competition. Then Olympic officials discovered that they'd "used a chemical to heat the runners of their toboggans to increase speed."
Reaction: They were disqualified and forfeited their medals. But the East German team never admitted guilt, blaming the incident on a "capitalist plot."

Bathroom delight: Americans bought $25 billion worth of books in 1995.

JOHN CARPENTER, American runner, 400-meter finals
Year: 1908
Place: London
What happened: Scottish champ Wyndham Halswelle, the fastest qualifier and the person favored to win, was rounding the final bend neck-and-neck with three U.S. runners when one of them—Carpenter—shoved him sideways. John Taylor, another of the Americans, "won" the race, but not before a British official broke the tape and declared "no race."
Reaction: Carpenter was disqualified; Halswelle and the other two American finalists were invited to re-run the race two days later, "this time in lanes separated by strings." The Americans refused. Halswelle re-ran the race alone and won the gold medal automatically, the only person ever to win the gold in a "walkover."

FRENCH OLYMPIC AUTHORITIES AND THE FINNISH OLYMPIC COMMITTEE
Year: 1924
Place: Paris
What happened: Finland's Paavo Nurmi was the world champion long-distance runner. But for some reason, French officials didn't want Nurmi to sweep the gold medals in the 1500-, 5000-, and 10,000-meter events. So they scheduled the 5000-meter final just 55 minutes after the 1500-meter final, hoping Nurmi would be too tired to win the second race. Then Finnish officials arbitrarily dropped Nurmi from the 10,000-meter race so Ville Ritola, Finland's second-best runner, would have a shot at a gold medal.
Reaction: Nurmi was furious, but there was nothing he could do about it. He ran the 1500-meter event…and won in record time. Then, less than an hour later, he ran the 5000 meter…and won that in record time. Finally, according to legend, "as Ritola won the 10,000 meters by half a lap in world record time, Nurmi ran a lone 10,000 meters outside the stadium and beat Ritola's time."

*   *   *

RANDOM THOUGHT: "It's strange that men should take up crime when there are so many legal ways to be dishonest."

Chopsticks are known as "quick little fellows" in China.

IN ONLY 66 YEARS...

This comparison of the Wright brothers' first flight and that of Apollo 11, only 66 years apart, was supplied to Uncle John by NASA back in 1980. Uncle John recently found it among some old research papers, and immediately took it to the bathroom. It's a fascinating reminder of how fast things have changed.

WRIGHT BROTHERS		APOLLO 11
December 17, 1903	**Date**	July 16-24, 1969
Kitty Hawk, NC	**Place**	Cape Kennedy, FL; moon; Pacific Ocean
Less than $ 1,000 (includingspare parts and round-trip rail tickets)	**Cost**	$355 million (Office of Manned Space Flight), or $375 Million (Manned Spacecraft Center)
12 seconds	**Duration**	195 hours, 19 minutes, 35 seconds
15 feet	**Altitude**	242,000 statute miles (210,000 nautical miles)
120 feet	**Distance**	952,700 miles, 363 feet
3 pounds, 3 ounces	**Fuel Weight**	6.6 million pounds
Gasoline	**Fuel**	Liquid oxygen, liquid hydrogen, and kerosene
12 horsepower	**Power**	192,000,000 horsepower (7,600,000 pounds of thrust)
605 pounds	**Craft Weight**	6.4 million pounds
10 feet/second (31 mph)	**Speed**	35,000 feet/second
5	**Witnesses**	500,000,000 (est.)

Most, if not all, polar bears are left-handed.

SHADES OF GREY

Queen Elizabeth always takes her own tea with her when she travels. And she insists on making it herself so that she can have it exactly the way she likes it. The blend? Earl Grey, of course.

How English can you get? Try a city called Newcastle-upon-Tyne on the northeast coast of England, which is where the hero of our story reigns, as still as a statue, on the top of a 135-foot column. It must be thirsty work up there with the pigeons. No doubt his lordship is gasping for a cup or two of that weak, world-famous, and oh-so-English bergamot-flavored tea—long known as "Earl Grey." (And, let us not forget, dear to the hearts of Trekkies as the favorite computer-generated drink of Captain Jean-Luc Picard: "Tea, Earl Grey, hot.")

NICE WORK, DAD
King George III had dished out the earldom to Charles Grey's father in 1806, when Charles was in his early forties, as a reward for Grey Senior's "brave and distinguished military career" which included dastardly doings in America in the 1760s and later in the French West Indies. His descendants have enjoyed the title ever since. Doubtless they've had to put up with 170 years of tea jokes.

EARLIE LIFE
The Earl Grey of our story received a gentlemanly education at Eton College—where to this day they still sing quaint boating songs and wear striped blazers. Then off to Trinity College, Cambridge, followed by a life in politics, first as a Member of Parliament, later as England's Prime Minister.

THE EARL AT WORK
Grey belonged to the Whig party, which made him a sort of an early Liberal. He argued for equal rights for Catholics, and as Prime Minister, he introduced the very radical "Great Reform Bill" which became law in 1832. That got rid of a lot of centuries-old corruption and made government more equitable and accountable. Before 1832 only nobs and toffs (those upper-class fellows) were eligible to vote. Grey's new law meant that many professional and working men (but not, alas, women for

On some Caribbean islands, the oysters can climb trees.

nearly another century) could vote. The next year he oversaw the passage of the 1833 Anti-Slavery Act that abolished slavery throughout the very sizeable British Empire…

EVENTS IN CHINA

Meanwhile, thousands of miles to the east, in China, a British diplomat—a representative of King William IV and, by extension, of Grey and the British government—was humanely intervening in the affairs of a wealthy Chinese dignitary who'd been wrongly accused of a crime and who was about to be put to death. The diplomat stepped in and the dignitary was reprieved. Result? One very grateful Chinese who wanted to thank the British government with some kind of gesture.

SOME OF THE TEA IN CHINA

So a special blend of tea was produced, flavored and scented with peel of bergamot—a pear-shaped orange named after the town of Bergamo in Italy. A generous consignment was sent to Earl Grey at 10 Downing Street in London, presumably with a thank-you note.

Grey liked the tea and shared it with friends and visitors. News of it got out and before you could say "Lemon or sugar?" people in high places were sipping it. Earl Grey tea became elegantly fashionable and has remained so all over the world for more than 17 decades. And if we're to believe Star Trek scripts, it still will be well into the 24th century.

* * *

AND NOW…BEHIND THE TITLE

GONE WITH THE WIND, by Margaret Mitchell
First the book was called *Pansy*, after the lead character. Then Pansy's name was changed to Scarlett and the title became *Tote the Weary Load*. That didn't last long, either—Mitchell decided on *Tomorrow Is Another Day* (Scarlett's famous line)…then backed away from it when she realized that more than a dozen books in print already started with the word "Tomorrow." Publication was imminent—and she needed a title. Finally, she just picked a line she'd used in the book.

The Wright brothers made four flights on December 17, 1903; the first was the shortest.

FAMOUS FOR BEING NAKED

We know—this sounds a little off-color. Butt...er...we mean but...it's just another way to look at history.

LADY GODIVA, wife of Earl Leofric, lord of Coventry, England, in the 1100s
Famous for: Riding horseback through Coventry, covered only by her long blonde hair.
The bare facts: Lady Godiva was upset by the heavy taxes her husband had imposed on poor people in his domain. When she asked him to give the folks a break, he laughingly replied that he'd cut the taxes if she would ride through the town naked. To his shock, she agreed. But she requested that townspeople stay indoors and not peek while she rode through the streets. Legend has it that they all complied expect for one young man named Tom, who secretly watched through a shutter...which gave us the term "peeping Tom."

ARCHIMEDES (287–212 B.C.), a "classic absent-minded professor" and one of the most brilliant thinkers of the Ancient World
Famous for: Running naked through the streets of ancient Syracuse, screaming "Eureka!"
The bare facts: Archimedes' friend, King Hieron II of Syracuse, Sicily, was suspicious that his new crown wasn't solid gold. Had the goldsmith secretly mixed in silver? He asked Archimedes to find out. As Peter Lafferty recounts in his book, *Archimedes:*

> Archimedes took the crown home and sat looking at it. What was he to do? He weighed the crown. He weighed a piece of pure gold just like the piece the goldsmith had been given. Sure enough, the crown weighed the same as the gold. For many days, he puzzled over the crown. Then one evening...the answer came to him.
>
> That night, his servants filled his bath to the brim with water. As Archimedes lowered himself into the tub, the water overflowed onto the floor. Suddenly, he gave a shout and jumped out. Forgetting that he was naked, he ran down the street to the palace shouting "Eureka" ("I have found it!")

Something's cooking: **More than 10 million Easy-Bake Ovens have been sold since 1964.**

Archimedes, presumably still wearing his birthday suit, explained his discovery to the king: "When an object is placed in water," he said, "it displaces an amount of water equal to its own volume."

To demonstrate, he put the crown in a bowl of water and measured the overflow. Then he put a lump of gold that weighed the same as the crown into the bowl. "The amount of water was measured," writes Lafferty, "and to the king's surprise, the gold had spilled less than the crown." It was proof that the goldsmith really had tried to cheat the king. The secret: "Silver is lighter than gold, so to make up the correct weight, extra silver was needed. This meant that the volume of the crown was slightly larger than the gold, so the crown spilled more water."

Archimedes became famous for his discovery. We can only guess what happened to the goldsmith.

RED BUTTONS, popular red-headed actor of the 1940s and 1950s
Famous for: Being the first person ever to appear naked on TV.
The bare facts: In the early 1950s, Red did a guest spot on the "Milton Berle Show," which was broadcast live. One skit featured Berle as a doctor and Buttons as a shy patient who wouldn't disrobe for his exam. Buttons wore a special "breakaway" suit—the coat, shirt, and pants were sewn together so they'd all come off when Berle yanked on the shirt collar. As he explained in *The Hollywood Walk of Shame:*

> When my character refused to get undressed, Milton was supposed to grab my shirt front and rip the entire thing off— and I'd be left standing there in old-fashioned, knee-to-neck piece underwear.
>
> Well, Milton reached for my shirt and accidentally grabbed me under the collar. And when he yanked at my breakaway suit, everything came off—including my underwear! We were on live television and there I stood—nude in front of a studio audience and all the people watching at home. When I realized what had happened, I got behind Milton, who was as shocked as I was, but had the presence of mind to announce the next act and have the curtain closed.

Buttons said he turned "as red as my hair."

Celebrated dropout: Mark Twain didn't even make it through elementary school.

BEHIND THE TITLE

What does it take to come up with just the right book title? Here are a few stories about famous titles that might give you an idea. For more of the same, read Now All We Need Is a Title, *by André Bernard.*

JAWS, by Peter Benchley
Benchley, a first-time author, struggled for months to come up with a title for his book about a man-eating shark. He tried hundreds—from *The Shark* and *Great White* to *A Silence in the Water*. His father, writer Nathaniel Benchley, suggested *What's That Noshin' on My Laig?* Finally, Benchley's editor said the only word he liked in any of the titles was "jaws." By then, Benchley didn't even care anymore: "Nobody reads first novels anyway," he said.

CATCH-22, by Joseph Heller
In 1961, Simon & Schuster was all set to publish Heller's first novel as *Catch-18*. Then another publisher protested that it was too similar to Leon Uris's new book, Mila-18—which they were about to release. Uris (who wrote *Exodus)* was a big name, Joseph Heller was an unknown. Simon & Schuster gave in and changed the title. Ironically, the phrase *Catch-22* has become part of the English language, and is arguably America's most famous modern book title.

BONFIRE OF THE VANITIES, by Tom Wolfe
During the 15th century, a monk named Savonarola inspired residents of Florence, Italy, to build a bonfire and burn all their worldly possessions—their vanities. After two such fires were built, the citizens built a third—this one for Savonarola. Tom Wolfe came upon the story during a trip to Italy. The idea of a bonfire for destroying one's "vanities" intrigued him.

SEX AND THE SINGLE GIRL, by Helen Gurley Brown
Cosmopolitan editor Helen Gurley Brown wanted to "write a book about sex being okay for single women." Her original title, *Sex for the Single Girl*, was considered immoral; she didn't want readers to think she was promoting sex after all. By changing one three-letter word, the title became morally acceptable. The book

---

Tsunamis travel as fast as jet planes.

was a huge bestseller and helped create the "sexual revolution of the 1960s."

THE POSTMAN ALWAYS RINGS TWICE, by James M. Cain

Cain has given two different versions. He's said that while he was working on the manuscript, the mailman would ring the bell twice when delivering bills, once for personal letters. He's also said that the mailman would ring twice when delivering rejection letters from publishers. (On the day Alfred Knopf decided to publish the novel, the postman only rang once.) Cain named the novel as a memorial to his early failures.

A MOVEABLE FEAST, by Ernest Hemingway

Hemingway spent over 30 years writing this memoir about his life as a struggling writer in Paris. He died before it was published, and still hadn't come up with a satisfactory title (rejects: *The Paris Nobody Knows; To Write It Truly*). Finally, Hemingway's widow thought of a letter he'd written a decade earlier: "If you are lucky enough to have lived in Paris as a young man," he wrote, "then wherever you go for the rest of your life, it stays with you, for Paris is a moveable feast."

THE MALTESE FALCON, by Dashiell Hammett

Hammett had this title before he had written the book. But his publisher, Alfred Knopf, tried to talk him out of it. "Whenever people can't pronounce a title or an author's name," he said, "they are…too shy to go into a bookstore and try." The word Knopf objected to? Falcon. Hammett stuck to his guns, and the title is a part of American pop culture.

CAT ON A HOT TIN ROOF, by Tennessee Williams

Williams created the character of Brick in a short story called "Three Players of a Summer Game." Later, he turned the story into a play, adding Brick's wife—Maggie the Cat. That reminded him of something his father always used to say: 'Edwina, you're making me as nervous as a cat on a hot tin roof!' "

WHO'S AFRAID OF VIRGINIA WOOLF?, by Edward Albee

Albee found the phrase scrawled on a mirror in a Greenwich Village bar.

Time yourself: If you're an average adult, you spend 11-13 minutes in the shower.

MARILYN'S SECRETS

Marilyn Monroe's life has been examined and re-examined so often, you may feel there's nothing you don't know about her...but thanks to the diligence of BRI member Jack Mingo, we're able to bring some interesting little-known facts to light.

Her mother was a film-negative cutter in Hollywood. Her father could have been any of several men her mother was sleeping with at the time, but later in life Marilyn Monroe convinced herself that Clark Gable was her biological father.

• Two weeks after her birth, she was placed with a religious foster family that taught her that going to movies was a sin.

• Her closest playmate was a stray dog she adopted. Just after her seventh birthday, a neighbor killed him with a shotgun. That same day, her mother suddenly appeared and took her back.

• Still working as a film cutter, her mom used movie houses as a form of day care, knowing her daughter would stay cool and safe while she worked. The devout seven-year-old spent hours praying that her shockingly amoral mother wouldn't be condemned to hell.

• When Monroe was 10, her mother was committed to a mental institution. She went to live with an aunt, who dyed young Marilyn's hair platinum blonde and bought her only white clothes.

• As a child, she vowed she would never get married. She was going to become a schoolteacher and have lots of dogs, instead.

• She quit high school at 16 to marry a 21-year-old. She took a job spraying varnish on fabric for airplanes, but soon became a model. Her agent said she was "too plump" and "smiled too high on her face," but two years later she had appeared on 33 magazine covers.

• As a young adult, she spent her small income on acting classes and rent. She filled the gaps by providing quick in-car sex in exchange for restaurant meals, and began getting movie parts by sleeping with movie executives.

• Monroe's beauty wasn't all natural. Her hairline was heightened by electrolysis, her teeth were bleached, and an overbite was corrected. A plastic surgeon removed a lump of cartilage from the tip of her nose and inserted a crescent-shaped silicone implant into her jaw to give it a softer line.

George Washington and Abraham Lincoln were both descended from England's King Edward I.

FOUNDING FATHERS

You already know the names. Here's who they belonged to.

Godfrey Keebler. Opened a bakery in Philadelphia in 1853. His family expanded it. Today, Keebler is second-largest producer of cookies and crackers in the U.S.

Linus Yale, Jr. Invented the first combination locks and the first flat-key cylinder locks, in the 1860s. In 1868, the Yale Lock Company was formed to mass-produce his creations.

Joseph Campbell. A fruit merchant, he opened a canning factory in 1869. His specialties included jellies, salad dressing, and mince-meat—but not soup. The company added condensed soup in 1897. (First variety: tomato.)

Pleasant and John Hanes. Brothers who built a tobacco business in the late 1800s, then sold it in 1900. Each invested his profits in a textile company. John's made socks and stockings; Pleasant's made new-fangled two-piece men's underwear. They were separate companies until 1962, when the families joined forces.

Carl Jantzen. Part owner of the Portland Knitting Mill. In 1910, at the request of a member of the Portland Rowing Club, he developed the first elasticized swimsuits. They became popular around the country as "Jantzens." In 1920, the company changed its name to Jantzen.

John M. Van Heusen. Started the Van Heusen Shirt Company. In 1919 it became the first to sell dress shirts with collars attached. Developed a way to weave cloth on a curve in 1920, which made one-piece collars possible…and revolutionized the shirt industry.

Arthur Pitney and Walter Bowes. In 1901 Pitney created a machine that could stick postage stamps on letters. In 1920 he joined forces with Bowes. Because of WWI, there was a letter-writing boom, and the post office needed a machine to keep up. In 1920 Congress passed a bill allowing the Pitney-Bowes machine to handle the mail.

Gas guzzlers: 76% of U.S. commuters drive to work alone.

FAMILIAR PHRASES

Here are the origins of some everyday phrases.

HIGHTAIL IT
Meaning: Leave quickly.
Origin: Dates back to the Old West. Cowboys on the Great Plains noticed that wild horses jerked their tails very high just before galloping off. Soon anyone who left quickly was said to have "hightailed it."

RED HERRING
Meaning: Distraction; diversionary tactic.
Origin: Comes from hunting. When herring is smoked, it changes from silvery gray to brownish red and gives off a strong smell. Hunters use red herrings to train dogs to follow a scent...and, by dragging a red herring across the trail, they can also throw a dog off a scent.

STUFFED SHIRT
Meaning: Braggart or pompous person.
Origin: In the days before mannequins, clothing shops displayed shirts in their windows by stuffing them with tissue paper or rags. The shirt looked broad-chested, like a strong man, but was really light and flimsy.

RIGHT-HAND MAN
Meaning: Important assistant.
Origin: In 17th-century cavalries, the soldier at the far right of a line of troops had a position of special responsibility or command.

AT THE DROP OF A HAT
Meaning: Quickly; without delay.
Origin: The term dates back to the days when races, prizefights, and other sporting events were literally started with the wave or the drop of a hat.

When he didn't wear a pocketwatch, George Washington used a small sundial to tell the time.

WIENERS ON WHEELS

Here's a BRI inside look at the Oscar Mayer Wienermobile,
perhaps the most popular pop-culture icon on four wheels.

THE EVOLUTION OF THE WIENERMOBILE

In the beginning, there was the "Weiner Wagon," a horse-drawn cart that the Oscar Mayer Company sent to Chicago-area butcher shops to promote its products. A German band rode on the back, oom-pahing for crowds wherever the wagon stopped.

Modern thinking. In the mid-1920s, Oscar's nephew, Charlie, joined the company right out of college. He came up with the idea of hiring a midget to dress up in a chef's uniform and make appearances with the band. Dubbed "Little Oscar, the world's smallest chef," the midget sang, plugged Oscar Mayer products, and gave away prizes at each stop.

Rolling along. In the 1930s, there was a nationwide craze for vehicles in the shape of products. There were milk bottle-mobiles, vacuum cleaner-mobiles, cheese-mobiles, and so on. Mayer's nephew decided to create a special vehicle for Little Oscar. He paid the General Body Company of Chicago $5,000 to convert an old car into a 13-foot, open-cockpit hot dog—the first "Wiener-mobile." It rolled off the assembly line in 1936.

Wieners everywhere. Putting the world's smallest chef behind the wheel of the World's Largest Wiener, as Oscar Mayer called it, generated plenty of publicity. In fact, it was such a good promotional gimmick that by the 1940s the company had an entire fleet of Wienermobiles. Every time they opened a new meat-packing plant, they commissioned a new Wienermobile to go with it. The vehicles were on the road continuously from 1936 to 1977, stopping only during World War II gasoline rationing.

Dead dog. By the mid-1970s, it looked like the Wienermobile's days were running out. Oscar Mayer wanted to move away from its regional meat plant promotions towards nationwide TV advertising campaigns...and who knows, maybe it thought the dogs-on-wheels were getting too dorky. So, in 1977, the entire wienie fleet was put up on blocks.

On a roll. The giant wieners might have stayed there forever. But in 1986, the company decided to commemorate the 50th anniversary of the original Wienermobile. As Wienermobile manager Russ Whitacre explains, "We brought the last working one out of storage and put it on the road, driven by two college students for the summer. We got a great deal of response…a lot of nostalgia. Boomers said it was a piece of their lives." When thousands of fans wrote to Oscar Mayer about the vehicles, company officials decided they had something worth preserving, and ordered a brand-new fleet of six to be built. They hit the road in 1988.

LAMBORWIENIE
The pre-1980s Wienermobiles had been pretty spartan as sausages go, but the 1988 models were genuine Wienerbagos, complete with microwave ovens, refrigerators, CB radios, cellular phones, and stereo systems capable of belting out 21 different renditions of the Oscar Mayer Wiener song, including country, rap, and rock 'n' roll versions. Even the car's exhaust system was improved—in addition to ordinary automobile fumes, the Wienermobiles give off a "fondly familiar hot dog scent" during appearances.

The car's V6 engine has a top speed of 110 mph. But the only person known to have driven the car that fast was A1 Unser Jr., who took one of the wienies for a spin at the Indianapolis Motor Speedway. Oscar Mayer hotdoggers (the company's name for Wienerdog drivers) are pretty much stuck driving at the legal speed limit. As Whitacre explains, "Because of the vehicle's visibility, we hear about it if someone drives a Wienermobile in an unsafe manner."

WIENERMOBILE 2000
By 1994, the new Wienermobiles had logged an average of 200,000 miles apiece on American highways and byways, so Oscar Mayer hired California auto designer Harry Bradley—creator of the original Mattel Hot Wheels—to design a Wienermobile for the 21st century. Among his improvements: He extended the wienie theme to the *inside* of the vehicle, giving it a hot dog dashboard and glove box, a condiment control panel, and relish-

25 hot dogs high, and 10 hot dogs wide, and weighs in at 10,000 lbs.

colored captain's chairs for the driver and passengers. Estimated total cost of each vehicle: $150,000.

WIENERMOBILE FACTS

• Nine different men played Little Oscar; the last one retired in 1971. Why wasn't he replaced? Oscar Mayer is mum on the subject. Our theory: As times changed, dressing midgets up as chefs could be considered "bad taste."

• What happens to old Wienermobiles? Most are sent to Canada, Mexico, and other countries where Oscar Mayer has affiliates, but at least one is always kept on hand as a "loaner wiener" in case any of the new ones break down.

• Which is harder to get into: Harvard Law School, or the driver's seat of the Wienermobile? Hint: Every year, more than 1,000 recent college graduates apply for the coveted position of "hotdogger"; only 12 get the nod. Oscar Mayer says "outgoing personalities and impressive academic credentials" are key qualities for the job.

• Once you're hired on as a hot dogger, you have to put in a week of on-the-dog training at Hot Dog High, the company's Wiener-dog training facility. "The curriculum takes about seven days," hotdogger Brian Spillane explains, "including one day to learn how to drive the 'Dog,' just so no one gets in a pickle when they miss a turn."

• Mastery of hot dog puns is another must. "Go ahead and grill us," Dan Duff, another hotdogger, challenges. "In this job, we're trained to cut the mustard. It's a job to relish…and that's no bologna."

• Wienermobiles log an average of 1,000 miles per week visiting baseball games, children's hospitals, grocery stores, etc. Even so, there have been very few traffic accidents involving the Wiener-mobile—although there was at least one accident involving a Wienermobile fan. As one hotdogger admits: "One guy saw the Weinermobile, and laughed so hard, his false teeth fell out—right into the big air vents on the buns. We never did find them. He really sank his teeth into our buns."

The Nestles haven't run Nestle since 1875.

THE FIRST PHONE BOOKS

Today, the phone directory is the most widely used book in America. Practically every household has at least one. Here's how they got started.

THE FIRST WHITE PAGES

The first personal phone directory was issued in 1878—just two years after Alexander Graham Bell invented the telephone—by Boston's Telephone Dispatch Company. It was different from today's White Pages in two major respects:

1. It was only one page long, because only 97 Bostonians owned telephones in 1878.

2. It didn't list any phone numbers. Why not? There weren't any. Direct dial hadn't been invented; you just picked up the receiver and turned a hand crank that rang a bell alerting the operator. When she came on the line, you told her who you wanted to talk to. That was it.

THE FIRST YELLOW PAGES

The first business directories were actually printed on white paper. The R.R. Donnelley Company, a Chicago printing firm, was already publishing listings of local companies with their addresses. When phones came along in 1877, Donnelley just noted which businesses had them.

The first Bell Telephone business directory followed almost immediately in 1878; like the first personal directories, it was only one page long. Businesses were divided into seven listings: Physicians; Dentists; Stores; Factories; etc.; Meat and Fish Markets; Miscellaneous; and Hack [horses for hire] and Boarding Stables.

The number of phone customers grew exponentially over the next decade, and as directories got larger, printing costs soared. In the late 1880s, telephone companies around the country began selling advertising space in their directories to defray expenses. Today the ads actually make money—a lot of it—for phone

Armadillos can get leprosy.

companies: U.S. businesses bought more than $10 billion worth of yellow-page ads in 1995.

THE COSMIC QUESTION

Of course, we still haven't answered the real question: why are yellow pages yellow? Well, research conducted by Bell Laboratories has shown that black ink on dark yellow paper is the second-most visible paper-and-ink combination—after black ink on white paper. But nobody knew that in 1881, when the first yellow pages were printed.

Here's what happened: The Wyoming Telephone and Telegraph Co. hired a printer in Cheyenne to print its first business directory. But he didn't have enough white paper to complete the job. So, rather than lose the phone company's business altogether, he used the stock he had on hand—yellow paper.

Like the first personal directories, the first "yellow pages" were actually a yellow page—a single sheet that contained only 100 business listings, under such headings as Boots, American Indian Jewelry, and Soda Water Companies. Most of the telephone numbers on it were just one, two, or three digits long.

*　　*　　*

PHONE PRANKS

In April 1996, some hackers tapped into the main number that directs callers to New York City's 76 police precincts and replaced the standard recording with the following message:

> You have reached the New York City Police Department. For any real emergencies, dial 911. Anyone else—we're a little busy right now eating some donuts and having coffee. (In the background, the *New York Post* reported, a second voice could be heard saying "A *big* cup of coffee. And masturbating.")

The recording ended, "You can just hold the line. We'll get back to you. We're a little slow, if you know what I mean. Thank you."

The average American female will have 3.3 pregnancies in her lifetime.

PRESIDENTIAL INFLUENCE

*Public service is only a part of our presidents' importance to us—
they're also pop icons. Their clothes, their hobbies, and so on
have an impact on our lives, too. Here are some examples.*

THE ROCKING CHAIR
President: JFK
Influence: Until the 1960s, Americans only thought of
rocking chairs as furniture for old folks or porches. Then
Kennedy's physician recommended he use a rocking chair whenever possible for back therapy. In 1961 he was photographed at
the White House sitting in an "old-fashioned cane-backed porch
rocker." Overnight, the company that made the chair was inundated with orders. Sensing a hot fad, furniture makers started
cranking out rockers. B. Altman, a New York department store,
even devoted an entire floor to them. The result: rocking chairs
became furniture for living rooms.

BROCCOLI
President: George Bush
Influence: In 1992, Bush commented that he didn't like broccoli
when he was a kid, and he didn't like it now. "I'm president of the
United States," he said, "and I'm not going to eat any more broc-
coli." The story was reported worldwide. Feigning outrage, a major
broccoli producer shipped the White House 10 tons of the veggie.
The arrival of the truck was carried *live* by CNN.

Campbell's Soups and *Women's Day* magazine co-sponsored a
recipe contest called "How to Get the President to Eat Broccoli."
With all the publicity, broccoli sales shot up 40%. "I can't begin to
tell you how wonderful this has been for us," a broccoli industry
spokesperson said. "The asparagus people were saying they wished
Bush had picked on them instead."

PAINT-BY-NUMBERS
President: Dwight D. Eisenhower
Influence: Painting-by-numbers was already becoming popular

Clothes horses: 9% of Americans buy their pets clothing on birthdays and holidays.

when Ike was elected in 1952. He helped turn it into a national craze. As the media reported, Ike loved to paint, but didn't care about originality (his paintings were copied from postcards, photos, etc.) or results ("They're no fun when they're finished," he said). Plus, he couldn't draw—so he often had other artists outline pictures on his canvas. Naturally, he thought paint-by numbers kits were great, and gave them his "official" endorsement in 1953 by handing out sets to his staff as Christmas presents. The craze peaked around 1954, but thanks in part to Ike, they're still with us.

GOING HATLESS
President: JFK
Influence: Believe it or not, kids, in 1960 "respectable" men were still expected to wear hats in public. (Not baseball caps but fedoras—the kind you see in old movies). JFK ignored tradition and usually went hatless. When other men began copying him, there were storms of protest from the fashion industry. The *New York Times,* for example, reported on July 6, 1963:

> A British fashion magazine today stepped up its campaign to persuade President Kennedy to wear a hat and pointedly asked him how a hatless man could properly greet a lady. "How does the president acknowledge such an encounter?" asked *Tailor & Cutter* in an editorial… "The deft touch of a raised hat, politely pinched between thumb and forefinger …would bring a bright spark of gallantry to modern diplomatic moves."

JFK ignored their entreaties, and the hat industry ultimately bowed to the inevitable.

THE SAXOPHONE
President: Bill Clinton
Influence: When he was running for office, Clinton played his sax on TV—and received a ton of favorable publicity. At his inauguration he did it again, playing "Your Mama Don't Dance." In 1993, the *Wall Street Journal* noted that "thanks in part to President Clinton's willingness to toot his horn on national television, sales of saxophones are way up." Music teachers also reported a big increase in sax students…and CD sales of sax music—from Kenny G to John Coltrane—have been booming.

Approximately 56,000 courier pigeons "fought" in World War II.

FASHIONABLE MATERNITY CLOTHES
First Lady: Jacqueline Kennedy
Influence: Before 1960, most pregnant women resigned themselves to staying out of the public eye, and to looking embarrassingly dowdy when they ventured out. In the early 1960s, Jackie Kennedy brought maternity clothes out of the closet. Although she was pregnant, she remained visible in public life, wearing stylish clothes adapted for her. As *Newsweek* commented:

> *Vogue* and *Harper's Bazaar* view [pregnancy] as mere plump frumpery, too impossibly unchic and rarely, if ever, mentionable. But with Jacqueline Kennedy being [as important as she is], the issue can hardly be obscured much longer. Pregnancy is fashionable; at the very least, it is no longer an excuse for looking unfashionable.

Clothesmaker Lane Bryant cashed in on the publicity with their new First Lady Maternity Fashion Ensemble. It was a hit, and maternity clothes have never been the same.

MISCELLANEOUS INFLUENCE
• George Bush loved playing horseshoes. During his presidency, sales of the game went up 20%.
• In 1962, *Newsweek* wrote: "When Jackie Kennedy sported Capri pants, women raced to buy them. When Jackie appeared in a roll-brimmed hat, millinery shops were rocked with orders for copies. So it was inevitable that when the president's wife took to wraparound sunglasses, a fad would follow. Indeed, despite a recent White House request that merchants not use the presidential family to push products, many of the fast-selling wraparounds still managed to focus their promotion on the First Lady. A big seller, for example, is the $15 Jaqui."
• President Eisenhower helped popularize TV trays. Every night, reporters told the nation, Ike and his wife "eat supper off matching tray-tables in front of a bank of special TV consoles built into one wall of the White House family quarters." Ordinary families followed suit.
• President Kennedy publicized the fact that he had taken the Evelyn Wood speed-reading course. For a time, enrollment at Evelyn Wood—and other courses—boomed.

There are 635,013,559,599 possible hands in a game of bridge.

FAMOUS INDIAN IMPOSTORS

*It's common for North Americans to romanticize the traditions
of Native Americans, so it shouldn't be surprising that the "Indian way"
is fertile ground for hoaxes and impostors. Here are two notable examples.*

GREY OWL

In the 1930s, Grey Owl was one of the most famous naturalists in the world. "He is no stuffed Indian," The New York Times reported at the time. "He is real and honest."

Who He Said He Was: Grey Owl claimed to be the son of a Scottish man and his Apache wife. At the age of 15, his story went, he went to live with the Ojibway tribe near Ontario, Canada. They named him Wa-Sha-Quon-Asin, which translates as "He-Who-Flies-by-Night" (an appropriate name), or "Grey Owl." They also taught him how to trap beavers...but when his traps killed a mother beaver and left its young as orphans, he decided to stop killing animals and start protecting them.

The Canadian government was impressed. They made a film about his work and gave him a job as a conservationist in their national parks. His fame grew; he wrote two bestselling books (in 1931 and 1935) and toured England twice, speaking in packed lecture halls to more than 250,000 people. He was even invited to meet with King George...whom he greeted as an equal, extending his hand and saying, "I come in peace, brother."

Who He Really Was: A few days after He-Who-Flies-by-Night died in 1938, an Ontario newspaper discovered that he was actually Archibald Stansfeld Belamey, an Englishman who'd moved to Canada at the age of 18. Once there, he quickly acquired four wives, several children, a police record, and a reputation for public drunkenness. He abandoned them all for the fantasy world of a half-Indian beaver lover.

What Happened: Belamey is still held in high esteem. As *History Today* reported in 1994, "Grey Owl has never been forgotten. His books remain in print. His cabins in the National Parks where he worked have been resorted, and some of his canoe routes have been mapped for park visitors."

LITTLE TREE

In 1976, Delacorte Press published *The Education of Little Tree,* by Forrest Carter. The book became a #1 bestseller on the New York Times nonfiction list. More than a million copies were in print by the late 1980s, and in 1991 the American Bookseller's Association voted it the book "they most enjoyed selling."

Who He Said He Was: Carter said *The Education of Little Tree* was an autobiographical account of the way his Cherokee grandmother and her Scottish husband taught him how to weave baskets, make moccasins, hunt wild game, and live off the land.

Who He Really Was: In 1991, an historian was researching a biography of segregationist Alabama governor George Wallace when he discovered Forrest Carter's true identity. Incredibly, he was really Asa Carter, a violent white supremacist and former speechwriter for Wallace. As the historian wrote in The New York Times:

> Between 1946 and 1973, [Asa] Carter carved out a violent career in Southern politics as a Ku Klux Klan terrorist, rightwing radio announcer, home-grown American fascist and anti-Semite. ...He even organized a paramilitary unit of 100 men that he called the Original Ku Klux Klan of the Confederacy.

In time, Carter became too bigoted even for the Wallace campaign. So he ran against Wallace for governor in 1970 (he got 15,000 votes out of more than 1 million cast). Then he dropped out of sight, moved to Texas, and began writing novels as Forrest Carter (after Nathan Bedford Forrest, the Confederate general who founded the Ku Klux Klan). His two most successful novels were *Gone to Texas,* which Clint Eastwood made into the film *The Outlaw Josey Wales,* and *The Education of Little Tree.* Carter died in 1979...and his true identity remained a secret until 1991.

What Happened: The New York Times Book Review moved *The Education of Little Tree* from its nonfiction list to its fiction list. Carter's books are still in print, and sales remain strong.

Three Mile Island is only 2 1/2 miles long.

SPEAK OF THE DEVIL

Here are some random bits of information about the Devil.

THE DEVIL YOU SAY

- The Devil as we think of him—with the horns, pitchfork, etc.—dates back to the 10th and 11th centuries; his popular image was not taken from the Bible. According to the New Testament, the devil takes the form of a lion, a wolf, a dragon, and a serpent. Early Christians sometimes thought of him as a three-headed dog.

So where does the Devil we know come from?

- His beard (goatee), horns, hooves, hairy legs, pointy ears, etc. were borrowed from the goat. Scholars cite two reasons:
1. "The domestic goat was renowned for the size of its phallus," writes historian J.C.J. Metford, and, according to legend, "tempted saints by whispering in their ears lewd details of the sexual pleasures they had relinquished."
2. One of the ways the Church discouraged interest in other religions was by literally "demonizing" gods that competed with theirs. So a lot of the imagery is derived from pagan sources: the goatlike features also come from Pan, the Greek god of shepherds, fertility, and nature.

- His red skin is the color of blood and fire.
- His three-pronged fork, or triton, was borrowed from Poseidon, the nasty-tempered Greek god of the sea and of earthquakes, whose main symbol was a three-pronged spear.

DEVOLUTION

- Modern mythology paints the Devil as the kind of all-powerful, evil being who possesses little girls in *The Exorcist* or tries to destroy the world in *The Omen*. But that hasn't always been the case.
- During the Middle Ages in parts of Europe, he was seen as more of a mean-spirited, clumsy, dimwitted lout with a fondness for pranks—like Bluto in the Popeye cartoons—that the wise and the holy could easily outsmart. "There was nothing grand about their Satan," historian Charles Mackay writes in his book *Extraordinary Popular Delusions and the Madness of Crowds*.

Henry Ford was Charles Lindbergh's first passenger in the *Spirit of St. Louis*.

On the contrary, he was a low, mean devil, whom it was easy to circumvent, and fine fun to play tricks with....It was believed that he endeavored to trip people up by laying his long invisible tail in their way, and giving it a sudden whisk when their legs were over it; that he used to get drunk, and swear like a trooper, and be mischievous. ...Some of the saints spat in his face, to his very great annoyance; others chopped off pieces of his tail, which, however, always grew on again.

• Of course, some countries were extremely serious about Satan. Historians estimate that from 1450 to 1750, more than 200,000 alleged witches were executed in Europe and America for "dealing with the Devil."

DEVIL'S FOOD
• How did devil's food cake get its name? One theory: The stuff was so tasty that people assumed that the inventors had to sell their soul to the Devil to get the recipe.
• You've probably eaten pumpernickel bread before...but did you know the word Pumpernickel means "Devil's fart" in German? Apparently, when German bakers invented the bread centuries ago, it was awful. The 1756 book *A Grand Tour of Germany* described it as bread "of the very coarsest kind, ill-baked and as black as coal, for they never sift their flour." Locals joked that it was so difficult to digest that even the Devil himself got gas when he ate it.
• In some countries, the Devil is nicknamed "the good man," "the old gentleman," and even "the great fellow." Why? Tradition had it that if you "spoke of the Devil," he would appear. So people didn't.

SATAN ON TRIAL
In 1971, a man named Gerald Mayo filed suit against Satan in the U.S. District Court in Pennsylvania, alleging that "Satan has on numerous occasions caused plaintiff misery and unwarranted threats, against the will of plaintiff, that Satan has placed deliberate obstacles in his path and has caused plaintiff's downfall. Plaintiff alleges that by reason of these acts Satan has deprived him of his constitutional rights."

The case, "Gerald Mayo v. Satan and His Staff." was thrown out of court after Mayo failed to provide the U.S. marshal with instructions on how to serve Satan a subpoena, and couldn't prove that Satan lived within the jurisdiction of the District Court.

Terminator 2 cost $647,000 per minute of film to make.

THE CREATION OF FRANKENSTEIN

You might assume that the flat-headed, bolts-in-the-neck monster we all know was taken directly from Mary Shelley's original novel. Nope. It was created specifically for the movies. Here's the story of how the world's most famous monster was born.

FIRST FRIGHT

History books credit Thomas Alva Edison with inventing the lightbulb, the phonograph, the movie camera, and many other things. But one invention they usually leave off his resume is the horror movie. His Edison Film Company invented it in 1910, when they put Mary Shelley's 1818 novel *Frankenstein* on film for the first time.

Edison's *Frankenstein* was barely 16 minutes long and was only loosely based on the original. The filmmakers thought the book was too graphic, so they eliminated "all the...repulsive situations and concentrated on the mystic and psychological problems found in this weird tale."

CREATIONISM

But one scene in Shelley's book wasn't graphic enough for Edison executives: the "creation scene" in which Dr. Frankenstein brings the monster to life. Shelley devoted only two sentences to it:

> I collected the instruments of life around me, that I might infuse a spark of being into the lifeless thing that lay at my feet. It was already one in the morning; the rain pattered dismally against the panes, and my candle was nearly burnt out, when, by the glimmer of the half-extinguished light, I saw the dull yellow eye of the creature open; it breathed hard, and a convulsive motion agitated its limbs.

That was all Shelley wrote. So the folks at Edison used their imagination and decided to make a "cauldron of blazing chemicals" the source of the monster's life. Edison's monster looked nothing like the Frankenstein we know. It was a white-faced hunchback with matted hair and a hairy chest.

ON THE ROAD

Following the success of Edison's *Frankenstein,* other studios filmed their own versions of the story. The first full-length Frankenstein film, called *Life Without a Soul,* hit the silver screen in 1916, and an Italian film called *Il Mostro di Frankenstein* followed in 1920.

But the Frankenstein monster might never have become a Hollywood icon if it hadn't been for Hamilton Deane, an English actor who ran (and starred in) a traveling *Dracula* show during the 1920s. Tired of performing *Dracula* night after night, Deane began looking for material he could use as an alternate. He settled on *Frankenstein.*

In 1927 he asked a member of the *Dracula* troupe, Peggy Webling, to adapt *Frankenstein* into a play. Like the folks at Edison, she got creative with the story. For example:

• Webling saw the monster—whom Mary Shelley called *Adam*—as an alter ego of Dr. Victor Frankenstein. She became the first person ever to refer to both the man *and* the monster as Frankenstein. To make the connection obvious, she dressed the characters in identical clothing throughout the play.

• She changed the ending. In the novel, Dr. Frankenstein pursues the monster to the Arctic circle, where the monster strangles him, jumps onto an ice floe, and drifts off to a sure death. The scene made good reading, but it was boring on stage. So Webling had the monster jump off a cliff instead

Unfortunately, Hamilton Deane, who played the monster, wasn't much of an athlete. As troupe member Ivan Butler recalled years later, the new ending was "very tame indeed, because of Deane's tentative jump." So Webling wrote a more exciting ending. "The final version was quite a bloodthirsty affair," Butler recalled, "with the monster apparently tearing his maker's throat out before being destroyed by lightning. Old Deanie reveled in it."

CLASSIC FRANKENSTEIN

Universal Pictures bought the screen rights to Deane's *Dracula* and cast Bela Lugosi in the starring role. Even before the film was released in 1931, studio executives knew it would be a hit. So they commissioned a *Frankenstein* film, too. They bought the rights to Webling's play, then hired fresh screenwriters to craft a brand-new script.

Mary Stuart became Queen of Scotland when she was six days old.

A WHALE OF A TALE

First, Universal hired director James Whale to work on the film. Whale had just finished work on *Hell's Angels* and *Journey's End*, two films about World War I, and Universal officials were so impressed with them that they offered Whale his pick of any of the dozens of film projects they had in the works. He chose Frankenstein. Why? As he later recalled:

> Of thirty available stories, *Frankenstein* was the strongest meat and gave me a chance to dabble in the macabre. I thought it would be amusing to try and make what everybody knows is a physical impossibility seem believable....Also, it offered fine pictorial chances, had two grand characterizations, and had a subject matter that might go anywhere, and that is part of the fun of making pictures.

And besides, Whale was sick of working on war movies.

BEG, BORROW, AND STEAL

Once again, writers changed Shelley's story. Universal's screenwriters followed the novels only loosely, adding and deleting details as they saw fit. They also appropriated ideas from other films:

* An early draft of the script said the lab should be filled with electrical gadgets that were "something suggestive of the laboratory in *Metropolis*," a 1926 German film about a mad scientist.
* Dr. Frankenstein's lab was moved from the top floor of his house to an old watchtower. This idea was taken from *The Magician*, a 1926 film in which a student of the occult finds "the secret of the creation of human life...in an ancient sorcerer's tower."
* *The Magician* was also an inspiration for the creation scene. As in *Frankenstein*, lightning bolts that strike the tower create life.
* Both *Metropolis* and *The Magician* provided ideas for the character of Igor, Dr. Frankenstein's assistant. In both films, the mad scientist has a dwarf for an assistant. Whale's scriptwriters changed him from a dwarf to a hunchback.
* Universal scriptwriters moved the final scene to an abandoned windmill, where angry peasants trap Dr. Frankenstein and the monster inside and burn it to the ground. Why was a

windmill chosen? Scriptwriter Robert Florey remembers, "I was living in a [Hollywood] apartment above a Van de Kamp bakery," which had a windmill as its company symbol. The sight of the company's "windmill rotating inspired me to place the final scene in an old mill."

• In Mary Shelley's *Frankenstein*, the monster is extremely articulate and drones on for entire chapters without stopping. But movie audiences were still getting used to the idea of people talking (and screaming) in movies, let alone monsters—so the scriptwriters decided to make the Frankenstein monster a mute. Throughout the film, all he does is grunt.

CREATING THE MONSTER

Whale cast an actor named Colin Clive to play Dr. Frankenstein and selected a woman named Mae Clarke to play Dr. Frankenstein's fiance. (Bette Davis was also considered for the part.)

Casting the monster turned out to be more difficult. Bela Lugosi, probably Universal's first choice for the part, filmed a full-dress screen test. But because the *Frankenstein* makeup hadn't yet been finalized, the makeup department gave Lugosi a big, fat head "about four times normal size," and "polished, clay-like skin."

Nobody knows if Lugosi's performance was any good; the screen test was lost shortly after it was filmed. But it didn't really matter—Lugosi figured the nonspeaking role was beneath him and worried that his fans wouldn't recognize him under all that makeup. The role went to someone else, someone who was almost completely unknown in Hollywood.

For Part II of the Frankenstein story, turn to page 642.

* * *

BLACKENSTEIN

In 1972, a "blaxploitation" version of *Frankenstein* was released—*Blackenstein*. The plot: Dr. Stein experiments on a black Vietnam vet. Something goes awry...and a "crazed monster with a square Afro" is created. A planned sequel, *Blackenstein Meets the White Werewolf*, was never made.

WARHOLISMS

Don't let the blank look fool you. Andy Warhol had insight.

"If a person isn't generally considered beautiful, they can still be a success if they have a few jokes in their pockets. And a lot of pockets."

"The most beautiful thing in Tokyo is McDonald's. The most beautiful thing in Stockholm is McDonald's. Peking and Moscow don't have anything beautiful yet."

"Good B.O. means good box office. You can smell it from a mile away."

"If the lines on your hands are wrinkles, it means your hands worry a lot."

"When I look around today, the biggest anachronism I see is pregnancy. I just can't believe that people are still pregnant."

"After you pay somebody back, you never run into them anymore. But before that, they're everywhere."

"In the '60s, everybody got interested in everybody. In the '70s, everybody started dropping everybody."

"They say that time changes things, but actually you have to change them yourself."

"People look the most kissable when they're not wearing makeup. Marilyn's lips weren't kissable, but they were very photographable."

"Changing your tastes to what other people don't want is your only hope of getting anything."

"Even beauties can be unattractive. If you catch a beauty in the wrong light at the right time, forget it."

"If people want to spend their whole lives creaming and tweezing and brushing and gluing, that's really okay too, because it gives them something to do."

"I really do live for the future, because when I'm eating a box of candy, I can't wait to taste the last piece."

"The best time for me is when I don't have any problems that I can't buy my way out of."

The potato chips Americans eat each year weigh six times as much the Titanic.

LUCKY FINDS

*Ever found something valuable? It's a great feeling. Here's
a look at a few people who found really valuable stuff...
and got to keep it. You should be so lucky.*

FLEA MARKET TREASURE
The Find: A copy of the Declaration of Independence,
printed on the evening of July 4, 1776
Where It Was Found: Inside a picture frame
The Story: In 1989, an unidentified "middle-aged financial
analyst from Philadelphia" paid $4 for a painting at a flea market.
He didn't even like the painting, but liked the frame, so he took
the picture apart...and when he did, a copy of the Declaration of
Independence fell out. "It was folded up, about the size of a busi-
ness envelope," says David Redden of Sotheby's Auction House.
"He thought it might be an early 19th-century printing and worth
keeping as a curiosity."

A few years later, the man showed the print to a friend, who
suspected it might be valuable and encouraged him to look into it.
He did, and learned that only hours after finishing work on the
Declaration in 1776, the Continental Congress had delivered the
handwritten draft to a printer with orders to send

> copies of the Declaration...to the several Assemblies, Conven-
> tions & Committees...and the Commanding Officers of the
> Continental troops, that it be proclaimed in each of the United
> States & at the head of the Army.

This was one of those original copies. No one is sure how many
were printed that night; today only 24 survive, and most are in
poor condition. But the one in the picture frame was in mint
condition, having spent the better part of two centuries undisturbed. In 1991, it sold at auction for $2.4 million.

UNCLAIMED MERCHANDISE

The Find: More than 20,000 previously unreleased recordings by
Bob Dylan, Elvis Presley, Johnny Cash, Roy Orbison, Frank Sinatra, Louis Armstrong, and other music stars.

In an average hour, there are 61,000 Americans airborne over the United States.

Where It Was Found: At a Nashville warehouse sale

The Story: In 1990, Douglas and Brenda Cole went to an auction in Nashville. On a whim, they paid $50 for the contents of a storage locker that a recording engineer had abandoned. Among the contents: boxes of used recording tapes that Nashville's Columbia Studios had apparently sold the engineer between 1953 and 1971 as scrap. "They were considered waste material, waste tape," an attorney explains. After listening to a few of them, the Coles realized they had something special, but they couldn't get Columbia Records interested. So, in 1992, they sold the tapes for $6,000 to Clark Enslin, owner of a small New Jersey—based record label.

Enslin contacted Sony Records (Columbia's parent company) about the tapes—and they filed suit against him, claiming he'd acquired the tapes illegally. The case was in court for three years and ended in a mixed verdict. Sony won commercial control over the 30% of the tapes recorded by artists who were signed with Columbia at the time the recordings were made; Enslin kept control of the remaining 70%—including songs by Presley, Sinatra, Williams, Armstrong, Orbison, and Jerry Lee Lewis. Actual estimated value of the tapes: $100 million. "It's very exciting," Enslin says. "It's hard to describe what it's like, knowing I have the best collection of recorded music in the world."

TREASURE IN THE TRASH

The Find: The $200,000 grand prize—winning cup in a Wendy's Restaurant fast food contest

Where It Was Found: In the garbage

The Story: In 1995, Craig Randall, a 23-year-old trash collector in Peabody, Massachusetts, noticed a Wendy's contest cup sitting in some garbage he was collecting. "I won a chicken sandwich the week before," he told reporters, "and I figured, hey, I'd get some fries to go with it." Instead, when he peeled off the sticker he saw: "Congratulations. You have won $200,000 towards a new home." The fact that he found the cup didn't matter; Wendy's gave him the money anyway. "I have no idea where it came from," he said. "It was just sitting there."

I'M GAME

You've played them. You've loved them.
Now here's a look at where they came from.

THE GAME OF LIFE

In 1860, young Milton Bradley's lithography company was in trouble; sales of his bestselling product, pictures of a clean-shaven Abraham Lincoln, had fallen off drastically when Lincoln grew a beard. Desperate, he printed up a board game called "The Checkered Game of Life." Players who landed on "Idleness" were told to "Go to disgrace"; the "Bravery" square led to "Honor"; and so on. It was perfect for the puritanical Victorian era, and sold so well that Bradley became America's first game mogul.

In 1960, the Milton Bradley Company came out with the 100th-anniversary "Game of Life." It became the second best-selling game of all time (after Monopoly).

PARCHEESI

In the late 1800s, a manufacturer approached Sam Loyd, one of America's premier game designers, with a problem: His company had a surplus of cardboard squares. Could Loyd devise some sort of game that would use the squares, so his company could get rid of them?

Borrowing from a centuries-old Indian game called pachisi, Loyd created a "new" game he called Parcheesi. It didn't take him very long. In fact, it was so easy that he only charged the manufacturer $10 for his services. Within a few years, the game became one of the most popular in the United States—but that $10 was the only money Loyd ever got for it.

TWISTER

In the early 1960s, Reynolds Guyer worked at his family's sales-promotion company designing packages and displays. He also created premiums—the gifts people get for sending in boxtops and proofs-of-purchase.

One day in 1965, the 29-year-old Guyer and his crew started work on a premium for a shoe polish company. "One idea," he says, "was to have kids standing on this mat with squares that told them where to put their feet....but I thought, this is bigger than

---

Medical Alert for Vince Lombardi: "Telesphobia" is the name given to "the fear of being last."

just a premium."

He expanded the mat to 4' x 6' and turned it into a game. "I got the secretaries and the designers and everyone together to play. You know, in 1965 no one ever touched. It really broke all the rules of propriety having people stand so close together."

At first it was a flop. No one knew what to make of a game where people were the main playing pieces. But when Johnny Carson and Eva Gabor played it on the "Tonight Show" in 1966, America got the point. Overnight, it became a runaway hit.

TRIVIAL PURSUIT

In December 1979, Scott Abbott, a sports editor with the *Canadian Press*, and Chris Haney, a photographer with the *Montreal Gazette*, sat down to play Scrabble. Then they realized their game was missing four pieces. Haney went out to buy a new game...and was astonished that he had to cough up $16 for it. Abbot suggested that they invent their own game. They tossed around some ideas until they came up with the magic word "trivia."

"I was the sports buff," Abbott remembers, "and Chris was the movie and entertainment buff. We sat down...and started doodling a game board. The whole thing was done in about 45 minutes."

They offered $1,000 shares in the game to friends and co-workers, but hardly anyone was interested. "I heard people call them small-time shysters," one colleague remembers. As Haney puts it, "Of course, it was no, no, no, and they all came to us later, and of course we said no, no, no." Abbott and Haney eventually raised the money to produce 20,000 games...and managed to sell them all, mostly in Canada. Still, according to Matthew Costello in *The World's Greatest Games:*

> Trivial Pursuit might have stayed just a moderate success if the daughter of the Canadian distributor for Selchow & Righter (ironically, the maker of Scrabble) hadn't discovered "this terrific new game." She told her father, and Selchow & Righter bought the rights to it. With their marketing push, North America was besieged by Trivial Pursuit.

Since then, more than 60 million sets—over $1 billion worth of the games—have been sold in 33 countries and in 19 languages around the world.

Mussolini dodged the Italian draft.

WOULD YOU BELIEVE?

According to Webster's Dictionary, *a cynic is "one who believes that human conduct is wholly motivated by self-interest." Does that describe you? Find out by taking this handy-dandy, 100% all-true quiz.*
(Answers on page 763.)

POLITICS
1. Presidential security advisor Oliver North testified in 1987 that information leaked by Congress had "seriously compromised intelligence activities" during an incident involving Egyptian terrorists. Actually...
a) North made the incident up.
b) North was the one who'd leaked the information.
c) Since Oliver North never lies, everyone believed him.

GOOD CAUSES
2. As a spokesperson for AIDS awareness, pop singer Madonna advised Americans that using condoms is "the best way to say I love you." However in her own life, she explained...
a) She never uses condoms.
b) She doesn't trust most condoms, so she has them custom-made.
c) When she really loves someone, she says, "The hell with the condom."

3. Candy Lightner founded Mothers Against Drunk Driving (MADD) in 1980 when her daughter was killed by a drunk driver. In 1994, she took a job as...
a) A paid lobbiest for a liquor industry trade group.
b) A nightclub comedian doing a "drunk" act.
c) An advisor to Seagram's.

EDUCATION
4. In May 1996, an 18-year-old crusader for sexual abstinence named Danyale Andersen was in the news. After spending more than 100 hours preaching abstinence to younger students in her school and appearing before the school board in her home-town to support an "abstinence-only health curriculum," she...
a) Posed for Playboy.
b) Became a nun.
c) Had a baby out of wedlock.

Q: Who invented the talking doll? A: Thomas Edison, in 1888.

SPORTS

5. Japan's Yasuhiro Yamashita overcame a torn leg muscle to win a gold medal in Judo at the 1984 Olympics. His opponent, Mohamed Ali Rashwan of Egypt, told reporters he hadn't attacked Yamashita's leg because "I would not want to win this way." For his sportsmanship, he received the 1985 Fair Play Trophy. Actually...
a) The first thing Rashwan did was attack Yamashita's leg.
b) Japanese businessmen had bribed Rashwan to lose.
c) He only found out the leg was injured *after* the match was over.

6. The National Football League presents itself as an advocate of "family values." So when David Williams, a lineman for the Houston Oilers, missed a game to be with his wife during the birth of their son, the Oilers' front office...
a) Gave him a special award.
b) Gave him two weeks of paternity leave.
c) Docked him a week's pay.

FINANCES

7. Benjamin Franklin, America's "apostle of thrift," coined phrases like "A penny saved is a penny earned." Historians now say that Franklin's own bank account...
a) Was with a Mafia bank.
b) Was perpetually overdrawn.
c) Had the lowest interest rate in the Colonies.

8. The IRS say it's every American's duty to keep good, accurate financial records. But a 1994 audit showed that...
a) No one understands what they're talking about.
b) Even the IRS's records are a mess.
c) Only about 47% of Americans keep any records at all.

THE NEWS MEDIA

9. *The New York Times*' well-known slogan is "All the News That's Fit to Print." But when the *Times* summarized the Supreme Court's decisions in 1973, it omitted one. Why?
a) It was a paternity suit brought against their publisher, Arthur Ochs Sulzberger.
b) It involved obscene grafitti, and they refused to print the four-letter words involved.
c) It was a libel suit against a major news organization, and they didn't want to publicize it.

Advanced civilization: In Italy, teachers get four months' vacation per year.

ANONYMOUS STARS

You've watched them work, you've heard them speak—but you've probably never heard their names. They're the actors inside the gorilla suits, the voices of talking animals, etc. We think they deserve a little credit.

THE VOICE OF E.T.

The voice of E.T.

• E.T.'s voice was created by combining the voices of three people, a sea otter, and a dog. But the person who spoke the most famous lines— "E.T. phone home" and "Be good"—was Patricia A. Welsh, a former radio soap opera star who'd only been involved in one other movie (*Waterloo*, with Robert Taylor, in 1940).

• By contract, she was forbidden to say her lines (which are copyrighted) even casually in conversation; Steven Spielberg said he "didn't want kids to get confused about E.T.'s image." Her name isn't even listed in the credits.

DARTH VADER

• David Prowse is a 6' 6", 266-pound former heavyweight wrestling champion. George Lucas saw him in *A Clockwork Orange* and offered him his choice between two parts— Chewbacca or Vader. Prowse chose Vader because he didn't like the idea of going around in a "gorilla suit" for six months.

THE "LOST IN SPACE" ROBOT

• Bob May, a stuntman, had a few small parts in a TV series called *Voyage to the Bottom of the Sea*. The producer, Irwin Allen, told May he was the right size for a part in a new TV series and asked if he'd be interested. May said yes; Allen said: "Fine, you have the part, go try on the robot costume."

• Cast members goofed on May a lot. One time they locked him in the robot suit and left him there during a lunch break. He tried yelling, but no one was around...so he had a cigarette. Irwin Allen wandered in, saw smoke coming from the robot and thought it was burning up. He went to get a fire extinguisher while May yelled from inside the suit. Later, Allen decided he liked the effect and had May smoke a cigar in the suit for a story about the robot burning out.

MR. ED'S VOICE

• When "Mr. Ed" debuted in 1960, the horse's voice was credited to "an actor who prefers to remain nameless."

• *TV Guide* sent a reporter to the studio to figure out who it was. The reporter found a parking space on the "Mr. Ed" set assigned to an old 1930s movie cowboy named Alan "Rocky" Lane.

• Lane admitted it was his voice (he'd been too embarrassed to let people know). He dubbed Ed's voice off-camera, while the horse was "mouthing the words." A nylon bit concealed in Ed's mouth made him move his lips.

R2-D2

• Kenny Baker, 3' 8" tall, was hired simply because he fit into the robot suit. "They made R2-D2 small because Carrie and Mark were small… My agent sent me down. They looked at me and said, "He'll do!"

• "I thought it was a load of rubbish at first. Then I thought, 'Well, Alec Guinness is in it; he must know what's going on.'"

THE VOICE OF THE DEMON IN *THE EXORCIST*

• Mercedes McCambridge, an Academy Award-winning actress, was a Catholic. So when she was offered the role, she was uncertain about whether to take it. She consulted Father Walter Hartke at Catholic University, and he approved.

• In the film, the demon's voice is heard as Linda Blair vomits green gunk. According to one report: "A tube was glued to each side of Blair's face and covered with makeup. Two men knelt on either side of Blair holding a syringe filled with the green stuff, ready to shoot on cue."

• "McCambridge had to coordinate her sound effects with the action. A prop man lined up a row of Dixie cups in front of her containing apple pieces soaking in water, and some containing whole boiled eggs. McCambridge held the soft apple chunks in her jaws as she swallowed a boiled egg. On cue, in precise coordination with the screen action, she flexed her diaphragm and spewed everything on the microphone… 'It was hard,' she said. 'I sometimes had to lie down after those scenes.'"

Ancient Egyptian tombs are decorated with pictures of watermelons.

CAB CALLOWAY'S JIVE DICTIONARY

In the '30s and '40s, Cab Calloway and his band were famous for tunes like "Minnie the Moocher" and "St. James Infirmary." But he was also known as a "hep-cat," identified with outrageous zoot suits and jive talk. His guide on how to talk like a hipster was published in the 1940s. It was unearthed by BRI member Gordon Javna.

APPLE: The big town, the main stem

BARBEQUE: The girlfriend, a beauty

BARRELHOUSE: Free and easy

BATTLE: Crone, hag

BEAT IT OUT: Play it hot

BEAT UP THE CHOPS: To talk

BEEF: To say, to state

BLIP: Something very good

BLOW THE TOP: To be overcome with emotion or delight

BUDDY GHEE: Fellow

BUST YOUR CONK: Apply yourself diligently, break your neck

CLAMBAKE: Every man for himself

COOLING: Laying off, not working

CORNY: Old-fashioned, stale

CUBBY: Room, flat, home

CUPS: Sleep

CUT RATE: Low, cheap person

DICTY: High-class, nifty, smart

DIME NOTE: $10 bill

DRAPE: Suit of clothes, dress

DRY GOODS: Dress, costume

DUKE: Hand, mitt

FALL OUT: To be overcome with emotion

FAUST: An ugly girl

FEWS AND TWO: Money or cash in small quantity

FRAME: The body

FROMPY: A frompy queen is a battle or faust

FRUITING: Fickle, fooling around with no particular object

GATE: A male person

GLIMS: The eyes

GOT YOUR BOOTS ON: You know what it is all about, you are wise

GOT YOUR GLASSES ON: You are ritzy or snooty, you fail to recognize your friends

---

Ouch! Pain travels through your body at a rate of 350 feet/second.

GUTBUCKET: Low-down music

HARD: Fine, good

HEP CAT: A guy who knows all the answers, understands jive

HOME-COOKING: Something very nice

ICKY: A stupid person, not hip

IN THE GROOVE: Perfect

JACK: Name for all male friends

JEFF: A pest, a bore

JELLY: Anything free, on the house

JITTER BUG: A swing fan

KILL ME: Show me a good time, send me

KILLER-DILLER: A great thrill

LAY YOUR RACKET: To jive, to sell an idea

LEAD SHEET: A coat

LILLY WHITES: Bed sheets

MAIN IN GRAY: The postman

MAIN ON THE HITCH: Husband

MAIN QUEEN: Favorite girl friend, sweetheart

MESS: Something good

METER: Quarter, twenty-five cents

MEZZ: Anything supreme, genuine

MITT POUNDING: Applause

MOUSE: Pocket

MURDER: Something excellent or terrific

NEIGHO POPS: Nothing doing, pal

OFF THE COB: Corny, out of date

OFF TIME JIVE: A sorry excuse, saying the wrong thing

PIGEON: A young girl

PINK: A white person

POPS: Salutation for all males

POUNDERS: Policemen

QUEEN: A beautiful girl

RUG CUTTER: A very good dancer

SALTY: Angry or ill-tempered

SEND: To arouse the emotions (joyful)

SET OF SEVEN BRIGHTS: One week

SHARP: Neat, smart, tricky

SLIDE YOUR JIB: Talk freely

SOLID: Great, swell, okay

SQUARE: An un-hip person

STAND ONE UP: To assume one is cut-rate

TAKE IT SLOW: Be careful

TOGGED TO THE BRICKS: Dressed to kill

TRILLY: To leave, to depart

TRUCK: To go somewhere

WHIPPED UP: Worn out, exhausted

WRONG RIFF: Saying or doing the wrong thing

Heavy thought: The average adult male has 40 lbs. of bone and 65 lbs. of muscle in his body.

WHO CRACKED
THE LIBERTY BELL?

*What do you know about the Liberty Bell? This piece, adapted
from* American Heritage *magazine and the Liberty
Bell website, might fill in a few details.*

THE FIRST CRACK

T• At a meeting of the Assembly of the Province of Pennsylvania in 1751, representatives decided to buy a bell to
hang in the belfry of the State House in Philadelphia.

• They ordered one from the Whitechapel Bell Foundry in
London. It arrived at Philadelphia in the late summer of 1752. But
when officials hung it "to try the sound," it "cracked at the first
stroke."

• They tried to send the bell back on the ship that had brought it,
but there was no room. So two local foundrymen—John Pass and
John Stow—were hired to recast it. "They made a mold from the
original bell to preserve the design, melted down the metal…and
recast. The bell that resulted, however, was judged to have poor
tone, and they tried again."

• The second time, they did a better job. The new bell "was
deemed acceptable if not altogether satisfactory," and that's the
one that was hung in the State House.

• Why did it become known as the Liberty Bell? Probably because
of the inscription on its crown:

> PROCLAIM LIBERTY THROUGHOUT ALL THE LAND UNTO
> ALL THE INHABITANTS THEREOF LEVITICUS. XXV VSX.

THE SECOND & THIRD CRACKS

• It's commonly believed that the Liberty Bell cracked a second
time when people enthusiastically rang it to celebrate the signing
of the Declaration of Independence in 1776. Actually, it broke in
1835— "either in July while tolling for Chief Justice John
Marshall's death, or on Washington's Birthday, when a group of
small boys pulled too energetically on the rope."

• The latter is more likely. In 1911, Emmanuel Rauch, one of the

---

The average housefly weighs 10 to 15 millionths of a pound.

boys, was interviewed, and he insisted that it was he and his friends who had cracked the bell. He pointed out that during Marshall's funeral "the bell's clapper would have been muffled and unlikely to cause damage."

• Eleven years later, in 1846, the bell cracked again. "An attempt was made to put the great bell in ringing order by drilling out the edges of the crack to prevent their rubbing together...[but]when the bell was rung on [Washington's Birthday], the crack suddenly split open farther. Since then the only sound heard from the bell has been a disappointing thunk created by tapping it gently with a small mallet on occasions like the invasion of Normandy in 1944."

WHY DID IT CRACK?

"But why did the bell crack in the first place? According to metallurgist Dr. Alan R. Rosenfield, an expert on metal fracture, it's no big deal: "Bells are necessarily made out of brittle metal, and they often break," he says, adding "even Big Ben is slightly cracked.' " Specifically, he notes:

1. "Pass and Stow were not skillful enough to produce a bell with a uniformly smooth surface: there are numerous pockmarks and some seams." On top of that, it contains too much tin and "many nonmetallic impurities, globs of lead, and small voids. Any of these irregularities...could have started the fatal crack."

2. "The Liberty Bell had a rough time during the Revolution." With the threat of British occupation of Philadelphia in 1777, [the bell was] removed from the City (so it wouldn't fall into British hands and be made into a cannon). "It was loaded on a wagon and jolted over bad roads to Allentown for safekeeping until 1778. It [was] dropped at least once en route, which may have produced an incipient, microscopic crack."

3. "Any big bell is subject to metal fatigue—the gradual deterioration of part of the bell under a repeated number of strikings." The Liberty Bell could have developed "a fatigue crack any time in its first 50 or 60 years of existence."

POSTSCRIPT: In 1943 the Whitechapel Bell Foundry, still in business in London, offered to melt down the bell and recast it. They were turned down. "The crack, it would seem," writes *American Heritage*, "has become as sacred as the bell itself."

Game maker Nintendo sold its one billionth video game in October 1995.

TRUE CONFESSIONS

A little bathroom pastime: Match the intimate revelation with the celebrity who said it. Inspired by Jon Winokur's book of quotes, True Confessions.

1. "Brain the size of a pea, I've got."

2. "I never wanted to be famous; I only wanted to be great."

3. "I learned the way a monkey learns—by watching its parents."

4. "If only I had a little humility, I would be perfect."

5. "The only reason they come to see me is that I know life is great—and they know I know it."

6. "It costs a lot of money to look this cheap."

7. "I guess I look like a rock quarry that someone has dynamited."

8. "Sometimes, at the end of the day when I'm smiling and shaking hands, I want to kick them."

9. "I left high school a virgin."

10. "I never had a date in high school or in college."

11. "I'm not smart enough to lie."

12. "I'm at the age where food has taken the place of sex in my life. In fact, I've just had a mirror put over my kitchen table."

13. "I pretended to be somebody I wanted to be until I finally became that person. Or he became me."

14. "Sitting on the toilet peeing—that's where I have my most contemplative moments."

A. Tom Selleck

B. Cary Grant

C. Sally Jesse Raphael

D. Charles Bronson

E. Richard Nixon

F. Ronald Reagan

G. Madonna

H. Ray Charles

I. Princess Diana

J. Clark Gable

K. Dolly Parton

L. Prince Charles

M. Ted Turner

N. Rodney Dangerfield

ANSWERS 1-I, 2-H, 3-L, 4-M, 5-J, 6-K, 7-D, 8-E, 9-A, 10-C, 11-F, 12-N, 13-B, 14-G

Poll results: 2% of Americans "always" tip a waiter/waitress; 70% say it "depends on service."

THE REMOTE CONTROL

*Over 400 million TV remote controls are currently in use in the
United States. Here's the story of their creation.*

THE FIRST TV REMOTE

T • Commander Eugene MacDonald, Jr., president of the
Zenith Radio Co., hated TV commercials. He figured
other Americans did too, so he told his researchers to create a
system that would mute all ads by remote control.
• Zenith wasn't the only one working on this idea. In 1953,
another company introduced a TV remote control that operated
with radio waves. Unfortunately, the waves traveled through walls
and down the street, and tended to operate neighbors' TV sets as
well.

TRY, TRY AGAIN

• In 1953 and 1954, Zenith developed two remote-control
systems, both of which flopped:
1. The "Lazy Bones" connected to the TV with a long cable. It
   worked, but among other problems, it kept tripping people.
2. The more advanced "Flashamatic" used four photo cells, one in
   each corner of the TV cabinet. Each cell controlled one function—volume, channels, etc. All a viewer had to do was aim a
   flashlight at the right cell. Unfortunately, first-generation couch
   potatoes couldn't remember which cell did what…and direct
   sunlight operated all of them at once.
• In 1955, Robert Adler, a Zenith acoustics expert, developed a
remote system using high-frequency sound. The device contained
an aluminum rod that rang when hit by a hammer. Called the
Space Command 200, it debuted in 1956. Retail price: $399.95.
Unfortunately, any noise produced by small pieces of metal, such
as jingling keys or dog chains, produced tones similar to the
remote's, so channels changed and sets turned on and off unpre-
dictably.
• By 1962, the kinks in the Space Command were worked out.
Bulky vacuum tubes were replaced with transistors, making the
remote smaller and cheaper. But Adler's development of ultra-
sound remained the technique for all remote controls until the
early 1980s, when new semiconductors make infrared remote
controls capable of transmitting digital codes.

The founding fathers' name for the American Revolution was "The War with Britain."

FAMILIAR PHRASES

More origins of everyday phrases.

START WITH A CLEAN SLATE
Meaning: Make a fresh start.
Origin: From the days when tavern keepers used slate blackboards to keep track of money owed by customers. When a person paid off a debt, their name was erased, and they literally got to "start with a clean slate."

HARP ON SOMETHING
Meaning: Dwell obsessively on the same topic.
Origin: The modern expression is a shortened version of the old phrase, "harping on one string," which meant playing the same note of a harp over and over.

BAIL OUT
Meanings: (1) Remove water from a ship; (2) pay to get someone out of jail; and (3) jump out of a plane in an emergency.
Origin: The expression and all of its meanings come from a time when English sailors used buckets known as beyles to remove unwanted water from their ships.

BIGWIG
Meaning: Important person.
Origin: Judges and lawyers have worn wigs in British courts since the 18th century. Lawyers wear short wigs, but the judge wears a long wig, sometimes down to his shoulders. That makes the judge—the most important person in the room—literally a "bigwig," because he wears the biggest wig.

CANARY / CANARY ISLANDS / CANARY YELLOW
Meanings: Species of bird; islands near Africa; a shade of yellow.
Origin: When ancient Romans first set foot on an archipelago off the coast of West Africa, they quickly discovered that the islands were crawling with wild dogs. They named the islands Canariae Insulae, "Dog Islands." In time, they became known as the "Canary Islands" and the small gray and green finches that lived

---

An adult giraffe's tongue is 17 inches long.

there became known as "canaries." When selective breeding resulted in a bright yellow variety of the bird, the color itself became known as "canary yellow."

THROW INTO STITCHES
Meaning: Make someone laugh hard.
Origin: This stitch has nothing to do with sewing: it comes from stice, an Old English word that means "to sting." When you throw someone into stitches, you make them laugh so hard that it hurts.

TURN A BLIND EYE
Meaning: Deliberately overlook something.
Origin: Goes back to the British admiral Lord Nelson, who was blind in one eye. In 1801, Nelson was second-in-command during a naval attack on Copenhagen. The commanding admiral signaled an order to cease fire. Rather than obey it, Nelson held his telescope up to his blind eye, turned toward the admiral's ship, and told a subordinate, "I don't see anything." The attack continued, and the Danish eventually surrendered.

EAT HUMBLE PIE
Meaning: Admit you're wrong; humiliate yourself.
Origin: In the Middle Ages, when the lord of a manor returned from deer hunting, he and his noble guests dined on venison (deer meat), considered the finest part of the deer. His servants and other commoners ate a pie made from the umbles—the heart, liver, entrails, and other undesirable parts. Originally, "umbles" and "humble" were unrelated words. But eating the pie was such a humble act that when the word umble disappeared, humble took its place in this expression.

FORK IT OVER
Meaning: Surrender something.
Origin: Centuries ago, most of the farmland in England was owned by great lords. Farmers were supposed to pay the lords their rent with silver coins. When the farmers had no coins, landlords took wagons into the fields and demanded that the farmers use pitchforks to "fork over some" of the crop instead.

Maine is the only U.S. state with a one-syllable name.

CELEBRITY MUMMIES

Here are a few contemporary mummies of note.

JOHN WILKES BOOTH (aka John St. Helen)
After he shot Lincoln, Booth was a fugitive for 12 days. The government said that federal troops tracked him down and shot him in a Virginia tobacco barn. Then, to prevent his gravesite from becoming a Confederate shrine, they quickly buried him in an unmarked grave at the Washington Arsenal. But this made people suspicious. Why so fast—were they hiding something? Was the man they buried really Booth...or had the assassin escaped?

Over the years, more than 40 people made deathbed "confessions" claiming they were Booth. One of these was John St. Helen. In 1877, thinking he was about to die, St. Helen confessed to a man named Finis L. Bates that he was Lincoln's assassin.

St. Helen actually survived and lived until 1903. When he finally died, Bates had St. Helen's body mummified and moved to his basement, where it was stored for the next 20 years. Then, when Bates died in 1923, his wife sold the mummy. It ended up in the hands of carnival operators who exhibited it as Booth until the mid-1970s. It then disappeared, and hasn't been seen since.

ELMER J. MCCURDY
In 1976, an episode of TV's "The Six Million Dollar Man" was filmed at the Nu-Pike amusement park in Long Beach, California. There was a dummy hanging from a fake gallows in the fun house; when a technician tried to move it out of the way, its arm came off at the elbow...exposing human bones. It was a mummy, not a dummy!

The film crew was horrified. The mummy's face had been painted and shellacked so many times that the amusement park owners thought it was made of wax. But who was the mummy? And how did it wind up in the park?

The L.A. County coroner had one clue: the mummy's mouth was stuffed with carnival ticket stubs. They were traced to Oklahoma, and, working with Oklahoma historians, the coroner finally identified the body as Elmer J. McCurdy, a long-forgotten bandit.

Q: How did Levi's 501 jeans get their name? A: The new denim's lot number was 501.

According to a 1993 *Wall Street Journal* article:

> Eighty years ago, [McCurdy] robbed the wrong train and rode off with $45 and a load of whiskey. When the posse caught him two days later, the whiskey was gone and he was having a nice nap. According to local legend, he decided to shoot it out anyway. That was another mistake. An…undertaker in Pawhuska, OK, mummified his body and put it on display for 5¢ a view until 1916, when two men posing as Mr. McCurdy's brothers claimed the corpse. They were actually carnival promoters. For decades, the unfortunate Mr. McCurdy criss-crossed the country as a sideshow attraction.

The town of Guthrie, Oklahoma, paid for McCurdy's trip back to the state and gave him a Christian burial. His grave (which has been sealed in concrete to ensure that it is his *final* resting place) is now the town's biggest tourist attraction.

EVA "EVITA" PERON

Juan Peron was the president of Argentina from 1948 to 1954. His wife, Eva, a former actress and a crusader for the poor, was extremely popular. When she died of cancer in 1952 at age 33, Peron had her mummified and put on public display. The procedure took about a year and cost $100,000.

Peron fell from power while his wife was still lying in state, and went into exile in Spain before he could arrange her burial. Evita was put in storage in Buenos Aires. Then her body disappeared.

It turned out that anti-Peronists—making sure the body was never again used as a pro-Peron political symbol—had stolen the coffin, sealed it in a packing crate, and eventually buried it in a Milan cemetery. In 1971—19 years later—a sympathetic Spanish intelligence officer told Peron where his wife was buried. Peron had her exhumed and brought to Spain. When the ex-dictator pried open the coffin, his wife was so well preserved that he cried out, "She is not dead, she is only sleeping!"

Rather than bury his Evita again, Peron kept her around the house; he and his third wife, Isabel, propped her up in the dining room and ate in her presence every evening, even when they entertained guests. The arrangement lasted until 1973, when Peron returned to power in Argentina and left his beloved mummy in Spain. Later, Evita was brought across the Atlantic and was buried in Argentina.

It must be cool: James Dean's favorite food was rice pudding.

GROUCHO SEZ...

A few choice words from the master, Groucho Marx.

"I've had a perfectly wonderful evening. But this wasn't it."

"I was married by a judge. I should have asked for the jury."

"Remember men, we're fighting for this woman's honor—which is probably more than she ever did."

"If I held you any closer, I'd be on the other side of you."

"Those are my principles. If you don't like them I have others."

"From the moment I picked up your book until I laid it down, I was convulsing with laughter. Someday I intend to read it."

"The husband who wants a perfect marriage should learn how to keep his mouth shut and his checkbook open."

"Oh, are you from Wales? Do you know a fellow named Jonah? He used to live in Wales for a while."

"Blood's not thicker than money."

"He may look like an idiot and talk like an idiot, but don't let that fool you. He really is an idiot."

"The secret of success is honesty and fair dealing. If you can fake those, you've got it made."

"Well, Art is Art, isn't it? Still, on the other hand, water is water! And East is East and West is West and if you take cranberries and stew them with applesauce they taste more like prunes than rhubarb does.... Now you tell me what you know."

"I've been around so long I can remember Doris Day before she was a virgin."

"Outside of a dog, a book is a man's best friend. Inside of a dog it's too hard to read."

"Who are you going to believe, me or your own eyes?"

"Well, I hardly know where to begin. I hardly know when to stop, either; just give me a few drinks and see for yourself."

Survey result: 70% of employers don't like hiring married couples to work in the same office.

SILENT PARTNERS

Everyone knows that Hollywood is a world of fiction and fantasy; even so, it's hard to believe that people who appear to like one another on TV and in film sometimes loathe each other in real life. Some examples:

FRED AND ETHEL MERTZ ("I LOVE LUCY")
How we remember them: Fred and Ethel (William Frawley and Vivian Vance) were like everybody's next-door neighbors. Both were frumpy and grumpy, but underneath, they had an abiding love for one another...at least in front of the cameras.
How they really were: Frawley and Vance could barely stand each other from the moment they began working on the show...and things got worse from there: Vance, who was 25 years Frawley's junior (39 to his 64), hated the idea that viewers believed she could be married to someone so old. "He should be playing my father, not my husband," she routinely complained. Another thorn in her side: there was a clause in her contract that allowed the show to dump her if Frawley died or became too ill to work.

Frawley wasn't any happier: his nicknames for Vance were "Old Fat Ass" and "that old sack of doorknobs," and he was famous for frequently asking Desi, "Where did you dig up that bitch?"
Silent treatment: Things came to a head near the end of the "I Love Lucy" run, when Desi Arnaz approached Vance about spinning off the Fred and Ethel characters into their own show. As Vance later recounted,

> I loathed Bill Frawley, and the feeling was mutual....There was no way I could do a series with him on our own, so when Desi asked me, I refused. I still wouldn't budge when he offered me a bonus of $50,000 just to do a pilot. When Bill found out, he was furious, not because he wanted to work with me any more than I did with him, but because he stood to earn a lot more money than he did on "Lucy." He never spoke to me again except when work required it.

A few years after "I Love Lucy" ended, someone asked Frawley if he'd kept in touch with Vance. "I don't know where she is now and she doesn't know where I am," he replied, "and that's exactly the way I like it."

The Pacific Ocean is twice as large as the Atlantic...and larger than all the continents combined.

ABBOTT AND COSTELLO

How we remember them: The quintessential buddy comedy team
of the 1930s, 1940s, and 1950s. Sure, they fought onstage, but that
was part of their act...and it never seemed to get in the way of
their warm friendship.

How they really were: According to Penny Stallings in *Forbidden
Channels*, Abbott and Costello's relationship deteriorated toward
the end of their careers. Abbott was one of showbiz's greatest
straight men, but Costello came to believe that he'd "carried"
Abbott for years. Mel Blanc, who worked on Abbott and
Costello's TV show in the 1950s, recalled, "They hated each
other. Especially Costello. Even at the end he was still trying to
get other straight men, but he could just never find one as good."

Silent treatment: The pair frequently hosted "The Colgate
Comedy Hour," but Costello stormed off the set after an argument
one day and never returned. Instead, he became a frequent guest
on a competing show hosted by Steve Allen. Abbott was so upset
by the split that he fell ill and had to check into a hospital. The
relationship remained troubled from then on: Costello later sued
Abbott for $222,000 in unpaid royalties, but he dropped dead of a
heart attack in 1959 before the suit was resolved.

SONNY AND CHER

How we remember them: The ultimate hippie power couple of
the 1960s and early 1970s, Sonny and Cher were a beacon of
stability at a time when people were questioning the merits of
traditional relationships. In their songs, on their show, and in
their marriage—or so we thought—Sonny and Cher proved that
two people didn't have to be square to be devoted to one another.

How they really were: Not long after they hit superstardom with
their variety TV show, Sonny and Cher's private life began to
crumble. In November 1972, Sonny says, Cher announced she
was having an affair with their guitarist. Sonny was devastated,
but within a few months, he realized their marriage was over for
good...at least behind the scenes. Public perception was another
story, as Bono recounts in his autobiography *And the Beat Goes
On.*

If you want to hardboil an ostrich egg, bring along something to do. It takes up to four hours.

Despite their differences, he and Cher decided to stay together for the sake of their bank accounts:

> I told Cher that she had to realize that we were involved in a business, a highly profitable business, and though the marriage was gone and the love lost, it was silly to give up the tremendous sums of money we were making. I'd come to terms with the reality of our situation. I accepted it...and I was OK with her pursuing whatever personal life she wanted. I'd do the same. But Sonny and Cher were names too valuable to simply walk away from. She agreed.

Silent treatment: For the last year of their marriage and their variety show, Sonny and Cher lived a lie: pretending to be happily married, they set up separate households in different parts of their 54-room mansion, Sonny with his lover in one corner and Cher with hers in another. The charade lasted until February 1974, when Cher moved out and filed for divorce on grounds of "involuntary servitude." They've been taking potshots at each other in the media ever since.

"Cher wants to run like a racehorse, but she can't find a track," Bono laments in his autobiography. "I used to be the jockey, but Cher quite nicely shoved the saddle up my ass."

SISKEL AND EBERT

How we think of them: The best film critics on TV. "The fat one" (Ebert) and "the other guy" (Siskel) seem to get along pretty well despite their different opinions about movies.

How they really are: As *Time* magazine reported in 1987, "The two have little in common outside the TV studio....They rarely socialize...Nor are their fights confined to the TV cameras. In the middle of an interview, for example, Ebert will complain that Siskel won't let him plug his books on TV. And Siskel will deride his partner for his "megalomania." "He thinks the world revolves around him," Siskel sneers to the reporter. Are they just kidding? No one knows.

Silent treatment: Siskel and Ebert don't even sit together during their film screenings. Siskel sits at the rear of the screening room, Ebert sits closer to the front, *Time* reports, "usually munching from a box of Good & Plenty."

I SCREAM, YOU SCREAM

*We've uncovered a lot of food origins in the Bathroom Readers,
but until now, we never got around to one of the best foods of all.*

ICE AGES

Which is oldest—ice cream, sherbet, or snow cones?
As far as anyone can tell, snow cones are the oldest: they date
back at least as far as Roman emperor Nero (37 A.D. to 68 A.D.),
who had snow brought down from mountaintops to cool his wine
cellars. On hot days he'd mix some of the extra snow with honey,
juices, and fruit pulps, and eat it as a snack.

Sherbet—which has more fruit and less milk or cream than
ice cream—came next. In the late 13th century, Marco Polo
brought a recipe for sherbet from China to Italy. Only a few
people knew about it. "Recipes [for sherbet] were secrets, closely
guarded by chefs to the wealthy," explains Charles Panati in *Extraordinary Origins of Everyday Things*.

Historians estimate that sometime in the 16th century one of
these chefs—no one knows who—increased the milk content in
the recipe and reduced or eliminated the fruit entirely…inventing
ice cream in the process.

RICH DESSERT

Iced dessert remained an inclusive, upper-class treat for over a
century. "With refrigeration a costly ordeal of storing winter ice in
underground vaults for summer use," Panati says, "only the
wealthy tasted iced desserts." Then, in 1670, a Sicilian named
Francesco Procopio dei Coltelli opened Paris's first coffeehouse,
Cafe Procope. It was the first business ever to make ice cream
available to the general public.

This inspired other coffeehouses around Europe to do the
same. By the mid-17th century, ice cream could be found in most
of the continent's major cities…and by the end of the century,
people were addicted to it. Beethoven wrote from Vienna in 1794:
"It is very warm here….As winter is mild, ice is rare. The Viennese are afraid that it will soon be impossible to have any ice
cream."

Why are all the continents wider in the north than in the south? Nobody knows.

ICE CREAM IN AMERICA

Meanwhile, ice cream had gotten a foothold in the New World. It was first brought over in 1690, and by 1777 it was being advertised in New York newspapers. Ice cream was popular with many of the Founding Fathers, including Alexander Hamilton, George Washington (who ran up a $200 ice cream tab with one New York merchant in the summer of 1790), and Thomas Jefferson (who had his own 18-step recipe for ice cream and is believed to be the first president to serve it at a state dinner). First Lady Dolly Madison's ice cream parties helped make ice cream fashionable among the new republic's upper crust.

CRANKING IT OUT

By the 1790s, ice cream was becoming more readily available in the United States, but it was still a rare treat due to the scarcity and high price of ice—and the difficulty in making it. Most ice cream was made using the "pot freezer" method: the ingredients sat in a pot that, in turn, sat in a larger pan of salt and ice. The whole thing had to be shaken up and down by one person, while another vigorously stirred the mixture.

Over the next 50 years, two developments made ice cream an American staple:

1. In the early 1800s, "ice harvesting" of frozen northern rivers in winter months, combined with insulated icehouses that sprang up all over the country, made ice—and therefore ice cream— cheap for the first time. By 1810, ice cream was being sold by street vendors in nearly every major city in the United States.
2. In 1846, Nancy Johnson created the world's first hand-cranked ice cream freezer. With this invention, ice cream was both affordable and easy to make for the first time. By 1850, it was so common that Godey's Lady's Book could comment: "A party without it would be like a breakfast without bread."

WE ALL SCREAM

By 1900, electricity and mechanical refrigeration had given rise to a huge domestic ice cream industry. And it had become so closely identified with American culture that the people in charge of Ellis Island, determined to serve a "truly American dish" to arriving immigrants, served them ice cream at every meal.

How about you? 37% of U.S. coffee drinkers use milk & sugar; 21% drink it black.

WEIRD BAR SPORTS

Here's a look at some of the more unusual ways that bar owners have tried to keep customers busy and entertained while they drink.

DWARF TOSSING
How It's Played: A dwarf dresses up in body padding, a crash helmet, and a harness. Then contestants hurl him across the room into a pile of mattresses. The "winner" is the person who throws the dwarf the farthest. In some contests, dwarfs have been thrown as much as 30 feet. Why do the dwarfs do it? They can make as much as $2,000 a night.

History: Invented at a Queensland, Australia, bar in 1985. It later produced an offshoot—dwarf bowling: "A helmeted dwarf is strapped to a skateboard or mechanic's creeper and rolled headfirst into bowling pins, which are made of plastic."

In 1987, a few American bars tried out this "sport," and it was a commercial success. But the bad publicity—combined with lobbying by groups like Little People of America—killed it.

THE HUMAN (BAR) FLY

How It's Played: Wearing a velcro suit, bar patrons sprint down a runway, leap on a small trampoline, and hurl themselves onto a wall covered with velcro hooks. First prize goes to the person whose feet stick highest on the wall. Getting off the wall can be fun, too. "One of our rules is that the men peel off the women, and the women peel off the men," says a bar owner. "Sometimes it takes three women to peel off one guy."

History: Inspired by David Letterman, who performed the stunt on his show in 1984. The Cri Bar and Grill in New Zealand began holding "human fly" contests in 1991, and other New Zealand bars followed suit. *Sports Illustrated* covered it in 1991; it quickly spread to the United States, where it flourished for a few years.

SUMO SUIT WRESTLING

How It's Played: Participants don 43-pound rubberized vinyl and nylon suits that make them look like 400-pound sumo wrestlers—

complete with the traditional Japanese sumo "diaper" and a crash helmet with a sumo wig glued on the outside. Then they slam into each other on a big padded mat. (Not to be confused with human cockfighting, in which—no kidding—people dress up in padded chicken costumes and peck, bump, and scratch each other.)

History: Englishman Peter Herzig invented the suits after seeing sumo wrestlers in a Miller Beer commercial. Miller then bought hundreds of the suits and began promoting the "sport" in nightclubs in the early 1990s.

HUMAN BOWLING

How It's Played: Like real bowling, you have to knock down as many pins as you can…but in this sport, the pins are five feet tall and made of canvas and styrofoam; the bowler is strapped inside a huge metal-frame bowling ball. A partner rolls them down the 30-foot lane toward the pins. "Just because you're in the ball doesn't mean you have no obligations to the team," says Lori Fosdick, a regular bowler. "I've seen some pretty maneuvers—but I've also seen people who seemed to be going straight and rolled right around the pin."

History: Creator Thomas Bell got the idea in the early 1990s after watching some gerbils running on an exercise wheel. He figured humans might enjoy doing the same thing. "Bowling has always been a competitive sport," he says straight-faced. "We're just taking it to a more competitive level."

GERBIL RACING

How It's Played: Eight gerbils race in a portable race track that's set up on the wall behind the bar. Betting is not allowed, but customers who pick the winning gerbil win free drinks.

History: Invented in 1992 by a bar in Alberta, Canada, with the blessings of the Canadian SPCA. "My gerbils live to the age of two, unlike wild gerbils, which have a lifespan of only eight months," says Morley Amon, owner of the Alberta track. "They aren't running against their will. They run just to see what's on the other side."

The average U.S. farm has 467 acres of land; the average Japanese farm has 3 acres.

BRAND NAMES

*Here's another look at brand names you
know and where they come from.*

Q-TIPS. In the early 1920s, the owner of the Gerstenzang Infant Novelty Company noticed that his wife cleaned their daughter's ears by wrapping cotton around a tooth pick. Inspired, he built a machine that made "ready-to-use cotton swabs." At first he called the product Baby Gays. In 1926, they became Q-Tips ("Q for Quality") Baby Gays…and finally just Q-Tips.

ZIPPO LIGHTERS. Introduced as a revolutionary windproof lighter in 1932 and named after another revolutionary invention of the time—the zipper.

MAYBELLINE. In 1915, Mabel Williams created an eye makeup for herself out of black pigment and petroleum jelly. Her brother decided to sell it in his mail-order catalog as Lash-Brow-Ine. It sold extremely well, and in 1920 he changed the name to Maybelline, as a gesture to her.

SARAN WRAP. In 1933, Dow researchers discovered a plastic called monomeric vinylidene chloride. They called it VC Plastic. In 1940, a salesman suggested they rename it Saran (the name of the tree in India). Dow liked the new name because it had only five letters and had no negative connotations. During World War II, Saran was used in everything from belts to subway seats. In 1948, it was marketed to housewives as a plastic film called Saran Wrap.

MAX FACTOR. In the early days of the movie industry, Max Factor devised a new makeup that made actors look natural on film. It established his reputation as Hollywood's premier cosmetics authority, which gave him cachet with the general public.

RAY-BANS. Originally called "Anti-Glare goggles" in 1936. Bausch & Lomb, the manufacturer, decided "anti-glare" would be too hard to protect as a trademark, so the glasses—designed to "inhibit ultraviolet and infrared rays"—were re-christened Ray-Bans.

End to end, the number of Crayola crayons made in a year would circle the globe 4-1/2 times.

MISS AMERICA, PART II:
The Early Years

Here's more of the history of the Miss America Pageant. (Part I is on page 418.) One aspect we find fascinating: The same "traditionalists" who call Miss America their own and fight to preserve it whenever it's threatened today were its biggest enemies in the 1920s and 1930s. It goes to show how transient some notions of "decency" and "morality" can be.

RAKING IN THE DOUGH

The 1921 Fall Frolic was such a moneymaker that the Atlantic City government increased its contribution from $1,000 to $12,500 the following year. The number of participating newspapers also increased in 1922, from 8 to 57 (this time the entire country was represented). As the pageant grew, so did the crowds that thronged to see it. In 1922, 250,000 people visited Atlantic City during the pageant; 300,000 came the following year.

To maximize the time (and money) that tourists spent in Atlantic City, organizers spread the events out over three days in 1922, and then to five days in 1924 and afterward. As A.R. Riverol writes in *Live from Atlantic City*:

> The ingenuity in the pageant was that it was structured to keep the people at the resort happily spending their money. Most events were scheduled either on separate days or on the same day but hours apart…To enjoy all of the offerings of the Miss America pageant, the day tripper would either have to wait for hours or travel to Atlantic City the next day. The answer? Stay overnight.

A MAJOR SETBACK

But as the Atlantic City festivities grew in popularity, they also attracted increasing opposition. Even in the "Roaring '20s," bathing suit contests were as controversial as wet T-shirt contests are today. Women's groups and civic and religious organizations condemned the pageant for being indecent, for exploiting women for money, and for corrupting the youthful contestants.

On top of the general criticism, there were also a number of "scandals" that muddied the pageant's reputation. In 1923, for example, Miss Brooklyn and Miss Boston turned out to be married; Miss Alaska was not only married, but also a resident of New York City—not Alaska.

As the '20s wore on, hotel owners began to lose faith in the pageant as a moneymaker. Frank Deford writes in *There She Is:*

> They became convinced that the pageant, for all its notice, was starting to give Atlantic City a bad name, and cost the hotels respectable cash-and-carry patrons.

HARD TIMES

Finally in 1928, after years of negative publicity and vehement opposition from conservative groups, the Atlantic City hotel operators decided to shut Miss America down, stating that it had degenerated into a "worn out and useless...cheap exploitation of physical beauty."

From the very beginning critics had charged that the pageant lured "bad" women to the boardwalk and turned innocent young girls into hussies; now the organizers believed it themselves. The Hotelmen's Association declared:

> There has been an epidemic recently of women who seek personal aggrandizement and publicity by participating in various stunts throughout the world, and the hotelmen feel that in recent years that type of woman has been attracted to the Pageant in ever increasing numbers...Many of the girls who come here turn out bad later and though it may happen in other cities, it reflects on Atlantic City.

SECOND TRY—THE 1933 PAGEANT

"Miss America" seemed to be dead and buried. But memories of the big bucks the pageant had brought in lingered on...and in 1933, in the middle of the Great Depression, a handful of organizers decided to bring it back to life.

The Hotelmen's Association and the Chamber of Commerce refused to support it, and the newspapers—who'd sponsored earlier beauty contests—declined to participate. So the pageant had to turn to carnivals, amusement parks, theaters, and other seedy businesses to find beauty queens to compete in the 1933 event.

There were so many problems during Pageant Week that the

In skywriting, the average letter is nearly 2 miles high.

1933 contest became, arguably, the biggest disaster in Miss America history. For example:

- Miss West Virginia had to drop out because of stomach pains after she ate lobster with her ice cream.
- Miss New York State collapsed onstage from an abscessed tooth.
- Miss Oklahoma was rushed to the hospital for an emergency appendectomy.
- Miss Arkansas was revealed to be married.
- Misses Iowa, Illinois, and Idaho were disqualified because they actually resided in neither Iowa, Illinois, nor Idaho.

The 1933 crown ultimately went to Miss Connecticut, 15-year-old Marian Bergeron, but her shining moment was tarnished. "The crown was so big it came right down over my eyes, and it made me look retarded," she recalled years later. The crown was stolen the day after and was never recovered.

IF AT FIRST YOU DON'T SUCCEED...

The 1933 pageant was such a loser that until the mid-'50s, organizers of the Miss America pageants never recognized it as an "official" pageant...or acknowledged Bergeron as a genuine Miss America.

Nonetheless, in 1935, "respectable" members of Atlantic City society decided to hold another one. Why? They were probably motivated by competition. In 1934 an "American Queen of Beauty" was crowned in Madison Square Garden. And a year later, a "Miss America" was named at the San Diego County Fair. These contests were even sleazier than their Atlantic City predecessor. According to There She Is, the San Diego crown was conferred upon the winner by "the two gentlemen who ran the midget and nudist concessions at the fairs." And the San Diego Miss America didn't get a cash prize, a college scholarship, or anything like that. Instead, she won "the right' to pose in the buff for two years."

Rather than let a good thing get away—and perhaps also to keep the Miss America name from sinking deeper into the muck, if such a thing were possible—Atlantic City decided to give the pageant one more chance in 1935.

Stay tuned—there's more on page 517.

CURSES!

Even if you're not superstitious, it's hard to resist tales of "cursed" ships, tombs, and so on. Who knows—maybe there's something to them. Here are some of our favorites.

THE CURSE OF JAMES DEAN'S PORSCHE
Curse: Disaster may be ahead for anyone connected with James Dean's "death car." It seems to attack people at random.

Origin: In 1955, Dean smashed his red Porsche into a another car and was killed. The wreckage was bought by George Barris, a friend of Dean's (and the man who customized cars like the Munsters' coffin-mobile for Hollywood). But as one writer put it, "the car proved deadly even after it was dismantled." Barris noticed weird things happening immediately.

Among Its Victims:
- The car slipped while being unloaded from the truck that delivered it to Barris, and broke a mechanic's legs.
- Barris put its engine into a race car. It crashed in the race, killing the driver. A second car in the same race was equipped with the Porsche's drive shaft—it overturned and injured its driver.
- The shell of the Porsche was being used in a Highway Safety display in San Francisco. It fell off its pedestal and broke a teenager's hip. Later, a truck carrying the display to another demonstration was involved in an accident. "The truck driver," says one account, "was thrown out of the cab of the truck and killed when the Porsche shell rolled off the back of the truck and crushed him."

Status: The Porsche finally vanished in 1960, while on a train en route to Los Angeles.

THE PRESIDENTIAL DEATH CYCLE
Curse: Between 1840 and 1960, every U.S. president elected in a year ending in a zero either died in office of natural causes or was assassinated. By contrast: Since 1840, of the 29 presidents who were not elected in the 20-year cycle, only one has died in office and not one has been assassinated.

Origin: The first president to die in office was William Henry

Harrison, elected in 1840. In 1960, when John Kennedy was shot, people began to realize the eerie "coincidence" involved.

Victims:

- William Henry Harrison, dead in 1841 after one month in office
- Abraham Lincoln (elected in 1860), fatally shot in 1865
- James Garfield (1880), assassinated in 1881
- William McKinley (re-elected in 1900), fatally shot in 1901
- Warren G. Harding (1920), died in 1923
- Franklin D. Roosevelt (elected for the third time in 1940), died in 1945
- JFK (1960), assassinated in 1963
- Ronald Reagan (1980) was nearly the eighth victim. He was shot and badly wounded by John Hinckley in 1983

Status: Astrologers insist that 1980 was an aberration because "Jupiter and Saturn met in an air sign, Libra." That gave Reagan some kind of exemption. They say we still have to wait to find out if the curse is over.

THE CURSE OF THE INCAN MUMMY

Curse: By disturbing a frozen mummy's remains, authorities brought bad luck to the region where it had been buried.

Origin: Three Andean mummies were discovered by an archaeologist/mountaineer in October 1995. They had been undisturbed in snow at the top of 20,000-foot Mount Ampato, in Southern Peru, for at least 500 years. Then an earthquake exposed them. One of the mummies was the remains of a young woman, referred to by local shamans as "Juanita." She had apparently been sacrificed to Incan gods.

Among Its Victims:

- Within a year of the discovery, a Peruvian commercial jet crashed and killed 123 people near the discovery site.
- Thirty-five people were electrocuted when a high-tension cable fell on a crowd celebrating the founding of the city of Arequipa (which is near the discovery site).

Status: Local shamans said these were the acts of the angered "Ice Princess." To break the curse, they gathered in the city of Arequipa in August 1996 and chanted: "Juanita, calm your ire. Do not continue to damn innocent people who have done nothing to you." Apparently it worked—we've heard nothing of it since 1996.

How were presidents Franklin D. Roosevelt and Theodore Roosevelt related? Fifth cousins.

THE ORIGINS OF HALLOWEEN

Where does Halloween come from? Here's what the experts say:

THE BASIC FACTS

• The holiday was first celebrated by the ancient Celts in Ireland in the fifth century B.C. November 1st was the first day of the Celtic new year; according to historian Virginia Franco, the festival commemorating it was called "Samhain" (pronounced sow-wen)—which means 'summers end.' "

• ABC News: "The Christians [co-opted] the festival in the seventh century A.D. by making Nov. 1 a celebration of all...saints and martyrs—hence the name All Saints Day or all Hallows Day." (According to the *Morris Dictionary of Words and Phrases*, " 'Hallow' is derived from an Old English word meaning 'holy person.' ")

• The night before All Saints Day was known as All Hallow E'en or Even (evening)—which was shortened to "Hallowe'en."

THE MYSTERY OF HALLOWEEN

What's Halloween's original connection to spirits and costumes? No one's sure...but here are three reasonable guesses.

• **According to Francis X. Weiser, *The Handbook of Christian Feasts and Customs*:**

"The Celts believed that the night [before] November 1 demons, witches, and evil spirits roamed the earth in wild gambols of joy, ready to greet the arrival of 'their season'—the long nights and early dark of the winter months. They had their fun with...mortals that night, frightening, harming them, and playing all kinds of mean tricks. The only way, it seemed, for scared humans to escape the persecution of the demons was to offer them things they liked, especially dainty food and sweets. Or, in order to escape the fury of these horrible creatures, a human could disguise himself as one of them and join in their roaming....They would take him for one of their own and he would not be bothered....That is what the ancient Celts did, and it is in this very form the custom has come to us, practically unaltered, as our familiar Halloween celebration."

Ben and Jerry's Ice Cream gives its ice cream waste to Vermont farmers, who use

- **According to ABC News:**

"Halloween traces its ultimate origins back to the Druids—a Celtic priestly class—who believed that the spirits of the dead would roam the earth at the turn of the new year on November 1st. According to Celt tradition, the veil between this world and the other was at its thinnest on this 'all souls' day and people would dress up and paint their faces to remove differences between the two worlds so they could better interact with the souls of the dead. Costumed villagers would offer up a feast and then parade to the outskirts of town leading the ghosts away."

- **According to Charles Panati, *Extraordinary Origins of Everyday Things*:**

"The Celts believed that on October 31, all persons who had died in the previous year assembled to choose the body of the person or animal they would inhabit for the next 12 months, before they could pass peacefully into the afterlife. To frighten roving souls, Celtic family members dressed as demons, hobgoblins, and witches. ...They extinguished the fires on their hearths to deliberately make their homes cold and undesirable to disembodied spirits....They paraded first inside, then outside, the fireless house, in as noisy and destructive a manner as possible. Finally, they clamored along the street to the bonfire outside town....

In time, as belief in spirit possession waned, the dire portents of many Halloween practices lightened to ritualized amusement....Irish immigrants fleeing their country's potato famine in the 1840s brought to America with them the Halloween customs of costume and mischief.

TRICK OR TREAT?

"The custom of trick-or-treating is thought to have originated not with the Irish Celts, but with a ninth-century European custom called souling. On November 2, All Souls Day, early Christians would walk from village to village begging for 'soul cakes,' made out of square pieces of bread with currants. The more soul cakes the beggars would receive, the more prayers they would promise to say on behalf of the dead relatives of the donors. At the time, it was believed that the dead remained in limbo for a time after death, and that prayer, even by strangers, could expedite a soul's passage to heaven." —*Archibald Bard*

DUMB CRIMINALS

*Many Americans are worried about the growing threat of crime.
Well, the good news is that there are plenty of crooks who are
their own worst enemies. Here are a few true-life examples.*

TAKE ALL YOU WANT

"SEATTLE—Police got an early morning call from the owners of a motor home parked on a Seattle street. When officers arrived, they found sewage and what looked like vomit on the ground. Nearby, they found a man curled up ill next to the car.

"The man admitted he had been trying to siphon gas and had plugged his hose into the motor home's sewage tank by mistake. The motor home's owner declined to press charges, calling it the 'best laugh he's ever had.'"

—**The Eugene *Register-Guard*, Aug. 6, 1991**
(Submitted by BRI member Karen Roth, Eugene, Oregon)

DOG YUMMIES

"SPRING VALLEY, Calif.—Thieves broke into a commercial meat freezer in Spring Valley and are not being pursued as a high priority. The freezer is located equidistant between two buildings. The thieves undoubtedly thought the freezer belonged to a restaurant and that they were stealing frozen steaks for resale; in reality, it belongs to the restaurant's next-door neighbor, the Paradise Valley Road Pet Hospital, which reported nine euthanized dogs missing."

—*News of the Weird*, **March, 1996**

MAKING TRACKS

"SPOKANE, Wash.—Police had little difficulty catching up with a woman who robbed the Five Mile branch of the Washington Trust Bank last Saturday. The woman, who walked into the bank and showed the teller what appeared to be the handle of a gun, was given an undetermined amount of cash. She then walked out of the bank, got into a waiting cab and left. Police traced the taxi and got the woman's address. She was arrested without incident.

—**Wire service story, March 8, 1996**

George Washington was named after King George of England.

EYE DID IT
"EL CERRITO, Calif.—Robbery suspect Aaron Lavell Harris has given new meaning to the word eyewitness. Police searching the scene of an aborted armed robbery last week found one clue—a glass eye with Harris's name stenciled on it Apparently, it popped out when Harris jumped from a second-story window to escape."
—*San Francisco Chronicle*, **March 24, 1993**

BALED OUT
"LANCASTER, Calif.—An inmate who fled prison by hiding in a garbage truck found himself trapped in a compacted bale of trash on Thursday. The prisoner thought he could escape the minimum security person by hiding in a trash bin. But the bin was collected by a truck that crushes garbage into a bale about one-fifth the size of the original load. The bale and prisoner were dumped at a landfill. He was discovered by the operator of a tractor breaking up garbage. He is listed in fair condition with broken bones."
—*The Oregonian*, **Jan 14, 1996**

THANKS FOR THE RIDE
"OSLO, Norway—Thomas Braendvik was walking to the local police station to report the theft of his bicycle, when a kind bicyclist headed his way offered him a lift. Braendvik accepted, and took a seat on the luggage rack.

"I thought the bike looked suspiciously like mine, so I asked if he minded me trying my key in the lock,' Braendvik told a reporter. The key fit, proving that the bike belonged to Braendvik. A policeman happened to have been watching the whole episode. He arrested the thief on the spot."
—*Associated Press*, **July 7, 1996**

WRONG BAR
"CHICAGO—Two would-be robbers could not have picked a worse place than Z's Sports Tap for their holdup attempt. Much to their chagrin, there was a retirement party going on…for a police officer. There were more than 100 cops in the bar. They quickly subdued the robbers and called on-duty police. 'That's what makes this job interesting,' said a police spokesman. 'Dumb people.'"
—**Wire service reports, December 21, 1995**

The average office worker spends 50 minutes a day looking for lost files and other items.

WILL ROGERS SAID...

A tiny piece of the rich legacy left by America's national humorist in the 1920s and early 1930s. (He died in 1935.)

"Even if you are on the right track, you'll get run over if you just sit there."

"If stupidity got us into this mess, why can't it get us out?"

"We can't all be heroes... because someone has to sit on the curb and clap as they go by."

"Alexander Hamilton started the U.S. Treasury with nothing—and that was the closest our country has ever been to being even."

"There's no trick to being a humorist when you have the whole government working for you."

"I belong to no organized party. I am a Democrat."

"You can't say civilizations don't advance...In every war they kill you a new way."

"The man with the best job in the country is the Vice-President. All he has to do is get up every morning and say, 'How is the president?' "

"Diplomacy is the art of saying 'Nice doggie' until you can find a rock."

"Nothing you can't spell will ever work."

"If you make any money, the government shoves you in the creek once a year with it in your pockets. All that don't get wet you can keep."

"Liberty don't work as good in practice as it does in speeches."

"I see we are starting to pay attention to our neighbors in the south. We could never understand why Mexico wasn't just crazy about us; for we have always had their good will, and oil and minerals, at heart."

"Half our life is spent trying to find something to do with the time we have rushed through life trying to save."

"I never expected to see the day when girls would get sunburned in the places they do today."

Q: Why do helium-filled balloons float? A: Helium is seven times lighter than air.

CELEBRITY SUPERSTITIONS

They're only human, after all.

Luciano Pavarotti: "I won't sing a note or act a word until I find a bent nail onstage. It's like a good-luck charm for me. If I can't spot my nail onstage, I search the wings."

Larry Bird (basketball player): Always makes sure to rub his hands on his sneakers before a game, to give him "a better feel" for the ball.

Lena Horne (Singer): Thinks peanut shells in her dressing room bring bad luck.

Winston Churchill: Thought it was unlucky to travel on Fridays. Tried to arrange his schedule so he could " stay put" on that day.

Tony Curtis (actor): Wears only slip-on shoes. Thinks laces are unlucky.

Cornelius Vanderbilt (America's richest man in the 1860s): Had the legs of his bed placed in dishes of salt, to ward off attacks from evil spirits.

Drew Barrymore (actor): Says "peas indicate good luck."

Jim Kelly (Buffalo Bills quarterback): Vomits for good luck before each game. He's been doing it since high school.

Queen Elizabeth II: Insists on making a token payment for scissors used to cut ribbons at official openings. (It's bad luck to accept scissors as a gift and return nothing.)

Babe Ruth: Always stepped on first base when he came in from his right field position.

Zsa Zsa Gabor: Thinks it's bad luck to have goldfish in the house.

Wayne Gretzky (the NHL's all-time leading scorer): Puts baby powder on his stick before every game, and tucks only one side of his jersey into his pants.

Joan Rivers: "I knock on wood so often I have splinters in all ten knuckles."

Princess Diana: Had a lock of hair sewn into her wedding dress. (For luck?)

A watermelon is 92% water; a raw apple is 84% water.

FAMILY REUNIONS

You know how strange it seems when you find out you have an unexpected connection to someone. But what if the person were closely related to you? These stories are almost too weird for words, but they're all true. Inspired by an article sent by BRI member Joann McCracken in Boston.

WHO: James Austin and Yvette Richardson / Brother and sister
SEPARATION: When Yvette was three years old and James was seven months old, their father and mother separated. The father took James; the mother took Yvette. That was the last time the siblings saw or heard of each other.
TOGETHER AGAIN: James went to school in Philadelphia and got a job at the main post office. He worked the 4 p.m. shift, along with 4,100 other people. One day, he was talking to his shop steward, Barrie Bowens, about his life. As the Boston Globe reported:

> Austin told her that his father died young and that he never knew his mother. Bowens asked his mother's name and realized it was the name of Richardson's mother, too.
>
> For two years, James and Yvette had worked side by side, shooting the breeze but never prying into each other's personal life....Now they discovered they were brother and sister.

They were stunned. "Working in the same department side by side," the 34-year-old Richardson said, shaking her head. " The same place, the same time, every day. What are the odds of that?"

WHO: John Garcia and Nueng Garcia / Father and son
SEPARATION: During the late 1960s, John Garcia was stationed in Thailand with the Air Force. He lived with a woman named Pratom Semon, and in 1969, they had a son. Three months later, Garcia was shipped back to the States; he wanted to take Semon, but she refused to go. For two years, Garcia regularly wrote and sent checks to support his son. Then Semon started seeing another man and told Garcia to end his correspondence. Garcia lost touch with his son. Although he tried to find him,

even sending letters to the Thai Government requesting an address, he was unsuccessful. He reluctantly gave up.

TOGETHER AGAIN: In 1996, John (who lived in Pueblo, Colorado) was driving through Colorado Springs when he decided to stop at a gas station. He filled up and bought two lottery tickets, than handed the clerk a check for $18. According to news reports, when the clerk saw the name on the check, the conversation went likes this: "Are you John Garcia?" "Yes." "Were you ever in the Air Force?" "Yes." "Were you ever in Thailand?" "Yes." "Did you ever have a son?"

"With that question," writes the *San Francisco Chronicle,* " the two stared at each other and realized at the same moment that they were the father and son who had been separated 27 years ago and half a world away." Nueng's mother, it turned out, had married an American and moved to Colorado in 1971.

Incredibly, the elder Garcia had never been to that gas station before and wasn't even particularly low on fuel. "I don't even know why I stopped for gas," he admitted on "Good Morning America." "I started thinking—this couldn't be. I was totally shocked."

WHO: Tim Henderson and Mark Knight / Half-brothers
SEPARATION: When Mark Knight was a year old, his parents divorced. His father remarried and had a son named Tim. His mother remarried, too, and Mark took his stepfather's last name. The brothers met once, when Mark was five and Tim three, but the families fought and never saw each other again.
TOGETHER AGAIN: In February 1996, Henderson had to travel from Newcastle, England, to London. He couldn't afford the train fare, so he called the Freewheelers Lift Share Agency, which matches hitchhikers and drivers. They have 16,000 names on file. The name they gave him was Mark Knight.

According to a report in the *Guardian:* " As they drove, they started talking about friends and relatives. 'There was a moment of complete silence as we both stared at each other in disbelief,' said Mr. Henderson. 'Then one of us said, "You must be my brother." It was pretty mind-blowing. I always knew I had a half-brother but never thought we would meet.'"

A female mackerel lays 500,000 eggs at a time.

A FOOD IS BORN

These foods are such a big part of our lives that sometimes it's hard to believe they weren't always around. Here's a brief history of how they got to your house.

HEINEKEN BEER. In the 1860s, a young Dutch man named Gerard Adriaan Heineken wanted to start his own business. He didn't have any money…but his mother did. Heineken knew she hated the way drunks wandered the streets of Amsterdam on Sunday mornings after all-night Saturday binges. So he suggested that if she helped him start a brewery, local men might drink beer all night instead of hard liquor, and public drunkenness might decrease. It was a pretty strange sales pitch…but it worked. Today, Heineken N.V. is the largest beer producer in Europe, and the second largest in the world.

MIRACLE WHIP. Early in the Great Depression, prepared mayonnaise went from a household staple to an expensive luxury item that few could afford. Kraft began researching ways to make an inexpensive substitute and eventually came up with something made of oil, egg yolks, cooked starch paste, and seasonings. It had less oil than regular mayonnaise, so it was cheaper to produce… but was also harder to make. Kraft invented a new mixer they called the "miracle whip" to give the product its creamy consistency. Then they named the product after the machine.

INSTANT COFFEE. In the early 1930s, Brazilian coffee harvests were so huge that the worldwide price of coffee nearly collapsed. In desperation, the Brazilian Coffee Institute started looking for new ways to use the coffee beans. They approached the Nestle Company with the idea for "coffee cubes," which would convert quickly into coffee when immersed in water.

Nestle took on the project…then gave up. But Max Morgenthaler, a company researcher, continued on his own time, using coffee he bought himself. In 1937, he finally found a way to turn coffee into powder without destroying its flavor. Nestle awarded him a gold medal and a percentage of the profits. They marketed

Great name: In some parts of England, garbage collectors are known as "swill solicitors."

the "instant" coffee under the brand name Nescafe, leaving it in powdered form (rather than cubes) so consumers could make their brew as strong as they wanted. It was issued to American GIs as part of their daily rations during World War II, and soldiers brought their taste for it home when the war was over.

BEN & JERRY'S ICE CREAM. In the late 1970s, Bennett Cohen and Jerry Greenfield, friends since high school, moved to Vermont to start a business. They weren't sure what kind of business, except that it would involve food. "We were both big into eating," Jerry says. Their first idea was bagels, but they gave that up when they learned that bagel-making equipment costs at least $40,000. So they paid $5 for a five-day ice cream–making correspondence course, rented an old gas station in Burlington, and began turning out ice cream by hand. Today, Ben & Jerry's ice cream is sold all over the world, and their factory in Waterbury is Vermont's leading tourist attraction.

CRISCO. You've probably seen "hydrogenated vegetable oil" on ingredients lists of cookies or crackers. It means that hydrogen was added to the oil to harden it. Crisco was the first food product to use this process: In the early 1900s, Proctor & Gamble experimented with hydrogenation to "harden" liquid cottonseed oil so it could be used as a substitute for lard. After they came up with a "creamy shortening" they could sell, they held an employee contest to name the new product. "Cryst" was rejected for religious reasons; "Krispo" was nixed because it was already trademarked. In the end, the company combined the two to get "Crisco," an acronym for "crystallized cottonseed oil."

ICED TEA. While tea drinking is a nearly 5,000-year-old pleasure that began in China," Maureen Sajbel writes in the *Los Angeles Times*, "Sipping iced tea is a fairly recent American invention. The story goes that on a hot, humid day at the St. Louis World's Fair, a discouraged vendor wasn't having much success in selling Indian hot tea. With a scratch of the head and a burst of American inventiveness, he added ice. Within hours, fair-goers were drinking glass after glass of the thirst-quenching iced drink."

The typical U.S. 18-year-old has spent 11,000 hours in school and 18,000 hours watching TV.

MYTH AMERICA

*Here are a few more stories about America
that we've been taught are true...*

THE MYTH: Jackie Robinson broke baseball's color barrier in 1947 when he joined the Brooklyn Dodgers.

THE TRUTH: Robinson was not the first black man to play major league baseball; in fact, he came along more than 60 years after Moses "Fleet" Walker, a catcher who played 42 games for the Toledo Mudhens of the American Association in 1884. Walker's brother joined him later in the season, but only played five games. When the season ended, both Walkers were gone. Apparently, a country with dozens of Jim Crow laws still on the books wasn't ready to integrate their national pastime just yet.

THE MYTH: Machine Gun Kelly coined the expression "G-men" (for government men). In 1933, the story goes, FBI agents surrounded him on a Tennessee farm. Rather than shoot his way out, Kelly threw up his hands and shouted to the government agents, "Don't shoot, G-men, don't shoot!"

BACKGROUND: FBI director J. Edgar Hoover recounted the tale in a 1946 issue of the *Tennessee Law Review.*

THE TRUTH: Hoover made it up to generate publicity for the Bureau and to give his agents a nickname. The FBI wasn't even responsible for capturing Kelly; he was actually caught by a posse of lawmen led by W. J. Raney, a Memphis police officer. And, according to contemporary accounts, what Kelly really said was, "Okay, boys, I've been waiting for you all night."

THE MYTH: "The Spirit of '76," the famous painting showing a flag-carrier, a drummer, and a man playing a fife (flute), was inspired by an actual scene in the Revolutionary War.

THE TRUTH: It started off as a Civil War painting. Archibald Willard, a Civil War veteran himself, first painted a cartoonish version, depicting three imaginary war recruits parading around "in lighthearted fashion." It wasn't until a friend talked him into painting a more somber version that he added the revolutionary themes and gave the painting its now-famous name.

THE MYTH: George Washington was a great military tactician.

THE TRUTH. "So notorious was his reputation for losing battles ineptly," writes Michael Korda in *Success*, "that John Adams called him 'an old muttonhead' and Jefferson commented, with great delicacy, that Washington was 'not a great tactician.' "

> As a young officer, he once constructed a fort at Great Meadows, Pennsylvania, on a swampy creek bottom, hemmed in on all three sides by wooded hills. This position for a fortress was so ludicrous that the French, in this case Washington's enemies, captured him immediately, and generously released him with the advice to take up some other line of work.
>
> Giving up fortifications, Washington then…became the personal aide to Lt. General Edward Braddock, whom Washington persuaded to divide the forces in the siege of Fort Duquesne. The result? Braddock lost the battle, his army, and his life.

After taking over the command of the Continental army,

> Washington proceeded through 1775 and 1776 to retreat from Long island to Brooklyn Heights, from Brooklyn Heights to Kips Bay, from Kips Bay to Washington Heights, from Washington Heights to White Plains, and from there across the Hudson into New Jersey. …It can be truly said that…Washington beat the British by retreating faster than they could advance.

THE MYTH: Geronimo was the name of a famous Apache chief.

THE TRUTH: His name was actually Govathlay, which doesn't sound anything like Geronimo. Mexican settlers, who couldn't pronounce Govathlay, referred to the chief as "Jerome," or "Geronimo" in Spanish. And there's nothing in the historical record to suggest that Govathlay ever shouted "Geronimo!" as he jumped from a cliff into a river to escape the U.S. Cavalry. That scene was invented for a 1940 movie, which probably led directly to the legend. (World War II paratroopers did, however, frequently shout "Geronimo!" when they jumped out of planes.)

DR. STRANGELOVE

Dr. Strangelove is considered one of the best satires of the Cold War era…if not one of the funniest movies ever made. Here are some little-known, behind-the-scenes details.

BUT SERIOUSLY, FOLKS

In the late 1950s, a 28-year-old film maker named Stanley Kubrick began reading up on the U.S.-Soviet arms race. He subscribed to *Aviation Week* and the *Bulletin of the Atomic Scientists*, and over the next six years read more than 70 books on the subject. As he read, he became fascinated by what he called "people's virtually listless acquiescence in the possibility—in fact, the increasing probability—of nuclear war."

One of the books Kubrick read was *Red Alert*, a novel about a paranoid U.S. military general who goes insane and launches an unprovoked nuclear attack on the Soviet Union. The book, by former Royal Air Force officer Peter George, was so intriguing that Kubrick bought the film rights and hired George to help him write a screenplay from the book.

BLACK HUMOR

The screenplay was supposed to be serious…but Kubrick's dark sense of humor kept intruding. Finally, he stopped fighting it and placed a phone call to satirist Terry Southern. Kubrick hadn't actually met Southern, but he'd read one of his books—*The Magic Christian*. A few years earlier, Peter Sellers had bought 100 copies of it and sent it to his friends…including Kubrick. Southern recalls Kubrick telling him on the phone that

> he had thought of the story as a "straightforward melodrama" until …he "woke up and realized that nuclear war was too outrageous, too fantastic to be treated in any conventional manner." He said that he could only see it now as "some kind of hideous joke." He told me he had read a book of mine which contained, as he put it, "certain indications" that I might be able to help him with the script.

So Southern became a co-writer on the world's first black comedy about nuclear war.

Mosquitoes aren't fond of citronella. Why? It irritates their feet.

A SELLERS MARKET

That wasn't Sellers's only behind-the-scenes contribution. For some reason, the corporate geniuses at Columbia Pictures decided that the movie *Lolita,* which Kubrick had directed in 1962, had succeeded because of "the gimmick of Peter Sellers playing several roles." So before Strangelove even had a title, they agreed to give Kubrick the green light for it…as long as it "would star Peter Sellers in at least four major roles."

Kubrick made that promise…but it turned out to be impossible to fulfill. Sellers did play three parts in the film brilliantly: Dr. Strangelove, President Merkin Muffley, and Group Captain Lionel Mandrake. Unfortunately, at the last minute, he was injured and had to give up the role of Major T. J. "King" Kong. Southern remembers:

> Kubrick's response was an extraordinary tribute to Sellers as an actor: "We can't replace him with another actor, we've got to get an authentic character from life, someone whose acting career is secondary—a real-life cowboy."…He asked for my opinion and I immediately suggested big Dan ("Hoss Cartwriter") Blocker…of the TV show Bonanza….
>
> [Kubrick] made arrangements for a script to be delivered to Blocker that afternoon, but a cabled response from Blocker's agent arrived in quick order: "Thanks a lot, but the material is too pinko for Dan. Or anyone else we know for that matter."
>
> As I recall, this was the first hint that this sort of political interpretation of our work-in-progress might exist.

It was only then that Slim Pickens, a former rodeo clown, was hired for the part. (Ironically, Pickens was more conservative than Blocker, even supporting presidential candidate George Wallace.)

MIXED REVIEWS

As the film progressed, Kubrick had a growing uneasiness about the reception that awaited it. At one point, Mo Rothman, the executive producer assigned by Columbia Pictures, called with the message that "New York does not see anything funny about the end of the world!" Ultimately, many critics agreed. When it premiered in January 1964, Bosley Crowther wrote in *The New York Times:*

> *Dr. Strangelove*…is beyond any question the most shattering sick joke I've ever come across…I am troubled by the feeling,

which runs all through the film, of discredit and even contempt for our whole defense establishment, up to and even including the hypothetical Commander in Chief...Somehow, to me it isn't funny. It is malefic and sick.

Columbia was spooked and distanced itself from the film. "Even when *Strangelove* received that infrequent good review," Southern wrote, "the studio dismissed the critic as a pinko nutcase." At one point, Columbia's publicity department called the film "a zany novelty flick which does not reflect the views of the corporation in any way." But of course, when the Library of Congress listed *Strangelove* as one of the "50 greatest American films of all time," former Columbia execs were "in prominent attendance."

THE LOST SCENE

Something to look for: In many of the scenes filmed in the Pentagon war room, a long table filled with cakes, pies, and other desserts can be seen off to one side. The table isn't there by accident—Kubrick originally intended to end the movie with a pie fight. He even filmed the scene, as set director Ken Adams remembers:

> It was a very brilliant sequence with a Hellzapoppin kind of craziness. Undoubtedly one of the most extraordinary custard pie battles ever filmed. The characters were hanging from chandeliers and throwing pies which ended up by covering the maps of the General Staff.... The sequence ended with the President of the United States and the Soviet ambassador sitting on what was left of the pies and building 'pie castles' like children on a beach.

But Kubrick removed the scene. Why? He forgot to tell the actors to play it straight. As the scene progressed, it was obvious that they were having a great time—which didn't fit with the rest of the film. Unfortunately, there was no time or money left to reshoot it.

FINAL THOUGHT

> "Confront a man in his office with a nuclear alarm, and you have a documentary. If the news reaches him in his living room, you have a drama. If it catches him in the lavatory, the result is comedy." **—Stanley Kubrick**

The average woman shaves 412 inches of skin on her body; the average man, 48.

LANGUAGE OF LOVE

They say that it's international, but a good vocabulary can help.
Here are some forgotten Victorian words that might come in handy.

THE GOOD:

Ravary: A fit of passion

Babies-in-the-eyes: The reflection of oneself in a loved one's pupils

Lavolt: A lively dance

Frike: Lusty, bawdy

Enterbathe: To bathe together, literally, to mix tears

Fairhead: A beauty

Amoret: A loving look, glance

Smick: To kiss

Fardry: To paint the face with white make-up for cosmetic benefit

Greade: A woman's bosom

Loveship: Act of love-making

Bridelope: Wedding

Frim: Fleshy, vigorous

Halch: To embrace tightly

Fucus: A kind of rouge made from lichen

Half-marrow: A husband or wife

Modesty-piece: A lace cloth that covers a woman's chest

Muskin: A term of endearment for a woman; sweetheart

THE BAD:

Curtain-sermon: A lecture given by a wife at bedtime

Grandgore: Infectious disease

Acharne: To thirst for blood

Chichevache: A thin, ugly face

Gandermooner: A man who chases other women during the first month after his wife has given birth

Clarty-paps: A slovenly, dirty wife

Delumbate: To sexually maim

Mormals: Inflamed sores

Winchester goose: A sexually transmitted disease

Fulyear: A man who dishonors women

Rush ring: To "Wed" without a ring; to convince a woman that a false marriage was legal

Bespawled: Covered with spittle and saliva

Flesh-shambles: A dirty, illreputed brothel

Stewed prune: Madam in a brothel

When your face blushes, the lining of your stomach turns red, too.

HONESTLY, ABE

A few random thoughts from our 16th president, Abraham Lincoln.

"It's better to be silent and thought a fool than speak and remove all doubt."

"People are just about as happy as they make up their minds to be."

"Whatever you are, be a good one."

"If I were two-faced, would I be wearing this one?"

"How many legs does a dog have if you call the tail a leg? Four. Calling a tail a leg doesn't make it a leg."

"If both factions, or neither, shall abuse you, you will probably be right. Beware of being assailed by one, and praised by the other."

"If you intend to go to work, there is no better place than right where you are."

"A woman is the only thing that I am afraid of that I know will not hurt me."

"The severest justice may not always be the best policy."

"Things may come to those who wait, but only the things left by those who hustle."

"The loss of enemies does not compensate for the loss of friends."

"If this country cannot be saved without giving up that principle [equality]....I would rather be assassinated on this spot than surrender it."

"A fellow once came to me to ask for an appointment as a minister abroad. Finding he could not get that, he came down to some more modest position.... When he saw he could not get that, he asked me for an old pair of trousers. It is sometimes well to be humble."

"It is said an Eastern monarch once charged his wise men to invent him a sentence...which should be true and appropriate in all times and situations. They presented him the words: 'And this, too, shall pass away.'"

"A universal feeling, whether well- or ill-founded, cannot be safely disregarded."

Only two words in the English language end in "gry"—angry and hungry.

TAKE ME OUT TO THE BORU GAME

This is a page for baseball fans.

The Japanese have adopted baseball as their national game. They've also taken a number of American baseball terms and made them Japanese. Here are some of the words, written phonetically. Some are easy, some confusing. See if you can tell what they mean. Answers are at the bottom of the page.

1. Batta
2. Boru
3. Kochi
4. Besuboru
5. Besu-ryne
6. Chenji appu
7. De Gemu
8. Era
9. Herumetto
10. Mitto
11. Maneja
12. Suisaido sukuiizu
13. Homuran
14. Auto
15. Fain Puray
16. Kyatcha
17. Pasu boh-ru
18. Sukoa bodo
19. Batta bokkusu
20. Kuriin hitto
21. Foku boru
22. Wairudo pitchi
23. Banto
24. Pitchingu sutaffu
25. Furu kaunto
26. Puray boru
27. Senta
28. Gurobu
29. Fauru
30. Pinchi ranna
31. Hitto endu ran
32. Battingu sutansu
33. Foa boru
34. Daburu Hedda
35. "Gettsu"
36. Katto ofu puray

ANSWERS: 1. Batter; 2. Ball; 3. Coach; 4. Baseball; 5. Baseline; 6. Change-up; 7. Day game; 8. Error; 9. Helmet; 10. Mitt; 11. Manager; 12. Suicide squeeze; 13. Home run; 14. Out; 15. Fine play; 16. Catcher; 17. Passed ball; 18. Score board; 19. Batting box; 20. Clean hit; 21. Fork ball; 22. Wild pitch; 23. Bunt; 24. Pitching staff; 25. Full count; 26. Play ball!; 27. Center field or center fielder; 28. Glove; 29. Foul ball; 30. Pinch runner; 31. Hit-and-run; 32. Batting stance; 33. Four balls (a walk); 34. Double-header; 35. "Get two" (double-play); 36. Cutoff play

---

Longest word in Shakespeare's plays: "honorificabilitudinitatibus" (*Love's Labour's Lost*)

LITTLE SHOP OF HORRORS

In this chapter, we feeeed you the story of one of the most unlikely—but most popular—cult films of all time.

ALL SET TO GO

A few days after he finished work on a film called *A Bucket of Blood* in 1959, director Roger Corman had lunch with the manager of Producers Studio, the company that rented him office space. The manager mentioned that another company had just finished work on a film, and the sets were still standing.

"I said, just as a joke, 'If you leave the sets up, I'll come in for a couple of days and see if I can just invent a picture, because I have a little bit of money now and some free time,'" Corman recalled years later. "And he said, 'Fine.' The whole thing was kind of a whim. I booked the studio for a week."

TO B OR NOT TO B

Corman, 32, had only been directing films for five years (*The Monster from the Ocean Floor* and *Attack of the Crab Monsters* were two early titles). But he was already developing a reputation for making profitable movies very quickly on minuscule budgets—a skill that would later earn him the title "King of the B films."

He had filmed *A Bucket of Blood*, a "beatnik-styled horror comedy" in only five days, a personal record. He bet his friend at Producers Studio that he could make this next film in 48 hours.

COMING UP WITH A SCRIPT

Corman called scriptwriter Chuck Griffith, who'd written *A Bucket of Blood*, and told him to write a new variation of the same story. The only limitations: it had to be written for the existing sets, and Corman had to be able to rehearse all the scenes in three days…and then film them in two.

Griffith took the assignment. He and Corman went bar-hopping to brainstorm an outline for the film. It was a long night: Griffith got drunk, then got into a barroom brawl.

Poll results: What kind of flowers do most U.S. women get on Valentine's Day? Roses.

Somehow, he and Corman still managed to come up with a story about a nerdy flower shop employee and his man-eating plant.

DEJA VU

Griffith turned in the final script a week later. It was essentially a warmed-over version of A *Bucket of Blood*.

• In A *Bucket of Blood*, a well-meaning sculptor accidentally kills his landlord's cat, then hides the evidence by turning it into a sculpture, which he titles *Dead cat*. When the sculpture brings him the notoriety he's always sought, he starts killing people and making them into sculptures, too.

• In *Little Shop of Horrors*, a well-meaning flower shop employee becomes a local hero after he accidentally creates a man-eating plant (which he names Audrey Jr., after his girlfriend) by cross-breeding a Venus flytrap with a buttercup. He then begins killing people to keep the plant—and his fame—alive.

LOW BUDGET

• The filming took place between Christmas and New Year's Eve 1959. Corman spent a total of $23,000 on the film, including $800 for the finished script and $750 for three different models of Audrey Jr.: a 12-inch version, a 6-foot version, and a full-grown 8-foot version.

• Corman pinched pennies wherever he could. Jack Nicholson, 23 years old when Corman hired him to play a masochistic dental patient named Wilbur Force, remembers that Corman wouldn't even spend money making copies of the script: "Roger took the script apart and gave me only the pages for my scenes. That way he could give the rest of the script to another actor or actors."

• Corman also paid a musician named Fred Katz $317.34 for the musical score…but as John McCarty and Mark McGee write in *The Little Shop of Horrors* book,

> Katz simply used the same score he'd written for A *Bucket of Blood*, which has also been used in another Corman film, *The Wasp Woman* and would be used yet again in Corman's *Creature from the Haunted Sea*. Whether or not Corman was aware he was buying the same score three times is unknown.

• Even if a shot wasn't perfect, Corman would use it if he could. In the first day of shooting, Jackie Haze and Jack Nicholson accidentally knocked over the dentist's chair, spoiling the shot and breaking the chair. When the property master said it would take an hour to fix the chair so they could reshoot the scene, Corman changed the script to read, "The scene ends with the dentist's chair falling over."

• Corman was legendary for getting as much work out of his actors and writers as he could. One example: Chuck Griffith, who wrote the script, also played a shadow on a wall, the man who runs out of the dentist's office with his ear bitten, and the thief who robs the flower shop. He also directed the Skid Row exterior shots and provided the voice for Audrey Jr. (Griffith's voice wasn't supposed to make it into the final film—he was just the guy who stood off camera and read the plant's lines so the actors would have something to react to. Corman had planned to dub in another actor's voice later. "But it got laughs," Griffith says, "so Corman decided to leave it the way it was.")

• Corman also saved money by filming all of the Skid Row exteriors actually in Skid Row, and using "real bums to play the bums." Griffith, who directed the scenes, paid them 10¢ per scene, using the change he had in his pocket.

THAT'S A WRAP

• Corman finished all of the interior shots in the required two days, then spent a couple more evenings filming the exterior shots. To this day, *Little Shop of Horrors* is listed in the *Guinness Book of World Records* for "the shortest shooting schedule for a full-length, commercial feature film made without the use of stock footage."

• In this original release, *Little Shop of Horrors* was only a modest success. It didn't develop its cult following until the late 1960s, when it became a Creature Feature classic on late-night TV. It was adapted into an off-Broadway musical in 1982, which was itself adapted into a new $20 million film in 1987.

• "*Little Shop of Horrors* is the film that established me as an underground legend in film circles," Corman says. "People come up to me on the street who have memorized parts of the dialogue. I suppose you could say it was *The Rocky Horror Picture Show* of its time."

A world record: Mrs. Myra Franklin saw the film *The Sound of Music* more than 900 times.

FAMILIAR PHRASES

More origins of everyday phrases.

RIDE PIGGYBACK
Meaning: Ride on the back of something.
Origin: "Piggyback" has nothing to do with pigs—it is a corruption of "pick-a-back"...which, in turn, came from "pick back" and "pick pack." All of these referred to packs that people threw on their back to carry things.

COAT OF ARMS
Meaning: Design showing a family crest.
Origin: In the Middle Ages, knights wore a special coat over their armor to keep it clean and protect it from the weather. The coat was usually decorated with the knight's family crest, showing that the knight was of noble birth and thus entitled to bear arms. As gunpowder made suits of armor obsolete, coats of arms became purely decorative.

HAVING A FIELD DAY
Meaning: Having a great time; easily overwhelming an opponent.
Origin: "Field days" began as special days set aside by the military for troop maneuvers and exercises. By the 19th century, the expression expanded to include civilian festivities as well. Eventually, it was used to mean any pleasurable experience.

GET COLD FEET
Meaning: Become wary; back out of a commitment.
Origin: In the early 17th century, having cold feet meant having no money (and thus no shoes). In the 18th century, the meaning changed, probably in reference to soldiers with cold or frozen feet, who are more likely to retreat than those with warm ones.

BEAT A HASTY RETREAT
Meaning: Leave quickly; back down.
Origin: In the 14th century, European armies used trumpets and other instruments to call troops back to camp. Centuries later, drums were used. Drummers literally "beat the signal to retreat."

In 1995, the bestselling adult Halloween costume was the Judge Ito robe and mask.

BUTTONHOLE A PERSON
Meaning: Stop a passer-by; detain someone.
Origin: The expression was originally "buttonhold" a person. It referred to the practice of grabbing a person by their buttons and holding on while you tried to sell them something.

HEARD THROUGH THE GRAPEVINE
Meaning: Heard some gossip.
Origin: During the Civil War, soldiers said that rumors came in "on the grapevine telegraph"—a reference to the fact that there were no real telegraph lines in camp to supply accurate information…just grapevines.

INDIAN SUMMER
Meaning: The period of warm weather after summer has gone and before fall has begun.
Origin: Dates back to the days of mistrust between settlers and Native Americans. The term "Indian" acquired a derogatory connotation and was used in expressions like "Indian giver" and "Indian summer"—weather that appeared to be summer but wasn't.

DRINK A TOAST
Meaning: Drink in honor of another person.
Origin: Literally comes from drinking toast. In the Middle Ages people added a piece of spiced toast to their tankards of ale to improve the taste. The practice was abandoned as brewing methods improved, but the term continued to apply to the practice of drinking to someone's health.

FLY IN THE OINTMENT
Meaning: One thing wrong with an otherwise-perfect situation.
Origin: Ointment used to mean a sweet-smelling cosmetic. The phrase comes from a verse in the Bible, Ecclesiastes 10:1: "Dead files make the perfumer's ointment give off an evil odor."

DRESSED TO THE NINES
Meaning: Well-dressed.
Origin: Probably comes from the Old English expression *dressed to then eyne,* which means "dressed to the eyes."

Why don't your eyes freeze in winter? There's lots of salt in your tears.

CELEBRITY SWEEPSTAKES

Celebrity endorsements are a multi-billion-dollar business. If you get the right celebrity to pitch your product, it can be worth millions. But if you pick wrong…well, take a look at these examples.

GERALDINE FERRARO

Pepsi hired the 1984 Democratic vice-presidential candidate—the first woman ever nominated by a major political party—to do a diet Pepsi commercial in 1985.

What they wanted: People "who represent America's new generation of leaders" to go with their "Choice of a New Generation" campaign. Roger Enrico, Pepsi's CEO, explained that "Ferraro is [no longer] a despised Democrat; she's a living symbol of woman's possibilities." He added, "As the first woman vice-presidential candidate, she'll get us on every news show in America."

What they got: Angry customers. Liberals attacked Ferraro for selling out, conservatives attacked Pepsi for promoting a liberal agenda. But the worst criticism came from anti-abortion protesters, as Enrico recalled in his book, *The Other Guy Blinked:*

> As the commercial started to air, a whole other kind of protest began. It was about "The Choice of a New Generation." No, it was about the word choice….Did it ever enter our minds that, in politics, that word has a very different meaning? Nope. So we were very, very surprised when we start getting letters. Angry letters. Letters that said, "Your commercials are 'poor-choice.' You favor the right of women to have abortions on demand."

What happened: Pepsi pulled the ads. "I felt sorry for Ferraro," Enrico writes, "but I learned to keep Pepsi's nose out of politics."

RUSH LIMBAUGH

In 1994, the Florida Citrus Department bought $1 million worth of ads on Limbaugh's show to get him to promote orange juice.

What they wanted: A big audience for their "health-oriented" ads. The 300-pound Limbaugh might not be a good spokesperson for health food, but he did have upwards of 15 million listeners. "True, Mr. Limbaugh is no plain-vanilla guy," wrote *Advertising*

Something to ponder: Elvis Presley got a "C" in his eighth grade music class.

Age in February. "He's popular because of his conservative opinions. And he dotes on baiting liberals. But that's a plus in today's market…where ad messages delivered by popular hosts carry extra weight with loyal listeners."

What they got: An instant public-relations disaster. Groups like the National Organization for Women (NOW) and the NAACP started a "Flush Rush–Drink Prune Juice" campaign. "Limbaugh's hate-mongering is being underwritten by state and federal tax dollars," NOW's president complained. And Democrats—particularly Florida's governor—were outraged. "We're looking for people who will present the best possible image for Florida citrus—not people who will engender hate, disregard for minorities or represent any political philosophy," said a Democratic state representative. Even the citrus commissioners' jobs wound up in jeopardy. The following month, Democrats held up the otherwise-routine appointment of three members of the Citrus Board in the Florida legislature as a protest.

What happened: Sales of orange juice dropped after the campaign went on the air, and the board dumped Limbaugh after his six-month contract expired. Limbaugh predictably blamed his firing on "liberals, both in government, in special interest groups like the "militant National Organization for Women, and in the press."

*　　*　　*

SELLING OUT?

Terri Garr on why she made a Yoplait commercial:

"They give you a lot of money, and I come from a …relatively poor background. So I go, '*That* much money for a day's work? Yessss!' But my management people said it's not enough. And I say, 'What do you mean it's not enough?' So they came back with even more money. It's crazy. But what am I going to do, be in the Motion Picture Country Home, 86 years old, saying to my pal, Farrah Fawcett: 'In 1986, I could have done a commercial for a million dollars but nooooo, I was too fine.' I don't want to be telling that story. I want to be on my own estate, in the south of France, telling my servants, 'I got this commercial….' "

Ho, ho, ho: More than 25 million kids visit Santa in malls nationwide year.

THE TRUTH ABOUT "KILLER BEES"

Since 1964 we've read news reports of "killer bees" working their way up from South America to the United States. They finally arrived in 1990 ...and nothing much happened. Is the killer bee crisis for real, or is it an example of media exaggeration fueling public hysteria?

IN THE BEEGINNING

In 1956, the Brazilian government wanted to improve Brazil's honey industry. Although Brazil is the fifth-largest country in the world, it ranked only 47th in world honey production. So it hired Dr. Warwick E. Kerr, an American entomologist. Kerr's solution was to import African honeybees, which produce far more honey than the European bees that had been brought to Brazil by Western colonists in the 16th and 17th centuries.

Because African bees are more aggressive than Brazilian bees, Kerr decided not to release the bees directly into the environment. Instead, he planned to interbreed them with the gentler Brazilian bees, then release their hybrid offspring.

Kerr's plan didn't work as he had hoped. About a year after he began the project, 26 swarms of the purebred African bees escaped from his laboratory in São Paulo and quickly began overrunning the Brazilian honeybee population. His efforts to create a kinder, gentler honeybee had failed—and the aggressive bees were taking over.

NO BEEG DEAL

No one was too excited by this development. True, Africanized bees are more aggressive than European honeybees—for instance, they attack by the hundreds instead of by the dozens when their hives are disturbed. But they can still only sting once before they die. Brazil actually had a larger problem with its native wasps, which can sting someone many times without dying. About the only people who noticed the difference were Brazilian beekeepers, who found the new bees harder to manage.

Largest 24-hour snowfall on record in the U.S.: Valdez, Alaska, in January 1990—47.5 in.

POLITICAL ANIMAL

For the next eight years, the Africanized bees attracted little or no attention at all. Then, on April 1, 1964, the Brazilian army over-threw president Joao Goulart and set up a military dictatorship. When Kerr spoke out against human rights abuses, the new regime used the government-controlled press to portray him as a modern-day mad scientist. Professor Robert Morse describes what happened next in his book *Bees and Beekeeping:*

> In an effort to discredit Kerr as a scientist, the military played upon the fear that many people have of stinging insects. Since most people do not know the difference between bees and wasps, any stinging incident, many of which were caused by wasps, was blamed on Professor Kerr's [accidental release of Africanized bees].
>
> The Brazilian military called the bees, in Portuguese, the language of Brazil, abelhas assassinas (killer bees). So far as I can determine, the first mention of the words "killer bees" in the United States was in *Time* magazine in the September 24, 1965, issue that picked up one of these military press releases.

Some Brazilian newspapers even claimed that Dr. Kerr had *taught* the bees to be mean.

Other magazines and newspapers followed *Time's* lead and printed the Brazilian junta's propaganda as if it were the truth. In the process, they created wave of hysteria that swept across South America, then Central and North America as the Africanized bees moved inexorably northward.

HARD TO BEELIEVE

When will the killer bees arrive in the United States? Actually, they've been here since 1959, thanks to a U.S. Department of Agriculture program that distributed—no kidding—Africanized bee semen to domestic beekeepers. "It's common knowledge among larger commercial beekeepers," says Dee Lusby, an Arizona beekeeper. "The USDA bee lab in Baton Rouge, Louisiana, received Africanized bee semen from Brazil 30 years ago and made the offspring available to beekeepers in this country and around the world. It was part of an ongoing program to breed superior honey-producing bees, just like Dr. Kerr's experiments in South America."

And that probably wasn't their first trip to the United States. According to *Bee World* magazine, other bee breeders may have brought them over from Africa as early as the mid-1800s. So the killer bees aren't coming, they're already here, and they've probably been here for over a century.

For that matter, most beekeepers say that the German bee, which has been in the United States for over two centuries, is even meaner than the Africanized bees. But even these extra-mean bees aren't much of a public nuisance, beekeepers note, and say many predict that the Africanized bees aren't either. "You're more likely to be killed by lightning than attacked by Africanized honeybees," says Dr. Anita Collins, a research geneticist with the Department of Agriculture.

SO WHAT'S THE DIFFERENCE?
• Anatomically speaking, Africanized bees are virtually indistinguishable from European bees, except that they're slightly smaller. Even the experts have a hard time telling them apart without studying them in a lab
• Africanized bee venom is no stronger than that of European bees. In fact, Africanized bees carry slightly less venom than European bees do.
• The only real difference is behavior: Africanized honey bees are much more active, both as honey producers and defenders of the hive. They're more easily angered, and, once agitated, take longer to calm down—sometimes as long as 24 hours. They also defend the hive in greater numbers than European bees do. "They get eight to ten times as many bees out to defend the colony and sting," Dr. Collins says. "It's not any different sting for sting," adds Stormy Sparks, a Texas A&M entomologist, "but there's just a much bigger potential for multiple stings."
• A positive note: Africanized bees evolved in a hot climate, so they have very little tolerance for cold compared to European bees, and will probably never go above the southern third of the United States.

OLYMPIC MYTHS

Every four years, we're treated to another round of Olympics. Whether you watch them or not, it's impossible to avoid all the hype—which, it turns out, isn't all true. Next time someone refers to "Olympic tradition," read them this.

THE MYTH: Athletes who competed in the ancient Greek Olympics were amateurs.

THE TRUTH: Technically, maybe. But in fact, they were handsomely rewarded for their victories. "Contrary to popular be- lief," says David Wallechinsky in his *Complete Book of the Olympics*, "the Ancient Greek athletes were not amateurs. Not only were they fully supported throughout their training, but even though the winner received only an olive wreath at the Games, at home he was amply rewarded and could become quite rich." Eventually, top athletes demanded cash and appearance fees—even back then.

THE MYTH: In ancient Greece, the Olympics were so important that everything stopped for them—even wars.

THE TRUTH: No war ever stopped because of the Olympics. But wars didn't interfere with the games because: 1) participants were given nighttime safe-conduct passes that allowed them to cross battlefields after a day's fighting was done and 2) the Olympics were part of a religious ceremony, so the four Olympic sites—including Delphi and Olympia—were off-limits to fighting.

THE MYTH: To honor ancient tradition and discourage commercialism, organizers of the modern Olympics decided that only amateur athletes could compete.

THE TRUTH: Not even close. It was "amateurs only" strictly to keep the riff-raff out. Baron Coubertin, the man responsible for bringing back the Olympics in 1896, was a French aristocrat who wanted to limit competitors to others of his social class. "He saw the Olympics as a way to reinforce class distinctions rather than overcome them," writes one historian. Since only the rich could afford to spend their time training for the games without outside support, the best way to keep lower classes out was to restrict them to amateurs.

Coincidence? William Shakespeare and Miguel De Cervantes died on the same day in 1616.

THE MYTH: The torch-lighting ceremony that opens the games originated with the ancient Greeks.
THE TRUTH: It has no ancient precedent—it was invented by the Nazis. The 1936 Olympics took place in Berlin, under Hitler's watchful eye. Carl Diem, who organized the event for the Führer, created the first lighting of the Olympic flame to give the proceedings "an ancient aura." Since then, the ceremony has become part of Olympic tradition…and people just assume it's much older than it really is.

THE MYTH: The 5-ring Olympic symbol is from ancient Greece.
THE TRUTH: The Nazis are responsible for that myth, too. According to David Young's book, *The Modern Olympics,* it was spread in a Nazi propaganda film about the Berlin Games.

THE MYTH: Adolf Hitler snubbed U.S. runner Jesse Owens at the 1936 Olympics in Berlin.
THE TRUTH: This is one of the enduring American Olympic myths. Hitler, the story goes, was frustrated in his attempt to prove Aryan superiority when Owens—an African American—took the gold. The furious Führer supposedly refused to acknowledge Owens's victories. But according to Owens himself, it never happened. Hitler didn't congratulate anyone that day because the International Olympic Committee had warned him he had to congratulate "all winners or no winners." He chose to stay mum.

THE MYTH: The Olympic marathon distance was established in ancient times to honor a messenger who ran from Marathon to Athens—about 26 miles—to deliver vital news…then died.
THE TRUTH: The marathon distance—26 miles, 385 yards—was established at the 1908 games in London. It's the distance from Shepherd's Bush Stadium to the queen's bedroom window.

THE MYTH: Drugs have always been taboo in the Olympics.
THE TRUTH: Drugs weren't outlawed until 1967. In fact, according to the *Complete Book of the Olympics,* drugs were already in use by the third modern Olympic Games: "The winner of the 1904 marathon, Thomas Hicks, was administered multiple doses of strychnine and brandy during the race."

The average 10-gallon hat holds only 3 quarts of water.

TEST YOUR GRAMMY I.Q.

Every year, the news media make a big deal about who won the Grammy
Awards. Have you been paying attention? Here's a little quiz to see
how much you really know about the "coveted" music awards.
(Answers on page 765.)

1. Which of these groups has never won a Grammy?
  a) Alvin and the Chipmunks b) The Beach Boys c) Aerosmith

2. An assassination ended the meteoric career of the 1962 winner
of Album of the Year. Who was it?
    a) Vaughn Meader b) Sam Cooke c) Clark Taylor

3. In 1965, the bestselling record of the year was "Satisfaction";
the Beatles recorded "Help!"; Motown was tearing up the charts.
The Grammy winner that year for Best Vocal Group was:
    a) The Beatles b) The Supremes c) The Anita Kerr Quarter
  d) Steve Brummet & His Polka Pals e) The Mamas & the Papas

4. When did Elvis win his first Grammy?
a) 1960, for "Are You Lonesome Tonight?" (Best Male Singer)
b) 1965, for *Blue Hawaii* (Best Movie Soundtrack)
c) 1967, for *How Great Thou Art* (Best Inspirational Performance)
d) 1974, for "In the Ghetto" (Song of the Year)

5. The first artist ever to refuse a Grammy was
    a) Nina Simone b) Bob Dylan c) Sinead O'Connor

6. In the decade following the Beatles break-up in 1970, each
member of the group won a Grammy for a non-Beatle
effort...except one. Which one?
    a) John b) George c) Ringo d) Paul

7. Although this rock group—considered one of the world's best
by most critics—had never won a Grammy, they received a Lifetime Achievement Award in 1985. "Thank you," said the group's

The French writer Voltaire drank 70 cups of coffee a day.

leader, "the joke's on you." What band was it?
a) The Doors b) The Rolling Stones c) The Who

8. What performer won a Best Vocalist Grammy for a song she'd written about not receiving the award a few years earlier?
a) Roseanne Cash b) Dolly Parton c) Carole King

9. Which Grammy winner told a reporter: "My nomination must have been an accident. Either that, or a lot of people have a perverse sense of humor."
a) Bobby McFerrin b) Bob Newhart c) Frank Zappa

10. What was notable about the Grammys won by Jimi Hendrix and Janis Joplin?
a) What Grammys?
b) They were withheld because of the artists' overt drug use.
c) They were given for a little-known duet they did of the Beatles' old hit, "She Loves You."

11. Who was the first African-American ever to win the Best New Artist award?
a) Chubby Checker, 1960   b) Little Stevie wonder, 1962
c) O. C. Smith, 1968   d) Natalie Cole, 1975

12. What was surprising about 1966's Best Folk Artist winner, Cortelia Clark?
a) It turned out he'd undergone a sex-change operation.
b) He couldn't afford to rent a tux to go to the awards ceremony.
c) There was no Cortelia Clark—it was really B. B. King, recording under a different name.

13. In 1996 John Popper, harmonica player for Blues Traveler, pulled off a Grammy first when he jumped out of his seat to get an award, and…
a) Tore a ligament in his leg
b) His pants fell down
c) He tripped and fell

No wonder they grunt: Most of a hog's sweat glands are in its snout.

THE CHEW-CHEW MAN

Where did the low-calorie diet come from? It started with a guy known as the "Chew-Chew Man" to critics and the "Great Masticator" to fans.

THE BIRTH OF "FLETCHERISM"

In 1895, 44-year-old Horace Fletcher was turned down for life insurance because he weighed 217 pounds (at 5'6" tall), and he drank excessively. "I was an old man at forty, and on the way to a rapid decline," he recalled years later.

In 1898, Fletcher performed an experiment on himself. He began chewing each bite of food 30 to 70 times—even milk and soup, which he swished in his mouth—and never ate when he was upset or wasn't hungry. After five months of "Fletcherizing" each morsel of food, he lost 60 pounds and regained his health. He also found that he could live happily on 1,600 calories a day, far less than the 3,500 to 4,500 calories recommended at the turn of the century.

THE GREAT MASTICATOR

The experience helped Fletcher find a new calling—pitching his chewing habits to the masses. His slogan: "Nature will castigate those who don't masticate." Fletcher's lecture tours and bestselling books attracted tens of thousands of followers, including John D. Rockefeller and Thomas Edison. Adherents formed "Fletcher clubs," where they met to eat slowly and chant ditties like:

> I choose to chew, Because I wish to do, The sort of thing that
> Nature had in view, Before bad cooks invented sav'ry stew;
> When the only way to eat was to chew! chew! chew!

Fletcher died from bronchitis in 1919 at the age of 69, and his chewing theories soon followed him to the grave. But one thing that did survive him was his low-calorie diet: In 1903, a Yale University professor named Russell Chittenden examined Fletcher, found him to be in excellent health, and decided to try the diet himself. Soon after, his rheumatic knee stopped bothering him and his chronic headaches went away, prompting Chittenden to launch a series of studies into diet and health. These and other pivotal studies led to a ratcheting down of the recommended calorie intake from 3,500 a day to the 2,000 recommended today.

If your stomach didn't produce a new layer of mucous every two weeks, it would digest itself.

MISS AMERICA, PART III:
Creating an Institution

Here's where Miss America starts to look like the pageant we know today. It's interesting that one person is so responsible for its success—which makes her either an unsung hero, if you like the pageant...or the culprit, if you don't. It's also interesting to see that the key to turning a "moneymaking scheme" into an "institution" is finding a way to make it seem patriotic.

WONDER WOMAN

The 1935 pageant would probably have been another dud. But Eddie Corcoran, the person in charge of organizing the event, had a stroke of luck: he read an article praising Lenora Slaughter, assistant to Florida Baseball Commissioner Al Lang. The article lauded Slaughter's work on the "Festival of the States" parade and pageant, in Saint Petersburg, Florida. Corcoran had never organized a pageant, and knew he needed help. He wrote a letter to Lang asking to "borrow" Slaughter for the six weeks leading up to the contest. He offered to pay her $1,000 for the work.

Slaughter hesitated...but Lang urged her to "go up there and show those damn Yankees how to do a *real* job with a pageant." Finally, she consented to go to Atlantic City. But only for the agreed-upon six weeks. She ended up staying for more than 30 years.

CULTURAL REVOLUTION

Slaughter had spent her career working with civic-minded, upper-crust society women, and she put this background to work on the Miss America Pageant's #1 problem: its reputation for sleaze. For the rest of the 1930s and into the 1940s, she tore the pageant down to its barest essentials and rebuilt it into the kind of event that even high-class society matrons could love. Or as Bess Myerson, Miss America 1945, put it, "She picked the pageant up by its bathing suit straps and put it in an evening gown."

One of the ways Slaughter cleaned up the contest's image was by drawing attention away from the swimsuit competition. She did this by adding a talent category to the competition, and by

---

The Sanskrit word for "war" also translates as "desire for more cows."

bringing back family-oriented events. She also excluded children from the competition for the first time, requiring that all entrants be 18 years old by the first day of competition.

MRS. ATLANTIC CITY

Despite all these changes, the pageant's survival remained in doubt. Conservatives and women's organizations kept up their criticism, and groups like the Federated Women's Clubs of New Jersey denounced the contest as "the work of the devil."

Her back to the wall, Slaughter made a brilliant move to stave off an attack by the Atlantic City government—then run by conservative Quakers. She asked the wife of Mayor C. D. White to head the pageant's hostess committee, which organized the chaperones and escorts for contestants during Pageant Week. Mrs. White, whom Slaughter described as "the Quakerest of Quakers," was perfect for the job. She recruited people from the "best" families in town to volunteer in the pageant. The 1935 and 1936 pageants were considered successes.

CLOSE CALL

Putting Mrs. White in charge of the hostess committee helped the pageant survive its next big scandal. In 1937, a 17-year-old girl named Bette Cooper won the Miss America crown before anyone realized she was too young to compete. Then, the morning she was supposed to be crowned, she ran off with her pageant-appointed escort—an Atlantic City man named Lou Off. Cooper never returned, and the title remained vacant for the rest of the year.

It turned out later that Cooper ran away simply because she didn't want to drop out of Junior College to fulfill her "queenly duties," and didn't know how else to get out of them. Even so, newspapers all over the East Coast covered the drama in lurid—and inaccurate—detail. Ordinarily, the pageant would have been doomed, but not this time. "The pageant escaped a lot of heat," Deford writes, "because nobody wanted to take on Mrs. White."

FOR WOMEN ONLY

After the scandal blew over, Slaughter and White took steps to make sure it would never happen again. They instituted a ban,

forbidding contestants from having any contact with any men—
even their fathers—during Pageant Week. The young women
were also barred from nightclubs, bars, and taverns, and had to
avoid any public events where alcohol was served. They had to
observe an ironclad 1:00 a.m. curfew, and even taxicabs were
declared off-limits except in emergencies, to avoid even the hint
of scandal. Nearly all of the rules set down in the 1930s are still in
effect today.

GOING FURTHER

Once Slaughter got the Miss America Pageant and its contestants
firmly under control, she set her sights on the pageant's other
major problem: the cheesy state and local "franchise" pageants
that fed their winners into the Miss America contest.

Over the next several years, Slaughter phased out contests
run by newspapers and amusement parks and began regulating
operators of the state and local pageants that were left. For-profit
pageants were out. One by one, Slaughter took control of them
and turned them over to local chapters of the nonprofit Jaycees
(Junior Chamber of Commerce) to run as a public service.

Today more than 300,000 volunteers around the country run
the 2,000 local contests that feed into the Miss America Pageant.

ALL THIS AND WORLD WAR II

Slaughter was still implementing her reforms when the Japanese
bombed Pearl Harbor and the United States entered World
War II. Once again, the future of the pageant seemed in doubt
(although this time, at least, it wasn't the pageant's fault). Who
could justify all of the effort and expense that went into the
pageant when America's sons were shipping off to war?

The federal government, that's who.

The War Finance Department, which had the power to
cancel frivolous and wasteful public events during wartime,
decided that the pageant could—and should—continue during the
war. Why? "They knew we could do a good job selling war bonds,"
Slaughter explained, "and agreed to pay $2,500 if I would chaper-
one Miss America on a trip around America selling war bonds in
1943."

For the next three months, Slaughter and that year's Miss

America, a 19-year-old UCLA coed named Jean Bartel, toured the United States selling bonds. They made 469 appearances in 24 different states and autographed 50,000 pictures.

When it was done, they'd sold $2.5 million worth of bonds—more than any other individual Americans during the war.

WRAPPED IN THE FLAG

This was an amazing accomplishment. But it was even more amazing to see who *bought* the bonds. More than 80% of Bartel and Slaughter's customers were women—a total surprise, since traditionally, women did not like swimsuit contests or beauty pageants.

This illustrated how effective the bond sales had been as an image-building tool. Before the drive, the pageant was generally seen as an overhyped swimsuit contest. Afterward, it was regarded as a wholesome search for the ideal American woman—a beauty pageant the entire family could enjoy.

More than all of Lenora Slaughter's reforms combined, wrapping the pageant in the flag had transformed Miss America into an "all-American" institution.

* * * * *

MISS AMERICA FACT

During a bond-selling visit to the University of Minnesota, the student council there approached Bartel and Slaughter with a suggestion. "I don't know any of the names," recalled Slaughter, "but I remember that an ugly little girl with spectacles—never a potential beauty—was at the head of it."

The ugly duckling noted that while plenty of scholarships were available for male students, there were almost none for females, and the pageant could help change that. Slaughter—always on the lookout for ways to improve the contest's image—was immediately enthusiastic.

Today, the Miss America Pageant is the largest source of scholarship money for U.S. women, handling over $25 million a year.

For Part IV of the story, turn to page 568

OOPS!

More examples of Murphy's law—anything that can goe wrong, will.

BORDER CROSSING
"If you closely examine a map of South Dakota, you'll see that the man-made western border of the state has a slight bump in it as it runs north-south. When the territory was being surveyed, the boundary was set to fall on the 27th meridian west from Washington, D.C. As the surveyors working down from the north met those coming up from the south, they missed each other by a few miles. This error remains on every map to this day."
—from *Oops*, by Paul Smith

HAPPY BIRTHDAY!
"A Dutch couple tried to have a baby for more than five years. Finally, they turned to the University Hospital at Utrecht, one of the Netherlands' most prestigious fertility clinics. An in-vitro fertilization took place in March, 1993; in December, the woman had twins—Teun and Koen.

"Apparently, however, the clinic made a mistake. 'Little Teun,' said news reports, 'is as white and blonde as his father and mother. Little Koen is black.' After first denying responsibility, the clinic had to admit they'd 'accidentally inseminated the mother's eggs with sperm from another man along with that of her husband.' "
—from the *San Francisco Chronicle*, 6/29/95

HEAR, HEAR
"In the 1950s Harold Senby of Leeds, England began experiencing difficulty hearing. He was fitted for a hearing aid, but his hearing did not improve.

In fact, he seemed to be hearing worse than before. During the next 20 years, he was refitted several times, but each time his hearing stayed the same. Finally, during a visit to his doctor in March 1978, the hearing aid was removed entirely.

Miraculously, Senby's hearing began to improve. After a closer medical examination, the doctor discovered that "in the 1950s,

U.S. physicians treat an estimated 4 million broken bones a year.

the hearing aid had been made for his left ear, not the right ear, which was the one giving him trouble."

—from *The Blunder Book,* by M. Hirsch Goldberg

FUNNY MONEY

In 1960, the Brazilian government discovered that the cost of printing a 1-cruziero note was 1.2 cruzieros. They immediately stopped issuing it.

—from *Oops,* by Paul Smith

GOOD BET

In 1995, Pizza Hut scheduled a commercial featuring Pete Rose. According to news reports, "a young boy asks Pete Rose about his accomplishments in baseball. At the end, Rose asks if the boy likes Pizza Hut pizza, and the boy replies, 'You bet!' " After reviewing the script, the company canceled its plans. "That's not the best choice of words," explained Rose.

—from the *San Francisco Chronicle,* 6/21/95

WHAT A GAS!

"When a cow has an attack of bloat (actually methane gas generated in the stomach), it must obtain relief promptly or die.

"A Dutch veterinarian was summoned recently to treat a cow suffering from this affliction, an agricultural news service reported. He tried a standard remedy, which is to insert a tube carefully up the beast's rear end.

"A satisfying rush of gas followed. With misplaced scientific zeal, the vet, perhaps seeking a source of cheap heat and light, then applied a match. The resulting torchlike jet set the barn ablaze. It burned to the ground. The flames spread to the nearby fields, which were consumed.

"The vet was convicted of negligence and fined. The cow remained serene."

—from *Remarkabilia,* by John Train

WHAT A DOLL!

*Here are five of the more usual
dolls sold in America in recent years.*

THUGGIES
Introduced in the summer of 1993, Thuggies came with
something that no dolls had ever had before—criminal
records. There were 17 different characters, with names like
"Motorcycle Meany," "Dickie the Dealer," "Bonnie Ann Bribe,"
and "Mikey Milk 'em." They were outlaw bikers, dope pushers,
white-collar criminals, even "check-kiting congressmen."

But despite their "personal histories," the dolls were designed
to discourage crime, not encourage it. Each one came packaged in
a prison cell and had its own rehabilitation program. Children
were supposed to set them on the straight-and-narrow. (Bonnie
Ann Bribe, for example, doing time for trying to bribe her way
through school, had to read to senior citizens one hour a day.) The
dolls even came with a gold star to wear when they successfully
completed rehab.

"It works, believe me," Carolyn Clark, co-founder of Thuggies, Inc., told reporters. "It's not going to turn the kid into a
criminal. ...It lets them know that they can correct this kind of
behavior."

TONY THE TATTOOED MAN
Comes with tattoos and a "tattoo gun," that kids can use to apply
the tattoos to the doll or to themselves. Additional tattoos—
including "brains, boogers, bugged-out eyes and other anatomical
atrocities"—are sold separately.

BABY THINK IT OVER
Like Thuggies, Baby Think It Over was designed to teach kids a
lesson—in this case, "Don't get pregnant." The dolls are issued to
junior-high and high school students so they can experience what
it's really like to have a baby. Each doll weighs 10 pounds, and
contains electronics that make it cry "at random, but realistic,
intervals, simulating a baby's sleeping and waking patterns to its

Congress has proposed 10,679 amendments to the U.S. Constitution since 1789; 27 made it.

demand for food," says Rick Jurmain, who invented the doll with his wife, Mary.

Like a real baby, there's no way to stop the doll from crying once it starts except by "feeding" it, which is done by inserting a special key into the baby's back, turning it, and holding the baby in place with pressure for as long as 15 minutes. The key is attached to the "parent's" arm with a tamper-proof hospital bracelet, which prevents them from handing off the responsibility to someone else. And the teenagers have to respond quickly— once the baby starts crying, a timer inside the baby records how long it cries. It also records any shaking, drops, or harsh handling that takes place. If the crying baby is left unattended for longer than two minutes, the timer registers that as neglect.

There's also a "drug-addicted" version that's more irritable, has a "higher pitch, a warbling cry," and a body tremor. Priced at $200 apiece, Baby Think It Overs are sold as instructional aids, not toys.

RHOGIT-RHOGIT

Sexual abstinence is simply not an option for Rhotig-Rhogit. "Elegant, intellectual, and extremely sexy, Rhogit-Rhogit will seduce you with his male prowess, his animal sexuality, his vision, and his depth," says the sales catalog from BillyBoy Toys, the Paris company that manufactures it. "He feels equally comfortable in butch, tough-boy clothes as he does in the most avant-garde French and Italian designer clothes and the most utterly formal attire."

Rhogit-Rhogit also has a male sidekick, Zhdrick, who, according to the catalog "is, perhaps, the most sophisticated, sensual, and provocatively sexual doll ever made." The dolls retail for $1,000 apiece, which includes one designer outfit and one condom. If you want wigs, jeans, lassos, boots, underwear, top hats, or other accessories from the company's "Boy Stuff" collection, you have to pay extra. (A lot extra—outfits run $600 to $900 apiece.)

TALKING STIMPY DOLL

From the cartoon series, Ren & Stimpy. "Yank the hairball in Stimpy's throat and he talks. Squeeze his leg and he makes 'rude underleg noises.' " Recommended for "ages 4 and up."

In 39 of the 50 U.S. states, the travel industry is the largest single employer.

UNUSUAL AWARDS

You've heard of the Oscars and the Emmys,
but how about these awards?

THE BOZOS

Awarded during the 1980s by Bozo the Clown (Larry Harmon) to the "biggest bozos in the news." Winners included Jim and Timmy Bakker, Oliver North, Vanna White, Geraldo Rivera (twice), and Cher. The prize: a Bozo telephone.

SITTING DUCK AWARD

Presented annually by the National Society of Newspaper Columnists to "the target most useful to a columnist on a slow news day." Winners include: Roseanne Arnold, O.J. Simpson's houseguest Kato Kaelin, and Millie, the dog belonging to former first lady Barbara Bush.

HARLON PAGE HUBBARD LEMON AWARD

Awarded annually by consumer, public health, and environmental groups to "the year's most unfair, misleading, and irresponsible advertising." Hubbard pioneered America's first nationwide advertising campaign for "Lydia Pinkham's Vegetable Compound," a cure-all health tonic with a 20% alcohol content. Winners include: Walt Disney's "movie news" ads, which look like real news reports, and GMC truck, for bragging about the safety of its Safari minivan when it actually ranked " near the bottom" in crash tests.

GOLDEN FLEECE AWARDS

Awarded from 1975 to 1988, by Senator William Proxmire, to government agencies that wasted the most money. Winners included the Department of Agriculture, which spent $46,000 to find out how long it takes to cook two eggs for breakfast, and the National Science Foundation, which awarded a $9,992 grant to an anthropologist to study the "political significance of bullfighting in Spain."

GOLDEN RASPBERRIES (RAZZIES)

Awarded by "460 film professionals, journalists, and fans for the worst films and performances of the year." Winners get a golf ball-sized raspberry glued to a film reel and spray-painted gold. "It costs us about $2 to make and is every bit as tacky as the movies and performances they are given to," says John Wilson, the ceremony' organizer. Winners include *Showgirls*, *Mommie Dearest*, *Howard the Duck*, and Sylvester Stallone (who's won eight times, including a special award for worst actor of the decade.)

MILLARD FILLMORE MEDAL OF MEDIOCRITY

Presented by "The Society for the Preservation and Enhancement of the Recognition of Millard Fillmore, the Last of the Whigs" to "recognize mediocrity in high places." The award is named after America's 13th president, who was denied his own party's nomination for re-election in 1852. "We felt that underachievers needed somebody to look up to, or down on, and that's Fillmore," says the group's president. "He was the Gerald Ford of the 19th century."

Winners include ex-President Bush (for winning a 90% approval rating at the end of the Gulf War...and then losing the 1992 election to the governor of Arkansas); Roseanne Arnold (for botching the national anthem at a baseball game in 1990); the canceled baseball season of 1995; former Vice President Dan Quayle (do we need to explain?); Billy Carter; Ed McMahon; Prince Charles and Princess Diana; and James Watt, Reagan's Secretary of the Interior.

* * * * *

BRI's nominee for the "Did-We-Really-Need-This Award?" Award: The Liberace Legend Award. Presented since 1994 by the Liberace Foundation, in "a gala benefit at the famed Liberace Mansion." Winners are selected "for major contributions to the community and the world of entertainment." They include Debbie Reynolds, Siegfried and Roy, and Liza Minelli. According to a press release: "The presentation is the highlight of a series of festivities surrounding the May 16 birthday celebration of Liberace."

Count 'em yourself: Ears of corn always have an even number of rows of kernels.

THE MYSTERIOUS OUIJA BOARD

*Why did Uncle John write this chapter? Maybe
his porcelain Ouija board told him to.*

GHOSTWRITER

In the 1890s, spiritualism was a big fad. In the midst of it,
someone came up with a new tool for communicating
with the dead: a small piece of wood called a "planchette." People
would gather around a table or other flat surface, place their hands
on the planchette, and watch how it moved. Some had pencils
attached that wrote out messages; others pointed at letters,
numbers, and words painted on the table and spelled out messages
that way. No one could explain why the planchette moved. Skep-
tics charged that the people who held the planchette were moving
it—perhaps unconsciously. But true believers insisted that spirits
guided the little thing across the table.

SPELLING IT OUT

William and Isaac Fuld thought the whole thing was a bunch of
nonsense, but wanted to cash in on it. They owned a toy company
in Maryland, and figured the planchette would make a good game.
So they took a board about the size of a cafeteria tray, painted
the letters of the alphabet across the middle, and put the numbers
0 through 9 underneath. They also put the words "Yes" and "No"
in the left and right corners, and the word "Goodbye" across the
bottom. Then they painted the name of the game, "Ouija"—a
combination of oui and ja, the French and German words for
"yes"—across the top. Their "Ouija Talking Board" was patented
in 1892.

DEAD SERIOUS

It wasn't until World War I that Ouija boards became a big
commercial success.

Company legend has it that not long before the war broke
out, William Fuld's favorite Ouija board told him to "prepare for

big business." So he expanded production...and sure enough, during the war people began using the Ouija to "keep in touch" with loved ones who'd been sent into battle. Sales skyrocketed, and the money poured in.

Since then, Ouija sales have always boomed in times of national crisis, tailed off when conditions improved, then increased again when the next crisis hit. The Ouija board sold well during World War II, the Korean War, and the Vietnam War, and dipped in between. The Fuld Family manufactured Ouija Boards until 1967, when they sold the rights to Parker Brothers.

OUIJA FACTS

• At the time World War I started, the IRS collected a 10% tax on every game sold in the United States and the Fulds didn't want to pay. So they declared the Ouija board to be a "scientific instrument" that didn't qualify for the tax. They fought the case all the way to the Supreme Court ...and lost.

• No one can explain how the Ouija planchette moves across the board. "There's nothing special about Ouijas to give it any supernatural powers," one Parker Brothers spokesperson insists. "It's simply a game."

• One reasonable theory: the game works through an "idiomotor action" in much the same way that a dowsing rod finds water. "Unconsciously picturing what you want to have happen can cause your muscles to make it happen," psychology professor Ray Hyman explains. "People think they're not doing anything and that some outside force is making it happen."

*   *   *   *   *

TRUE STORY

At age 47, the Rolling Stones' bassist, Bill Wyman, began a relationship with 13-year-old Mandy Smith, with her mother's blessing. Six years later, they were married, but the marriage only lasted a year. Not long after, Bill's 30-year-old son Stephen married Mandy's mother, age 46. That made Stephen a stepfather to his former stepmother. If Bill and Mandy had remained married, Stephen would have been his father's father-in-law and his own grandpa.

WEIRD TALES OF THE OUIJA BOARD

*Here are some of the strangest stories
from the annals of the Ouija board.*

GHOST WRITING?

The most famous Ouija board user in history was Pearl Curran, a St. Louis, Missouri, housewife. She was playing the game with some friends in 1913 when, legend has it, the planchette began moving around the board with surprising strength. It spelled out this message: "Many moons ago I lived. Again I come, Patience Worth my name." The "spirit" identified itself as a woman who'd been born in 1625 in Dorsetshire, England, and had migrated to New England...where she was murdered by an Indian.

For the next six years (according to Curran), the spirit fed her poems, aphorisms, and other works through the Ouija board. Paul Sann writes in *Fads, Follies and Delusions of the American People*,

> Between 1913 and 1919 the pent-up Patience transmitted to Curran no less than 1,500,000 pearls of wisdom heavy with moral and religious dissertations, garnished with 2,000 items of blank verse and six novels. Mrs. Curran said that in one busy ten-day stretch alone her whirling planchette recorded 30,000 words. She said she could take 2,000 words an hour off the board when both she and the virginal puritan were on the right wavelength.

One thing that made Curran's story believable was the fact that while she'd had no formal training as a writer, the prose she produced was surprisingly good, often using very antiquated language. All of it was "far beyond the ken of Mrs. Curran, who," one critic wrote, "has never exhibited a shred of literary talent or enthusiasm," Curran's story was still intact when she died in 1937 at the age of 46—although many psychology experts explained away her writings as either a fraud or the product of an "alternating personality," the same phenomenon that causes people to speak in tongues.

COMMAND PERFORMANCES
A handful of people have actually committed murder when their Ouija boards "told" them to.

• In the early 1930s, for example, a 15-year-old girl named Mattie Turley murdered her father with a shotgun, apparently with the help of her mother, Dorothea Turley, who wanted to leave Mattie's father for another man. "The Ouija board told me to do it so that Mama can be free to marry a handsome cowboy, that's all that happened," the 15-year-old testified at her trial, "Mother told me the Ouija board couldn't be denied and that I would not even be arrested for doing it." Both mother and daughter were convicted of murder: Mrs. Turley's 10-to 25-year sentence was overturned three years later, and she was freed, but Mattie Turley didn't get out until she was 21.

• In 1932, a 77-year-old railroad worker named Herbert Hurd murdered his wife after their Ouija board falsely accused him of having an affair. As he later testified:

> The spirits told her through her Ouija board that I was too fond of another woman and had given her $15,000 of a hidden fortune. The Ouija board lied. I never was friendly with another woman and I never had $15,000, but Nellie beat me and burned me and tortured me into confessing all those lies, so I finally had to kill her.

• In 1956, a wealthy Connecticut woman named Helen Dow Peck left nearly her entire $178,000 estate to John Gale Forbes, a name her Ouija board had spelled out in 1919. The only problem: There was no John Gale Forbes—a court-ordered search failed to turn up a single person by that name in entire United States.

OUIJA BOARDS IN THE NEWS
"Britain's Appeal Court was asked today to review a murder trial because three jurors allegedly used a Ouija board to contact one of the victims before finding a man guilty. Lawyers for Stephen Young told the court they had received information from another juror about a seance in the hotel where the jury stayed the night before they found Young guilty of shooting newlyweds Harry and Nicola Fuller. The three jurors 'contacted' Harry Fuller, who named Young, 35, as the killer, they said. The jury went on to convict Young unanimously."—*San Jose Mercury News*, 1994

The country of Brazil is named after the Brazil nut.

BRAND NAMES

Here are more origins of commercial names.

ADIDAS. Adolph and Rudi Dassler formed Dassler Brothers Shoes in Germany in 1925. After World War II, the partnership broke up, but each brother kept a piece of the shoe business: Rudi called his new company Puma; Adolph, whose nickname was "Adi," renamed the old company after himself—*Adi Dassler*.

PENNZOIL. In the early 1900s, two motor oil companies—Merit Oil and Panama Oil—joined forces and created a brand name they could both use: Pennsoil (short for William Penn's Oil). It didn't work—consumers kept calling it Penn-soil. So in 1914 they changed the *s* to a *z*.

DIAL SOAP. The name refers to a clock or watch dial. The reason: It was the first deodorant soap, and Lever Bros. wanted to suggest that it would prevent B.O. "all around the clock."

WD-40. In the 1950s, the Rocket Chemical Company was working on a product for the aerospace industry that would reduce rust and corrosion by removing moisture from metals. It took them 40 tries to come up with a workable Water Displacement formula.

LYSOL. Short for *lye solvent*.

MAZDA. The Zoroastrian god of light.

NISSAN. Derived from the phrase *Nissan sangyo*, which means "Japanese industry."

ISUZU. Japanese for "50 bells."

MAGNAVOX. In 1915 the Commercial Wireless and Development Co. created a speaker that offered the clearest sound of any on the market. They called it the Magna Vox—which means *great voice* in Latin.

FAMOUS TIGHTWADS

Who are the cheapest guys around? Often, the richest ones.
Here are more examples of extreme tightfistedness.

JOHN D. ROCKEFELLER, founder of Standard Oil. Gave a groundskeeper a $5 Christmas bonus…then docked it from the man's pay when he took Christmas Day off to spend with his family.

WALT DISNEY. Timed employees' trips to candy and soda machines.

CLARK GABLE, movie star. Often argued with his grocer about the price of jelly beans.

PAUL VOLCKER, chairman of the Federal Reserve Board. Rather than pay for a laundromat, he packed dirty laundry into a suitcase every week and drove it to his daughter's house.

TY COBB, baseball legend. As an early investor in Coca Cola stock, he was extremely wealthy—but still collected bars of soap from locker room showers and hotel rooms and sent them back to his Georgia farm.

J. PAUL GETTY, oil baron.
• When his son was kidnapped and held hostage, he refused to pay ransom money until the kidnappers sent the boy's ear to him in the mail.

• He calculated the wages of his gatekeeper by counting the number of times the main gate of his estate was opened and closed on a given day, then multiplied the number "by some minute sum" to arrive at a salary.

CALVIN COOLIDGE, U.S. president. Personally oversaw and approved all White House expenditures; reportedly bought food for state dinners at the local Piggly Wiggly.

ARTHUR FIELDER, conductor of the Boston Pops. Rather than repair the holes in the walls of his home, he stuffed them with "moldering bits of carpet." He was also famous for skipping out on the tab when dining with his musicians.

When a cat died in ancient Egypt, its owners shaved off their eyebrows as a sign of mourning.

THE PINBALL STORY

If you like pinball (and who doesn't), here's the next best thing to actually having a machine in the bathroom. Hmm…interesting idea. Imagine what it would sound like to people waiting to use the toilet. "What are you doing in there? What's that noise? Hey, are you playing pinball?!!?"

ROLLING STONE

Have you ever heard of a game called Bagatelle? No one plays it anymore, but for centuries it was one of the most popular pastimes of the European upper classes. Originally, it was played outside. People threw stones up a hill and hoped that, as the stones rolled down, they'd fall into holes that had been dug in the hillside.

By the middle of the 17th century, the game was played indoors. Players pushed small balls up an inclined felt board with a stick, then let the balls go. Again, the object was to get the balls to drop into holes. But now each hole was surrounded by small pins (actually brass nails) to make it harder. The more points a hole was worth, the more pins were nailed around it. That, of course, is how *pinball* got its name.

THE NEXT STEP

Bagatelle remained popular in various forms for centuries. But modern pinball didn't evolve until 1931, when game manufacturer David Gottlieb created a version called Baffle Ball. He made two important changes to Bagatelle:

> 1. He incorporated a spring-loaded mechanism (virtually indistinguishable from modern-day pinball shooters), so balls were launched rather than pushed or dropped.
> 2. He made it a coin-operated machine, designed to sit on retailers' countertops.

There weren't any lights, bells, mechanical bumpers, or even flip-pers. Players shook and jostled the machine (technically, they weren't even supposed to do *that*) to get the ball into one of the high-scoring holes.

But it was an appealing diversion during the Great Depres-sion, and was very popular.

The average caterpillar has 2,000 muscles in its body; the average human, 700.

As Russell Roberts wrote in the *Chicago Tribune*:

> To an American public haunted by economic disaster, facing day
> upon dreary day of hanging around street corners with nothing to do
> and no hope in sight, the new games were a welcome respite. For ei-
> ther a penny or a nickel (for which you got 7 or 10 balls, respective-
> ly), you could forget, for a few minutes anyway, the world and all its
> troubles. Soon every drugstore, bar and candy store had at least one.

Baffle Ball was also a source of employment. The games sold
for only $16. Anyone who had the money could buy one, put it in
a store, and split the profits with the store owner. "Pinball route-
men," explains Candice Ford Tolbert in *Tilt: The Pinball Book*,
"were anyone and everyone who could come up with a little cash
and who had the time to service and collect from machines out on
locations."

THE BIG THREE

Demand for Baffle Ball was so great that Gottlieb couldn't fill all
his orders. So some of his distributors started to build their own
games. In 1932, Gottlieb's biggest distributor, Ray Moloney,
invented a game called Ballyhoo. It was so successful that he
formed the Bally company and began designing games full-time.

Another distributor—an aspiring Disney cartoonist named
Barry Williams—came up with so many innovations that Gottlieb
offered him a royalty for his designs. (Later, Williams formed his
own company.) Their first joint venture was a game called
Advance. Roger Sharpe writes in *Popular Mechanics*:

> One of the breakthrough attractions of Advance was its delicately
> counterbalanced gates, which were vulnerable to jabs and nudges
> from players. One day, in 1932, Williams went to a drugstore and
> saw a player hit the bottom of Advance to score points without
> hav-ing to aim. This so enraged Williams that he took the game off
> location and hammered five nails through the bottom of the
> machine. In William's words, "Anybody who tried to affect the play
> of the game by slapping the flat of his hand against the game's under
> surface, would now think twice before trying it again."

> However, Williams knew this was a cruel and temporary
> solution.So, he developed a simple, effective device that stopped
> play if the machine was handled roughly. The device consisted of a

small ball balanced on a pedestal. If the game was shaken or pounded, the ball fell from the pedestal and struck a metal ring that immediately stopped play.

Williams called the device a stool pigeon…but not for long. "I never quite liked the name 'stool pigeon,' " he recalled years later, "but I just couldn't come up with anything else." So he set one of the games up in a nearby drugstore and waited to watch the response. Sure enough, a player came along and handled the game too roughly, setting off the stool pigeon. "Damn, I tilted it!" he exclaimed. From then on, the mechanism was known as the tilt.

OTHER MILESTONES

There were four other important steps in creating the pinball machine as we know it:

1. Themes. In 1933, David Rockola (later a jukebox tycoon) came up with *Jigsaw*. Players could put a puzzle together by hitting certain targets and holes. Its popularity showed that the public wanted variety and novelty in their pinball games.

2. Electricity. Williams introduced *Contact*, the first pinball game to use electricity, also in 1933. It had an electrified "kick-out hole" that returned a ball to play after awarding points, and a bell that rang every time a player scored. Features like automatic scoring and "lighted back glass" quickly appeared on new machines.

3. Bumpers. Bally introduced *Bumper* in 1937. It used the first "electrically operated wire and spring bumpers."

4. Flippers. The first flippers appeared in a Bally game called *Humpty Dumpty*, in 1947. Before this breakthrough—created by accident when a technician touched two loose wires together— pinball machines were almost entirely games of chance. In *Humpty Dumpty*, the balls jumped around at the player's command. This feature quickly became indispensable on the machines…and turned pinball into a worldwide phenomenon. "In most of Europe, in fact, they're called flipper games and flipper machines," Roger Sharpe writes in *Pinball!* "Today, we have ramps, drop holes, underground networks, multiball games, drop targets and spinners, but they all don't necessarily have to be on every game. A flipper does."

PINBALL AND THE LAW

In 1933, pinball manufacturers made a mistake that would haunt them for decades. They decided to compete directly against slot machines, electronic bingo, and other gambling machines by building "payout" pinball machines, which rewarded successful players either with cash or tokens that could be redeemed for cash.

To many people, the move made pinball machines synonymous with gambling. And when communities outlawed other types of gambling machines—before and after World War II—they often got rid of all types of pinball machines as well.

Fighting Back. Pinball manufacturers countered by introducing "free play," machines that rewarded players with extended games instead of cash. But even these were controversial. Free games are objects of value, and therefore a kind of gambling payoff. Tamer add-a-ball" features were condemned, too. In fact, it wasn't until America was exposed to the excesses of the 1960s that pinball finally regained acceptance as the lesser of many evils.

Believe it or not, however, many cities and states still have anti-pinball laws on the books, although they're seldom enforced anymore. Ironically, Chicago—home of Gottlieb, Bally, and Williams, the big three manufacturers of pinball machines—is one of the cities that had a long-term ban on the game. It wasn't until 1976 that pinball was finally legalized in its own hometown.

PINBALL FACTS

• David Gottlieb may have invented pinball, but he didn't have much faith in it. His second game was called *Five Star Final*, supposedly named after his favorite newspaper, the *Chicago Tribune*'s end-of-the-day edition. Actually, though, Gottleib figured the pinball "fad" was over and this was his "final" game. A few decades later, in the "golden Age" of pinball, new machines were being designed and shipped every *three weeks*.

• It takes a team of six designers about nine months to invent and perfect a pinball game.

• Pinball designers work toward these ideals: the game should be easy enough to keep novices from getting discouraged, yet challenging enough to keep "wizards" interested; the average game should last from 2 1/2 to 3 minutes, or roughly 47 seconds a ball; and the player should get one free game for every four played.

At birth, a Panda is smaller than a mouse.

MAKING HIS MARK

Mark Twain is one of America's greatest humorists…and maybe one of our great philosophers, too. Here are examples of what we mean.

"A banker is a fellow who lends you his umbrella when the sun is shining and wants it back the minute it begins to rain."

"Clothes make the man. Naked people have little or no influence on society."

"Every time you stop a school, you have to build a jail. What you gain at one end you lose at the other. It's like feeding a dog on his own tail. It won't fatten the dog."

"If you pick up a starving dog and make him prosperous, he will not bite you. This is the principal difference between a dog and a man."

"The human race has one really effective weapon, and that is laughter."

"The man who sets out to carry a cat by its tail learns something that will always be useful and which never will grow dim or doubtful."

"The surest protection against temptation is cowardice."

"There is no distinctly native American criminal class…except Congress."

"Keep away from people who try to belittle your ambitions. Small people always do that, but the really great make you feel that you, too, can become great."

"The rule is perfect: in all matters of opinion our adversaries are insane."

"It usually takes more than three weeks to prepare a good impromptu speech."

"The best way to cheer yourself up is to try to cheer somebody else up."

"Nothing so needs reforming as other people's habits."

"Put all your eggs in one basket and WATCH THAT BASKET!"

CRANK CALLS

*Ever make a "phony phone call"? What if you tried it and reached
the president or vice president...and they took you seriously?
Here are a few times when it really happened.*

THE PRESIDENT IS DEAD!

Call for: Vice President Thomas Marshall

What happened: Marshall was in the middle of a speech
at Atlanta's Civic Auditorium on November 23, 1919, when he
was interrupted by a member of his staff. They'd just received a
call from the White House telling them that President Woodrow
Wilson, who'd recently had a stroke, had died. "I cannot continue
my speech," the stunned vice president told his shocked audience,
"I must leave at once to take up my duties as chief executive of
this great nation."

Aftermath: Marshall was stunned again when he found out the
call was a fake. He denounced it as a "cruel hoax."

WE WANT TO NEGOTIATE

Call for: President George Bush

What happened: In March 1990, an Iranian official called the
White House to say he'd been instructed to set up a phone conference between Bush and Iranian president Ali Akbar Hashemi
Rafsanjani concerning U.S. hostages held in Lebanon. Bush took
the call "on the off chance that it might be real." Two days later,
when the White House tried to return the call, they realized it
had been a put-on.

Aftermath: Even the Iranians thought the Bush administration's
response to the crank call was a little weird. "Can it be that such a
global power, with all its intelligence capabilities, talks to a person
it cannot identify?" the real President Rafsanjani asked in
Teheran. "This is a strange occurrence."

THE PRESIDENT IS DEAD!

Call for: CNN (Cable News Network)

What happened: In 1992, three hours after President Bush had
collapsed during a banquet in Tokyo and vomited in the Japanese
prime minister's lap, the CNN newsroom got a call from the president's personal physician, who was with Bush in Japan. He had

terrible news: the president had just died. CNN staffers thought the story was real and typed it into their news computer. Fortunately for them, the caller had left his phone number...and they traced it to Idaho, not Tokyo.

The story was quickly wiped off the computer and never made it onto CNN's main news channel. But downstairs at Headline News, staffers saw it moments before it was erased. They rushed the tragic information to anchor Don Harrison. "This just in to CNN Headline News!" he told viewers urgently. Then, as he opened his mouth to read the bulletin, he heard someone off-camera yell, "No! Stop!" "We are now getting a correction...," he ad-libbed.

Aftermath: The call was traced to the Garden City, Idaho, home of James Edward Smith, 71, who was arrested and placed in a mental hospital.

WHAT DO YOU THINK OF QUEBEC?

Call for: Queen Elizabeth
What happened: In October 1995, Pierre Brassard, a disc jockey at Montreal's Radio CKOI, called Buckingham Palace and said he was Canadian Prime Minister Jean Chretien; he asked to speak to the queen. Palace officials checked with Chretien's office to verify that the call was genuine, but Chretien wasn't in. Still, an official said that Chretien "probably wanted to speak with her."

So Queen Elizabeth got on the line...and chatted for 17 minutes. She didn't realize it was a prank, even when Brassard "started talking about Halloween and suggesting she put on a nice hat."

Aftermath: The English public was not amused. "We think it's annoying," a palace spokesperson said. In retaliation, one British newspaper published Radio CKOI's phone number and urged readers to call when Brassard was on the air. Another paper had a reporter call Brassard, posing as a Scotland Yard detective, and threaten legal action. But the London tabloid *News the World* got the best revenge: it offered Brassard an $80,000 trip to London for an exclusive story...then reneged on the deal when he accepted, telling him it was a prank.

The most popular Campbell's soup in Hong Kong is watercress and duck gizzard.

ALL ABOUT CHESS

For chess lovers, books about how to play the game are essential bathroom reading. For the rest of us, three pages about chess—one of the oldest and most popular board games in history—are plenty.

FIRST MOVES
• Chess began in northern India sometime before 500 A.D. and was probably based on an Indian military game called *chaturanga—chatur* meaning "four," and *anga* meaning "parts of an army." Like real Indian armies of the day, the game had four types of pieces: elephants, chariots, cavalry, and infantry. It was largely a game of chance; how well you did depended on how well you rolled the dice.

• Chaturanga was later combined with *petteia*, a Greek game of reason. The result was a game close to modern chess. The dice were eliminated, and the emphasis of the game shifted from chance to strategy. There were 16 pieces per player, just like in modern chess: one king, one vizier, or adviser, two elephants, two horses, two chariots, and eight foot soldiers.

• The new game became a worldwide phenomenon. By 800 A.D., it had spread east to China, Korea, and Japan...and west to the Arab world. In Persia, the game was known as *shah mat*—"the king is dead." This is the direct linguistic predecessor to the English word "checkmate."

• When the Moors conquered Spain in the ninth century, they brought chess with them. From there it spread all over Europe, and continued to evolve into the game we know today.

THE PIECES
How did the game go from the original pieces to what we have now?

• **The elephant.** According to The Greatest Games of All Time, Arabs didn't approve of the elephant piece because "physical representations are forbidden in the Islamic religion." They replaced it with "a minaret-shaped piece with a nick cut into it." Later, when Europeans saw it, the pointed top with a nick reminded them of a bishop's hat...so they called it a bishop.

Spinach consumption in the U.S. rose 33% after the Popeye comic strip became a hit in 1931.

• **The chariot.** Hadn't been used for centuries in European warfare. It was changed to something more familiar: a castle (or rook).

• **The vizier.** Never a part of European culture, it was replaced by the queen—a king's most important unofficial advisor.

• **The cavalry pieces and foot soldiers.** Stayed the same—the names were simply changed to knights and pawns.

SLOW MOTION

About the only thing that separated medieval chess from today's version was the way the pieces moved. Most were considerably weaker. The queen, for example—the most powerful piece today— could only move one space at a time. But in the 15th century, the rules abruptly changed.

• The queen was suddenly able to go any distance in any direction, as long as she wasn't blocked by other pieces.

• The bishop became able to move any distance diagonally, as long as no one was in the way.

• Even the pawns were strengthened a little: they became able to move two spaces on the first move.

Chess historians believe these changes were connected to the introduction of artillery into modern warfare. Artillery enabled armies to shoot weapons over previously unthinkable distances, so the short distances traveled in chess no longer made military sense. When the game was brought up to date, pieces naturally became more powerful.

THE RIGHT MOVES

Today, the way some pieces move seems pretty arbitrary. For example, the pawns can only move straight ahead, except when they are attacking; then they can only move diagonally. And the knight (horse) can jump over other pieces. But these moves actually made a lot of sense when they were introduced:

• The pawn is based on a soldier known as a pikeman. As pikemen marched forward into battle, they held their shields directly in front of them and stuck their pikes (spears) out on either side. The shield was so bulky that it was literally impossible for the pikeman to attack anything directly in front of him. That's why a pawn can only attack pieces that are diagonally to the left or right.

• Knights were the only people in the battlefield on horseback—and thus are the only ones who can leap over their opponents.

CHESS AND REVOLUTION

Because many court officials—kings, queens etc.—are represented in chess, the pieces have traditionally been seen as symbols of the establishment. This has made them unpopular with revolutionaries. Often, when a king was overthrown, the people who toppled him would try to replace the country's chess pieces as well.

• After the Revolutionary War, for example, many American chessmakers replaced kings with acorn-shaped pieces. One editor who hoped to make chess "better adapted to our feelings as citizens of a free republic," suggested calling the kings, queens and pawns *governors*, *generals*, and *pioneers*. The idea never caught on.

• At the beginning of the French Revolution, the Convention decreed that kings, queens, knights, rooks, bishops, and pawns would henceforth be known as *flags*, *adjutants*, *dragoons*, *cannons*, *volunteers*, and *troops of the line*. These changes were rejected by chess players...although many French sets still contain crownless queens.

CHANGING SIDES

The most bizarre example of "revolutionary chess" came in the late 1920s, when the Marx and Engels Institute in Moscow invented a communist chess board for the USSR. The board was divided into red and white teams, with Joseph Stalin serving as the red king and other prominent Communists filling out the ranks of the red queen, bishops, knights, and rooks. Prominent opponents of the Communists filled out the white ranks.

But as Stalin began wiping out his political enemies in the purges of the 1930s, many Communists represented by the red pieces fell out of favor—which meant they could no longer be represented on the red side. These "enemy of the people" pieces had to be bleached white and moved to the other side of the board; owners who didn't comply risked being sent to Siberia. As the purges progressed, it became so difficult to keep track of who belonged on which side of the board that the chess sets had to be abandoned.

IS *THIS*
BATHROOM READING?

Here's a surprise entry—the Bill of Rights. Actually, Uncle John's been thinking about including this for some time. After all, what better chance to read the document than in the bathroom? You know, you can read one of the Amendments, then flip to the history of bubblegum or something. If they'd taught it that way in school, we'd all know it by heart now. We at the BRI like to think that the Founding Fathers would be proud of us.

BILL OF RIGHTS

Here's the complete text of the first 10 Amendments to the U.S. Constitution.

1. Congress shall make no law respecting an establishment of religion, or prohibiting the free exercise thereof; or abridging the freedom of speech, or of the press; or the right of the people peaceably to assemble, and to petition the Government for a redress of grievances.

2. A well regulated militia, being necessary to the security of a free State, the right of the people to keep and bear Arms, shall not be infringed.

3. No Soldier shall, in time of peace be quartered in any house, without the consent of the Owner, nor in time of war, but in a manner to be prescribed by law.

4. The right of the people to be secure in their persons, houses, papers, and effects, against unreasonable searches and seizures, shall not be violated, and no Warrants shall issue, but upon probable cause, supported by Oath or affirmation, and particularly describing the place to be searched, and the persons or things to be seized.

5. No person shall be held to answer for a capital, or otherwise infamous crime, unless on a presentment or indictment of a Grand Jury, except in cases arising in the land or naval forces, or in the Militia, when in actual service in time of War or public danger; nor shall any person be subject for the same offence to be twice put in jeopardy of life or limb; nor shall be compelled in any criminal case to be a witness against himself, nor be deprived of life, liberty, or property, without due process of law; nor shall private property be taken for public use, without just compensation.

6. In all criminal prosecutions, the accused shall enjoy the right to a speedy and public trial, by an impartial jury of the State and district wherein the crime shall have been committed, which district shall have been previously ascertained by law, and to be informed of the nature and cause of the accusation; to be confronted with the witnesses against him; to have compulsory process for obtaining witnesses in his favor, and to have the Assistance of Counsel for his defence.

7. In Suits at common law, where the value in controversy shall exceed twenty dollars, the right of trial by jury shall be preserved, and no fact tried by a jury, shall be otherwise re-examined in any Court of the United States, than according to the rules of the common law.

8. Excessive bail shall not be required, nor excessive fines imposed, nor cruel and unusual punishments inflicted.

9. The enumeration in the Constitution, of certain rights, shall not be construed to deny or disparage others retained by the people.

10. The powers not delegated to the United States by the Constitution, nor prohibited by it to the States, are reserved to the States respectively, or to the people.

* * * * *

FOOD FOR THOUGHT

In a recent survey, a randomly selected group of American citizens were shown a list of freedoms. Then they were asked by pollsters if they would vote for those rights. Not only did many respondents fail to recognize that the freedoms on the list were already guaranteed by the Bill of Rights—they said they'd vote *against* the rights if they were on the ballot.

There are more fatal traffic accidents in July than any other month.

BRAND NAMES

You already know these names. Now you know where they come from.

KOOL-AID. Originally named Kool-Ade, until bureaucrats in the Food and Drug Administration banned the use of "ade" because it means "a drink made from…" So inventor E.E. Perkins simply changed the spelling to "aid," meaning "help."

SONY. Originally called Tokyo Tsushin Kogyo. Founder Akio Morita wanted a name he could market internationally. He looked through a Latin dictionary, picked out the word *sonus* (sound), and combined it with "sunny."

CHEERIOS. Originally Cheery Oats. In 1946, Quaker Oats threatened to sue, claming it had exclusive rights to the name "Oats." Rather than fight, General Mills switched to Cheerios.

BISSELL CARPET SWEEPER. Melville Bissell owned a crockery shop in Grand Rapids, Michigan. He was so allergic to the straw his crockery was packed in that he started sneezing whenever he had to sweep it up. So he invented—and ultimately manufactured—the first carpet sweeper.

HAMILTON-BEACH. L. H. Hamilton and Chester A. Beach perfected a "high-speed, lightweight universal electronic motor" and used it in the first commercial drink mixer in 1912. They went on to build small appliances for home use.

GREY POUPON DIJON MUSTARD. Sound classy? Actually, it's named for the Briton who invented it—a Mr. Grey—and his French business partner—Monsieur Poupon—who put up money to open a mustard factory in (where else?) Dijon, France.

CARNATION. In 1901, while walking down a street in Seattle, the head of the Pacific Coast Condensed Milk Company noticed a box of Carnation Brand cigars in a store window. He decided it was a good name for his milk, too. With a picture of a flower on the label, it would be recognizable even to children.

FAMILIAR PHRASES

More origins of everyday phrases.

TURN OVER A NEW LEAF
Meaning: Start over.
Origin: Trees have nothing to do with it—the leaf in the expression is actually the page of a book. Just as the plot of a novel changes from page to page, so too can people change their lives.

IN THE DOLDRUMS
Meaning: Unhappy or depressed; sluggish.
Origin: *Doldrum* is believed to be a corruption of the word *dullard*—meaning "dull or sluggish person." Early cartographers applied it to the dullest areas of the ocean, near the equator, where the waters are calm and winds are very light. With little or no wind in their sails, ships might literally spend weeks "in the doldrums."

WORKING FREELANCE
Meaning: Working independently, for more than one employer.
Origin: The novelist Sir Walter Scott first used this term to describe soldiers-for-hire in the Middle Ages. Because they owed loyalty to no one, he reasoned, they were *free* to hire out their skill with *lances* to anyone who could afford them.

PUT SOMEONE ON THE SPOT
Meaning: Put someone in a difficult position.
Origin: Gangster slang from the 1920s. A person on the spot was marked for execution. Probably originated in reference to witnesses, who were "on the spot" where a crime was committed.

ON THE NOSE
Meaning: Perfect; right on time.
Origin: In the early days of radio broadcasting, directors used hand signals to communicate with announcers in soundproof studios. A finger across the throat meant "cut," and a finger on the nose meant that the show was right on schedule.

Sound like someone you know? An ostrich's eyes are bigger than its brains.

PLEASE LEAVE A MESSAGE...

Telephone answering machines are a bathroom reader's friend. We owe the inventor a debt of gratitude, because they let us read in peace. After all, who wants to jump off the toilet and race madly for the phone every time it rings?

THE FIRST EFFORT

You may not know this, but when Thomas Edison played "Mary Had a Little Lamb" on his first crude recording device in 1877, he was really trying to create a telephone answering machine. The problem with the telephone, he reasoned, was that—unlike the telegraph—it didn't take messages. Unfortunately, the Wizard of Menlo Park couldn't come up with a viable answering device; he had to "settle" for the phonograph instead.

THE FIRST MACHINE

A Danish technician named Valdemar Poulsen invented the answering machine in the summer of 1898. Polusen's device, called the "telegraphone," was meant to be used exclusively as an answering machine, but was actually the world's first magnetic recorder—the direct precursor to the tape recorder. In 1903, his company, the American Telegraphone Company, tried to crack the U.S. Market. It failed miserably, for three reasons:

1. Poor sound quality.

2. It was too expensive for most homes or businesses.

3. The Bell companies refused to allow "outside" machines to be hooked up to their phone lines—which virtually eliminated the entire U.S. market.

American Telegraphone then tried to market their machine as a dictaphone instead, but that failed, too. They went bankrupt in 1919.

THE PHONEMATE

Then, in the late 1960s, Neal Buglewicz, a California inventor, decided to buck the phone company. He developed an answering

The man who created the Thighmaster was once a Bhuddist monk.

machine that used two tape recorders and called it the Phonemate 700. His second version, the "streamlined" Phonemate 400, became the first answering machine made widely available to consumers. By today's standards, it was laughably primitive: It weighed 10 pounds, used reel-to-reel tapes, could only record voice messages 30 seconds long, and required earphones to retrieve messages. But it opened the door for other designs. Soon other companies were offering similar machines.

AT&T did what it could to prevent the answering machine from succeeding. In 1972, they announced that phone customers had to buy special equipment to connect answering machines to the telephone company network. But Phonemate and its competitors went to court to have the regulations thrown out, and in 1976 they won.

*   *   *   *   *

FARTS IN THE NEWS

• Frank Lathrop is the proud inventor of the TooT TrapperR, a special seat cushion that instantly absorbs the odor of unwanted gas. Lathrop got the idea after too many complaints from his wife. "You just sit on it, and it goes to work," Lathrop explains. "We call this the perfect thing for the person who has everything, including gas." The TrappeR's air filter "uses the same technique that was used in gas masks during the Desert Storm War."

• Biologist Dr. Colin Leakey has devoted his entire career to figuring out what makes people pass wind. "We believe that by looking at chemicals in the flatus, we can look at what is being broken down and where these particular chemicals come from," he says. To accomplish this, Leakey (*Leakey?!!?*) has invented the *flatometer*, a device that measures flatulence.

• Johnson & Johnson, which produces drugs for gas and indigestion, once conducted a survey and found that almost one-third of Americans believe they have a flatulence problem. However, according to Terry Bolin and Rosemary Stanton, authors of *Wind Breaks: Coming to Terms with Flatulence*, most flatulence is healthy. What is unhealthy, the authors argue, is that we spend too much time dwelling on it.

Male hospital patients fall out of bed twice as often as female patients.

THE ODD TITLE AWARD

Q: What do the Pulitzer Prize and the Odd Title Award have in common? A: None of Uncle John's Bathroom Readers have won either of them. Here are some real-life books that have won Bookseller *magazine's annual award for the most unusual book title.*

THE NAME GAME

Every year, tens of thousands of new books are published. Some are pretty strange…and in 1978, the staff at *Bookseller* magazine decided to honor a few with the Odd Title of the Year Award. Every year, they give a bottle of champagne to the person who finds the most unusual book title of the year. The only rules: the book itself has to be serious, and "gratuitously eye-catching academic works" are automatically disqualified. The title has to be weird without trying to be. (That's why *New Guinea Tapeworms & Jewish Grandmothers; Tales of Parasites and People*, lost out in 1994.) Here are all the winners. Remember: These are *real* book titles!

1978: *Proceedings of the Second International Workshop on Nude Mice* (Also won the Oddest of the Odd Book Title Award, given in 1994 to the oddest title in the contest's 15-year history)

Runners-up:
• *Cooking with God*

• *Iceberg Utilization*

• *Fight Acne and Win*

1979: *The Madam as Entrepreneur: Career Management in House Prostitution*

Runners-up:
• *Macrame Gnomes*

• *100 Years of British Rail Catering*

1980: *The Joy of Chickens*

Runner-up:
• *Children Are Like Wet Cement*

1981: *Last Chances at Love: Terminal Romances*

Runner-up:
• *Waterproofing Your Child*

1982: Two winners: *Braces Owners' Manual: A Guide to the Care and Wearing of Braces*, and *Population and Other Problems*

Runners-up:
• *Tourist Guide to Lebanon*

• *Scurvy Past and Present*

• *Keeping Warm with an Axe*

1983: *The Theory of Lengthwise Rolling*

Runners-up: • *Practical Infectious Diseases*
• *Nasal Maintenance: Nursing Your Nose Through Troubled Times*

• *Atlas of Tongue Coating*

1984: *The Book of Marmalade: Its Antecedents, Its History and Its Role in the World Today*

• *Big and Very Big Hole Drilling*

• *Picture Your Dog in Needlework*

• *Napoleon's Glands and Other Ventures in Biohistory*

1985: *Natural Bust Enlargement with Total Power: How to Increase the Other 90% of Your Mind to Increase the Size of Your Breasts*

Runner-up:
• *Anorexia Nervosa in Bulgarian Bees*

1986: *Oral Sadism and the Vegetarian Personality*

1987: No prize awarded

1988: *Versailles: The View from Sweden*

Runner-up:
• *Detecting Fake Nazi Regalia*

1989: *How to Shit in the Woods: An Environmentally Sound Approach to a Lost Art*

1990: *Lesbian Sado-masochism Safety Manual*

1991: No prize awarded

1992: *How to Avoid Huge Ships*

Runner-up:
• *Watermark Diseases of the Cricket Bat*

1993: *American Bottom Archaeology*

Runner-up:
• *Liturgy of the Opening of the Mouth for Breathing*

• *The Complete Suicide Manual*

1994: *Highlights in the History of Concrete*

• *Septic Tanks and Cesspools: A Do-It-Yourself Guide*

• *Butchering Livestock at Home*

• *Best Bike Rides in the Mid-Atlantic*

• *Gymnastics for Horses*

• *Psychiatric Disorders in Dental Practice*

1995: *Reusing Old Graves* ("a study of cemetery etiquette")

Runner-up:
• *Amputee Management: A Handbook*
• *Mucus and Related Topics*
• *Simply Bursting: A Guide to Bladder Control*
• *Fun Games and Big Bangs: The Recreational Use of High Explosives*
• *Rats for Those Who Care*
• *Teach Your Cat to Read*
• *Virtual Reality: Exploring the Bra*

"Aglet" is the plastic or metal tip of a shoelace.

INCOME TAX TRIVIA

You may not like to pay them, but reading about them isn't so bad.
And when you're done with the page, you can always tear it out and...

AUDIT INFO
Do you worry about being audited? Actually, the odds you'll be audited are pretty low: In 1994 the IRS audited about 93,000 individual income tax returns out of 114 million submitted, or about .08% of all returns filed. That's way down from 1914, when every single one of the 357,598 tax returns submitted was audited. The IRS didn't take any chances with the signatures that year, either: each taxpayer had to sign their return under oath in the presence of IRS officials.

KISS & TELL
Believe it or not, the IRS actually pays people to tattle on tax cheats. In fiscal year 1993, for example, it paid out $5.3 million to tipsters. The money was rewarded to more than 14,000 different informants, whose tips led to the collection of $172 million in previously unpaid taxes. The most "useful" tattlers earned an average of $1,772 apiece. But they had to file Form 211, the official IRS informer form, to claim their "reward."

TAX RANKINGS
Sweden has the highest taxes of any modern economy on earth—its taxes make up 56.9% of the country's total income. The United States comes in ninth behind Sweden, France, Italy, Germany, Canada, Britain, Switzerland, and Japan. Taxes make up about 29.9% of its total income.

LEGAL DEADBEATS
According to a 1990 IRS study, 1,219 taxpayers with incomes over $200,000 legally paid no federal income tax at that year—and 1,114 of these people paid no income taxes anywhere else in the world, either.

The U.S. Post Office sold a record 123 million Elvis Presley commemorative stamps in 1993.

DEDUCTIONS

According to the 1995 tax code, Nobel Prize money is exempt from taxation, and the cost of a police officer's uniform can be deducted. But the meals a firefighter eats in the firehouse are taxable, because the IRS considers the fire station to be a "home."

THE FIRST "LOOPHOLE"

In 1915 a U.S. Congressman, complaining about the increasing complexity of the tax code, lamented, "I write a law. You drill a hole in it. I plug the hole. You drill a hole in my plug." His words were reported in newspapers all over the country, and a new word—loophole—was born.

IT'S OUR TIME, TOO

How much time do you spend each working day to pay your federal income taxes? Over the years the National Tax Foundation, an income tax lobbying group, has kept track of how much of the average American's working day is used to earn enough to make payments to Uncle Sam. Their findings:

1929:19 minutes per day	1969: 1 hour, 48 minutes
1939: 40 minutes	1979: 1 hour, 48 minutes
1949: 1 hour, 16 minutes	1989: 1 hour, 47 minutes
1959: 1 hour, 36 minutes	

CHANGING VIEWS

In a 1972 poll by the Advisory Commission on Intergovernmental Relations, Americans ranked the federal income tax as "the fairest of all taxes." In a similar study in 1989, American taxpayers ranked the tax as "the least fair of all taxes."

THE DREADED DATE

In 1954, the IRS moved the deadline for filing tax returns back a month, from March 15 to April 15. Reason: The tax code had become so complicated that Americans needed more time to fill out the forms.

AS SMART AS BAIT

A lot of stuff on the internet makes great bathroom reading. For example: Here's a list of "35 Politically Correct Ways to Say Someone's Stupid," taken off the Internet and sent to us by BRI member John Dollison.

1. A few clowns short of a circus.
2. A few fries short of a Happy Meal.
3. An experiment in Artificial Stupidity.
4. A few beers short of a 6-pack.
5. Dumber than a box of hair.
6. A few peas short of a casserole.
7. Doesn't have all his corn flakes in one box.
8. The wheel's spinning, but the hamster's dead.
9. One Fruit Loop shy of a full bowl.
10. One taco short of a combination plate.
11. A few feathers short of a whole duck.
12. All foam, no beer.
13. The cheese slid off his cracker.
14. Body by Fisher, brains by Mattel.
15. Has an IQ of 2, but it takes 3 to grunt.
16. Warning: Objects in mirror are dumber than they appear.
17. Couldn't pour water out of a boot with instructions on the heel.
18. Too much yardage between the goal posts.
19. An intellect rivaled only by garden tools.
20. As smart as bait.
21. Chimney's clogged.
22. Doesn't have all his dogs on one leash.
23. Doesn't know much but leads the league in nostril hair.
24. Elevator doesn't go all the way to the top floor.
25. Forgot to pay his brain bill.
26. Her sewing machine's out of thread.
27. Her antenna doesn't pick up all the channels.
28. His belt doesn't go through all the loops.
29. If he had another brain, it would be lonely.
30. Missing a few buttons on her remote control.
31. No grain in the silo.
32. Proof that evolution can go in reverse.
33. Receiver is off the hook.
34. Several nuts short of a full pouch.
35. He fell out of the Stupid tree and hit every branch on the way down.

The oldest pig in the world lived to the age of 68.

THE ROOSEVELTS

The Roosevelt family has been a big part of the American 20th century. They're quotable, too.

"The best executive is one who has sense enough to pick good people to do what he wants done, and self-restraint enough to keep from meddling."

—*Theodore Roosevelt*

"A conservative is a man with two perfectly good legs who has never learned to walk forward."

—*Franklin D. Roosevelt*

"No man is justified in doing evil on the ground of expediency."

—*Theodore Roosevelt*

"No one can make you feel inferior without your consent."

—*Eleanor Roosevelt*

"To destroy our natural resources, to skin and exhaust the land instead of using it so as to increase its usefulness, will result in undermining, in the days of our children, the very prosperity which we ought by right to hand down."

—*Theodore Roosevelt*

"Every time an artist dies, part of the vision of mankind passes with him."

—*Franklin D. Roosevelt*

"I think we consider too much the good luck of the early bird, and not enough the bad luck of the early worm."

—*Franklin D. Roosevelt*

"If you can't say something good about someone, come and sit by me."

—*Alice Roosevelt Longworth* (Theodore's daughter)

"My father gave me these hints on speechmaking: Be sincere…be brief…be seated."

—*James Roosevelt* (FDR's son)

"Never underestimate a man who overestimates himself."

—*Franklin D. Roosevelt*

"Calvin Coolidge looks like he was weaned on a pickle."

—*Alice Roosevelt Longworth*

"When they call the roll in the Senate, the Senators do not know whether to answer 'Present' or 'Not guilty.' "

—*Theodore Roosevelt*

"The gains of education are never really lost. Books may be burned and cities sacked, but truth…lives in the hearts of humble men."

—*Franklin D. Roosevelt*

"The Alphabet Song," "Twinkle, Twinkle Little Star," and "Baa, Baa Black Sheep" are

THE ICEMAN COMETH

*Not all mummies are wrapped in bandages. Here's one
who was buried in ice, fully clothed, for 5,000 years.*

SURPRISE ENCOUNTER

On September 19, 1991, some people hiking in the Alps along the Austrian/Italian border spotted a body sticking out of a glacier. The corpse was brown and dried out and looked like it had been there for a long time. But neither the hikers nor the Austrian officials who recovered it four days later had any idea how long.

When scientists carbon-dated the remains, the "Iceman" (as he was dubbed in the press) turned out to be more than 5,300 years old. It was the world's oldest fully preserved human body, and the first prehistoric human ever found with "everyday clothing and equipment"—including an axe, dagger, and bow and arrows. Other bodies that have been found were either buried following funerals or sacrificed in religious ceremonies…which means they had ceremonial objects and clothing that didn't shed much light on what everyday life was like.

CLOSE CALL

Because no one realized how old or valuable the Iceman was until five days after he was discovered, no one took any precautions to ensure he wasn't damaged during removal and shipment to the morgue. In fact, it seems they did just about everything they could to damage him. An Austrian police officer tried to free the Iceman from the ice by using a jackhammer—shredding his garments and gashing his left hip to the bone. He probably would have done more damage, except that he ran out of compressed air for the jackhammer and had to quit.

Next, as word of the unusual discovery spread, locals and gawkers traveled to the site to view the remains. Many pocketed the Iceman's tools and shreds of garment as souvenirs. And when forensics experts finally removed the body from the ice, they did so using clumsy pickaxes, destroying the archaeological value of the site in the process.

---

all sung to the same music: a 1765 French song titled *"Ah! Vous Diraije Maman."*

By now the Iceman, clothed from the waist down when initially discovered, was buck naked save for pieces of a boot on his right foot and shards of clothing strewn around the body. Even worse, his private parts were missing, perhaps stolen by one of the visitors to the site. They were never recovered.

MODERN PROBLEMS

When scientists did get around to studying him, they found a dark-skinned male between the ages of 25 and 40 who stood 5'2" tall. The Iceman surprised archaeologists with his shaved face, recently cut hair, and tattoos; experts thought that people did not "invent" shaves, haircuts, and tattoos until thousands of years later.

He also suffered from some surprisingly modern ailments. A body-scan revealed smoke-blackened lungs—probably from sitting around open fires, but definitely not from smoking—as well as hardening of the arteries and blood vessels. He also had arthritis in the neck, lower back, and hip. But he didn't die from any of them.

CAUSE OF DEATH

The fact that the Iceman's body survived so long may provide a clue about how he died. Most bodies recovered from glaciers have literally been torn to pieces by slow-moving ice. But the Iceman's wasn't. He was found in a small protective basin, 10 to 15 feet deep, that sheltered him as glaciers passed overhead. This leads archaeologists to speculate that he sought shelter in the basin when a surprise winter storm hit. "He was in a state of exhaustion perhaps as a consequence of adverse weather conditions," a team of experts theorized in Science magazine in 1992. "He therefore may have lain down, fallen asleep, and frozen to death." Snow covered the body, the glacier eventually flowed over it...and the body remained completely preserved and undisturbed for the next 53 centuries.

FINAL RESTING PLACE

The Iceman now resides in a freezer in Austria's Innsbruck University, kept at 98% humidity and 21°F, "the glacial temperature he had grown accustomed to over more than 5,000 years." Scientists only examine the body for 20 minutes every two weeks—anything more than that would cause the mummy to deteriorate.

Not party animals: 76% of Americans celebrate New Year's Eve in groups of less than 20.

FOOD FLOPS

How can anyone in the food industry predict what people will buy, when Frankenberry Cereal and Cheez Whiz are wild successes? It's anyone's guess what America will eat... which is how they come up with clunkers like these.

LA CHOY "FRESH AND LITE" EGG ROLLS. A quick snack? Not exactly. The big, fat egg rolls took half an hour to thaw and eat, so by the time the center was hot, the shell was damp and gooey. Even the name "Fresh and Lite" was half-baked. "It sounded like a feminine hygiene product," one of the company's ad executives admitted. "And it was hard to say it was fresh anyway, because it was frozen."

McDONALD'S McLEAN DELUXE. In 1991, McFood scientists were ordered to come up with a burger that even health nuts could love. Their solution: to replace most of the fat with carrageenan (seaweed extract) and water to create the "91% fat free" McLean Deluxe. It was a product with no market: health-conscious eaters still avoided the Golden Arches; fast-food aficionados were revolted by the concept of a seaweed burger. After years of slow sales, McDonald's finally threw in the towel in 1996.

WINE & DINE. According to *Business Week* magazine, Wine & Dine was "the upscale answer to Hamburger Helper—noodles and a sauce mix bundled with a tiny bottle of Chianti. Sad to say, the labeling didn't make it clear that the Chianti in that bottle was salty cooking wine. Consumers thought they had bought a little vino for dinner. When they discovered their error, they took their wining and dining elsewhere."

I HATE PEAS. If kids won't eat peas in their natural shape, why not mash them into a paste and make them look like French fries? Answer: Because, as one kid put it, "they still taste disgusting." Consumer researcher Robert McMath summed it up: "Kids said, 'A pea is a pea is a pea.....I don't like peas. In fact, I hate peas, even if they're in the shape of French fries." I Hate Beans also flopped.

About 75% of U.S. families put up a Christmas tree; 54% of the trees are artificial.

MILLER CLEAR BEER. In the wake of huge publicity generated by Crystal Pepsi, Tab Clear, and other colorless soft drinks (most of which flopped), Miller came up with this clearly stupid idea. Unlike soft drinks, which are artificially colored, a beer's color is *natural*. So it's just about impossible to remove the color without destroying the flavor and body at the same time. One newspaper critic described Clear Beer as "a lager the color of 7-up, with little head and a taste like sweetened seltzer...with the faintest touch of oily, medicinal hoppiness in the finish." Born: 1994; died: 1996.

NESTEA'S TEA WHIZ. World you give a "yellowish, carbonated, lemon-flavored drink" a name like *Whiz?*

VIN DE CALIFORNIE. "For the first time in history, American wines will cross the sea to France!" boasted three California winemakers in 1966. The ship might as well have sunk on the way over. Novelty shops were the only stores willing to stock "Vin de Californie" (the brand name they marketed it under)—and even there, sales were poor. "French customers approached the displays gingerly," Newsweek magazine reported, "almost as if they were afraid the wines might explode."

Critics considered the wine a joke. And the Californians unwittingly seemed to agree. "Vin de Californie," it turned out, is French slang for Coca-Cola.

JUMPIN' JEMS. The soft drink equivalent of the lava lamp. Introduced in 1995 by Mistic Brands, it was supposed to have "jelly balls" floating in the liquid. A major flaw: The "jelly balls" settled to the bottom of the bottle. Consumers figured the product had gone bad and wouldn't touch it. "Even I didn't drink it," admitted Mistic's president.

• Okay, then. A year later, the Clearly Canadian Beverage Company tried again with Orbitz. This time, the "flavored gel spheres" stayed suspended in the drink and were small enough to fit through a straw, but large enough so they "didn't look like a mistake." Reaction: "I think it's gross," one consultant told reporters. "It's like, when you drink a glass of milk, do you want to find lumps?"

REVENGE!

"Don't get mad, get even" was John F. Kennedy's motto. All of us want to get back at someone, sometime. Here are six reports we've found about people (and a rabbit) who actually did.

TRIGGER HAPPY

"Two gangsters, James Gallo and Joe Conigliaro, set about to murder a stoolpigeon, Vinny Ensuelo, alias Vinny Ba Ba. On November 1, 1973, they jumped him on Columbia Street, Brooklyn, and took him for a ride. Gallo pointed a gun at his head from the right; Conigliaro covered him from the left. The car swerved violently. The two gangsters shot each other."

As the New York *Daily News* described it:

> Conigliaro, hit in the spine, was paralyzed. Every year after that Vinny Ensuelo sent wheelchair batteries to Conigliaro. A small card with the batteries always said, " Keep rolling, from your best pal, Vinny Ba Ba."

—*Remarkable Events*, by John Train

COMMON CENTS

"A shabbily dressed man went up to a teller yesterday at the U.S. Bank of Washington in Spokane, and asked her to validate his 60¢ parking ticket. She refused. The man asked to talk to a bank manager about the matter. The manager also refused. So 59-year-old John Barrier withdrew all the money he had on deposit—$1 million—and took it down the street to the Seafirst Bank. 'If you have $1 in bank, or $1 million, I think they owe you the courtesy of stamping your parking ticket,' he said."

—UPI, Feb. 21, 1989

MASHED

In 1974, after three seasons as Col. Henry Blake on "M*A*S*H" (CBS), McLean Stevenson suddenly announced he was leaving to star in a sitcom for NBC.

The show's producers paid him back in kind. "One story around Hollywood," wrote Tom Shales in the *Washington Post*, "was that Stevenson was so disliked on the set that Blake's death was written in to make sure there was no way he could ever come back."

The average color TV lasts for 8 years.

John Carman updated the story 20 years later in the *S.F. Chronicle*:

> To be *McLeaned* is to be blotted out fully and finally and with extreme TV prejudice.
>
> Reserved for actors who've been naughty and unappreciative, the process is named for McLean Stevenson, who wanted off M*A*S*H and saw his wish come all too true. His irate producers packed Stevenson's character, Henry Blake, into a helicopter and had it plunge from the sky. Message to McLean: You're crop dust now. You can't come home again.

LETTERS FROM HELL

"When attorney Theresa McConville sold her vacant lot in Ventura Country in 1985, a losing bidder was Reynaldo Fong, a local anesthesiologist. Fong, embittered by the loss, devised a novel form of revenge. Over ten years he took out nearly 100,000 magazine subscriptions in her name, asking in each case that the magazine bill McConville. He also sent McConville a refrigerator—C.O.D. McConville spent $50,000 to straighten out the mess."

—*Forbes* **magazine, June 5, 1995**

FROM THE X-(RATED) FILES

"An employee of the St. Louis Blues apparently couldn't resist a parting shot at the team after he was fired.

"On the page listing playoff records in the hockey team's media guide, between the date of the Blues' last overtime game on the road and their overtime loss at home, the anonymous employee slipped in a crudely worded 'record' for sexual favors.

"The red-faced Blues have recalled the guide and will have to amend it, at a reported cost of $70,000."

—**L. A. *Times*, Oct. 16, 1995**

I'M GAME

"Near Louisville, Kentucky, a rabbit reached out of a hunter's game bag, pulled the trigger of his gun, and shot him in the foot."

—**New Yorker, May 1947**

TREK WARS!

As "Star Trek" creator Gene Roddenberry conceived it, the Starship Enterprise was a metaphor for an ideal world—a multiracial, multinational crew working together to achieve humanity's highest goals. In real life, however, the crew of the Enterprise was bogged down in typical 20th-century politics. Here are four examples.

CAPT. KIRK VS. EVERYBODY

William Shatner (Capt. Kirk) was originally intended to be the only star of "Star Trek." That meant he made a lot more money than everyone else—$5,000 per episode, compared to Leonard Nimoy's $1,250, and $600 to $850 for the other actors. And it meant he got what he wanted, even at other cast members' expense. In virtually every script, for example, he had more lines than any other actor. But that didn't stop him from taking other people's lines if he felt like it. As George Takei (Mr. Sulu) writes in his book *To the Stars:*

> [The script consultant] would occasionally give us an advance peek at an early draft of a script, which might contain a wonderful scene for our respective characters or even a fun line or two of dialogue…. But when the final shooting script was delivered, the eagerly awaited scene or line would now be in someone else's mouth, and invariably, it was Bill's… Even if an idea had originated with one of us, if Bill wanted it, he got it.

CAPT. KIRK VS. MR. SPOCK

Spock was conceived as a minor character, but Leonard Nimoy was so good in the role that the part kept growing. This apparently drove Shatner nuts, as J. Van Hise writes in *The History of Trek:*

> Shatner was so concerned over the situation that he counted his lines in each new script to be certain that he had more than Nimoy. If he didn't, either more were added for him at his insistence, or Nimoy's lines were cut….[One scriptwriter] witnessed the director trying to come up with an alternative way for Nimoy to react to Shatner in a scene, because for Nimoy to utter a line would have given him one line too many as far as Shatner was concerned.

The rivalry started interfering with production schedules. During the first season, for example, *Life* magazine decided to shoot a photo essay on Spock's makeup. They sent a photographer to the set, and everything went smoothly until Shatner arrived. When he saw what was going on, he turned and walked away. Shortly afterward, a production assistant insisted that the photographer leave. Takei writes:

> Leonard, understandably, was livid. He got up and refused to have his makeup completed until the photographer was allowed back. Until then, he announced, he would wait in his dressing room with his makeup only half done. And with that, he exited.

For the next few hours, studio executives shuttled back and forth between Nimoy's and Shatner's dressing rooms trying to resolve the dispute. The photographer was finally allowed to finish the job, and the article appeared in *Life* as planned. By then, however, half a day's shooting had been lost.

LT. UHURA VS. NBC
Nichelle Nichols (Lt. Uhura) was the only main character who wasn't signed to a contract when she was hired. In her autobiography, *Beyond Uhura*, Nichols writes that contract talks broke down when NBC executives found out she was a black woman:

> ["Star Trek" creator Gene Roddenberry] told the network that he wanted to add a little "color" to the bridge. They assumed he was merely redecorating the set....The network men had a fit when they saw that not only was there a woman in the command crew and on the bridge, but a Black one! When they realized that Uhura's involvement would be substantial and her lines went beyond "Yes, Captain!" they furiously issued Gene an ultimatum: Get rid of her!

Roddenberry refused to fire Nichols, but couldn't get the network to hire her as a permanent cast member. So he hired her as an uncontracted "day player" for each episode. Ironically, thanks to the union wage scale, Nichols made more money than she would have under contract. "Not only did Gene get what he wanted," Nichols writes, "he made sure NBC paid—literally and dearly—for it."

AN UNLIKELY FAN
By the end of the first season, Uhura was nearly as popular as Capt. Kirk and Mr. Spock—and got nearly as much fan mail. But Nichols

didn't know it. Studio officials had ordered that she not receive her fan mail. Near the end of the first season, a mailroom employee finally told her of the embargo. "To say I was stunned does not even begin to convey how I felt," she writes in *Beyond Uhura*.

In fact, she was so upset that she decided to quit. The following evening, however, she met Dr. Martin Luther King at an NAACP fundraiser. He turned out to be an fan of the show and urged her to stay on, arguing that "Uhura was the first non-stereotypical black character in television history"...and that *white* Americans, as well as black Americans, needed to see that character. Nichols agreed to stay and fight it out.

MR. SPOCK VS. GENE RODDENBERRY

What about the Great Idealist himself? It turns out that the creator of "Star Trek" could be just as much of a pain to work with, especially when money was involved. "My business dealings with him were always miserable," Nimoy recalled in 1994. "Gene always had an agenda—his own." One example: Early in the show's history, a Connecticut amusement park offered Nimoy $2,000 to make a personal appearance on a Saturday morning. But the only flight available was on Friday evening—which meant Nimoy had to get permission from Roddenberry to leave work a few hours early.

Rather than give Nimoy a direct answer, Roddenberry mentioned he was forming "Lincoln Enterprises," his own talent agency, and he wanted to represent Nimoy when he made public appearances. Nimoy wasn't interested; he already had an agent and didn't want someone else getting a percentage of his salary. But Roddenberry pressed the issue, as Joe Engel writes in *Gene Roddenberry: The Myth and the Man Behind Star Trek*:

> "The difference between your agent and Lincoln Enterprises," Roddenberry said, "is that Lincoln can get you off the lot at five p.m. every Friday."

> "Gene," Nimoy said, "I already have the job. I'm asking if you can help me out of here so I can pick up two thousand dollars this week-end."

> "The problem with you," Roddenberry said, "is that you have to learn to bow down and say 'Master.' "

PRACTICALLY FUNNY

Mark Twain said, "The first of April is the day we remember what we are the other 364 days of the year." Here's a short history of some practical jokes and jokesters.

Modern man may think he invented humor, what with vaudeville, stand-up comics, and *Everybody Loves Raymond*. But the fun started way before that.

A YEAR BY ANY OTHER NAME
In France, New Year's celebrators used to get out the party hats—and later in the evening the lampshades—on April 1. But then, in 1582, Pope Gregory had a brainstorm: he put 12 sheets of paper together, with spaces too small to write in, and cute pictures of puppies and kittens, and called it the Gregorian calendar. And the Pope said it would all begin on January 1. And it was good. Except for those who hadn't heard about it, or didn't want to go along with it. When they continued to party on April 1, others called them "April Fools." Which led to the tradition of telling people things that weren't true, so they could be April Fools, too.

A TOWN BY ANY OTHER COLOR
On April 6, 1837, after a day of galloping over hill and dale (and probably drinking way too much sherry), the foxhunting crowd had some time—and paint—on their hands. The eccentric Marquis of Waterford and a few of his cronies decided the town should match their hunting "pinks," which is what they called their bright red hunting jackets. Thus was born the phrase "painting the town red."

BLESS YOU!
In 1905, a coal tar product salesman named Soren Sorenson Adams (Sammy to his friends) noticed that the leavings of his goods—black dust—had the power to invoke earth-shattering sneezes. He tested the dust's giggle potential by blowing it through hotel keyholes. Convinced of his sneezing powder's value, he marketed it under the name "Cachoo." A Philadelphia buyer purchased 70,000 bottles in the first three months, and Sammy was on his way.

He devoted the rest of his life to practical jokes; in fact, he invented over 700 of them, including squirting flowers, "snakes" that jump out of cans, hot pepper gum, the joy buzzer, and the dribble glass. All the classics. Gee, thanks, Sammy!

When boxer dogs get excited, they stand on their hind legs and jab the air with their front paws.

FART FACTS

You won't find trivia like this in any ordinary book.

THE NAME

The word *fart* comes from the Old English term *foertan*, to explode. *Foertan* is also the origin of the word *petard*, an early type of bomb. *Petard*, in turn, is the origin of a more obscure term for fart—*ped*, or *pet*, which was once used by military men. (In Shakespeare's *Henry IV*, there's a character whose name means fart—Peto.)

WHY DO YOU FART?

Flatulence has many causes—for example, swallowing air as you eat and lactose intolerance. (Lactose is a sugar molecule in milk, and many people lack the enzyme needed to digest it.) The most common cause is food that ferments in the gastrointestinal tract.

• A simple explanation: The fats, proteins, and carbohydrates you eat become a "gastric soup" in your stomach. This soup then passes into the small intestine, where much of it is absorbed through the intestinal walls into the bloodstream to feed the body.

• But the small intestine can't absorb everything, especially complex carbohydrates. Some complex carbohydrates—the ones made up of several sugar molecules (beans, some milk products, fiber, etc.) can't be broken down. So they're simply passed along to the colon, where bacteria living in your intestine feed off the fermenting brew. If that sounds gross, try this: the bacteria then excrete gases into your colon. Farting is how your colon rids itself of the pressure the gas creates.

FRUIT OF THE VINE

So why not just quit eating complex carbohydrates?

• First, complex carbohydrates—which include fruit, vegetables, and whole grains—are crucial for a healthy diet. "Put it this way," explains Jeff Rank, an associate professor of gastroenterology at the University of Minnesota. "Cabbage and beans are bad for gas, but they are good for you."

• Second, they're not the culprits when it comes to the least

An estimated 405, 000 U.S. homes still lack indoor plumbing.

desirable aspect of farting: smell.

• Farts are about 99% odorless gases—hydrogen, nitrogen, carbon dioxide, oxygen, and methane (it's the methane that makes farts flammable). So why the odor? Blame it on those millions of bacteria living in your colon. Their waste gases usually contain sulfur molecules—which smell like rotten eggs. This is the remaining 1% that clears rooms in a hurry.

AM I NORMAL?

• Johnson & Johnson, which produces drugs for gas and indigestion, once conducted a survey and found that almost one-third of Americans believe they have a flatulence problem.

• However, according to Terry Bolin and Rosemary Stanton, authors of *Wind Breaks: Coming to Terms with Flatulence*, doctors say most flatulence is healthy. What's unhealthy is worrying about it so much.

NOTABLE FARTERS

• Le Petomane, a 19th-century music hall performer, had the singular ability to control his farts. He could play tunes, as well as imitate animal and machinery sounds rectally. Le Petomane's popularity briefly rivaled that of Sarah Bernhardt.

• A computer factory in England, built on the site of a 19th-century chapel, is reportedly inhabited by a farting ghost. Workers think it might be the embarrassed spirit of a girl who farted while singing in church. "On several occasions," said an employee, "there has been a faint girlish voice singing faint hymns, followed by a loud raspberry sound and then a deathly hush."

• Joseph Stalin was afraid of farting in public. He kept glasses and a water pitcher on his desk so that if he felt a wind coming on, he could mask the sound by clinking the glasses while pouring water.

• Martin Luther believed, "on the basis of personal experience, that farts could scare off Satan himself."

Science fact: City dwellers have longer, thicker, denser nose hairs than country folks do.

LITTLE THINGS MEAN A LOT

"The devil's in the details," says an old proverb. And in the profits too. The littlest thing can mean big bucks. Here are a few examples.

A MINUS SIGN

The story: In 1962, an Atlas-Agena rocket that was carrying the Mariner 1 satellite into space was launched from Cape Canaveral. Unfortunately, the rocket went off course and ground controllers had to push the self-destruct button. The whole thing exploded. Investigators found that someone had left a minus sign out of the computer program. Cost to U.S. taxpayers: $18.5 million.

A LETTUCE LEAF

The story: In 1993, Delta Airlines was looking for ways to reduce costs to compete in the cutthroat airline industry. They discovered that by just eliminating the decorative piece of lettuce served under the vegetables on in-flight meals, they could save over $1.4 million annually in labor and food costs.

A SHOE

The story: On September 18, 1997, the Tennessee Valley Authority had to close its Knoxville nuclear power plant. The plant stayed shut for 17 days, at a cost of $2.8 million. Cause of the shutdown: "human error." A shoe had fallen into an atomic reactor.

A DECIMAL POINT

The story: In 1870, the government published a table of nutritional values for different foods. According to the charts, spinach had ten times as much iron as other vegetables. Actually, a decimal point had been misplaced; spinach has about the same amount as other veggies. But a popular misconception had already taken hold that spinach promotes strength. Long-term benefit: It ultimately gave us Popeye the Sailor, who's "strong to the finish,'cause I eats my spinach."

Stretched end-to-end, the blood vessels in your body would go around the equator 2-1/2 times.

MISS AMERICA, PART IV:
There She Is…

When you think about it, the Miss America contest is more a TV show than a pageant. Sure, we get a national figure (or figurine) out of it —but the thing that keeps it going is ratings. So just like any sitcom or talk show, it has to have a theme song. Here's how Miss America got hers.

ON THE AIR

After the war, the Miss America Pageant was flying high. It was oh-so-respectable, financially sound, and as popular with women as with men. Its survival was no longer in doubt.

In fact, thanks to strong media coverage, it was regarded as a national institution. Millions of Americans followed the contest in the newspapers, on the radio, and in movie newsreels. But if they wanted to watch the pageant in its entirety, they had to go to Atlantic City and view it in person. There was no other way.

Then in 1953, the fledgling American Broadcasting Company (ABC) offered $5,000 to broadcast the event over its small network of TV stations. Miss America officials seriously considered the offer, but turned it down when ABC refused to black out the broadcast in nearby Philadelphia. (The Pageant had just doubled its ticket prices and was afraid too many people would stay home and watch it on TV.)

The next year, ABC upped the ante. It doubled the offer to $10,000, and lined up the Philco Television Company as a sponsor. Philco even offered to introduce a new line of "Miss America" television sets. This time pageant officials accepted. The Miss America Pageant was broadcast live on September 11, 1954; a record breaking 27 million people—39% of the viewing audience—tuned in to watch. All through the '50s, TV ratings were astronomical.

MUSIC MAN

One of the people who got caught up in the excitement was Bernie Wayne, a songwriter. He learned about the first TV broadcast in a newspaper article, and it inspired him to write a song. "Although I

Science fact: Goldfish remember better in cold water than in warm water.

had never seen a pageant before," he explained years later, "some how the words and melody for the song suddenly came into mind....I just sat down in my little office, and started writing. I wrote the whole song in the space of an hour...I just tried to put myself in the place of the lucky girl—walking down the runway— an ideal, walking on air." He called his song "There She Is."

Wayne performed the song for the pageant's producer and musical director. "They loved it," he says, and told him they would use it in the pageant. Wayne phoned his mother and told her to watch for the song during the broadcast.

Then the producer called him over during final rehearsals and said they'd changed their minds—they weren't going to use the song. The reason: Bob Russell, host of the broadcast, wanted some songs he'd written, "This Is Miss America" and "The Spirit of Miss America," included—and he got his way. "I was brokenhearted," Wayne recalled years later....The next night I was too disappointed to go see the show. I watched it on TV from some broken-down bar."

LUCKY BREAK

"There She Is" might never have made it into the pageant, if Wayne hadn't been invited to a Park Avenue party a few months later. While performing a piano medley of his songs, he sang "There She is." "As I sang, the place quieted down like magic. When I finished, there was such a hush I thought I'd laid an egg." Someone in the audience asked him, "Why haven't I heard this song before!

He was Pierson Mapes, the advertising executive in charge of both the Philco account and the upcoming 1955 pageant. Mapes pressured Miss America officials to make the song a centerpiece of the broadcast—a task made all the easier by the fact that host Bob Russell did not return in 1955. Crooner Bert Parks took his place, and both Parks and "There She Is" became hits.

Still interested? We continue the story on page 622.

Oldest ex-president: John Adams, America's second president, was 90 years old when he died.

FAMILIAR PHRASES

More origins of everyday phrases.

IN ONE FELL SWOOP
Meaning: All at once.
Origin: Falling has nothing to do with it. *Fell* comes from the Middle English word *fel*, meaning "cruel, deadly, or ruthless" and is related to the word *felon*. The expression "one fell swoop" first appeared in *Macbeth* (Act 4, Scene iii), when Shakespeare compares the sudden death of a character's family to an eagle *swooping* down on some chickens and carrying them off.

HAVE YOUR WORK CUT OUT FOR YOU
Meaning: Have a difficult task ahead.
Origin: According to Christine Ammer in *Have a Nice Day—No Problem!*, the term refers to "a pattern cut from a cloth that must be then made into a garment." When the easier task of cutting out the cloth is finished, the more difficult job of sewing the garment is still left.

CALLED ON THE CARPET
Meaning: Admonished or reprimanded by a superior.
Origin: In the 19th century, carpets were prohibitively expensive, so usually, only the boss's office was carpeted. When employees were "called on the carpet," it meant the boss wanted to see them—which frequently meant they were in trouble.

SIGHT FOR SORE EYES
Meaning: Welcome sight.
Origin: According to ancient superstition, unpleasant sights could make eyes sore…and pleasant sights made sore eyes feel better.

TEN-GALLON HAT
Meaning: Big cowboy hat.
Origin: Measurements have nothing to do with it. The name comes from sombrero galon, which means "braided hat" in Spanish.

"Vodka" is Russian for "little water."

MORE OLYMPIC CHEATERS

*Here are four Olympians who might have cheated...and then
again, maybe they didn't. We'll never know.*

HAMMOU BOUTAYEB AND KHALID SKAH,
members of the Moroccan track team
Year: 1992
Place: Barcelona, Spain
What Happened: Boutayeb fell so far behind in the 10,000-meter
event that the two front-runners, Khalid Skah and Kenya's
Richard Chelimo, were about to lap him. Rather than let them
pass, Boutayeb blocked Chelimo for an entire lap before officials
finally dragged him from the track and disqualified him. But by
then it was too late—he'd allowed his teammate, Khalid Skah, to
sprint past Chelimo into first place and win the race.
Reaction: Skah's excitement was short-lived. Spectators booed
loudly and pelted him with garbage as he made his victory lap; 30
minutes later, Olympic officials disqualified him and took away his
gold medal, figuring that he and Boutayeb had been in cahoots.
Skah appealed the decision...and won: the next day the appeals
committee took the gold medal back from Chelimo and returned
it to Skah.

STELLA WALSH, Polish 100-meter runner
Years: 1932 and 1936
Place: Los Angeles and Berlin
What happened: Walsh won the gold medal in the 100-meter
race in Los Angeles and a silver medal in Berlin. But she aroused
suspicions. "She ran like a man," says Roxanne Andersen, a
women's track coach in the 1930s, who also noted that at the 1936
Olympics, Walsh appeared to have a "five o'clock shadow."

Walsh's victories went unchallenged until 1980, when she was
gunned down by a man robbing a Cleveland, Ohio, discount store.
An autopsy revealed that she had a genetic condition known as
mosaicism, which gave her "traces of male *and* female genitalia,"
as well as male and female chromosomes. Walsh had kept her
condi-tion secret her entire life and would probably have taken it

to the grave had she not been murdered. If people had known about her condition in the 1930s, she would almost certainly have been barred from competing as a woman. "Maybe that's why she refused to room with anybody else," Andersen remarked to reporters.

Reaction: In 1991, the U.S. Women's Track & Field Committee decided not to strip Walsh of her titles, concluding that her gender identity was more complex than it seemed, and that "allegations Walsh either masqueraded as a woman or was definitely a man were unfair." (Gender testing of female athletes has been standard since 1966.)

BORIS ONISCHENKO, member of the USSR pentathlon team
Year: 1976
Place: Montreal
What happened: The defending silver medalist was in the middle of the fencing competition, when the British team noticed that he scored points even when his sword didn't touch his opponent's body. Olympic officials examined his sword...and discovered it had been rigged with a "hidden push-button circuit-breaker" that enabled him to score a hit every time he pushed the button.
Reaction: Soviet officials initially protested, but later "admitted" Onischenko's guilt and apologized. "He lost many of his privileges and his career was left in ruins," says Carl Schwende, fencing director for the Montreal Games. "I heard he was working as the manager of an aquatic center in Kiev...Then I learned he was found dead at the pool. Drowning, suicide, accident? My Soviet colleagues won't talk about it."

Onischenko denied any knowledge of the rigging for the rest of his life, and no one knows if he really was responsible. The sword may not even have been his: "This Russians had about 20 identical looking weapons lined up for their use," Schwende says. "A fencer is handed his mask and weapons by a coach only when his name is called....It's possible someone else rigged the weapon, but we had no proof. If we had, we would have disqualified the entire Soviet team." One theory: Onischenko was sacrificed by the Soviets to save the rest of the team. But no one will ever know.

MORE LUCKY FINDS

Here are more examples of valuable things that people have stumbled on—including one that Uncle John found...and lost.

BURIED IN THE LIBRARY

The Find: The Inheritance, Louisa May Alcott's first novel

Where It Was Found: On a shelf in a Harvard University library.

The Story: The manuscript, hand-written by Alcott, represents one of the grossest oversights in Western literature: it was listed in the Harvard card catalog under "The Inheritance, a manuscript; Boston, 1849; 166 pages, unpublished, her first novel."

Even so, probably fewer than a dozen people even knew it existed, and it didn't occur to any of them to publish it. At least five people had checked it out since the library acquired it, and a microfilm copy was made for a scholar. But that was it—the manuscript sat virtually ignored for nearly 150 years, until Joel Myerson and Deniel Shealy, two professors researching a book on Alcott, came across it in the late 1980s. They made a Xerox copy of it, took it home, and transcribed it. In 1996, they submitted it to an agent...who began shopping it to publishers and movie studios. Estimated worth: $1 million.

MESSAGE IN A BOTTLE

The Find: The will of Daisy Singer Alexander, of the Singer Sewing machine family

Where It Was Found: In a bottle on a beach near San Francisco.

The Story: In 1937, the eccentric Alexander, who lived in England, made out her will, stuffed it into a bottle, and tossed it into the Thames River in London. The will read:

To avoid any confusion, I leave my entire estate to the lucky person who finds this bottle, and to my attorney, Barry Cohen, share and share alike—Daisy Alexander, June 20, 1937.

Almost 12 years later, in March 1949, a unemployed man named Jack Wrum (or Wurm, depending on which version you read) was wandering along a San Francisco beach when he found the bottle. To his credit, he not only opened it and read its contents, he also took it seriously enough to find out if it was real. It was—Wrum inherited $6 million up front, and $80,000 year in income from Alexander's Singer stock.

UNCLE JOHN'S CONFESSION

The Find: A first edition of Dr. Seuss's first book, *To Think That I Saw It on Mulberry Street*…inscribed to the mother of the boy who inspired Seuss to write it

Where It Was Found: In a farmhouse in Worcester, Vermont.

The Story: In the 1970s, Uncle John rented a woodworking shop from a woman named Phyllis Keyser. It was located next to her house, and occasionally John would wander in to chat. One day, he picked up a copy of To Think That I Saw It on Mulberry Street from her coffee table and noticed an inscription that read something like: "*To* ——, *the real Marco's mother. Thanks for the inspiration. From your neighbor, Ted Geisel.*" Uncle John knew that Dr. Seuss's real name was Theodore Geisel and that the boy in the story was named Marco. He asked Phyllis for an explanation.

"Oh," she replied, "that's my sister. She lived next to Ted Geisel in Boston. Her son, Marco, used to make up these wild stories every day when he came home from school, and that gave Geisel the idea for the first book he ever published."

Apparently, she didn't have any idea of the book's value. Uncle John offered to check it out, but the used bookstores he talked to wouldn't touch it. "You've got to bring it to a rare book dealer," they said. Unfortunately, Uncle John dropped the ball. Keyser died a few years later, and her possessions were disposed of.

First editions of Dr. Seuss's books (as well as Dr. Seuss memorabilia) have become extremely collectible since then. And until now, most experts weren't aware that this "first of the first" edition ever existed.

So, if someone out there in Bathroom Readerland has picked it up at a garage sale, you may have something worth tens of thousands of dollars!

Flamingoes can only eat with their heads upside down.

THE EVOLUTION OF THANKSGIVING

In "Thanksgiving Myths" (see page 380), you read about how the pilgrims ate deer, not turkey, at the first Thanksgiving celebration. So how did turkey become the food of choice? Here's more info on how Thanksgiving, as we know it, came to be.

GOING NATIONAL

As late as the 1860s, Thanksgiving was exclusively a Yankee holiday. Every Northern state celebrated it (not all on the same day), but no Southern states did. There had been several efforts to make it a national holiday—the Continental Congress tried in 1777, and George Washington proclaimed a National Day of Thanksgiving in 1789. But it never caught on, thanks to people like Thomas Jefferson, who denounced the idea as a "monarchical practice" unfit for the new republic.

Early presidents occasionally proclaimed their own days of thanksgiving to mark victories on the battlefield or other good fortune. But such occasions were one-time affairs, not annual events.

ABE STEPS IN

Then, in 1863, President Abraham Lincoln proclaimed two national days of Thanksgiving: one on August 6, to honor Union victories at Gettysburg and Vicksburg, and one on November 26, the last Thursday of the month, to celebrate a year "filled with the blessings of fruitful fields and healthful skies."

Lincoln didn't intend to make Thanksgiving an annual event, but when General Sherman captured Atlanta in September 1864, the president declared the last Thursday in November a day of thanksgiving for the second year in a row. And after Lincoln was assassinated, succeeding presidents turned it into a tradition in his honor. As the wounds of the Civil War healed, the popularity of the holiday grew. By the 1890s, the last Thursday in November was celebrated as Thanksgiving by nearly every state in the Union.

A "beer can fancier" is called a canologist.

THE BUSINESS OF THANKSGIVING

The Pilgrims aren't responsible for making turkey the center of the Thanksgiving feast (see page 381), so who is? Business historian Thomas DiBacco believes that poultry companies deserve the credit. "There is no rhyme or reason for us to have turkey on Thanksgiving, except that business promoted it," he says, adding that poultry producers in New Jersey, Pennsylvania, and Maryland began promoting turkey as Thanksgiving food after the Civil War. Why? Because at 10¢ a pound, it was more profitable than any other bird.

Illustrators followed their lead and painted Pilgrim dinners with roast turkey on the table. Soon a brand-new "tradition" was born.

The next group of businesses to cash in on Thanksgiving were turn-of-the-century retailers, who used the holiday to jump-start Christmas sales. Newspaper ads began counting down the number of shopping days until Christmas, and in 1921, Gimbel's department store in Philadelphia came up with a retailer's tour-de-force: they held the first Thanksgiving Day parade, designed to kick off the shopping season. By 1930, department stores all over the country sponsored parades to get shoppers into their stores.

FRANKSGIVING

By the late 1930s, Thanksgiving was as much the start of the Christmas shopping season as it was a holiday in its own right. That's why retailers—still trying to dig their way out of the Great Depression—were worried in 1939. Thanksgiving was traditionally the last Thursday of the month, and since there were five Thursdays in that November instead of the usual four, Thanksgiving fell on the very last day of the month. That meant only 20 shopping days until Christmas. In the Spring of 1939, the National Retail Dry Goods Association lobbied President Franklin Roosevelt to move Thanksgiving back one Thursday to November 23, arguing that it would boost retail sales by as much as 10%. Roosevelt agreed, and announced the change during the summer.

The decision made headlines around the country. It became a political issue as traditionalists (unaware of the day's true roots) and Republicans both condemned it. "What in the name of common sense has Christmas buying to do with it?" the Rev. Norman Vincent Peale bellowed from his pulpit. "It is questionable thinking and contrary to the meeting of Thanksgiving for the president of this great nation to tinker with a sacred religious day on the specious excuse that it will help Christmas sales. The next thing we may expect Christmas to be shifted to May 1 to help the New York World's Fair of 1940."

Like the proclamations that had proceeded it, Roosevelt's Thanksgiving proclamation was only binding with federal employees and in the District of Columbia—the governors of individual states had to ratify the decision for it to apply to their own states. Usually this was only a technicality...but Republican governors seized on the issue as a means of discrediting Roosevelt. As Diana Carter Applebaum writes in *Thanksgiving: An American Holiday, an American History*:

> Politician watchers...began to call November 23 the Democratic Thanksgiving and November 30 the Republican Thanksgiving Day...Colorado law required that the state observe both holidays, 23 rd. Republican Senator Styles Bridges of New Hampshire said that he wished that while he was at it, "Mr. Roosevelt would abolish winter; and Republican Governor Nels Hanson Smith of Wyoming commended Roosevelt for finally instituting a change "which is not imposing any additional tax on the taxpayers."

FINAL SETTLEMENT
In the end, 23 states celebrated Thanksgiving on November 23 and another 23 celebrated it on November 30, with Texas and Colorado celebrating it on both days and the city of Minneapolis celebrating it from 12:01 a.m. November 23 to 11:59 p.m. November 30. The controversy might have continued to this day if retail sales had gone up as predicted. But they didn't—some retailers even suspected that the confusion caused sales to drop. So in May 1941, President Roosevelt announced that, beginning in 1942, Thanksgiving would again be held on the last Thursday in November.

Several congressmen, who feared that future presidents might pull similar stunts, introduced legislation to make the change permanent. On November 26, 1941, Roosevelt signed a compromise bill: Thanksgiving would always fall on the fourth Thursday in November, whether it was the last Thursday of the month or not. (Five years out of seven, it is the last Thursday of the month). Thanksgiving has been celebrated on that day ever since.

Driving tip: The worst day for automobile accidents is Saturday.

DOLL DISASTERS

Some dolls, like Barbie and Cabbage Patch Kids, are enormous successes. Others seemed like good (even brilliant) ideas at the time, but they fell on their little plastic butts. Here are some "sure things" that bombed.

THE "MOST WONDERFUL STORY" DOLL

Background: In 1957, Ben Michtom, president of the Ideal Toy Company, had a brainstorm: why not sell a Jesus doll? The majority of kids in America were Christian, so he figured parents would jump at the opportunity to make playtime a religious experience. Other Ideal executives were horrified, but Michtom was convinced it was a great idea. To prove it, he took his case to a higher authority; while on vacation in Italy, he got an audience with the Pope and pitched the idea to him. The Pope gave his blessing, as did every other Christian leader Michtom consulted.

What Happened: Unfortunately for Ideal, Michtom didn't consult any parents, who probably would have told him the idea was a loser...which it turned out to be. As Sydney Stern describes the doll in *Toyland: The High-Stakes Game of the Toy Industry:*

> No one bought them because parents were horrified at the idea of undressing the Jesus doll, dragging it around, sticking it in the bathtub. Nothing sold. Ordinarily, there is a no-return policy on products already shipped. But in this case it was such a horrible mistake that Ideal took them back....It appears that what Ideal did with them was give each of its employees a doll and then ground up the rest and put them in landfills.

Jesus dolls—packaged in a box that looked like the Bible—were probably the biggest doll flop in American toy history.

THE JOEY STIVIC DOLL

Background: In 1976, Ideal came out with another product that it thought was a sure thing: the "drink-and-wet" baby Joey Stivic doll, based on Archie Bunker's grandson in TV's "All in the Family." The show was the most popular sitcom of the decade, and Ideal officials figured the hype surrounding Joey's birth (on an episode of the show) would be as huge as when Lucille Ball had her TV baby on "I Love Lucy" in the 1950s.

What Happened: "All in the Family" was daringly realistic—the first of its kind on TV, and Ideal execs decided to be just as realistic with the Joey doll. They gave him something that few little boy dolls had in the 70s: a penis. Big mistake. America was not ready for reality-based "anatomically correct" male dolls.

CHAIRMAN MAO DOLL

Background: In 1968, a U.S. company tried to import Chairman Mao dolls into the country. The dolls—manufactured in Ireland, not China—were really a joke: they showed Mao holding a copy of his little red book in front...and a bomb behind his back. Furthermore, Newsweek magazine reported, "each doll comes with twelve voodoo pins, just in case anyone misses the point."

What Happened: They never got off the boat. Figuring the dolls were part of a subversive plot, the Longshoreman's Union refused to unload the shipping crates. "That's definitely Communistic!" a union member exclaimed when a U.S. Customs official opened the crate, "We'd rather lose work than handle this cargo."

"I don't believe these dolls come from Ireland," one union official told reporters. "This stuff is being pushed through by some subversives—but we're on the lookout."

THE "HAPPY TO BE ME" DOLL

Background: If Barbie were life-sized, her measurements would be 38-18-28—an outrageously impossible role model for girls. That's what prompted Cathy Meredig, a 38-year-old software designer, to develop her own doll, "Happy to Be Me," in 1989. It has measurements of 36-27-38, with "rounded tummies and hips, normal sized waists, legs, chest, neck and feet." Traditional toy manufacturers balked at selling the doll, so Meredig founded High Self-Esteem Toys and began marketing it herself.

What Happened: Happy to Be Me was the toy equivalent of boiled carrots. Grown-ups loved them, but kids overwhelmingly preferred Barbie...no matter how much their parents tried to get them to switch. Meredig's company was still in business as late as 1994, but by then the dolls were only available by mail.

In 1994, $25,285,127 in counterfeit U.S. bills were found circulating here and abroad.

ZAPPED!

Irreverent comments from the late, great Frank Zappa.

"It would be easier to pay off our national debt overnight than to neutralize the long range effects of our national stupidity"

"Remember, there's a big difference between kneeling down and bending over."

"Life is like high school with money."

"It is always advisable to become a loser if you can't become a winner."

"There will never be a nuclear war—there is too much real estate involved."

"The whole universe is a large joke. Everything in the universe are just subdivisions of this joke. So why take anything too seriously?"

"Anything played wrong twice in a row is the beginning of an arrangement."

"Seeing a psychotherapist is not a crazy idea–it's just wanting a second opinion of one's life."

"Bad facts make bad laws."

"Politics is the entertainment branch of industry."

"Thanks to our schools and political leadership, the U.S. has an international reputation as the home of 250 million people dumb enough to buy 'The Wacky Wall Walker.' "

"Stupidity has a certain charm. Ignorance does not."

"Without music to decorate it, time is just a bunch of boring production deadlines or dates by which bills must be paid."

"The only thing that seems to band all nations together is that their governments are universally bad."

[*When asked by Tipper Gore whether he feels music incites people toward deviant behavior.*] "I wrote a song about dental floss, but did anyone's teeth get cleaner?"

"People who think of music videos as an art form are probably the same people who think Cabbage Patch Dolls are a revolutionary form of soft sculpture."

Psst! 68% of gossip columnists say the best place to interview a celebrity is

THE 10 WORST SNAKES TO BE BITTEN BY

In his book, Dangerous to Man, *Roger Caras included a list of the 10 snakes he'd least like to be "trapped in a phone booth with." Here's the list, with some extra info gathered by our own herpetologists.*

1. KING COBRA

The largest poisonous snake in the world. According to many experts, it's also the most dangerous. Its venom is so powerful, it can kill an elephant…and in some known instances, it actually has. Adults measure 14 feet (longest on record is 18 feet). When angered, its hoodspring expands and it "stands" with its head 5-6 feet in the air. It's found in Southeast Asia, southern China, and India.

2. TAIPAN

A 10-footer from Australia. There's enough venom in one Taipan bite to kill 100,000 mice. Also known as the "Fierce Snake," it is normally shy and prefers to escape rather than attack. Fortunately, it lives in sparsely populated areas. A person bitten by a Taipan will die in a matter of minutes.

3. MAMBA

A black or green snake from Africa. The 10- to 14-foot black mamba, which lives among rocks and in tall grass, is the largest and most feared snake in Africa. It is the world's fastest snake (burst of speed up to 15 mph) and may be the only poisonous snake known to stalk humans. Two drops of black mamba venom can kill a person in 10 minutes. The green mamba is about half as long and spends most of its life in trees. But it's just about as deadly.

4. BUSHMASTER

The world's largest viper. Found mostly in Central America, where it occupies the abandoned burrows of other animals. Particularly dangerous because, when confronted, it attacks people rather than

in their kitchen; 13% say their bedroom; 4% say the yard.

fleeing from them, as most snakes do. Has one-inch fangs and carries enough poison to kill several people.

5. WESTERN DIAMONDBACK RATTLER

The name comes from diamond- or hex-shaped blotches on its skin. Measures anywhere from 3 to 8 feet. Because it's aggressive and abundant, it's the cause of more serious bites and deaths than any other snake in North America. Its poison can kill a mouse in a few seconds, and a person within an hour.

6. FER-DE-LANCE

Also known as the Terciopelo (Spanish for "velvet"), it is relatively small (about 4 feet), but especially dangerous to humans because it's nervous and quick to bite. Its venom spreads through the body and causes internal bleeding. Found in tropical areas in the Americas, such as Martinique.

7. TROPICAL RATTLESNAKE

Has venom 10 times more potent than its cousin, the Western Rattler. This variety is found predominantly in Central and South America.

8. TIGER SNAKE

Named for the yellow stripes covering its body. Usually feeds on mice, frogs, and rats. Occasionally, this 6-footer also dines on Australians. A single dose of venom induces pain, vomiting, and circulatory collapse. Mortality rate from a bite is 40%. Considered the most dangerous reptile Down Under.

9. COMMON COBRA

Also known as the Indian Cobra. It's the kind of snake tamed by Indian snake charmers and is normally a shy hunter that eats frogs and rats. However, because it lives in populated areas, it is actually more dangerous than the King Cobra. Just one bite has enough venom to kill 30 people. It grows to 4 to 5 feet long.

10. JARRACUSSU

An aquatic snake from South America with a deadly bite. Usually, a bite from one of these water-dwellers isn't necessarily fatal. But it *will* cause blindness and tissue damage.

THE HISTORY OF THE INCOME TAX

"In this world," Benjamin Franklin wrote in 1789, "nothing can be said to be certain, except death and taxes." We at the BRI have written about death once in a while, but never about taxes. We figure it's time to make amends.

Abraham Lincoln isn't remembered as the "Father of the Income Tax"…but he could be. In 1862, in order to raise money to pay for the Civil War, he signed the country's first income tax into law.

However, under this law, only people with an income over $800 a year had to pay any tax. And only1% of the American people made more than $800 a year in 1862…so the government wound up having to look elsewhere for a source of money to finance the war (they borrowed it.)

TAX CONTROVERSY

From the start, the income tax was very controversial. No one was even sure if it was legal. The Constitution had authorized the federal government to collect taxes "to pay the debts and provide for the common welfare of the United States"—but it didn't explicitly state that the government had the right to levy taxes on income. And as this was hotly debated, public opposition grew. The first income tax was repealed in 1872.

But it wasn't dead. By the 1890s, an overwhelming majority of Americans supported re-establishing an income tax—as long as it applied only to the super-rich. Farm, labor, and small-business interests promoted it as a means of taking money away from millionaires and robber barons and redistributing it for the common good.

In 1894, they succeeded in passing a 2% tax on all personal and corporate net income over $4,000. Few Americans were in that income bracket…but those who were had the incentive and resources to oppose the tax. They battled it all the way to the Supreme Court, and in 1895 the Court declared that an income tax was unconstitutional.

Australia is the only continent where poisonous snakes outnumber nonpoisonous kinds.

THEODORE ROOSEVELT

Opinion was divided along party lines—Democrats and Populists supported the income tax; Republicans opposed it. But in 1908, outgoing Republican president Theodore Roosevelt broke with his party and called for both an income tax and inheritance tax. He wasn't able to enact either before his term ran out, but the momentum had shifted.

In the election of 1908, America sent a pro-tax Congress and an anti-tax president—Republican William Howard Taft—to Washington. Taft tried to derail the issue by proposing a Constitutional amendment permitting the personal income tax. He figured the hurdles for such an amendment were so great that the amendment would fail and the income tax issue would go away.

But he was wrong. By February 1913, less that four years after it was introduced, 36 states had ratified the 16th Amendment to the Constitution. For the first time in U.S. history, income taxes were indisputably constitutional. On October 3, 1913, President Woodrow Wilson signed the first modern income tax into law.

POPULAR TAX?

The 1913 tax was simple—the entire tax code was only 16 pages long (compared to 9,100 pages today). The rate was 1% on income over $3,000 for a single person and $4,000 for a married person, with "super taxes" as high as 6% applied to income over $500,000. In general, the tax was popular with just about everyone…because it applied to almost no one.

The few Americans who were required to pay income taxes in 1913 paid an average of $97.88 apiece.

WEAPON OF WAR

But America's entry into World War I in 1917 changed everything. The federal budget shot up from $ 1 billion in 1916 to $19 billion in 1919. Faced with enormous, unprecedented expenses, the Wilson administration was forced to raise the tax rate…and to broaden the tax base to include millions of Americans who had never before paid income taxes.

To insure that the new taxes were paid promptly and in full, Wilson expanded the IRS. The agency's total number of employees mushroomed from 4,000 workers in 1913 to 21,300 in 1920.

Weird coincidence: Ex-presidents Thomas Jefferson and John Adams both died on July 4, 1826.

Compared to earlier income taxes, Wilson's were pretty severe. The top tax rate, applied to income over $1 million, was 77%. These taxes revolutionized the finances of the federal government; its total tax revenue went from $344 million to $5.4 billion…and the percentage of government revenues collected from income taxes went from 10% to 73%.

In the 1920s, income taxes were cut five different times, but they would never again be as low as they were before the war.

WORLD WAR II

The 1930s, too, were a period of relatively low taxes. The Great Depression had wiped out the earnings of most Americans. In 1939, for example, the average blue-collar employee paid no taxes, the average doctor or lawyer paid about $25 a year, and a successful business person earning $16,000 paid about $1,000. But taxes changed once more when America began gearing up for World War II.

Like the previous "Great War," World War II was a budget buster. Government expenses rose from $9.6 billion in 1940 to $95 billon in 1945—prompting the government to raise the tax rate again (the highest bracket rose to 94%).

The tax base broadened, too. In 1939, before the war, there were 6.5 million Americans on the tax rolls; they paid about $1 billion a year. By the end of the war in 1945, 48 million Americans paid $19 billion annually. To handle this, the IRS nearly doubled in size, going from 27,000 employees in 1941 to 50,000 in 1945.

For the first time, even people with ordinary incomes had to pay taxes. As the Chicago Times put it, World War II transformed America's income tax "from a class tax to a mass tax."

WITHHOLDING BEGINS

Another development that came about as a result of World War II was income tax withholding, which enabled the government to collect estimated taxes every pay period, not just once a year. The federal government's cash needs were so great during the war that it couldn't wait until the end of the year, and it began withholding estimated taxes from every paycheck. Similar "pay-as-you-go" plans had been used during the Civil War and World War I, but they were abandoned. This time the change was permanent.

A year on the planet Jupiter is 12 times longer than a year on Earth.

There was a second reason for withholding: Taxes were collected from so many new taxpayers that the IRS could no longer handle the flood of tax payments that came in on tax day. It had no choice but to spread the payments out over the entire year.

INCOME TAXES TODAY

By the end of World War II the pattern for taxation had been set: wars and other crises pushed taxes up, peace and prosperity sent them back down, although rarely to where they had been before. Today's taxes seem higher than ever, but believe it or not, when you correct for inflation they're about the same as they were in the 1960s.

On the other hand; the IRS's job is bigger than ever—it is now the world's largest law-enforcement agency, with more than 115,000 employees. In fiscal year 1993 it processed more than 207 million tax returns, collecting more than $586 billion in personal income taxes and $ 1.2 trillion in other taxes. It also paid out more than $84 billion in personal refunds, and cost taxpayers more than $7.1 billion to operate. That comes to about 60¢ for every $100 collected.

*　　*　　*

TAX QUOTES

"A hand from Washington will be stretched out and placed upon every man's business; the eye of the federal inspector will be in every man's counting house....The law will of necessity have inquisitorial features, it will provide penalties, it will create complicated machinery. Under it men will be hauled into courts distant from their homes. Heavy fines imposed by distant and unfamiliar tribunals will constantly menace the tax payer. An army of federal inspectors, spies, and detectives will descend upon the state."

—**Virginian House Speaker Richard E. Byrd,
predicting in 1910 what would happen if
a federal income tax became law**

"Those citizens required to do so can well afford to devote a brief time during some one day in each year to the making out of a personal return…willingly and cheerfully."

—**The House Ways and Means Committee,
recommending passage of the landmark
1913 income-tax law**

"The hardest thing in the world to understand is income taxes."

—**Albert Einstein, 1952**

*   *   *

─────── **BY THE YEAR 2000…** ───────

For decades, "experts" made predictions about what the year 2000 would be like. Here are a few, from *The Bathroom Reader's Guide to the Year 2000*.

"A trip down an air street to see a neighbor may be on top of an individual flying platform; a trip to Europe by rocket may take only half an hour."

—*The New York Times, 1967*

"Housewives [will] wash dirty dishes—right down the drain! Cheap plastic would melt in hot water." And homes will be waterproof, so "the housewife of 2000 can do her cleaning with a hose."

—*Popular Mechanics, 1950*

"We will press a button to formulate our clothing. We will have alternatives: what color, should it give off steam, do we want it to light up, do we want it to sparkle or do we prefer a matte finish, do we want it to glow in the dark, do we want an invisible shield?"

—**Betsey Johnson, fashion designer**

"Men of the year 2000 could enjoy exotic extras like orgasmic earlobes, replaceable sex organs, electronic aphrodisiacs, ultrasensory intercourse, and a range of ecstasy options that would make current notions of kinkiness look sedate by comparison."

—**Howard Rheingold, *Excursions to the Far Side
of the Mind: A Book of Memes* (1988)**

TAKE A DRINK

The background info on three of America's favorite drinks.

MOUNTAIN DEW. Invented in the 1940s by Ally Hartman of Knoxville, it was intended as a chaser for Tennessee whiskey. The original version looked and tasted like 7-Up, but after Hartman sold the formula in 1954, a succession of new owners tinkered with it. According to one account, credit for the final version goes to William H. Jones, who bought the formula in 1961 and sold it to Pepsi three years later. "He fixed it so it had just a little more tang to it, mainly by adding citrus flavoring and caffeine," a business associate recalls. "He'd take little cups marked A, B, C and D around to high schools and factories and ask people which mixture tasted best. That's how he developed his formula."

V-8 JUICE. In 1933, W.G. Peacock founded the New England Products Company and began manufacturing spinach juice, lettuce juice, and other vegetable juices. Even though the country was in the midst of a health craze, few people wanted to drink Peacock's concoctions. So he began mixing the drinks together, hoping to find something more marketable. It took about a year, but he finally came up with a drink he called Vege-min—a combination of tomato, celery, carrot, spinach, lettuce, watercress, beet, and parsley juices. The label had a huge V for Vege-min and a large 8 listing the different juices. One day, as he gave a free sample to a grocer in Evanston, Illinois, a clerk suggested he just call the product V-8.

A &W ROOT BEER. Roy Allen made a living buying and selling hotels...until he met an old soda fountain operator who gave him a formula for root beer. "You can make a fortune with a five-cent root beer," the guy told him. It was during Prohibition when beer was illegal, so Allen decided there was a market for a root beer stand that looked like a Wild West "saloon"—including a bar and sawdust on the floor. The first stand, opened in Lodi, California, in 1919, did so well that Allen opened a second one in nearby Stockton and made one of his employees, Frank Wright, a partner. In 1922, they named the company A & W, after their own initials.

55% of the world's milk drinkers drink goat's milk.

MOVIE RATINGS

This page is rated PG for reading by general audiences.
Parental Guidance is advised.

NEW KID IN TOWN

In 1966, Jack Valenti quit his job as a senior White House aide to become president of the Motion Picture Association of America. Three weeks into his new job, he attended a meeting with studio head Jack Warner concerning some foul language in Warner Bros. upcoming film, *Who's Afraid of Virginia Woolf*.

At issue were the expressions "Screw you" and "hump the hostess," which had never been heard in films before. Valenti—whose job was to protect Hollywood's image—wanted the words taken out of *Virginia Woolf;* Warner—whose job was to make money—wanted to leave them in. After three hours of arguing, Warner agreed to substitute "goddam you" for "screw you," but insisted on keeping "hump the hostess." He also agreed to include the words "Suggested for Mature Audiences" in ads promoting the film.

"As I listened to Jack Warner and his associates debate whether they should cut a 'screw' and leave in a 'hump the hostess' or vice versa," Valenti recalled years later, "it dawned on me that...the old Production Code wasn't adequate to deal with these changes anymore."

SPEAKING IN CODE

Valenti was referring to the Motion Picture Production Code, established by Hollywood executives in 1930 to keep the government from getting involved in movie censorship. The Hollywood Code served as the official list of filmmaking dos and don'ts—complete with taboo subjects like extramarital sex—for nearly 40 years. At first, if you followed The Code, your film made it into theaters. If you didn't, your film was shut out and nobody saw it. It was that simple.

But while the Production Code remained static over the next 35 years, the world had changed dramatically. In fact, it became such a ridiculous standard by which to judge films that even the censors began to ignore it. By the early 1960s, movies like the double-entendre-laden James Bond films sailed through the censorship process virtually untouched, when in earlier years they would have been banned.

As the film industry's censorship powers waned, increasingly controversial films made it into the theaters. The result was the movie industry's worst nightmare—local censorship groups began to spring up all over the country. The industry challenged these groups...and lost. In April 1968, the U.S. Supreme Court handed down two rulings guaranteeing the legality of state and local censorship efforts.

LETTERS OF APPROVAL

As Valenti saw it, Hollywood had to act. If local groups began setting different standards all over the country, it would be impossible to make and market films to national audiences. Movies that were acceptable in one community would be illegal to show in others. The film industry stood to lose millions.

"It didn't take long," he recalled in 1978, "to figure out that the movies would be inundated by classification systems....We could see 200 to 300 regulating bodies across the country, each with its own ideas of what was obscene and what wasn't....So we started discussing a self-regulatory system in May 1968, and had it put together by the fall."

THE ORIGINAL CODE

After more than 100 hastily called meetings, the MPAA announced its ratings system on November 1, 1968. It included four categories:

G: General audiences, all ages admitted

M: Mature audiences, parental guidance suggested, but all ages admitted

R: Restricted, children under 16 not admitted without an accompanying parent or adult (the age was later lifted to 17)

X: No one under 17 admitted

PARENTAL GUIDANCE

Now that there was a ratings system, who would rate the films? Valenti and other Hollywood executives figured that since the

---

Actor Sean Connery was once selected Scotland's "Mr. Universe."

ratings were designed primarily with parents in mind, parents should be the ones to rate the films. The MPAA set up a board of 13 parents to watch and issue ratings on an estimated 1,200 hours' worth of films per year. This board is still in effect today: People who serve on it are paid for their time, and for some of them, it has become a full-time career. After the board rates a film, the producer can withdraw it from release for 90 days and then re-submit it for rating, with or without re-editing.

CHANGES

• Not all the original ratings survived. When the MPAA discovered that parents mistakenly thought M was stricter than R they changed it to GP (*General audiences, Parental guidance suggested*)...then to PG (*Parental Guidance*). When parents expressed concerns that PG had become too broad a category, they split it into PG and the stricter PG-13 (*Not recommended for children under 13*).

• The X rating posed another problem. The MPAA intended that it be used for "serious" films with adult themes, such as *Midnight Cowboy, A Clockwork Orange*, and *Medium Cool*. But when they trademarked all of the other motion picture codes in 1968, the Association either declined or forgot to trademark the X rating. This left filmmakers free to use it however they wanted. It quickly became synonymous with pornography, which made it virtually useless to the MPAA and the kiss of death to serious filmmakers. Even so, the MPAA didn't change it until 1990, when it replaced X with NX-17, "No Children Under17"—which it trademarked.

MOVIE MISCELLANY

• How successful has the ratings system been? When it was introduced in 1968, there were more than 40 local censorship boards around the country. By 1996, there were none—the last one, in Dallas, Texas, closed up shop in 1993. The City council of Dallas abolished it, saying that the movie industry does a better job.

• Unlikely the original Motion Picture Code, the MPAA's rating system is entirely voluntary, with the exception that members agree not to release films that haven't been rated. Exhibitors are responsible for enforcement; an estimated 80% to 85% follow the guidelines and keep children out of R and NC-17 films.

The Statue of Liberty's index finger is eight feet long.

IRONIC DEATHS

Here's a look at more ironic deaths.

MAJOR GENERAL JOHN SEDGWICK, *commander of the Sixth Army Corps during the Civil War*
On May 9, 1864, he was sitting under a tree making battle plans with an aide when he observed that some of his soldiers were not properly positioned for the upcoming battle.

As Sedgwick got up and started walking toward the men, a lone Confederate sniper opened fire. Rather than return fire, most of the soldiers ducked or ran for cover, which made Sedgwick laugh. "What, what men!" he told them, "Dodging for single bullets? I tell you they could not hit an elephant at this distance."

Final Irony: One of Sedgwick's aides later recounted,

> before the smile which accompanied these words had departed from his lips…there was a sharp whistle of a bullet, terminating in a dull, soft sound; and he fell slowly and heavily to the earth.

Sedgwick was killed instantly.

ALAN SIMPSON, *a U.S. airman during World War II*
In 1942, he was shot down off the coast of Sicily. He was captured and spent three years in a German prisoner-of-war camp, where he was "starved, tortured, and tossed in isolation for months at a time." According to his daughter Catherine, "He always hated the Germans for what they did to him."

Final Irony: In 1989, the 67-year-old Simpson went to London, England, for a reunion with his POW buddies. As he was crossing the street on his way to the meeting place, he was run down by a bus…filled with West German tourists.

"It took forty years, but they finally got him," his daughter was quoted as saying. "He took all the punishment they could dish out during World War II, but now they've nailed him with a bus."

Pierre Michelin, inventor of super-safe Michelin tires, died in a car accident.

JEAN BAPTISTE LULLY, *orchestra conductor*
Lully liked to stamp out the beat of the music on the floor with a long, pointed staff as he conducted.

Final Irony: According to one account, "One time he missed the floor, hit his own foot, got blood poisoning from the accident, and died."

RICHARD VERSALLE, *opera tenor*
In January 1996, the 63-year-old Versalle joined the cast of New York's Metropolitan Opera House to perform in a Czech opera called *The Makropulous Case.* He played an elderly law clerk who sings about a legal case that's nearly a century old.

Final Irony: In the opening scene, Versalle climbed a 10-foot ladder to reach a file cabinet in the "law office." As he reached the top, he sang the words "You can only live so long." At that moment, he fell backward from the ladder to the stage. According to the Associated Press:

> Many of the 3,000 spectators at first thought the seemingly graceful drop from the ladder was deliberate. But admiration quickly gave way to gasps and murmurs of alarm as he lay motionless on his back with his arms outstretched.

In fact, Versalle had died from a heart attack.

JIM FIXX, *author*
Fixx, who almost single-handedly started the jogging craze of the 1970s with his 1977 bestseller *The Complete Book of Running,* ran an average of 10 miles a day. He championed its health benefits: "Research has repeatedly shown that with endurance training such as running, the heart becomes a distinctly more efficient instrument."

Final Irony: In July 1984, he had just started off a run when he suffered a massive heart attack. An autopsy revealed that two of his arteries "were sufficiently blocked to warrant a bypass operation." He was 52.

The word "television" means to "see at a distance."

YOU'RE MY INSPIRATION

Often, fictional characters are around long after the people who inspired them have been forgotten. Ever heard of these three people, for example?

FRANCES "FRANKIE" BAKER
Inspired: The song "Frankie and Johnny"
The Story: In 1899, when she was 22 years old, Frankie shot and killed her boyfriend, Allen (not Johnny). She pled self-defense and was acquitted. But that was just the beginning of her problems. When "Frankie and Johnny" became a popular tune, she was the talk of St. Louis. She tried to get away by moving to Omaha, then to Portland. But when *Frankie and Johnny* was released as a film in 1936, she sued the film studio for defamation of character. Ironically, she lost because she convinced jurors she was *not* a "woman of easy virtue," like the character in the film. She was committed to a mental hospital in 1950 and died two years later.

GEORGE TRAIN
Inspired: *Around the World in 80 Days*
The Story: In 1890, wealthy American businessman/eccentric George Frances Train made a highly publicized trip around the world in only 80 days—an incredible speed for that time. Two years later, Jules Verne published his acclaimed novel, but called his hero Phileas Fogg. Train, the self-described "advocate of speed," was incensed. "Verne stole my thunder," he complained. He made the round-the-world trip three more times, finally breaking his own record by completing the journey in a mere 60 days.

DENNIS PATRICK CASEY
Inspired: The poem "Casey at the Bat"
The Story: Baseball fans have long wondered about the hero in Ernest L. Thayer's 1888 poem. Who was he? Convincing evidence points to Dennis P. Casey, a popular star with the Baltimore Orioles at the time. Casey's pitching and hitting elevated the team into "First Division" in the American Association, a feat no Baltimore team had accomplished.

The first Chamber of Commerce in the U.S. was organized in 1912.

THE MUNSTERS

Here are some things you didn't know about
TV's weirdest sitcom family.

HOW IT STARTED
In 1963, Joe Connelly and Bob Mosher were considering ideas for a new sitcom. Their 1950s hit *Leave It to Beaver,* was about to go off the air. Their 1961 sitcom *Ichabod & Me* had flopped.

Universal Pictures had recently dusted off its classic horror films—*Frankenstein, Dracula, The Mummy,* etc.—and sold them to TV. Monsters had quickly become a fad, with baby boom kids buying monster models, wallets, cards, toys, and dozens more products.

Connelly and Mosher saw a chance to bring back the Cleavers: turn them into monsters. A family of middle-class monsters in a typical suburb would make the same old sitcom plots seem new.

They were excited about the prospect, but weren't sure how the networks would react. So they assembled a crew of experienced actors—including Fred Gwynne and "Grandpa" Al Lewis (both fresh from *Car 54, Where are You?*), and shot a 15-minute pilot episode. "It was pretty bizarre" Gwynne recalled. "They hadn't figured out the costumes or the laughs. God only knows how they ever sold it on those fifteen minutes, because it was just awful."

But they did sell it—right away. According to Norman Abbot, who directed the pilot: "We had everybody from the studio at the soundstage watching the filming. Somebody called the people from the head office and told them to come down and see it. It was wild. Jim Aubrey, [president of] CBS, bought it instantly."

INSIDE FACTS

Start and Stop
The Munsters premiered on April 30, 1964—the same week that ABC first aired its own monster sitcom, *The Addams Family.* And it was cancelled in 1966—ironically, the same week *The Addams Family* was dumped. Which show was more popular? *The Munsters.* It ranked #18 on the list of the most popular shows of 1964-5. The

The average human sheds 40 lbs. of dead skin in their lifetime.

Addamses ranked 23rd. By the second season, however, the novelty of both shows had worn off, and ratings were only mediocre.

Making the Monster
It took two hours to transform the bony 6'5", 180-pound Fred Gwynne into Herman Munster. His face was covered with grease, balloon rubber, and yellow-green makeup (even though the show was filmed in black-and-white).
•He wore pants stuffed with foam and a shrunken jacket stuffed with foam in the shoulders and arms. The costume was so heavy and hot that he lost 10 lbs. during the first weeks of shooting.
•Gwynne's boots had 5" heels and weighed 10 lbs. They were intentionally hard to walk in, so he'd have a clumsy, "lurching" walk.

Yvonne to Be Alone
Yvonne De Carlo's (Lily's) makeup wasn't as difficult as Gwynne's, but she hated it as much—and had five different hairdressers fired during the show's two-year run. She complained that her makeup made her look older, and even tried to paint out the grey streak that ran though her wig (the producers made her put it back in).
•She also refused to paint her own nails black, which meant she had to have fake nails glued on every day. They wouldn't stay attached; often shooting had to be suspended while De Carlo and the crew looked around the set for the nails that had fallen off.
•De Carlo didn't even want the part. "I did the show in the beginning for one reason only—I needed money at the time." Her husband, a stuntman, had been critically injured during the filming of How the West Was Won, and De Carlo had exhausted her savings nursing him back to health.

THE COFFIN CAPER
•Grandpa's car, the *Dragula,* was a dragster with a real coffin as a body. It wasn't easy to build. When George Barris, the car's designer, tried to buy a coffin for it, he couldn't find a funeral home that would cooperate. "They wouldn't sell one unless you were dead." Finally, Barris had someone leave an envelope full of money at a funeral home while "my guys picked up a casket and walked out with it. We literally spooked off with the casket."

Sarah Josepha Hale's 1830 poem "Mary Had a Little Lamb" was inspired by a little

THE 10 MOST-WANTED LOST FILMS

Only about 20% of the silent movies made between 1895 and the late 1920s. (when talkies began) still survive. Many were discarded as worthless. Others, made on fragile films, have crumbled into dust. Today people are searching for—and sometimes finding—masterpieces of the silent era. In 1980, the American Film Institute (AFI) compiled this list of the 10 most historically and artistically significant "lost films." It is supplied by Gregory Lukow at AFI.

THE LIST, IN ALPHABETICAL ORDER

1. CAMILLE (1927). Norma Talmadge played the title role in one of her last triumphs. A legend of the silent screen, Talmadge watched her career all but vanish with the arrival of the "talkies." Apparently her voice did not match her image, and when audiences stopped buying tickets, the studios—which she'd helped to build—unceremoniously dropped her. Not a frame of this film (which was remade in 1937 with Greta Garbo) is known to exist.

2. CLEOPATRA (1917). This lavish half-million dollar epic featured Theda Bara, the original vamp of the silent era, as the sexy queen of the Nile. Sadly, only two of Bara's 38 films have survived. Her body of work is considered one of the lost treasures of the silent era, with *Cleopatra* the crown jewel.

3. THE DIVINE WOMAN (1928). Greta Garbo starred in 10 silent films before shifting to sound in 1930. *The Divine Woman* was her first starring role, and the only one of her films that hasn't survived, One reel was recently located in the former Soviet Union; the rest is still missing.

4. FRANKENSTEIN (1910). The first horror film (see p. 80). This version, made by Thomas Edison, has turned up in a private collection. But because the American Film Institute has no access to the film, they keep it on their list.

5. GREED (1925). Scholars and film critics consider this the Holy Grail of lost films. The original version—40 reels and 10 hours—was the masterpiece of one of film's most talented directors, Erich von Stroheim. It was released in a butcher version over von Stroheim's vociferous protests. The rest of the film was discarded. No one knows what happened to it.

6. THE KAISER, BEAST OF BERLIN (1918). Part of a series of short anti-German propaganda films made during the World War I period. Directed by and starring Rupert Julian as the Kaiser. U.S. historians are especially interested in this one.

7. LITTLE RED RIDING HOOD (1922). This was Walt Disney's first cartoon, produced six years before the introduction of Mickey Mouse in *Steamboat Willie*. Posters and a few sketches are all that remain.

8. LONDON AFTER MIDNIGHT (1927). Produced at the height of horror star Lon Chaney's short career, and hailed as a masterwork when it was released. Chaney stars as a detective who turns into a vampire at night. The false teeth he wore caused him so much pain that he was unable to keep them on for more than a few minutes at a time. Directed by Tod Browning.

9. THE ROGUE SONG (1930). Would be considered just another forgettable operetta, if it didn't contain a few non-musical scenes of Laurel and Hardy in their only known color film. It's also Laurel and Hardy's last short film. (In the '30s, they worked exclusively in features.) A three-minute segment, the original trailer, and the soundtrack (which was released as an album in 1980) are all that remain.

10. THAT ROYLE GIRL (1925). The story of an innocent girl saved from her accusers by a loving district attorney was the second film that legendary director D. W. Griffith made with W. C. Fields. Griffith was reportedly uncomfortable with the contemporary setting (he liked historical epics). However, given his status as one of the great directors of all time, and Fields's as a great comedian, film scholars would love to get another chance to see this.

Of the top 10 moneymaking Hollywood films, only *Forrest Gump* won the Best Picture Oscar.

FAMILIAR PHRASES

More origins of everyday phrases.

THAT'S A LOAD OF BULL
Meaning: It's a lie or exaggeration.
Origin: It's logical to assume that this phrase started with cow-chips…but it turns out that *boule* is an Old French verb meaning "to lie."

CLAP-TRAP
Meaning: Meaningless talk; empty speech.
Origin: "Claptrap" comes from the theater. It describes any line that the playwright inserts—often knowing it's terrible—just to get applause. It's literally "a trap to catch a clap."

RED-LETTER DAY
Meaning: Special occasion or day.
Origin: As far back as the Middle Ages, Christian church calendars and almanacs had feast days, saint days, and other holy days printed in red ink; everything else was printed in black ink.

IF YOU CAN DO IT, I'LL EAT MY HAT
Meaning: I don't believe you can do it.
Origin: Why would anyone offer to eat a hat under any circumstances? Answer: The original hat in this expression was "hatte," an English dish that contained eggs, veal, dates, saffron, and salt. Over time, the meaning of the phrase evolved into the ridiculous proposition it *sounded* like.

MY BETTER HALF
Meaning: My spouse.
Origin: The Puritan view of people was that we're made up of two halves: a body and a soul. The soul—our spiritual side—was considered our better half. In the 16th century, the English writer Sir Philip Sidney became the first person to apply the term to the union between a married couple. By the 18th century, his use of the expression had become the most common.

Average jury award to plaintiffs in medical malpractice suits in 1994: $977,392.

CELEBRITY SWEEPSTAKES

Three big stars—three big products. What could go wrong with these endorsements? Try divorce, sex, and alcoholism. Here are more surefire celebrity promotions that didn't quite turn out as expected.

MADONNA
In January 1989, Pepsi agreed to pay Madonna $5 million for a two-minute commercial featuring her brand-new single, "Like a Prayer."

What they wanted: Publicity. Pepsi planned to show its "Like a Prayer" ad the night *before* the world premier of Madonna's video on MTV. So it was the first chance for Madonna fans to see her sing it. Madonna was so popular—and the deal so unusual—that Pepsi's "coup" became front-page news. They showed the ad simultaneously on all three TV networks, and in 40 countries.

What they got: A scandal. Incredibly, nobody at Pepsi previewed Madonna's video before they built their campaign around it. Their ad featured Madonna going back to her eighth birthday. But the *video* was full of sexually suggestive scenes and provocative religious symbolism—including "a scantily clad Madonna singing in front of burning crosses, suffering wounds on her hands like Jesus and kissing a saintly statue that turns into a man."

What happened: Pepsi had purposely linked its ad campaign to the video, and they were stuck with it. Fundamentalist Christians turned their wrath on the "blasphemous" soft drink company. Sensing a consumer boycott in the making, Pepsi cancelled the whole deal within 24 hours. Madonna cried all the way to the bank. "It's just what I'd expect from her," a friend said, "She doesn't have any obligations to Pepsi…and still gets to keep their money."

BURT REYNOLDS
In 1992, the Florida Department of Citrus hired Reynolds to promote Florida orange juice in a $16 million ad campaign.

What they wanted: A believable spokesperson. Reynolds was a native Floridian with a pleasant, good ol' boy image. Plus, he and his

---

Sure, and they can quit any time: 21% of U.S. smokers say they don't believe nicotine's addictive.

wife, actress Loni Anderson, had actually *left* Hollywood to live in the Sunshine State. "I'm kind of Mr. Florida," he told reporters modestly. "I know a lot of the growers, and I'm proud to speak for them."

What they got: "The world's ugliest and most public divorce." Anderson filed for divorce in June 1993, and nearly every detail of the split was played out in the tabloids. Most accounts blamed Reynolds for the breakup. And he didn't do much to help the situation when he admitted to the National Enquirer that he'd had a two-year affair with a Florida cocktail waitress.

What happened: The Citrus commission pulled the ads. "What was happening in his personal life, at the level it was being played out, overshadowed the message we were trying to communicate," a spokesman told reporters. Reynolds no longer drinks Florida orange juice, and blames the Florida Citrus commission for cashing in on his failed marriage. "They took the opportunity…to cash in on the P.R. from my divorce, saying I wasn't the right image for them. Yeah, like Anita Bryant is. Or Rush Limbaugh."

BRUCE WILLIS

In the mid-1980s, Willis was hired to plug Seagram's Wine Coolers for an estimated $2 to $3 million a year.

What they wanted: A macho, good-time spokesman to make their wine coolers acceptable to young cable drinkers.

What they got: A huge success—albeit with some bad publicity. Seagrams' brand-new product quickly became the best selling cooler in the country. Then, in May 1987, Willis was arrested for "scuffling" with police officers who were called to his home to break up a loud, drunken party. The charges were dropped after Willis apologized to his neighbors and promised to move away.

What happened: Seagrams stuck by its man, apparently thinking that his drunk and disorderly behavior was *good* for their product—or at least didn't hurt it.

But Willis was finally dumped in 1988 after:

1. The *National Enquirer* ran a story saying he had an alcohol problem, and

2. His wife, Demi Moore, began a public campaign against alcohol abuse.

New York's Central Park is almost twice as big as the entire country of Monaco.

TOY FACTS

The BRI takes a look at random info on some childhood (and adulthood) classics.

NERF BALLS

After successfully inventing the game Twister (see p. 87), Reynolds Guyer decided to become a full-time toy designer. He quit his family's business and formed his own toy design firm. One of his company's first efforts was a game based on a caveman theme. It involved hiding money under foam rubber rocks and defending the loot by throwing some of the rocks at an opponent.

"Pretty soon," Guyer recalls, "we found we really enjoyed throwing the rocks. Then someone decided that the rocks were not as round as they would like, so they began shaping them, cutting them with scissors," until they were balls. Guyer soon abandoned the caveman theme entirely and focused on the balls. He made up the name "Nerfs" to communicate what he thought of as their "soft, friendly nature." Within a decade Nerf became one of the largest lines of sports/action toys on earth.

MAGIC SLATE

In the early 1920s, R. A. Watkins, owner of a small printing plant in Illinois, was approached by a man who wanted to sell him the rights to a homemade device made of waxed cardboard and tissue. You could write on it, but the messages could be easily erased by lifting up the tissue. Watkins couldn't make up his mind; he told the man to come back the next day.

In the middle of the night, Watkins's phone rang; it was the man calling from jail. He said that if Watkins would bail him out, he'd *give* Watkins the rights to the invention. The printer agreed. He wound up getting a patent for the device—which he called Magic Slate. Since then, tens of millions have been sold.

PICTIONARY

Robert Angel, a Seattle waiter, used to entertain his friends at parties by selecting a word from the dictionary, drawing it, and having them guess what it was. He didn't think about developing it into a game until Trivial Pursuit became popular. Then he spent eight months looking up 6,000 words in the dictionary (2,500 made it into the game) while a friend designed "word cards" and the board. He borrowed $35,000 to manufacture the game and started selling it to stores in Seattle out of the trunk of his car.

He got his big break when Nordstrom ordered 167 games. They didn't even have a game department. "They let us set up a table in the accessories department," Angel recalls. "If anybody glanced in our direction, we would yell at them to come and watch us play the game." Tom McGuire, a salesman at Selchow & Righter (manufacturer of Trivial Pursuit), played Pictionary at Nordstrom with his family. He was so impressed that he quit his job and began marketing it full time. By the end of 1987, over $90 million worth of Pictionary games had been sold in the United States alone.

* * * *

MISCELLANY

• Tonka Toys was originally called the Mound Metalcraft Company. It was renamed *Tonka* after Lake Minnetonka, which dominated the scenery around their factory.

• Mattel got its name from its two founders—Harold *Mat*son and *El*liot Handler. Handler was in the picture frame business in L.A. In 1946 he had a bunch of extra frame slats, so he and Matson built doll furniture out of them.

• Mattel was the first toy company to advertise on national TV. In 1955 they sold toy burp guns on "The Mickey Mouse Club."

• Mr. Potato Head used to come with a pipe—which bugged anti-smoking activists. "It's not only dangerous to his health," complained Surgeon General C. Everett Koop, "it also passes on the message to kids that smoking is okay." In 1987, Hasbro gave in; after 35 years of smoking, Mr. Potato Head surrendered his pipe to the Surgeon General. Koop was so pleased that he named Mr. Potato Head "Official Spokespud" for the Great Smokeout.

• World record: A game of Twister was played by 4,160 participants on May 2, 1987 at the University of Massachusetts.

There are more bagpipe bands in the U.S. than there are in Scotland.

MORE STRANGE LAWSUITS

Here are more real-life examples of unusual legal battles

THE PLAINTIFF: Mary Verdev, a 73-year-old Milwaukee resident
THE DEFENDANT: St. Florian Catholic Church
THE LAWSUIT: In 1990, the church's 300-pound electronic bingo board fell on Verdev. She sued, claiming it had caused $90,000 worth of injuries. She also said that as a result of the accident, she now found herself sexually attracted to women and had begun to experience spontaneous orgasms, "sometimes in clusters"
THE VERDICT: Verdev wouldn't undergo a psychological exam ordered by the judge. He dismissed the case.

THE PLAINTIFF: Three-year-old Stacy Pavnev
THE DEFENDANT: Three-year-old Jonathan Inge
THE LAWSUIT: In February 1996, the two children were playing in the sandbox at a local park in Boston. Jonathan apparently kicked Stacy, and the parents argued heatedly. Then Stacy's mom went to court and asked that Jonathan be restrained from using the playground when Stacy was there. "Maybe it's a little emotional, maybe it's overprotective, but you do what you can," she said.
THE VERDICT: Amazingly, Superior Court Judge Charles Spurlock actually granted a temporary restraining order. Then he called the families to court and ordered them to stay separated at the playground.

THE PLAINTIFF: Richard Loritz
THE DEFENDANT: San Diego County
THE LAWSUIT: Loritz was imprisoned for three months in 1995. During that time, he says, he asked for dental floss and was refused. As a result, he developed four cavities. He sued for $2,000 in dental expenses.
THE VERDICT: The case was thrown out of court.

President Lyndon Johnson used to give electric toothbrushes with presidential seals as gifts.

THE PLAINTIFF: Sharon Silver
THE DEFENDANT: Gerald Pfeffer, her ex-husband
THE LAWSUIT: After the couple divorced in 1985, Silver moved out of state. Pfeffer stayed in their St. Paul, Minnesota, home. In 1988, the reunion committee of Silver's high school class sent an "update" questionnaire to her old address. Pfeffer filled it out and returned it. A sample of his answers:

> **Current occupation:** "Retired on third husband's divorce settlement."
> **Current interests/hobbies:** "Night clubbing and partying. Looking for new and wealthier husbands."
> **Recent outrageous/unusual/interesting experience:** "Going to W. Virginia on the job and having an affair with two different guys while my third husband was in Minnesota working two jobs."

The committee printed these (and other) answers in its newsletter. Silver sued for libel; her ex-husband argued that it was all true.
THE VERDICT: After three years of litigation, the case was settled out of court for $75,000—$50,000 from Gerald, $25,000 from the Harding High School Class of 1958. "Well, I thought they were pretty good answers at the time," Pfeffer commented afterward.

THE PLAINTIFF: Kenneth Parker
THE DEFENDANT: Nevada State Prison
THE LAWSUIT: Parker was an inmate, serving 15 years for robbery. He wanted to buy two jars of chunky peanut butter from the prison canteen. (Cost: $5.) But the canteen had only one jar of chunky peanut butter. When they had to substitute a jar of creamy for the second one, Parker sued for "mental and emotional pain," asking for $5,500 and the imprisonment of a prison official.
THE VERDICT: The case went on for two years. It was finally dismissed.

THE PLAINTIFF: Jeannine Pelletier and her husband
THE DEFENDANT: Fort Kent Golf Club in Portland, Maine
THE LAWSUIT: Pelletier hit a golf ball in the spring of 1995 that bounced back and bonked her on the nose. She and her husband sued—she for physical damages, he for "lost of consortium."
THE VERDICT: The Maine Supreme Court awarded her $40,000. Her husband got zilch.

In his entire lifetime, King Louis XV bathed three times.

CELEBRITY GOSSIP

A few bits of gossip you've probably never heard. They're supplied by Jack Mingo, whose book The Juicy Parts *is full of great tidbits like these.*

MICK JAGGER

"About the time Mick started dating girls, his mother started selling Avon. When his parents were out, he would invite a girl to the house where they would sit at his mother's dressing table trying on her makeup. One of his dates remembers, 'He just seemed happy letting me put lipstick and mascara on him. Then he'd do the same for me. It did strike me as very strange at the time, but it was all in fun. Dating Mick was more like being with one of the girls.'"

HENRY FORD

"The automobile tycoon believed in reincarnation. Since he was born a few weeks after the battle of Gettysburg, he decided he had been a solider killed in that battle. And later in life, he decided his niece was really the reincarnation of his mother."

W. C. FIELDS

"He didn't like to carry a lot of cash while on the road, so wherever he was, he opened a bank account. He claimed to have 700 of them in banks all over the world—including London, Paris, Sydney, and Cape Town. Usually these accounts were open under his real name, but sometimes he used odd aliases like Figley E. Whitesides, Sneed Hearn, Dr. Otis Guelpe, and (in Madrid, Spain), 'Señor Guillermo McKinley.' After his death, only about three dozen accounts were located."

MICHAEL JACKSON

• "What started him on plastic surgery? According to one report, it was because he hated the fact that he was growing up to look like his father."

• "He once met Andy Warhol and Alfred Hitchcock and thought, for some reason, that they were brothers."

• "He's been reported as saying he believes human beings can fly."

HARPO MARX

"In Harpo's professional debut with the Marx Brothers, he looked out at the audience…and immediately wet his pants."

WALT DISNEY

• "The animator shared an apartment with his brother Roy until Roy got married. Then Walt, feeling abandoned, decided that he (as he put it) 'needed a new roommate' and three months later, took a bride himself. His honeymoon night was spent on a train from Idaho to California; his behavior was strictly Mickey Mouse: he developed a 'toothache' and spent the entire night shining shoes in the porter's car 'to keep his mind off the pain.'"

• Walt's famous 'trademark' signature was designed by a studio artist. He often had to insist he really was Walt Disney to auto-graph seekers who thought he was putting them on."

RICHARD NIXON

• "In first grade, his mother made a point of telling his teacher, 'Never call him Dick—I named him Richard.' Every day he wore a freshly starched white shirt with a black bow tie and knee pants, and his teacher was quoted as saying later that she could not remember him ever getting dirty."

• "He took great pains in brushing his teeth, was careful to gargle, and before he left for school asked his mother to smell his breath to make sure he would not offend anyone on the bus. He didn't like to ride the school bus, because the other children didn't smell good."

THE BEATLES & MUHAMMAD ALI

"In 1963, during their first American tour, the world-famous Beat-les tried to meet heavyweight boxing champion Sonny Liston, who was going to fight Cassius Clay (later known as Muhammad Ali) for the championship in a few days. He refused to have anything to do with 'a bunch of faggots.' Instead, they met Clay. He bossed them around for the photographers, commanding them to the canvas with 'Get down, you little worms!'

"Lennon, however, got the last laugh. While Clay was talking with them, he used one of his favorite lines: 'You guys ain't as dumb as you look.' John Lennon looked him in the eye and said, 'No, but you are. "

Is it us, or do they have good noses? Polar bears can smell a human from 20 miles away.

MUCH ADO ABOUT SNORING

They say that if your spouse snores loudly enough to keep you awake, one of the best things to do is lay down on the living room couch and read until you fall asleep. Uncle John suggests saving this chapter for just such an occasion.

A SNORE BY ANY OTHER NAME

There's an old saying: "Laugh, and the world laughs with you, Snore, and you sleep alone." But you won't snore alone. It's estimated that every night, as much as half the population of the world is snoring, too.

What, exactly, is snoring?

• When you go to sleep, the muscles that control the soft tissue in your mouth—your tongue, soft palate, uvula (the piece of flesh hanging down in the back of your mouth), tonsils, and adenoids—begins to relax.

• The deeper you sleep, the more these soft tissues relax. In some people, they actually begin to obstruct the airway. When this happens, the air that flows in and out of your mouth makes the tissues vibrate, causing the snoring sound.

WHO SNORES?

• Anyone can snore; doctors estimate that as many as 910 million Americans over the age of 18 do. But the problem is worst among people over sixty (65% of people over 60 snore), especially for males.

• For that matter, men snore more than women in just about every age group. Men have more muscles in their necks and throats than women, which means they have more to go flabby as they age.

• Girth is a factor, too People who are overweight are three times more likely to snore than people who aren't. Why? Sleep experts point to two causes.

1. Overweight people generally have less muscle tone than people of average weight—including in their mouths. Poorly toned flesh

According to the record books, an Englishman named Melvin Switzer is the world's loudest snorer.

flaps around more than toned flesh, which increases the likelihood of snoring.

2. Overweight people actually gain weight inside their mouths; and the more fleshy tissue in the mouth, the more likely you are to have a snore-causing obstruction.

There are also external reasons for snoring:
• Colds, allergies, nasal infections, and anything else that stops up the nose can cause snoring. Why? The sufferer has to breathe more forcefully than normal through the mouth—which increases the chance of blockage.
• People who take depressants—including alcohol and sleeping pills—snore more than people who don't, because of the relaxing effect they have on the body.
• Smoking doesn't usually cause snoring, but can aggravate the condition because it irritates the pharynx and causes mucous membranes to swell.

SNORE CURES
Quick Fixes
• Snoring is usually worst when you sleep on your back, because the soft tissue in your mouth slumps backward, blocking the airway. That's why many traditional cures aim at preventing people from sleeping on their backs. During the Revolutionary War, soldiers forced to bunk together sometimes sewed small cannonballs to the backs of the nightshirts of anyone who snored to keep them off their backs. Not much has changed—a common cure for snoring today is the "snore ball," a tennis ball in a sock that snorers fasten to the back of their pajama tops.
• Another trick that may help: raising the head of your bed four inches by placing bricks, phone books, etc., under the bed. Sleeping with more than one pillow won't do the trick. In fact, it'll .probably make snoring worse by bending your body either at the neck or the waist, both of which can increase snoring. (Switching from feather to synthetic pillows can also help, if snoring is caused by allergies.)
• A preventative: Chewing two or three pieces of gum at a time may help, some sleep researchers think, by reducing flab and increasing muscle tone inside your mouth.

He has been recorded snoring as loudly as 91 decibels, more noise than is made

• If snoring is really serious, there are plenty of high-tech solutions. Tongue retainers and other appliances are available. Or you can try a "continuous positive air pressure" (CPAP) pump that blows a steady stream of air into your nostrils while you sleep. And if nothing else works, there's surgery: Surgeons can, for example, move your tongue forward and stitch the underlying muscle to the chin bone, so that nothing flops back into the airway during sleep.

DEADLY SNORES

• Snoring can actually be fatal. More than half of all chronic snorers over age 40 suffer from "sleep apnea." In these people, the airway becomes totally obstructed, cutting off the oxygen supply to their brain for as long as sixty seconds before they wake up enough to clear the obstruction. Not all sleep apnea sufferers survive. Every year, more than 2,500 of them die from cardiac arrest brought on by the condition.

• Sleep apnea may have other unfortunate side effects. It is believed to cause high blood pressure, an increased pulse, and an enlarged heart, and may also increase the risk of strokes.

• And because it disrupts the deep sleep that provides the most rest, sleep apnea also poses indirect health risks: Sufferers are often physically exhausted during the day, thus more prone to on-the-job accidents and other injuries. More than 20% of sleep apnea victims have been in car accidents caused when they fall asleep at the wheel.

LIFE SAVERS

To be fair, we should also point out that snoring can also save lives. This article, reported by Reuters News Service, appeared in newspapers recently:

> A London undertaker was terrified when he heard snores coming from a coffin in which 85-year-old Rose Hanover had been laid out for burial....She had collapsed and apparently died in her home. Two hours after arriving at the parlor, Mrs. Hanover began to snore, even though she had been pronounced dead by a doctor using the normal breathing and heart tests. Last night she was sitting up in a hospital bed and was reported to be much improved.

by a power lawnmower. (Big surprise: His wife is deaf in one ear.)

SHAKESPEARE'S INSULTS

Shakespeare was a master at hurling off an insult or two. Here are some of his meanest, wittiest, and cruelest.

"The tartness of his face sours grapes."

—*Coriolanus*

"[You] leather-jerkin, crystal-button, knot-pated, agate-ring, puke-stocking, caddis-garter, smooth-tongue, Spanish pouch!"

—*Henry IV, Part 1*

"You are as a candle, the better part burnt out."

—*Henry IV, Part 2*

"He never broke any man's head but his own, and that was against a post when he was drunk."

—*Henry V*

"[Your] face is not worth sunburning."

—*Henry V*

"You blocks, you stones, you worse than senseless things!"

—*Romeo and Juliet*

"Your horrid image doth unfix my hair"

—*Macbeth*

"His brain is as dry as the remainder biscuit after a voyage."

—*As You Like It*

"It is certain that when he makes water, his urine is congealed ice."

—*Measure for Measure*

"I durst not laugh, for fear of opening my lips and receiving [your] bad air."

—*Julius Caesar*

"Thy food is such as hath been belch'd on by infected lungs."

—*Pericles*

"[Your] face is Lucifer's privy-kitchen, where he doth nothing but roast malt-worms."

—*Henry VI, Part 2*

"He has not so much brain as ear-wax."

—*Troilus and Cressida*

"Though [he] is not naturally honest, [he] is so sometimes by chance."

—*The Winter's Tale*

"He's a most notable coward, an infinite and endless liar, an hourly promise-breaker, and the owner of no one good quality."

—*All's Well That Ends Well*

When migrating birds fly in a "V" formation, it increases their range by as much as 70%.

MORE TAXING TRIVIA

Here are a few additional ways that income tax has shaped our culture.

H & R BLOCK

Encouraged by their mother to go into business together, Henry Bloch and his brother Richard formed the United Business Company in 1946. They planned to provide bookkeeping, management, and other services to businesses, but they spent so much time helping their customers fill out tax forms that they decided to focus on tax preparation exclusively.

To give their business a more personal touch, they decided to name it after themselves. But rather than have customers mispronounce their name as "blotch," they changed the spelling to match the way the name is pronounced. Today, H&R Block preparers fill out one of every ten income tax returns filed with the IRS.

BOOSTING THE CREDIT CARD

In 1958, the IRS began requiring taxpayers with expense accounts to list each of their unreimbursed expenses on their tax returns. To avoid this extra record keeping, many employers issued credit cards—which itemize all purchases in the monthly billing statement—to employees with expense accounts. Result: Credit card companies reported the largest sales increases in history.

HISTORIC SWITCH

Ronald Reagan made so much money as a Hollywood actor that he ended up in the 94% tax bracket. In his autobiography *An American Life*, he revealed that the tax was instrumental in converting him from a New Deal Democrat to a conservative Republican.

"The IRS took such a big chunk of my earnings," he wrote, "that after a while I began asking myself whether it was worth it to keep on taking work. Something was wrong with a system like that."

"When you have to give up such a large percentage of your income in taxes, incentive to work goes down."

25% of the 206 bones in your body are in your feet.

BATHROOM NEWS

Bits and pieces of bathroom trivia we've flushed out over the years.

WORLD NEWS
• **In Paris:** Concerned about the estimated 500,000 tons of poop that Parisian dogs deposit on city streets each year, Pierre Pascallon, Conservative member of Parliament, introduced a bill in the National Assembly requiring the installation of dog *toilets*—to be known as *canisettes.* To pay for it, he proposed that dog owners pay a graduated tax in proportion to how much their dogs weigh.

• **In Malaysia:** The government announced that it is now illegal for restaurants to substitute toilet paper as table napkins. Punishment: $80 in fines (with jail time for repeat offenders).

• **On Mt. Everest:** A state-of-the-art, $10,000 outhouse is being erected about 4 miles up the side of Mount Everest. "Until now, climbers and Sherpas have had to go off and find boulders and bushes to hide behind," a spokesman for the company doing the installation told reporters. The outhouse will help control Mt. Everest's growing waste problem. Since Sir Edmund Hillary first scaled the 29,000-foot summit in 1953, hundreds of Everest climbers have discarded tons of garbage and "other" waste—which decomposes very slowly in the frigid, low-oxygen environment.

AN HISTORIC MOMENT
What was it like to be the second person to walk on the lunar surface? Astronaut Edwin "Buzz" Aldrin, who followed Neil Armstrong moments after Armstrong made his famous first step, described the experience in an interview for British television: "I held onto the near edge of the landing gear and checked my balance and then hesitated a moment....I am the first person to wet his pants on the moon."

THE BATHROOM CRIME BLOTTER
• In 1993, Barry Lyn Stoller, a Seattle drywall installer, took some Ex-Lax to cure his constipation…and when it didn't work, he wrote the folks at Ex-Lax demanding a refund. The company mailed him a check…with his *zip code* entered as the dollar

amount. Stoller deposited the $98,002 in the bank, withdrew it a few days later…and hasn't been seen since.

• In 1994, Milton Ross was videotaped urinating into his office's coffeepot, part of an "an ongoing feud" he had with a co-worker. (Office employees had installed the video camera after noticing that their coffee tasted funny.) Ross's co-workers turned the tape over to the police…*and* the media, which broadcast it all over the world. Ross pled guilty to third-degree assault. He was sentenced to 100 hours of community service, which the judge stipulated had to be spent cleaning public restrooms.

• In October 1995, Gerald Finneran, described as "one of the world's leading authorities on Latin American debt," exploded into rage on a United Airlines flight from Buenos Aires to New York, after a flight attendant refused to serve him another drink. According to witnesses, Finneran assaulted the flight attendants, then "defecated on a serving cart, cleaned himself with the airline's first class linens, and thus left an odor that remained in the cabin for the remaining four hours of the flight." Ordinarily, such a flight might have been diverted to a closer airport. But the president of Portugal was on board, which made a detour impossible.

PUBLIC SERVICE ANNOUNCEMENT

Do toilet seat covers really protect us against anything? According to David Feldman, in *Why Do Clocks Run Clockwise and Other Imponderables:* "Not only are venereal diseases not spread by toilet seats, but nothing else is, either. Although there was one report suggesting that the herpes virus may survive briefly in such an environment…doctors we spoke to [all said], 'There is no scientific evidence of disease transmitted from toilet seats.'"

THE FINAL FRONTIER

According to *Buzz* magazine, William Shatner, who played *Star Trek*'s Capt. Kirk, had his bathroom remodeled to resemble the bridge of the starship *Enterprise*. *Buzz* reports that he even had his toilet "custom-made in the shape of the fabled vessel."

RAMBO: THE MOVIE

Here's the second installment of our story about the fictional Vietnam vet who became one of the most enduring pop icons of the 1980s. (Part I is on page 411).

S AVED!!
First Blood, the story of Rambo, had been bouncing around Hollywood for years when it was rescued by two film distributors who wanted to be producers. Andrew Vajna and Mario Kassar were rummaging through unused film properties at the Warner Bros. lot, looking for an action film they could sell internationally, when they stumbled on Morrell's story.

They immediately bought the movie rights. Then they hired Kirk Douglas to direct it, and picked Sylvester Stallone—whose only commercial success up to that time was *Rocky*—to star.

CHANGING THE STORY
To make the story more suitable for an action film, they changed the plot. In the novel, Rambo becomes a psychopathic killer, while the sheriff, also a veteran, is shown in a sympathetic light. For the film, however, they shifted all the sympathy to Rambo, and made the sheriff into the villain. "The portrayal of the sheriff bothered me," Morrell says. "In the novel both the police chief and Rambo had to die to show how pointless everything was.... My intent was to transpose the Vietnam war to America, whereas the film's intent was to make the audience cheer for the underdog."

PROBLEMS
Making *First Blood* quickly became difficult and expensive. Then Kirk Douglas—whom the producers were counting on to help sell the film to distributors and investors—dropped out. That left Stallone as the only well-known person connected to the film...and all of his non-*Rocky* films had been box-office disappointments. There was no reason to assume his next film would make money either, so no one was interested in the distribution rights. Kassar recalls, "Here I was $14 million in the red, and nothing was sold." Things were looking bad.

Every day, Americans use 4.8 billion gallons of water flushing the toilet.

BREAKTHROUGH

In desperation, Vajna and Kassar spliced together 55 minutes of the unfinished film and presented it at the American Film Market convention. "Even today," the *Los Angeles Times* wrote in 1990, "distributors remember the buzz that film clip generated. Within hours, rights to *First Blood* were sold out."

First Blood's timing was perfect. The bad memories of Vietnam were fading, Ronald Reagan was in office, and the country was becoming more conservative and isolationist at the same time. The increasing threat of terrorists was making the country nervous. Morrell says. "Like Rambo, Americans felt backed into a corner by hijackers and terrorists, and they were ready to strike back, if only in fiction."

First Blood, which even Stallone feared would be a flop (he called it "the most expensive home movie ever made"), did $9 million worth of business during its opening weekend in October and went on to gross $120 million worldwide.

FIRST BLOOD PART II

Two weeks after First Blood premiered, Vajna and Kassar decided to make a sequel—*Rambo: First Blood Part II*. In it, Rambo returns to Vietnam to obtain proof that the Vietnamese are still holding American MIAs and ends up single-handedly liberating an entire prison camp full of U.S. soldiers. Sylvester Stallone, who wrote the script, got the idea for the plot after receiving a letter from a Virginia woman whose husband had been missing for 16 years.

First Blood Part II hit American theaters in the summer of 1985 and was an even bigger hit than the first movie: it was the third most successful launch in Hollywood history. "Sequels usually do about 60% of the original," Vajna told interviewers. "With *Rambo*, we are doing 300%, maybe 400%." By the time it finished its run, *First Blood Part II*, which cost $27 million to make, grossed more than $390 million at the box office.

POP GOES THE SYMBOL

First Blood Part II did more than just make piles of money—it turned Rambo into a household word. This was partly due to the movie, and partly due to merchandising (Rambo posters, T-shirts, action figures, collectors' knives, toy guns, toy bow-and arrow sets, vitamins...and even Wrigley's Rambo Black Flak bubble gum, black raspberry-flavored gum shaped like shrapnel.)

It was also helped along by the Reagan administration's foreign policy, the most assertive and controversial since the end of the Vietnam War. When President Reagan ordered air strikes against Libya, the London Times headline screamed "RAMBO JETS BOMB LIBYA"; and when Nicaraguan president Daniel Ortega made a speech at the United Nations, he urged President Reagan to remember "that Rambo exists only in the movies."

U.S. Army recruiting centers hung *Rambo* posters in their windows, and there was even a poster of President Reagan's head grafted onto Rambo's body. It was a bestseller.

People speculated that Rambo might become as enduring a character as James Bond. But times changed: *Rambo III*, released in 1988, was a critical and box-office flop. Vajna and Kassar's studio, Carolco Pictures, Inc., ran into financial trouble beginning in 1991 and limped along for several years before finally filing for bankruptcy in 1995.

MORE RAMBO FACTS

• Rambo got a first name in *Rambo II*—Johnny, from the song "When Johnny Comes Marching Home Again." By strange coincidence, there really was a John Rambo who fought in Vietnam. But Arthur John Rambo of Libby, Montana, didn't come back— he was killed by enemy fire in 1969.

• Morrell was earning $1,000 a month as a college professor when he sold the rights to his *First Blood* novel in 1971. His lawyer charged him $500 to revise the contract's fine print to include sequels and merchandising rights, and at the time, Morrell felt ripped off. "I told my lawyer, 'What sequels? Everyone's dead at the end of the novel. Merchandise? Who's going to bring out dolls and lunch-boxes for a movie about a psychopathic killer?' He said, 'You don't understand Hollywood. They can change anything they want. They could make it into a musical.'" It was the best $500 Morrell ever spent; the contract changes earned him millions.

• How does Morrell feel about the way his anti-war novel was changed to a violent thriller? He likes it. "The *Rambo* films are marvelous special effects movies....like cartoons. When Sylvester comes down the trail with his machine gun, I laugh."

LUCKY FINDS

In an earlier Bathroom Reader, *we included a section about valuable things people have found. Since then we've found many more stories. Hey—maybe it's not such a rare occurrence. It could happen to you!*

GARAGE SALE TREASURE
The Find: Two Shaker "gift" paintings
Where They Were Found: Inside a picture frame
The Story: In 1994, a retired couple from New England bought an old picture frame for a few dollars at a garage sale. When they took the frame apart to restore it, two watercolor drawings—dated 1845 and 1854—fell out.

A few months later, the couple was traveling in Massachusetts and noticed a watercolor on a poster advertising the Hancock Shaker Village Museum. It was similar to the two they'd found. Curious, they did some research and found out the works were called "gift paintings."

It turns out that the Shakers, a New England religious sect of the 1800s, did not allow decorations on their walls; Shaker sisters, however, were permitted to paint "trees, flowers, fruits and birds...to depict the glory of heaven." The paintings were than "gifted" to other sisters and put away as holy relics. And one of the couple's paintings was signed by the most famous of all "gift" artists, Hannah Cohoon.

They called a curator of the Hancock Museum with the news, but he didn't believe them. Only 200 Shaker "gift" paintings still exist...and very few are of the quality they described. Moreover, all known paintings were in museums—none in private hands. Nonetheless, in January 1996, the couple brought the paintings to the museum, where they were examined and declared authentic. A year later, in January 1997, Sotheby's sold them for $473,000.

BIZARRE BITE
The Find: A diamond
Where It Was Found: In a plate of pasta
The Story: In October 1996, Liliana Parodi of Genoa, Italy, went to her favorite restaurant for some pasta. The meal was uneventful...until she bit down on something hard and it wedged

painfully between her teeth. She complained to the management, then left. The next morning, she went to a dentist, who extracted the object—a one-carat, uncut diamond worth about $3,000. Parodi took it to a jeweler and had it set in a ring. How it got into the pasta is still a mystery.

A BEATLE'S LEGACY
The Find: Dozens of sketches by John Lennon
Where They Were Found: In a notebook
The Story: In 1996, a man named John Dunbar—who'd been married to British singer Marianne Faithfull in the 1960s—was going through some old belongings and came across a notebook he hadn't seen in over 25 years. He'd had it with him at a London party in 1967, on a night when he and his friend John Lennon were taking LSD together. But he'd stashed it away and forgotten about it.

During that week in 1967, Lennon had seen an ad in the newspaper offering "an island off Ireland," for about $2,000. At the party, the drugged-out Beatle suddenly decided to buy it. He and Dunbar immediately flew to Dublin, traveled across Ireland in a limousine, and hired a boat to get there. "The island was more like a couple of small hills joined by a gravelly bar with a cottage on it," Durbar recalled. "When we got there, John sat down and started drawing." The pair stayed on the island for a few days. Lennon did buy it, but never lived there. (In fact, he gave it away a few years later, to a stranger who showed up at Apple Records.)

Dunbar kept the notebook as a memento of the trip, and today, experts estimate the drawings at about $165,000. The incredulous Dunbar can always look as it as a belated "thank you"—he was the fellow, it turns out, who introduced Lennon to Yoko Ono.

LOTTERY TICKET
The Find: A wallet with $224.
Where It Was Found: On a street in Adelaide, Australia
The Story: In the 1970s, Joan Campbell found a wallet and tracked down the owner, hoping for a nice reward. She was disappointed—all the man gave her was a 55¢ lottery ticket. Later, she cheered up: the ticket paid $45,000.

ACCIDENTAL HITS

*Here are a few improbable-but-true stories that show how musicians
can become stars overnight...or write hit songs without knowing it.*

G **ET TOGETHER (1967/1969), by the Youngbloods**
Background. In 1967, a group called the Youngbloods put
out their first record on RCA, "Grizzly Bear." It was a
modest hit. But the follow-up, a peace and love anthem called
"Get Together" ("Come on people, smile on your brother / Everybody get together, try to love one another"), bombed. It reached
#62 on the charts and died.
Lucky Break. Two years later, the National Conference of Christians and Jews put together a package of information for TV and
radio stations to read on the air during National Brotherhood
Week. They included a copy of the obscure "Get Together" in
each package for the stations to use as background music.
It's a Hit! People may not have paid attention to the message, but
they listened to the song. Radio stations all over the country were
flooded with calls asking what that record was and where they
could get it. Stations began playing their copies of "Get Together,"
turning it into a Top 10 song that sold over 2 million copies.

HUMAN NATURE (1982), by Michael Jackson
Background. Steve Porcaro was a member of the group Toto. One
day his daughter came home upset about a fight she'd had with
some friends. "Why do they do that?" she asked. "It's just human
nature," her father said...and then decided that was a good song
title. So he went into Toto's studio and put a melody on tape,
occasionally singing the line, "It's just human nature." Then he
left the cassette lying around and forgot about it.
Lucky Break. Michael Jacksons's producer, Quincy Jones, was
looking for material to use on Jackson's new album. He asked
another member of Toto, David Paitch, for some songs. Paitch
went into their studio, put three tunes on a tape and sent it to
Jones...who didn't care for them. But he said he loved the other
song at the end of the tape.

What song? It turned out Paitch had accidentally picked up

the tape on which Porcaro had recorded "Human Nature."

It's a Hit! Jones hired a lyricist to finish the song and included it on Jackson's album—called "Thriller"—which turned out to be the bestselling album in history. Porcaro earned millions for it. On top of that, the single of "Human Nature" reached #7 on its own.

HANKY PANKY (1966), by Tommy James & the Shondells

Background. In 1963, Tommy Jackson, a 16 year-old Michigan high school kid, recorded "Hanky Panky" with his band, the Shondells. It was a regional hit in Michigan, Illinois, and Indiana. Then it disappeared. A year and a half later, Jackson graduated from high school and the Shondells disbanded.

Lucky Break. Jackson was at his family's house one evening in 1965 when he got a phone call from a guy calling himself "Mad Mike" Metro.

"He said, 'I'm a deejay in Pittsburgh, and your record's number one. Can you come here?'" recalls Jackson. "I said, 'What record? Who is this? What's your name?' I thought it was one of my friends pulling my leg." But it was true. A disc jockey had found "Hanky Panky" in a 10¢ bin and started playing it on the air. Soon, every station in Pittsburgh was playing it.

It's a Hit! Jackson's old band wasn't interested in getting back together, so he flew to Pittsburgh alone and began making appearances with a new group. Meanwhile, Roulette Records released "Hanky Panky" nationally. It became the #1 song in the country, and Tommy Jackson—now known as Tommy James—became one of the biggest pop stars of the late 1960s.

OH HAPPY DAY, (1967), The Edwin Hawkins Singers

Background: Edwin Hawkins assembled the 46-piece Northern California State Youth Choir in 1967. To raise money, he picked out eight members of the choir and recorded an album in the basement of a local church. It was never intended for any audience except the limited gospel market. When they sold 600 copies they were pleased.

Lucky Break: A San Francisco rock promoter found the album in a warehouse and gave it to popular S.F. deejay, Abe "Voco" Kesh.

It's a Hit! Kesh loved it. He played it so often that it became a local hit. Then it went national and sold over a million copies.

Ramses condoms are named after Ramses II, an Egyptian pharoah who fathered 160+ children.

MISS AMERICA, PART V: THE 1960s

For a brief spell during the '60s, Miss America became a political as well as cultural symbol, caught in the crossfire between forces for change that saw it as an embarrassing relic, and traditionalists who saw it as a comforting connection to the "Leave It to Beaver" years.

MIDDLE AGE

The Miss America Pageant was tremendously popular in the 1950s and early 1960s....But by the late 1960s, it began to show its age. One of the problems was that the various pageant committees had become top-heavy with stodgy Atlantic City businessmen and society matrons, who had virtually nothing in common with the young women of the sixties. After decades of innovation, the pageant officials—many of whom had run the show since the 1930s and were defensively proud of their accomplishments—had become the greatest obstacle to further change.

Out of Fashion

Pageant director Lenora Slaughter's sense of fashion was the most visible manifestation of the problem: She fought nearly every new style in clothing, hair, shoes, and swimsuits that developed in the 1960s, and banned many of them outright, including miniskirts and bikinis. The "fashions" that were permitted were so out-of-date that many were nearly impossible to find in stores, as Miss New York 1969 recounted to Frank Deford in *There She Is:*

> We spent days shopping....There weren't many of the one-piece swimsuits around—I mean, you had no choice—and the shoes with the three-inch spiked heels, they were virtually impossible to find. The clothing styles had to reach within two inches of the knee, and they just weren't selling any dresses like that....All we could do was lengthen the dresses that we bought, but the problem was that we couldn't even find dresses long enough so that when we let them down they were long enough for the pageant.

By 1969 the pageant had gone from a fashion trendsetter to "nearly a complete laughingstock," Deford writes. Contestants

---

Dieter's delight: The average stamp, when licked, has 1/10th of a calorie.

quickly discovered that they were not buying a wardrobe for a pageant; they were buying one for a weeklong costume party."

WHITES ONLY

Like many American cultural institutions, the Miss America Pageant had a history of tokenism and outright racism that caught up with it during the Civil Rights movement. From the very first pageant, Native American and Puerto Rican contestants—when they were allowed to participate at all—had been shunted off to the sidelines in noncompetitive "official guest" roles. Blacks were excluded entirely, except for the 1926 pageant, when a handful of black women played slaves on the King Neptune float in the Fall Frolic.

This began to change in the mid-1950s, when the pageant quietly dropped its whites-only clause—Rule No. 7. But that only applied to the national pageant. Left to their own devices, many state pageants (at least unofficially) continued to discriminate.

A TURNING POINT

Finally in the late 1960s, the pageant began to tackle its problems. This change was partly due to the fact that Lenora Slaughter retired in 1967 after 32 years as Pageant Director, and partly to the fact that the pressures for change had become overwhelming:
• In 1967 civil rights groups threatened demonstrations to protest the fact that there were no black pageant organizers, judges, or contestants more than 10 years after the whites-only rule was abandoned. In response, the pageant agreed to institute reforms.
• A year later Pepsi, a pageant sponsor since 1957, pulled its sponsorship out of concern that the pageant had lost touch with teenagers and young adults. One Pepsi spokesman told reporters, "Miss America as run today does not represent the changing values of our society." (Pepsi's slogan at the time: "Now it's Pepsi for those who think young.")
• Beginning in 1967, the National Organization of Women (NOW) and other feminist groups organized protests at the pageant, charging that the pageant was demeaning to women, racist, and pro-war. Or as one protester put it:

Maine is the only U.S. state with a one-syllable name.

It has always been a lily-white racist contest. The winner tours Vietnam entertaining the troops as a murder mascot. Where else could one find such a perfect combination of American values? Racism, militarism, and capitalism—all packaged in one "ideal" symbol: a woman.

The 1968 protests were the most colorful. According to Anne Marie Bivans in *Miss America: In Pursuit of the Crown*, "the feminists…marched on the Boardwalk, where they refused to speak with male reporters, chanted anti-pageant slogans, and tossed bras, girdles, makeup, and hair curlers into a 'freedom trashcan.'" Rumors also circulated that a feminist had infiltrated the pageant and would reveal herself onstage as soon as she was out of the running for the crown, but no one ever did.

The protests generated huge publicity, but after 1969 most feminist organizations backed off, as Deford explains: "The women had received so much serious attention that, practically speaking, they did not need Miss America any more. For one thing, the were beginning to get the uncomfortable feeling that they were becoming part of the show, halfway between the parade and the evening gown competition."

And now, here it comes…the last section, on page 661.

*　　*　　*　　*

And Now for Something Completely Different: Ping Pong

• Lawn tennis has been popular with upper-crust Englishmen for centuries, but it can't be played in the rain. That's why someone invented "table tennis" in the 1890s.
• Because it was cheaper than regular tennis, it was also more accessible, and quickly became more popular than tennis had ever been. Parker Brothers brought it to the United States in 1902.
• Thanks to the Doppler effect, which changes the sound of an object as it travels toward or away from you, the sound a table tennis ball makes when it moves away from you is different from the sound it makes when it moves toward you. Because of this, early players nicknamed the game Wick-Wack, Click-Clack, Whiff-Whaff, and Flim-Flam, before finally settling on Ping-Pong.

Illegible handwriting is known as "griffonage."

THE FORTUNE COOKIE

Confucius says: "Good book in bathroom is worth ten on library shelf."

HISTORY
• "Legend has it," a TV reporter told CNN viewers recently, "that the first secret message was sent hundreds of years ago during the Tang Dynasty. A pastry chef was in love with the daughter of the Lotus Queen, and slipped her rice-paper love notes in baked wontons."
• It's a romantic idea—but fortune cookies are actually American, not Chinese. They were invented by George Jung, a Los Angeles noodlemaker, in 1916, who gave them to customers at his Hong Kong Noodle Company to distract them while they waited for their orders.

HOW THEY'RE MADE
• A mixture of rice flour and other ingredients is squirted onto small griddles and forms a little pancake. While it's still pliable, it's taken off the grill and folded around a paper fortune.
• Traditionally, it was folded by hand. But in 1967 Edward Louie, owner of the Lotus Fortune Cookie Co., invented a machine that automatically inserts the fortunes as the cookies are folded. The strips of paper are sucked in by a vacuum.

THE FORTUNES
• The first fortunes were sayings from Confucius, Ben Franklin, etc. But today they're upbeat messages. "Basically," says Edward Louie's son Gregory, "we're in the entertainment business. We give people what they want."
• Edward Louie was once asked the secret of his success. He answered: "Nobody can resist reading their fortune, no matter how corny it is."
• Louie's favorite fortunes were, "If you see someone without a smile, give them one of yours" and "Don't wait any longer, book that flight."
• Overall, the ten most popular fortunes are: 1. You will have

If a child ate as much, comparatively, as a growing bird, he'd eat 3 lambs and 1 calf each day.

great success; 2. You will soon be promoted; 3. You will step on the soil of many countries; 4. Your destiny is to be famous; 5. Your love life will be happy and harmonious; 6. Your present plans are going to succeed; 7. Good news will come to you from far away; 8. Now is the time to try something new; 9. Be confident and you will succeed; 10. You will be rich and respected.

A REAL FORTUNE COOKIE
• Some fortunes have lottery numbers on the other side. Believe it or not, some people have played those numbers and won.
• According to one account: "In March 1995, Barbara and Scott Turnbull got a fortune cookie at a China Coast restaurant in the Texas town of McAllen. They both bought tickets with the same numbers—and won $814,000 each. Meanwhile, Nealy LaHair got a fortune cookie with the same numbers from a China Coast restaurant in Dallas. She played the numbers and won $814,000 for herself."

BACK IN ASIA...
• In 1989 an entrepreneur in Hong Kong began importing fortune cookies and selling them as luxury items. They were offered as "Genuine American Fortune Cookies."
• On Dec. 27, 1992, the Brooklyn-based Wonton Foods signed a joint venture agreement with a company in mainland China to build a fortune cookie plant there. The cookies had never been sold there before! Chinese fortunes are less direct than American ones. So instead of predictions, they offer comments like "True gold fears no fire," "The only way to catch a tiger cub is to go into the tiger's den," and "Constant grinding can turn an iron rod into a needle."

THE UNFORTUNATE COOKIE
• In the 1970s, a company in New England called the Unfortunate Fortune Cookie Company offered "dismal forebodings...for misanthropes, masochists or what some might regard simply as realists."
• What happened to them? They went out of business.

Do you dream in color? According to one source, only 5% of Americans do.

GROUCHO GETS ELECTED—ACT II

Here's more from Five Star Theater, *the 1933 radio show starring Groucho as Waldorf Flywheel, and Chico as his sidekick, Ravelli.*

Outside. Milling crowd. Car noises.

GUARD: You guys can't come in this door. If you wanta hear the Flywheel-Maxwell political debate, you've got to go around to the main entrance.

REPORTER: But we're from the press. We want to talk to one of the candidates, Mr. Flywheel, about tomorrow's election.

GUARD: Okay, come on in. Waldorf Flywheel's in that room down the hall. First door to the right.

PHOTOGRAPHER: Thanks.

REPORTER: Funny how this man Flywheel has jumped into prominence so suddenly.

PHOTOGRAPHER: Well, when Big Boss Plunkett gets behind a candidate, he's as good as elected. Here's the room.

Knocks.

GROUCHO: Come in.

Door opens, closes.

PHOTOGRAPHER: Good evening, Mr.Flywheel, we're from the press.

GROUCHO: Good. You can press my pants.

REPORTER: No, we're from the newspaper. We want your views on tomorrow's election.

RAVELLI (runs in): Hey boss!

GROUCHO: What's the matter, Ravelli?

RAVELLI: There's some big crowd outside. When I tried to come in here, a policeman wanted to hit me.

GROUCHO: How do you know he wanted to hit you?

RAVELLI: Because he hit me. Whatta you gonna do about it, boss?

GROUCHO: I'm busy now, but I'll thank him later.

REPORTER: Mr. Flywheel, our paper would like to get a record of all that you've done in this town.

RAVELLI: Come on, don't bother my boss. You can get his record at the police station.

GROUCHO: Shut up, Ravelli. Reporter, I'd like to say that everything I am I owe to my great-grandfather, old Cyrus Tecumseh Flywheel. If he were alive today, the whole world would be talking about him.

REPORTER: Why, Mr. Flywheel?

GROUCHO: Well, if he were alive today, he'd be a hundred and forty years old.

REPORTER: But...

RAVELLI: Excuse me, please, Mrs. Reporter. I got-a something important to ask my boss. Hey, Flywheel, was that hair tonic you had in the bottle on your desk?

GROUCO: No, it was glue.

RAVELLI: Glue? (Laughs) No wonder I can't get my hat off! ...Hey, here comes Big Boss Plunkett. He looks-a mad.

PLUNKETT: Flywheel!

GROUCHO: Just a minute, old boy, I want you to meet the reporters. Reporters, this is my friend and manager, Big Boss Plunkett. There are two things I want to say about Plunkett. First, he's never been in prison. And second, I don't know why.

PLUNKETT: See here...

PHOTOGRAPHER: Sorry to interrupt, but we've got to get back to the paper. And we'd like a photograph of Mr. Flywheel. Hold that smile, Mr. Flywheel. Here goes...Thank you! Goodbye!

Door shuts...followed by a knock.

PLUNKETT: Come in.

GUARD: Time for the debate.

PLUNETT: Come on, boys... right through this door. This is a shortcut to the platform. Remember, Ravelli, I had a tough time getting you the job as chairman of this debate. Do you know anything about a debate?

RAVELLI: Ah-h, sure! I explain it to you. When you wanta catch de fish, you use-a debate.

GROUCHO: There you are, Plunkett. You'd have to go pretty far to find a better chairman than Ravelli. And I wish you had!

PLUNKETT: Come on!— right through this door.

Door opens, crowd is cheering, "We want Flywheel," "Hooray for Maxwell," etc.

ANNOUNCER: Ladies and gentlemen. The debate on judicial reform between Judge Herbert Maxwell and Waldorf Tecumseh Flywheel is about to begin. I now present the chairman of the meeting, Mr. Emmanuel Ravelli.

(Applause.)

RAVELLI: (in formal speaking voice): Alright, everybody...The foist guy I want to introduce is a man everybody is-a crazy about. A man who's good to little kids— and to big kids too...And he ain't afraid of nothin'! Ladies and gentlemen, that man is...me!

(Crowd claps loudly.)

Now I gonna call on Judge Maxwell.

JUDGE: Mr. Chairman, ladies and gentlemen. I was born in this city forty-eight years ago. I studied law here. I married here. And in all my forty-eight years, I...

GROUCHO: Just a minute, chairman.

RAVELLI: What you want, boss?

GROUCHO: If this guy's gonna talk only about himself, I'm going home.

JUDGE: Please, Mr. Flywheel, you'll get your chance later. Ladies and gentlemen, my candidacy is being fought by a group of men who are dishonest, grafting and meretricious!

RAVELLI: Tanks, judge. I wish you da same.

JUDGE: Wish me what?

RAVELLI: A meretricious. A meretricious and a Happy New Year!

JUDGE (furious): Mr. Chairman, will you let me go on with my speech? Fellow citizens, I...

RAVELLI (pounds gavel): At's-a all, Judge. Your time is up.

JUDGE: My time is up? Why, how long have I talked?

RAVELLI: I don't know. I haven't got a watch. You sit down. And now, people, you're gonna hear from my boss, Mister Flywheel, the winner of this debate.

GROUCHO: Well, folks, I'm sorry my speech had to be delayed, but Maxwell insisted on talking. (Formal voice) Fellow citizens, I'm here to tell you that a vote for Flywheel means a vote for free speech, free press, free-wheeling and free cheers for the red, white and blue. (*Crowd claps.*)

My esteemed opponent...is all steamed up. And why? Because I broke a few promises. Well, I can make new ones just as good. And to you women in the audience, I can only say that there's one thing I'll never forget, as long as I can remember it... and that is, that the mothers of some of our greatest men were women.(Crowd claps.)

JUDGE: Flywheel, I'd like to ask a question. Is it true your organization has bought 20,000 votes to swing tomorrow's election?

GROUCHO: I'm glad you brought that up. We did buy 20,000 votes.

JUDGE: What?

GROUCHO: But don't get excited. I've got good news.

JUDGE: Good news?

GROUCHO: Yes, we bought five thousand more votes than we need, and we'll sell 'em to you at cost price.

Who's the new judge? For election results, turn to page 658.

"Gilligan's Island" was inspired by Daniel Defoe's *Robinson Crusoe*.

CELEBRITY TAX TROUBLES

It's not easy being famous, particularly if you haven't been paying your taxes properly. Here's a look at some rich and famous people who have fallen to earth with a thud, courtesy of the IRS.

WILLIE NELSON

Tax Troubles: In 1990, the IRS slapped the country singer with a bill for $32 million in delinquent taxes, penalties, and interest—one of the biggest in history—after it disallowed his heavy tax shelter investments. Nelson blamed his Price Waterhouse accountant, saying that their bad advice caused the underpayments.

What Happened: Nelson's lawyers argued that since the accountants were to blame for his troubles, he should only be required to pay the original taxes owed. The IRS ultimately agreed to charge Nelson only $9 million, and gave him three years to pay it. He raised the money by auctioning off property, signing over the rights to an album called *Who'll Buy My Memories: The IRS Tapes*, handing over the proceeds from his lawsuit with Price Waterhouse, and accepting donations from fans. "Willie is happy to be done with it," his lawyer told reporters after the last payment was made. "He has a very good relationship with the IRS now."

PRESIDENT BILL CLINTON

Tax Troubles: In December 1993, the *Washington Post* revealed that then-Governor Clinton had donated his underwear to the Salvation Army and claimed the donations as charitable deductions on his income taxes. The deductions included $1 apiece for under-shorts donated in '84, $2 apiece for 3 pairs of underwear donated in '86, and $15 for a single pair of long underwear donated in '88.

What Happened: Making deductions for underwear donated to charity is perfectly legal, provided you don't claim more than the "fair market value" of the garments. That's where Clinton ran into trouble: he claimed too large a deduction on his knickers. The actual fair market value of underwear for tax purposes is 5¢-6¢ a *pound*, even for skivvies worn by governors. (No word on whether he ever made good on the overstated deductions.)

LEONA HELMSLEY

Tax Troubles: A few years after telling an employee that "only the little people pay taxes," the hotel queen was indicted on charges that she and her husband, hotel magnate Harry Helmsley, evaded $1.2 million in income taxes by billing their business for "personal items ranging from a marble dance floor to girdles."

What Happened: Harry was eventually deemed too incompetent to stand trial because of failing health, but Leona was convicted of tax evasion in December 1989, fined $7.1 million, and sentenced to four years in federal prison. She was paroled in October 1993 and began three years of probation, which included 250 hours of community service per year.

In 1995, Helmsley's employees complained to reporters that they were the ones performing community service. Helmsley, they said, forced them to do the court-assigned work—wrapping gifts and stuffing envelopes for charity. "We sat around our staff dining table like field hands shucking peas," one anonymous employee complained, "but instead of shucking, we were wrapping presents in between our regular duties." The judge tacked an additional 150 hours of community service on to Helmsley's sentence.

JOE LOUIS, "THE BROWN BOMBER"

Tax Troubles: Louis was heavyweight boxing champ from 1937 to 1949, a national hero who held the title longer than any boxer in history. Like many of us, he didn't fill out his own tax forms. His manager did…and he underpaid Louis's taxes so much that by the time the champ retired in 1949, he owed more than $1.25 million. Louis was forced to come out of retirement in 1950 and try to box his way out of his IRS troubles.

What Happened: Louis fought 10 times over the next year, but never recaptured his title and never made enough money to pay off the IRS. The agency filed liens against all of his assets, and even seized the $667 he inherited from his mother when she died. But it didn't come close to paying what he owed; he had to stoop to pro-wrestling to pay the bill. This helped him settle the tax issue, although not in the way he'd expected. As *Sports Illustrated* recounted in 1985:

Sympathy for him grew as the public came to believe that the

Franklin Roosevelt referred to World War II as "the War for

IRS had hounded the former heavyweight champion into a degrading career in wrestling. After considerable frustration, the IRS agreed in the early 1960s to limit its collections to an amount [that] did not even cover the interest on his debt.

The IRS never officially closed the books on the case, it just stopped trying to collect. As the commissioner of the IRS explained it, "We have gotten all we could possibly get from Mr. Louis, leaving him with some hope that he can live." Nearly bankrupt, Louis spent much of the 1970s working as a "greeter" at Caesar's Palace in Las Vegas. He died in 1981.

MARVIN MITCHELSON

Tax Troubles: When Mitchelson, divorce attorney to the stars and Hollywood's "Prince of Palimony," dumped a client-turned-lover, she got revenge by contacting the IRS. In 1993, he was formally indicted for filing false returns between 1983 and 1986, during which he allegedly hid more than $2 million in income.

What Happened: Mitchelson filed for bankruptcy and was convicted on charges of tax fraud, for which he was sentenced to 30 months in prison and ordered to pay more than $2 million in back taxes. "This is the second-saddest day of my life," he told the judge on the day of sentencing. "My mother's death was the first."

JERRY LEE LEWIS

Tax Troubles: The IRS nailed the '50s rock star for non-payment of back taxes in the late '70s. They seized real estate, vehicles, and other assets, but his tax bill continued to grow. By 1994, the amount due had grown to $4.1 million.

What Happened: Lewis worked out a deal to pay only $560,000, less than 15¢ on the dollar. His secret: He didn't have any money.

Lewis raised the cash through a concert tour, a record, a biography, and by temporarily opening his home in Nesbit, Mississippi, to tourists. The tours were conducted by friends or Lewis's wife and included visits to the living rooms, den, and piano-shaped swimming pool in back—but not the bedrooms. Price of admission: $5, not bad considering that every once in a while the tour offered something Graceland didn't—a live rock star. "At least once a week," Mrs. Lewis explained, "Jerry Lee forgets they're there and walks out in his robe or wearing jeans and a T-shirt."

UNCLE ALBERT SEZ...

Albert Einstein had a few things to say that even we bathroom readers can understand. Like these....

"If a cluttered desk is a sign of a cluttered mind, of what, then, is an empty desk?"

"Only two things are infinite, the universe and human stupidity, and I'm not sure about the former."

"Sometimes one pays most for things one gets for nothing."

"Problems cannot be solved at the same level of awareness that created them."

"To make a goal of comfort or happiness has never appealed to me; a system of ethics built on this basis would be sufficient only for a herd of cattle."

"Education is what remains after one has forgotten everything he learned in school."

"When the solution is simple, God is answering."

"What does a fish know about the water in which he swims all his life?"

"Knowledge is limited. Imagination encircles the world."

"Common sense is the collection of prejudices acquired by age eighteen."

"My religion consists of the humble admiration of the illimitablesuperior spirit who reveals himself in the slight details we are able to perceive with our frail and feeble minds."

"Peace cannot be achieved through violence, it can only be attained through understanding."

"Gravitation cannot be held responsible for two people falling in love."

"He who joyfully marches to music in rank and file has already earned my contempt. He has been given a large brain by mistake, since for him, the spinal cord would fully suffice."

"The answer is 'yes' or 'no,' depending on the interpretation."

"Nothing will benefit human health and increase the chances for the survival of life on Earth as much as the evolution to a vegetarian diet."

Believe it or not: If a man's tie is too tight, his vision gets worse.

"LIFE" AFTER DEATH

Here's an interesting question: If you make it big after you're dead, is it really you who's succeeding? After all, you—at least theoretically—don't exist anymore. Woody Allen, reflecting on this, said: "I don't want to achieve immortality through my work...I want to achieve it through not dying." Our sentiments exactly. Here are 4 examples of folks who hit it big after death. Enjoy it...while you can.

JONATHAN LARSON

In 1992, Larson wrote a musical about New York artists struggling with AIDS. He sent the script and songs to the New York Theater Workshop. The artistic director was so impressed that he spent the next four years helping Larson develop the work, called *Rent*, for the stage. It was finally scheduled to open on January 26, 1996, and would have been the biggest moment of Larson's life. But he couldn't make it—he was found dead in his apartment on January 25, a few hours after the final dress rehearsal. Cause of death: an aortic aneurysm. He was 35.

Life After Death: The show opened to rave reviews and quickly became the hottest theater ticket in town; within weeks, the New York press was printing lists of celebrities—including Woody Allen—who wanted tickets but couldn't get them. *Rent* later moved to Broadway and won the 1996 Pulitzer Prize for drama.

JOHN KENNEDY TOOLE

During the 1950s, while he was in the army, Toole wrote a novel called *A Confederacy of Dunces*. For years he tried to get it published. Finally, in 1967, Simon and Schuster expressed some interest; he was ecstatic. Unfortunately, in 1969—after Toole had spent two years on rewrites—the publisher rejected it. Toole, 31, didn't wait to see what happened next. He committed suicide.

Life After Death: Toole's mother found the manuscript among his belongings and spent the next seven years trying to get it published. In 1976, she convinced novelist Walker Percy to read it...and he convinced Louisiana State University to print 2,500 copies. An inauspicious beginning, but the novel got glowing reviews, and a major publisher picked it up. It went on to sell more than 650,000 copies and win the 1981 Pulitzer Prize for fiction.

OTIS REDDING

One of pop's great singers, Redding had never had a Top 10 hit, and he was determined to break into the mainstream market. So in 1967 he went to the Monterey Pop Festival and triumphantly performed with people like Janis Joplin and Jimi Hendrix. Afterward, Redding spent a week on a houseboat outside of San Francisco, "just wastin' time." He dreamed up a little pop tune called "Dock of the Bay," brought it back to Memphis, and put it on tape, planning to get back to it when he returned from a tour. Three days later, he died in a plane crash.

Life After Death: Redding's co-writer, guitarist Steve Cropper, went back into the studio and finished the record. It became the first posthumous #1 record in history.

HANK WILLIAMS

In 1952, a singer named Big Bill Lister got his first contract with a major record company. He knew country star Hank Williams, and asked if Williams had any songs he could use. To help Lister out, Hank gave him "There's a Tear in My Beer," a song he'd just written and recorded on a single acetate demo record. Lister included the tune on his album. A few months later, the 29-year-old Williams died from alcohol poisoning.

Life After Death: Lister lost track of Williams's acetate recording until 1988, when he found it while cleaning out his house. He sent it to Hank Williams, Jr. The younger Williams, now a country star in his own right, had been only three years old when his father died, so he'd never had the chance to record with him…until now. He took "There's a Tear in My Beer" into the studio, cleaned it up, and created a duet by mixing his own vocals with his father's.

Hank Jr. even made a video of "There's a Tear in My Beer." He took a film of his father singing a different song and superimposed someone else's lips onto the face. Both the song and the video became huge bestsellers, even winning the Country Music Association's Vocal Event of the Year award.

Note: Since then, other "direct from the grave" duets have been hits. Natalie Cole even won a Grammy singing with her dead father, Nat "King" Cole.

The song "You're a Grand Old Flag" was originally called "You're a Grand Old Rag."

WEIRD DOLLS

Here are a few more unusual dolls that you could have bought at your local toy store…but probably didn't.

EARRING MAGIC KEN

In 1993, Mattel decided to give Barbie's boyfriend a new look: it introduced "Earring Magic Ken" to its line of Ken dolls, complete with two-tone hair, a pink mesh shirt, a lavender "leather" vest, a plastic ring around his neck, and a single earring in one ear. "Ken's still a clean-cut guy," a Mattel spokesman explained to reporters. "He's just a little more contemporary."

Yeah, sure. "You can't look at Earring Magic Ken and not think gay," Chicago gay rights advocate Rick Garcia told reporters. "He's stereotypically gay—it's what you saw men wearing a few years back. And that plastic ring that Ken wears around his neck looks an awful lot like what gay men were buying at sex shops."

Retailers agreed. "We sold out in less than a month and we had to reorder them," one toy salesperson told reporters. "And it's primarily gay men who are buying them. Most customers just ask specifically for 'The Gay Ken Doll.'"

Mattel was shocked. "We gave him an earring and two-tone hair to make him look cool and hip," protested one company official, "and lavender clothing because it's a girl's second favorite color after pink."

THE J. J. ARMES DOLL

Ideal Toys had a big success with its Evel Knievel line of toys in the mid-1970s, so in 1976, they based another toy on a real-life human being—Jay J. Armes, a multimillionaire Texas private eye.

The real Armes was the James Bond of El Paso, complete with a karate blackbelt, a bomb-detecting Cadillac, a smoke-screen-spewing Corvette, and a walled-in estate that he patrolled himself with a 750-pound Siberian tiger on a leash. He'd built one of the most successful detective agencies in the country, commanding fees as high as $250,000 per assignment from clients like Elvis Presley, J. Paul Getty, and Marlon Brando.

Perhaps even more interesting to the folks at Ideal was the fact that the real Armes had no hands—he had lost both of them at the age of 11 playing with dynamite blasting caps in his backyard and had worn prosthetics ever since. Most of the time he wore steel hooks, but he also had custom-made prosthetic guns that shot real bullets. Ideal figured that Armes would make a perfect action figure, and sold the J. J. Armes doll with a large suitcase full of interchangeable prosthetic machetes, magnets, suction cups, and other gadgets.

It was a flop. Ideal speculates that the doll bombed for a number of reasons: (1) kids had never heard of Armes; (2) the adventures of a real-life detective can actually be pretty boring; and (3) a lot of youngsters were spooked by the idea of pretending to be a man with hooks for hands. "Kids would find it very difficult to role-play a man with two artificial arms," one (former) Ideal executive admitted afterwards. "I don't even think you'd want to. I would be kind of squeamish about it myself."

THE PET CONGRESSMAN

Described in press reports as a "fuzzy little bow-tied lawmaker doll," it was introduced in 1992 by a Maryland businessman after he noted the similarities between his pet dog and his representatives in government. "I realized congressmen are like pets," he told interviewers. "They wet the rug, and you get mad at them. But you still elect them and keep them."

The dolls were packaged in a "dome-shaped wire cage" designed to resemble the U.S. Capitol and came with a 15-page owner's manual that explained that the pint-sized politico "expects to be entertained frequently by his owner, but will rarely offer to pick up the tab." Not surprisingly, former President Ronald Reagan bought one for his Los Angeles office. But not everyone thought the dolls were funny. One chain store refused to carry them because they were "an inappropriate way to recognize a congressman."

MARYBEL GET WELL

The hypochondriac doll from Madame Alexander came with crutches, a cast for her leg, bandages, pills, quarantine signs, and measles spots.

---

2 years before he made his first flight, Wilbur Wright told friends, "man won't fly for 50 years."

COURT TRANSQUIPS

We never imagined that court transcripts would make good bathroom read-
ing. But that was before we read Humor in the Court *and* More Humor
in the Court, by Mary Louise Gilman, editor of the National Short-
hand Reporter. *Here are a few excerpts from these two funny volumes of*
"courtroom bloopers." Remember—these are actual courtroom transcripts.

THE COURT: "Now, as we begin, I must ask you to banish all
present information and prejudice from your minds, if you have
any."

Q: "What is your brother-in-law's name?"
A: "Borofkin."
Q: "What's his first name?"
A: "I can't remember."
Q: "He's been your brother-in-law for years, and you can't remem-
ber his first name?"
A: "No. I tell you I'm too excited."
    [Rising from the witness chair and pointing to Mr. Borofkin.]
    "Nathan, for God's sake, tell them your first name!"

Q: "Did you ever stay all night with this man in New York?"
A: "I refuse to answer that question."
Q: "Did you ever stay all night with this man in Chicago?"
A: "I refuse to answer that question."
Q: "Did you ever stay all night with this man in Miami?"
A: "No."

Q: "What is your name?"
A: "Ernestine McDowell."
Q: "And what is your marital status?"
A: "Fair."

Q: "Doctor, how many autopsies have you performed on dead
people?"
A: "All my autopsies have been performed on dead people."

Q: "Are you married?"
A: "No, I'm divorced."
Q: "And what did your husband do before you divorced him?"
A: "A lot of things I didn't know about."

Q: "How did you happen to go to Dr. Cherney?"
A: "Well, a gal down the road had had several of her children by Dr. Cherney, and said he was really good."

Q: "Do you know how far pregnant you are right now?"
A: "I will be three months November 8th."
Q: "Apparently then, the date of conception was August 8th?"
A: "Yes."
Q: "What were you and your husband doing at that time?"

Q: "Doctor, did you say he was shot in the woods?"
A: "No, I said he was shot in the lumbar region."

Q: "Mrs. Smith, do you believe that you are emotionally unstable?"
A: "I should be."
Q: "How many times have you committed suicide?"
A: "Four times."
Q: "Were you acquainted with the deceased?"
A: "Yes, sir."
Q: "Before or after he died?"

Q: "What happened then?"
A: "He told me, he says, 'I have to kill you because you can identify me.'"
Q: "Did he kill you?"
A: "No."

Q: "Mrs. Jones, is your appearance this morning pursuant to a deposition notice which I sent to your attorney?"
A: "No. This is how I dress when I go to work."

On just one square inch of your skin, there are 20 million microscopic animals.

JESSE'S BIG NUMBERS

Uncle John's six-year-old son, Jesse, has been asking questions about numbers lately, like "What comes after a trillion?" and "What's a billion billion?" We'd never thought much about that before, but it's pretty interesting. Here's a page that Jesse will enjoy.

HOW MUCH IS A BILLION?

Depends on where you are. In the United States, 1,000 is used as a multiplier for big numbers: a million is 1,000 thousands; a billion is 1,000 millions; a trillion is 1,000 billions, and so on.

But in many other places (Britain, Spain and Latin America, for example), they use 1,000,000 (one million) as the multiplier. A million is still 1,000 thousands. But a billion is one million millions; a trillion is one million billion, and so on. Big difference.

WHAT COMES AFTER A TRILLION?

Uncle John's standard answer: a trillion and one. But there's a whole universe of numbers that most of us have never heard of which follow a million, a billion, and a trillion. Here are some, in U.S. numerical terms:

Quadrillion: 1,000 trillion   **Tredecillion:** 1,000 duodecillion
Quintillion: 1,000 quadrillion   **Quattuordecillion:** 1,000 tredecillion
Sextillion: 1,000 quintillion   **Quindecillion:** 1,000 quattuordecillion
Septillion: 1,000 sextillion   **Sexdecillion:** 1,000 quindecillion
Octillion: 1,000 septillion   **Septendecillion:** 1,000 sexdecillion
Nonillian: 1,000 octillion   **Octodecillion:** 1,000 septendecillion
Decillion: 1,000 nonillion   **Novemdecillion:** 1,000 octodecillion
Undecillion: 1,000 decillion   **Vigintillion:** 1,000 novemdecillion
Duodecillion: 1,000 undecillion

• How do these numbers look on paper? To give you a sense of scale:

Trillion: 1,000,000,000,000

Quadrillion: 1,000,000,000,000,000

Septillion: 1,000,000,000,000,000,000,000,000

Quattuordecillion:
1,000,000,000,000,000,000,000,000,000,000,000,000,000,000,000

The word "furniture" originally applied to portable military equipment.

WHAT'S THE BIGGEST NUMBER?

Theoretically, you could probably keep going forever. But practically speaking:

• According to *The Mathematics Calendar 1996*, by Theoni Pappas, the "illions" haven't really been used beyond vigintillion. Why? "Perhaps," suggests one mathematician, "most everyday phenomena can be covered by these huge numbers."

• Nonetheless, books list some bigger numbers. Among the "illions," for example, is the number *centillion*—1,000, followed by 300 zeroes, or:

1,000,000,000,000,000,000,000,000,000,000,000,000,0
00,000,000,000,000,000,000,000,000,000,000,000,000,
000,000,000,000,000,000,000,000,000,000,000,000,000
,000,000,000,000,000,000,000,000,000,000,000,000,00
0,000,000,000,000,000,000,000,000,000,000,000,000,0
00,000,000,000,000,000,000,000,000,000,000,000,000,
000,000,000,000,000,000,000,000,000,000,000,000

• To deal with the "biggest number" question, one mathematician created a sort of catch-all number that has come into general use—the *googolplex*. By his reasoning, a googol is a one followed by 100 zeroes. And a googolplex is a one followed by a googol of zeroes. Presumably, we don't need any number larger than that.

HOW MUCH IS A ZILLION?

As one mathematician writes: "A zillion falls into the same category as a few, some, a lot, many. A zillion is deceiving since it ends in -illion, but it is no more specific than saying 'a tremendous amount.'"

WHERE DOES INFINITY FIT IN?

When exact numbers aren't big enough, there's always infinity, defined as "a concept of limitlessness." Or, practically speaking, a number too big for our minds to grasp or our language to describe.

When Uncle John was a kid, his sister asked: "What's bigger than infinity?" This stumped Uncle John. The answer was "infinity, +1." That sounded pretty clever, and Uncle John repeated it for years. But the truth is that since infinity goes on forever, you can't stop it at a single digit. Infinity +1 still equals infinity.

According to the Bible, there were two windows on Noah's Ark.

THE MONSTER LIVES!

*When Universal Pictures coined the term "horror movie" in
1931, it was because of this film...and Boris Karloff, the actor
who brought the monster to life. As one critic puts it: "Just as the
monster of the story was stitched together from pieces of the dead,
Universal's cinematic Monster was stitched together from the
genius of Jack Pierce's makeup, James Whale's direction, and
Boris Karloff's performance. The results were so perfect that the
image of the Frankenstein monster, as seen in this classic film, has
become ingrained into the fabric of our culture."*

LUCKY BREAK

Have you ever heard of William Henry Pratt? Most people
haven't. In late 1920s he was an unemployed actor, making
ends meet by driving a truck for a lumber yard. In 1931, he landed
a small part playing a gangster in a movie called *The Criminal
Code*. It happened to premiere just as director James Whale began
his search for someone to play the monster in *Frankenstein*.

A friend of Whale's saw the film, noticed Pratt, and suggested
that the director take a look at him. So Whale went to see *The
Criminal Code*. He was impressed with Pratt's work...but more
important, he recognized that Pratt's gaunt features, exaggerated
with lots of makeup, would make an excellent monster-face.

Whale drew some preliminary sketches of Pratt as the
monster and showed them to Jack Pierce, head of Universal's
makeup department. Then he approached Pratt about playing the
part. Years later, Pratt recalled how he learned about the role:

> I'd spent 10 years in Hollywood without causing the slightest
> stir. Then one day I was sitting in the commissary at Universal,
> having lunch, and looking rather well turned out, I thought,
> when a man sent a note over to my table, asking if I'd like to
> audition for the part of a monster.

THE NAME GAME

Pratt took a screen test and got the job on the spot. But he didn't
get public *acknowledgment* for the role until much later. He wasn't
considered an important member of the cast, so the studio didn't

---

What do pediatricians do when their kids get colds? 63% say they "let them run their course."

even bother to list his name in the credits. Only a question mark appears next to the words "The Monster"

Within a year, however, Pratt's name would become a household word....Or at least his *stage* name would: Universal Pictures thought that "William Henry Pratt" sounded too ordinary for such an exotic monster and asked him to change it to something a little more unusual. Pratt picked a name that would be synonymous with horror for over 35 years—*Boris Karloff*.

MAKEUP

Universal put Jack Pierce, head of the studio's makeup department, in charge of creating Karloff's makeup. He prepared for the job by studying anatomy, surgery, electrodynamics, and criminology. It was this research that led to the monster's unusual flat-topped skull, as Pierce later related to The *New York Times:*

> My anatomical studies taught me that there are six ways a surgeon can cut the skull in order to take out or put in a brain. I figured that Frankenstein, who was a scientist but no practicing surgeon, would take the simplest surgical way. He would cut the top of the skull off straight across like a pot-lid, hinge it, pop the brain in, and then clamp it on tight. That is the reason I decided to make the Monster's head square and flat like a shoe box and dig that big scar across his forehead with the metal clamps holding it together.

Pierce also added a caveman-like protruding brow to suggest de-evolution, and Karoly Grosz, a Universal poster illustrator, came up with the idea of putting steel bolts in the monster's neck.

FACE FACTS

Karloff had several false teeth on the right side of his mouth; these were removed to give his already gaunt face an even more hollow appearance. This look was further accentuated when Karloff himself suggested to Pierce that his eyelids be heavily puttied with embalmers' wax, which gave the monster a sense of pathos.

The rest of the facial makeup was applied to accent rather than cover up Karloff's natural features, so that his face would retain its expressiveness. "We were all fascinated by the development of Karloff's face and head," Mae Clarke later recalled.

Mark your calendar: Mother-in-Law Day was 1st celebrated on Mar. 5, 1934, in Amarillo, TX.

"White putty on the face was toned down to a corpse-like gray. Then there was a sudden inspiration to give the face a green tint. It awed us and gave Boris and the rest of us a different feeling about the whole concept." The movie was filmed entirely in black and white (that's all there was back then) but in some prints of the film, Universal had Karloff's face tinted green by hand before they were distributed to theaters.

BODY LANGUAGE

"Karloff's face fascinated me," James Whale would recall years later. "His physique was weaker than I could wish, but that queer, penetrating personality of his, I felt, was more important than his shape, which could be easily altered." And alter it they did:
• Karloff's frame was stiffened by a five-pound spinal brace that ran up his back and steel struts in his legs.
• He also wore platform asphalt spreader's boots, which weighed twelve and a half pounds apiece.
• On top of the braces, Karloff wore padding and on top of that a thick, double-quilted suit that added tremendous bulk to his frame; its sleeves were cut short to make his arms appear longer than they really were. All in all, the braces, struts, boots, and costume weighed more than forty-eight pounds.

TEST RUN

Even after Karloff was fully made up, he wasn't sure whether the makeup was truly scary or not—would it frighten people, or just make them laugh? As he recounted years later,

> I was thinking this while practicing my walk, as I rounded a bend in the corridor and came face-to-face with this prop man. He was the first man to see the monster—I watched to study his reaction. It was quick to come. He turned white—gurgled and lunged out of sight down the corridor. Never saw him again. Poor chap, I would have liked to thank him—he was the audience that first made me feel like the monster.

IN THE THEATER

When Universal previewed *Frankenstein* before test audiences in Santa Monica, they noticed two important things:

One ounce of gold can be beaten thin enough to cover an entire acre of ground.

1. It was Karloff's monster, not the other characters, who made the film work. This was real horror for panicked Universal execs. They'd considered Karloff unimportant and neglected to put him under contract. They quickly called his agent and signed him up. Karloff's response: "After more than 20 years of acting, for once I'll know where my next breakfast is coming from."

2. The film made people fidgety and squeamish. Rather than downplay the response, the studio decided to publicize it. They added a prologue, warning filmgoers what they were in for. Edward Van Sloan, who played Dr. Frankenstein's mentor, Dr. Waldman, told audiences:

> Mr. Carl Laemmle [head of Universal] feels it would be a little unkind to present this picture without a word of friendly warning….[Frankenstein] is one of the strangest stories ever told….It will thrill you,…It may shock you. It might even—horrify you! So, then, if you feel that you do not care to subject your nerves to such a strain, now is your chance to—well, we've warned you!

Theaters around the country added to the hype by posting nurses in the lobby, making free "nerve tonic" available to those who needed it, and other gimmicks. One movie house in Texas even hired a woman to sit in the empty theater and watch the film alone. But the publicity wasn't necessary—*Frankenstein* was one of the biggest hits of 1931 and went on to become one of the all-time classic Hollywood films. To this day, Boris Karloff's sensitive portrayal of the monster is the performance by which all other monster movies are measured.

GONE TO PIECES

By the late 1930s, it seemed like a *Frankenstein* might finally be dying. Boris Karloff, who'd played the monster in *Frankenstein* (1931), *Bride of Frankenstein* (1935), and *Son of Frankenstein* (1939), hammered the first nail in the creature's coffin when he announced that he'd grown weary of the role. As David Skal writes in *The Monster Show*, Karloff "suspected that the monster would be increasingly relegated to the role of prop or buffoon" and didn't want to be part of it.

It didn't take long for Karloff's prediction to come true. With each new film Universal released—*Frankenstein Meets the Wolf Man* (1943), *The House of Frankenstein* (1944), and *The House of Dracula* (1945), the monster became less frightening. The studio finished the job in 1948, when it ended its Frankenstein series with *Abbott and Costello Meet Frankenstein*. Karloff agreed to help promote that film…as long as he didn't have to watch it.

KID STUFF

But even as familiarity worked against Frankenstein films, demographics were working in their favor. Thanks to the post-World War II baby boom, younger viewers were making up an increasingly large share of the movie audience. By 1958, 72% of all moviegoers were between the ages of 12 and 25.

Hollywood started making movies especially for teenagers—and they quickly found out that teenagers loved horror films. Sticking a monster, vampire, or werewolf into a film became an easy way to increase ticket sales.

Low-budget studios like American International Pictures (*I Was a Teenage Werewolf*) couldn't use Karloff's familiar monster because Universal Studios owned a copyright on *that* Frankenstein "look." But they could use the *name* Frankenstein because it was in the public domain (which means no one owns it).

And they did use it—hundreds of times. "Frankenstein" became a generic term for any manmade monster. He showed up in theaters as an alien, a sex fiend, a "demon of the atomic age," a resurrected teenage auto wreck victim, and so on; 65 years later the Frankenstein movies keep on coming. As *The Videohound's Complete Guide to Trash Pics and Cult Flicks* says:

> Frankenstein lives in the movies better than anywhere else. With dozens of films based directly on characters from the novel, not to mention the hundreds with at least a tenuous connection to it, it may be the single most adapted work in all of cinema. No other name draws audiences so well.

Boris Karloff, the man who made *Frankenstein*—and horror films—a part of our culture, died in 1969. But he's been granted a weird kind of immortality. Every time a mad scientist builds a monster onscreen, it's an homage to Karloff's genius.

Ethiopia and Somalia switched Cold War sides in the 1970s.

FRANKENSTEIN MEETS THE SPACE MONSTER

Some of these Frankenstein films are pretty watchable. Others are so bad, only a dedicated fan could even consider sitting through them. These are real movies—we didn't make them up!

1. Frankenstein Meets the Space Monster (1965)
NASA builds a robot named Frank and sends it into space, where it meets a space monster and goes berserk.

2. Assignment Terror (1971)
An alien lands on Earth, brings Frankenstein, Dracula, the Mummy, and other monsters to life, "but is thwarted by the socially aware Wolf Man."

3. Jesse James Meets Frankenstein's Daughter (1965)
Frankenstein's granddaughter, Maria, tries to capture Jesse James and his sidekick to turn them into monsters.

4. I Was a Teenage Frankenstein (1957)
A descendant of Dr. Frankenstein moves to America, where he sets up a lab and begins building monsters out of the bodies of hot rod racers killed in car accidents.

5. Frankenhooker (1980)
After a woman dies in a freak lawnmower accident, her mad-scientist boyfriend brings her back to life by sewing her head onto body parts taken from prostitutes on New York's 42nd Street.

6. Frankenstein General Hospital (1988)
Frankenstein's 12th grandson tries his experiments in the basement of a modern hospital.

7. Frankenstein Conquers the World (1964)
"A boy eats the radioactive heart of the Frankenstein monster and begins to grow into an ugly giant that watches Japanese teenagers do the Twist" (*The Frankenstein Movie Guide*). Japanese title: *Frankenstein vs. the Giant Crab Monster*.

Elephants can run 20 miles per hour; hummingbirds can fly 60 miles per hour.

8. *Frankenstein Campus* (1970)
A college student plots to turn his fellow-students into monsters. "If you can sit through this tripe, go to the head of the class." (*Creature Features Movie Guide*)

9. *Frankenstein Island* (1981)
"A group of balloonists crash on a mysterious island populated by bikini-clad warrior-women descended from aliens....Frankenstein's great-great granddaughter Sheila, is around...experimenting on captives." (*Frankenstein Movie Guide*)

10. *Frankenstein Created Woman* (1966)
"Male spirit is transplanted into the body of a beautiful woman with a heaving bosom, who then goes around stabbing respectable folks with a knife." (*Creature Features Movie Guide*)

11. *Frankenstein 1970* (1958)
A descendant of Dr. Frankenstein sells the TV rights to his famous ancestor's story and uses the money to build an atomic-powered Frankenstein monster. The studio thought a futuristic-sounding title would help at the box office.

12. *Frankenstein's Daughter* (1958)
Frankenstein's grandson tests a drug called degeneral on a teenage girl, and it "degenerates her into a bikini-clad creature running through the streets."

13. *Frankenstein '80* (1979)
Dr. Otto Frankenstein puts together a sex-crazed monster who goes on a killing spree. Lots of blood, including real surgical footage.

14. *Frankenstein's Castle of Freaks* (1973)
Using his "Electric Accumulator," Count Frankenstein brings back Goliath the caveman, Kreegin the Hunchback, and Ook the Neanderthal Man! South Pacific star Rossano Brazzi—"sounding like a cross between Chico Marx and Bela Lugosi"—plays the Count.

15. *Frankenstein's Great-Aunt Tillie* (1983)
Victor Jr. and his 109-year-old aunt "search for the family fortune and become involved with women's emancipation." (*The Frankenstein Movie Guide*)

Long wait: The "longest recorded interval" between the birth of twins was 136 days.

THE WORLD'S MOST FAMOUS CORPSE

More people have seen Lenin's mummy than any other mummy in history. It's a tourist attraction, a cultural artifact, and as you'll see, a political gimmick. How did this weird monument—denounced by Lenin's official historian as an "absurd idea"—come into being? Here's the full story.

Lenin's tomb in Moscow's Red Square is the best-known landmark in the Soviet Union, as well as the spiritual center of Soviet political ideology. Some 150 millionpeople have visited the mausoleum since it was first built....There are always long lines, but you should expect to be descending the gloomy stairs into the tomb within 20-30 minutes. Without stopping, you walk around three sides of the glass case in which Lenin lies, stubbly and ashen-faced, wearing a jacket and polka-dot tie.
                    —***Travel Guide to the Soviet Union***

DEATH OF A LEADER
At 6:50 p.m. on January 21, 1924, Vladimir Ilyich Lenin, first leader of the Soviet Union and father of his country, suffered a stroke and died.

No one was sure how to handle it. Lenin had asked for a simple funeral. He wished to be buried next to his mother and sister in the family burial plot. But when Soviet leaders met to discuss the matter, they came up with another idea—turn the funeral into a "propaganda event" that could help legitimize the Communist regime. They decided to embalm him so he could lie in state for a while.

Then, only three days after his death, the Politburo began discussing the idea of saving the body "a little longer." Lenin's relatives balked at the idea...but Joseph Stalin insisted. As Dmitri Volkogonov writes in *Lenin: A New Biography*, Stalin "came to see [preserving Lenin's body] as the creation of a secular Bolshevik relic with huge propaganda potential." A short time later, the Politburo issued the following orders:

Q: How many times does One appear on a dollar bill? A: 16

1. The coffin containing V. I. Lenin's corpse is to be kept in a vault which should be made accessible to visitors;
2. The vault is to be formed in the Kremlin wall on Red Square among the communal graves of the fighters of the October Revolution. A commission is being created today for the construction of a mausoleum.

A burial vault was dug along the Kremlin wall, a wooden hut was built over it to keep out the elements, and Lenin's body was placed inside following the funeral.

CORPSE OF ENGINEERS
Meanwhile, the secret police were rounding up the country's top scientists to put them to work figuring out how to embalm Lenin for eternity. A streetcar was towed into Red Square and fitted with beds, hot plates, and washbasins; it served as the terrified scientists' home for the rest of the winter.

But restoring Lenin to his former glory was not so easy. Illness had ravaged him in the final years of his life, leaving him frail-looking and emaciated. And since permanent, *lifelike* embalming had never been attempted before, research on how to accomplish such a task had to begin from scratch. In the meantime, the body continued to deteriorate.

Lenin's cadaver was packed in ice to slow the decay, and by June the scientists finally succeeded in "stabilizing" the body. By then, however, it was a mess. "In those four and a half months," historian Robert Payne writes in *The Life and Death of Lenin*, "remarkable changes had taken place: he was waxen gray, wrinkled, horribly shrunken." Nonetheless, by August 1924, Lenin's body had been cleaned up enough to put on public display.

STAYING IN SHAPE
Work on *improving* Lenin's after-death appearance would continue for more than 25 years. The task was handled by the Research Institute for "Biological Structures" (a Soviet euphemism for cadaver) and its Lenin Mausoleum Laboratory—both of which were so secret that the West did not learn of their existence until after thecollapse of the Soviet Union. Part of the routine that was worked out over the years:

• To prevent Lenin from decomposing, the temperature in the mausoleum is kept at precisely 59°F. The humidity is also kept constant.

• Every Monday and Friday, the mausoleum is closed and a senior official of the institute's "body brigade" (most of whom log 20 years or more on the job before they are allowed to touch the corpse) removes Lenin's clothing and examines the cadaver for any signs of wear and tear. Any dust that has accumulated is carefully brushed away; then a special preservative ointment is applied to the skin. The corpse is then re-dressed and put back on display.

• Every 18 months, the cadaver is bathed in preservatives and injected with chemicals, which displace both water and bacteria in the cells and prevent the tissues from decomposing. Which chemicals are used in the process? Hardly anyone knows—even today, the "recipe" is as closely guarded a secret as the formula for Coca-Cola. Only the eight most senior members of the institute know the precise formula. When the process is completed, the cadaver is given a brand-new, hand-tailored suit.

KEEPING THE FAITH

As of 1996, more than five years after the collapse of the Soviet empire, Lenin's body was still on display in Red Square. Keeping the mausoleum open is no empty gesture—the corpse requires constant attention and a lot of money to keep it in good condition. But for many, it has become the political shrine that Stalin envisioned...and the Russian government fears that giving Lenin a regular burial will create a political backlash. Seventy-two years after he died, Lenin is still—literally—a political presence to be reckoned with.

MUMMIFIED FACTS

• **Wasted effort.** Soviet scientists continued perfecting their embalming techniques until the 1950s...just in time for the death of Joseph Stalin. He, too, was embalmed, then laid to rest alongside Lenin. But *that* turned out to be a waste of time. Eight years later, Nikita Khruschev ordered Stalin's body removed and buried in a more modest grave along the Kremlin wall.

• **Mummies for sale.** Budget cuts brought on by the collapse of the Soviet Union have forced the Research Institute for Biological

A giraffe's neck has 7 vertebrae; a bird's has 14; a person's has 26.

Structures to make its services available to the public. The mummification process takes a full year, requires the removal of all organs, and costs around $500,000. "The precise cost depends on the condition of the body," an official explains. "But our work is the best." The $500,000, by the way, only covers the cost of the embalming—you still have to build a mausoleum with temperature and humidity controls, which the institute estimates will cost as much as $5 million…not including the cost of staffing it forever.

• **No-brainer.** In 1924, Lenin's brain was removed and handed over to the Soviet Brain Institute—an organization founded specifically to determine whether the Leader's brain was superior to other human brains. Not surprisingly, they reported in 1936 that the brain "possessed such high organization that even during Lenin's illness, it continued to function on a very high level." Alas, it was just propaganda. In 1994, the Brain Institute's director admitted that "in the anatomical structure of Lenin's brain, there is nothing sensational."

CADAVER CONSPIRACY?

Is the body on display in Lenin's Tomb really his body? The official word is yes. But throughout the late 1920s, and 1930s, rumors spread that the embalmers had actually failed in their task. According to the story, the body in the mausoleum is a wax dummy.

This rumor is so widely accepted that the Soviet government opened an official "investigation" into the matter and invited a German doctor to participate and report his findings to the world. But the inquiry only heightened suspicions. As Payne reports, the German doctor

> was not permitted to make more than a cursory examination. He reported that he had observed frostbites on the skin, felt the cheeks, and lifted one of Lenin's arms….He inquired about the techniques and was told they were secret but would be fully revealed in three or four years' time when they had been proved effective; and nothing more was ever heard about the secret formula.

Even after the fall of Communism in Russia, no one (except for the government) knows for sure whether the corpse is real.

VICTORIAN PECULIARITIES

*Queen Victoria sat on the English throne from 1837 to 1901.
And during that time the rules of behavior were as
restrictive as the corsets.*

Was there ever a way of life among the upper-classes that was more constricted? More cramped, squeezed, pinched? Herewith, some Victorian rules of the road.

MORNING, MY DEAR

- The Mister will rise in his own chamber (how did they manage to have all those children?) and retire to the dressing room to suit up for the day.

- The lady of the house will have early tea in bed, perhaps with a newspaper to peruse (freshly ironed, to remove excess ink), before brushing her hair and saving any leftover strands in a jar called a hair retainer, for later use as toy stuffing, or the making of pictures and jewelry. She would not dream of putting on her pearls or diamonds in the morning. (And you've been wearing them to walk the dog. We've seen you.)

- After breakfast, each will go about their own daily occupations, the lady to her household, the man to his "business," a wonderful male euphemism for a day at the club smoking cigars and hanging out with the guys.

- Madam may, if she dares, invade the kitchen, where cook presides over the other servants and the monstrous coal stove that burns 24 hours a day heating water, cooking meals, and blowing most of its warmth up the chimney.

OUT AND ABOUT

Men were expected to do a little bit of everything. "It is the duty of a gentleman to know how to ride, to shoot, to fence, to box, to swim, to row and to dance. He should be graceful. If attacked by ruffians, a man should be able to defend himself, and also to

---

You can't take it with you: When Empress Elizabeth of Russia died in 1762, she owned 15,000 dresses.

defend women from their insults." So says "Rules of Etiquette and Home Culture," published in 1886. (And nowhere does it mention watching football on TV all day.)

Men were also directed:

- Never to let a lady of acquaintance stand in the street, but to walk with her while conversing, even if the gentleman isn't going in that direction.
- Not to tip their hats to a lady until she nodded in their direction. (Today they'd have to tip their Mohawk or waggle a nose ring.)

Women were actually allowed out of the house, but they were admonished:

- Never to call alone on a gentleman, unless it be for business reasons. (This in an age when it was assumed women had no head for business…hah!)
- If under 30, never to be out walking unaccompanied, except to go to church.

HER MAIN SQUEEZE

The ladies of the day were eye-catching, even if they couldn't catch their breath. Fashion in dresses bounced around more than their bustles. In 1873 "the look" was a high bodice and fat waist with bustle. This morphed into a longer torso bodice and narrow, tight sleeves. Forms bustled out again in 1883, and ended up as "hourglass" figures in the 1890s. (We should really pity the lady for whom the sands of time had run out.)

The most voraciously consumed fashion item was the bridal gown description. In some newspaper accounts, the rundown of a girl's trousseau could take several columns. Occasionally a groom was mentioned, somewhere.

WHO YOU CALLING A LADY?

Women's rights were a hot topic. In 1839 women were finally granted the right to custody of children under seven. But the next year, a court upheld a husband's right to lock up his wife and "beat her in moderation." Queen Victoria called the women's rights movement "mad, wicked folly...with all its attendant horrors." This from a woman who ruled the largest civilized empire on earth for 63 years?

COME INTO MY PARLOR...

You're probably thinking that Victorians didn't know how to have a good time. Some parlor games were the perfect cure for repression.

- Blind Man's Bluff (and don't tell us there weren't some "accidental" collisions.)

- Change Seats (a combo of Mother May I and Musical Chairs. Tame enough.)

- Squeak, Piggy, Squeak. In this daring game, a blindfolded person held a pillow, while standing in a circle. They were spun around till dizzy, then had to place the pillow on someone's lap, saying "squeak, piggy, squeak," and then they sat on their lap. And had to guess who it was. (Shameful...absolutely shameful.)

TEA TIME

For the tender souls who couldn't take that much excitement, there was always tea. By the late 1880s, this had become a major event. The ladies wore long gowns while presiding over the silver tea service and the gossip of the day. "High tea" was held later in the evening; the dishes were a bit more elaborate, but less than a full dinner. This was a nice, economical entertainment for down-on-their-luck widows.

There were tea gardens, too, where a few coins in the box marked T.I.P.S (to insure prompt service) got you piping hot pekoe, and started the tradition of tipping in public eateries.

NIGHT FALLS ON THE EMPIRE

Dances were always popular, but governed by the strict rules on:

- Who to invite

- How to make out the invitations

- What to do about wallflowers

At least at a dance, you might get the chance to study early

The Nobel Prize was first awarded in 1901.

semaphore communications, otherwise known as the "language of the fan."

- Resting on the right cheek: yes.
- On the left cheek: no.
- Fanning slowly: I'm married.
- Fanning faster: I'm engaged.
- Fan held behind the head with finger extended: Goodbye.

A MARTHA STEWART CHRISTMAS

Everyone enjoyed Christmas but Scrooge and the housewife who cursed the needle-droppings on the carpet (courtesy of Victoria's husband, Prince Albert, who introduced the Germanic custom of an indoor Christmas tree in 1841). A lot of the ornaments were edible: net bags of sweetmeats, and nuts or apples and oranges suspended from ribbons. Lighting was more dicey; they didn't have to worry about tripping over electrical cords, but they kept buckets of sand or water handy for fires set off by the real, genuine candles that lit up a Victorian tree.

WHERE'S MY PRESENTS?

Little boys might get wooden horses, guns, or wagons. Girls would get dolls with porcelain heads and hands that were not for playing with, just looking at. The more practical dolls were made out of cloth to practice future motherhood on.

A typical gift for a man might be pearl studs or gold waistcoat (vest) buttons. Ladies got brooches or lockets. Ladies also often "worked" gifts of slippers or purses with their own little hands.

ON YOUR WAY OUT...

The end of each person's personal Victorian era was serious business:

- A black wreath was placed on the door.
- Shades were drawn in the house of mourning.
- The deceased went to his Maker's consecrated ground on a wagon drawn by black horses (plumed and beribboned according to his status).
- The family wore black...nothing but. And would continue to do

A newborn baby's heart beats twice as fast as an adult's.

so for varying lengths of time, dictated by their closeness to the deceased.

- Before the casket was closed, a lock of hair might be snipped from the head of the dearly departed, to be worn enclosed in a mourning ring or woven into a wreath.

- Rushes were often strewn in the street to deaden...er, that is, quiet the sound of horses passing by.

Queen Victoria greatly influenced funeral customs by her inconsolable grief at the death of Prince Albert in 1861. Only when the ladies of her court sank into despair, did she relent after the first year and allow them to wear white or purple. Men of the household were required to wear black armbands until 1869.

At the time, Harrods, the elegant London department store, not only sold funeral fabrics and black-edged stationery...but they offered no less than seven different funeral packages! Today the store sports a sushi bar and a counter where you can buy a bagel topped with Parmesan and sun-dried tomatoes.

It's almost enough to make you nostalgic for the old days of silk and lace instead of polyester and octopus wrapped in seaweed.

* * *

PRESENTING...THE FEJEE MERMAID

Background: In 1842 P.T. Barnum began displaying the body of what he claimed was an actual mermaid, which he said had been found by sailors near the faraway island of "Feejee." (That's how Barnum spelled Fiji.) He put the mermaid on display in August 1842, printing up more than 10,000 handbills, leading up to opening day.

What Happened: The "mermaid," one of the biggest hoaxes of Barnum's long career, was actually "an ingenious sewing together of a large fish's body and tail with the head, shoulders, arms, and rather pendulous breasts of a female orangutan and the head of a baboon." But it did the trick—at the peak of New York's "mermaid fever," ticket sales at Barnum's Museum hit nearly $1,000 a week. "In truth, by the close of 1843," says a biographer, "with the help of...a dried up old mermaid, Barnum had become the most famous showman in America."

Medical update: Men get more ulcers; women get more migraine headaches.

ACT III:
JUDGE GROUCHO

Here's the final episode of a 1933 radio show starring Groucho as newly elected Judge Waldo Flywheel, and Ravelli (Chico) as his sidekick.

BRUMMET: Well, Judge Flywheel owes a lot to you.

PLUNKETT: Yeah, we ran away with the election.

BRUMMET: It's lucky for you that your trial's coming up in his court.

PLUNKETT: Lucky? What do you think I got him put in office for? Judge Maxwell would've given me twenty years on this bribery charge. But with Flywheel on the bench, I ought to get off in a couple of hours.

BRUMMET: What about that lawyer you got—Ravelli? He don't look too smart to me.

PLUNKETT: Oh, Ravelli's all right. Flywheel asked me to hire him. I guess they got the whole thing worked out between them. I ain't even demandin' a jury. I'm leaving it all in Judge Flywheel's hands. Let's go in. The courtroom's filling up.

BAILIFF: Hear ye, hear ye. Court is now in session. Everybody rise. His honor, Judge Flywheel.

GROUCHO: Never mind.

Where's the court stenographer? I want him to take a letter to my wife.

BAILIFF: Why, he can't do that.

GROUCHO: He can't? Better look for a new stenographer. What's the first case?

BAILIFF: It's the case of Steve Granach, charged with making too much noise in his apartment, and operating a poolroom within three hundred feet of a schoolhouse.

GROUCHO: A poolroom three hundred feet from a schoolhouse? That's a disgrace. Have them move the schoolhouse. I don't want those little kiddies walking that far. Now then, it's time I went to lunch.

BAILIFF: But Judge Flywheel, you haven't tried any cases yet.

LIFF: Next case is the trial of John H. Plunkett, charged with bribing public officials.

GROUCHO: Where's your lawyer, Plunkett?

RAVELLI: Here I am.

GROUCHO: Ravelli, are you the lawyer for the defendant?

When asked what they think is the most stressful event of the year, 20% of Americans

GROUCHO: Ravelli, are you the lawyer for the defendant?

RAVELLI: No, I'm the lawyer for this crook, Plunkett.

PLUNKETT: Say! What do you mean saying I'm a crook?

RAVELLI: Alright, alright. I didn't know it was a secret.

DISTRICT ATTORNEY: Your honor!

GROUCHO: What is it?

DISTRICT ATTORNEY: The state is prepared to proceed with the trial of John H. Plunkett. Our first witness is Leo Greenbury.

GROUCHO: Greenbury can't be a witness in this court.

DISTRICT ATTORNEY: Why not , your honor?

GROUCHO: Well, he told my wife's butcher that he didn't vote for me. The sneak!

DISTRICT ATTORNEY: I regret to say, your honor, that I consider your remark most unbecoming to a judge.

GROUCHO: What did you say?

DISTRICT ATTORNEY: I said your remark was most unbecoming to a judge.

GROUCHO: Hey, that's the second time you said that. Just for that I fine you a hundred bucks. I dare you to insult me again.

DISTRICT ATTORNEY: Oh, never mind.

GROUCHO: Oh, come on. I'll let you have this insult for fifty bucks.

RAVELLI: Come on, Plunkett, get on the witness stand, I ask you questions.

PLUNKETT: Alright, Ravelli. (gets on stand)

RAVELLI: How old are you?

PLUNKETT: I'm forty-five.

RAVELLI: Hey, Judge, I object.

GROUCHO: You object to your own witness's answer? On what grounds?

RAVELLI: I dunno. I couldn't think of anything else to say.

GROUCHO: Objection sustained!

DISTRICT ATTORNEY: On what grounds?

GROUCHO: I couldn't think of anything else to say either. Ravelli, proceed.

DISTRICT ATTORNEY: If your honor pleases, the state...

GROUCHO: Oh, pipe down and give somebody else a chance. You talk more than my wife. That's why I never got married.

DISTRICT ATTORNEY: The state objects, your honor. This is not a divorce case! John H. Plunkett is charged with bribery!

GROUCHO: Bribery? Why wasn't I told about that? I don't count, do I? Oh, no. I'm just judge here, that's all. Plunkett, I'm going to give you your choice of sentences: 10 years in Leavenworth, or 11 years in twelve-worth.

PLUNKETT: What?

GROUCHO: All right. We'll make it 5 &10 in Woolworth.

PLUNKETT: Wait a minute, your honor. The state ain't proved that I'm guilty of bribery.

GROUCHO: The state doesn't have to. I know you're guilty.

PLUNKETT: Say, how do you know I'm guilty?

GROUCHO: Are you kidding? Don't you remember? You bribed me. That's how I become a judge.

PLUNKETT: You double-crosser!...

RAVELLI: (Looking at the door): Boss, here comes Judge Maxwell.

MAXWELL: Mr. Flywheel, we have just come from the election board. Your sitting on the bench is absolutely illegal. We've just discovered that Emmanuel Ravelli voted more than once.

GROUCHO: Is that right, Ravelli? Did you vote more than once?

CHICO: Well, let me see. (Thinking) Mm-m. Maybe I did.

GROUCHO: (Upset): Well, did you or didn't you? Think, man.

RAVELLI: (Still thinking): I voted one...two...YEP, I voted three thousand times.

*   *   *   *

MORE "TRANSQUIPS"

Real courtroom conversation from Humor in the Court *and* More Humor in the Court, *by Mary Louse Gilman.*

(*see page 638 for more*)

Q: Now, Mrs. Johnson, how was your first marriage terminated?
A: By death.
Q: And by whose death was it terminated?

Q: And who is this person you are speaking of?
A: My ex-widow said it.

Q: Officer, what led you to believe the defendant was under the influence?
A: Because he was argumentary and he couldn't pronunciate his words.

Literary pretensions: The TV show "The Love Boat" was based on a novel.

MISS AMERICA TODAY, PART VI

Like all social institutions, the Miss America Pageant has had to become a bit of a cultural chameleon to survive. It doesn't change drastically—it has to be true to its roots as a traditional beauty contest, after all. But when the pressure gets strong enough, it seems to creak forward. Here's an update on the state of the pageant today:

NEW AND IMPROVED

The protests of the late 1960s and early 1970s over the Miss America Pageant's alleged anti-feminist and racist attitudes launched an era of gradual change for the pageant that continues to this day. For example:

√ In 1968, the pageant named a black clergyman to its board of directors and nominated two African American women to the hostess committee; a year later Dr. Zelma George became the pageant's first African American judge. The first African American contestant was Cheryl Brown, Miss Iowa 1970.

√ The most crassly sexist components of the pageant (except the swimsuit contest, of course) were quietly done away with. The "Neat as a Pin Award," created in 1969 to reward $250 to the tidiest contestant, was abandoned in 1973; the Miss Congeniality Award bit the dust two years later. In 1986 the pageant abandoned the practice of publishing contestants' bust, waistline, and hip measurements.

√ Contemporary issues were given greater attention beginning in 1974. Contestants had to answer "controversial, issue-oriented questions dealing with topics ranging from rape to prostitution." But the questions were asked offstage, away from the audience and TV cameras, to avoid the possibility of embarrassing the contestants or the pageant. The TV audience had to settle for short rehearsed issue speeches, which were made during the evening gown competition. Eventually, the pageant came up with a "platform" that the new Miss America agreed to support.

How long does it take a frozen sandwich to thaw at room temperature? Our sources say about 3 hours.

THERE HE GOES...

By the 1980s, nothing was sacred. In its endless quest for relevance and higher ratings, the pageant began leading its most sacred cows to slaughter. In 1980 it was announced that Bert Parks, who'd hosted every broadcast since 1955, was "retiring." (Pageant chairman Albert Marks later claimed that sponsors had been urging him to get rid of Bert for more than a decade.)

The move was handled shabbily—Parks learned of the firing from a reporter—and the publicity that resulted was disastrous. Miss America fans bombarded the pageant's Atlantic City headquarters with thousands of angry phone calls and letters, and "Tonight Show" host Johnny Carson, no spring chicken himself, waged an on-air campaign to have the crooner reinstated.

It didn't work. Marks stuck to his guns and replaced Parks with actor Ron Ely in 1980...then with Gary Collins in 1982...then with Regis Philbin and Kathie Lee Gifford in 1991. So far, however, no one has been able to fill Parks's shoes. (Parks made a guest appearance at the 1990 pageant—which some insiders claim was possible only because Marks had died in September 1989—but he made a lot of gaffes during the live broadcast and did not return in subsequent pageants. He died in 1992.)

There It Ain't

The axe fell again in 1982, when the Miss America Pageant failed to agree with composer Bernie Wayne on a price for using the song "There She Is" in the pageant. Wayne wanted a 15-year, $25,000 contract, but pageant officials refused, and the song was cut. As with Parks's firing, public response was negative and overwhelming...and this time it actually worked. Three years later, the pageant put "There She Is" back in the show.

THE HOLY OF HOLIES

The biggest change of all came in 1994, when the Miss America Pageant—after suffering the lowest TV ratings in 20 years—announced that it was considering dropping the swimsuit competition altogether. This idea was hardly a new one; in fact, the swimsuit competition was as unpopular with top officials at the Miss America Pageant as with the pageant's protesters. Lenora Slaughter had spent years lobbying to dump the swimsuits,

5 most common American last names: 1. Smith 2. Johnson 3. Williams 4. Jones 5. Brown

but pressure from traditionalists and swimsuit fans had proved too great.

Now, rather than make the decision itself, the pageant left it up to viewers. And to milk the maximum amount of publicity from the event, the vote was held *during* the 1995 Miss America broadcast. Viewers could call a 900 number and cast their votes while watching the show. The vote was updated throughout the program; the final tally was to be announced toward the end of the show. Just in case the vote was in favor of axing the suits, the pageant had another "mystery" event waiting in the wings to take its place.

The mystery event wasn't needed—the suits won 60% to 40%. The live vote was the biggest pageant publicity stunt since the 1920s, and it had the desired effect: 2.1 million more people watched the broadcast in 1995 than did in 1994.

THE END?
Will the pageant survive? Maybe not as the major cultural institution that it was in the 1950s, but if the pageant's ability for reinventing itself in a crisis is any guide (and the TV ratings don't slip much further), it will probably be around for decades to come

*   *   *   *

MISS AMERICA BEAUTY SECRETS
How do makeup artists affiliated with the Miss America Pageant keep America's beauties beautiful? Here are a few of their tricks.

Dirty hair. One of the pageant's hairstylists admits, "Dirty hair is more manageable. I can make a style fuller and stay better."
Face Putty. Used to cover up lines, scars, and pockmarks, and to create "porcelain" complexions. One makeup artist says: "I've even gone so far as to use mortician's wax mixed with the makeup."
Vaseline. Smeared on the teeth so that contestants can smile easily—even if their mouths dry up from nervousness.
Preparation H. The hemorrhoid ointment is smeared on eyelids and under the eyes. According to one makeup artist, "It smells pretty bad, but it removes puffiness."

There are ten million bricks in the Empire State Building.

MISS AMERICA SCANDALS

The Miss America Pageant has never had a scandal big enough to destroy it…but a bunch of middle-sized controversies have made headlines over the years. Here are a few of the juicier ones that we haven't already covered.

VANESSA WILLIAMS, *Miss America 1984*
Scandal: It was a big deal when Williams became the first African American Miss America. And there was just as much publicity when, 10 months later, *Penthouse* magazine announced that it had obtained a series of nude pictures Williams had posed for years earlier (including photos in suggestive poses with another woman)…and was planning to publish them in its September 1984 edition. Pageant officials immediately pronounced the photos "inconsistent with the Miss America image"and gave Williams 72 hours to resign her crown.
What Happened: It was the biggest scandal ever involving a reigning Miss America. But if anything, it *boosted* Williams's career. Since 1984, she's appeared on Broadway and recorded million-selling singles and Grammy-winning albums. Ironically, she's now the most successful ex-Miss America in the history of the pageant.

VENUS RAMEY, *Miss America 1944*
Scandal: A few days after she won the title, Ramey, 19, revealed that she'd forged her mother's name on the contract binding her to the pageant's scheduled promotional appearances—so it was legally unenforceable. Her reason for the stunt: She wanted to negotiate her own deals directly with advertisers.
Pageant officials "invited" Ramey to New York's Waldorf-Astoria hotel, where they held her while they tried to persuade her to honor the contract. When that failed, they flew in Ramey's mother to sign the contract for real. She also refused to cooperate.
What Happened: Ramey never did honor the contract. She embarked on her own tour—which bombed. She earned only $8,500 for an entire year on the road. (By comparison, Miss America 1941 earned an estimated $150,000 during her reign.) "I wanted to get into show business," Ramey complained afterward. I thought the pageant would be a good entree. It is, all right—an

Chicago is called "The Windy City"…but Bule Hill, Mass. is actually America's windiest city.

entree into oblivion. Forever afterward, you're like a broken-down actress trying to make a comeback."

CLAIRE JAMES, *Miss California 1938*
Scandal: James made it all the way to First Runner Up, then lost out to Marilyn Meseke, Miss Ohio, when judges "disapproved of her use of mascara."
What Happened: James was furious. Her promoter, theatrical producer Earl Carroll, denounced the judges as "incompetents," and the day after the pageant called a press conference to crown James the "people's choice" for Miss America. It was a publicity stunt, but James took it seriously, often identifying herself as Miss America in commercials and in speaking tours around the country. She finally backed off after Meseke, the real Miss America, took her to court.

B. ("BILLY") DON MAGNESS, *Chairman of the Board, Miss Texas pageant, 1970-1990*
Scandal: In September 1990, *Life* magazine alleged in an article on Magness—whose nicknames included "Mr. Miss Texas" and "God"—that, among other things, he:

• Held private swimsuit modeling sessions with Miss Texas contestants at his house.
• Made "very pointed hints" to a number of contestants over the years.
• Regularly kissed contestants on the lips.
• Telephoned contestants and asked them questions like "Wanna get nekkid?"
• Gave contestants obscene T-shirts, including one that read, "In case of rape, this side up."
• Referred to contestants as "sluts" during the *Life* magazine interview.

"While I make an attempt at appearing to be a dirty old man," Magness explained in an interview, "I make double that attempt to be sure that I'm not. Does that make sense? It's just kind of fun. You can be too clean and pure. Some of the girls just need to be dirtied up a little. It's just a continuance of their education."
What Happened: The article quoted Miss America CEO Leonard Horn as saying Magness "has lots of elegance and class. I think B.

Don really cares about these kids." But after reading the Life article, Horn quickly changed his tune. He ordered Texas pageant officials to investigate Magness, then threatened to keep the next Miss Texas out of the Miss America pageant unless Magness resigned.

YOLANDE BETBEZE, Miss America 1951
Scandal: The day after her coronation, Betbeze announced at a breakfast meeting that she would not pose in swimsuits during her reign. An earlier Miss America had taken the same stand and gotten away with it, but this time the Catalina Swimsuit Company was sponsoring the pageant, and had already booked Betbeze on a nationwide swimsuit tour.
What Happened: "The coffee cups rattled, let me tell you," Betbeze recalled years later. "The man from Catalina bathing suits stood up and fumed. He was furious. He looked at me and said, 'I'll run you off the news pages. I'll start my own contest. You'll see.' "

"I said, 'That's splendid. Good luck to you.' Anyway, he did, indeed, start the Miss USA and Miss Universe Pageants. So people can thank me—or blame me—for that."

BESS MYERSON, Miss America 1945
Scandal: In 1987, Myerson, then New York City's Commissioner of Cultural Affairs, was indicted for conspiracy, bribery, and fraud after she allegedly helped her boyfriend, a millionaire sewer contractor with reputed mob ties, lower his alimony payments by giving a judge's daughter a $19,000-a-year job in city government.

That was only the beginning of Myerson's legal troubles: In May 1988, she was arrested for shoplifting after she walked out of a New York department store without paying for the six bottles of nail polish, five pairs of earrings, one pair of shoes, and the flashlight batteries she'd stuffed into her purse and shopping bag. "I was leaving the store to lock my car and come back and pay for the merchandise," she explained to reporters after her arrest. Total value of the merchandise: $44.07. (Myerson was carrying $160 in cash.)
What Happened: Myerson was eventually acquitted on the alimony fixing charges, but pled guilty to shoplifting and paid a $100 fine, plus court costs.

There are more people of Irish descent in Boston and surrounding New England than in Ireland.

SUSAN AKIN, Miss America 1986

Scandal: Within a month of her crowning, the story broke that Akin's father and grandfather had been arrested in connection with the Ku Klux Klan murders of three Mississippi civil rights workers in 1964. Neither man was convicted.

What Happened: Miss America officials didn't learn of the story until it was reported in the media, but insisted that Akin had no responsibility to disclose the family connection. Akin—who was born a month after the murders—admitted she was hurt by the revelations, but refused to let her family's past affect her reign. "They're not Miss America," she told reporters, "I'm Miss America. …You're not going to hold it against me….I don't even know the facts about these things because I don't want to know."

TONI GEORGIANA, Miss New Jersey 1985

Scandal: Shortly after Georgiana won the New Jersey title, first runner-up Laura Bridges filed a lawsuit saying that Georgiana was actually a Pennsylvania resident, had competed twice in the Miss Pennsylvania pageant (and lost), and that she wasn't really a New Jersey student because she'd only enrolled in a single two-week education course at a state college, had not attended a single class, and had failed the course.

What Happened: New Jersey pageant officials sided with Georgiana, arguing that even if it was true, she had met minimum residency requirements set by the national pageant. Bridges lost the case.

STACY KING, Miss Louisiana 1989

Scandal: In 1989, the Miss Louisiana pageant director filed a protest, alleging that King was unfairly excluded from the Top 10 contestants in the national pageant because she was white and non-disabled. "It appeared that if you were black, ethnic, or had some kind of medical problem you had overcome, you stood a better chance of getting into the Top 10," he told reporters. "Two of the Top 10 were ethnic—one black and one Oriental—and there was one contestant who had a kidney transplant and another one who was deaf….It was just awful odd the way it worked out."

What Happened: The media had fun with the "anti-politically correct" protest, but pageant officials ignored it.

THE

"EXTENDED SITTING" SECTION

A Special Section of Longer Pieces

Over the years, we've gotten
numerous requests from BRI members to
include a batch of long articles—
for those times when you know
you're going to be sitting for a while
Well, the BRI aims to please…
So here's another great way
to pass the…uhh…time.

THE PUPPET-MASTER

Harry Reichenbach is largely forgotten today, but he was one of the most influential people of the 20th century. Along with a few cohorts, he virtually created the public relations field in the early 1900s. His specialty was movie publicity—he didn't usually try to manage cultural forces, the way contemporaries like Edward Bernays did—but his success at manipulating the press to further his clients' commercial interests was amazing. This selection, taken from Reichenbach's 1931 book Phantom Fame, *presents an early, unselfconscious account of the way publicity firms and the media deceive the public—wittingly or unwittingly. Their "news" is fun and harmless—but not real.*

NOTE: Before 1920, when the movie business was still young, there was no "studio system." Dozens of small film companies struggled to find some way to attract audiences to their latest silent movie. They began hiring publicity specialists...who went to extraordinary lengths to get attention for the films. The most successful was Harry Reichenbach, a legendary press agent who learned his craft from carnivals and circuses...and transferred the art of P.T. Barnum to movies.

This tale is not about one of his greatest triumphs—like saving Tarzan, outwitting super-censor Anthony Comstock, or helping to sell World War II to the American public. But it was a favorite story, because the "stunt" worked so well...and because it revealed the innate character of the American press and public. It's a true story—and if you were reading the daily newspapers in 1919, you would have believed it was really happening. Here's his version.

A NEW PROJECT
"In 1919, Universal Studios produced *The Virgin of Stamboul* [Ed. note Stamboul=Istanbul], a costume picture starring [then-famous] Priscilla Dean. It was the entirely unoriginal story of a Turkish maiden abducted by a villain...and rescued by a hero.

"Costume pictures at the time had become [box office poison], and Universal feared that this latest and most expensive of their dress parades would never bring back even the cost of the celluloid.

"It was up to me to save it.

"Preparations for the publicity stunt were almost as elaborate as the production of the picture. I took a trip to New York's 'Little Turkey,' east of Chatham Square, and found that though there were plenty of Armenians and Greeks, there were few Turks. So I befriended an Assyrian, Khalie Ossmun, who promised to dig up eight Turks…and he did. They looked as if he had dug them out of sewers. Two were ex-dishwashers, one was a pastry cook, another a porter and two sold home-made lemonade out of huge brass tureens strapped to their backs like papooses. The seventh was a fierce-looking Mussulman with an ugly scar that almost cut his face in two, and the eighth was a pedigree who kept mumbling all the time that his brother was a 'pasha.' I found out later that a 'pasha' was a rubber in a bath."

TAKING THE PARTS

"My Assyrian friend Khalie being the most personable, I appointed him chief Sheik Ali Ben Mohamed, ruler of this motley band. The knife-scarred Turk whom we called 'Goom' became lord high aide-de-camp and the white-haired old mumbler I turned into the Grand Caliph Shafkrat. The pastry cook became his lordship, the Effendi Houssien, the two ex-dishwashers acquired the titles of Generals Haedan and Rafkhat respectively, and the lemonade peddlers became the grand eunuchs of the Sheik's harem, Jamil and Abdul Halsh.

"After freely distributing these high ranks and titles, I let them spend a night at the Turkish bath, which was something new to the Turks, and then transformed my mob of eight into a high diplomatic body on a secret mission from the East. A theatrical costumer dressed them in lavish splendor from sea-green trousers to gold-crescented turbans.

"The next thing was to teach the Turks the manners and customs of their native land. I persuaded a friend of mine, Alexander Brown, who had spent many years in Constantinople as general representative of the American Licorice Company, to show them how to act with true Turkish elegance. For an entire week he drilled them in handling table service. He taught them how to wear their decorations, how to salaam, and how the eunuchs were to taste all food before their masters would take the chance.

"Another week passed rehearsing the Sheik on the story he would have to tell the newspapermen, while all the other members of this august body were warned to keep their mouths shut. For many hours I would sit around with my Turks in a rehearsal hall and hurl questions at them which I thought that reporters might ask…and to all inquiries, they were to give but a single answer: 'I cannot talk. You must ask the master.' The master knew his speech by heart, and would say nothing he hadn't memorized."

THE BIG DAY

"Finally, we were ready to make our 'arrival' into New York from Turkey. I had my secretary telephone the Hotel Majestic and say, 'Montreal is calling.' I spoke to the hotel manager, Jack Heath, in a tortured dialect explaining very dimly that 'We are the Turkish mission that comes to your country on a very secret importance. Please reserve for us the best rooms of the suite and protect us please from the newspaper reporting!'

"Two days later our royal party arrived at the Majestic.

"At four o'clock that afternoon, the Grandees of the Porte made their first public appearance in full regalia, going into the hotel tearoom in state according to all the rules of Turkish royalty laid down by the American Licorice Company's manager. Ossmun the Sheik acted as if cameras were turning in all corners. As I passed through the lobby, John MacMahon, New York dramatic critic, confided in me, 'I understand this is a Turkish war mission.'

"O. O. McIntyre, the Majestic's press agent, tipped off the newspapers reticently as if they were being let into a secret of international significance. That night the royal suite was a reporters' convention. The next morning the newspapers throughout the country and throughout the world gave major coverage to the story of Sheik Ali Ben Mohamed's strange and mysterious mission in America."

TAKING IT SERIOUSLY

"Our rented costumes received the most minute and painstaking descriptions in the press. *The New York Tribune* pictured my Chatham Square Assyrian as follows:

> There was Sheik Ali Ben Mohamed of Hedjaz, which all students of the League of Nations know to be a newly formed kingdom of Arabia, the subjects of which bear no love for the Turkish Empire, from which it was dismembered.

The phrase "It's Greek to me" first appeared in Shakespeare's *Julius Caesar*.

A burnous of maroon, margined with a wide band of yellow silk and piped with peagreen, partially hid more gorgeous garments of the Arab nobleman, His fez kept shape to the white folds of linen that draped over it and swathed about his neck. The linen was bound closely about his head by a turban of orange pattern that revealed the Sheik as a Holy Man.

"Even the Prince of Wales's latest clothes were never more faithfully reported than these gaudy theatrical garments. Then Khalie Ossmun recited with a marvelous memory the little speech we had rehearsed in the hall on Sixth Avenue:

> Gentlemen, I come to this country, which to my desert-trained eyes is like the heaven promised in the Koran, to seek the betrothed of my younger brother. She is Sari, so beautiful that in all Turkey there was none like her. She was known as the Virgin of Stamboul."

HOW DO YOU SPELL GULLIBLE?

"Then the Sheik proceeded to give a complete summary of the plot of the movie starring Priscilla Dean. But the reporters swallowed every word avidly as news of the first magnitude.

'Her father was very rich,' murmured the Sheik, raising a weary hand to shield his piercing black eyes. 'Her mother too was of royal blood. Sari had an English governess. The American soldiers came to Stamboul. They saw Sari. One of them she saw. They spoke together, she proud of her few words in English. Then she disappeared. That same day the American transport sailed for this country. Sari's mother died of grief. Then her father. We had established that she was not dead. We knew all too surely that it was a love affair that had caused the Virgin of Stamboul to disappear.'

"All this the reporters copied verbatim. Then the Sheik told them that the Burns and Val O'Farrell Detective Agencies had been retained to aid in the worldwide search. He made them print an offer of ten thousand dollars reward for information leading to Sari's discovery. He told them that she was an heiress to about a hundred million. He didn't even forget the detail that her English governess, after weeping many days, had drowned herself in the Bosporus.

"By killing off the entire household in Turkey we eliminated the possibility of anyone calling there for confirmation."

American chickens are direct descendants of the ones brought over by Columbus.

UH-OH!

"As soon as the Sheik had completed his tale, the reporters returned to describing the garments. Even that lynx-eyed newspaper man, Boyden Sparkes, devoted half a column to the costumes. He reported the silver-mounted scimitar with ebony hilt and the maroon burnous that only partially concealed a robin's-egg blue tunic braided with lavender. He noted the purple jacket lined with ver-million silk and striped with gold braid.

"But he also detected what he told me later was the first hint of what was really going on. Because beneath all this majesty of attire peeped out the starched cuffs of a shirt, a bit soiled, that might have been made in Troy, New York!

"Up to that point the Sheik had been doing splendidly. But the starched cuffs bothered Sparkes. He asked the Turkish lord whether he knew any Americans and Ossmun answered promptly, 'I know your Mr. Henry Morgenthau very well [Ed. Note: A wealthy and prominent businessman of the time] I am to have dinner with him.' I had anticipated that question and the day before I learned from Morgenthau's secretary that he would be away for the weekend. It was therefore safe to use his name.

"When the interview ended, none of the reporters questioned the Sheik's story in the slightest. They ran out into the hall, hugged each other with delight and dashed to the nearest telephone to report the greatest romantic news scoop in years. Only Boyden Sparkes seemed worried. He hesitated, then went into the manager's office and we heard him call up Morgenthau. To my amazement, Morgenthau was in. I vanished. So did McIntyre."

IT JUST KEEPS GOING AND GOING...

"The next day Sparkes wrote just as elaborate and full an account of the story as all the others, but near the end he added:

> Mr. Morgenthau said Sheik Ben Mohamed was a blasted liar.
> Mr. Morgenthau said more. He said the Sheik's costume was too
> good to be true. He made a solemn statement that he wasn't
> going to let the Sheik dine with him, and was unkind enough
> to call him a fake. But that won't interfere with the early
> release of that thrilling picture, The Virgin of Stamboul.

"In view of Morgenthau's statement it seemed that the stunt was over. But it wasn't. There was a quality of fascination about the story that made it almost better than truth. It had become romance, illusion. It was one of those episodes that gave the public and press alike the feeling that if it didn't happen, it should have happened!

"Besides getting its quota of coverage in every daily newspaper, the stunt got the attention of three newsreel companies—Fox, Kintograms and Pathe Weekly. Each paid the Sheik fifty dollars to go to Central Park and pose for their films. The Hippodrome Theater gave a box party to the royal visitors and even spread a carpet from the curb to the lobby that the holy feet of the dishwashers and lemonade peddlers should not touch unhallowed ground. Many night clubs invited the Sheik and his party and undoubtedly recognized among them some of their former help."

IT'S A HIT!

"A few days later, when Sari was found by Val O'Farrell in a rooming house on Kenmare Street, newspapers again covered the story. The reporters swarmed into the royal suite at the Majestic and were treated to a stirring Oriental scene. Through an open door they saw a young hysterical girl tossing in a bed surrounded by the Sheik and five kneeling turks, while a physician stood near her, constantly jabbing hypodermics into the mattress, and a nurse anxiously made notes on a chart. The Sheik, deeply touched and distracted, still found time to come out and tell reporters that Sari had been saved and the party would sail Saturday on the White Star Line.

"In everyone's presence he handed ten $1,000 bills to Val O'Farrell, who returned them later when nobody was around. The Sheik thanked the U.S. press for its cooperation and said that it was no wonder, judging by its press, that the American people were the most enlightened in the world. An agent of the White Star Line entered with nine first-class tickets. Not a single cue went wrong.

"The girl who played Sari was an accomplished actress, but as she could speak neither Turkish nor French, we did not allow the reporters to interview her. We told them she was delirious. The press reported every detail faithfully to the end and *The Virgin of Stamboul* scored a record at the box office.

"It didn't surprise me that wise newspapermen were so gullible. My capacity for surprise had been exhausted long ago."

Most earthworms like to eat ice cream.

HOLLYWOOD SCANDAL: 1921

*A woman is found dead…a well-known celebrity is charged with
murder…the whole world follows the trial. O. J. Simpson?
Nope—Fatty Arbuckle. In its day, the Arbuckle trial
was as big as the Simpson trial. Here's the story.*

A KNOCK AT THE DOOR

On the morning of Saturday, September 10, 1921, two
men from the San Francisco sheriff's office paid a visit to
Roscoe "Fatty" Arbuckle, then Hollywood's most famous comedian, at his home in Los Angeles. One of the men read from an
official court summons:

"You are hereby summoned to return immediately to San
Francisco for questioning…you are charged with murder in the
first degree."

Arbuckle, thinking the men were pulling a practical joke, let
out a laugh. "And who do you suppose I killed?"

"Virginia Rappé."

Arbuckle instantly knew that this was no joke. He'd just
returned from a trip to San Francisco, where he'd thrown a party
over the Labor Day weekend to celebrate his new $3 million
movie contact—then the largest in Hollywood history—with
Paramount Pictures. A 26-year-old bit actress named Virginia
Rappé had fallen ill at the party, presumably from drinking too
much bootleg booze. Arbuckle had seen to it that the woman
received medical attention before he returned to L.A., but now
Rappé was dead—and Arbuckle had somehow been implicated in
her death. Whatever doubts he may still have had about the
summons vanished the following morning as he read the three-
inch headlines in the *Los Angeles Examiner*:

ARBUCKLE HELD FOR MURDER!

The autopsy report showed that Rappé died from acute peritonitis,
an inflammation of the abdominal lining brought on by a ruptured

bladder. Why was Arbuckle a suspect in the death? Because Maude "Bambina" Delmont, another woman at the party, had filed a statement with San Francisco police claiming that she had seen Arbuckle drag Rappé into his bedroom against her will and assault her. As she later explained to newspaper reporters,

> I could hear Virginia kicking and screaming violently and I had to kick and batter the door before Mr. Arbuckle would let me in. I looked at the bed. There was Virginia, helpless and ravaged. When Virginia kept screaming in agony at what Mr. Arbuckle had done, he turned to me and said, 'Shut her up or I'll throw her out a window.' He then went back to his drunken party and danced while poor Virginia lay dying.

The 265 pound comedian had supposedly burst Rappé's bladder with his weight during the assault. And because the injury had gone undiagnosed and untreated, it developed into a massive abdominal infection, killing Rappè.

Pressing Charges
After Delmont's statement was filed, San Francisco District Attorney Matthew Brady had ordered Arbuckle's arrest and had issued a public statement to the press:

> The evidence in my possession shows conclusively that either a rape or an attempt to rape was perpetrated on Miss Rappè by Roscoe Arbuckle. The evidence discloses beyond question that her bladder was ruptured by the weight of the body of Arbuckle either in a rape assault or an attempt to commit rape.

FALSE WITNESS
Brady's case was based almost entirely on Delmont's police statement. And the case certainly appeared substantial—at least until Brady looked into Maude Delmont's background after she gave her statement. Then he discovered a police record containing more than 50 counts of bigamy, fraud, racketeering, extortion, and other crimes (including one outstanding bigamy warrant, which Brady would later use to his advantage.)

WHAT REALLY HAPPENED
Brady later learned from other guests at the party that a very drunk Maude Delmont had actually been locked in a bathroom

with Lowell Sherman, another party guest, during the entire time that she claimed to have witnessed Arbuckle with Rappé. She could not have seen any of the things she claimed to have seen—and if that were not bad enough, Brady later discovered that on Wednesday, September 7, Delmont had dashed off the following telegram to two different friends as Virginia Rappé lay dying at the St. Francis Hotel:

> WE HAVE ROSCOE ARBUCKLE IN A HOLE HERE
> CHANCE TO MAKE MONEY OUT OF HIM

Blind Ambition

District Attorney Brady had no case—there wasn't a shred of physical evidence to indicate that Arbuckle had committed any crime against Rappé; his only "witness" was a woman with a long criminal record; and the telegrams demonstrated clearly that Delmont's police statement was part of an attempt to blackmail Arbuckle.

Despite all this, Brady decided to bring the case to trial. Why? One theory: Brady, whom acquaintances described as a "self-serving, arrogant, ruthless man with blind ambition and a quick temper," was gearing up to run for governor of California. He probably figured that winning a murder conviction against Hollywood's biggest comedian would score points with the public.

Judge Not

Still, the case could not have gone to trial if the police judge, Sylvain Lazarus, had dismissed the case due to lack of evidence. But Judge Lazarus refused to throw it out, citing the "larger issues" surrounding the case:

> I do not find any evidence that Mr. Arbuckle either committed or attempted to commit rape. The court has been presented with the merest outline….The district attorney has presented barely enough facts to justify my holding the defendant on the charge which is here filed against him.
>
> But we are not trying Roscoe Arbuckle alone; we are not trying the screen celebrity who has given joy and pleasure to the entire world; we are actually, gentlemen, trying ourselves.
>
> We are trying our present-day morals, our present-day social conditions, our present-day looseness of thought and lack

Most of the villains in the Bible have red hair.

of social balance....
I have decided to make a holding on the ground of manslaughter.

The judge suspected Arbuckle was innocent, the district attorney knew Arbuckle was innocent, and yet the case still went to trial.

EXTRA!
Much like the Menendez brothers trials and the O.J. Simpson trials of the 1990s, the media—which in the 1920s consisted mostly of newspapers—had a field day with the Arbuckle trial. Unlike the Simpson trial, however, the lack of evidence in the Arbuckle trial led most newspapers to conclude that Arbuckle was innocent. Most papers, that is, except for those owned by media baron William Randolph Hearst. His papers loudly attacked Arbuckle's character, insinuated his guilt, and ran as many as six special editions per day to keep readers up-to-date on the latest developments in the case.

The Hearst papers published the most lurid accounts of the crime and the trial, and even stooped to publicizing totally unsubstantiated rumors about the case—the most famous of which was that Arbuckle, supposedly too impotent from booze to rape Rappé himself, had used a Coke bottle (some accounts said it was a champagne bottle) instead, causing her bladder to rupture. "Nowhere in any testimony in the court transcripts, police reports, or personal interviews did this story appear," Andy Edmonds writes in *Frame Up! The Untold Story of Roscoe "Fatty" Arbuckle*. "Everyone connected with the case vehemently denied it, yet it is the most popular story, and one of the most ugly lies, still connected with the ordeal. The fabrication haunted Roscoe throughout the remainder of his life."

GOING TO COURT
As Brady prepared his case, one of the first things he did was see to it that Maude Delmont would not be able to testify. He knew that the other witnesses would prove she had lied in her police statement. Furthermore, Delmont had changed her story so many times that Brady knew she would be caught in her own lies during cross-examination. Rather than let that happen, Brady had her arrested on an outstanding charge of bigamy. Delmont—the only

person who claimed that Arbuckle had committed a crime—spent the next several months in jail, where Arbuckle's attorneys could not get at her.

THE TRIAL

The People v. Arbuckle lasted from November 14 to December 4, 1921. More than 60 witnesses were called to the stand, including 18 doctors. According to Bernard Ryan in *Great American Trials:*

> Through defense witnesses, lawyer Gavin McNab revealed Virginia Rappé's moral as well as medical history: As a young teenager, she had had five abortions in three years, at 16, she had borne an illegitimate child; since 1907, she had had a series of bladder inflammations and chronic cystitis; she liked to strip naked when she drank; the doctor who attended her in the several days before she died concluded that she had gonorrhea; when she met Arbuckle for the first time on Monday, she was pregnant and that afternoon had asked him to pay for an abortion; on Wednesday, she had asked her nurse to find an abortionist….Medical testimony proved that Virginia Rappé's bladder was cystic—one of the causes of rupture of the bladder.

Arbuckle Takes The Stand

The climax of the trial came on Monday, November 28, when Arbuckle testified in his own defense. He recounted how he had found Rappé in his bathroom vomiting into the toilet, and how he had helped her into the next room when she asked to lie down. Arbuckle testified that he spent less than 10 minutes alone with Rappé before summoning Maude Delmont, who took over and asked him to leave the room. He stood up well under cross-examination; and the final testimony, in which expert witnesses testified that the rupture of Ms. Rappé's bladder was not caused by external force, seemed to cinch the case for Arbuckle.

THE VERDICT

As the case went to the jury, both sides appeared confident of victory. But on December 4th, after 44 hours of deliberation, the jury announced that it was hopelessly deadlocked, and the judge declared a mistrial.

One juror, a woman named Helen Hubbard—whose husband was a lawyer who did business with the D.A.'s office—held out for a conviction throughout the entire deliberations.

The three best-known western names in China: Jesus Christ, Richard Nixon, and Elvis Presley.

The Second Trial

The case went to trial a second time, beginning on January 11 and lasting until February 3. The second trial was much like the first, only this time the defense introduced even more evidence concerning Ms. Rappé's shady past. But Arbuckle's lawyers, confident they would win handily, did not have Arbuckle take the stand in his defense. That was a huge mistake—this time the jury deadlocked 9-3 in favor of conviction.

The Third Trial

The case went to trial a third time on March 13. This time, Arbuckle's defense left nothing to chance: it provided still more evidence questioning both Rappé's physical health and her moral character, and it brought Arbuckle back to the stand to testify on his own behalf.

FINAL VERDICT

The case went to the jury on April 12, 1922. They deliberated for less than 5 minutes, then returned to court and read the following statement:

> We the jury find Roscoe Arbuckle not guilty of manslaughter.
>
> Acquittal is not enough for Roscoe Arbuckle. We feel that a great injustice has been done him. We feel also that it was only our plain duty to give him this exoneration, under the evidence, for there was not the slightest proof adduced to connect him in any way with the commission of a crime.
>
> He was manly throughout the case, and told a straightforward story on the witness stand, which we all believed.
>
> The happening at the hotel was an unfortunate affair for which Arbuckle, so the evidence shows, was in no way responsible.
>
> We wish him success….Roscoe Arbuckle is entirely innocent and free from all blame.

THE AFTERMATH

Roscoe Arbuckle was a free man, but his life was in tatters. The trials had cost him more than $750,000, wiping out nearly his entire life savings (the $3 million Paramount contract had fallen through when the scandal broke). As if that wasn't bad enough,

---

In the novel Frankenstein, the monster's name was Adam.

the IRS went after him a few months later, when it seized the remainder of his estate to collect more than $100,000 in back taxes. It also obtained a court order to attach whatever wages he earned in the future until the entire tax debt was paid back.

THE HAYS OFFICE

Things got even worse for Arbuckle. Largely because of the scandal, 12 of Hollywood's top studio moguls hired William Hays, chairman of the Republican National Committee and a former postmaster general, to become America's "movie czar." His job: Keep Hollywood's image clean. His first task: Deal with Arbuckle.

Hatchet Job

Six days after Arbuckle was acquitted, the "Hays Office" (as it came to be known) banned him from the screen. The public was led to believe it was a moral issue. Actually, Hays was doing the bidding of Paramount heads Adolph Zukor and Jesse Lasky, who no longer wanted to work with Arbuckle, out of fear that he was box office poison. But they didn't take any chances; rather than risk losing Arbuckle to a competing studio, they lobbied the Hays Office to ban him from the film industry entirely.

COMEBACK

The ban was lifted eight months later, but the taint remained and Arbuckle had trouble finding work. He began work on a short subject film called *Handy Andy*, but was so hounded by reporters that he gave up on the project.

Over the next decade he appeared in stage shows, ran a Hollywood nightclub, and directed a number of films under the pseudonym William B. Goodrich (Will B. Good). But it wasn't until 1932—more than 10 years after the trials—that he had a chance to return to the screen. Studio head Jack Warner hired him to act in a film called *Hey, Pop!* It was a box office success, and Arbuckle was signed for six more films. He only completed three—*Buzzin' Around*, *Tamalio*, and *In the Dough*. The evening *In the Dough* finished shooting, Arbuckle celebrated at dinner with his wife and went home to bed. He died in his sleep at about 2:30 a.m., leaving an estate value at less than $2,000.

LIFE IN THE WHITE HOUSE

Just about everyone has wondered what it would be like to live at 1600 Pennsylvania Ave...but most of us will never know. Judging from the experiences of people who have lived there, maybe that's not such a terrible thing...

JAMES MADISON (1809-1817)

The first and so far the only president to be burned out of (white) house and home, was James Madison, president during the War of 1812. On August 24, 1814, four thousand British troops marched on Washington, D.C., setting fire to the Capitol Building, the White House, and just about everything else they could torch. Madison wasn't home at the time—he was either out directing troops, or running away. But his wife, Dolly Madison, hung in there and managed to remove the Gilbert Stuart portrait of George Washington before the British arrived and gutted the building.

Washington, D.C. suffered so much damage that there was serious talk of moving the capital to some other city. It stayed put, of course, and the White House was rebuilt. But not before Madison left office. For about a year, he ran the country from Octagon House, the residence of the French Minister; and later from a house at 19th St. and Pennsylvania Avenue. Madison's successor, James Monroe, moved back into the White House in 1817.

MARTIN VAN BUREN (1837-1841)

President Van Buren had the misfortune of being the person who moved into the White House right after it was vacated by President Andrew Jackson—probably the most raucous president ever to live there.

He inherited a White House "in a pretty sorry state of repair," Ethel Lewis writes in *The White House*. "The walls were all grimy with smoke, the floor coverings had had more than their share of tobacco juice, and most of the china and silver and glass had been broken."

Van Buren spent $60,000 on cleaning, whitewashing, and

Americans recycled enough paper in 1990 to make 100 billion pizza boxes.

furniture repairs for the White House…only to have Congressman Charles Ogle from Jackson's own Whig party attack the newfound "regal splendor of the Presidential Palace," citing such wretched excesses as bracket lights, "ice cream vases," and the president's private bathtub. Van Buren spent less on the White House than Jackson had, but Ogle's attacks contributed to his losing the 1840 presidential election to William Henry Harrison.

JAMES BUCHANAN (1857-1861)

By the middle of the 19th century, Washington, D.C. had grown into a city with 50 thousand people. But it had no sewage treatment facilities, which resulted in serious sanitation problems for the city. The problem was so bad near the White House, Ethel Lewis writes, that:

> There was serious consideration of removing the President's house to a more salutary place and using the present building for offices only. Up to 1850, sewers from public buildings emptied onto the open ground south of the White House. There the water stagnated and made a marsh. Immediately following Buchanan's Inauguration, several residents of the National Hotel and its neighborhood died as the result of poison gases from obstructed, inadequate sewers.

CHESTER A. ARTHUR (1881-1885)

President James A. Garfield lived long enough to install the White House's first elevator for his mother, Grandma Garfield, but that was about it: he was assassinated four months into his term and Vice President Chester A. Arthur became president.

Unlike his plain predecessor, Arthur was a dandy who kept up with the latest fashions. He was so appalled at the condition of the White House that he refused to move in—even in time of crisis (Garfield's death)—until the White House was redecorated to his taste. On April 15, 1881, 24 wagonloads of White House furnishings were carted away and sold at auction to the highest bidder. Items sold included cuspidors, hair mattresses, marble mantles, a globe that had belonged to President Grant's daughter, and a pair of Lincoln's pants. Arthur then hired New York artist and decorator Louis Comfort Tiffany to redecorate from floor to ceiling. "Tiffany transformed the old mansion into an art nouveau palace," Kenneth Leish writes. "Throughout the house, everything

---

Americans bought almost a billion pounds of unpopped popcorn in 1990.

that could be sprayed with gold, was; everything that could be overstuffed, was; and every space that could hold a potted plant, held two." Arthur finally took up residence in the White House in December 1881.

BENJAMIN HARRISON (1889-1892)

Living in the White House must have been particularly difficult for Harrison, who shared the five-bedroom residence with his wife, her 90-year-old father, her sister, a niece, the Harrisons' two daughters and son, the son's wife and daughter, and two other infants. There were five bedrooms in the residence at the time, so it's not surprising that First Lady Caroline Harrison was a strong proponent of enlarging the White House.

In 1891, Mrs. Harrison had an architect draw up plans adding an enormous wing to each end of the White House. The ends of the two wings would be connected by a long conservatory, creating an enclosed courtyard in back of the White House. Inside the courtyard, Mrs. Harrison proposed, would be a fountain commemorating both Columbus' discovery of the New World, and the laying of the White House cornerstone 300 years later. And the best part of all, at least as far as Mrs. Harrison was concerned, was that there would be plenty of room on the upper floors of the new wings for additional bedrooms and office space.

Mrs. Harrison's plans might well have succeeded if President Harrison hadn't offended Speaker of the House Thomas Reed, the "Czar" of Capitol Hill, by refusing to appoint one of Reed's cronies to a government job. Reed was so angry that he prevented the White House bill from ever coming to a vote. The Harrisons, all twelve of them, stayed put for four years.

THEODORE ROOSEVELT (1901-1908)

Roosevelt, who became president when McKinley was assassinated, was determined to enlarge the White House to suit the needs of both the growing country and his growing family—which numbered six children. Roosevelt added the West Wing, which houses the Oval Office, the Cabinet Room, the White House press office, and other Executive offices. Because the West Wing was built only one story high and was separated from the rest of the mansion by a long corridor, the appearance of the White House changed very little. Roosevelt's distant cousin, Franklin

Roosevelt, added the East Wing during World War II. It contained three stories of office space, including new offices for the First Lady, and the White House's first bomb shelter.

HARRY TRUMAN (1944-1952)

In 1948, Harry Truman authorized an expenditure of $10,000 to have a balcony installed on the south side of the second floor of the White House. He'd barely gotten around to enjoying it when he became the first president since James Madison to evacuate the White House out of fear for his life. "Found the White House 'falling down,'" he wrote in his diary. "My daughter's sitting room floor had broken down into the family dining room."

Truman had lived in the White House long enough to know that it wasn't in the best of shape—the floor in the upstairs study swayed and creaked when he walked across it, and the chandelier in the Blue Room swung back and forth for no reason. But he was astonished at what structural engineers told him: The beams that held the building up had been cut into so many times, and were carrying so much more weight than they had been designed to carry, that they had begun to split under the strain. The entire building was on the verge of collapse. The family quarters on the second floor were in particularly bad shape—they were being held up "purely by habit," the engineers told Truman.

Truman had three choices: (1) move away and have the White House designated a museum; (2) tear the White House down and build a replica in its place; and (3) save the exterior walls, tear down everything else, and replace it with an exact replica of the original interior. Truman chose the third option, and moved across the street to Blair House, normally the government's guest house for visiting heads of state. According to Kenneth Leish:

> Mantelpieces, wall paneling, fixtures, moldings—all were taken apart and stored away for later reinstallation. Then the whole interior was demolished....Steel beams were erected to support the new interior. The entire structure was fireproofed and air-conditioned. And the...outer walls were shored up....It took four years and more than $5 million, but when Truman moved back, in 1952, the presidential mansion was, as Abigail Adams had said too optimistically 150 years earlier, "built for ages to come."

THE ANATOMY
OF LAUGHTER

And you thought reading the funny stuff we put in the Bathroom
Reader *was just a way to kill time. Well, it's not—while you're
giggling at Uncle John's prose, you're actually getting some exercise
and improving your health. Don't believe it? Here's proof.*

HARDEE HAR HAR
Even after centuries of scientific research, no one knows
for sure why human beings (plus a few other primates,
including chimpanzees, apes, and orangutans) laugh.
People have ideas, though.

*"A 2-pound turkey and a 50-pound cranberry—
that's Thanksgiving dinner at Three Mile Island."*

—Johnny Carson

• Charles Darwin speculated that laughter, which begins in
infants as young as three months old, served as an evolutionary
"reward" to parental care-giving. Laughter in infants sounded and
felt so different from crying, he believed, that even prehistoric
parents must have interpreted it as a sign of well-being, kind of
like the purring of a kitten. The parents enjoyed the laughter,
which encouraged them to continue caring for the child.
• Sigmund Freud believed (of course) that laughter was closely
intertwined with lust.

*"[On old age:] First you forget names, then you
forget faces, then you forget to pull your zipper up,
then you forget to pull your zipper down."*

—Leo Rosenberg

• Contemporary theorists believe that laughter evolved as a
means for primates to diffuse tension and reduce the likelihood of
confrontation when meeting and interacting with others.

FUNNY BUSINESS

Even if scientists still don't know why we laugh, they've learned a lot about it. For example:

• You use 15 different muscles in your face to laugh.

• The sound of laughter is created when you inhale deeply and then release the air while your diaphragm moves in a series of short, spasmodic contractions.

• The typical laugh is made up of pulses of sound that are about 1/15th of a second long and 1/5th of a second apart. When tape recorded and played backward, laughing sounds virtually the same as it does when it's played forward.

• Hearty laughter produces physical effects similar to those resulting from moderate exercise: The pulse of the person laughing can double from 60 to 120, and the systolic blood pressure can increase from 120 to 200—about the same thing that happens when you exercise on a stationary bicycle. Stanford University researcher Dr. William Fry even refers to laughter as "a kind of stationary jogging."

> "I saw a TV commercial that said, 'Kiss your hemorrhoids goodbye.' Not even if I could."
> **—John Mendoza**

• When people stop laughing, just as when they stop exercising, the muscles in the body are more relaxed than they were before the laughing started. Heartbeat and blood pressure are also lower. This leads scientists to believe that laughing is a means of releasing stress and pent-up energy.

THE BEST MEDICINE

One of the most interesting things researchers have learned is the powerful healing effect of laughter.

Well, actually they're re-learning it after centuries of neglect: In the Middle Ages, doctors "treated" their patients by telling them jokes, but modern medicine discounted the curative properties of laughing.

That began to change in 1979, when editor Norman Cousins wrote *Anatomy of an Illness*, in which he credited watching humorous videos with helping him reduce pain and recover from ankylosing spondylitis, a life-threatening degenerative spinal disease. The book inspired researchers to look into whether laughter really did aid in healing and recovery from illness.

THE LAUGH TEST

In 1995, two researchers at the Loma Linda University School of Medicine had 10 medical students watch a 60-minute videotape of Gallagher, a stand-up comedian famous for smashing watermelons and other objects with a sledgehammer.

The researchers found that after watching the video, there was a measurable decrease in stress hormones, including epinephrine and dopamine, in the students' blood, plus an increase in endorphins, the body's natural painkillers. But the most changes were found in the students' immune systems. These included:

√ Increased levels of gamma interferon, a hormone that "switches on" the immune system, and helps fight viruses and regulates cell growth

√ Increased numbers of "helper T-cells," which help the body coordinate the immune system's response to illness

√ More "Complement 3," a substance that helps antibodies destroy infected and damaged cells

√ An increase in the number and activity of "natural killer (NK) cells," which the body uses to attack foreign cells, cancer cells, and cells infected by virus

Some of the levels even began to change before the students watched the video—just from the expectation that they were about to laugh. "Say you're going to your favorite restaurant," Dr. Berk explains. "You can visualize the food; you can almost taste it. You're already experiencing the physiology of enjoying it. Your immune system [also] remembers…By using humor to combat stress, you can condition yourself to strengthen your immune system."

> *"Everything is drive-through. In California they even have a burial service called Jump-in-the-Box."*
>
> **—Wil Shriner**

GETTING THE JOKE

In 1995 Peter Derks, a psychologist at the College of William and Mary, tested how laughter stimulates the brain. He hooked research subjects up to an EEG (electroencephalogram) topographical brain mapper, then told the subjects jokes. His findings:

• At the start of the joke, the brain processes the information in the left lobe, the analytical side that processes language.
• As the joke progresses, the primary activity shifts to the frontal lobe, where emotions are processed.
• Just before the punch line is delivered, the right side of the brain, which controls the perception of spatial relationships, begins coordinating its activity with the left side of the brain. This is the point where the brain is trying to "get" the joke.
• "What humor is doing," Derks says, "is getting the brain into unison so it can be more efficient in trying to find explanations for—in this case—the punch line. Laughter may also have long-term therapeutic effects." Derks suspects that joke-telling may even help stroke victims and the elderly recover lost brain function.

> *"I date this girl for two years—and then the nagging starts: 'I wanna know your name.'"*
>
> **—Mike Binder**

THE LAUGHTER GENDER GAP

Robert Provine, a psychology professor at the University of Maryland, has studied the laughter that takes place in conversations between men and women. (How? He and his assistants eavesdropped on more than 1,200 conversations that took place on the street and in offices, shopping malls, cocktail parties, and other public places around Baltimore.)

> *"My father's a strange guy. He's allergic to cotton. He has pills he can take, but he can't get them out of the bottle."*
>
> **—Brian Kiley**

His findings:

• "We found that far and away the most laughter takes place when males were talking and females were listening, and the least took place when females were talking and males were listening. Male-male and female-female conversations fell somewhere in between." Provine believes that this is because females are better listeners and are more encouraging in conversation.

• Men are more likely to make jokes than women are, and women are more likely to laugh at them than men are. These differences, Provine says, are already apparent when children begin telling their first jokes, usually around the age of six.

> *"I feel good. I lost 20 pounds on that deal a meal plan.*
> *Not that Richard Simmons plan. This is where you play*
> *cards, lose, and don't have enough cash to eat."*

—John McDowell

ANIMAL LAUGHTER

Chimpanzees, apes, orangutans and a few other primates laugh, but no other animals do. Chimps laugh at the relief of tension, when tickling each other, and when playing chasing games. Their laugh sounds like rapid panting, but unlike humans, they are unable to regulate or control the air as they breathe out, which means they can't change the way it sounds. This lack of ability to control airflow is the same thing that deprives them of speech.

Just because primates can't talk, it doesn't mean they can't share jokes. Chimps and gorillas that have learned sign language have been known to sign one another for laughs. Sometimes they give incorrect signs in "conversation," and then laugh audibly with each other; other times they urinate on humans and then sign "funny."

Ninety percent of all animal species in the history of the Earth are now extinct.

A BRIEF HISTORY OF THE JUKEBOX

Most of us think of jukeboxes as frivolous (or nostalgic) entertainment, but once they were considered mechanical marvels. They played a critical role in developing popular music; in the early 20th century, they were the first phonographs most people saw, and the only ones people could afford. Without them, there would have been no market for blues, jazz, or "hillbilly" music, and the record industry might not have survived. Hard to believe? Read on.

THAT'S AN EARFUL

When Thomas Edison invented the "Edison Speaking Phonograph" in 1877, it was an accident—he was actually trying to create a telephone answering machine. When that didn't work, he suggested a new use for it: a dictation machine for business executives.

The one thing Edison did not want his proud machine used for was entertainment. But that's precisely what happened.

THE MUSIC MACHINE

On November 23, 1889, a man named Louis Glass bought an Edison machine, installed a coin slot, and set it up inside the Palais Royale Saloon in San Francisco. Glass's phonograph didn't have much in common with 20th century jukeboxes: it played a wax cylinder; it had no electric amplifiers—just four listening tubes, so only four people could use it at a time—and it could only play a single song over and over.

But most people had never even seen a record player...so it was quite a novelty. The machine—which cost a nickel for a two-minute song—reportedly brought in more than $15 a week, big money in 1889. Glass set up a dozen more around San Francisco, and raked in the profits.

A NEW BUSINESS

Word of the money-making machine quickly spread. Dozens of saloons around the country copied the idea, and within a year a whole new industry had sprung up to capitalize on the fad.

Long-distance travelers: Hummingbirds can fly 500 miles without stopping.

THE AMERICAN ENTERTAINER

Seventeen years later, the first true "juke box" was introduced. It was called the "Automatic Entertainer"—a slightly misleading name, since it had to be cranked by hand. But it did play the new 10-inch discs instead of wax-and-cardboard cylinder recordings. It also offered more than one selection; it had a huge 40-inch horn instead of listening tubes (though you still couldn't hear it unless you were standing nearby); and it could even tell the difference between "slugs" and real coins.

Its most impressive feature, however, was its record-changing mechanism. This was mounted inside a glass cabinet at the top of the machine, and customers could actually watch the machine pick their record and play it. For most people, that was worth a nickel by itself. They would stand and gawk as the machine performed for them. Thereafter, the jukebox was as much of an attraction as the music it played.

AN ELECTRIFYING DEVELOPMENT

The Automatic Entertainer and its descendants dominated the industry for the next 20 years. But they were still missing something: volume.

In 1927—at about the same time that the electric guitar was being developed—the Automatic Music Instrument Company (AMI) changed that. They introduced the world's first electrically amplified music-playing machine.

"Electrical amplification was the single most important technical improvement in the history of the machine," Vincent Lynch writes in *Jukebox: The Golden Age.* "Suddenly the jukebox was capable of competing with loud orchestras. It could entertain large groups of people in large halls, all at once, for a nickel."

MUSIC NOT PROHIBITED

The timing couldn't have been better. In the late 1920s and early 1930s, radio was the hot new medium. It threatened to make both jukeboxes and phonographs obsolete.

But as soon as jukeboxes could be heard in crowds, they found a profitable new home: speakeasies. Alcohol had become illegal in 1920, and rather than stop drinking, millions of Americans started frequenting these illegal bars. They needed entertainment.

When snakes are born with two heads, they fight each other for food.

"Automatic phonographs" were the perfect solution: they were cheaper and less risky than big bands, and more entertaining than a piano player.

In small, low-rent speakeasies, they were also the only way to get around the prejudice and elitism of radio. Network radio—as powerful an influence on music trends in the 1930s as MTV is on rock today—shunned most "race" music such as jazz, rhythm and blues in favor of classical and mainstream pop hits.

Because of this, black speakeasies—known as juke joints (originally slang for prostitution houses, juke came to mean "dance")—preferred to get their music from automatic phonographs. "For all practical purposes," says one music critic, "there was no place a black musician could have his records heard on a large scale but the jukebox." In time, the machines became so closely associated with juke joints that they became known as jukeboxes.

Well…To be fair, it wasn't just booze that saved the jukebox. Because of the Great Depression in the 1930s, most families couldn't afford their own Victrola phonographs and records. But they could afford to pop an occasional nickel into a jukebox.

THE GOLDEN AGE

Jukeboxes were a thriving industry in the late 1930s; their impact on the recording industry is hard to imagine today. In 1939, jukeboxes used 30 million records. In 1942, that number was up to about 60 million—half of all records produced that year.

But competition from network radio, home phonographs, and other sources grew increasingly fierce. One way jukebox manufacturers distinguished themselves was by making their machines as pleasing to the eye as they were to the ear. As late as 1937, jukeboxes had been virtually indistinguishable from the large wooden radios of the day. "But from then on," says Charles McGovern of the Smithsonian Institution, "the jukebox was more than a source of music. It was a showpiece, a spectacle with lights, color, and observable mechanical motion."

Manufacturers experimented with new designs involving glass, chrome, ornate metals, bubble lights, mirrors, special lighting, and plastics—which had just been invented—to give their machines beautiful new art deco designs that would stand out in any environment. Even the names of the machines were flashy: some popular models included Singing Towers, the Throne of Music, the Mother of Plastic, and the Luxury Light-Up.

The Wurlitzer 1015

But the most famous design of all was the Wurlitzer 1015, better known as "The Bubbler," thanks to its famous bubble tubes, which was introduced in 1946. In the next two years the company manufactured and sold more than 60,000 of them, making it the most popular jukebox in history and establishing Wurlitzer as the industry giant. "In most peoples' minds," says McGovern, "the 1015 is the Jukebox."

THE END OF AN ERA

Post-war sales of all jukeboxes were enormous: by the late 1940s there were more than 700,000 of them in the U.S., filling nearly every bar, bowling alley, malt shop—even gas stations and schools—with music. But mechanically they weren't all that different than the ones that had been around in the 1930s. Most jukeboxes contained about 20 records and played between 20 and 40 songs (depending on whether they could play the "B" sides).

The Seeburg

That changed in December 1948, when the Seeburg company introduced the Model M100-A, a jukebox that wasn't nearly as nice looking as the competition, but had a whopping 100 selections. Because it offered so many musical choices, it had the potential to make a lot more money than any other jukebox on the market. The golden age of jukeboxes was over—beauty would never again count as much as performance and profitability.

THE JUKEBOX BUST

The market for jukeboxes grew through the 1960s, but by the 1970s, it started to decline. There were lots of reasons: alternative rock, FM radio, cassette tapes, the rising cost of records (which forced operators to charge more for each play), and even drunk driving laws. "That was a 'problem' I heard about from Virginia to Mississippi," says a veteran jukebox distributor. "The fact that the drunk driving laws were being enforced, that they got a little stricter, meant that bars started closing down. Took away a big market."

A recent U.S. Army study estimates that 25% of U.S. troops cannot be taught to use a map.

By 1992, there were fewer than 180,000 jukeboxes in America. Recently, compact-disc technology has created a new market for them—and there's talk of developing "digital" jukeboxes....But none of them is likely to be as exciting or important as the originals. To most of us, the machines that shaped pop music in America are just collector's items or curiosities.

* * *

OFF THE WALL

In 1937, the Seeburg Jukebox Co. introduced a machine that didn't have a record-changing mechanism exposed—so people couldn't watch the machine play their selection. Watching was such a big part of the jukebox experience that Seeburg, fearing customers would turn away, invented the "Wall-o-Matic" for diners and restaurants to install at every table, so customers didn't have to leave their seats to play music. They were a huge success. Other companies attempted variations, as Jack Mingo writes in *The Whole Pop Catalog*:

> Until 1941, Wurlitzer made an oversized counter-top jukebox that housed an entire phonograph. Another company put wheels on large wireless units, enabling waitresses to roll jukebox selectors up to their patrons. Neither overtook the Wall-O-Matic, which remains an integral part of diner decor today.

How did those wall units work? Nothing complicated—they were basically just speakers plugged into ordinary A/C outlets. When you choose your song, the box sends electrical impulses through the electrical wiring to the main jukebox—which registers the musical selection and returns it to the speaker the same way.

There are an estimated 508,000 metric tons of tea in China.

GREASE IS THE WORD

More than $400 million and counting—that's what the movie Grease *has grossed worldwide. Not bad for a film that reviewers dismissed as "a thin joke" when it was released in 1978. Here's the story behind one of the most successful musicals of all time.*

DOO-WOP

In 1970, a Chicago advertising copywriter named Jim Jacobs threw a party for the cast of an amateur theater group he worked with.

"I [went] into my closet and dragged out all my old 45 records from the 1950s—Little Richard, Dion and the Belmonts, The Flamingos," he told Didi Conn in her book, *Frenchy's Grease Scrapbook.* "I started playing them in the midst of all the acid rock and psychedelic. Everyone at the party was going, 'What's this stuff?' And I said, 'Doo-wop. Don't you just love to doo-wop?'"

At some point during the party, Jacobs remarked to his friend, Warren Casey, that he thought it would be fun to write a 1950s musical about the kinds of kids he knew in high school…and score it with doo-wop. He even had a title—"Grease"—because in the 1950s "everything was greasy," he says. "The hair, the food, the cars, you know, everything."

THE MORNING AFTER

It was just a passing thought; Jacobs immediately forgot about it but Casey didn't. He'd just been laid off from his job and had always envied the freedom Jacobs seemed to have as a writer. So he bought a typewriter and started pounding away. Two weeks later, he showed up at Jacobs's apartment with a scene he'd written for their musical. Jacobs was dumbfounded. "What musical?" he asked.

Then Jacobs read what his friend had written (it was the pajama party scene) and liked it so much that he agreed to collaborate on the play.

THE REAL THING

Grease debuted on February 5, 1971, in an old Chicago trolley barn that had been converted into a theater. (There's a story that it was originally five hours long—which we printed in our

Queen Elizabeth and Prince Philip of Great Britain are 2nd, 3rd, 4th, and 5th cousins.

Ultimate Bathroom Reader. But Jacobs says that's not true—it was two hours long.) Their timing was perfect—a wave of '50s nostalgia was about to sweep America.

One night not long after it opened, two New York producers happened to catch the play. They realized how on-target it was and bought the rights. Then they helped rewrite it and took it to New York. *Grease* opened off-Broadway in early 1972...and was so successful that it moved to Broadway by June. It ran there for 3,388 performances. When it closed on April 13, 1980, it was the longest running musical in Broadway history (*A Chorus Line* broke its record shortly after).

GOING TO THE BIG SCREEN

In the summer of 1974, a film producer named Allan Carr saw *Grease* on Broadway. He was so impressed that he called the next day to see if the film rights were still available. They weren't—someone was already planning to turn *Grease* into a feature-length cartoon.

Two years later, Carr went to the New York opening of Bette Midler's *Clams on the Halfshell.* "I'll never forget it," he says. "I was on the escalator going down to the lower lobby and realized that right in front of me were Ken Waissman and Maxine Fox, the producers of *Grease.* I tapped them on the shoulder and said, 'By the way, what ever happened with the film rights to *Grease?*'"

"'Funny you should ask,' Ken said. 'The rights lapsed today and the owners didn't pick up their option, so the film rights are available again.'"

Ugly Duckling

Grease was a legitimate Broadway hit by 1976, but newer, more serious plays like *Man of La Mancha and Company* were getting all the respect. *Grease* was considered the "bastard child of Broadway," Carr says, kind of like *The Beverly Hillbillies* on stage. That may have helped keep the film rights affordable—Carr got them for a paltry $200,000.

There was only one problem: Carr didn't have $200,000. As he tells Conn:

> I asked if I could pay it on an installment plan, like I was
> buying a used car, and surprisingly, and happily for me, they

agreed. And even more important, they also agreed that if some of the music from the stage musical wasn't quite right for the movie, we had the right to add additional songs to the picture. Without that interpolation clause, something that composers for the legitimate theater never agree to, "You're the One That I Want," "Grease," "Sandy," and "Hopelessly Devoted" could never have been in the movie.

Carr was a big believer in the film, but Paramount Pictures wasn't convinced. "Hollywood had stopped making musicals at that point," he says, "and they didn't think audiences wanted to see them. Paramount agreed to do it, but at a very modest budget." The studio coughed up $6 million, about half the usual budget for a feature film in the late 1970s.

CASTING ABOUT
Here's who would've been in the movie if Carr had landed his first choices.

• Henry Winkler as Danny Zuko. The Fonz from *Happy Days* was the logical choice for the part. And, as far as Winkler was concerned, that was exactly the problem. "I play this every week on TV," he told Carr. "Why would I do this as a movie?"

• Susan Dey as Sandy. *The Partridge Family* regular (later star of L.A. Law) turned it down. She was tired of playing a teen.

• Stephen Ford (President Gerald Ford's son) as Tom, Sandy's jock boyfriend. The aspiring actor made everyone jittery, including himself, when he showed up on the set with enough bodyguards to take on the Rydell High basketball team. A bad case of nerves wouldn't allow him to step in front of the camera.

• Dick Clark as Vince Fontaine, host of *National Bandstand.* Clark's price was too high. "He wanted more money than Travolta was getting," recalled Carr.

• Cheryl Ladd as cheerleader Patty Simcox. Not yet famous, Ladd was the wife of one of Carr's friends. She didn't mind being asked to be in the movie, but she'd already committed to replacing Farrah Fawcett on *Charlie's Angels.*

• Lucie Arnaz as Rizzo. Lucie's mom, Lucille Ball, was insulted when Carr requested a screen test. "I'm not letting my daughter do a screen test," she fumed. And that was that. Three days later, Stockard Channing was hired.

• Andy Warhol as Rydell High's art teacher. Carr's "one and only regret" was that a studio executive shot down this idea. "I will not have that man in my movie," said the bigwig.

ENTER TRAVOLTA

After Winkler turned him down, Carr started looking for the right Danny again. He found his man by accident. Years earlier, a casting director had sent him a photo of an attractive young actor who was also an excellent singer and dancer. Carr didn't have any roles for the young man at the time, so he shoved the photo in a drawer. He found the photo—of John Travolta (then playing Vinnie Barbarino on *Welcome Back Kotter*)—and auditioned him.

Travolta had played Doody in the touring company of *Grease*. When he got the part as Danny, Carr arranged for Paramount to sign him to *Grease* as part of a three-picture deal; *Saturday Night Fever* was one of them.

Travolta was supposed to film *Grease* before he filmed *Saturday Night Fever*. But there was a clause in the contract that said *Grease* couldn't begin filming until the play ended on Broadway. "Well, the play went on for nine years," Carr says. "So we had to buy that part of the contract out. In the meantime, *Saturday Night Fever* came along….We finished in September, and *Saturday Night Fever* came out in late December, so by the time *Grease* was released, we did have a superstar." Travolta's celebrity helped turn *Grease* into the most profitable movie musical in Hollywood history.

ENTER NEWTON-JOHN

Meanwhile, Allan Carr set about finding another actress to play Sandy. He couldn't find anyone…until one evening when singer Helen Reddy invited him over for dinner. Pop singer Olivia Newton-John was the other invited guest. Carr was impressed by her innocent beauty, and he offered her the part. Newton-John agreed to have a look at the script, and by the time she got it, Sandy Dumbrowski from Chicago had been rewritten into Sandy Olsen from Australia. (Carr figured changing the script would be easier than changing Newton-John's accent.)

A strong bolt of lightning can contain as much as 100 million volts of electricity.

Newton-John was still smarting from her first film role, in a movie called *Tomorrow*. She hated the film and didn't want to be trapped in another film she didn't like. So she insisted on filming a screen test for *Grease*, and she reserved the right to turn down the part if she didn't like herself in the test. The test went fine, and she took the part.

CHECK THEIR I.D.'S

Dinah Manoff (Marty) was the only real teenager among the cast. She was 19. Travolta was 24, Newton-John 29, Jeff Conaway (Kenicke) 27, Didi Conn (Frenchy) 26, Barry Pearl (Doody) 27, Michael Tucci (Sonny) 28. Stockard Channing (Rizzo) was the oldest. She was 34.

BOOM AND BUST

Film critics hated *Grease* as much as the fans loved it. *The New Yorker*, for example, called it "a bogus, clumsily jointed pastiche of late 1950s high school musicals." Yet it was the #1 moneymaking film of the year and has since become the highest-grossing musical flick ever ($400 million worldwide).

In 1998, the critics greeted the 20th anniversary reissue of the film with their usual chorus of boos. "No revival, however joyously promoted, can conceal the fact that this is an average musical, pleasant, upbeat, and plastic," said one. "Because she looks genetically engineered," snapped another, "Newton-John didn't bring much life to the party."

Yet *Grease* keeps rolling on.

• The play has been staged an estimated 90,000 times by amateur and stock companies.

• The video of the movie has sold more than 11 million copies since its release in 1983, making it one of Paramount's top ten best-selling videos of all time.

• The soundtrack—with its three former Top Ten hits—still sells about 9,000 copies per week in this country. Total copies sold around the world: 20 million.

J. EDGAR HOOVER'S BIGGEST BLUNDER

Ever since the Japanese attacked Pearl Harbor in 1941, people have wondered if the U.S. could have prevented it. In our 7th Bathroom Reader, we reprinted an article that speculated on whether President Roosevelt knew it was coming, and let it happen anyway, to draw America into World War II. (Answer: probably not.) In another volume, we told the story of how radar operators mistook Japanese planes on their screen for a mechanical malfunction. Now we have the ultimate story—the tale of how FBI Director J. Edgar Hoover had advance information about Pearl Harbor...and ignored it.

POPOV...DUSKO POPOV

In 1940, agents for the Abwehr, Nazi Germany's military intelligence service, approached a 30-year-old Yugoslavian playboy named Dusko Popov, and asked if he'd like to become a spy for Hitler's war machine.

Popov detested the Nazis. But he accepted their offer...and then turned himself in to MI-6, the British counterintelligence agency. "Following intensive training by both the Germans and the British," Curt Gentry writes in *J. Edgar Hoover: The Man and the Secrets*, "Popov became one of Britain's most successful double agents, the misleading information he fed the Nazis resulted in a number of major intelligence victories."

Helping Out

Popov betrayed every German agent with whom he came into contact. As Ernest Volkman writes in *Spies: The Secret Agents Who Changed History*, because of Popov's work, the British "were able to identify every single agent or asset dispatched from Germany. Those sent to British territory were rounded up and evaluated as possible double [agent]s; those who either refused or did not seem suitable for the task were executed."

And because the British had cracked the Abwehr's secret codes, they could even monitor how well Popov's steady stream of misinformation was influencing decision-making in Berlin.

Name mentioned most frequently in the Bible: David. (Jesus is second.)

...On Second Thought, Let's Not Invade

Popov's efforts may have even altered the course of the war by saving Great Britain from invasion and defeat at the hands of the Nazis. According to Volkman, Popov's greatest achievement was to convince the Germans, via cooked documents, that the British were militarily much stronger than the Germans assumed (although, in fact, Britain had no real power to halt a German attack in 1940). The deception played no small role in Hitler's eventual decision to abandon Operation Sea Lion, the planned invasion of the British Isles.

COMING TO AMERICA

The Abwehr was so completely fooled by Popov's deception, and so impressed with his work, that it gave him one of the most important intelligence assignments of the war. Suspecting that the United States would soon enter the war on the side of the British, the Abwehr ordered Popov to travel to New York and set up a spy ring that would study and report back on the size and strength of the U.S. military.

The assignment represented an incredible opportunity—not for the Nazis, but for the U.S. and Britain: With Popov's help, the U.S. government, acting through the FBI, might be able to monitor, mislead, and ultimately destroy all Nazi espionage efforts in the United States for the remainder of the war.

Meeting with the FBI

There was more: When Popov met with agents in the FBI's New York field office, he took with him two items of interest to the bureau.

The first was samples of the Abwehr's new "microdot" technology, which was capable of shrinking an entire page of text to a tiny dot the size of the period at the end of this sentence. The microdot could then be glued on top of a comma or a period in an ordinary typed letter and sent back to Germany through the regular mail. Even if the letter were intercepted and read, it was unlikely the microdot would be discovered because Great Britain and the United States had never seen anything like it.

The second item of interest was a 97-line questionnaire listing the information that Germany's ally, Japan, hoped to obtain with the help of Popov's spy ring. Most of the questions were general in

An estimated 70% of the hats sold in the United States are baseball caps.

nature, but four addressed military installations on the Hawaiian Islands, and five additional questions, the most specific of the list, asked about a naval base called Pearl Harbor. Here's the questionnaire that the FBI was handed:

Hawaii—Ammunition dumps and mine depots.
1. Details about naval ammunition and mine depot on the Isle of Kushua [sic] (Pearl Harbor). If possible, sketch.
2. Naval ammunition depot Lualuelei. Exact position? Is there a railway line (junction)?
3. The total ammunition reserve of the army is supposed to be in the rock of the Crater Aliamanu. Position?
4. Is the Crater Punchbowl (Honolulu) being used as an ammunition dump? If not, are there other military works?

Naval Strong Point Pearl Harbor.
1. Exact details and sketch about the situation of the state wharf, of the pier installations, workshops, petrol installations, situations of dry dock No. 1 and of the new dry dock which is being built.
2. Details about the submarine station (plan of situation). What land installations are in existence?
3. Where is the station for mine search formations? How far has the dredger work progressed at the entrance and in the east and southeast lock? Depths of water?
4. Number of anchorages?
5. Is there a floating dock in Pearl Harbor or is the transfer of such a dock to this place intended?

BOMBS AWAY!
Popov had learned from a friend named Johann Jebsen, also a double agent, that the Japanese foreign minister and several top naval officials had taken an unusual interest in a stunningly effective attack by the British navy on the Italian port of Taranto. Using only 19 bombers launched from a single aircraft carrier more than 170 miles out to sea, the British navy had knocked nearly half the entire Italian fleet out of commission.

Jebsen himself had escorted the Japanese officials to Taranto, and he noted that they were particularly interested in the success of the British technique of dive-bombing the naval targets. When he learned of the questionnaire that the Abwehr had given Popov, he was convinced that the two were connected. "If my calculated opinion interests you," Jebsen told Popov, "the Japanese will attack the United States." Most likely at Pearl Harbor, most likely using dive-bombers.

STUCK IN NEW YORK

Popov told the FBI everything he knew. His information was good...perhaps too good. Percy "Sam" Foxworth, the FBI's Agent in Charge of the New York office, was skeptical from the start. "It all looks too precise, too complete, to be believed," he told Popov. "The questionnaire plus the other information spell out in detail exactly where, when, how, and by whom we are to be attacked. If anything, it sounds like a trap."

Popov was under orders from the Abwehr to go immediately to Hawaii, but the FBI vetoed the trip and ordered him to remain in New York until Director J. Edgar Hoover decided whether to approve the Nazi spy ring. So Popov took up residence in an exclusive Park Avenue penthouse, where he resumed his passions for women (his British code name was "Tricycle," reportedly because of his penchant for taking two women—preferably twins—to bed at the same time), alcohol, and the good life while waiting for Hoover to make up his mind.

Keeping an Eye on Things

Unfortunately for Popov and the Allied war effort, Hoover ordered Popov's penthouse placed under surveillance. Heavy surveillance. "If I bend over to smell a bowl of flowers," Popov later complained, "I scratch my nose on a microphone."

When word of Popov's lavish accommodations and lurid lifestyle found its way to Hoover's desk, the director was furious. Any link with Popov, if exposed, could sully the FBI's carefully constructed, squeaky-clean public image. What would happen to the Bureau's reputation if the public learned that it couldn't catch Nazi spies on its own without the help of a womanizing foreigner who wore too much cologne and smoked cigarettes out of an ivory holder?

Australia has more sheep than any other country on Earth.

MEETING MR. HOOVER

Popov spent more than five weeks in New York before J. Edgar Hoover finally agreed to meet with him.

The meeting did not go well. "There was Hoover," Popov wrote in his autobiography, "looking like a sledgehammer in search of an anvil."

> "I can catch spies without your or anybody else's help," Hoover barked. "What have you done since you came here?"
>
> "Nothing but wait for instructions, which never came," I answered. Hoover breathed in deeply and noisily. It seemed to calm him. "What kind of a bogus spy are you?" he said accusingly...."You're like all double agents...."You're begging for information to sell to your German friends so you can make a lot of money and be a playboy...." He turned to [an assistant] and said, "That man is trying to teach me my job."
>
> ....I recognized the futility of it all. "I don't think anyone could teach you anything," I told the FBI chief, and walked toward the door.
>
> "Good riddance," he screamed after me.

Hoover vetoed the German spy ring. That was just the beginning. He also confiscated the funds Popov received from Germany and nearly arrested his Abwehr handler, which would have exposed him as a double agent and made him useless to the British; and then he forced the British to withdraw Popov from the U.S. Not that Popov minded—as Curt Gentry writes, Popov wasn't unhappy about leaving. The trip had, he felt, been a waste of time—with one extraordinarily important exception. When the Japanese launched their "surprise" attack on Pearl Harbor, Popov knew, the United States would be ready and waiting.

MISSED OPPORTUNITY

Did Hoover's insecurities cost the United States the most important intelligence coup of the war? Popov wasn't alone in thinking so. In 1945, Rear Admiral Edwin Layton, the Fleet Intelligence Officer at Honolulu during the bombing of Pearl Harbor, published a report on the attack. He found that where Popov's warning was concerned, Hoover "dropped the ball completely.... His failure," Layton concluded, "represented another American fumble on the road to Pearl Harbor."

Secret stash: FBI director J. Edgar Hoover kept a collection of pornography locked in his desk.

KING KONG

King Kong was one of the most influential movies of all time. As both entertainment and a vehicle for special effects, it was unsurpassed. Even its promotion foreshadowed modern advertising techniques. We all know the character, but few of us know anything about how the film was made.

PART I: ADVENTURE FILMS

The early 1900s were years of discovery in which transcontinental railroads, steamships, and airplanes were opening up the last unexplored corners of the world.

- In 1909 U.S. explorer Robert Peary became the first person to reach the North Pole.
- In 1911 Roald Amundsen was the first to step foot on the South Pole.
- In 1927 Charles Lindbergh made the first nonstop flight across the Atlantic Ocean from New York to Paris.

Thanks to the new medium of motion-picture film, it was now possible for explorers to take cameras with them and bring back footage of an exotic world that audiences at home would otherwise never see.

The Partners

Merian C. Cooper and Ernest Schoedsack were part of the new breed of filmmaker/explorer. Cooper, a former fighter pilot, and Schoedsack, a combat photographer, had met during World War I. In 1925 they reunited and traveled to Persia (now Iran) to film a feature-length documentary about the migration of 50,000 Bhaktiari tribesmen over a 12,000-foot mountain range and across the Karun river in search of grazing land for their herds.

Even today, the film—called *Grass*—is considered a classic. "The crossing of the torrential Karun river," Eric Barnow writes in *Documentary*, "with loss of life among men, women, children, goats, sheep, donkeys, and horses, provided one of the most spectacular sequences ever put on film."

Cooper and Schoedsack followed up with *Chang*, a film about tribal life in the remote jungles of Siam (now Thailand). Like *Grass*, it was a critical success that also made money at the box office. One critic called it "the most remarkable film of wild beast life that has reached the screen…Man-eating tigers, furious

There are no words in the English language that rhyme with purple.

elephants in thundering stampedes, leopards, bears, monkeys, snakes, and other animals are shown in…one tense thrill after another."

Chang was popular with theater *audiences*, but theater *owners* complained that the movie would have played to larger audiences if it had contained a love story. Cooper took their message to heart.

PART II: GORILLA MY DREAMS

In 1929 Cooper and Schoedsack split up: Cooper stayed in New York to tend to his investments in the fledgling aviation industry; Schoedsack and his wife shot another film in the Dutch East Indies.

While he was stuck behind his desk in New York, Cooper began reading up on the newly discovered Komodo dragons. The world's largest species of lizards, they are found in only one place on earth: the island of Komodo in the South Pacific.

The Island That Time Forgot

The dragons gave Cooper the idea for another film, set on an imaginary island "way west of Sumatra." It would be about modern man's discovery of the island, and an encounter with huge "prehistoric" animals there. As the plot developed in Cooper's imagination, he explained,

> I got to thinking about the possibility of there having been one beast, more powerful than all the others and more intelligent. Then the thought struck me—what would happen to this highest representative of prehistoric animal life in our materialistic, mechanistic civilization? Why not place him at the pinnacle of the tallest building, symbol in steel, stone and glass of modern man's achievement and aspiration, and pit him against modern man?

Evolutionary Thinking

That central character, Cooper decided, should be a gigantic ape. An ape would be better at approximating human emotions than an elephant or dinosaur.

He wrote up a proposal for the film in 1931 and pitched it to Paramount and Metro-Goldwyn-Mayer. He suggested filming the jungle scenes on location in Africa and on Komodo Island, and casting a real ape in the lead—a character he named "Kong." The

Pop singer Michael Jackson collects mannequins.

studios liked the concept, but the Great Depression was underway, and they refused to risk so much money on a film that relied on animal actors and expensive on-location filming. Cooper put the idea aside.

PART III: THE SPECIAL EFFECTS MAN

In 1932 David Selznick, head of production at RKO studios, hired Cooper as his executive assistant. Like many Hollywood studios in the 1930s, RKO was on the verge of bankruptcy. Cooper's job was to help Selznick review studio projects to see which ones were likely to make money, and which ones should be scrapped.

One project that Cooper looked over was test footage from *Creation*, a movie about shipwrecked sailors who land on an island of prehistoric animals. The dinosaur footage was created by Willis O'Brien, a former cowboy, prize-fighter, and newspaper cartoonist who was now a pioneer in trick photography.

Stop-Motion Animation

As a feature film, *Creation* didn't work because the footage was boring—Cooper called it "just a lot of animals walking around"— and there wasn't much of a plot. But Cooper was still amazed by what he saw: the dinosaurs were lifelike and huge, and the backdrops were incredibly realistic.

It turned out that the creatures were less than eight inches tall. O'Brien had made the footage with miniature models on a tabletop in his garage, using a procedure called "animation in depth" (now known as *stop-motion animation*). O'Brien filmed the animation frame by frame: he took pictures of his models, then moved them slightly and photographed them again. He repeated this painstaking process again and again, 24 times for each second of animation. When played back at ordinary speed, the models appeared to move by themselves.

O'Brien also knew how to combine the footage with human action sequences, making it appear as if dinosaurs and humans were in the same scenes.

Cooper had stumbled onto someone who could actually make his Kong movie work. With animation in depth, he wouldn't need a real ape, and he wouldn't need to film on location—he could film all of the ape sequences right on O'Brien's workbench for a fraction of the original cost.

PART IV: GOING APE

RKO agreed to pay for a test reel of animation footage showing Kong in action, and O'Brien's assistant, Marcel Delgado, was assigned the task of designing the ape model that would make or break the film. Cooper told him to make it look somewhat human, so audiences would feel sorry for it at the end of the movie.

The first model was apelike, but still too human; so was the second model. So Cooper changed his instructions. "I want Kong to be the fiercest, most brutal, monstrous damned thing that has ever been seen." O'Brien argued that if the ape was too apelike, no one would sympathize with it, but Cooper disagreed. "I'll have women crying over him before I'm through, and the more brutal he is, the more they'll cry at the end."

What a Doll!

The test Kong was 18 inches high and covered with sponge rubber muscles and trimmed rabbit fur. "I never was satisfied with the fur," Delgado later recalled, "because I knew it would show the fingerprints of the animators." (He was right—even in the finished film, Kong's fur "bristles" as if it is being blown by the wind; an unintentional effect caused by the animators' fingers disturbing the fur as they move the model between shots.)

RKO executives watched the footage… and immediately commissioned the film. Cooper called Schoedsack in, and the two became partners again.

PART V: WRITE ON

Finding someone to write a satisfactory script proved as hard as building a good ape: The first writer died of pneumonia before he could start work, and the second couldn't figure out how to make some of the key parts of the plot seem believable, such as how Kong gets to New York.

Finally Schoedsack turned to a real adventurer to write the story: his wife Ruth Rose. She had never written a screenplay in her life, but her travel experiences as an explorer made her perfect for the job. "Put us in it," Cooper and Schoedsack told her. "Give it the spirit of a real Cooper-Schoedsack expedition."

The Story

The finished version of the story did just that: it featured a crazed documentary filmmaker named Carl Denham (Robert Armstrong)

Dwight Eisenhower hated cats so much he ordered that any found on his property be shot.

who learns of Skull Island from a Norwegian skipper and plans an expedition to the island to make the ultimate travel-adventure film. With him on the voyage is Ann Darrow (Fay Wray), a beautiful but desperate young woman he rescues from the mean streets of New York City only hours before the ship sets sail. Hired to add "love interest" to the documentary, Darrow delivers more than expected when she captures Kong's heart.

PART VI: SPECIAL EFFECTS
Like the *Star Wars* films that would follow four decades later, *King Kong* was a milestone in special effects filmmaking. Willis O'Brien and his crew performed camera miracles the like of which no one had ever seen.

Making the Monkey
All of the ape sequences were made using models. There isn't a single man-in-an-ape-suit scene in the entire film (although at least two actors would later claim to have been the "man inside Kong").

O'Brien and Delgado made the ape footage in total secrecy, with only Cooper, Schoedsack, and top RKO executives allowed to monitor their progress. The secret was kept for several years after the film was released, and few people had any idea at all how the ape scenes had been created. One rumor had it that RKO had built a full-sized, walking robot ape that was controlled by several men who rode inside. The reality was much different.

Kong was billed as a 50-foot-tall ape. Actually, he was portrayed as much smaller than that in the film.
• The ape model used in the jungle scenes was only 18 inches tall; the one used in the Empire State Building Scenes was 24 inches tall.
• Since the modelers were working on a scale of 1 inch as equaling 1 foot, that means Kong was 18 feet tall in the jungle and 24 feet tall in the city.

Why the difference in sizes? Cooper wanted Kong large enough to be terrifying, yet small enough to take a believable love interest in tiny Fay Wray. Eighteen feet was initially set as the standard... but when work began on the Empire State Building scenes, he and Schoedsack saw that Kong looked too small against the skyscrapers. "We realized we'd never get much drama out of a fly crawling up the tallest building in the world," Schoedsack said later.

Julius Caesar was epileptic.

You Big Ape

There were no full-scale models of the complete ape, although the studio did make full-size models of the body parts that had contact with human actors. A huge hand suspended from a crane was made to lift Fay Wray aloft; and a huge foot and lower leg were made for the scenes in which Kong stomps natives to death.

The most complicated piece of all was the full-sized head-and-shoulders model, which was made of a wood and metal skeleton covered with rubber and carefully trimmed bearskins. The plaster and balsa wood eyeballs were as large as bowling balls, and the mouth, complete with a full set of huge balsa wood teeth, opened wide enough for Kong to chew on the natives.

The head-and-shoulders unit was large enough to hold the three men who controlled Kong's facial expressions using levers and compressed-air hoses connected to the movable mouth, lips, nostrils, eyes, eyelids, and eyebrows.

PART VII: THE VOICE

Sound effects were also a challenge: in some scenes Kong roared for as long as 30 seconds and though RKO had a sound effects library with more than 500,000 different animal sounds, even the longest elephant roars only lasted 8 seconds.

RKO sound man Murray Spivack went to the zoo at feeding time to get his own sounds. He got Kong's sounds from the lion and tiger cages, as he later recounted:

> The handlers would make gestures like they were going to take the food away from them and we got some pretty wild sounds. Then I took some of these roars back to the studio and put them together and played them backward. I slowed them down, sort of like playing a 78-rpm record at 33, until the tone was lowered one octave, then I re-recorded it. From this we took the peaks and pieced them together. We had to put several of these together in turn to sustain the sound until Kong shut his mouth, because Kong's roars were many times longer than those of any living animal.

For the affectionate sounds Kong makes when he's with Ann Darrow, Spivack grunted into a megaphone, then slowed the recording down until he thought it sounded like a big ape.

PART VIII: THE SCENERY

Their revolutionary approach to special effects included innovation with scenery. The "location" sequences were filmed on miniature sets that used a combination of special effects:

- The background details were painted on glass.
- Objects in the foreground, such as trees, rocks, and logs, were modeled in miniature using clay, wire, and even toilet paper.
- Sometimes the human footage (a person crouching in a cave, for example) was shot in advance. Then, in a process known as "miniature projection," a tiny screen would be set up in the tabletop jungle set where the ape animation was filmed. The human footage was then projected onto the screen frame by frame, making it seem as if the cave was part of the jungle. In the finished film, Kong appears to be towering over someone hiding in a cave.

PART IX: KONG ON THE RAMPAGE!

Cooper and Schoedsack wanted a powerful, one-word title for their film, so they named it *Kong*. But David Selznick was afraid that *Kong* would be mistaken for just another travel film (like *Grass* or *Chang*). So just before the film was released, he changed the name to *King Kong*.

When work on the film began, everyone in Hollywood thought it would fail. But when RKO showed the finished film to theater owners, the response was so enthusiastic that the studio launched the biggest promotional campaign in its history. "THE PICTURE DESTINED TO STARTLE THE WORLD!," advertisements blared in national magazines.

The promotions paid off—in New York City, *King Kong* was booked at both the Radio City Music Hall and the New Roxy, the city's two largest theaters, with a total of more than 10,000 seats.

Even that wasn't enough. It made no difference that the Depression was on—as Goldner and Turner write in *The Making of King Kong,* "in the first four days of its run, *King Kong* set a new all-time world attendance record for any indoor attraction, bringing in $89,931...To accommodate the crowds it was necessary to run ten shows daily."

The movie made so much money that it lifted RKO out of debt for the first time in its history.

THE WOLFMAN AT THE MOVIES

The werewolf is one of the most recognized movie monsters in history, thanks in large part to the 1941 film The Wolf Man, *starring Lon Chaney Jr. Here's a behind-the-scenes look at the making of that classic film.*

FRIGHT FACTORY

The early 1930s was the golden age of movie monsters. In 1930, Universal released the classic *Dracula*, starring Bela Lugosi; a year later it had another huge hit with Boris Karloff's *Frankenstein*. Inspired by their success, Universal decided to make a movie about a werewolf. In 1931, they handed writer/director Robert Florey a title—*The Wolf Man*—and told him to come up with an outline.

A few months later, Florey submitted notes for a story about a Frenchman who has suffered for 400 years under a witch's curse that turns him into a werewolf during every full moon...unless he wears a garland of wolf-bane around his neck.

The studio approved the idea and scheduled the movie as a Boris Karloff vehicle for 1933. A shooting script was written...and rewritten...and rewritten several more times. By the time it was finished, the script was about an English doctor who is bitten by a werewolf in Tibet, then turns into one himself on his return to London. Universal renamed the picture *Werewolf of London*.

BAT MAN

By now, however, Boris Karloff was too busy to take the part....So it went to a Broadway actor named Henry Hull. *Werewolf of London* hit theatres in 1935.

The movie wasn't very good: One critic has called it "full of fog, atmosphere, and laboratory shots, but short on chills and horror." That was largely because Hull didn't look scary. He refused to cover his face with werewolf hair, complaining that it obscured his features. Makeup man Jack Pierce—already a legend for creating Bela Lugosi's Dracula and Boris Karloff's

Frankenstein—had no choice but to remove most of the facial hair, leaving Hull looking like a demonic forest elf. *Werewolf of London* was a box office disappointment. It was also Hull's last werewolf film.

SECOND TRY

In the early 1940s, Universal launched a second wave of horror films featuring Dracula, Frankenstein, and other classic monsters. They decided to give the werewolf another try, too.

This second werewolf film started the same way the first one did: with the title *The Wolf Man*. This time the scriptwriter was Curt Siodmak. He started from scratch, researched werewolf legends himself, and used what he learned to write the script. The story he concocted was about an American named Lawrence Talbot who travels to his ancestral home in Wales and is bitten while rescuing a young woman from a werewolf attack.

Once again, the studio wanted to cast Karloff in the lead…and once again, he was too busy to take it. They considerd Bela Lugosi, but he was too old for the part. So they gave it to newcomer Lon Chaney, Jr., son and namesake of the greatest horror star of the silent movie era. Chaney, Sr. was known all over the world as "the Man of 1000 Faces," for his roles in *The Phantom of the Opera* and *The Hunchback of Notre Dame*. Chaney, Jr. had recently starred in *Man Made Monster,* and Universal thought he had potential in horror films.

THE MAKEUP

Jack Pierce was still the makeup artist at Universal, and he welcomed the chance to use his original design: a hairy face complete with fangs and a wolfish nose, plus hairy hands and feet. The makeup took a total of four hours to apply, most of which was spent applying tufts of fur—authentic yak hair imported from Asia—one by one, and then singeing them to create a wild look. Chaney's wolfman didn't talk—all it did was grunt, growl, and howl—and that was no accident: when Chaney was fully made up, he couldn't talk and could only eat through a straw. As he recounted years later, the only thing worse than wearing the makeup was taking it off:

Ronald Reagan is the only U.S. president to have performed in Las Vegas.

What gets me is when it's after work and I'm all hot and itchy and tired, and I've got to sit in that chair for forty-five minutes more while Pierce just about kills me ripping off the stuff he put on in the morning! Sometimes we take an hour and leave some of the skin on my face!

THANKS, DAD
Most actors would probably have refused to wear such difficult makeup, but Chaney (whose real first name was Creighton) had no choice: he was desperate to make it in the film business.

While he was alive, Lon Chaney, Sr. had fought Creighton's attempts to become an actor. He even forced his son out of Hollywood High and into a plumbing school when he asked to take acting lessons. As Chaney, Sr.'s career soared to its heights in the late 1920s, Chaney, Jr. was working as a boilermaker.

The elder Chaney died of throat cancer in 1930; Creighton Chaney signed with RKO studios two years later. After moving from bit part to bit part for more than two years, he reluctantly changed his name to Lon Chaney, Jr., to cash in on his father's fame. "They had to starve me to make me take his name," he groused years later.

Finally, in 1939—only days after his car and furniture were repossessed by a furniture company—Chaney scored a hit in a stage version of *Of Mice and Men*. That led to a starring role in the movie version, and in 1940, a contract with Universal.

ALL THIS AND WORLD WAR II
The studio had modest hopes for *The Wolf Man*. They scheduled its release for December 11, 1941, right before Christmas. But on December 7, Japan bombed Pearl Harbor and the United States entered World War II. Universal was sure the movie would become a box office disaster. After all, who was going to take time out for the movies when they were going to war?

Good vs. Evil
To their surprise, it was a hit. The film played to packed movie houses all over the country, and was the studio's biggest money-maker of the season. It established the Wolf Man as an important movie monster, along with Dracula and Frankenstein. It almost

In 1980, a Las Vegas hospital suspended workers for betting on when patients would die.

singlehandedly made werewolves a part of the popular culture, and it turned Lon Chaney Jr. into one of the best known actors in the country.

World War II probably had more to do with making *The Wolf Man* a hit than any other factor. What Universal had failed to realize was that the war fueled a need for the kind of escape that horror films provided. Inside a darkened theater, moviegoers could forget their troubles, at least for a while, as they watched ordinary mortals triumph over seemingly insurmountable evil. As David Skal writes in *The Monster Show: A Cultural History of Horror,*

> Talbot's four-film quest to put to rest his wolf-self is, in a strange way, an unconscious parable of the war effort. The Wolf Man's crusade for eternal peace and his frustrated attempts to control irrational, violent, European forces....The Wolf Man's saga was the most consistent and sustained monster myth of the war, beginning with the first year of America's direct involvement in the war, and finishing up just in time for Hiroshima.

WOLF MAN FACTS

• The hardest scene to shoot was the final "metamorphosis" scene, in which Chaney turns from a werewolf to a human as he dies. Chaney describes the process:

> The way we did the transformation was that I came in at 2:00 a.m. When I hit the position, they would take little nails and drive them through the skin at the edge of my fingers, on both hands, so that I wouldn't move them anymore.
>
> While I was in this position, they would take the camera and weigh it down with one ton, so that it wouldn't move when people walked. They had targets for my eyes.
>
> Then, they would shoot five or ten frames of film in the camera. They'd take the film out and send it to the lab. While it was there, the make-up man would come and take the whole thing off my face and put on a new one. I'm still immobile. When the film came back from the lab, they'd put it back in the camera and then they'd check me.
>
> They'd say, "Your eyes have moved a little bit, move them to the right...." Then they'd roll it again and shoot another 10 frames. Well, we did 21 changes of make-up and it took twenty two hours. I won't discuss about the bathroom...

• For the rest of the cast and crew, the worst part of filming *The Wolf Man* was breathing the special effects fog that was used in the outdoor scenes. "The kind of fog they used in those days was nothing like the kind we have today," cameraman Phil Lathrop remembers. "It was greasy stuff made with mineral oil. We worked in it for weeks and the entire cast and crew had sore eyes and intestinal trouble the entire time. Besides that, we were all shivering with cold because it was necessary to keep the temperature below 50 degrees when using the fog." Female lead Evelyn Ankers fainted on the set after inhaling too much fog during a chase sequence.

• *The Wolf Man* made a lot of money for Universal, but not much of it filtered down to the writers and actors who actually brought it to life. "My salary was $400 a week," scriptwriter Curt Siodmak recalls. "When the picture made its first million, the producer got a $10,000 bonus, the director got a diamond ring for his wife, and I got fired, since I wanted $25 more for my next job.

LON CHANEY'S WOLFMAN SEQUELS

Chaney made four wolfman movies for Universal during the war years…more than Universal made of *Dracula* or *Frankenstein*. The others were:

• *Frankenstein Meets the Wolfman* (1943). Chaney travels to Castle Frankenstein to see if he can find a cure for his wolfman condition in Dr. Frankenstein's notes. All he finds is the Frankenstein monster, played by Bela Lugosi, who had turned down the original *Frankenstein* in 1931 because there wasn't any dialogue. Movie Note: Lugosi played a particularly stiff Frankenstein, not just because he was growing old, but also because in the original version of the film, Frankenstein is left blind and mute after a botched brain transplant. In the version released to theaters, all references to blindness, muteness and the brain transplant were removed, so he just looks old.

• *House of Frankenstein* (1944). Mad scientist Dr. Gustav Niemann (Boris Karloff) escapes from an insane asylum with the help of his hunchback assistant Daniel (J. Carrol Naish) and flees to Castle Frankenstein. There he teams up with Dracula (John Carradine), Frankenstein (Glenn Strange), and the Wolfman

(Chaney) to terrorize the countryside until they are finally killed by villagers.

• **House of Dracula (1945)**. Dr. Franz Edelman (Onslow Stevens) finds a way to cure Dracula (John Carradine) of his vampirism, but Dracula refuses to submit. Instead, he bites Dr. Edelman and turns him into a vampire; then Edelman raises Frankenstein from the dead, just as the Wolfman arrives on the scene.
Movie Note: Originally titled *The Wolfman vs. Dracula*, the movie had to be renamed because the Wolfman and Dracula do not actually meet in the film.

• **Abbot and Costello Meet Frankenstein (1948)**. Bud Abbott and Lou Costello team up with the Wolfman to prevent Dracula (Lugosi) and a mad female scientist (Lenore Aubert) from transplanting Costello's brain into the Frankenstein monster. Critics say the film is symbolic of the decline of Universal's horror classics in the late 1940s—fans say it is one of the best films Abbot and Costello ever made.

THE END
Chaney would reprise the wolfman role in movies and in television for the rest of his life, including appearances on *The Pat Boone Show*, and *Route 66*. He also played the Frankenstein monster in *The Ghost of Frankenstein* (1942), Count Dracula in *Son of Dracula* (1943), and the Mummy in three Mummy movies. A heavy drinker, by the 1960s he was reduced to appearing in low-budget schlock like *Face of the Screaming Werewolf* (1965); *Hillbillies in a Haunted House* (1967); and *Dracula vs. Frankenstein* (1970). He died of a heart attack in 1973. But the wolfman lives on.

The Legend Lives On.
Like all classic Hollywood monsters, the werewolf was spun off into dozens of movies, many of them low- budget, some just plain unusual. Take these, for example:

• **I Was A Teenage Werewolf (1957)**
The original "teenage" horror film, *I Was a Teenage Werewolf*, was filmed in seven days at a cost of $125,000…and made $2,000,000.

It launched an entire genre of low-budget, B-movie films, including *I Was a Teenage Frankenstein*, *I Was a Teenage Zombie*, and *I Was a Teenage TV Terrorist*.

The movie stars a young Michael Landon (of *Bonanza* and *Little House on the Prairie* fame) in his first feature film role. He plays an emotionally disturbed teenager seeking treatment for his problems. A mad scientist hypnotizes him and he "regresses" so far back in time that he becomes a prehistoric werewolf. Landon's girlfriend is not amused, and neither are the police. They gun him down at the end of the film.

• The Mad Monster (1942)
Dr. Cameron, a mad scientist, injects a handyman with the blood of a wolf, "turning him into the prototype for an army of wolfmen to battle the Nazis." In the end, however, Dr. Cameron succumbs to pettiness and uses the werewolf "to kill the men he believes responsible for destroying his reputation." The film, banned in the UK until 1952, was finally released with an X rating and a medical disclaimer touting the safety of blood transfusions.

• Werewolf In A Girl's Dormitory (1961)
When a series of ghastly murders take place at a correctional school for wayward girls, investigators discover that Mr. Swift, the school's superintendent, is a werewolf.

• Werewolves On Wheels (1971)
"With surfing music blaring on the soundtrack, motorcycle gang members curse, attend impromptu orgies, drink barrels of beer and rough up some monks. In retaliation, cyclists are cursed with lycanthropy [they're turned into werewolves]. What follows is some very unintentional comedy and some very unnecessary nudity."

—The Creature Feature's Movie Guide

• Leena Meets Frankenstein (1993)
"A hardcore remake of *Abbot and Costello Meet Frankenstein* (1948), which changes from black and white to color for the sex scenes. When their car breaks down, two street-wise babes are stranded at a time-share condo with the classic monsters—the

Wolfman, Dracula, his vampire wives, and the Frankenstein monster."

—The Illustrated Werewolf Movie Guide

• *The Rats Are Coming! The Werewolves Are Here!* (1972)
"When a newly married man discovers that his inlaws are incestuous werewolves, he and his wife set out to break the family curse. The characters include a 108-year-old family patriarch and the wife's brother Malcolm, who is kept in shackles in a locked room, where he commits unspeakable crimes against chickens and mice. "To pad its short running time, producer Andy Milligan filmed a subplot of man-eating rats in Milligan's hometown of Staten Island. Ads offered: 'Win a live rat for your mother-in-law.'"

—Cult Flicks and Trash Pics

• *Night Stalkers* (1995)
A private detective stumbles onto a society of werewolves while investigating the murder of someone who was skinned alive. Probably the world's first all-deaf werewolf film, directed by a deaf director and "shot on video in London and Liverpool with an all-deaf cast for an incredible $600, utilizing sign language, subtitles, and voice-over for the hearing impaired."

—The Illustrated Werewolf Movie Guide

• *Werewolf Of Woodstock* (1975)
A few days after the Woodstock festival, a beer-drinking, hippie-hating farmer (Tige Andrews from TV's *The Mod Squad*) who lives next to the farm, is struck by lightning and turns into a beer-drinking, hippie-hating werewolf who preys on slow-to-leave concert-goers. *The Creature Features Movie Guide* describes it as "undoubtedly one of the dumbest lycanthropy [werewolf] movies ever produced."

• *Curse Of The Queerwolf* (1987)
"A straight man is bitten on the butt by a gay werewolf(!) and transforms into the title character. When the moon is full, he finds himself turning into a werewolf—and gay! [Director Michael] Pirro takes advantage of the outrageously funny idea of turning homophobia into a horror movie."

—Cult Flicks and Trash Pics

• *The Werewolf And The Yeti* (1975)
A man on a Tibetan expedition in search of the Yeti is bitten by
two cannibalistic sisters he finds in a cave. He becomes a werewolf
during the next full moon, and battles the abominable snowman.

• *Full Moon High* (1981)
A 1950s high school student (Adam Arkin of TV's *Chicago Hope*)
is bitten by a werewolf while on a trip to Armenia with his CIA
agent father. Forever young, he returns to Full Moon High twenty
years later disguised as his own son.

• *Blood!* (1974)
Dracula's daughter Regina meets the son of Laurence Talbot (the
Wolfman) and falls in love. "They get married, move to America,
and attempt to raise flesh-eating plants to cure their respective
curses."

—*The Illustrated Werewolf Movie Guide*

*   *   *

ASK THE EXPERTS

Q: *Why is it considered bad luck for a black cat to cross one's path?*
A: "[This superstition] is probably a survival of the medieval belief
that Satan often assumed the form of a black tom-cat when he
sallied out upon an excursion for mischief. The ancient Egyptians
regarded the cat as sacred, but during the Middle Ages this animal
fell into bad repute among Europeans, who associated black speci-
mens especially with the devil and darkness. In some countries it
was believed that all black cats were transformed into evil spirits
at the end of seven years. Up until a few hundred years ago all
witches were supposed to have black cats as familiars, and in
popular representations at Halloween time witches are still shown
accompanied by black cats while on their nocturnal journeys.
Strangely enough, the appearance of a stray cat of any color into a
home has always been regarded as a sign of good luck, especially if
it remains." (From *Why Do Some Shoes Squeak?*, by George W.
Stimpson)

According to zoologists, deer like to play tag. They tag each other using their hooves.

TARZAN OF THE MOVIES: HERE'S JOHNNY!

Besides Edgar Rice Burroughs, the person most associated with the character of Tarzan is a swimmer-turned-actor named Johnny Weismuller. In fact, it wasn't until 1932, when Weismuller took on the role, that Tarzan developed a stable personality and face the public could get used to. But to Johnny, it was just a job. Here's the story.

AFRICA SPEAKS

In 1927, MGM bought the film rights to *Trader Horn*, the memoirs of an African adventurer, and assigned director W.S. "Woody" Van Dyke to the picture. The studio originally planned to make it as a silent film, but then decided that *Trader Horn* would be their first talkie.

Making the leap from silent films to sound is considered the biggest technological advance in the history of filmmaking. MGM understood the significance of the coming of sound and wanted its first talkie to be larger than life. Money was no object—*Trader Horn* was going to be the best film possible.

On the Road

Van Dyke persuaded the studio that the only way to do the film justice was to film it on location. So in March 1929, Van Dyke—along with 35 cast and crew members, three sound trucks, and 90 tons of equipment—set sail for Africa. Over the next seven months, they (and 200 African natives) traveled more than 10,000 miles through Africa, shooting more than a million feet of film. Needless to say, the production ran over budget.

'The expense was worth it," John Taliaferro writes. "When *Trader Horn* was released in 1931 it was a huge hit and helped rekindle public interest in the continent of Africa. Even Ernest Hemingway credited *Trader Horn* with giving him his Africa 'bug.'"

MGM had more than just a hit film on its hands: It had thousands and thousands of feet of unused African film footage and the studio began looking for ways to put it to good use.

"Inevitably," Taliaferro says, "someone suggested Tarzan."

Mighty Mouse's girlfriend was named Pearl Pureheart.

TOUGH BREAK

By 1931 MGM had bought the rights to *Tarzan the Ape Man* and hired Van Dyke to direct it. For the first time in the history of the Tarzan franchise, a movie studio was simply buying the right to make a movie about Burroughs's character and was free to come up with its own story.

Having Van Dyke direct the film was a good idea from a stylistic point of view: he was considered Hollywood's finest nature filmmaker. But it made casting the film more difficult, because Van Dyke was a perfectionist who wasn't afraid to turn down Tinseltown's biggest stars if he felt they weren't right for the role. Clark Gable was one of the first actors rejected. "He has no body," Van Dyke complained. "What I want is a man who is young, strong, well-built, reasonably attractive, but not necessarily handsome, and a competent actor. The most important thing is that he have a good physique. And I can't find him."

STROKE OF LUCK

Meanwhile, screenwriter Cyril Hume was hard at work in his hotel room cranking out the Tarzan screenplay. One afternoon he stepped out for a minute and happened to notice a powerfully built young man swimming in the hotel pool. It was 27-year-old Johnny Weissmuller, the greatest amateur swimmer the world had ever seen.

Between 1921 and 1928, Weissmuller had won 52 national titles, held every freestyle record, and broken his own records dozens of times. Weissmuller won three gold medals at the 1924 Olympics and two more at the 1928 games. Not long afterward he gave up his amateur status and signed on as the national spokesman for BVD swimwear and underwear. He was still modeling for BVD when Cyril Hume discovered him.

MR. NATURAL

Hume was so impressed by Weissmuller that he arranged a meeting with Van Dyke. However, rather than give him a formal screen test, they just had him strip to his shorts to get a sense of what he'd look like in a loin cloth. Two things immediately struck them: 1) Weissmuller clearly had the right build for the part, and 2) he seemed perfectly at ease stripping down to his underpants in front of two men he hardly knew. He actually appeared comfortable in his skivvies, something almost unheard of in an age where most men still wore two-piece, shirt-and-shorts bathing suits on the beach. In fact, Weissmuller had spent so many years modeling underwear and wearing skimpy one-piece racing trunks that he was completely uninhibited about appearing semi-nude on film. Even though he was nearly naked, he somehow seemed wholesome.

"Other Tarzan actors, when they wore loincloths and leopard skins, seemed merely undressed," Taliaferro writes. "Weissmuller, by contrast, was clean-limbed in every sense. He gave the impression that he could have sold Bibles door to door wearing nothing but a G-string...There was no hint of either embarrassment or braggadocio in his comportment."

Weissmuller won the part hands (and pants) down...and just in case anyone failed to notice his unique abilities, in the publicity leading up to *Tarzan the Ape Man*'s premiere, MGM's publicity agents billed Weissmuller as "the only man in Hollywood who's natural in the flesh and can act without clothes."

A CHANGED MAN

Weissmuller still didn't have much acting experience, but it didn't really matter—rather than change Weissmuller to make him better fit the role, MGM simply adjusted the Tarzan character to fit Weissmuller's strengths and weaknesses: the Tarzan of the Edgar Rice Burroughs novels was a self-educated, cultured gentleman who spoke several languages; the Tarzan of the Weissmuller films was someone who spoke very little and swam surprisingly often for a guy who lived in the middle of a jungle. "The role was right up my alley—it was just like stealing," Weissmuller recounted years later.

Not much of Burroughs's original Tarzan character had ever made it to the screen. But by the time MGM was through, the few remaining vestiges had been swept away. The screenplay made absolutely no mention of Tarzan's noble origins and didn't even bother to explain how he'd ended up in the jungle. Even the sound of Tarzan's name was changed: Burroughs had always pronounced it as TAR-zn, but MGM changed it to TAR-ZAN; and TAR-ZAN it would stay. Burroughs had always resisted changes to his character in the past; this time he just accepted it.

"I don't give a damn what they call him," he told a friend, "as long as their checks come regularly."

FINDING HIS VOICE

Because this was the first true Tarzan talkie, the filmmakers had to figure out what Tarzan's jungle yell would sound like. Nobody really knew what to do…until Weissmuller came up with the yell on his own. He recalled:

> When I was a kid, I used to read the Tarzan books, and they had kind of a shrill yell for Tarzan. I never thought I'd ever make Tarzan movies, but when I finally got the part, they were trying to do yells like that. And I remembered when I was a kid I used to yodel at the picnics on Sundays, so I said, "I know a yell!"

Nobody gave Weissmuller's yell much thought until after the film opened and MGM realized just how popular the yell was. They quickly invented a story that it was created by sound engineers who blended Weissmuller's voice "with a hyena's howl played backward, a camel's bleat, the pluck of a violin string, and a soprano's high C."

"It was a commentary on the mystique of talkies and the bizarre singularity of the yell itself," John Taliaferro writes in *Tarzan Forever*, "that the public accepted the studio's fib as fact."

LOVE INTEREST

MGM knew pretty quickly what Jane would look like—they cast a contract actress named Maureen O'Sullivan to play her. But it took a while to decide what she should wear. "First," O'Sullivan recalled, "they had the idea of having Jane wearing no bra—no brassiere at all—and she would always be covered with a branch. They tried that, and it didn't work. So they made a costume and it wasn't that bad at all. There was a little leather bra and a loin-cloth."

THE FILMING

The stage was set. Filming of *Tarzan the Apeman* began on October 31, 1931, and finished eight weeks later. Total cost, even with the free leftover jungle footage from *Trader Horn*, was just over $650,000. The film had not come cheap, but it turned out to be worth every penny: *Tarzan the Ape Man* opened to huge crowds and rave reviews in March 1932 and went on to become one of theTop 10 box-office hits of the year. The movie's success helped increase the popularity of the Tarzan novels and comic strips, whose sales had started to suffer in the grip of the Great Depression.

Weissmuller didn't have a lot of dialogue in the film, but his acting was surprisingly authentic. He became the hottest new star of 1932. "However credible or interesting Tarzan may be on the printed page," Thorton Delehanty wrote in the *New York Evening Post*, "I doubt very much if he emerges in such splendor as he does in the person of Johnny Weissmuller... With his flowing hair, magnificently proportioned body, catlike walk, and virtuosity in the water, you could hardly ask anything more in the way of perfection."

Maureen O'Sullivan also won high praise for her performance and, like Weissmuller, set the standard by which all future Janes would be judged; to this day the six movies she made with Weissmuller are considered the best Tarzan films ever made.

THE SEQUEL

When *Tarzan the Ape Man* became a runaway hit, MGM paid Burroughs for the right to make a sequel called *Tarzan and His Mate*. They signed Weissmuller and O'Sullivan for an encore. Influenced by the success of *King Kong* the year before, the makers of *Tarzan and His Mate* spent a lot of money on animal and special effects, including a 20-foot-long, steel-and-rubber mechanical crocodile that Weissmuller wrestles and kills in the film, and a live hippopotamus that was imported from a German zoo so that Weissmuller could ride on its back. Even Cheetah the chimp was given an expanded role to take advantage of the public's newfound fascination with primates.

BIG GAMBLE

The film ultimately cost $1.3 million, nearly double what *Tarzan the Apeman* cost and a huge sum for a Depression-era film. But like its predecessor, it played to packed theaters all over the country—and, when it was released to foreign markets, all over the world. It's considered the best of the Weissmuller Tarzan films and proba-bly the best Tarzan film of all time.

It is also famous for another reason: It features the most

nudity of any of Weissmuller's Tarzan films. O'Sullivan wears a skimpy leather top and a loincloth comprised of one flap of leather in front and one in back, leaving her thighs and hips fully exposed. It "started such a furor," O'Sullivan remembered years later. "Thousands of women were objecting to my costume." MGM finally caved in and changed O'Sullivan's costume from "something suitable for the jungle" into "something resembling a suburban housedress," a la Wilma Flintstone. Even Weissmuller had to cover up for the next film in the series: he went from a revealing loincloth to what looked like "leather gym shorts."

BIG BUDGET

In July 1935, MGM began work on *The Capture of Tarzan*, its third Tarzan film. They planned to make it the most elaborate, most expensive, and (they hoped) most profitable one yet.

Set designers built a six-room treehouse for Tarzan and Jane that the Flintstones would have envied, complete with running water, an oven for baking, overhead fans operated by Cheetah, and an elevator powered by an elephant.

The Capture of Tarzan was also supposed to be much more graphic than the earlier films. In one scene, a safari party is captured by the Ganeolis tribe of natives and the captives are spread-eagled on the ground "to be butchered in a two-part ritual: a savage cutting with knives followed by a rock-swing to the head, cracking the skull open," but are rescued by Tarzan just in time. In another scene, the party crosses into a foggy marshland where they're attacked by pygmies, giant lizards, and vampire bats.

Unfortunately, when *The Capture of Tarzan* was shown to preview audiences in 1935, it "terrified children and brought outraged complaints from irate mothers and women's organizations," Gabe Essoe writes. "Afraid that *Capture* would alienate more people than it would attract, studio bosses ordered all gruesome scenes cut out and replaced with re-takes." When director Jim McKay objected to the changes, he was fired and replaced with John Farrow, who was himself later fired. (But not before falling in love with Maureen O'Sullivan and eventually marrying her, and fathering seven children—one of whom is actress Mia Farrow.) Next in line for director was Richard Thorpe, who stayed on as director for the rest of the MGM series.

WATCH OUT FOR THAT TREE!

Thorpe spent months shooting new scenes "as necessary" to make the film "appeal" to young and old alike, and changed the name to *Tarzan Escapes*. Thorpe also began the tradition of reusing scenes from older Tarzan films—in this case cutting out the vampire bat attack scene and replacing it with the crocodile fight from *Tarzan and His Mate*—and cheapening what had been considered a top-notch motion picture franchise. "In essence, this film marked a major step in lowering the Tarzan series to the child's level," Essoe writes.

With all of the rewriting, refilming, and reediting, *Tarzan Escapes* took 14 months to finish and cost more than the first two MGM Tarzan films combined. That would have been okay if it was a good film. But when it finally opened in New York in November 1936, it ran into harsh reviews and lousy ticket sales. "The tree-to-tree stuff has worn pretty thin for adult consumption," *Variety* complained, "While at first the sight of Tarzan doing everything but playing pinochle with his beast pals was a novelty, it's all pretty silly now. Derisive laughter greets the picture too often."

JUNGLE FAMILY VALUES

Johnny Weissmuller was content to continue as Tarzan, but Maureen O'Sullivan wasn't. When she learned that a fourth Tarzan film was in the works, she insisted on being written out of it. MGM offered to let her take a leave of absence, but she insisted on leaving permanently. So screenwriter Cyril Hume decided to kill her off with a spear wound at the end of the fourth film.

This created a problem: the female character helped attract women and families to Tarzan pictures, and the studio was afraid that if Tarzan went solo his audience would shrink. So they gave the couple a son—Boy. And to avoid controversy from censorship groups (because MGM's Tarzan and Jane never married), Boy was adopted. Tarzan and Jane find a baby in the jungle following a plane crash and raise him as their own.

MGM ran an ad in the *Hollywood Reporter* asking readers, "Do you have a Tarzan, Jr., in your backyard?" and auditioned more than 300 boys for the part before finally settling on seven-year-old

---

Emergency rooms treat twice as many left-handed people for accidents as right-handed people.

Johnny Sheffield. (Sheffield's stunts were performed by a 32-year-old midget named Harry Monty, who billed himself as the "Midget Strong Man.")

BACK FROM THE DEAD

Edgar Rice Burroughs was furious when he learned MGM wanted to kill off his second-most important character. "MGM reminded Burroughs that while their contract forbade them to kill, mutilate, or undermine the character of Tarzan, it didn't mention Jane," Essoe writes. "MGM was free to rub her out and Burroughs was powerless to stop them."

In the end, though, MGM didn't "rub Jane out." Preview audiences were so upset at the prospect of Jane dying that the studio felt compelled to re-film the ending so that she survives. Not only that, O'Sullivan went on to play Jane in two more films before finally hanging it up for good.

TRAPPED IN THE JUNGLE

O'Sullivan made an average of three other films for every Tarzan she made, but Weissmuller wasn't that lucky. MGM wouldn't let Weissmuller play any other roles, fearing they'd damage his screen image. So although Johnny had been compared to Clark Gable in 1932, by the late 1930s he was hopelessly typecast.

Another thing that irked Weissmuller was that although he'd done so much to bring millions of dollars into MGM's coffers, the studio refused to give him a share of the profits. When MGM used up the last of its Tarzan movie rights making *Tarzan's New York Adventure* (1942) it decided not to buy any more, and let Weissmuller's option expire. Weissmuller moved over to RKO Pictures, the new owner of the Tarzan film rights, and made *Tarzan Triumphs*—the first of six RKO Tarzan films. But his deal there was the same as at MGM: no profit-sharing. Weissmuller earned his salary and nothing more.

LARGER THAN LIFE

In the years that followed, the Tarzan film budgets shrank as RKO relied more and more on reusing footage from earlier Tarzan movies, and the films themselves became shorter as they slipped from top billing to second place in double features. About the only thing that grew during the 1940s was Weissmuller's waistline: Now in his early 40s, his svelte swimmer's build had long since

In 1992 former Panamanian pres. Noriega's wife was arrested in Miami for shoplifting buttons.

given way to the barrel-chested brawn of a middle-aged man who was having trouble staying in shape. Weissmuller gained as much as 30 pounds between Tarzan films, and he wasn't always able to take it all back off.

In 1948, Weissmuller finished *Tarzan and the Mermaids*, his 12th Tarzan film in 17 years. When talk of a 13th film began, Weissmuller again asked for a percentage of the profits. Rather than give it to him, producer Sol Lesser let Weissmuller go.

It wasn't the end of his career, though. Weissmuller wound up with the lead in a new series—Jungle Jim, based on a comic strip by the same name. This time he talked and wore clothes. He made 20 Jungle Jim films between 1948 and 1956, and when he finished he began looking around for new roles to play. But no one would have him—after spending 26 years in the jungle, no one could see him playing any other kind of part. "Casting directors wouldn't even talk to him," Essoe writes. "After kicking around Hollywood for awhile, Weissmuller went into a forced retirement."

After more than a quarter century in the movie business, Weissmuller had only one non-jungle film to his credit: the 1946 film *Swamp Fire*. "I played a Navy lieutenant in that one," he joked later, "I took one look and went back to the jungle."

Weissmuller died on January 20, 1984, at the age of 79. At his request, a tape recording of his famous Tarzan yell was played as his coffin was lowered into the ground.

* * *

MONKEY MISCELLANY

• The chimpanzee is also one of the few animals that uses tools. In the forest a stick is used to extract termites or honey from nests, and in captivity to reach objects which are beyond the reach of its arms.

• According to some reports, chimpanzees have been taught to play tic-tac-toe. In September 1971, it was reported that "Washoe," the most advanced of a group of chimpanzees being taught to communicate by signs at Norman, Oklahoma, knew 200 words and could construct simple sentences.

Aztec emperor Montezuma had a nephew, Cuitlahac, whose name meant "plenty of excrement."

THE TARZAN AWARDS

Here's a look at some of the more notable—and notorious—
Tarzan films that have made it onto the big screen:

TARZAN TRIUMPHS (1943)

Claim to Fame: Most political Tarzan movie ever.
Details: Johnny Weissmuller never fought in World War II, but he
used his star power to contribute to the war effort in a number of
ways, including making the anti-Nazi propaganda film *Tarzan
Triumphs* in 1943. The film was a commentary on the dangers of
isolationism in the face of Nazi agression: When the Germans
invade the jungle and enslave the people of the hidden city of
Palandria, Tarzan's first impulse—presumably like that of many
people in his audience—was not to get involved, as long as the
Germans left him alone. In one scene, he bellows, "Nazi go
away!"…only to change his tune when the Germans kidnap Boy:
"Now Tarzan make war!"

The film ends with a scene of Cheetah playing with the two
way radio while someone is broadcasting from Berlin. "Idiot!" the
voice screams, "this is not von Reichart! This is der Fuhrer!"

TARZAN THE APE MAN (1959)

Claim to Fame: Cheesiest Tarzan special effects ever.
Details: Rather than go to the unnecessary trouble and expense of
hiring actors and shooting lots of new footage to make his film,
producer Al Zimbalist cast Denny Miller, a UCLA basketball star
with no acting experience, as Tarzan…then larded the film with
as much stock jungle footage from the 1950 film *King Solomon's
Mines* as he could. And when that ran out, he used footage from
the original 1932 classic *Tarzan the Ape Man* starring Johnny
Weissmuller.

Of course, there was the small problem that Zimbalist's film
was filmed in color, and Weissmuller's was shot in black and
white…but Zimbalist got around this (or so he thought at the
time) by having the black-and-white footage tinted to make it
appear as if it had been filmed in Technicolor, like the rest of the
movie. No dice—the 1932 footage didn't look like Technicolor,
and didn't even look like Denny Miller. "In one scene," David
Fury writes in *Kings of the Jungle*, "you can actually see Johnny
Weissmuller's face clearly as he fights the crocodile."

What little footage Zimbalist did bother to film was awful. In one important action sequence, real footage of an animal trainer dressed as Tarzan wrestling with a live leopard was combined with shots of Miller wrestling with a large stuffed animal. "This was passable," Fury writes, "but the movie then cut to two separate close-ups of the face of the stuffed animal, resplendent with its plastic fangs and button eyes."

TARZAN AND THE GREAT RIVER (1968)

Claim to Fame: Tarzan film most likely to have been plagued by some kind of jungle voodoo curse.

Details: *Tarzan and The Great River* was the second Tarzan film to star Mike Henry, star linebacker for the L.A. Rams who signed on as the Ape Man after producer (and Rams fan) Sy Weintraub promised to make Henry "wealthier than the whole backfield."

Shot in the jungles of Brazil, things were troubled from the start: during filming of one scene in a downtown park in Rio de Janeiro, a 500-pound trained lion named Major got loose and wandered the streets of Rio, scattering passersby until the trainer was finally able to get it back under control.

The worst moment came during filming of a scene with Mike Henry and Dinky, the chimpanzee who played Cheetah. "Dinky seemed uneasy in his new environment," Henry recalls. "I was supposed to run over to the chimp and pick him up, but when I did he bit me on the cheek and ripped my jaw open. I was in a 'monkey fever delirium' for three days and nights, and needed twenty stitches to put my face back together. It took me three weeks to recuperate."

And that was only the beginning—Henry later contracted food poisoning and dysentery...and when the months-long jungle shooting schedule was abruptly expanded to squeeze in a second feature film before the start of the rainy season, he came down with a serious ear infection and then a liver virus. After that, there was rain. "It rained torturously for two weeks," Henry recalls. "The Amazon River swelled and overflowed, and then a typhoon struck, bringing the worst floods Rio had experienced in nearly a century." Soon afterwards, a typhoid fever epidemic swept the city.

At that point Henry had spent nearly a year filming in the jungle, and one year was enough. He returned to the United

States, where he promptly sued the producers for $875,000 alleging "maltreatment, abuse, and working conditions detrimental to my health and welfare."

TARZAN'S DESERT MYSTERY (1943)

Claim to Fame: Worst of the Johnny Weissmuller Tarzan films.
Details: The film featured Tarzan and Boy, but no Jane—Maureen O'Sullivan was pregnant and bowed out of the film to have her child. There was still some hope she would return in a future film, so MGM left the role unfilled. Actually, there isn't a whole lot of Tarzan in the picture, either. Weissmuller spends most of the film locked away, off camera, in a prison cell; and even when he is free the most exciting scene is his battle with a man-eating plant.

Keeping Tarzan off screen may have been a good idea, though: Weissmuller, trapped in the role of Tarzan, was in the middle of one of his periodic career funks, and it shows on film. "Admittedly, Johnny had let himself get out of shape for this picture," David Fury writes. "At age 39, the years and a few too many pounds were starting to show."

THE ADVENTURES OF TURKISH TARZAN (1944)

Claim to Fame: Worst Tarzan ripoff ever.
Details: "While in New York on business in 1944, Tarzan producer Sol Lesser was called by a Turkish film distributor who told him that he had a Turkish Tarzan film for sale. Intrigued by the idea, Lesser set up a screening of the film, after which he confiscated it legally. The film was one of Lesser's own productions, *Tarzan's Revenge* (1938). The Turks had dubbed it and ingeniously cut in the face of a Turkish actor whenever there was a closeup." —*Tarzan of the Movies*, by Gabe Essoe

* * *

"The most bizarre permutation of the Tarzan character has to be *Jungle Heat*, an X-rated, interactive CD-ROM, in which, according to those who have viewed it before Burroughs, Inc.'s lawyer had it quashed, Tarzan plays 'the wrong kind of swinger.'"

—*Tarzan Forever,* by **John Taliaferro**

NAZIS INVADE AMERICA!...A TRUE STORY

In June 1942, J. Edgar Hoover claimed credit for the FBI's capture of eight Nazi saboteurs who were deposited by submarine along the New York and Florida shores. Here's what really happened....

ALONG THE WATERFRONT

Not long after midnight on June 13, 1942, a Coast Guardsman named John Cullen saw four men struggling with an inflatable raft in the heavy surf off the town of Amagansett, on the eastern coast of Long Island.

Cullen stopped to investigate. The men told him they were fishermen, and Cullen might have believed them...except that the men were armed (fishermen at sea usually aren't), and they offered him $260 to forget he'd ever seen them. Why would fishermen do a thing like that?

Plus, when Cullen looked out to sea, he thought he saw a long, flat shape about 150 feet offshore, kind of like a submarine.

Getting Help

Cullen was alone and unarmed. He suspected the men were foreign agents (this was World War II, after all), but there wasn't much he could do about it by himself, and he feared that more foreign agents might be on the way. So he pretended to accept the bribe and then ran back to base to get help.

Cullen's superiors were skeptical, not to mention afraid of what would happen if they sounded a false alarm. So they did nothing...until just before dawn, when they sent Cullen and several other armed men to investigate. The "fishermen" were gone and so was the submarine (it was beached on a sandbar when Cullen first saw it, but had since freed itself). But the men left behind several hastily and poorly concealed caches containing explosives, timers, blasting caps, incendiary devices, cigarettes, brandy...and German uniforms.

Henry Ford was America's first billionaire.

The Nazis had landed on U.S. soil and nobody knew where they were.

SOUNDING THE ALARM

The FBI didn't learn of the incident until noon and didn't arrive at the scene until a couple of hours later; by then the saboteurs had already slipped into New York City and checked into a hotel.

J. Edgar Hoover was immediately informed of the landing. "All of Hoover's imaginative and restless energy was stirred into prompt and effective action," Attorney General Francis Biddle recalled years later. "His eyes were bright, his jaw set, excitement flickering around the edge of his nostrils....He was determined to catch them all before any sabotage took place."

After alerting President Roosevelt to the crisis, Hoover put the Bureau on full alert and launched the largest manhunt in FBI history. He also ordered a news blackout, for three reasons: (1) he didn't want the saboteurs to learn that they had been discovered; (2) he wanted to avoid a public panic; and (3) he wanted to avoid public embarrassment in the event that the FBI could not catch the German agents.

Secret Heroes

Nobody knew it at the time, but Hoover had nothing to worry about. Colonel George John Dasch, the leader of the Nazi saboteurs, had lived in the U.S. for twenty years before the war and secretly hated the Nazis. The only thing he wanted to sabotage was his own mission, and he had talked one of his compatriots, a naturalized U.S. citizen named Ernst Peter Burger, into joining him. Their plan: Surrender to the FBI.

CRAZY

The two men telephoned the FBI's New York City Field Office (NYFO) and tried to turn themselves in. It didn't work, as Curt Gentry relates in *J. Edgar Hoover: the Man and the Secrets:*

> In most of the large bureau field offices there is what the agents themselves refer to as the "nut desk." The special agent who had the unwelcome task of manning it that day at NYFO listened skeptically to Dasch's tale and observed, "Yesterday Napoleon called," and hung up. Although the whole bureau was on alert, nobody had informed him. He thought the call so

Chickens can live as long as 14 years.

ridiculous he didn't even bother to log it.

With no luck on the phone, Dasch decided to take a train to Washington, D.C., and turn himself in to J. Edgar Hoover at FBI headquarters. He brought with him a suitcase containing $84,000 in U.S. currency, the money his team was supposed to use to fund their sabotage efforts. Burger stayed behind in New York.

HOOVER'S HELPERS

The trip to FBI headquarters didn't work, either: Nobody believed Dasch's story, and he was passed from one bureau official to another like a hot potato. No one he talked to would let him speak with Hoover.

Finally, Dasch landed at the desk of D. M. "Mickey" Ladd, head of the bureau's Domestic Intelligence Division and the man leading the hunt for the Nazi saboteurs. Ladd didn't believe Dasch either—he figured the strange man with the German accent was some kind of kook who'd somehow learned of the landing at Amagansett and wanted to hone in on the excitement. He listened to Dasch for about five minutes and then showed him the door. After all, Ladd had Nazis to catch.

Surprise!

Dasch lost his patience. As he later wrote in his memoirs: "I seized the suitcase that had been lying on the floor, tore its snaps, and dumped the contents on the desk. The three feet of polished wood were too narrow to hold the eighty-four thousand dollars in cash. Packets of bills cascaded over the sides to create the illusion of a miniature waterfall."

"Is this stuff real?" Ladd asked.

SPILLING HIS GUTS

Once Ladd confirmed the money was real, the FBI sprang into action. It arrested Dasch and interrogated him for eight days. He told them how he'd been trained, who his contacts were in the U.S., and what his targets were (they included the New York City water supply and the hydroelectric plant at Niagara Falls). He told the FBI where to find Burger and the two other men on his sabotage team.

The landings, Dasch explained, were the first of several

scheduled to land every six weeks. The sabotage campaign had two goals: the disruption of vital war industries, and the launching of a wave of terror by leaving time bombs at railway stations, department stores, and other public places.

Acting on Dasch's information, the FBI picked up Burger and arrested the remaining saboteurs. Burger, like Dasch, cooperated immediately. He volunteered that a second team of saboteurs had landed along the coast of Florida, and FBI agents in Florida began their own roundup. They captured their last man on June 27, two weeks to the day after the landing at Amagansett. Neither sabotage team had been able to attack a single target.

SHHHH!

Hoover decided to keep the details of the arrests under wraps. The official explanation given was that if Dasch's and Burger's defection were kept secret, Hitler might think that the East Coast was so heavily guarded that further landings would be futile, not to mention a waste of valuable agents.

Fooling FDR

"This explanation makes of the FBI's decision an ingenious disinformation ploy," Gentry writes in *J. Edgar Hoover: The Man and the Secrets*. "It fails to account, however, for why Hoover also felt it necessary to deceive the president of the United States."

In the two weeks between the Amagansett landing and the capture of the last saboteur, Hoover sent FDR three different "personal and confidential memos" keeping the president updated on the progress of the manhunt. None of the memos mentioned the fact that Dasch had turned himself in or that he and Burger were cooperating fully, nor did they admit that the arrests of the Florida saboteurs were possible only because of the information Burger had volunteered to the FBI.

Instead, in the memos Hoover moved the date of Dasch's "arrest" to two days after that of his compatriots to make it look like their capture had led to his, and not vice versa. The director gave all of the credit to the FBI, which had nearly blown the case.

Joe Louis was the world heavyweight boxing champ for 11 years and 252 days.

GOING PUBLIC...SORT OF

Hoover announced the arrests—his version, anyway—in a public press conference on June 27. The story made headlines across the country:

FBI CAPTURES 8
GERMAN AGENTS
LANDED BY SUBS

As the New York Times reported at the time, Hoover "gave no details of how the FBI 'broke' the case. That will have to wait, FBI officials insist, until after the war." The press had little choice but to speculate on how the arrests had been made, and much of the speculation erred on the side of the FBI, according to then-Attorney General Francis Biddle:

> It was generally concluded that a particularly brilliant FBI agent, probably attending the school in sabotage where the eight had been trained, had been able to get on the inside, and make regular reports to America. Mr. Hoover, as the United Press put it, declined to comment on whether the FBI agents had infiltrated not only the Gestapo but also the High Command, or whether he watched the saboteurs land.

THANKS, GUYS

What did Dasch and Burger get for: (1) singlehandedly destroying Hitler's entire North American sabotage program; and (2) handing Hoover his biggest intelligence coup of the war? (Dasch was hoping for a Congressional Medal of Honor.)

Not much. Like the other six saboteurs, they were hauled before a military tribunal, tried, found guilty, and sentenced to death. Acting on the recommendation of military commission, however, President Roosevelt commuted Dasch's sentence to 30 years of hard labor and Burger's to life at hard labor. Everyone else was executed within a month.

Dasch and Burger languished in prison until 1948, when President Truman pardoned both men and ordered them deported to Germany. There, according to Gentry, "they were treated as traitors who not only had betrayed the fatherland, but also were responsible for the deaths of six of their comrades."

URBAN LEGENDS

Word to the wise: If a story sounds true, but also seems too good to be true, it's probably an "urban legend." Here's the inside poop.

GUESS WHAT I JUST HEARD?

At one time or another, just about everyone has heard about the poodle that exploded when its owner tried to dry it in a microwave...or the person who brought home a strange-looking chihuahua puppy from Mexico, only to learn it was really a rat.

Most of us now know these stories are urban legends—but only because they've been around a while. When individual stories become widely discounted as fables, new ones spring up to take their place.

WHAT MAKES A GOOD URBAN LEGEND?

People who study urban legends point to several characteristics that contribute to their believability and chances of survival.

√ They contain "details" that create the impression the story is true. Take the story about the woman who tries on an imported coat at the mall, feels a sting on her wrist...and later dies from the bite of a poisonous baby snake that had hatched in the lining of the coat. The name of the mall (it's almost always nearby), the item of clothing, its price, and other seemingly corroborative details are usually included in the story.

√ They may contain a grain of truth, which implies that the entire story is true. No word on what would happen if someone really did put a dog in a microwave oven, but if you've ever tried to hardboil an egg in one, you know it would probably be ugly.

√ The story reflects contemporary fears. The poodle-in-the-microwave story dates back to the days when few people owned microwaves, and fewer still understood how they worked. Other legends may be inspired by fear of attack, embarrassment, ghosts, or science.

Every day, 46 million Americans buy books.

√ The person telling the story believes he knows the person who knows the person who witnessed or is involved in the story. The listener thereby accepts it on faith, and when they tell the story, they can also claim a personal connection that makes the story more believable.

√ The story is reported in the media, either as fact or a rumor. It doesn't really matter whether the news story gives it credibility or labels it a myth; either way, the legend is often given new life. In 1917, columnist H.L. Mencken published a fictional history of the bathtub in the *New York Evening Mail* that claimed President Millard Fillmore installed the first White House bathtub in 1851. The story isn't true—Andrew Jackson installed the first indoor plumbing, complete with bathtub, in 1833. Mencken later admitted the hoax. But it continues to appear in print to this day.

SIX URBAN LEGENDS

The Story: On October 10, 1995, the U.S. Chief of Naval Operations released the following transcript of what the story claims is "an actual radio conversation."

NAVY: Please divert your course 15 degrees to the north to avoid a collision.

CIVILIAN: Recommend you divert YOUR course 15 degrees to south to avoid a collision.

NAVY: This is the captain of a U.S. Navy ship. I say again, divert YOUR course.

CIVILIAN: No, I say again, you divert YOUR course.

NAVY: THIS IS THE AIRCRAFT CARRIER ENTERPRISE. WE ARE A LARGE WARSHIP OF THE U.S. NAVY. DIVERT YOUR COURSE NOW!

CIVILIAN: This is a lighthouse. Your call.

How It Spread: On the Internet.

The Truth: According to Patrick Crispen, who co-writes *The Internet Tourbus* (http://www.tourbus.com), "It turns out the Navy story is a very old urban legend," made fresh by new exposure on the Internet.

The Story: A traveler visiting New York City meets an attractive woman in a bar and takes her back to his hotel room. That's all he remembers—the next thing he knows, he's lying in a bathtub filled with ice; and surgical tubing is coming out of two freshly stitched wounds on his lower chest. There's a note by the tub that says, "Call 911. We've removed your left kidney." (Sometimes both are removed). The doctors in the emergency room tell him he's the victim of thieves who steal organs for use in transplants. (According to one version of the story, medical students perform the surgeries, then use the money to pay off student loans.)

Note: Uncle John actually heard this from a friend, Karen Pinsky, who sells real estate. She said it was a warning given by a real estate firm to agents headed to big cities for conventions.

How It Spread: French folklorist Veronique Campion-Vincent has traced the story to Honduras and Guatemala, where rumors began circulating in 1987 that babies were being kidnapped and murdered for their organs. The alleged culprits: wealthy Americans needing transplants. From there the story spread to South America, then all over the world. Wherever such stories surfaced—including the U.S.—newspapers reported them as fact. The New York version surfaced in the winter of 1991, and in February 1992, the *New York Times* "verified" it. Scriptwriter Joe Morgenstern, thinking it was true, even made it the subject of an episode of the NBC-TV series "Law and Order."

The Truth: National and international agencies have investigated the claims, but haven't been able to substantiate even a single case of organ theft anywhere in the world. The agencies say the stories aren't just groundless, but also implausible. "These incredible stories ignored the complexity of organ transplant operations," Jan Brunvald writes in *The Baby Train and Other Lusty Urban Legends*, "which would preclude any such quick removal and long-distance shipment of body parts."

*   *   *   *

The Story: One of the most potent forms of marijuana in the world is "Manhattan White" (also known as "New York Albino"). The strain evolved in the dark sewers of New York City as a direct result of thousands of drug dealers flushing their drugs down the toilet during drug busts. The absence of light in the sewers turns the marijuana plants white; raw sewage, acting as a fertilizer, makes it extremely potent.

The Truth: Most likely an updated version of the classic urban myth that alligators live in the New York sewers.

* * * *

The Story: A young woman finishes shopping at the mall and walks out to her car to go home. But there's an old lady sitting in the car. "I'm sorry ma'am, but isn't your car," the woman says.

"I know," the old lady replies, "but I had to sit down." Then she asks the young woman for a ride home.

The young woman agrees, but then remembers she locked the car when she arrived at the mall. She pretends to go back into the mall to get her sister, and returns with a security guard. The guard and the old lady get into a fight, and in the struggle the old lady's wig falls off, revealing that she's actually a man. The police take the man away, and under the car seat, they find an axe. (The story is kept alive by claims that the mall has bribed reporters and police to keep the story quiet.)

The Truth: The modern form of the tale comes from the early 1980s and places the action at numerous malls...New York, Las Vegas, Milwaukee, Chicago, and even Fresno, California, depending on who's telling the story. Folklorists speculate the tale may date all the way back to an 1834 English newspaper account of "a gentleman in his carriage, who on opening the supposed female's reticule [handbag] finds to his horror a pair of loaded pistols inside."

* * * *

The Story: Two young men are driving home from a party one rainy night and notice a beautiful young woman standing by the side of the road. She doesn't have a raincoat or umbrella, so they stop and offer her a ride. She accepts, and while they drive her to her house, one of the young men gives her his jacket to wear.

About a block from the young woman's house, they turn around to say something to her...but she is gone. They drive to

In 1955 a book was returned to the Cambridge University library that was 288 years overdue.

her house anyway, knock on the door, and the woman who answers tells them, "that was my daughter. She was killed two years ago on the same spot you picked her up. She does this all the time."

The next day the young men look up the girl's obituary in the library. There it is—complete with a picture of the girl they picked up. Then they go to the cemetery...and find the jacket she borrowed resting on her tombstone.

The Truth: Another oldie-but-goodie. According to folklorist Richard Dorson, it predates the automobile. The story "is traced back to the 19th century," he writes, "in America, Italy, Ireland, Turkey, and China; with a horse and wagon picking up the benighted traveler." In the Hawaiian version, the girl hitches a ride on a rickshaw.

*   *   *   *

The Story: A woman catches a cockroach and throws it in the toilet. Rather than drown it, she decides to kill it quickly with bug spray. Her husband comes home a few minutes later, sits down on the toilet, and drops his lit cigarette into the bowl. Kaboom!

Burned on his behind and on his private parts, the man calls 911. As the paramedics are carrying him to the ambulance, he tells them what happened...and they laugh so hard they drop the stretcher, breaking his arm.

How It Spread: It apparently began in Israel: The *Jerusalem Post* reported the story in August 1988...then retracted it a few weeks later because it could not be substantiated.

The Truth: Urban legends featuring broken arms brought on by paramedics laughing at the embarrassing way in which a patient has injured himself, are so numerous they're practically a category unto themselves. The storyteller's fear of being embarrassed in a similar way is what keeps them alive.

*   *   *   *

"A lie can travel halfway around the world before the facts have even put their boots on."

—*Mark Twain*

THE STORY OF LITTLE LEAGUE

*If you're into baseball, chances are you've had something
to do with Little League. It's an American tradition
now, but it started out as one man's obsession.*

ACCIDENT OF FATE

One afternoon in 1938 a man named Carl Stotz went out into his Williamsport, Pennsylvania, yard to play catch with his two nephews. They would have preferred to play baseball, but the yard was too small to use a bat.

On one throw, a nephew tossed the ball so far that Stotz "had to move to the neighbors' side of the yard," he recalled years later. "As I stretched to catch the ball, I stepped into the cut off stems of a lilac bush that were projecting several inches above the ground. A sharp stub tore through my sock and scraped my ankle. The pain was intense."

The Good Old Days

As Stotz sat nursing his ankle, he was suddenly reminded that he had played on the same kind of rough turf when he was a kid…and he remembered a promise he'd made to himself when he was a young boy. Back then, equipment was scarce—he and his friends hit balls with sticks when they didn't have any bats, and used baseballs until the threads unraveled and the skins came off. Then they patched them up with tape and used them until there wasn't anything left to tape back together. Some of his friends had even played barefoot because they didn't have any shoes.

"I remembered thinking to myself, 'When I grow up, I'm gonna have a baseball team for boys, complete with uniforms and equipment. They'll play on a real field like the big guys, with cheering crowds at every game.'"

DOWNSIZING

Stotz didn't have any sons of his own, but he decided to fulfill his promise by organizing his nephews and the other neighborhood boys into baseball teams. That way, they could experience the

Every year, 5% of Americans go on cruises.

thrill of playing real games on real fields, wearing real uniforms—not just play stickball in open fields and abandoned lots.

He spent the next few months organizing teams and rounding up sponsors to pay for the equipment. At the same time, he set about "shrinking" the game of baseball so 9–12 year-old kids could really play. "When I was nine, nothing was geared to children," Stotz explained in his book A *Promise Kept.* "Take bats, for example: We'd step up to the plate with a bat that was both too heavy and too long. Choking up on the bat merely changed the problem. The handle would then bang us in the stomach when we lunged at the ball. We didn't have the strength or leverage for a smooth, controlled swing."

TRIAL & ERROR

Stotz finally found child-sized bats and equipment for his teams, and at every team practice he adjusted the distances between the bases and between the pitcher's mound and home plate, trying to find the ideal size for a field.

"I was trying to find out what distance would enable the boys to throw a runner out from third base or shortstop while still giving the batter a fair chance to beat it out, depending on where he hit the ball," he later wrote. "When I finally had what I thought was the ideal distance, I stepped it off and used a yardstick at home to measure my strides. The distance was so close to sixty feet that I set that as the distance we would use thereafter."

About the only thing Stotz didn't change was the size of the baseball itself. He figured it would enable kids to practice with any baseball they already had on hand. "Remember, this was 1938 when I was making these decisions, and the Great Depression was still with many families," he wrote. "I was afraid the expense of buying special-size balls would be too much for some families and might keep boys from becoming Little Leaguers."

SPONSORS

Shrinking the game turned out to be a lot easier than finding sponsors willing to pay for uniforms and equipment for the three teams in the league. "Ten prospects turned me down," Stotz wrote. "Then 20...40...50." Finally, two and a half months after he'd started, Stotz made his 57th sales pitch at the Lycoming Dairy Farms. He landed his first sponsor; they chipped in $30.

Fifty-eight percent of Americans believe they have above-average IQ's.

A LITTLE PROBLEM

Stotz used the money to buy uniforms at Kresge's 25¢-to-$1 Store, and set the date of the league's first game for June 6, 1939. He paid a visit to the offices of *Grit*, Williamsport's Sunday paper, and asked them to mention the league's first game in the paper.

Bill Kenoe, *Grit's* sports editor, asked Stotz what the league was called, but Stotz didn't know yet. "I'd been thinking of calling it Junior League Baseball," he explained, "until I remembered there's a woman's organization named 'Junior League.'" Because he'd modeled his kids' league after the "big leagues," he'd considered calling it either the Little Boys' League or the Little League. But he couldn't decide between them. He didn't like the sound of "Little Boys' League," but was worried that people would think the "Little League" meant the size of the league, not the size of the boys. In the end, he let Kehoe choose between the two names... and Kehoe picked Little League.

OUT OF THE PARK

Little League grew slowly over the next several years. As late as 1946, there were only 12 local leagues in the entire United States—all in Pennsylvania.

The turning point came in 1947, two years after the end of World War II. America's fighting men were back home, settled into their new lives, and they finally had time to participate with their sons in Little League.

In 1947, Little League, now up to 17 independent leagues, held its first "World Series"—an event that was covered by the Associated Press and other wire services. Stories and photographs appeared in hundreds of newspapers...and soon Little League headquarters was deluged with letters from all over the country, asking how to set up their own leagues.

MAKING NOISE

As Little League grew, it began to experience a problem: adults were taking the competition more seriously than the children did. In 1947, parents and other spectators began routinely booing players and officials during games.

"Some of them seemed unable to see the games as simply little boys having fun in a structured...athletic program," Little League's founder Carl Stotz wrote in *A Promise Kept*. "After all, many of the 8-to-12-year-old boys had played baseball less than a year. There was certainly no valid excuse for such adult criticism. And it was becoming quite discouraging to some of the boys."

Stotz and other Little League officials complained, and newspaper editorials condemned the conduct. "Fortunately," he wrote, "the booing fad of 1947 faded out." It was one of Little League's first brushes with controversy…but certainly not its last.

LITTLE LEAGUE, INC.
By the beginning of 1950 Little League had grown to more than 300 local leagues all over the United States; by the end of the year it had more than doubled in size to 776 leagues. There was even one in British Columbia, the first outside the U.S. The organization had grown so much that it could no longer be managed effectively by part-time volunteers. So in 1950 Little League voted to incorporate itself and began hiring a paid, full-time staff. Carl Stotz was appointed president and commissioner of the League. He didn't realize it, but his Little League days were numbered.

AND NOW A WORD FROM OUR SPONSOR
A year earlier, in 1949, the U.S. Rubber Corporation had become Little League's first national sponsor. In return, they wanted to help determine the direction of the organization—so executives of the company approached Stotz to discuss it. "Essentially," Stotz wrote, U.S. Rubber "proposed a national body that would have total control of the leagues that evolved from it. That body would own every Little League playing field and every Little Leaguer would be a paying member."

U.S. Rubber's plan was exactly the opposite of Stotz's vision; he favored completely autonomous local leagues, joined together in a national organization that would be run by representatives elected from the ranks of the local leagues.

The discussions broke off without any change in the direction of Little League…yet. "Our discussion ended amicably," Stotz later wrote. "In retrospect, though, I can see that it was the beginning of a deep philosophical conflict."

THE LITTLE SCHISM
By the early 1950s, Little League was doubling in size every couple of years. It was an enormous success, but Stotz wasn't satisfied; he

If you're average, your feet hit the floor 7,000 times a day.

was concerned about the increasing commercialism that accompanied Little League's rise to national prominence.

Another concern was the prominence placed on the Little League World Series, which was played every year in Williamsport, Pennsylvania. U.S. Rubber and the Little League board of directors wanted to maximize the importance and the publicity value of the event; but Stotz wanted to de-emphasize the series. He feared that teams trying to "win their way to Williamsport" would encourage cheating at the expense of good sportsmanship and fair play. The lure of the national spotlight, he worried, would encourage teams to recruit players who were ineligible either because they were too old or lived outside their league's territorial boundaries.

Yet another controversy erupted when Stotz tried to invite legendary pitcher Cy Young, then in his 80s, to come to the 1951 Little League World Series. "Two members of the board sought to veto Carl's suggestion," Kenneth Loss writes in A Promise Kept. One director "said Cy Young was an old man who probably couldn't control his bladder, and would embarrass Little League." Stotz invited Young anyway (nothing happened), but his differences with Little League Inc. continued to fester.

YOU'RE OUT!
In 1952, Stotz stepped down as the president of Little League, but remained as commissioner of the league. He was replaced as president by a U.S. Rubber executive named Peter McGovern. Stotz still retained a great deal of power...but not for long. In 1954 the board of directors adopted a new set of bylaws that effectively stripped the office of commissioner of much of its power and gave it to McGovern. Then, in 1955, McGovern fired Stotz's secretary while Stotz was out of town promoting Little League, and replaced her with one of his own aides.

That was it—a few months later Stotz resigned as commissioner and filed suit against McGovern, alleging that he was ignoring Little League volunteers. When Stotz lost the suit he cut all ties to Little League forever. A few teams left with him to form the unaffiliated Original Little League, which played their games in a field not far from where Stotz had founded Little League in 1939. Stotz boycotted every Little League Inc. World Series game

First million-selling album in U.S. history: the soundtrack to Oklahoma, 1958.

until 1990, when, at age 79, he attended a game to honor the 50th anniversary of the founding of Little League. He died two years later.

∗ ∗ ∗

LITTLE LEAGUE BASEBALL: GOOD, CLEAN FUN?
Did Stotz's fears come true? These news reports are food for thought.

OUT OF CONTROL
"In June, 1992, the Little League season in Albuquerque, N.M., was cut short because of hostility and fighting among adults. A postgame fight that sent one person to the hospital included a group of parents, a league director, a coach and even the coach's mother.

"That same year, a coach in Whiteville, N.C., used a pocketknife to slash the throat of another coach in front of 100 Little Leaguers, spattering blood on one boy's jersey."

—Los Angeles Times, **1994**

FAIR PLAY
"Taiwan and the Dominican Republic were disqualified Wednesday from tournaments leading to the Little League World Series because they violated rules involving player eligibility....Taiwan, which reportedly drew its all-star team from a population pool more than twice the legal limit this year, has won 14 Little League World Series titles since 1969. 'This has to taint all the victories they've had the last 20 years,' Little League coach Larry Lewis said."

—Long Beach Press-Telegram, **1993**

A HARD FALL
"A 46-year-old Federal Way man has died from injuries after being punched and hitting his head on concrete bleachers during a Little League baseball game last week....Ralph Baldwin, the father of a player on the Federal Way team, died Saturday at Harborview Medical Center....Several witnesses told police Baldwin and his friend were drunk and ill-behaved during the game. After the men

On any given day, 60 million U.S. females and 41 million U.S. males are dieting.

ignored requests to be quiet, several fans asked them to leave, the police report said....Baldwin and his friend left but returned a short time later, the report said. An Everett man, who had a son on the opposing team, asked Baldwin to quiet down, and Baldwin started moving toward him, prompting the punch, witnesses told police. Baldwin fell several rows and hit his head."

—The Seattle Times, 1994

YOU'RE OUTTA HERE!
"Stories of bizarre parental behavior at Little League games abound. For example, a pitcher's mother was convicted in Texarkana, Ark., of assault, disorderly conduct, resisting arrest and making 'terrorist threats' after she pulled a knife on two women during an argument at a game. The boy's father was found guilty of disorderly conduct. Reportedly, the women who were threatened had made derogatory comments about the pitcher."

—The Los Angeles Times, 1985

THE GANG'S ALL HERE
"Two baseball coaches trade insults. Someone throws a punch. Before it's over, five guys pile on in a no-holds-barred brawl....A major league scuffle? No, it happened in Garden Grove on Tuesday night when a meeting of parents who coach 11-and 12-year-old Little League players turned violent in a dispute over whether a hotshot pitcher is too old to play in the league.

"By the time police arrived, one team manager was on his way to the hospital—gouged with a set of keys....And mothers at the league meeting were clutching their children and screaming for their husbands to stop slugging it out."

—The Los Angeles Times, 1998

SWINGING FOR THE GRAVEYARD
"A wild brawl after a weekend Little League baseball game in Castro Valley has left a 17-year-old spectator dead, the suspected bat-wielding assailant struggling for consciousness and the umpire the target of a death threat. Joseph Matteucci, 17, of Castro Valley died Monday after being struck with a bat allegedly swung by

catcher Antonio John Messina of San Lorenzo during a melee involving players and spectators at Proctor School. Messina, 18, tried to escape but he was felled by a rock thrown by the Castro Valley pitcher, whose identity has not been revealed. The cause of the melee remained unclear yesterday, but it appeared to start as players and spectators were filing away from the field after a tense game. It was the first game-related homicide in the organization's history, according to Dennis Sullivan of the national Little League Inc. office in Williamsport, PA. There were signs yesterday that tensions continue to run high. The umpire was the target of attempted arson and a death threat early yesterday."

—*The San Francisco Chronicle*, 1993

YOU'RE FIRED!
"Flaming newspapers were tossed through the smashed window of a Little League umpire's home Tuesday in Castro Valley, Calif., igniting a fire apparently connected to a baseball brawl that killed one teenager and put his attacker in the hospital."

"A brick bearing a note reading 'Talk and Your (sic) Dead' was found outside the home of Robert Lloyd, a key witness in weekend violence after a game between 16-to-18-year-olds in the Big League Division of Little League....Lloyd was threatened after identifying a player who threw a rock that struck and seriously hurt another player suspected of killing Joseph Matteucci, 17. Antonio Messina, 18, suspected of swinging the bat, was in 'stable but guarded' condition at Highland Hospital in Oakland."

—*USA Today*, 1993

STOTZ'S REVENGE
"Little League...suffered the most embarrassing moment in its history in September when it...stripped Zamboanga City of the Philippines of its World Championship title....Although 12 is the official age limit, the team from the Philippines used players as old as 15 in its 15–4 victory over Long Beach in the Major Division World Series final."

—*Los Angeles Times*, 1993

THE ANSWER ZONE

It isn't over yet…not
until we give you
the answers to the
brain teasers, puzzles
and quizzes.

If those are your
favorite part of the
Bathroom Reader,
you might want to
mark this page with
a Post-It note
[to read about
how they were
invented, go
to page 54].

HITS OF THE 1970S: A QUIZ (from page 44)

1 — a

In 1978, Gary Guthrie, a disc jockey for WAKY AM in Louisville, Kentucky, was in the process of breaking up with his wife. One night, a friend played them the new Neil Diamond album, Guthrie recalls: "When it got to 'You Don't Bring Me Flowers,' my wife started crying and this other lady started crying. I knew it was special, but I couldn't help feeling there was something missing. I just couldn't figure out what. A few days later, the new Barbra Streisand LP came into the radio station, and she was doing the song too. It set off this image in my mind, in *The Sound of Music*, when Christopher Plummer and Julie Andrews were onstage singing 'Edelweiss' at the Austrian Music Festival… and a light-bulb! It needed two people singing it to each other."

The Diamond and Streisand versions happened to be in the same key. Guthrie had a brainstorm. "I went into the studio, and after sixteen hours and five days of putting things together, I came out with my finished product of 'You Don't Bring Me Flowers.'" Guthrie had spliced the songs together to create a duet.

"I put it on the radio as a going away present for my wife," he continues. "I called her up and played it for her, and the phones started going crazy: 'What is that song?'" So many people asked for it at local record stores that the stores finally demanded the station stop playing it.

When Columbia Records got wind of the uproar in Louisville, they got the two stars together to duplicate Guthrie's recording. The "official" duet version reached #1 in five weeks. Guthrie ended up without a wife…or a song. Claiming he'd been wronged by the company after selling them the idea for the duet, he filed a $5 million breach of contract lawsuit against CBS.

2 — a

The session in which Led Zepplin recorded "Stairway to Heaven" was pretty spontaneous. Drummer John Bonham worked out his part on the spot…and singer Robert Plant made up the lyrics as he was getting set to record them. Although he later cited a book called *Magic Arts in Celtic Britain* by Lewis Spence as the inspiration for the words, Plant also admitted that he didn't really know what they meant. They were just words he put together in a hurry.

Do you close your eyes when you dive? So does a frog.

"Really," he said, "I have no idea why 'Stairway to Heaven' is so popular. No idea at all. Maybe it's because of its abstraction. Depending on what day it is, I still interpret [the song] a different way—and I wrote those lyrics."

How do people turn that into devil-worship? Simple— "automatic writing." The reason, some people say, that Plant doesn't know the meaning of his own song is that Satan guided his hand when he was writing it, and if you play it backwards (who'd want to play a record backwards?), you can hear evil messages.

For the Record: It wasn't released as a single—a decision which boosted the sales of the album by an estimated 500,000 copies.

3 — c

The group, four Americans from Rockford, Illinois, had been trying to get some recognition in the U.S. for several years. They'd released three albums, all of which bombed. They couldn't make it in Europe, either. In fact, the only place they were popular was Japan.

There, they were heroes with hit singles and tremendously successful tours. When the group's third album flopped in the States, they headed for Japan to tour again. Their record company, Epic, decided to tape their performances in Osaka and Tokyo and come out with a quickie "live" album exclusively for the Japanese market. "Some of the songs," their lead singer said, "were single takes." But for some reason, *Live at Buddokan*—which wasn't released anywhere except Japan—caught on in America, and the live version of "I Want You To Want Me," complete with screaming, became Cheap Trick's first hit. It was a twist on a classic rock 'n' roll story. Jimi Hendrix and the Stray Cats had to go to England to become popular in America; Cheap Trick went to Japan.

4 — a

It seemed so tailored to The Captain and Tennille that no one thought to ask what it was really about. Actually, it had a very different origin. For over twenty years, Neil Sedaka had co-written songs with his high school buddy, Howard Greenfield. Their hits included "Calendar Girl" and "Breaking Up Is Hard to Do." But by 1973, their Midas touch had worn off and they decided to

---

Over 6 billion copies of the Bible have been sold.

break up the team. "Our last song together was called 'Love Will Keep Us Together.' says Sedaka. "It was actually written about us and our collaborating."

5 — b

"Brand New Key" was banned from some radio stations for being "too suggestive." It was interpreted as promoting drug use (a "key" being a kilo of marijuana) or sexual freedom (a wife-swapping club in L. A. used it as a theme song). Actually, the inspiration was an impulsive visit to McDonald's.

Melanie's search for enlightenment and purification had inspired her to go on a twenty-seven day fast in which she drank nothing but distilled water. Coming off the fast, she was eating transitional food—grated raw carrots, a sip of orange juice—when suddenly she felt an incredible urge, like an "inner voice," telling her to go out and get a McDonald's hamburger and french fries. After three years of following a strict vegetarian diet and a month spent cleansing her body, she gave in to what she "assumed to be the voice of spiritual awareness." "I ran down," she says, "and got the whole meal. And then on the way home, in the car, I started to write 'Brand New Key.' So if you are what you eat...(laughs)... I totally connect the McDonald's meal and the song.

6 — b

The Bee Gees had a #1 record in 1972. But by 1974, they had released two stiff albums in a row and two years passed without a single in the Top 40. They had fallen so low that they were relegated to the oldies circuit when they toured.

Arif Mardin, Atlantic's superstar producer, had produced their "Mr Natural" album. It flopped (peak: #178 on the charts), but the band developed a good rapport with him and requested that he produce their next album as well. Mardin accepted. His first advice to the band this time was to listen to the radio and get back in touch with what was happening in pop music. Open their ears. Then he said, "I'm going away for a week. I want you to write while I'm away." It was a "do or die" situation.

Luckily, Barry Gibb's wife, Linda, took Mardin's advice and kept her "ears open." "We used to go over this bridge every night on the way to the studio," she told a critic later. "I used to hear this "hunka-chunka-chunka' just as we went over the railroad tracks. So I said to Barry, 'Do you ever listen to that rhythm when we go across the bridge at night?' He just looked at me." That night, as they crossed the Sunny Isles Bridge headed for Miami's Criterion Studio, Linda brought it up again.

"I said, 'Listen,' and he said, 'Oh, yeah.' It was the chunka-chunka. Barry started singing something and the brothers joined in." It became "Drive Talking," which became "Jive Talkin," which became a #1 record and the first step in the Bee Gees' astounding comeback.

7 — a

The song was originally written as "Le Moribund" (literal translation: "The Dying Man") by Jacques Brel in 1961, and adapted to English by Rod McKuen in 1964. Jacks heard it on a Kingston Trio record, and in 1972, he took it to a Beach Boys' session he was involved with. The Beach Boys recorded it but didn't release it, so Jacks, who was distraught over a friend's death, decided to do his own version of it. He rewrote the last verse.

One day a year later, he was playing his recording of it when the boy who delivered his newspapers overheard it; the boy liked it so much that he brought some friends over to Jacks' house to listen to it, and their enthusiastic response inspired him to release it on his own Goldfish label.

AUNT LENNA'S PUZZLERS (from page 325)

1. Utopia   2. Nymphs   3. Nausea

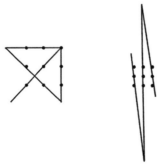

Got beef? Americans, on average, eat 100 lbs. of beef a year—about 50% of it as hamburger.

BRAIN TEASERS (from page 168)

1. They were at a drive-in movie.

2. The poison was in the ice cubes. When the man drank the punch, the ice was fully frozen, but as it melted, it poisoned the punch.

3. The twins were born while their mother was on an ocean cruise. The older twin, Terry, was born first—on March 1. The ship, traveling west, then crossed a time zone and Kerry, the younger twin was born on February 28. In a leap year, the younger twin celebrates her birthday two days before her older brother.

4. Not a single word in this paragraph uses the most common letter in the alphabet: "e."

5. It's the bottom of the ninth. The score is tied; a runner is on third—and the batter hits a foul ball. If the right fielder catches it, the runner will tag up, score and win the game.

6. John.

7. The math does add up—the question is just worded in a misleading way. Look at it like this: The $27 spent by the men includes the $2 kept by the bellhop. Thus, the men paid $27 (the bellboy kept $2, and $25 went to the desk clerk).

8. The women paid $28 (the bellboy kept $3, and $25 went to the desk clerk). You subtract the bellhop's tip from what the guests paid; you don't add it.

9. The "bicycles" are Bicycle playing cards. The guy was cheating; when the extra card was found, he was killed by the other players.

10. Alice is a gold fish; Ted is a cat.

11. The blind man says, "I'd like to buy a pair of scissors."

Ouch! A typical porcupine has about 30,000 quills.

THE POLITICALLY CORRECT QUIZ (from page 287)

1 — c) "The real-life sexual harassment problems the Army was having kind of spilled over onto us," Walker told reporters. "Some editors felt that although we weren't condoning it, we were on the edge. So Halftrack went off to a training course. When he returned, he apologized to the women in his office: "Y'know, I never meant to offend you with sexist remarks....I like and respect both of you."

2 — a) The ACLU and NOW each informed the school board that the move was illegal and would probably threaten their federal funding. The board decided to deal with it on a case-by-case basis. What we at BRI are curious about is this: if 25% of your cheerleaders are pregnant, doesn't that suggest some lack of sex education?

3 — c) In 1998, a group of meat shop owners in France announced they were "hurt by reporters who routinely refer to vicious murderers as butchers." The group insists that butchers are "gentle, peace-loving artisans."

4 — b) It's not an issue anymore, because Sears is out of the catalog business. But because of the letter, all the maternity models wore rings the following year.

5 — b) In February, 1996, a guy named John Howard opened an apparel store called The Redneck Shop, in Laurens, South Carolina. The problem was that he sold Ku Klux Klan apparel. Also in the store: a Klan museum. When a reporter asked how people in town had responded, he said: "The only people I've had a problem with, who took it as an insult and a racial situation, have been blacks. I didn't know blacks here were so prejudiced." It didn't last long. Someone rammed the store with a pickup truck and closed it down.

6 — b) Apparently it made sense to the women to discriminate in the name of anti-discrimination. The director of the University of Pennsylvania Women's Center, which co-sponsored the event, told reporters: "[Racism] is a white problem and we have a responsibility as white women in particular to do what we can to eradicate [it]."

7 — b) What can we say?

THE "ODD ELVIS" QUIZ (from page 402)

1. c. He thought he could heal the sick. For example: One time Dean Nickopolous, son of Dr. Nick (Elvis' personal physician), injured his leg sledding in the snow. It hurt so badly that he thought it was broken. Elvis's bodyguard recalls: "Then old psychic healer Elvis comes along. He starts 'laying on the hands' and grabbing the leg. Poor old Dean is nearly passing out with pain." Later in the hospital, the doctor told Elvis and his friends that the leg was only bruised, not broken.

"When Elvis heard from the doctor that the leg wasn't broken, he gave one of those satisfied little know-all smiles," the bodyguard says. "He said, 'I know, it isn't broken. It's okay now.' He was taking credit for the fact that the leg wasn't broken."

2. b. Elvis' vegetarian friend Larry Geller recounts in *If I Can Dream: Elvis' Own Story:*

> Out went the brownies, the ice cream, the chicken-fried steak, the burgers. Elvis ate only fresh, nutritious, healthy foods—for two days. Then it was back to the same old nonsense.

3. c. Elvis hated the show because Karl Malden's character was named Mike Stone. When Priscilla Presley separated from the King, she left him for a karate instructor named Mike Stone. A different Mike Stone to be sure, but that didn't matter to Elvis.

4. a. "Dr. Nick said he didn't recommend the surgery, merely mentioned it as a possibility," Jerry Hopkins writes in *Elvis: The Final Years*, but "Elvis, no stranger to rapid and extreme weight loss schemes, said he wanted the operation that night." Dr. Nick finally talked the King out of the procedure by explaining that if he had it, Elvis would have to stick to a strict diet for the rest of his life. "To celebrate the decision not to have the operation," Hopkins writes, Elvis "had one of his boys go to a fast-food place in the neighborhood and sneak back with a sack of bacon cheeseburgers and fried potatoes."

5. b. Elvis loved mortuaries. As we told you in *Uncle John's Sixth Bathroom Reader*, Elvis liked to wander through the Memphis funeral home where his mother had been laid out before her burial. "I don't mean he would just go there during the day and look around," Elvis' friend Sonny West recounted to Steve Dunleavy in *Elvis: What Happened?* "I mean he would go there at three in the morning and wander around the slabs looking at all the embalmed bodies. It scared the sh—out of me."

When his friend on the police force died, the King wanted to be there at the mortuary when they worked on him. "I'm sure Elvis was sad about the whole thing, but do you know what he did, man?" says a member of the Memphis Mafia. "He watched the mortician embalm his friend…Can you imagine that? Someone watching someone else slicing into the body of a friend…Elvis could tell us details about embalming that would impress a doctor."

6. a. A friend recalls: "I remember Jimmy Dean, a nice guy, was waiting for him one night. Elvis came out of his bedroom after keeping Jimmy out there for an hour. Jimmy greeted Elvis with a big hello and said jokingly, 'I oughta rip a yard from your ass, keeping me waiting.' And Elvis whipped out his .22 revolver and stuck it under Jimmy's chin and said, 'And I ought to blow your head off for talking to me like that.' "

7. b. His manager, Colonel Tom Parker, botched the invitation by demanding $25,000 for the King to appear. As Jerry Hopkins writes, "The man in the White House was dumbfounded. Finally he regained his composure and said, 'Why, Colonel parker, no one ever gets paid to perform in the White House.'

" 'Well,' said the Colonel, 'no one ever asks Elvis to play for free'" Elvis lost the gig…and was never invited back.

8. b. "There's all kinds of speculation about what book Elvis was reading when he died," says his cousin Billy Smith. "It was *The Scientific Search for the Face of Jesus*, the Shroud of Turin book, by Frank Adams."

"WOULD YOU BELIEVE..."(from page 456)

1. b) North was testifying before the Iran-Contra investigating committee, and in a supremely cynical gesture, presented the incident as an example of why Congress can't be trusted with secrets. It was too much for Newsweek, which had been the recipient of the leaked information. They revealed that the sources of their info had been "none other than North himself."

2. c) In an interview with Norman Mailer in *Esquire*, she said: "I think you get to a point with a person that you say, 'I live this person...enough that I don't give a damn what happens to me, I'm willing to take the chance.' "

3. a) Lightner, who was fired by MADD in 1985, began work for the American Beverage Institute—which represents restaurants and breweries. "I assume some people will say, 'Gee, what's she doing working for the industry, the other side,' " she told a reporter, adding: "I don't see it was the other side. They're just as affected by drunk driving as anyone else." Lightener's first project, according to *The New York Times*, was "working against state laws tightening the standards for drunk driving."

4. c) "Her beliefs remain unshaken," said news reports, "even though she had a baby during spring break." The report went on:

> The baby's father was a short-term boyfriend...and the athletic teenager gained only seven pounds during her pregnancy. So she was able to conceal her condition from family and friends until she went into labor during a trip with her present boyfriend. He had planned to take her hang-gliding, but ended up rushing her to a hospital maternity ward at 3 a.m. She told her mother the news the day after the baby was born. Danyale plans to attend college next year and the child probably will live with her grandmother. When the time comes, the baby will be taught about abstinence. "I still believe in it," Danyale said.

5. a) When Rashwan didn't show up to receive his Fair Play Trophy, David Wallechinsky, author of a definitive book on the Olympics, "went back and looked at the tape of the match and discovered that Rashwan had attacked the injured leg. In fact, it was his first move, 10 seconds into the match."

Father of his own country: President John Tyler (1841–45) had 15 children by 2 wives.

6. c) "Football and family values—a great marketing concept," wrote columnist Joe Urschel in *USA Today*. "Too bad David Williams was dumb enough to fall for it." He went on:

> First, they threatened to fine and suspend him. Then they decided to withhold $111,111 of Williams' pay instead.
> Williams' immediate supervisor, offensive line coach Bob Young, took a more personal view of the situation...."Shoot, I had a baby when I was playing," Young said. "Ninety percent of the guys have babies when they are playing, but you never miss games. My wife told me she was having a baby, and I said, 'Honey, I've got to play a football game.'"

7. b) Scot Morris writes in *The Emperor Who Ate the Bible*: "Benjamin Franklin saved his well-earned pennies at Philadelphia's Bank of America. In 1940, accountants audited all of the bank's records—including the earliest transactions. According to their findings, Benjamin Franklin...was overdrawn on his account at least three times each week."

8. b) In 1994, the General Accounting Office of Congress did an audit of the IRS and found that "the agency did things with its books that would put ordinary people in jail." According to one news report, for example:

• The IRS's "inventory records are so poorly maintained that it said a $752 video display terminal had cost $5.6 million."
• "Auditors couldn't account for two-thirds of the money [the IRS] spent in one recent year."
• "When federal investigators wanted to see records for several billion dollars' worth of transactions, the paperwork couldn't be found. So [IRS] employees doctored files to fit."

9. a) According to an account in *If No News, Send Rumors*: "In a summary of Supreme Court actions in 1973, *The New York Times* omitted one Court decision. The Justices had announced that they would not revive a paternity suit in which the defendant was Times publisher Arthur Ochs Sulzberger."

Why sled dogs don't scratch: There are no fleas in the Arctic.

TEST YOUR GRAMMY I.Q. (from page 514)

1. b) The Beach Boys. They were nominated for Best Vocal Group in 1966, along with the Association and the Mamas & the Papas. But all lost to the Anita Kerr Quartet, a nondescript middle-of-the-road group. (Anita Kerr just happened to be the vice president of the Nashville chapter of the National Academy of Recording Arts and Sciences—the organization that gives out the Grammys.)

"Good Vibrations" was nominated for 1966's best rock & roll recording...but lost to "Winchester Cathedral." In 1988, the Beach Boys were nominated (and lost) again—this time for "Kokomo."

On the other hand: The Chipmunks won in 1958, for Best Comedy Record and Best Children's Record. Aerosmith was named Best Rock Group in 1990.

2. a) Vaughn Meader did a great impersonation of President John F. Kennedy, and his First Family record, which gently spoofed life at the Kennedy White House, was Album of the Year in 1962. In fact, at one point was certified by the Guinness Book of World Records as the fastest-selling album in history. Thomas O'Neil writes in The Grammys:

> Meader is remembered in comedy circles today as one of its most tragic figures. He was clearly America's leading political satirist of his day, but [his] career was...shot down the same day the gunfire made history in Dallas on November 22, 1963....
>
> When Kennedy was assassinated in Dallas, the album was tossed out of homes and record stores across America. While other comics [who] lampooned Kennedy in the past...were able to prevail professionally after his death, Meader was unable to rescue his career, despite countless comeback tries that even included changing his name.

3. c) Yep, it's the Anita Kerr Quartet again, for their immortal album, *We Dig Mancini*. Probably the most scandalous award in Grammy history, because they beat out the Beatles, who were in their prime. The Beatles were nominated for nine awards—and got none. Bob Dylan didn't even get a nomination.

4. c) 1967, for *How Great Thou Art*. In fact, the only Grammys

Elvis ever won were for religious music. He was given the 1972 and 1974 Best Inspirational Performance awards, too.

5. c) Sinéad O'Connor. In 1990, she was nominated in four categories, and said: "If I win, I won't accept it and I wouldn't want it near me. As far as I'm concerned, it represents everything I despise about the music industry." She did win a Best Alternative Music award, and turned it down.

6. a) John. George and Ringo won in 1972 for their performances on the Concert for Bangladesh album, Paul won one in 1972 for Uncle Albert and one in 1974 for Band on the Run. Remarkably, the most creative of the quartet got nothing for his solo efforts while he was alive. After (and perhaps because) he was assassinated, he and Yoko won an Album of the Year award for Double Fantasy.

7. b) The Rolling Stones. But the Who and the Doors never won anything, either.

8. a) Roseanne Cash. She was nominated for 1982's best female country singer, and didn't get it. After the show, driving down Hollywood Boulevard, she wrote a "tongue-in-cheek...little ditty" that went, "I got my new dress, I got my new shoes/ I don't know why you don't want me." She recorded it, and it won her the award for Best Female Country Vocalist in 1985. "I wrote it out of self-pity," she said in her acceptance speech. "How ironic to win with it!"

9. c) Frank Zappa. When he was nominated in 1987 for *Jazz from Hell* (which won Best Rock Instrumental, he said, "I have no ambiguous feelings about the Grammys at all. I know they're fake. I find it difficult to believe that Whitney Houston is the answer to all of America's music needs."

10. a) What Grammys? Each was nominated once—Hendrix in 1970 for an instrumental of "The Star Spangled Banner" and Joplin in 1971 for "Me & Bobby McGee" And that's it.

11. d) Natalie Cole, 1975. It took 17 years. Among the winners in that stretch: Tom Jones, the Carpenters, and Marvin Hamlishch.

In her entire lifetime, a female hummingbird will lay at most 2 eggs.

12. b) He couldn't afford to rent a tux to go to the awards ceremony. It's a bizarre story. Clark, a blind Nashville street singer, recorded an album for RCA, called *Blues in the Street*. It didn't sell well, but did get a Grammy nomination. For some reason, RCA wasn't interested in promoting it; they didn't even loan him the money to go across town and attend the ceremony. So he wasn't there when he beat out Peter, Paul & Mary and Ravi Shankar for Best Folk Recording. In fact, he never recorded again.

According to Thomas O'Neil in *The Grammys:*

> The day after the Grammy ceremony, he was seen still hustling spare change on the sidewalks of the honky-tonk capital. Two years later, he died when a kerosene stove exploded in his trailer home.

13. a) "I tore a ligament in my leg, jumping out of my seat," Popper said; he had to limp up to the stage. What was he going to do with his trophy? "I got a lovely spot for this," he said, as he waved it around. "There's this door that keeps closing…"

*   *   *

DOCTOR'S ORDERS

Recently, BRI member Jack Miller sent us this amusing story.

"My friend's dad was an ear-nose-and-throat doctor on the upper West Side, in New York City. He treated a lot of well-known singers, including many from the Metropolitan Opera. He was a very proper old Viennese gentleman.

"One day in the late 1960s, who should walk into the office but Janis Joplin. Dr. Reckford doesn't know her from Adam, but he examines her and delivers his diagnosis:

'Young lady, I don't know what you do for a living, but you've got to stop drinking and shouting so much.' "

Takin' it easy: The top speed of a 3-toed sloth is .12 miles per hour.